Teaching Aboriginal Studies

2nd Edition

Edited by Rhonda Craven

LONDON AND NEW YORK

First published 2011 by Allen & Unwin

Published 2020 by Routledge
2 Park Square, Milton Park, Abingdon, Oxon OX14 4RN
605 Third Avenue, New York, NY 10017

First issued in hardback 2021

Routledge is an imprint of the Taylor & Francis Group, an informa business

This work contains images of deceased Aboriginal and Torres Strait Islander people. We regret any sadness this may cause relatives and community members.

Cover photo: Students from Derby Youth Services celebrate on stage at the Halls Creek Croc Festival 2005. Courtesy Indigenous Festivals of Australia. Photographer Wayne Quilliam.

Copyright © Rhonda Craven, 2011

All rights reserved. No part of this book may be reprinted or reproduced or utilised in any form or by any electronic, mechanical, or other means, now known or hereafter invented, including photocopying and recording, or in any information storage or retrieval system, without permission in writing from the publishers.

Notice:
Product or corporate names may be trademarks or registered trademarks, and are used only for identification and explanation without intent to infringe.

Publisher's Note
The publisher has gone to great lengths to ensure the quality of this reprint but points out that some imperfections in the original copies may be apparent.

Copyright of individual chapters remains with individual authors.
Cataloguing-in-Publication details are available
from the National Library of Australia
www.trove.nla.gov.au

Index by Garry Cousins

ISBN 13: 978-0-367-71956-2 (hbk)
ISBN 13: 978-1-74175-475-9 (pbk)

Dedicated to the memory of
Oodgeroo of the tribe Noonuccal,
Custodian of the land Minjerribah,
who proved that one person
can make a difference

Teaching Aboriginal Studies (2nd edition)

A resource of 'Teaching the Teachers': Indigenous Australian Studies' project

A project of National Significance funded by:

Department of Employment, Education, and Training

with assistance from:

Council for Aboriginal Reconciliation

and developed by:

The Steering Committee: Indigenous Australian Studies for Teacher Education Courses

Editor:

Professor Rhonda Craven, Head, Educational Excellence and Equity (E³) Research Program, Centre for Educational Research, College of Arts, University of Western Sydney

Pictorial Editor

Nigel Parbury

Project Management

Lisa Car

Nyrie Nalbandian

Educational Excellence and Equity (E3) Research Program
Centre for Educational Research, College of Arts, University of Western Sydney

Foreword

The New South Wales Review of Aboriginal Education (2004), conducted by the New South Wales Aboriginal Education Consultative Group (AECG) Inc. with the Department of Education and Training, was told time and again: 'Aboriginal students must have the right to be Aboriginal.' And, years ago, Aboriginal students in western Sydney defined a good teacher as: 'Someone that likes us and is fair'. Relationships are critical in Aboriginal culture; that includes schools. Teachers must be empowered to understand and appreciate Aboriginal students and know how to develop their talents—and at the same time teach *all* students about Aboriginal Australia.

The New South Wales Aboriginal Education Consultative Group Inc. has always believed that teacher education is critical to achieving the twin goals of Aboriginal education: appropriate education for Aboriginal students and teaching all students about Aboriginal Australia, history, culture, and issues now. One cannot be achieved without the other. We have always maintained that a major reason for the failure of Aboriginal students by education systems in the past—and the wastage of Aboriginal talents and lives—has been the failure of teacher education institutions to prepare student teachers to be able to teach Aboriginal students effectively and to educate all students about the real Australia.

Teaching Aboriginal Studies is the text of 'Teaching the Teachers Indigenous Australian Studies', funded through the 1990s by the then Department of Employment, Education, and Training (DEET) as a Project of National Significance. The New South Wales AECG Inc. was Principal Consultant to the project, and as such *Teaching Aboriginal Studies* was launched at the AECG Secretariat in 1999.

Quality teaching is the name of the game. Teachers' understanding of Aboriginal history, cultures and contemporary issues is critical to improving the schooling outcomes of Aboriginal students and educating all Australian students about Aboriginal Australia. Teachers have the right to understand Aboriginal students and be empowered to do the right thing by them. Universities have a duty to provide this knowledge, understanding and empowerment.

The New South Wales AECG Inc. commends this revised and updated edition of *Teaching Aboriginal Studies* to teacher educators, to student teachers and to all teachers. We hope *Teaching Aboriginal Studies* will make a difference by empowering teachers to make a difference in schools, by being able to understand and appreciate Aboriginal students, to develop their talents, and at the same time educate other Australian students about Aboriginal Australia. This is the way we can put an end to the wastage of Aboriginal talent, and tell the truth about this country in order to achieve the vision of the Council for Aboriginal Reconciliation: 'A united Australia that respects this land of ours, values the Aboriginal and Torres Strait Islander heritage, and provides justice and equity for all.'

Cindy Berwick,
President, New South Wales Aboriginal
Education Consultative Group (AECG) Inc.

The Teaching the Teachers story

Nigel Parbury

In 1990, Oodgeroo Noonuccal, aka Kath Walker, the famous Aboriginal poet who changed her name in protest at the Bicentennial, was engaged as Artist in Residence at the University of New South Wales (UNSW). Not so many people know Oodgeroo was passionate about education, and in fact always described herself as an educator.

Rhonda Craven, then a young teacher education lecturer at the St George (Oatley) campus of the University of New South Wales, was delegated to look after Oodgeroo. Rhonda and Alan Duncan, Oodge's old mate from their FCAATSI days, met her off the plane and took her to UNSW's International House where she was booked to stay. Oodgeroo took one look at that, said it would be like living in a gaol, and said to Rhonda: 'Let's go to your place.' So Alan drove them out to Riverwood. Rhonda's house was just bought, and a bombsite, but Oodgeroo walked through the door, (stepping over the sander in the hallway), dumped her bag on the sleepout bed at the back and moved in. For the rest of her life, Riverwood was her Sydney home, and she took Rhonda to her heart as the daughter she never had.

Oodgeroo always described herself as an educator as much as a poet (not many people know that most of her early poems were written for the Referendum movement, to educate people). Rhonda was deeply involved in educating student teachers about Aboriginal history, culture and issues, and believed that Aboriginal Studies should be mandatory in all teacher education. Seeing this passion, Oodgeroo rang Robert Tickner, the federal Minister for Aboriginal Affairs, and talked him into a seeding grant to develop a mandatory subject for universities. This turned into 'Teaching the Teachers: Indigenous Australian Studies for Primary Pre-service Teacher Education Programs', funded by the then Department of Education, Employment, and Training (DEET) as a Project of National Significance.

Rhonda's home in Riverwood—where Teaching the Teachers happened from the start, round the kitchen table and out the back—was a fitting place for an Aboriginal education project.

Oodgeroo speaking to students at Oatley Campus, University of NSW; a young Rhonda Craven looking on. Photo courtesy Rhonda Craven.

Bert Groves, a pioneer in the early struggle, had lived round the corner. Down the way was Salt Pan Creek, where Aboriginal activists in the 1930s camped, walking up to Hurstville to shop or catch the train into town to talk up Aboriginal rights in the Domain on Sundays.

The New South Wales AECG had always stressed the need for Aboriginal Studies in teacher education, in order to make a difference in schools, and was right behind Teaching the Teachers from the start. Aunty Ruth Simms and Aunty Mae Robinson represented the AECG on the Steering Committee. As AECG Research Officer ('Mr AECG' behind my back), I represented the views of the AECG as Assistant Coordinator. I thought we should call it 'Teaching the Teachers' (as in, keep it simple and straight-out).

Successive drafts of the project were workshopped at AECG state meetings for several years—Teaching the Teachers took so much time and effort that Linda Burney used to refer to it, through her teeth, as 'that project'. With 'doorstop' consultation drafts lobbing across the country, and workshops at Aboriginal Studies Association conferences, Teaching the Teachers was said to be the most consulted project ever. The Council for Aboriginal Reconciliation kicked in funding for publication. Two folders of sample lecture and tutorial notes, four videos, a project summary and a booklet, *Using the Right Words,* were produced. The whole Teaching the Teachers package was launched at the AECG in 1996, by Sonya Link of the Human Rights and Equal Opportunity Commission, then mailed to universities across the country and sold at cost.

Oodgeroo chaired the Steering Committee for the project, and stayed with Rhonda periodically for the rest of her life, which was cruelly cut short by cancer in 1993. Rhonda and I visited her at Moongalba, her 'bush school' home on Stradbroke Island. Her last wish was that Teaching the Teachers succeed and make a difference in schools. She nominated Bundjalung Elder Uncle Charles Moran to chair the Steering Committee in her place.

Teaching the Teachers has been around. When the University of New South Wales cancelled its primary teacher education program, Rhonda Craven took a position in the School of Education at Sydney University and took the project with her, as well as the ASA which she drove from the start, convening twelve national conferences. In 1999, she moved homeward to the University of Western Sydney as Deputy Director of the Self-Concept Enhancement and Learning Facilitation (SELF) Centre; again, she took Teaching the Teachers and *Teaching Aboriginal Studies* with her, and directed the Aboriginal Studies Association from there.

Teaching the Teachers was led from the front and driven by (now Professor) Rhonda Craven. When the late Rick Farley launched the first edition of *Teaching Aboriginal Studies* at the AECG home in Stanmore, he said it should be in every home in the country; his partner Linda Burney, MC for the night, introduced Rhonda as 'the woman who drove me nuts and drove the team to a wonderful conclusion'.

Oodgeroo always said one person can make a difference. Her own life showed exactly that. Teaching the Teachers made a difference. Team Rhonda has made a difference, recognised in her Director-General's medal for her outstanding contribution to Aboriginal education. This updated edition of *Teaching Aboriginal Studies* is to take the momentum onward. As the reconciliation poster said, together we can't lose.

Teaching the Teachers video Munyarl Mythology. 'Munyarl' is Bundjalung for 'gammon', 'not even', 'not true', 'a lie or a pack of lies'. The triple-tick 'Teaching the Teachers' logo was designed by Peter Yanada McKenzie.

Members of the Steering Committee of the Teaching the Teachers Project working on materials. Left to right: Aunty Ruth Simms, Nigel Parbury, Adrian Tucker, Aunty Mae Robinson, Rhonda Craven and Linda Burney.

Contents

Foreword *Cindy Berwick*		v
The Teaching the Teachers story *Nigel Parbury*		vi
Acknowledgements		x
Contributors		xi
1	Why teach Aboriginal Studies? *Rhonda Craven*	1
2	Living cultures *Uncle Charles Moran, Uncle Norm Newlin, Terry Mason and Rhoda Roberts*	22
3	Misconceptions, stereotypes and racism: Let's face the facts *Rhonda Craven and Kaye Price*	42
4	*Terra nullius*: Invasion and colonisation *Nigel Parbury*	68
5	A history of special treatment: The impact of government policies *James Wilson-Miller*	90
6	Discovering shared history: Moving towards new understanding in Australian schools *Paddy Cavanagh*	110
7	A history of Aboriginal education *Nigel Parbury*	132
8	Reconciliation matters *Nina Burridge*	153
9	Educating for the future *Rhonda Craven*	172
10	Community involvement *Bev Smith*	194
11	What research can tell us *Rhonda Craven and Gawaian Bodkin-Andrews*	210
12	Closing the gap *John Lester and Geoff Munns*	229
13	Working with Aboriginal students *Christine Halse and Aunty Mae Robinson*	257
14	Teaching resources *Rhonda Craven, Mark d'Arbon and Sharon Galleguillos*	273
15	Developing teaching activities *Rhonda Craven, Mark d'Arbon and James Wilson-Miller*	289
16	Together we can't lose *Rhonda Craven*	315
References		330
Index		343

Acknowledgements

With special thanks to:

- the late Oodgeroo of the Tribe Noonuccal and the New South Wales Aboriginal Education Consultative Group (AECG) Inc. (Joint Principal Consultants), the Elders Committee and Steering Committee, who inspired and guided Teaching the Teachers from which this book was developed;
- Cindy Berwick, President, New South Wales AECG Inc.;
- Indigenous and other Australian educators and community members who have contributed their wisdom and knowledge to this work;
- academics, teachers, student teachers and schools who have provided valuable insights on what seeds success;
- the College of Arts, University of Western Sydney, which provided funding for research assistance;
- Elizabeth Weiss and Lauren Finger (Allen & Unwin), whose expertise, patience and understanding represent a shining light in proactive reconciliation;
- staff and students of the Educational Excellence and Equity (E^3) Research Program, Centre for Educational Research, College of Arts, University of Western Sydney;
- Virginia O'Rourke and Nyrie Nalbandian for their professional research assistance; and finally
- two people without whom this long-awaited update could not have been possible: Lisa Car for meticulous project management, caring and proactive support of authors, and all-round helpful goodwill—nothing was ever too much trouble; and Nigel Parbury, for his knowledge and wisdom, inspiration and painstaking guidance, relentless editing and striking placement of amazing images!

Contributors

Gawaian Bodkin-Andrews is of the Dharawal nation and is currently an Indigenous Research Fellow in the Educational Excellence and Equity (E³) Research Program, Centre for Educational Research (CER), University of Western Sydney. His research focuses on advancing understandings of Indigenous education and psychology, with a particular emphasis on the validity of both qualitative and high-level quantitative research methodologies. His key research interests include addressing racial discrimination targeting Indigenous Australian students; and enhancing Indigenous students' self-confidence and motivation. His research is often conducted in close collaboration with the Dharawal Traditional Descendants and Knowledge Holders' Council.

Nina Burridge holds the position of Senior Lecturer in the Faculty of Arts and Social Sciences at the University of Technology, Sydney. She has been involved in tertiary education since 1991 in education faculties at Macquarie University and Sydney University. Her main research interests and publications centre on Indigenous education with reconciliation as a key theme, educating for human rights, and ethno-cultural diversity in schools and community settings. She sees herself as an activist professional whose involvement in community organisations and social action groups informs her academic work in education.

Paddy (Pat) Cavanagh has worked either in Aboriginal education or developing his professional interest in the history of contact since 1982. While working in the New South Wales Aboriginal Education Unit, he assisted in the development and implementation of the New South Wales Aboriginal Education Policy, the first in Australia, and helped develop the original Two-unit HSC syllabus in Aboriginal Studies. He was the first Research Officer for the New South Wales Aboriginal Education Consultative Group (AECG) and taught courses in the history of contact at Macquarie University and the Australian Catholic University. He was also involved in developing Indigenous teacher training programs at the Australian Catholic University.

Rhonda Craven is an inaugural Professor of the Centre for Educational Research, College of Arts, University of Western Sydney, and leads the Educational Excellence and Equity (E³) Research Program. She is a highly accomplished researcher, having successfully secured over $6 million in nationally competitive funding for 36 prestigious large-scale research projects. This performance is arguably one of the strongest for an Australian education researcher. She was the National Project Coordinator of the Teaching the Teachers: Indigenous Australian Studies Project of National Significance, which has resulted in the development of sound models for the teaching of Aboriginal Studies in Australian teacher education courses and schools. She is the recipient of the Meritorious Service to Public Education Award, the Betty Watts Award and the Aboriginal Studies Association Life Achievement Award.

Mark d'Arbon has been a teacher for 40 years. He has been involved in Aboriginal education since the early 1970s and has presented in-services courses and professional development workshops in Aboriginal Studies at the school, system and tertiary levels. From 1992 to 1995, he was a curriculum officer in Human Society and its Environment (HSIE) at the New South Wales Board of Studies. He is a lecturer in social and environmental studies and critical literacy for preservice teachers at the University of Newcastle, Ourimbah Campus. He maintains a lively interest in Indigenous perspectives in education, particularly in the primary curriculum.

Sharon Galleguillos is an Indigenous educator with wide professional experience in tertiary, secondary and primary school teaching. Sharon graduated as a primary teacher in Queensland in 1976 and taught extensively in Queensland and New South Wales. She worked for six years as a Senior Education Officer in the Aboriginal Education Unit in the New South Wales Department of Education and Training, helping to develop the 1996 Aboriginal Education Policy. She is an active facilitator and mentor, and has presented on Indigenous research and education at numerous conferences. She works intensively with Indigenous communities and student bodies and is a board member of the Aboriginal Education Council. She is also known in Sydney fundraising circles as the Trivia Queen.

Christine Halse is Professor and Director of the Centre for Educational Research at the University of Western Sydney. She is a sociologist in education whose doctoral research involved working with remote Indigenous communities and survivors of the first 'Stolen Generations' on oral histories of their experiences of the European invasion. Her current research focuses on narrative research methods, and the implications of social and cultural diversity for schooling. Her book, *A Terribly Wild Man: The Life of the Rev. Ernest Gribble* (Allen & Unwin, 2002) documented the life of an important fighter for Aboriginal rights, as well as the impact of the missionary invasion on Indigenous people in northern Australia.

John Lester is a strong Wonnarua man who has played a pivotal role in Aboriginal Education for over 30 years at the school, TAFE and university levels. One of the architects of the New South Wales Aboriginal Education Consultative Group, and a Life Member, he has been a leading policy innovator and pioneer of community empowerment. Career highlights include being first Executive Officer of the New South Wales AECG, a member of the National Aboriginal Education Committee, the first Aboriginal head of Aboriginal Units in the Department of Education and TAFE, the first Aboriginal TAFE principal, the inaugural Chair of Aboriginal Studies at the University of Newcastle and inaugural Director Aboriginal Education and Training in the New South Wales Department of Education and Training.

Terry Mason is from the land of the Awabakal language group and works in the Badanami Centre, University of Western Sydney. He is a former Academic Coordinator of the Aboriginal Rural Education Program (AREP), is currently chair of the National Tertiary Education Union Indigenous Policy Committee and serves on the Board of the Welfare Rights Centre. Terry was a reader of written submissions to the 2004 New South Wales Review of Aboriginal Education, a key researcher in the Successful Transition Programs from Prior-to-School to School for Aboriginal and Torres Strait Islander Children project, and has contributed to Australian and overseas publications in the areas of transition, starting school and student support.

Uncle Charles Moran is a Bundjalung Elder, educated in culture and language by initiated Elders. An arduous working life as a farm labourer, timber-cutter, boundary rider, stockman, cane-cutter, fettler, builders' labourer and miner has given him wide experience of Australian bush life. He initiated the Beaudesert Aboriginal Housing Cooperative to provide basic housing for families living in extreme poverty; set up the New South Wales Asbestos Ex-Miners' Aboriginal Corporation to fight for justice for asbestos miners; and in 1992 was inspirational in the rescue of the *Koori Mail*. He is a leader in Aboriginal education and promotes greater understanding of Aboriginal people and history. He succeeded Oodgeroo Noonuccal as Chair of the Teaching the Teachers Elders Committee.

Geoff Munns is an Associate Professor and lectures in pedagogy and curriculum in the University of Western Sydney's School of Education. He has more than 25 years' teaching experience in primary schools, including executive roles as Assistant Principal and Principal. His research interests focus on improved educational outcomes for students from educationally disadvantaged backgrounds, including Indigenous students. In particular, he is interested in how these students can become engaged in their classrooms and subsequently develop a long-term commitment to education.

Uncle Norm Newlin is a Worimi Elder. He is an experienced educator who has conducted Aboriginal Studies lectures and workshops in universities, schools and prisons for many years. He is now accredited as a Visiting Elder for gaols in New South Wales. He was the first Aboriginal person to complete an Associate Diploma in Adult Education and a BA in Communications at the University of Technology, Sydney and first Aboriginal writer in residence at Charles Sturt University, Bathurst. His poetry has been acclaimed internationally and published widely. He is often sought by the media for his views on Aboriginal issues and to discuss his work.

Nigel Parbury was a teacher, taxi driver and radio operator in a previous life. He was Research Officer for the New South Wales AECG from 1990 to 1999. A founding member and a former President of the Aboriginal Studies Association, he is also Vice-President of the Aboriginal Education Council and a director of the Inner City Education Centre. On behalf of the New South Wales AECG, he was Assistant Coordinator of Teaching the Teachers and edited the school musical resource kit *1788: The Great South Land* and Diana Kidd's *The Fat and Juicy Place*. He is the author of *Survival: A History of Aboriginal Life in New South Wales* (1986, 2005), the ten-year commemorative book *Croc Festival* (2007) and a history of the New South Wales AECG, *The Education Movement: A people's history of the AECG* completed in 2010.

Kaye Price is Director of the Ngunnawal Indigenous Higher Education Centre at the University of Canberra, recently moving from a Lecturer position within the Education faculty. A doctoral graduate from the Australian National University, she has also studied at the University of South Australia, Edith Cowan University and Hobart Teachers College. She was the Tasmanian Aboriginal Centre's nominee on the National Aboriginal Education Committee. Kaye has worked with Curriculum Corporation and on *What Works*, and recently led a team that produced *Stepping Up: What Works in Teacher Education*. She is a fellow of the Australian College of Educators and was named an Education Warrior at the World Indigenous Peoples Conference Education (WIPCE) 2008.

Rhoda Roberts is a member of the Bundjalung nation, Widjebal clan, of Northern New South Wales and Southeast Queensland. Over more than three decades, Rhoda's involvement in the arts has been extensive. She was a co-founding member of the Aboriginal National Theatre Trust (ANTT)—Australia's first national Aboriginal theatre company. As an actor/producer and director, she continues to work on a freelance basis as a consultant and performer in theatre, film, television and radio. She was the first Aboriginal person to front a mainstream TV show (*Vox Populi*, SBS), and has directed key events and celebrations like Yabun, the Dreaming Festival, the Woggan-ma-gule mourning ceremony at the start of every Australia Day in Sydney's Botanic Gardens and Sydney's New Year's Eve fireworks 2009. She is now fronting the Vibe health show, *Living Strong*.

Aunty Mae Robinson is an Elder and a highly respected educator in the Metropolitan South West community of Sydney. She is a life member of the New South Wales AECG. Aunty Mae taught in New South Wales departmental schools for over fifteen years and has held the position of Regional Aboriginal Education Consultant for eight years in the Metropolitan South West region, where she was also regional rep for the AECG. She has served on the executive of the AECG and as a senior education officer in the state office responsible for Aboriginal education. In 2010 she was named UWS Woman of the

West. Currently, she is assisting the University of Western Sydney to develop its Aboriginal Attributes program, between other engagements—Aunty Mae is in high demand!

Bev Smith is an experienced Aboriginal educator and secondary teacher. She was closely involved in the New South Wales AECG for well over a decade, and in that role served on syllabus committees for the Board of Studies New South Wales, and in policy and resource development for the Department of Education and Training. More recently, she has taught on the North Coast of New South Wales. She has recently retired from teaching and can devote more time to her art and her passion for diving and marine environments.

James Wilson-Miller is Section Head and Curator of Koori History and Culture with the Powerhouse Museum in Sydney, a position he has held for fifteen years. Over that time, he has curated over 20 permanent and temporary Koori-inspired exhibitions, both in Sydney and overseas, while including Koori perspectives in many others. He is a former school teacher and university academic with over three decades of experience teaching Koori history, studies, culture and issues. He is an experienced researcher, and became this country's first published Koori historian in 1985 with his seminal work *Koori: A Will to Win*. He is an experienced musician, and sang with the Silver Linings—one of Australia's first Aboriginal bands.

1 Why teach Aboriginal Studies?

Rhonda Craven

Aboriginal Charter of Rights

We want hope, not racialism,
Brotherhood, not ostracism,
Black advance, not white ascendance:
Make us equals, not dependants.
We need help, not exploitation,
We want freedom, not frustration;
Not control, but self-reliance,
Independence, not compliance,
Not rebuff, but education,
Self-respect, not resignation.
Free us from a mean subjection,
From a bureaucrat Protection.
Let's forget the old-time slavers:
Give us fellowship, not favours;
Encouragement, not prohibitions,
Homes, not settlements and missions.
We need love, not overlordship,
Grip of hand, not whip-hand wardship;
Opportunity that places
White and black on equal basis.
You dishearten, not defend us,
Circumscribe, who should befriend us.
Give us welcome, not aversion,
Give us choice, not cold coercion,
Status, not discrimination,
Human rights, not segregation.
You the law, like Roman Pontius,
Make us proud, not colour-conscious:
Give the deal you still deny us,
Give goodwill, not bigot bias;
Give ambition, not prevention,
Confidence, not condescension;
Give incentive, not restriction,
Give us Christ, not crucifixion.

Reconciliation Day at Penshurst West Public School, Sydney. An Aboriginal girl (the author's daughter) and a non-Aboriginal boy get into the spirit. Photo: Lisa Car.

Though baptised and blessed and Bibled
We are still tabooed and libelled.
You devout Salvation-sellers,
Make us neighbours, not fringe-dwellers;
Make us mates, not poor relations,
Citizens, not serfs on stations.
Must we native Old Australians
In our land rank as aliens?
Banish bans and conquer caste,
Then we'll win our own at last.

—'Aboriginal Charter of Rights', Oodgeroo Noonuccal
(2007, p. 36)

Oodgeroo (aka Kath Walker) wrote 'Aboriginal Charter of Rights' to present to the fifth Annual General Meeting of the Federal Council for the Advancement of Aborigines and Torres Strait Islanders (FCAATSI) in Easter 1962. This poem contributed to providing a voice for Aboriginal Australians and helped to educate other Australians about the critical need for social justice for Aboriginal Australians. Oodgeroo said it was her most expensive poem ever, as a public reading resulted in her home being invaded and her clothes and blankets slashed. This did not deter Oodgeroo from being a spokesperson for her people, an activist for social justice and a committed Aboriginal Studies educator. In fact, her life story (see Cochrane 1994; Shoemaker 1994) is a striking testimony to why implementing Aboriginal Studies is a national priority, and why educators should be committed to teaching this subject area. 'Aboriginal Charter of Rights' expresses poignantly Aboriginal people's pleas that their human rights be respected. It also shows clearly that Aboriginal people's basic human rights were not given sufficient respect, and calls for attention to social justice issues. In a nation that pays homage to the principle of a 'fair go for all', we can see that in Oodgeroo's eyes this ethos clearly did not extend to Aboriginal Australians.

Aboriginal Studies is about social justice for all Australians—equity, human rights, a fair go and mutual respect for our fellow Australians. It is hard to define social justice but everybody knows what it is, particularly when it is missing. Mick Dodson famously described social justice as:

> what faces you in the morning. It is awakening in a house with an adequate water supply, cooking facilities and sanitation. It is the ability to nourish your children and send them to a school where their education not only equips them for employment but reinforces their knowledge and appreciation of their cultural inheritance. It is the prospect of genuine employment and good health: a life of choices and opportunity, free from discrimination. (Mick Dodson, 1993, p. 8)

Consultations across Australia have stressed that social justice is not so much about the expenditure of vast sums of money on Indigenous programs; rather, it is about changing systems and mindsets, to recognise Aboriginal and Torres Strait Islander cultures and knowledge as being of equal validity to non-Indigenous cultures, and to secure Indigenous Australia in the frame of reference of mainstream Australia. Clearly, all schools have a critical role to play in promoting this recognition.

How many Indigenous Australians?

A total of 455 028 people identified themselves as 'Indigenous' in the 2006 Census. (Australian Bureau of Statistics, 2008a, p. 25). Of these, 409 525 were Aboriginal, 27 302 were Torres Strait Islanders and 18 201 identified themselves as both Aboriginal and Torres Strait Islander. Overall, 2.3 per cent of the total population of Australia in 2006 identified themselves as Indigenous, an increase of 11 per cent since the 2001 Census (Australian Bureau of Statistics, 2008a, p. 25). The Australian Bureau of Statistics recommends the estimated resident population (2008a, p. 9) of 517 174 as the official measure of the Indigenous population—this is higher because it has been adjusted for a net undercount of Indigenous people and occasions where Indigenous status is unknown (Australian Bureau of Statistics, 2008a, p. 8). In 2006, the estimated resident population of people of Torres Strait Islander origin was 53 300 (10 per cent of the Indigenous population and 0.3 per cent of the total Australian population (Australian Bureau of Statistics, 2008a, p. 168). As a whole, the Indigenous population is much younger than the non-Indigenous population: 56.5 per cent of the Indigenous population in Australia are aged under 25 compared with 32.9 per cent of the non-Indigenous population (see Figure 1.1, Australian Bureau of Statistics, 2008a, p. 17). Figure 1.1 shows double the proportion of Indigenous people up to the age of 14, and still way more in the 15–24 age group. This means there will be more and more Indigenous students in Australian schools and the Indigenous proportion of Australian population will keep on increasing, especially as their birthrate is higher.

Figure 1.1 Proportion of Indigenous and non-Indigenous population in specific age groups, 2006

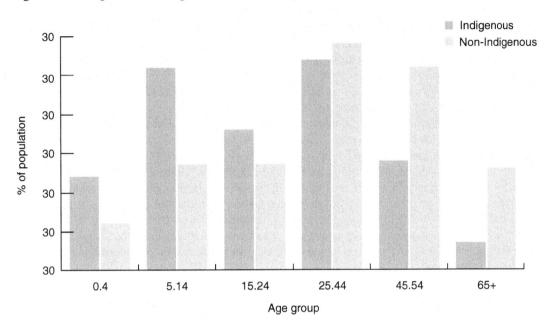

Source: Australian Bureau of Statistics, *Population Characteristics: Aboriginal and Torres Strait Islander Australians*, Catalogue No. 4713, Table 2.3. *Estimated Resident Population*, (27 March 2008), p. 17.

What is Indigenous Studies?

Content

Aboriginal Studies and Torres Strait Islander Studies is the study of Aboriginal societies or Torres Strait Islander societies past and present, including histories, cultures, values, beliefs, languages, lifestyles and roles, both prior to and following invasion. This study of Torres Strait Islander people and Aboriginal people presents an accurate history of Australia, and is studied in a context that:

- is central to Aboriginal societies and Torres Strait Islander societies and relevant to the total Australian community;
- presents Torres Strait Islander people and Aboriginal people within an accurate and culturally inclusive history of Australia;
- acknowledges the sophistication and complexity of Aboriginal and Torres Strait Islander kinship and social structures;
- promotes respect for the integrity of all people;
- emphasises an understanding of spiritual, political, economic and environmental issues;
- affirms the diversity of cultures within Aboriginal societies and Torres Strait Islander societies (Oliver, 1995, p. 1).

We as teachers can feel overwhelmed by the breadth and depth of this subject area as described in definitions like the one above. However, such feelings diminish when we come to understand the content and recognise that our role is to facilitate learning in this area, as opposed to being experts on all facets of the subject-matter.

Indigenous Studies comprises both Aboriginal Studies and Torres Strait Islander Studies—by definition, Indigenous Studies includes Torres Strait Islander Studies. Torres Strait Islander people are indigenous to Australia and are culturally distinct from all Aboriginal peoples. Therefore, Indigenous Studies is the study of Aboriginal and Torres Strait Islander history, societies and cultures, both as a subject in its own right and as content incorporated into all curriculum areas at all levels of education. Indigenous Studies is not just an isolated unit of

Aboriginal Studies was an experience

When I first enrolled in Aboriginal Studies at the end of Year 10, I didn't know what to expect. I wondered how I could gain an adequate understanding of Indigenous issues in an environment as sterile as a high school. Little did I know that Aboriginal Studies was not your generic HSC subject. It was an experience.

There was always a bit of excitement upon entering Room L14. Would there be a guest hiding away in a corner? Was there a heated discussion about to break loose, unleashing passion for the issues in the people who always put on the most apathetic of fronts? The diversity of the subject was a highlight for me. We studied Indigenous culture through many forms of media. Film, documentaries, art, internet, newspaper articles and so on. Not only did you feel constantly interested and enlightened, the subject kept us, the typical cut-off-from-the-world HSC student, a little in contact with what was actually going on outside of school. Cathy Russell, our teacher, inspired and motivated us with her obvious love for the subject. Her undeniable passion for Indigenous issues also proved a very valuable source for the HSC. Visits from Uncle Larry, an Indigenous liaison officer, were definitely a class favourite. Somehow, he always managed to hold the whole room captive for 53 minutes with his first-hand accounts and leave us feeling as though we had a real insight into the lives of the Indigenous population.

The study of Indigenous culture in regards to music, art, dance and Dreaming was what I found most interesting. Also, it was just so liberating to finally have an Indigenous perspective on the events of Australian history, something previously untouched in my school career. Participating in reconciliation walks, attending cultural days, making presentations to the school and embarking on a trip to Dubbo kept the sentiment for the subject alive in our class. The major work component of the course brought people together, allowed us to interact with members of the local Indigenous community and create a work we were really proud of.

Although I wish to pursue a career in magazine writing and editing, the course did in fact alter my choice of further study. Instead of choosing a journalism major in communications, I decided on a writing and cultural studies major, which allows Aboriginal Studies electives and allows me to both further my knowledge in regards to Indigenous issues and leaves my options a little more open-ended for the future.

Honestly, Aboriginal Studies changed my view on life and Australia forever. It is more than an HSC subject. I can no longer tell you the heating system used in the public baths in Herculaneum and Pompeii, but rest assured, I can talk for hours on the lack of Indigenous perspective in the education system, how I can see the crucial understanding many people lack and most importantly, how the subject should be compulsory, at least for one year in junior school where tie-dyeing an apron and making a barbecue fork are considered more valuable life skills.

Speech by Emma Stewart, Kiama High School, top HSC Aboriginal Studies student, 2008

Left to right: Cindy Berwick, President New South Wales AECG; Maquilla Brown, top Aboriginal student, HSC Aboriginal Studies, 2008; Hon. Linda Burney MP, Minister for Community Services; Emma Stewart, top student HSC Aboriginal Studies; Dr John Bennett, President, New South Wales Board of Studies. Photo: Kevin Lowe, Aboriginal Inspector, New South Wales Board of Studies.

work, as it also involves Indigenous perspectives across all curriculum areas. It is about teaching *with* Indigenous people in contrast to teaching *about* Indigenous people. It requires an ongoing school commitment to community consultation and involvement (see Chapter 10).

The subject is designed to focus on understanding today's society and addressing current social concerns. History is utilised as a vehicle to examine how today's society and concerns emerged, since it is not possible to comprehend the complexity of today's society without understanding how it was shaped by historical influences. History also provides a basis for empowering children to imagine and create preferred futures. That is, this subject area—like other social studies areas—empowers children to think about current issues, feel concerned about these issues, recognise Australian achievements and take social action to create a better society.

Some teachers still think the subject is of relevance only to Indigenous children and are reluctant to introduce Aboriginal and Torres Strait Islander Studies and perspectives into schools with predominantly non-Indigenous student populations. That is wrong. This subject is of critical interest to all Australian students because Indigenous Studies is about Australian people, Australian history and critical Australian social justice concerns of our time. In practical terms, this means that whether there are 30 Indigenous pupils in a class, or none, all Australian students have the right to be taught Indigenous Studies, as this is an essential part of Australian Studies.

The political context

Education must be seen in the political context of contemporary Australia. Because Australia was colonised on the basis of the legal fiction (white lie) of *terra nullius*—'land belonging to no one'—all the institutions of Australia, including education, have been European based. Australian education systems have been key tools of colonisation and agents for assimilation (see Chapter 4). Until the 'White Australia' policy was abolished in 1972, Australia was officially defined as white. Aboriginal and Torres Strait Islander people were not part of White Australia, and Indigenous Studies was not required in the school curriculum. This meant schooling was culturally inappropriate for Indigenous students. In addition, the curriculum did not educate other Australian students to appreciate either past or living Indigenous cultures (see Chapter 7). Misconceptions and stereotypes about Indigenous Australia have persisted, based on historical attitudes that were not even correct at the time (see Chapter 3). Many of my teacher education students have been shocked to discover that some of their attitudes were not really their own but based on past misinformation and prejudice, passed on and accepted without question. Many have also been outraged to discover that their own schooling, even in recent times, has continued to omit Indigenous Studies and contributed to the continuance of this problem.

Closing the gap

Closing the Gap is a great national challenge, but also a great national opportunity to achieve lasting change and ensure that future generations of Indigenous Australians have all the opportunities enjoyed by other Australians to live full, healthy lives and achieve their potential. (COAG, 2009, p. 33).

The Council of Australian Governments (COAG) in 2009 committed all Australian governments collectively to overcoming Indigenous disadvantage. Six key targets form COAG's Closing the Gap objective:

1. Close the life expectancy gap within a generation.
2. Halve the gap in mortality rates for Indigenous children under five within a decade.
3. Ensure access to early childhood education for all Indigenous four-year-olds in remote communities within five years.
4. Halve the gap in reading, writing and numeracy achievements for children within a decade.
5. Halve the gap for Indigenous students in Year 12 attainment or equivalent attainment rates by 2020.
6. Halve the gap in employment outcomes between Indigenous and non-Indigenous Australians within a decade. (COAG, 2009).

A regular public report on progress—the *Overcoming Indigenous Disadvantage:*

Table 1.1 Age specific death rates, 2005–2007[a, b]

	Males			Females		
	Indigenous[b]	Non-Indigenous	Race ratio[c]	Indigenous[b]	Non-Indigenous	Race ratio[c]
		NSW/QLD[d]				
0[e]	11.1	5.2	2.2	7.7	4.1	1.9
1–4	51.8	23.9	2.2	29.3	19.3	1.5
5–14	20.4	11.3	1.8	11.6	8.4	1.4
15–24	94.1	59.2	1.6	48.6	23.5	2.1
25–34	191.2	85.0	2.2	111.1	33.8	3.3
35–44	462.1	128.1	3.6	269.6	68.7	3.9
45–54	862.3	278.9	3.1	506.6	167.9	3.0
55–64	1675.8	674.8	2.5	1143.3	400.0	2.9
65 and over	5091.4	4217.6	1.2	4173.9	3681.2	1.1
		SA/WA/NT[f]				
0[e]	14.0	3.6	3.9	10.1	3.8	2.6
1–4	79.9	25.4	3.1	67.9	15.0	4.6
5–14	36.5	7.8	4.7	28.2	7.7	3.6
15–24	260.2	67.1	3.9	113.8	26.6	4.3
25–34	503.6	100.4	5.0	264.8	37.5	7.1
35–44	1080.6	139.3	7.8	578.8	73.3	7.9
45–54	1565.2	282.3	5.5	972.1	167.1	5.8
55–64	2682.7	660.9	4.1	2022.0	376.0	5.4
65 and over	6729.5	4190.4	1.6	5334.1	3625.9	1.5

a Deaths per 100,000 population, except age 0.
b Indigenous rates are based on registered deaths and are therefore likely to be underestimated.
c Indigenous rate divided by the non-Indigenous rate.
d Data for New South Wales and Queensland combined.
e Infant deaths per 1000 live births
f Data for South Australia, Western Australia and the Northern Territory combined.

Source: ABS (2008b) *Deaths Australia 2007*, Cat. no. 3302.0.

Key Indicators report—is published by the Productivity Commission to inform policies to address disadvantage. This report in 2009 shows how much remains to be done to close the gaps on key social indicators. As we all know, education is the key—it all starts in schools.

Life expectancy

Based on combined data for Australia for 2005–07, life expectancy for Indigenous males was 67 years versus 79 years for non-Indigenous males, and for Indigenous females, 73 years versus 83 years for non-Indigenous females (see Figure 1.2). This represents a gap in life expectancy of twelve years for males and ten years for females. Furthermore: 'Indigenous death rates were nine times as high as non-Indigenous rates for diabetes, six times as high for cervical cancer, four times as high for kidney diseases and three times as high for digestive diseases.' (Productivity Commission, 2009, p. 12).

Child mortality

Indigenous perinatal and infant (within one year) mortality rates are two to three times higher than the non-Indigenous rates. Indigenous child mortality rates for the 1–4 years and 0–4 years age groups for 1997–99 to 2005–07 were between two and four times the non-Indigenous rates (see Figures 1.2 and 1.3).

Academic achievement

Literacy and numeracy have been shown to have a significant impact on the completion of Year 12 and on employment prospects (ACER). It is disappointing that the Productivity Commission (2009) had to acknowledge that in general no significant changes showed up between 1999 (2001 for Year 7 students) and 2007 for Indigenous students' performance in Years 3, 5 and 7 against the national benchmarks for reading, writing and numeracy. Fewer Indigenous students than other Australian students at all year levels achieved the national benchmarks for:

- reading (e.g. for Year 3, 68.3 per cent of Indigenous students versus 93.5 per cent of non-Indigenous students);
- writing (e.g. for Year 3, 78.8 per cent of Indigenous students versus 96.4 per cent of non-Indigenous students); and
- numeracy (e.g. for Year 3, 78.6 per cent of Indigenous students versus 96 per cent of non-Indigenous students; see Table 1.1).

As remoteness increased, the gap between Indigenous students and all students increased. Similarly, as Indigenous students progressed through school, the proportion who achieved the national benchmarks decreased for reading (from Year 3 to Year 5) and numeracy (from Year 3 to Year 5, and Year 5 to Year 7). Disparity in performance is evident from Year 1 onwards, and is maintained for Indigenous students compared with non-Indigenous students until the mid-secondary school years (Zubrick et al., 2006). These statistics show we have a long way to go to achieve equity in academic outcomes.

Year 12 attainment

On 2006 figures, fewer than half of Indigenous 19-year-olds (36 per cent) compared with non-Indigenous 19-year-olds (74 per cent) complete Year 12 or its equivalent. Based on current trends, this gap is widening (COAG, 2009, p. 16; see Figure 1.4).

Figure 1.2 Life expectancy at birth, 2005–2007

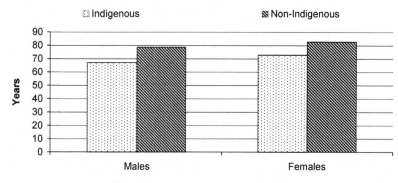

Source: ABS (2004); table 3A.1.1.

Figure 1.3 Perinatal mortality by Indigenous status, 2003–05[a]

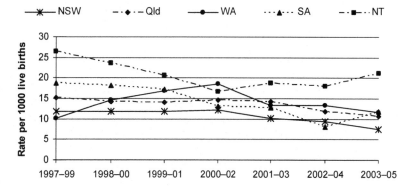

a The perinatal mortality rate is defined as the death of an infant within 28 days of birth (neonatal death) or of a fetus (unborn child) that weighs at least 400 grams or that is of a gestational age of at least 20 weeks.

Source: ABS *Deaths Australia* (unpublished); table 4A.2.3.

Other factors affecting academic performance

Absenteeism affects academic performance. In Western Australia, Zubrick et al. (2006) found that, on average, Indigenous students miss around 26 days of school per year compared with eight days for all students. They also found that the level of absenteeism increases for Indigenous students living in remote and very remote locations.

Emotional distress also affects academic performance. Zubrick et al. (2006) found that Aboriginal students at high risk of clinically significant emotional or behavioural difficulties were almost three times more likely to have low academic performance compared with Aboriginal students at low risk.

Table 1.2 Comparison of Indigenous and non-Indigenous students who achieved the national minimum standard by learning domain

Year	Reading Indigenous %	Reading Non-Indigenous %	Writing Indigenous %	Writing Non-Indigenous %	Numeracy Indigenous %	Numeracy Non-Indigenous %
3	68.3	93.5	78.8	96.4	78.6	96.0
5	63.4	92.6	69.7	93.9	69.2	94.0
7	71.9	95.4	67.9	93.2	78.6	96.4
9	70.7	94.2	59.7	88.8	72.5	94.8

> **'Things that work': Early literacy engagement**
>
> The MULTILIT pilot program improved the reading ability of Indigenous children at Coen State School in Cape York in Queensland. The program involved taking the 15 least proficient readers and giving them intensive, systematic instruction in phonics for 17 to 18 weeks by specialist teachers (IRUA, 2006; Devine, 2006). Since the Coen pilot, MULTILIT has been expanded as part of the broader Cape York Welfare Reform Trial, which began on 1 July 2008, to Hope Vale and Mossman Gorge (OATSIP, 2008), and was rolled out in Aurukun in Term 1, 2009 (Queensland Government unpublished). In addition, the MULTILIT program provided assistance to Indigenous students at the Redfern Tutorial Centre in NSW, under the auspices of the Exodus Foundation. Results for the second intake of MULTILIT students under the 2007 program at the Centre showed that after 18 weeks of instruction the cohort made average gains of: 13 months in reading accuracy; 7 months in comprehension; and 15 months in spelling.
>
> MINILIT, a modified version of MULTILIT, was offered to younger students in Years 1 and 2 at the Redfern Tutorial Centre. Results for the second intake of MINILIT students showed that, after 15 weeks of instruction, the cohort made average gains of: 8 months in single word recognition and 11 months in spelling.
>
> The National Accelerated Literacy Program (NALP) is an enhancement of the Scaffolding Literacy Program initially introduced at the Kulkarriya Community School. More than 70 schools across the NT participate in the NALP. There have been significant improvements in literacy outcomes for the students involved in the program. An evaluation by Charles Darwin University found that the 2007 average progress rate for NT Accelerated Literacy students was 1.18 reading year levels per year (on average one reading level per year is expected of students) (SSPR, 2008).
>
> The Finding Your Pathway into School and Beyond program was introduced at Port Dalrymple and South George Town Primary Schools in Tasmania in 2007. The aim of this program was to improve Aboriginal students' literacy. Computers and specialised software were bought, which enabled students to undertake self-paced learning. Home usage and loan of the computers was used as an incentive to encourage participation. There has been an increase in school attendance and a decrease in suspension rates. The project is assisting 55 Aboriginal students, and attendance rates have increased to 95 per cent.
>
> *Source:* Productivity Commission (2009, p. 34).

Moorditch Mob at Wesley

Moorditj, a Nyoongar (south-west Western Australia) word meaning excellent, strong, good, was adopted as the name for Indigenous education at Wesley College, Perth. Wesley had admitted Aboriginal boys on scholarship since the late 1950s, but in 2006 it began a bursary program for Aboriginal boys from regional and remote Western Australia. By 2009, the Moorditj Mob had grown to 20, and 32 Aboriginal boys had passed through the doors.

Moorditj Mob students generally arrive at Wesley with both positive and negative experiences from their communities. They have a strong sense of belonging to group and to place (country), of responsibility, identification with Indigenous culture, a strong commitment to family, values of sharing, resilience and fairness, respect for Elders and strategies to resist racism. They know about culture and what it means to be Indigenous. On the other hand, many of these boys have grown up in a vastly different world to most Wesley students. Over half of the current body of Indigenous students have experienced family breakdown, family in prison, family affected by drugs and alcohol, and domestic violence. These boys are usually the first in their communities to not only access private education, but to even attempt to complete their schooling.

Wesley's Moorditj Mob Program seeks to revive the Warrior spirit within these boys—an ancient way of being Men—through rekindling the spirit in each boy and returning the young warrior as a leader for his community. It aims to reawaken their sense of identity as young Indigenous men who are Moorditj: strong and proud to be Wesley Indigenous students. It gives them the opportunity to reconnect to ancestral knowledge and be able to pass on knowledge and skills—rekindling the lines of transmission in schools, often the places where the flame was snuffed out in the past.

Moorditj learning is based on traditional ways of learning. It is not about knowledge for the individual but for the group, the mob—learning together, performing together, and sharing skills and knowledge which belong to all. They learn language (Nyoongar as well as their own), ceremonies, didgeridoo, songs in language, painting and art, bush knowledge, lore and Dreaming, spirituality, and about other Indigenous groups, Aboriginal history and pathways for Aboriginal youth. They learn from Nyoongar men who come in to instruct, and who act as role-models and mentors to the students. Younger boys learn from older boys. Everyone has a leadership role. Other schools invite Moorditj Mob boys to perform and present Indigenous cultural lessons. Moorditj Mob dancers and didgeridoo players have performed in many places. Older boys teach didg to all Year 5 students.

Indigenous boys between the ages of 12 and 18 can be 'lost between worlds' and the rite of passage for some boys to become a man can involve car stealing, breaking and entering, or

Moorditj Mob Aboriginal dancers from Wesley College Perth performing at Notre Dame University in 2009. 'Moorditj' is Noongar for 'very strong, great', and the name 'Moorditj Mob' was adopted by Aboriginal boarders and day boys on scholarship at Wesley. Photo courtesy Lynn Webber, Indigenous Student Coordinator, Wesley College.

doing time in juvenile detention. Indigenous people are 3 per cent of Western Australia's population, but Indigenous youth incarceration rates at the two state detention centres have been 60 to 80 per cent for fifteen years, by far the highest in Australia.

At this fundamental stage of their lives, belonging to the Moorditj Mob offers boys a stable, pathway to manhood, a vision for a new way of being as Indigenous men. It allows them to re-learn the meaning of manhood by offering them strong Indigenous and non-Indigenous male leaders and mentors from within the school (teachers) and the broader community.

What also works for Aboriginal students at Wesley is having an Indigenous student support teacher, staff committed to their well-being and education, their own Moorditj room, an Indigenous tutoring program, Wesley's zero-tolerance of racism and its Indigenous Youth Leadership Program (which, in 2009, eleven of the 20 boys in Moorditj Mob were selected to participate in).

Wesley has forged bonds with Aboriginal organisations in the Pilbara and these now fund scholarships for boys to attend Wesley and more

Deadly VIBE *October 2009: Jessica Mauboy with her four Deadly awards. Jessica grew up in Darwin. She went from never putting up her hand in school to winning the* Road to Tamworth *country music competition, being the 2006 Australian Idol runner-up, winning APRA and ARIA awards and four Deadlys. She had a lead role in the film* Bran Nue Dae *and is taking the world by storm. Courtesy Vibe.*

'Things that work': Increasing secondary school participation and attainment

Deadly Vibe is a magazine for Indigenous students published by Vibe Australia (an Aboriginal media agency) with funding from the Australian Government. The magazine promotes positive self-image and healthy lifestyle messages through articles focusing on the achievements of Indigenous people in sport, music, the arts and education. The target audience for the magazine is schoolaged children (6 to 18 years old). The magazine has been evaluated three times since 2002, most recently in 2006 by the Cultural and Indigenous Research Centre Australia (CIRCA). A survey of young people and readers of the magazine showed that:

- *Deadly Vibe* was the most popular magazine/newspaper they read
- 83 per cent had read the magazine, with 23 per cent of respondents reading it regularly
- 75 per cent of readers of *Deadly Vibe* assessed it as 'deadly'
- 85 per cent agreed that *Deadly Vibe* magazine made them feel proud to be Indigenous
- 83 per cent agreed that the magazine taught them about being healthy.

The Cape York Institute's Higher Expectations Program (HEP) and St Joseph's Indigenous Fund are examples of non-government sponsorship of programs for students to board at private schools. The HEP provides Indigenous students living in the Cape York region with access to secondary education at Queensland's most academically successful boarding schools. The HEP provides both financial assistance and ongoing support from a program administrator and student support officer, who maintain regular contact with students, school staff, parents/guardians and home communities, and assist students and their families with transition and communication issues. The HEP has expanded from 6 scholarships in 2005, to 24 in 2006, 25 in 2007, 33 in 2008 and 38 from 15 communities enrolled in 2009. There are currently nine partner schools located in Brisbane, Rockhampton, Townsville, Charters Towers and Cairns. The Australian Government contributes funding [for 9 students in 2008 and 29 students in 2009] and funding from Macquarie Group Foundation has been approved for 2009–2011.

HEP's success is partly due to individual case management of students and extra activities to increase motivation, develop life skills and leadership. Though only a fraction of Cape York students will participate in the HEP, their success (completion of secondary school and enrolment in tertiary studies) will greatly influence Cape York educational statistics and provide Cape communities with a pool of talented and educated future leaders. In 2007, four students finished Year 12 and three of those students enrolled in university and, in 2008 two students graduated from Year 12 and enrolled in university.

The St Joseph's Indigenous Fund offers scholarships to Indigenous boys to attend St Joseph's College at Hunters Hill in Sydney. Started in 1998 with one Year 7 student from Walgett, the program has more than 40 Indigenous students whose fees are paid through assistance from the Australian Government, parents, the school and other donors. Six boys have already completed their Higher School Certificate.

Information on remote schooling in the NT has been included in previous reports. The focus has been on increasing access to secondary education for students in remote and very remote communities in the NT. Across the NT, the number of Indigenous students completing the Northern Territory Certificate of Education (NTCE) increased from 126 in 2007 to 157 in 2008. In 2008, 45 students achieved the NTCE in their home communities. The individual schools that are producing graduates are increasing in number and support structures include a dedicated NTCE implementation officer to work with remote schools that offer NTCE, and professional development opportunities for senior years teachers including a remote schools conference held annually.

Source: Productivity Commission (2009, p. 52).

scholarships are being negotiated. Wesley has also established links with Curtin University, promoting university pathways and helping with transition issues.

In 2009, Moorditj Mob, working with local Aboriginal artists transformed their *Wagyl* (Rainbow Serpent) painting into a mosaic in the Middle School atrium. The Cullacabardee (Nyoongar for meeting place) Indigenous Cultural Centre will cater for meetings, teaching culture, didg and dance, and parents' meetings. It will be a place for all classes to learn about Indigenous culture and history, for the school community to gain cultural awareness, for the Aboriginal community to gain skills, and for NAIDOC and other celebrations. There are plans to set up a relationship with a remote-area Aboriginal school and to present Aboriginal prizes on speech night: for most outstanding or most improved Aboriginal student and for working for reconciliation in the community.

Moorditj Mob is a liberating revolution for those who risk walking this road together. Both the oppressed and those labelled as oppressors discover the freedoms and sometimes the pain in taking risks, dreaming a common dream and discovering human wealth that can only truly be found in going beyond cross-cultural boundaries and deconstructing what has separated them and us. It takes great courage for a privileged school like Wesley to open its doors and share its resources with those who too many in our society still dismiss as drunks, thieves or violent misfits.

Lynn Webber, Indigenous Student Coordinator, Wesley College

Post-secondary attainment

In 2006, Indigenous people had significantly lower rates of post-secondary attainment to Certificate Level III or above compared with other Australians (see Figure 1.4). In 2006, Indigenous people aged 20–24 years attended university at about one-fifth the rate of other Australians (5 and 24 per cent, respectively) and attended Technical and Further Education (TAFE) at two-thirds the rate of other Australians (5 and 8 per cent, respectively).

Senior Moorditj Mob boys teach didgeridoo to Year 5 boys at Wesley. The college runs five-week dance, didgeridoo and cultural classes for 'the Mob', taught by Aboriginal teachers. Photo courtesy Lynn Webber, Indigenous Student Coordinator, Wesley College.

Figure 1.4 Attainment of Certificate III or above by age, 2001 and 2006

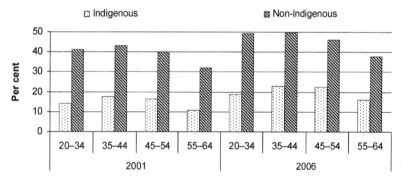

Source: Figure 4.7.5 *Overcoming Indigenous Disadvantage*, p. 223.

Employment

Between 2001 and 2006, the employment-to-population ratio increased for Indigenous people from 43 per cent to 48 per cent, and for non-Indigenous people from 68 per cent to 72 per cent. The gap in employment to population ratio for Indigenous people compared with non-Indigenous people is large (24 percentage points, see Figure 1.5). These statistics are worrisome

Figure 1.5 Rate of Indigenous and non-Indigenous employment to 2006

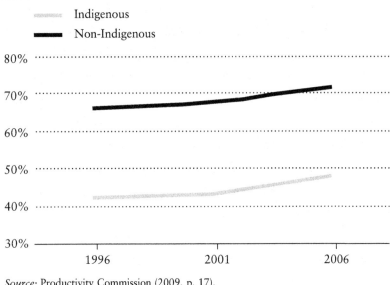

Source: Productivity Commission (2009, p. 17).

given that being employed leads to enhanced life opportunities and increased community capacity.

Child abuse and neglect

The rate of substantiated notifications for child abuse or neglect has increased for both Indigenous and other Australian children from 1999–2000 to 2007–08 (see Figure 1.6). Over this period, the rate for Indigenous children has more than doubled from sixteen to 35 per 1000 children compared with five to six per 1000 non-Indigenous children: 'Indigenous children were more than six times as likely as non-Indigenous children to be the subject of a substantiation of abuse or neglect in 2007–08 . . . 41 out of every 1000 Indigenous children were on care and protection orders, compared to 5 per 1000 non-Indigenous children at 30 June 2008.' (Productivity Commission, 2009, p. 23)

Statistics of shame

I have only highlighted some of the statistics that demonstrate the gap in relation to basic human rights for Indigenous Australians compared with other Australians. There are so many more.

Figure 1.6 Children aged 0–16 years who were the subject of substantiations

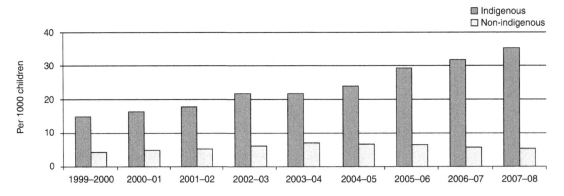

Source: Figure 4.10.1 Productivity Commission, p. 26.

Things that work
- **Follow the Dream**, run by the Western Australia Department of Education and Training, targets high achieving Aboriginal students enrolled in Years 6 to 12, and aims to increase the number of Aboriginal students completing Year 12 and gaining university entrance.
- The **Will and a Way** program (New South Wales) addresses barriers that prevent 'at risk' students from completing Year 12 and gaining entry to university. The program provides individualised support to 'at-risk' Indigenous and non-Indigenous youth in Years 10 to 12.

Source: Productivity Commission (2009, p. 43).

> **Things that work**
> - The **Workstart Program** is an intensive, self-paced, thirteen-week pre-employment program for Indigenous trainees in the Pilbara (Western Australia). It includes literacy, drivers' licence, alcohol and drug training, fitness for work, safety training, self-development and personal financial management.
> - **Rio Tinto Indigenous employment programs** have helped increase the proportion of Indigenous employees at Rio Tinto from 0.5 per cent to 8 per cent. Rio Tinto has included education and training as part of employment, helping Indigenous employees overcome educational barriers. Rio Tinto is also involved in the Australian government's National Indigenous Cadetship Project.
> - The **Learning to Earning** program (Western Australia) is a twelve-week pre-vocational course that includes structured workplace experience with industry as part of accredited Certificate I training in engineering and plant processing.
> - The **Aboriginal Employment Strategy**, established in Moree in 1997, now provides tailored employment services to unemployed Indigenous Australians in eleven sites in New South Wales, the Northern Territory, Western Australia and Queensland, utilising the Australian government's Structured Training and Employment Projects program.
> - The **Accor Asia Pacific Corporate Leaders for Indigenous Employment Project** encourages private-sector companies to generate job opportunities using elements of the Australian government's Indigenous Employment Program.
> - The **ACT Indigenous Traineeship Program** provides opportunities for Indigenous youth to commence twelve-month traineeships, with a view to permanent full-time employment with Australian Capital Territory government agencies on completion.
> - The **VicRoads Indigenous Traineeship Program** operates in fourteen rural and metropolitan Customer Service Centre locations across Victoria where there is a local Indigenous community.
> - **Warakurna Artists** in remote Western Australia has 150 artists on its registry and provides significant benefits to the community, with approximately $500 000 turnover per year and a range of social welfare outcomes.
>
> *Source:* Productivity Commission (2009, p. 63).

What is clear is that, across all socio-economic indicators in one of the richest nations on earth, Indigenous Australians remain the most disadvantaged Australians. In the land of the 'fair go for all', closing these gaps is one of our greatest challenges. I believe that what can make the biggest difference is the quality of our teachers, who quietly close the classroom door, develop genuine relationships with Indigenous students, focus on culturally appropriate education, and ensure Indigenous students achieve the same achievement and psycho-social educational outcomes (e.g. academic self-concept, motivation and engagement) as their non-Indigenous peers. It seems that the Productivity Commission (2009) agrees, in that it asserts: 'The quality of teaching is a key determinant of student outcomes.' (2009, p. 38).

> **Things that work**
> - **Rekindling Indigenous Family Relationships in the Riverland**, an early intervention project in South Australia, is assisting the Aboriginal community to resolve family violence and child abuse issues.
> - The **Family and Community Healing Program** (Adelaide, South Australia) aims to equip Aboriginal women, men and youth with the skills for effective communication and conflict-resolution.
> - The **Kalparrin Spirited Men's Project** (South Australia), a program for male perpetrators, aims to encourage positive parenting and educate Indigenous men about the detrimental effects of family violence.
>
> *Source:* Productivity Commission, (2009, p. 27).

Compounding disadvantage

The New South Wales Legislative Council report *Overcoming Disadvantage* was told many programs targeting disadvantage expected Aboriginal people to adhere to mainstream values. Dr Gaynor Macdonald, Senior Lecturer in Anthropology at Sydney University, said such programs were:

> not only assimilationist, they can be demeaning or disrespectful of Aboriginal difference. This compounds Aboriginal disadvantage because it renders them 'in the wrong', as not complying or succeeding, as second-rate citizens.

Jack Beetson told the committee:

> It is putting it mildly to say that language can be a barrier. It can be the most disempowering and disenfranchising tool available to some people when they come into communities.

Aboriginal people, he said, tend to cop the blame for communication problems—compounding disadvantage again—when really the fault is with the 'communicators'.

Dr Bob Boughton, Adult and Workplace Education, University of New England, was told time and again of 'consultations' where bureaucrats would simply ask someone else if they didn't get the answer they wanted. The Aboriginal Justice Advisory Council spoke of 'head-office mentality'—wanting to run everything—and one-size-fits-all—'whenever you try to work with Aboriginal people, you have to stop using a broad approach'.

Witness after witness, especially Elders, spoke with feeling of their frustration at endless meetings with every agency involved in Indigenous affairs or services, with no confidence that anything they said made any difference. As AECG President Cindy Berwick told the committee:

> [T]he perception in the community is we tell you all our problems, we often tell you what we need and all it does is go into a little booklet somewhere and nothing gets done about it. So I think the perception of overconsultation, when I hear people say that, is not that we are being asked too much about these things, it is the fact

---

Things that work

- The **Dare to Lead** program challenges school principals to take the lead to foster Indigenous education programs in schools throughout Australia. Over 5000 schools have signed up. In 2005, the Bendigo Senior Secondary College in Victoria was one of six national winners of the Excellence in Leadership in Indigenous Education awards established under the program.
- The **Broulee Public School Dhurga Djamanji** language program in New South Wales has successfully integrated Aboriginal language into everyday classroom activities and has received strong support from the school and local communities.
- **Specialist language training** to teach Aboriginal languages in New South Wales public schools is being provided by the New South Wales Department of Education and Training's Aboriginal Education and Training Directorate, in collaboration with the University of Sydney's Koori Centre.
- A **Stage 4 Aboriginal language program** in place in ten New South Wales schools means that the local Indigenous language can be studied to meet the mandatory language requirement for the School Certificate.
- The **Teacher Education Scholarship Program** ('Join Our Mob', New South Wales) encourages and supports Aboriginal people to become secondary or primary teachers.
- The **Connecting with Country, Culture and Community** program (Tasmania) engages Indigenous students with their culture through meaningful and relevant cultural learning experiences as part of their academic schooling.
- The Tasmanian **Aboriginal Sharers of Knowledge (ASK)** program provides cross-cultural training for teaching and education staff and equips teachers and students with awareness and understanding of Tasmanian Aboriginal peoples and their cultures.

Source: Productivity Commission (2009, p. 40).

that we are asked all the time. We tell you all the time but nothing gets done.

A woman in Griffith told a researcher, 'You give us the pilot but where is the plane?'

Equity in education

A national policy

On 5 December 2008, state, territory and Commonwealth Ministers for Education met as the Ministerial Council on Education, Employment, Training, and Youth Affairs (MCEETYA) and released the Melbourne Declaration on Educational Goals for Young Australians (MCEETYA, 2008). The Declaration sets the direction for Australian schooling for the next decade. The goals were developed by Education Ministers in collaboration with the Catholic and independent school sectors, following public consultation.

The opening of the declaration states: 'As a nation Australia values the central role of education in building a democratic, equitable and just society—a society that is prosperous, cohesive and culturally diverse, and that values Australia's Indigenous cultures as a key part of the nation's history, present and future.' (MCEETYA, 2008, p. 4) The declaration also acknowledges that: 'Educational outcomes for Indigenous children and young people are substantially behind those of other students in key areas of enrolment, attendance, participation, literacy, numeracy, retention and completion.' (2008, p. 15) Furthermore, the declaration emphasises that: 'Australia has failed to improve educational outcomes for many Indigenous Australians and addressing this issue must be a key priority over the next decade.' (2008, p. 5).

The Melbourne Declaration (MCEETYA, 2008) commits all Australian governments to taking actions that include 'closing the gap' for young Indigenous Australians; developing stronger partnerships with Indigenous communities based on cross-cultural respect (see also Chapter 10); improving educational outcomes for Indigenous youth; and providing all Australian students with the opportunity to access Indigenous content (2008, pp. 14–15). Fundamental to the successful achievement of these actions is quality education that results in Indigenous students achieving educational outcomes that are commensurate with those of their non-Indigenous peers.

> **A People's Survival**
> That education is seen to be entirely central to the reconciliation agenda is entirely justified. Aboriginal disadvantage in employment, housing and, ultimately, life expectancy can be removed only if education is fixed up. Patently, it is the key to inclusion in the real economy.
> —Noel Pearson (2009, p. 1)

Education is the key

Education is the key to equity in socio-economic outcomes for Indigenous Australians. Improving the quality of teaching for Indigenous students in our schools is critical to address the appalling literacy, numeracy and other educational outcomes of so many Indigenous students. Education is also fundamental to enabling full potential, enhancing community capacity and adding materially to national well-being. Jackie Huggins (2009), the former Co-Chair of Reconciliation Australia, emphasises that education:

> provides the tools and self esteem to triumph over disadvantage in other areas of people's lives—in employment, for instance, and in health ... Education is the key to reconciliation because it's hard to achieve any measure of equity or self worth, any sense of belonging in the real economy, without education. (Huggins, 2009)

Huggins also advocates that teachers need to promote reconciliation and suggests:

> Those teachers who have no Indigenous pupils enrolled in their schools can commit to ensuring that students develop an informed understanding of Australia's Indigenous peoples and their cultures, and of the importance of reconciliation. They can promote face-to-face contact between young people from different backgrounds, **probably the best stimulus for reconciliation**. (Huggins 2009)

Principals Australia (formerly the Australian Principals Association's Professional Development Council) also realises that education is the key. Its 'Dare to Lead' project (Dare to Lead, 2005) calls on principals to commit to a 10 per cent improvement in primary Indigenous students' literacy levels and a 10 per cent improvement in Year 12 retention rates for Indigenous students. Huggins (2009) notes that '"Dare to Lead" resources recognise that improving outcomes for Indigenous students is not rocket science. Getting them to attend school is already a big step in the right direction.'

> **Gumala Mirnuwarni Project**
>
> Gumala Mirnuwarni is an education project in the Pilbara in Western Australia, with another six replica models currently being trialled around the state. It grew out of the wish of Hammersley Iron to offer skilled work opportunities to Aboriginal people.
>
> Developed in partnership with the Graham (Polly) Farmer Foundation, a small charitable body, Gumala came about by bringing all relevant stakeholders to the table—everyone who might share an interest in seeing the local children succeed. They included parents, government and school authorities, three resource companies who wanted to engage with the Aboriginal community and the Polly Farmer Foundation.
>
> In the first five years, seven students have matriculated and gone on to university, fifteen have entered traineeships and not one of the 70 participants has been in trouble with the police. Attendance figures for the Aboriginal students are now comparable with those of the rest of the school community.
>
> The thinking behind Gumala involves understanding and taking into account where students come from and the other factors in their lives that are affecting their schooling. This might involve home support, access to homework centres, help when problems emerge, teacher belief and a clear explanation of the rewards on offer through educational success.
>
> *Source:* Huggins (2009).

> **Educating Indigenous people is an obvious area of failure**
>
> Australian school education is generally very good. It is humane, it has substance, and it is conducted by people who, in the main, believe that their work is full of purpose. Nevertheless, the education of young Indigenous people is the most obvious area of failure, and for many reasons—for the possible futures of those kids, for reasons of professional responsibility, and not least for the quality of our nation—that must be changed. That process begins at the dawning of cross-cultural awareness.
>
>
>
> **David McRae** *is an education consultant, researcher, writer and one of the founders of the national* What Works *and* Dare to Lead *programs.*

David McRae, educational researcher and writer, was a driving force behind the development and establishment of Dare to Lead and continues to support the project through his role with sister project What Works: The Works Program.

Teaching the teachers

Years of government reports stressed the need for teachers to be instructed in teaching Indigenous Australian Studies and to be empowered with the pedagogical knowledge and skills to do so. For example, in 1975 the Schools Commission's Aboriginal Consultative Group recommended to the Commonwealth that 'all teacher trainees in Australia should study courses relating to Aboriginal society' (1975, p. 26). In 1979, the Australian Education Council endorsed the principle that there should be promotion of Aboriginal and Torres Strait Islander Studies as core units of all pre-service and in-service education programs. In 1985, the House of Representatives Standing Committee on Aboriginal Affairs found a strong case for 'including Aboriginal Studies at the tertiary level and, in particular, in teacher training courses' (*Aboriginal Education* 13.15). In 1986, the National Aboriginal Education Committee (NAEC) stressed the need for 'at least one compulsory component of Aboriginal Studies/Aboriginal Education in every pre-service teacher education course, and in general in all inservice courses' (1986, p. 28). In 1992, the Schools Council of the National Board of Employment, Education, and Training recommended that 'all teachers, through their initial training, should experience a compulsory component of Aboriginal Studies and education' (NBEET, 1992, p. 31). In 1998, the Australian Council of Deans of Education developed 'National Standards and Guidelines for Initial Teacher Education'. Its very first guideline on curriculum content was that: 'Graduates should have developed the knowledge, understandings, capabilities and dispositions to effectively teach Indigenous students, and to teach all students about Indigenous issues.' (Australian Council of Deans of Education 1998, p. 11).

However, despite these urgings, and the dire situation faced by Indigenous people, many teacher education institutions have still not responded to the call to introduce core Indigenous Australian Studies into the teacher education curriculum to assist teachers to understand and teach. It is time for all our teacher education institutions to be proactive in curriculum reform. Teachers cannot be expected to teach Indigenous Studies and Indigenous students effectively without prior teacher education courses in this vital field. Teacher education is a critical key to addressing Indigenous disadvantage and enhancing life opportunities for Indigenous Australians.

Some rationales for teaching Indigenous Studies

Given all these recommendations, it would be easy to assume that, as teachers are now being encouraged to teach Aboriginal Studies, our problems are over. This is far from the case, as many teachers still do not even understand why they should teach this content. As Cindy Berwick, President of the New South Wales AECG points out:

> A policy is just words on paper. It is how these words are translated into action and practices that make the difference ... let's work together to effectively implement this policy ... so that education continues to not just be a dream to Aboriginal people but a reality. (Berwick, 2008, p. 3)

Given that Indigenous Australian Studies is a relatively recent addition to Australian curricula, it is important for our profession to develop and promote rationales for teaching this content. It is equally important that each of us develops our own personal teaching philosophy so that we can convey to parents and children our professional views on the importance of this aspect of the curriculum.

I have met student teachers and teachers who initially were most reluctant to teach Indigenous Studies—some because their own educational experiences did not include the subject and therefore they felt ill-equipped to convey key knowledge and understandings. Others with some knowledge of the subject-matter have been reluctant to implement what they do know for fear they may make a mistake. Still other teachers hold racist views—usually based on

Leading the way

In New South Wales, the inquiry of the Legislative Council's Standing Committee on Social Issues, Overcoming Indigenous Disadvantage in New South Wales, was told by the Director-General of Education and Training, Michael Coutts-Trotter, that competence in Aboriginal Studies is now a mandatory component of programs for beginning teachers, is required by the Institute of Teachers' Policy for Approval of Initial Education Programs and is part of interviews for applicants for teaching positions. The committee recommended:

Recommendation 17

That the NSW Department of Education and Training liaise with representatives of the Aboriginal Education Consultative Group and teacher education institutions in NSW to ensure that:
- there are sufficient teachers, both Indigenous and non-Indigenous, qualified to teach those compulsory elements of the primary and secondary schools' curricula that relate to Aboriginal history and culture;
- extensive and intensive inservice training is given to existing teachers so that they meet the standards required to effectively understand and teach Aboriginal culture and history.

Recommendation 18

That comparative studies of Australian history and culture be included as a mandatory core subject within all NSW educational institutions and that sufficient teachers are trained to ensure that it is taught effectively.

ignorance—and strongly resist understanding the rationale for teaching the subject area. Others have initially held misconceptions but after learning more have come to appreciate the need to challenge their knowledge base and their attitudes. Many of the latter have become some of the best Indigenous Studies teachers I have worked with.

No syllabus is 'teacher-proof'. Ultimately, each teacher will develop their own rationale as to why they will, or even will not, teach Indigenous Studies. Some of the strong teachers of this subject area that I have met started developing their teaching skills based on the firmly held belief that this was a critical component of the curriculum. This was what led them to develop themselves as outstanding teachers in the field. There are a wealth of important reasons why we as teachers should teach Indigenous Studies.

Cindy Berwick (2009) wrote about the proposed national curriculum:

> In NSW we have a framework for Aboriginal consultation on the syllabus in place already. Nationally we don't have that.

We've fought hard here in NSW to have the word 'invasion' included in the syllabus. We need to ensure a focus on Indigenous history remains in the national curriculum.

The *Overcoming Indigenous Disadvantage* report tabled in NSW Parliament in January 2008 said a rejection of *terra nullius* and recognition of prior occupation of Australia was crucial to tackling disadvantage—that's pretty important.

These things must be taught properly if we are to move forward as a society and achieve reconciliation.

The national curriculum must be underlined by values of social justice and equity.

Contributing to social justice

Teaching Indigenous Studies is critical to achieving social justice. Many people embark on a teaching career because they are committed to social justice and to creating a better nation. That is, they make a difference to the world in which we live by helping the next generation to shape today's society and create preferred futures. They recognise that education can be a panacea for many of today's social concerns. For such teachers, our appalling record as a nation in relation to Indigenous affairs, endemic racism and the need for social justice for Indigenous Australians is ample rationale for teaching Indigenous Studies.

Teaching the truth

Linda Burney (quoted in Craven, 1996) says there is an easy answer to the question, 'Why teach Indigenous Australian Studies?', and that is to teach the truth about Australia's history:

> To teach all children, both Aboriginal and non-Aboriginal, about the real history of this country and the role that everyone has had to play in that history is incredibly important so that we don't continue to ... pursue the myth that somehow or other Australia started in 1770.

Indigenous Studies is Australian Studies

Nigel Parbury (quoted in Craven, 1996) claims it is essential to teach Aboriginal Studies in our schools for one simple, fundamental reason: and that is because this is Australia. Australia has always been Aboriginal land. The racist lies of *terra nullius* and White Australia have to be countered by teaching Aboriginal Studies in schools. Teaching Aboriginal Studies is the only way all students can learn the real nature and the real history of this country.

It benefits all children

> Appropriate education will assist in providing young, active, developing minds, Aboriginal and non-Aboriginal, with a basis from which can grow cultural awareness, understanding and respect. (New South Wales AECG pamphlet)

Teaching Indigenous Studies benefits both non-Indigenous and Indigenous students. Every Australian child has the right to learn about this country's rich cultural heritage and be challenged by the social issues facing all Australians today. Every Australian child also has the right to be empowered to act on social issues in order to create a better society.

Teaching students Indigenous Studies will enhance their appreciation of Aboriginal and Torres Strait Islander cultures and history. Understanding can foster cultural respect, which is an essential value for all Australians, given the multicultural nature of Australian society today. Cultural respect can contribute to the eradication of racism in Australian society and lead to a more socially just society for all Australians.

Australia needs informed citizens. Indigenous Studies can help children to understand the truth about Australia's history and how our history still affects Indigenous Australians. It is not a 'guilt trip'; rather, it is about comprehending the forces that have shaped Australian society. The subject allows children a knowledge base from which to comprehend the historical causes of Indigenous issues in this country and to appreciate and contribute to recent initiatives on these issues. Understanding the full complexity of social issues in terms of their historical causes and consequences for Australians today enables students to plan and implement strategies for a better future for all Australians.

Learning about Indigenous Studies allows Australian students to acknowledge their rich cultural heritage. It helps children to recognise the achievements of Indigenous Australians, both in the past and today, promoting respect and understanding in the wider community. The end result can be a more tolerant and richer Australian society.

Benefits to Indigenous children

Teaching Indigenous Studies benefits Indigenous children. For example, some years ago I was assigned to teach a Year 3 class in Western Sydney. In my class was an Aboriginal child whom various executive staff in the school saw as a difficult pupil—always misbehaving in class and the playground. As a partial intervention to deal with his behaviour, I implemented a unit of work on Indigenous Studies in consultation with the local Indigenous community.

Once the unit had begun, the child offered to teach the class how to throw a boomerang. He told me that he was very good at this but some of the children in the class did not think that he could do it because he was not brought up in the bush. He was able to contribute to the unit by inviting some members of the local Aboriginal community to explain aspects of his culture to the class. This improved his self-concept. He became quite popular with his peers over the school year and increased his persistence on academic tasks. This behaviour continued throughout his primary school years. Supporting Aboriginality in the classroom and the school can promote Aboriginal students' sense of identity and pride in their Aboriginality and lead to long-term benefits.

This child's non-Indigenous peers developed respect for both the Indigenous student and his culture. They learnt that it could not be assumed that Indigenous children today could not do some of the things their ancestors could and that Indigenous children, like other Australian children, had different skills depending on their learning environment. The class also acknowledged that stereotyping of Indigenous children was not appropriate, given that some children such as their classmate could throw a boomerang but other Indigenous children might not be able to do this simply because, like most other Australian children, they had not had the opportunity to learn.

> Australia's past Indigenous history can be avoided no longer. Both Indigenous and non-Indigenous people today have inherited that history. However, it is not up to the present generation of Australians to feel guilty or ashamed of that history, but more importantly, develop an understanding of, and work to positively address, the many legacies still evident today, which reflect the past treatments of Australia's Indigenous peoples. If we, the present generations of Australians, can do this, then we will make this country a great country, not because we avoided the past, but we confronted it and overcame it. Australia is far better than it once was for its Indigenous peoples, but not as good as it might become.
> —James Wilson-Miller

> Rejecting and belittling Aboriginal culture and antiquity has deprived Australians of a rich source of meaning in defining what it is to be an Australian spiritually and culturally. Most Australians are indeed poorer for being aliens to an indigenous culture uniquely shaped by this continent and for being ignorant of the greater part of Australia's . . . history.
> —Robert Tickner (1993)

2007 Young Australian of the Year, Tania Major, with former prime minister John Howard. Courtesy National Australia Day Council.

> I bloody love this country and the only way we're ever going to heal in this country is to face up to reality. Face up to the fact that there was a Stolen Generation . . . people weren't paid right. My mother was denied an education cos she was black. And I want people to realise that so they understand how to interact with Indigenous people. Cos not many people know how to interact with Indigenous people. And I really want that for the future generation and for my kids to sit in a classroom and do talk about the worries and do talk about the massacres, because we've got to heal, we've got to get over this. We've got to say, 'Hey it's happened, why are we denying it?' And that's what I want.
> —*Enough Rope*, ABC TV, 27 August 2007

Tania Major, a Kokoberra woman from Kowanyama, western Cape York, was the first from her community to complete Year 12, at boarding school in Brisbane. She graduated in criminology and was the youngest ever ATSIC regional councillor at 21. She was Queensland's Young Australian of the Year for 2006, then national Young Australian of the Year 2007, won Young Leader of the Year at the 2007 Deadly Awards, plus the Political-Legal-Government-Affairs section of Outstanding Young Persons of the World held in India in 2007. After four years working with Noel Pearson at the Cape York Institute, she now works in consultancy and advocacy, has set up a youth foundation and has completed her Masters in Public Policy. She is now national spokesperson for Generation One.

'Who was here first?' *Australia opens for business as usual: Aboriginal people down the back, out-of-sight-out-of-mind, as shown by the shocked looks of the 'big boys'. Aboriginal Studies is about changing that mindset to give Aboriginal issues their rightful space at the heart of Australia. Courtesy Bruce Petty.*

Teaching Indigenous Studies is also essential to counteract the generational effects of our history on today's Indigenous children. Critical issues in Indigenous education are the participation of Indigenous people in education to achieve the same outcomes for Indigenous students as for their non-Indigenous peers. Statistics show that significant proportions of Indigenous Australians do not have proper access to education or do not participate in available education. The development of culturally relevant curricula in schools is critical. Indigenous children should experience an education that is relevant to their needs. They have the right to be taught how Australia's history has affected Indigenous people. Schools should be perceived as places where Indigenous culture is respected and celebrated.

Aboriginal and Torres Strait Islander Studies and perspectives are important areas that historically have been ignored or treated in a superficial manner. Teachers need to understand the critical need for teaching in this area in order to develop a commitment. Developing effective Indigenous Studies activities can: build Indigenous students' self-concepts and promote their identity; ensure that all Australian students are provided with an education that includes all of Australian history; assist all Australians to imagine social justice; contribute to the process of reconciliation between Indigenous and other Australians; end the structural prejudice fostered by the omission of Aboriginal Studies and Torres Strait Islander Studies; and demonstrate a commitment to a better future by initiating curriculum reform.

In the future, I hope not to hear teachers saying: 'I don't teach Indigenous Studies because we don't have any Indigenous children in our school'—clearly Indigenous Studies is for all Australians—or 'I did Indigenous Studies last term'—Indigenous Studies needs to permeate Key Learning Areas. The new generation of teachers educated in Indigenous Studies will be able to tell their colleagues why teaching

Indigenous Studies to all children is a national priority and be professionally committed to this goal. I also hope to see more and more teachers choosing to join the growing movement of Australian teachers committed to closing the gap for Indigenous students and leading the way. The future of our nation rests on the quality of our teachers, and their willingness and ability to make a real difference.

An Appeal

Statesmen, who make the nation's laws,
Will power to force unfriendly doors,
Give leadership in this our cause
That leaders owe.

Writers, who have the nation's ear,
Your pen a sword opponents fear,
Speak of our evils loud and clear,
That all may know.

Unions who serve democracy,
Guardians of social liberty,
Warm to the justice of our plea,
And strike your blow.

Churches, who preach the Nazarene,
Be on our side and intervene,
Show us what Christian love can mean
Who need it so.

The Press most powerful of all,
On you the underprivileged call:
Right us a wrong and break the thrall
That keeps us low.

All white well-wishers, in the end
On you our chiefest hopes depend;
Public opinion's our best friend
To beat the foe.

—Oodgeroo Noonuccal (2008, p. 3)

Living cultures

Uncle Charles Moran, Uncle Norm Newlin, Terry Mason and Rhoda Roberts

Dancer from Djilpin Arts at the 2009 Festival of the Dreaming, Woodford, Queensland, showing the mystery and spirituality of Aboriginal dance which has wowed audiences all over the world. Djilpin Arts, based in Beswick in the Northern Territory, presents the 'Walking With Spirits' festival with the Australian Shakespeare Company. Courtesy Festival of the Dreaming.

Bangarra

Bangarra—dance like the fire
flickering in the night
You weave your spell,
the audience is mesmerised
by an inner feeling
that's alien to them.
Your dance reaches—touches
and embraces their souls.
They are stunned
as you tantalise—hypnotise,
with a spirituality
born of our Mother,
our Spirit Creators,
living on and on
infinitely to you.
Bangarra—you've danced
your way to freedom,
broken the chains of oppression,
sung and chanted in time
until you've unlocked the prison
whiteman's imposed on our minds.
Let your flame leap higher
fill us all with warmth.
Show the world our beauty,
our peace and serenity.
Our Ancestors from the Dreaming
are smiling in your glow.
They know, they told me.
You've embodied our truth
to care, share and teach.
Dance Bangarra dance,
dance with cultural pride.
Your flame burns eternally,
as you glow into the night.

—Burraga Gutya, in Canning (1990, p. 51)

Who are Australia's Indigenous peoples?

The standard definition of Aboriginal and Torres Strait Islander people is that developed by the Commonwealth government:

> An Aboriginal or Torres Strait Islander person is a person of Aboriginal or Torres Strait Islander descent who identifies with and is accepted by the Aboriginal or Torres Strait Islander community in which they live or have lived. (Dept. of Aboriginal Affairs, 1981)

There are some problems with this definition. Some Indigenous people regard the term 'descent' as offensive. It has been suggested that a more culturally appropriate definition could include the spirituality of Aboriginal identity. The definition can also be seen as failing to address the issue of those Aboriginal people whose identity has been taken from them by assimilation and child-removal policies. When Australia was defined as white (until 1972), Aboriginal people were excluded from society and all its benefits, and were actively discriminated against. Assimilation policies increased the pressure to conform to White Australia. So many Aboriginal people learnt not to identify; the way to 'get on' was to 'pass as white'. Many Elders decided not to pass on languages and traditions. Children were taken away to be 'brought up white' and many never found their families again. Related issues include: Do Aboriginal or Torres Strait Islander people have to be accepted by the 'community' to be Aboriginal? And who is 'the community'?

The government definition, despite the issues raised above, does have some strengths. It requires descent and that gives recognition of connection to the land to which we belong. Identifying is important in declaring the sharing of a set of values recognised by the individual and the community. These are the lived and experienced cultural expressions that are understood and shared by the community. During the last decade, the definition of culture has been challenged by many from outside the Indigenous community. This encompasses what it is to be Aboriginal and how culture should be practised. At the same time, a continuous push toward assimilation has seen the withdrawal

Identity

Aboriginal identity is layered; it's colour blind; it's about our relationships to country, our ancient moieties and kinship systems. With the arrival of the whites to the east coast, there was mixing of the races; this has led to many Australians who are members of first nations looking very different to, say, our brothers and sisters in the north.

In the past, offensive terminology was used to describe the amount of Aboriginal blood in a person, and still today the government defines who is a member of the first nations of this country with its three-part definition of Aboriginal identity.

However, this definition has omitted the integral component of Aboriginality: the spiritual connection to land, our ancient ancestral beings, rituals and belief systems of our moieties, and stories. Often oral stories are regarded as myths; labelling them as such diminishes their worth in a cultural and social system that has been practised and will be practised continuously for thousands of years. Aboriginal spirituality is our religion, but has never been recognised as a religion.

Spirituality empowers the believer to continue ancient annual song cycles, and environmental maintenance of sacred country through varying rituals, traditions, and knowledge.

But consider this: Australia's east coast Aboriginal nations began intercultural and mixed marriages with the arrival of the First Fleet. Arnhem Land and northern communities for centuries developed exchange, trade and intermarriage with, for example, the Macassan from Sulawesi. The Burrawanga family live at Bawaka. Their traditional language includes many Macassan words; their graves and ritual are similar. Their great-great-grandmother as a young woman was taken to Sulawesi where she married. While the government banned trading in the twentieth century, the moiety, culture exchange and relationships through kinship continue today, with many Yolngu proud of their Macassan heritage. However, there are few in Australia who would quantify Arnhem Land Aboriginal blood simply because they intermarried with another dark race rather than a white one.

Aboriginality is not about blood quantums; it's about kinship, country and traditional obligations that have been carried through maternal or paternal bloodlines. Your grandmother's country is your country. It's family and you have a place in that community. It is not about the colour of your skin.

But identifying as an Aboriginal does require an integrity of the individual and a knowledge that those who do identify have a moral, cultural responsibility, and a spirituality that encompasses knowledge of country and community history. Today there are layers to identity for those who have grown up in community and/or have returned having spent time on country and understanding their connection. There are also many Australians who more recently are discovering an Aboriginal bloodline in their family histories but have not been associated with their Aboriginality.

It is something about which we will all be proud in years to come, but the question I pose is: Is it ethical to identify without having lived and or obtained connection to country and nationhood of your family's clan and language groups? Can one become Aboriginal overnight?

—Rhoda Roberts

of self-determination in the Northern Territory and to a lesser degree in North Queensland. Funding for communities in the rest of Australia has been diverted to 'traditional' areas. Treaties, sovereignty, self-determination and successful initiatives such as the recognition of traditional lore in circle sentencing programs and many other expressions of culture existing in a modern situation have been 'sidelined' rather than celebrated. In the twenty-first century, Australia stands on the threshold of an opportunity to embrace the robustness, the connectedness and the spirituality of the oldest living culture in a modern world.

A living culture

Aboriginal people have changed with the passing of time; policies in the past have imposed lifestyles and social outcomes that have had a major impact on the way we live and express our culture. We cannot go hunting through the bush; we are not allowed to fish freely; and our bush food is being wiped out by clearing of land. For generations, Aboriginal pride has been challenged. Many people think we have no culture, no language, no land—so what have we got to look forward to in life? They think that because the land is our mother, and we have lost our land, we are lost. Even some Aboriginal people think things like that because living with racism and inappropriate education means they have grown up learning to despair. But those people do not understand that Aboriginal culture is a living culture. Now we have to rebuild.

Blacktracks

The days of old they seem so good my land was full of mulga wood
Boomerangs and spears my life was easy
Song and dance it all made sense no land was owned by cash or fence
The people then their hearts was not so greedy

City lights they get me down seeing fences all around
Near makes me feel like crying
The land I love and know so much I only look but I can't touch
Feels like a part of me is dying

But now as I drift and stray and if I seem to lose my way
I'll always have that life deep down inside me
And as I get to live my days and fate sees me in different ways
I won't forget my blacktracks left behind me

With a different life enforced on us they thought our lives were out of touch
Clear the land and show them how to use it
With sugar tea and rationings they'll teach us all the white mans things
But through it all the black man he survived it

Our kids today they'll grow as one black skin red land and yellow sun
A common ground that keeps us all united
Although we're classed as a minority our blood it flowed through history
And through the years we never stood divided.

And now as you drift and stray and if you seem to lose my way
You'll always have that life deep down inside you
And as you get to live your days and fate sees you in different ways
Don't forget my blacktracks left behind you

© Charles Trindall

Family turtle dinner on the seashore at Galiwin'ku, Elcho Island, featured in the VIBE Living Strong health promotion show on NITV. The program has a big focus on healthy eating. Courtesy Vibe Australia.

Aboriginal and Torres Strait Islander Australia comprises living cultures from the point of view of Indigenous Australians. People live diverse lifestyles in a range of urban, rural and remote communities. It is often said that there are no strictly 'traditional' communities left in Australia. It is true that no Aboriginal or Torres Strait Islander community in Australia now lives exactly the life of Indigenous people before the invasion. But what many people fail to recognise is that Aboriginal and Torres Strait Islander people have maintained our worldview, our respect for our land and sea, and our interrelated social systems with their reciprocal kinship obligations and rights. These relationships are at the core of Aboriginal and Torres Strait Islander life. They provide a foundation of support and survival. In the ABS National Aboriginal and Torres Strait Islander Survey (2004), 90 per cent of Indigenous people stated that they could get support outside their immediate household in a time of crisis. One in four Indigenous Australians live in remote locations, but the largest Indigenous population is in Western Sydney and two states—New South Wales (29 per cent) and Queensland (27 per cent)—comprise over half of the Indigenous population. There is still a robust nature to the cultural continuum that is lived around the country.

The National Survey (2004) found no decline in the maintenance of culture since 1994:

> A similar proportion (just over half) of Indigenous people continued to identify with a clan, tribal or language group, as was the case in 1994, despite there being a decline in the proportion (29% to 22%) of people who lived in homelands and traditional country. Almost seven out of ten Indigenous people aged 15 years and over had attended cultural events in the previous 12 months, similar to the situation in 1994.

Also, 46.6 per cent had attended a funeral, 23.6 per cent a ceremonial activity, 45.9 per cent a festival or carnival, 68.1 per cent a cultural event and 26.1 per cent were involved in a community organisation over a twelve-month period. The increasing involvement of people in events such as the football knockout, Crocfest, and careers markets as a means of maintaining social and community contact helps foster cultural practice in a contemporary setting. There is still men's business and women's business. Funerals are still important occasions in communities.

The Return of our Human Remains

The return of our human remains from all corners of the western world to our people will represent to us: spiritual, cultural, historical and political reconciliation.

Because of current thinking and the learning that has taken place in recent times both Aboriginal and non-Aboriginal people understand that both sides have spiritual connection to the remains of the human body.

The difference here is that one group, the non-Aboriginal group, talks of the here and now and the afterlife and religious beings as being separated by time and space and eternity, whilst the Aboriginal group refers to the spiritual connections over several generations and are not separated by space from our ancestors, and spiritual connections. We share the same space they do. We are them and they are us.

It is the spiritual, cultural and ecological balance coupled with the emotional wellbeing and peace that policies should address for future repatriation and this is the reason why the remains of Aboriginal people should be given the same respect as other peoples who die within our own life time. Not to mention that such a small act of kindness, in the spirit of cooperation would mean so much to us. It would serve to:

- Close that chapter in our families' history with the respect and humanity that they deserve and without further anguish
- Give honour to the deceased who have been separated from their countries for so long.
- Lie to rest some of the pain and bitterness of the past.
- Return our dead stolen from us for the sake of science at a time when all efforts were being made to exterminate us.

Professor Mary Ann Bin-Sallik is a Djaru woman from the Kimberley, WA. She is the Dean of Indigenous Research and Education at Charles Darwin University and holds the Ranger Chair in Aboriginal Studies. She holds a Masters Degree in Educational Administration and a Doctorate in Teaching and Learning from Harvard University, USA. She is a mother of two and grandmother of six.

Sand goanna man

Bawili yugal yurrundali man
He's now in the dreamtime in Biami's hand
The mayarr still blowing
Across his ancient sands
With them blows his wandabaa
With a barran in his hand

Bawili yugal yurrundali man
Bawili yugal yurrundali man
Bawaili yugal yurrundali man
Bawaili bawili yugal

I will sing my song for the sand goanna man
He's now in the heavens in our creator's hand
The winds there still blowing

Dreaming is continuous and present, a cycle of life without beginning or end, a parallel and all-inclusive reality. It is something mystic and beyond words—a feeling of the harmony of the universe, in tune with the rhythm of the land. Dreaming is the life of the spirit and the imagination, expressed in art and poetry, music, drama and dance. Most of all, Dreaming is the religious experience, the spiritual tie that binds Aboriginal people to the land that owns them.

The Dreaming is the spirit of the land. In most of modern Australia, the Dreamtime was the web of life, the harmony of all things that was shattered by the white invasion.

—Nigel Parbury (2005, p. 10).

Darug tree ceremony. A funeral ceremony revived after generations in memory of Ken Upton, who dedicated his life to reviving Darug culture. His sisters (from left) Fay Richards, Patricia Jarvis and Edna Watson apply white ochre to the carving. By permission of the Upton family. Photo: Caroline Davy, courtesy University of New South Wales.

Across his ancient sands
With them blows his spirit
With a boomerang in his hand

I will sing my song for the sand goanna man
I will sing my song for the sand goanna man
I will sing my song for the sand goanna man
I'll sing I'll sing my song

(Music break)

We will sing my song for the sand goanna man
He's now in the heavens in our creator's hand
The winds there still blowing
Across his ancient sands
With them blows his spirit
With a boomering in his hand

We will sing our song for the sand goanna man
We will sing our song for the sand goanna man
We will sing our song for the sand goanna man
We'll sing we'll sing our song
We'll sing we'll sing our song

© Charles Trindall

All over Australia, kinship, relationships and belonging to the land remain the basis of Aboriginal life. In Indigenous communities, Elders are respected. Elders have always been the keepers of knowledge and the Law in Aboriginal Australia. The Elders in Council have been the final authority in Aboriginal societies. There is a view that Elders in Council should still be regarded as the body to make all decisions in Aboriginal communities. In much of Australia now, these councils have not survived due to the impact of invasion and colonisation, and cultural erosion. There are other structures and Indigenous organisations which provide advice and direction. However, Councils of Elders are being revived in some areas, and across Australia individual Elders are respected as custodians of culture and for their wisdom and experience. Respect for Elders is fundamental to our society. The establishment of relevant local decision-making processes has become even more important since the abolition of ATSIC.

All over Australia, Aboriginal people still know their Dreamings and many practise the ceremonies associated with their totem. Being rural or urban does not exclude Aboriginal people from carrying out ancient rituals. We still carry out certain rituals when approaching a special area, such as clapping our hands, putting ochre on our arms and face or speaking to the guardian spirits of the sites. Many urban and rural Aboriginal people will still smoke a house where a family member has died or before moving into a new place. This is to get rid of any bad spirits that may linger. Some Christian people will get a house blessed for the same reason.

All over Australia, Aboriginal people have set up cooperatives and other organisations to help our communities. These organisations identify as Aboriginal. Many have Indigenous names, such as the local tribal area or language of the Aboriginal area, or use an Aboriginal place name to identify their organisation as Aboriginal. As well as providing services, these bodies are a place to be Aboriginal, to be ourselves; they reinforce our identity and encourage us to express our culture. The many Aboriginal government agencies across the country, many with traditional names, also provide space for us to be blackfellas, as well as serving our needs.

Many Aboriginal people wear colours that are identifiable as the Aboriginal colours: black for the original people, gold or yellow for the sun as giver of all life, and red for the land (and the blood that has been shed). These colours are worn in the form of beads, wristbands, headbands, jewellery, t-shirts with the land rights flag, or in the colours, plus other accoutrements. Many t-shirts have slogans, such as 'White Australia has a Black History'—because being Aboriginal is political. Aboriginal people—and increasing numbers of other Australians—also wear Aboriginal designs from the growing range of Aboriginal designers who are now cornering their rightful share of the market—in all colours, not just red, yellow and black or ochres. These designs signify Aboriginal, belonging to the land, spirituality—and for whitefellas, belief in all of that.

Survival Days

On 26 January every year—Australia Day, also known as Invasion Day—Aboriginal people hold different forms of celebrations all over this country to commemorate the resistance and survival of the oldest living culture in the world. After the 1988 'Long March of Freedom, Justice and Hope' during the Bicentennial, it became evident that many Australians saw the injustices

Countrymen. *Mornington Island Elders meet at Aurukun on Cape York, Queensland. A powerful image of the closeness of Aboriginal relationships; the word means men of the same country, being related through that country—'country' in Aboriginal English means so much! Photo by Juno Gemes, reproduced in Marcia Langton's photo-book* After the Tent Embassy *(Valadon Publishing, 1983). © Juno Gemes Archive.*

and wanted to celebrate a future together. That year the inaugural Survival Concert was held at La Perouse, celebrating diverse cultural dance and music. Survival has become an annual event now staged in the City of Sydney's Victoria Park; it previously was held at La Perouse and then at Waverley Oval, Bondi. More recently, it has been renamed Yabun. Yabun means 'songs with a beat' (Wiradjuri). Similar events are held across Australia, celebrating Indigenous culture—mainly music, but also dance, poetry and all forms of art—for Aboriginal people and also for our fellow travellers across the country. They have been so successful that the day is now widely known as 'Survival Day'. Survival personally means that the oldest race has a tenacity and a powerful resilience to maintain identity, and we celebrate the country's national day through celebrating our survival, language and unique culture in our own way from our own perspective.

In 2000, Rhoda Roberts developed the Woggan ma Gule mourning ceremony to begin Australia Day events. It was based on the traditional practice of smoking, cleansing and acknowledging past ancestors, and research into William Cooper's idea of a National Day of Mourning. The ceremony is held on the

Deadly VIBE, *February 2010:* Preston Campbell: GAME ON! *On 13 February 2010—the second anniversary of the National Apology—the National Rugby League held a match between the Indigenous All-Stars, led by Preston Campbell (pictured) and a team of NRL All-Stars, led by Australian captain Darren Lockyer. The game was the brainchild of Campbell. Courtesy Vibe Australia.*

> **Deadly Vibe**
>
> Vibe Australia Pty Ltd (Vibe) is an Aboriginal multimedia and events management company focused on getting the right messages to Indigenous people, especially youth. Every month, *Deadly Vibe* spotlights achievers in music, entertainment and sports, a mix of social issues and a big focus on education. Eight times a year, an *Invibe* insert targets youth in institutions and at risk with straight-out messages on issues of concern to them. Another string to Vibe's bow is the *Deadly Sounds* radio program, networked across the country, with presenters like Rhoda Roberts, hip-hop guru Munkimunk and Casey Donovan. In 2009, Vibe's fifteenth Deadly Awards were held at Sydney's Opera House, with awards for all facets of contemporary Indigenous life, and the inaugural Deadly Dressed award for the audience. Vibe also runs three-on-three basketball events promoting sport, health and education across Australia. *VibeBlog* helps people connect and network. *VibeAlive* is role models talking up education, like 'Grey matter builds bridges between black and white', 'Get on board the brain train to a brighter future' and 'Be a smart part of the Education Generation'—look out, Australia! *VibeHealth* is all about healthy living—healthy body, healthy mind and substance abuse. Vibe is living culture in action, presented in living colour, with a strong focus on community and education. All of this can be found on the Vibe website, <www.vibe.com.au> and on Vibe's own YouTube page, with clips from *VibeAlive*, the three-on-three basketball Indigenous events all over the country.

original shoreline of Farm Cove in the Botanic Gardens in Sydney. It pays respect to those who lost their lives during the invasion and ongoing struggle while honouring cultural ancestral traditions and celebrating the survival of our next generations of Aboriginal and Torres Strait Islander peoples. It is a ceremony for all Australians that celebrates and informs about cultural richness and differences. The New South Wales Governor—Professor Marie Bashir—pays respect at Woggan ma Gule.

Belonging to the land

Red

Red is the colour
of my Blood;
of the earth,
of which I am a part;
of the sun as it rises, or sets,
of which I am a part;
of the blood
of the animals,
of which I am a part;
of the flowers, like the waratah,
of the twining pea,
of which I am a part;
of the blood of the tree
of which I am a part.
For all things are a part of me,
and I am a part of them.
—W. Les Russell, in Gilbert (1988, p. 2)

Aboriginal people have always believed that we are descendants of the land. By that we mean we believe we were formed out of the land at the beginning of time. That is why we class the land as our mother. Aboriginal people care for the land by not destroying it. The land is important to us because it gives us life, it provides food for survival, it supplies oxygen to breathe, and without the land there would not be any life. Since time began, Aboriginal people have lived

Shakaya singing on stage at the Yabun (song with a beat) Festival in Redfern Park, Sydney, Survival Day 2004. Photo © Mervyn Bishop/Viscopy. Courtesy Gadigal Information Service.

40,000 years (Awakening). *Paintings by Terry Shewring, visual arts student and later art teacher at the TAFE Eora Centre, Redfern (NSW). This painting is an expression of the belief of most Aboriginal peoples that they came from the land.*

with this land. We have hunted and gathered, lived off the land by living with the land. The land has provided everything we have needed. In return, we have looked after our land because we belong to the land. We used to pity the European 'pioneers' who were so dependent on getting supplies from far away, because we had everything we needed right there where we were.

Aboriginal people used the land but did not abuse it. By not abusing, we mean our people never stripped the land by taking everything that was edible in a particular area. We would kill some of the game in the area. Once there was a shortage of food and game in one particular area, we would move on to another, following the cycle of maintaining our environment. Burning off was controlled burning; this was done by choosing an area that had not too much dry grass. Burning off was necessary to give animals young shoots of green grass and to control fires when the fire season came around. It also was a way we used to look after the land, our mother. Aboriginal people did not waste or kill unnecessarily—we ate what we killed; we gathered from the land yams, nuts, berries and fruits. The sea was a rich resource for coastal Kooris, giving us a rich range of food—fish, crabs, shellfish and lobsters. All waterways had resources for us. Geoffrey Blainey, in *The Triumph of the Nomads* (1976), said that Aboriginal people at the time of the invasion ate better than all but the very rich in Europe.

We were the first conservationists. We looked after this land and managed its resources. Years ago, in her book *Old Days, Old Ways*, Dame Mary Gilmore (1934) wrote that most of the

> This is my home. I can't go back to Bateman's Bay. I suppose I could go back there, but I don't identify with Bateman's Bay. I identify with Redfern. This is where I come from, Redfern, and most of my grandchildren and my children. I always come back here, had to come back like a calling.
>
> —Joyce Ingram, in Rintoul (1993, p. 21)

> For our survival and for our history we must hold on to our Aboriginal laws. It is for us to learn white man's way as well, but never to forget the Aboriginal way, for this is what makes us uniquely Aboriginal Australians.
>
> —Rosalie Kunoth-Monks, in Rintoul (1993, p. 336)

dams in eastern Australia were the same places where we had dams and water traps. Her father told her: 'When the blacks went, the fish went.' Because we managed the water as well as the land. Mary Gilmore also recorded the conservation areas Aboriginal people had. Finally, people are starting to realise that Aboriginal people know about managing the Australian environment. Parks authorities have started to use our 'firestick farming' (mosaic burning) techniques and Aboriginal rangers are employed in all states. Co-management of parks has been beneficial in sharing knowledge and culture, and developing skills and employment, in communities. But too many people still think that Western science has all the answers. They do not recognise our science, our knowledge. Fortunately, Australians are learning—but it can be a slow process.

Colonial history is full of land-use conflicts. Aboriginal fishermen had nets with a large mesh;

this allowed small fish to swim through the big mesh. They took only what was needed for the day. English fishermen, with their small-mesh nets, caught all sorts of small fish and left them to rot on the sand. Aboriginal people were very upset at this disrespect for the sea and its resources. At first Aboriginal people had thought the invaders were Aboriginal people returned from the dead, but when they refused to share what they caught and cleared the bush, this kind of ignorance and disrespect made it clear that these pale people could never have been Aboriginal. Shell middens left by coastal Kooris were destroyed by being burnt in lime pits or used as back cargo to Sydney. Sydney Town's mortar was Aboriginal history destroyed. Whenever you come across a town or area called Lime Kilns, it was named from the burning of shells for lime.

To Aboriginal people, the land is so important. It is everything because without the land we would not survive. Food comes from the land, wildlife comes from the land, everything we eat comes from the land; it governs people's lives. The land also holds Dreaming places, totems (or Dreamings) that are sacred to Aboriginal people. These are the key to Aboriginal identity. Sacred sites are places where Aboriginal people go to communicate with ancestral spirits, the spirits of the land, and to ask for guidance. This would have been done by Elders of a community. Elders are men and women of knowledge or high degree. To communicate with spirits you have to be initiated. To be initiated you have to be chosen by Elders of the clan, after a long education and training process.

> The fight for me now is to save our little bit of land... we've only got a small corner left. The mining company CRA wants to put a slurry through that land, and one of the Gungalidda clan areas is where the pipe's gunna go through, and it's the dingo Dreaming. We see it as our last struggle: to hold on to our spirituality, our connection to the land, and we see it as a race of people struggling on a reserve where there's alcohol, there's violence; everything's going wrong for us. We're very oppressed and there's so much confusion, so then black people just drink to choke down the forget.
> —Wadjularbinna, Doomadgee, Gulf country, in Rintoul (1993, p. 153)

The land is:

- the basis for kinship, providing the links between families, clans and tribes, and between the people and the whole of creation;
- the basis of the people's life, identity and spirituality;
- a surface on which has been written the story of the people's spiritual understanding and belief. The land, with all its special features, is associated with events of the Dreaming, which are kept alive by oral traditions in myths, ceremony and painting; and
- home.

New Tomorrow

Our trees are dying, the land is choking from disease
There's children crying and streets of beggars on their knees
The earth is warming and from the ice comes flowing streams
Can't see the warnings, or hear Earth Mother's silent screams.

A new tomorrow is what our children really need
World without sorrow
More care and sharing and less greed
Where black and white, red and yellow can be free
To never fight, no more battles – land, air or sea

A world of hunger, it always comes from want and greed
And crime it thunders, a common sight on city streets
Killing for pleasure, our animals that should be free
Our only treasure seemed to be financially

Through drugs and drinking, our roads turn into killing fields
There's no more thinking, technology now turns the wheels
With rapid changes to our lifestyle and ideals
Through the ages, our cultural ways they tend to steal.

© Charles Trindall

The Land is our Body

For the Aboriginal people, land is a dynamic notion, something creative. Land is not bound by geographical limitations placed on it by a surveyor, who marks out an area and says, 'This is your plot'. Land is the generation point of existence.

Land is a living place made up of sky, clouds, rivers, trees, the wind, the sand and the spirit has created all these things, the spirit that planted my own spirit here, my own country.

It is something—and yet it is not a thing—it is a living entity. It belongs to me, I belong to the land. I rest in it. I come from there.

Land is a notion that is most difficult to categorise in English law, but it is something that is very clear in Aboriginal law. The limitations of my land are clear to me and to those people who belong in my group. Land provides for my physical needs and provides for my spiritual needs. It is a regeneration of stories.

New stories are sung from contemplations of the land, stories are handed down from spirit men of the past who have deposited the riches at various places—the sacred places . . .

The sacred places are not simply geographically beautiful. They are holy places, even more holy than shrines, but not commercialised. They are sacred. The greatest respect is shown to them and they are used for the regeneration of history—the regeneration of Aboriginal people, the continuation of their life. That is where they begin and that is where they return.

—Patrick Dodson, in Catholic Commission for Justice and Peace et al. (1987)

Disturbing sacred sites and land is agony for our people. Land and mountains and spring water—the heart of the sacred sites—is really our body. Grader, bulldozer and pressing down on our body, liver, kidney, bleeding. The spirit of the landowners is sickened. Graders are scraping the skin off our flesh—a sore that will not heal up: in my language, WILU, killing us.

—David Mowaljarlai, in Roberts (1981)

No English words are good enough to give a sense of the links between an Aboriginal group and its homeland. Our word 'home', warm and suggestive though it be, does not match the Aboriginal word that may mean 'camp', 'hearth', 'country', 'everlasting home', 'totem place', 'life source', 'spirit centre', and much else all in one.

—W.E.H. Stanner (1968)

Land was an economic unit, whose significance lay to its capacity to provide for the community. Its real importance, however, was that it was sacred land, the bearer of the religious faith of the community. Land was to be cared for, not controlled or exploited, for it carried the presence of the creative beings of the Dreamtime. The 'owners' of the land were those who possessed correct knowledge of the sacred sites on the land, and the dances, songs and stories tied to those sites.

Aboriginal women, as well as men, had a close relationship with the land. It was women who harvested the food the land gave them, women who knew where to find the variety of edible roots hidden in the earth, women who recognised the valuable fruits the land yielded. Women also had their own sacred sites and their own secret traditions about the land. They, like the men, lived in close contact with the land and depended on it for their life, identity and spirituality. Aboriginal people did not worship the land or the sacred sites. Rather, sacred sites were revered for their ability to reveal the sacred: they are symbols of a deeper spiritual reality.

This understanding of the land lives on. It is the understanding of many Aboriginal people today.

—Catholic Commission for Justice and Peace et al. (1987, p. 19)

> **Living on country**
>
> Many nations make up Australia but each nation has a number of specific clan groups and with this structure, through our custodians and knowledge-keepers, come obligation and maintenance of country. Our nations and clan groups are diverse for many reasons, including geography and topography, such as saltwater peoples or rainforest peoples or stone country peoples or grasslands peoples. Foods, dance, song cycles, language, instruments, implements and body ornamentation can be vastly different, which is why songlines and trade routes were important in Aboriginal life across the country. However, there are more similarities than differences and one specific commonality is our respect for country, the wisdom of our Elders and the knowledge of our lore.
>
> While many communities have Elders who indeed are respected, the knowledge-keepers, as they are now often referred to, are our custodians of lore, dance and song cycles, and are the most highly regarded people in Aboriginal society. Many remain on country and do not move from country (or their region). Our keepers live across the country; they are not divided by geography. They live in urban, remote and regional sectors. It's a handing down for thousands of years of the knowledge, and while suburbia might have developed around their specific clan lands, they do not move on as they are connected to that place.
>
> Specific custodians are both male and female, and they play specific roles as custodians and in particular in ceremony; this, however, does vary greatly between countries. Today, with the advent of Western dominance, they are also leaders in our communities. A knowledge-keeper's wisdom is not about age; rather, it is about an inheritance, and some regions—particularly in the north, where key dance custodians and lore men can be much younger than their Elders. However, they have been handed the secret knowledge and education about how to carry out customary practice and lore. Today, for example, some of our great writers and visual artists are seen as knowledge-keepers as they continue to pass on stories; it's just in a new medium. But using new technologies does not make the practice of tradition and customary obligation less Aboriginal.
>
> Lore was handed down through the Dreaming and the knowledge continues to be passed on through oral stories, ceremony, song and dance. As the oldest living adapting culture in the world, we have also adapted elements of our rituals, traditional lore and protocol practice to fit into our new environs.
>
> —Rhoda Roberts

Indigenous achievers

> Aboriginal achievement
> is like the dark side of the moon,
> For it is there
> But so little is known.
>
> —Ernie Dingo, in Gilbert (1988, p. 29)

In the 20-odd years since Ernie Dingo wrote these lines, Aboriginal achievement has blossomed. It is no longer possible to be unaware of Aboriginal successes. Aboriginal achievers have always been there, but they did not always get positive coverage in the old days. Back in the 1930s, Sir Douglas Nicholls said Aboriginal athletes had to be not just as good as non-Aboriginal athletes but better—to even be noticed. In 1993, Collingwood was playing St Kilda in the AFL competition. Nicky Winmar, an Aboriginal player and one of St Kilda's best, was being taunted by racists in the crowd. He lifted his jumper and pointed to his skin to say, 'I'm black and proud of it!' The Secretary of the Collingwood Club stated that if Nicky had 'acted like a white man' he would not have been abused. When challenged, he backtracked to say he really meant Aboriginal people should act like human beings if they wanted respect—which was even worse.

Often when Aboriginal people come to the fore in any field they will be knocked by the media or politicians. The wider community is fed biased reports about Aboriginal communities and people. Albert Namatjira was not considered a great painter because he never attended any art schools and his colours were 'wrong'. But Albert's colours were not wrong—people who had never seen the different shades of the McDonnell Ranges condemned them out of hand. Today, Namatjira is recognised as one of Australia's greatest artists.

Then there are the Aboriginal artists of our modern era—artists such as Bronwyn Bancroft, who has exported fashion materials and designs, as well as her paintings, posters and book cover designs; Jimmy Pike with his well-known Desert Designs; Sally Morgan, author as well as artist; Jeffrey Samuels; Arone Raymond Meeks; and Fiona Foley, whose work was included in the 1989 Aboriginal art exhibition at the Australian National Gallery. That is without even mentioning the work of more recognised Aboriginal artists, such as Clifford Possum Tjapaltjarri, Michael Nelson Tjakamarra (whose work is in the forecourt of Parliament House, Canberra), Yirawala, David Malangi, Rover Thomas and many other artists from Northern and Central Australia. More recently, these famous male artists have been joined by increasing numbers of women—the late Emily Kame Kngwarrye is now regarded as one of Australia's greatest artists. The work of major Aboriginal artists now commands very high prices and is regarded as among the most exciting art on the international art scene. In 1988, one of the biggest art exhibitions in New York was *Dreamings: The Art of Aboriginal Australia*. In 2009, Hettie Perkins opened a Papunya Tula exhibition in New York.

While we may not have a presence on some of Australia's mainstream exports such as the popular soap *Neighbours*, Aboriginal and Torres Strait Islander arts and culture represent one of Australia's great tourism experiences, and certainly visual arts are one of the Northern Territory's great export products.

There have been incredible artists who have told and retold their Dreaming stories through the visual arts. It is this art form that has encapsulated the globe, achieving an incredible profile on the world's fine arts market. In 2006, leading Indigenous art curators Brenda Croft and Hettie Perkins commissioned visual artists including Lena Nyadbi, Judy Watson, Michael Riley, Paddy Bedford, Gulumbu Yunupingu, John Mawurndjul and Tommy Watson for the opening of the Musee du Quai Branly, with the largest overseas collection of Aboriginal art. Under the creative direction of Rhoda Roberts, 20 dancers performed a smoking and cleansing ritual featuring performers from the significant clans of the artists involved, developing a new song cycle. The gallery was opened by M. Jacques Chirac, President of the French Republic. He addressed an audience that included Kofi Annan, Secretary-General of the United Nations. During his talk he invited our artists to join and wept as he stated:

> The 'first peoples' possess a wealth of knowledge, culture and history. They are the custodians of ancestral wisdom, of refined imagination, filled with wonderful myths, and of high artistic expression whose masterpieces rival the finest examples of Western art.

Music is another art form that has allowed the expression of political, cultural and social dialogue to reach a broader market on the international and national music circuits, challenging stereotypes. From the formation of the missions, traditional practice and rhythms were mixed with introduced instruments such as the

> To be a Noongah man today is to be someone very proud. I am a lot more proud of being a Noongah man today than I possibly would have been during my father's era, because they didn't talk openly in front of white people about being a Noongah. I am frustrated because of the fact that I can't do lots of the things that middle-class Australians can do in this society because I am black. I feel frustrated because I know there is a lot of racism that is under the carpet that we will never get rid of. I am frustrated because ultimately the people who are making policies in Australia are white people. I have big frustrations about Aboriginal rights.
> —The late Ted Wilkes, Director, Aboriginal Medical Service, Perth and Trustee, Museum of Western Australia, in Rintoul (1993, p. 75)

Christopher (Wirriimbi) Edwards

Chris (Wirriimbi) Edwards is a descendant of the Gumbaynggir people from Nambucca Heads in northern New South Wales. His work is inspired by the landscape of Nambucca Heads where he grew up. Chris has been painting for five years and draws his inspiration for his paintings from significant places and stories told him by his Elders of his Koori heritage such as the Nambucca fish traps. Chris has developed a unique style of painting where he mixes sand from a sacred beach in Nambucca Heads with modern materials like acrylic paint to tell his stories. Through his work the Gumbaynggir stories will stay entrenched in the community for generations to come.

Chris has been successfully exhibiting his work over the past few years and has had sellout shows in Sydney, the Blue Mountains, the Southern Highlands and Melbourne. Chris was a finalist at the Parliament of New South Wales Indigenous Art Award in 2007 and 2008 and was also invited to exhibit at Gallerie Figure in Paris in September 2007. His mural at the Department of Housing in Parramatta winds around the counter, hand painted and constructed in five sections before being put in place and covered with perspex. He has also run workshops for NAIDOC and pre-schools and after-school care.

violin and jug bands. Singers emerged, such as Jimmy Little, the Mills Sisters, Auriel Andrews and Wilma Reading, who toured the States with Duke Ellington and had a residency at New York's Copacabana Club. Jimmy Little's recording of 'Royal Telephone' topped the charts in the 1960s, and he has been singing ever since. At the 1994 Country Music Festival at Tamworth, New South Wales, he was inducted into the Country Music Roll of Renown. That was a big improvement on the 1950s when Harold Blair was singing with the Australian

Opera Company, but was still expected to carry his Exemption Certificate in his home state of Queensland.

There were gumleaf bands in the 1920s and 1930s. More recently, Herb Patten played gumleaf at the 2005 World Indigenous Peoples' Conference: Education in Hamilton, New Zealand, then brought his instrument to national attention on *Australia's Got Talent*, and again at the 2008 World Indigenous Peoples' Conference in Melbourne. Slim Dusty was taught guitar by an Aboriginal musician, the late Clive Kelly of Bellbrook, New South Wales, and performed in many communities throughout his career. Many mainstream country classics are said to have been written by Aboriginal musicians like Dougie Young. Mainstream bands such as Midnight Oil, Goanna and Gondwanaland have made a business out of Aboriginal-inspired music, and brought it to all Australians.

In the 1960s, music became more accessible and political bands started to form across the country. The success of Aboriginal musicians today is built on the work of people like the late Harry Williams's band Country Outcasts, the Silver Linings (later Black Lace) and other Aboriginal music pioneers. Yugal Band began playing blues. In the 1970s there were Us Mob and No Fixed Address led by Bart Willoughby (Mixed Relations in the 1980s), who supported Peter Tosh on his world tour. No Fixed Address is famous for the Aboriginal anthem 'We Have Survived [the White Man's World]—And You Can't Change That!' Many other bands followed, such as Coloured Stone and Mop and the Drop Outs. By the 1980s, there were groups and artists performing across many genres, including the Warumpi Band, Tiddas, the Pigram Brothers, Kuckles and Blek Bela Mujik to name just a few. In 1986, Yothu Yindi arrived, and literally overnight their song *Treaty* changed the perception of Aboriginal music.

Archie Roach, one of the 'Stolen Generations', sings of his pain and lost years—but also of the children coming back. Archie made us think in 1992 with his ARIA Award-winning album *Charcoal Lane* and the Deadly Award single, 'Took the Children Away'—the nation listened and was moved by a new way of telling history with music.

Kev Carmody's political lyrics touched the activist in all of us. He sang of the hardships of Aboriginal stockmen, black history and social problems. He is highly respected as a musician's musician. Most importantly, he is an inclusive singer who showed that collaboration of musicians from varying backgrounds could change the mainstream. He collaborated with Jimmy Little to re-establish their careers in the mainstream on the albums *Messenger* and *You Cannot Buy My Soul*. Other highlights in Aboriginal music include Casey Donovan winning *Australian Idol*, Gurrumul Yunupingu and Troy Cassar-Daley winning ARIA Awards (he won six Golden Guitar awards at Tamworth in 2010), Shellie Morris on the international circuit, and some of the latest rock acts—The Medics, out of Cairns, or ARIA winner Dan Sultan from Victoria—or *Idol* runner-up (and ARIA winner) Jessica Mauboy. What has become evident is that Indigenous music celebrated to the highest possible professional standard is a symbol of resilience and hope in the spirit and action of reconciliation. One of the most successful albums of 2009, *Cannot Buy My Soul: The Songs of Kev Carmody*, saw other leading Australian artists singing Kev Carmody songs on one CD, and Kev Carmody singing his own songs on the other. In 2008, the media music sensation was Geoffrey Gurrumul Yunupingu, the blind singer from Yothu Yindi who won two ARIAs with his beautiful voice singing his songs in language.

MC Wire works with young Aboriginal people across New South Wales, adding a particular Indigenous 'flavour' by the inclusion of language and cultural expressions, to reflect Indigenous community relationships and social issues. Rap and hip-hop have been taken up by many young people, and also express cultural resistance to the 'white man's world'. Today we have so many bands and individuals playing an eclectic mix of music with representation in just about every genre of musical practice. A recent breakthrough project promoted by then federal Arts Minister Peter Garrett (formerly the lead singer of Midnight Oil) awarded five groups support to promote and develop a major album. The groups were Busby Marou from Queensland, the Leah Flanagan Band from Darwin, and Microwave Jenny, Stiff Gins, and Street Warriors, all from New South Wales.

Extending into musical theatre, one of the success stories of Australian live entertainment

Thursday Island singer Seaman Dan holding his Deadly Award for contribution to music at the 15th Annual Deadly Awards, 2009. Courtesy Vibe Australia.

in the 1990s was *Bran Nue Dae*, the living history musical by Jimmy Chi and the band Kuckles, followed up by *Corrugation Road*. In late 2009, *Bran Nue Dae* hit the screens as a joyous film musical of Aboriginal life, directed by Rachel Perkins. In the same year, *Samson and Delilah*, by debut Aboriginal director Warwick Thornton, featuring unknown 15-year-old boy and girl leads, won the Camera d'Or (Gold Camera) prize at the Cannes Film Festival and took out several Australian Film Industry (AFI) Awards and was in competition for an Oscar. Meanwhile, Richard Frankland's *Stone Bros*, previewed to gales of helpless laughter at WIPCE in Melbourne 2008, was released nationally, also highlighting the edgy humour of Aboriginal life in one of the funniest films ever made in this country.

Yothu Yindi is a household name, our most famous band internationally. Yothu Yindi is also the perfect example of what living culture is all about—adapting to the contemporary world on Indigenous terms, as well as being a shining example of reconciliation in action. As noted above, Yothu Yindi band member Geoffrey Gurrumul Yunupingu is a cult favourite across Australia as a solo artist, with two ARIA awards in 2008. His portrait won the 2009 Archibald Prize. Mary G (a character created by Mark Bin Bakar, now chair of the Arts Board) and Sean Choolburra light up the TV screen with their comedy and there is now an Aboriginal stand-up comic industry—it's about time people saw the humour in Aboriginal life! The *Black Olive* TV cook show has hit the screens, and we had an Aboriginal contestant on *Masterchef*.

Although Aboriginal people were denied education for generations, then got second-class schooling, more and more Aboriginal writers are now achieving in the literary world. Following

Deadly Funny

There is a widespread, often well-meaning, assumption that Aboriginal lives are all sadness and tragedy. But there has always been lots of laughter in Aboriginal life—comedy based on sharp observation, mimicry and mime, plus lateral thinking—making connections and seeing comic possibilities. Many people say their humour—'black humour'—is a main reason for the survival of Aboriginal people through the dark times of invasion, colonisation, segregation, assimilation and all that.

In the 1980s, Ernie Dingo with his quick wit and cheeky smile introduced Aboriginal comedy to the mass market. More recently, Sean Choolburra won Sydney's Raw Comedy title in 2002. Mary G (aka Dr Mark Bin Bakar, Chair of the Australia Council's Aboriginal and Torres Strait Islander Arts Board) is one of the funniest people on Indigenous airwaves (or any other)—a riot in the road-movie comedy *Stone Bros* (2009).

In 2006, the Melbourne International Comedy Festival started its *Deadly Funny* stand-up-comic competition, with sponsorship from the Australia Council. The *Deadly Funny* program sent established comics like Judith Lucy out to Aboriginal communities to conduct mentoring workshops for aspiring Aboriginal comics.

It turns out that many Aboriginal people are 'natural' stand-ups, with individuality and ability to tell stories against themselves and laugh at anything. In every community *Deadly Funny* mentors have visited, they have been told 'so-and-so is funny'; 2010 winner Denise McGuiness's kids told them, "Mum thinks she's funny". *Deadly Funny* has been described as 'Indigenous humour at its rapidfire best'.

GJC Vibe CEO Gavin Jones says 2009 Deadly Funny winner Kevin Kropinyeri is not just a side-splitter, but also an insightful artist with true talent. From large-scale events to intimate gatherings, Kevin has the whole crowd laughing within seconds. That laughter keeps coming as Kevin shares his unique blackfella view of the world. He has the crisp, polished delivery to rival the best comedians, while his style is more like someone who has dropped in to share a few hilarious yarns.

Kevin Kropinyeri leads a new generation of Indigenous Australian stand-up talent. He is a master storyteller with a keen sense of humour. The world is just discovering how funny he is and boy, does it need to.

Winner: Tiarna Mason. How much athletic talent was wasted in the 'dark days' of white Australia? Courtesy Terry Mason.

Actor, singer and writer Leah Purcell on the cover of Black Chicks Talking, *the book of her interviews with Aboriginal women achievers from across Australia (2002).*

in the footsteps of David Unaipon, Kevin Gilbert and Oodgeroo of the Tribe Noonuccal (Kath Walker) were the pioneers of Aboriginal literature, even though Oodgeroo's work was said to be 'too political' to be 'real poetry'. As Aboriginal people have gained access to education, there has been an explosion of Aboriginal publications. Authors include Sally Morgan, Archie Weller, Colin Johnson (Mudrooroo Narrogin), Eric Willmot, Jack Davis—playwright and one of our greatest poets—Ruby Langford-Ginibi, Eva Johnson, Kim Scott, Richard Walley, Robert Bropho, Phillip Pepper, Philip McLaren, the late Margaret Tucker, the late Ella Simon, James Wilson-Miller—our first Aboriginal historian—plus a long and growing list of others. That's not even counting all the Aboriginal writers of children's books or the growing list of authors, such as the late Pat Torres, who have published with Magabala Books in Broome. Twenty years ago you could have counted Aboriginal authors on one hand. Now there are hundreds, and their numbers are growing. Some are winning wide acclaim, such as Anita Heiss (winner of the 2007 Deadly Award for outstanding achievement in literature) and Alexis Wright, who won the 2007 Miles Franklin Award with her epic novel of Aboriginal life, *Carpentaria*.

We have Aboriginal achievers in the media, law and business; we have actors and filmmakers. Luke Carroll, Ivan Sen, Aaron Pederson, Debra Mailman, Stan Grant, Karla Grant, Hettie Perkins, Rachel Perkins, Brenda Croft, Tracey Moffatt, Aden Ridgeway, Ernie Dingo, Warwick Thornton, Leah Purcell and the Page brothers are just some of them—the list goes on. Many of these are not just Aboriginal stars but stars in the mainstream of Australian life. Major movies such as *Samson and Delilah* and *Radiance*, TV programs like *Message Stick*, *Speaking Out* on ABC radio, *Living Black* on SBS, Imparja and National Indigenous Television, the *Koori Mail* and the *National Indigenous Times* as national newspapers, plus *VIBE Australia* for youth show just how much Indigenous creativity is contributing to the cultural life of Australia.

There have always been Aboriginal achievers in sport, but not so many people know this. The first Australian cricket team to tour England in 1868 was Aboriginal, yet few Aboriginal cricketers have played even at state level (in 2010 Dan Christian played for Australia). Aboriginal people have always tended to go for sports which could provide a living. In the late nineteenth century, professional foot-races were dominated by Aboriginal runners—until many of them were barred. Charlie Samuels beat three world champion sprinters and was timed over 100 yards at nine seconds flat! Kyle Van Der Kuyp, Patrick Johnson and Joshua Ross have performed with distinction in worldwide competition. Cathy Freeman famously won gold at the Sydney 2000 Olympics.

Now there are Aboriginal stars in all the football codes, boxing, athletics, netball and basketball, plus growing numbers of other sports. In the past—and still even now—'low-budget' sports tend to fit better with Aboriginal economic realities than sports like yachting or motor racing, where money plays a big part in participation. Years ago, Sir Douglas Nicholls was asked why he played football rather than, say, cricket—his answer was that the gear was a lot cheaper!

Up to 1980, 15 per cent of Australian boxing champions were Aboriginal; it was said that the boxing ring was the only place where 'a blackfellow could flatten a whitefellow and get paid for it instead of shot!' Anthony Mundine holds world champion status in boxing. The big-money sport in recent years has been football, and Aboriginal players are now over-represented in AFL (Australian Rules) and NRL (Rugby League), and there are Aboriginal stars in football (soccer). The biggest Rugby League competition in the world now is the New South Wales Koori Knockout. NITV now has two football shows, the *Barefoot Rugby League Show* and the *Marn Grook Show* (AFL).

Aboriginal women have also achieved in sport, but have faced the double barriers of racism and sexism. A few big names have broken the barriers: tennis star Evonne Goolagong Cawley won Wimbledon twice, was the first woman to win after having a baby, and became a household name. One of the biggest names in Australian sport in recent times has been Cathy Freeman, who is said to have made a bigger contribution to reconciliation than all the politicians put together when she ran a victory lap at the 1994 Commonwealth Games with both the Australian and Aboriginal flags draped over her. She made a similar statement at the Sydney 2000 Olympics, when the roar

The first Australian cricket team (and first Australian team) to tour England (1868) in front of the Melbourne Cricket Club pavilion, 1867. They played better than early white Australian teams, but there was no future for them back home. Courtesy Melbourne Cricket Club; Mitchell Library, State Library of New South Wales.

from the stadium across the water was like nothing a waterpoliceman had ever heard. Cathy Freeman and Nova Peris have both excelled at Commonwealth and Olympic level, and after retiring from sport have continued to work in developing mentor programs, television shows with a positive image and political lobbying—Evonne Goolagong-Cawley works with youth all the time, as does Sharon Finnan; both have been heavily involved in Croc Festivals in rural and remote areas across the country.

Communities and initiatives

Since the 1967 Referendum gave recognition to Aboriginal people, we have achieved much: the land rights demonstrations of the early 1970s; the Aboriginal Tent Embassy on the lawns of Old Parliament House; the promise of land rights by the Federal Government; the *Aboriginal Land Rights (Northern Territory) Act* in 1976; and Prime Minister Kevin Rudd's apology to the 'Stolen Generations' in 2008. Aboriginal people in some states still do not have land rights and, across the country, many Aboriginal people have gained little or nothing from native title. Where there *are* land rights, people have to fight government agencies to claim unalienated Crown land—land that was

> Blackfellas are 'people people', naturally gifted in human professions, making a difference in social work, nursing, teaching, hospitality. Aboriginal services break ground for the mainstream, establishing the first women's refuges, the first community legal service, first work-for-the-dole and inaugurating community consultation. And they add value: the best of Aboriginal education, for example, works better for all kids, while the connectedness and compassion of Aboriginal thinking could transform government.
>
> —Nigel Parbury (2005, p. 216)

ours in the first place. Due to a lack of funding for government services to process land claims, in 2009 over $1 billion of New South Wales land claims were granted that could not be transferred and a total of 57 per cent of claims remained unresolved.

Few people realise how many Aboriginal organisations there are in Australia. The Redfern Aboriginal Medical Service in inner Sydney was the forerunner to many Aboriginal medical services. At the same time, the first Aboriginal Legal Service was set up, and this also has developed into a nationwide network. There are also other community-based Aboriginal services, such as Aboriginal children's services.

There are many Aboriginal community enterprises that are thriving, from pre-schools to nightclubs, bush tucker shops to security services, plant nurseries, farm enterprises and

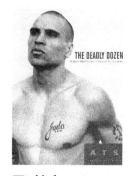

World champion boxer and role model Anthony Mundine on the cover of the VIBE Deadly Dozen calendar, 2003. Photo: Jason Loukas. Courtesy Vibe Australia.

Gavin Andrews, with permission from Bidigal Dharawal knowledge-holders, and accompanied by the Yandel'ora Women's Dance Group, leads the Gawura (Whale) Song Ceremony at a community event in the Royal National Park, Sydney, 2008. Dharawal people regularly sing to the whales during their migrations up and down the coast to wish them a safe journey and warn of nearby dangers. Many coastal Aboriginal communities have similar ceremonies. Photo: Gawaian Bodkin-Andrews.

tourist operations. The Aboriginal Land Council network in New South Wales has promoted a wide range of successful Aboriginal enterprises using the land tax funding paid as compensation under the *Land Rights Act* 1983 (NSW). In 2007, the Land Council created a $30 million endowment fund to fund 200 scholarships of $10 000 each in perpetuity. A major objective of the Land Council is to achieve total economic autonomy, self-sufficiency, and self-determination—to restore to Aboriginal people the economic base that was taken from them by the invasion and gain economic equity for New South Wales Aboriginal people. In Central and Northern Australia, where Aboriginal land has been returned, communities have been able to negotiate with mining companies and generate business enterprises with royalties income. Scholarships, training, jobs and services have been a beneficial part of many of these agreements.

Community Development Employment Projects (CDEP), the first work-for-the-dole scheme in Australia, was a program that created jobs through community development activities. Incorporated organisations in Aboriginal communities in the CDEP received grants approximately equivalent to the total social security entitlements of members of the community. People involved in the scheme undertook work for the community and received a wage similar to welfare payments. The success of this scheme demonstrated that our people did not want handouts ('sit-down money'); we wanted jobs, so we could earn our own money. Unfortunately, many of these positive programs were scrapped by the Howard government, although they survive in some remote areas and there is talk of replacing them with other schemes in the future.

Aboriginal people have achieved much in the short space of time in which we have been able to develop and grow. We are still very thin on the ground in the medical field, but we now have 90 Indigenous doctors around the country and over a hundred medical students. There are six dentists with three dental scholarships per year under the Puggy Hunter Memorial Scholarship Scheme. Faye McMillan graduated as the first Bachelor of Pharmacy from Charles Sturt University in 2001. The number of nurses is growing, but retention at university is a problem in this area as it is in all areas of study. Tenured Aboriginal academics are also scarce. There is an increasing number of Aboriginal mental health workers, and Charles Sturt University has introduced a degree program. Many are working in specific programs to attend to the outcomes of generations of trauma.

The future looks brighter. Every Australian university—though not yet every university campus—has an Indigenous Education Centre to support our students. There are now Aboriginal students in universities and they are studying across more faculties, not just the 'traditional' Aboriginal degrees such as welfare and teaching. However, we cannot afford to be complacent, because Indigenous people on the whole are still way behind the wider community on all social, economic and political indicators—particularly in education, which is essential to full participation in Australian society.

Although in recent years there has been a decrease in the number of Indigenous students at tertiary level, the future promises to be more positive. We now have proactive bodies such as the Aboriginal Studies Association, the Indigenous Advisory Council (to the Federal Minister of Education), the National Indigenous Higher Education Network, the National Tertiary Education Union Indigenous Policy Committee, AECGs (Aboriginal Education Consultative Groups) and other Indigenous Education Consultative Bodies (IECBs). From such organisations comes a steady flow of research, policy papers and lobbying. This has given ongoing support to the maintenance of 'block release' programs for remote students, secondary scholarships and employment strategies for Indigenous staff in universities.

We have educators and PhDs, many postgraduate students and a growing number of Aboriginal people who have achieved in business. There are also the ordinary Aboriginal community people whose achievement is rarely recognised, let alone honoured. Few people realise how difficult it can be even to survive as an Aboriginal person, let alone the effort that is required to battle bureaucracy and racism. These people are the true quiet achievers.

Maintaining the Dreaming

To maintain the Dreaming, first Aboriginal and Torres Strait Islander children need to see their culture reflected in their schooling—otherwise that schooling will be alien or irrelevant. Indigenous students can no longer be expected to participate in an education that fails to include their culture and heritage. Second, Education Departments have to educate all Australian students about Aboriginal and Torres Strait Islander Australia. Every Australian student has the right to learn the real nature and the real history of this country. This is the only genuine basis for achieving reconciliation and it is essential to achieving social justice for Indigenous people, which is a prerequisite to reconciliation as there can be no reconciliation without justice.

Schools without a significant number of Aboriginal or Torres Strait Islander students will have more difficulty in funding Aboriginal cultural input than schools with significant numbers of Indigenous students. Obviously, it is no longer reasonable to expect Aboriginal people to give their time and expertise for nothing—especially given the levels of unemployment and

---

First nations gatherings

Traditionally, clans gathered at significant sites and places of abundance during varying seasonal cycles such as the Bunya Festivals, where clans from across Southeast Queensland and Northern New South Wales gathered and held cultural ceremonies when the bunya pines were in harvest and food was plentiful.

Be it through visual arts, writing, major events or traditional rituals, ceremony, or public festivals celebrating music and dance, Aboriginal people are controlling our own stories and destiny. Things have moved forward for our custodial song men and women, and our artists since the time of David Unaipon, who is celebrated on the $50 note. He was an inventor who never had the money to develop his ten inventions, including a shearing machine. He was also one of our first writers—he wrote down his oral stories of his Ngarrindjeri people, which were later published without acknowledging him.

Some of our festivals, modern-day corroborees, produced by Indigenous Australians are:

The Dreaming, Australia's International Indigenous Festival (Queensland)

This is a four-day event held annually at Woodford, a celebration of global first nations, all art forms and cultural practices.

Laura Dance Festival (Queensland)

This biennial event showcases Cape York's rich and diverse Aboriginal song and dance traditions.

Garma Festival (Northern Territory)

One of Australia's leading cultural exchange events, Garma is held annually in August at Gulkula in Northeast Arnhem Land.

Yarnballa Cultural Festival (South Australia)

Staged on the edge of the outback and set by the sea in Port Augusta, Yarnballa showcases proud and strong Indigenous culture, with a giant dance and story ground, a spectacular opening ceremony, a huge community concert, a big family day, and comedy and film through the days and nights of the festival.

Walking with Spirits (Northern Territory)

Beswick Community's annual celebration of its people's culture and heritage. Using fire, puppetry, images and music to reinterpret the concepts within the traditional dances, Walking With Spirits presents corroborees from four Arnhem Land language groups.

Spirit Festival (South Australia)

Held at Elder Park in the heart of Adelaide, this free community event showcases the richness and diversity of Aboriginal cultures from around South Australia.

—Rhoda Roberts

Premier Aboriginal dancer and choreographer Matthew Doyle performs in Wirid-Jiribin *(The Lyrebird) in the Dharawal language of southern Sydney, as part of the Festival of the Dreaming, 1997. Photo: Maurice Ortega.*

poverty in Indigenous Australian communities. Equity programs can be used, but these usually have other objectives.

Over the last decade, there has been a gradual but clear loss of funding and positive programs in schools. The Aboriginal Student Support and Parent Awareness (ASSPA) program has gone—its guaranteed support funds replaced by a time-consuming and cumbersome application process, though the new Parent and Community Engagement (PaCE) program looks easier to get into. Some homework centres have lost funding, replaced with in-class tuition support. Indigenous Education Workers are not as numerous as they need to be, and the funding model for placing them tends to be based on a student numbers formula rather than being needs-based, leading to disadvantage to students in some areas.

Programs to bring Indigenous arts and culture into schools must play a large part in achieving the twin aims of Indigenous education: appropriate education for Aboriginal and Torres Strait Islander students; and educating all students about Aboriginal and Torres Strait Islander Australia. Indigenous cultural programs in schools can make some kind of reparation for all the years of assimilation in education—when Indigenous culture was seen as something worthless, to be got rid of before any 'progress' could be made in 'education'. Indigenous and non-Indigenous children also need to see examples of positive contributions to the shared history of Australia. Bennelong and Bungaree need to be celebrated as companions to the Governor's households in which they lived and served as ambassadors, advisers between two cultures, trusted public servants. Bungaree must be recorded in curriculum as the first Aboriginal person to circumnavigate Australia on Matthew Flinders' voyages with a recognised role in the success of the venture. Maria Lock 'duxing' the Anniversary Schools Examination in 1819 is a fine role model of educational achievement. All Australians should know the large contribution of Indigenous people in the establishment of rural industries and should recognise the achievement of David Unaipon as a writer, speaker and inventor who improved the mechanical shears that were so important to the wool economy. The contribution of Indigenous servicemen and nurses in overseas conflicts, and the current contributions in all areas of community, social, sporting, arts and political life in contemporary times, are essential knowledge at all levels. Through the presentation of examples of positive contributions, Indigenous students have their identity and self-esteem boosted and reflected in a cultural continuum that matches their current life in Australia. Non-Indigenous children also learn of these achievements and appreciate the strength of the Indigenous cultural continuum. Concepts of equity will develop from pre-school age growing towards achieving reconciliation.

Finally, programs in schools can play a major role in maintaining and fostering Indigenous cultures—not least by their demonstration that Indigenous cultures are of value. The development of an Aboriginal languages syllabus is a positive development. For Indigenous people, education is inseparable from culture: culture is the basis of Indigenous education and we cannot have Indigenous education without Aboriginal and Torres Strait Islander culture.

Unity

I am the land
I am the trees
I am the rivers
that flow to the seas
joining and moving
encompassing all
blending all parts of me
stars in my thrall
binding and weaving
with you who belong
sometime discordant
but part of my song
birds are a whisper
the four breezes croon
raindrops in melody
all form the tune
of being belonging
aglow with the surge
to life and its passions
to create its urge
in living expression
its total of one
and the I and the tree
and the you and the me
and the rivers and birds
and the rocks that we've heard
sing the songs we are one I'm the tree you
    are me
with the land and the sea
we are one life not three
in the essence of life
we are one.

—Kevin Gilbert (1994, p. 74)

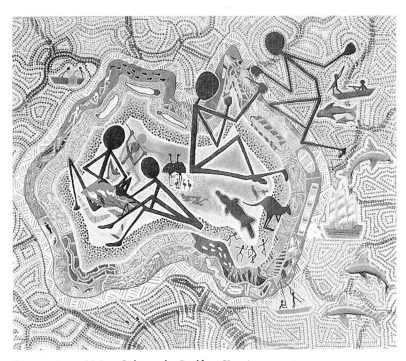

Discovering a Living Culture, *by Redfern Koori artist James P. Simon, 1985. This painting features a double discovery: Captain Cook's original 'discovery' in 1770 (the little white ship off Botany Bay) and people now rediscovering 'the power of the Dreaming'. Note the figures in the 'map' are artists and musicians representing the power of the Dreaming. Courtesy the artist.*

Misconceptions, stereotypes and racism: Let's face the facts

3

Rhonda Craven and Kaye Price

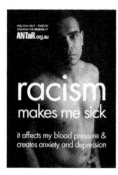

Courtesy ANTaR

Intolerance

When the white glug contemptuously
Says 'nigger', it is plain to me
He is of lower grade than we.
When the dark stockman, used to hate,
Is not accepted as mate,
Democracy is empty prate.
When we hear from the white elite
'We won't have abos in our street,'
Their Christianity's a cheat.
When blacks are banned, as we know well,
From city cafe and hotel,
The stink of Little Rock we smell.
Dark children coming home in tears,
Hurt and bewildered by their jeers—
I think Christ weeps with you, my dears.
People who say, by bias driven,
That colour must not be forgiven,
Would snub the Carpenter in heaven.

—Oodgeroo Noonuccal (2008, p. 28)

'Intolerance', by Oodgeroo, portrays the irrational and unfair nature of racism. Racism is often fuelled by misconceptions and stereotypes that are products of historical ethnocentric attitudes. Misconceptions are misunderstandings of the truth or specific concepts. Often misconceptions give rise to myths about groups of people that are based on misinterpretations rather than facts. Stereotypes are fixed impressions of groups of people, generalised to an entire race so that individuality is not considered. Many Australians believe that the attitudes of a number of non-Aboriginal people are a major obstacle to achieving social justice for Indigenous Australians. These attitudes also roadblock the process of reconciliation (see Chapter 8). Negative attitudes are often based on historical misconceptions and stereotypes that were not even true at the time. Often, when people come to understand how misconceptions and stereotypes have evolved, they become empowered to address negative attitudes they or others may hold.

This chapter is about Munyarl mythology—stereotypes and irrational beliefs about Aboriginal and Torres Strait Islander people. Munyarl is a Bundjalung word that is best translated as pretend, make-believe (not true), a lie—or a pack of lies.

What is racism?

Generally, racism is a set of beliefs, often complex, that asserts the natural superiority of one group over another, and which is often used to justify differential treatment and social positions. This may occur at the individual level, but often occurs at a broader systemic or institutional level. (Multicultural & Community Affairs Group, 2004, p. 4)

Racism is usually based on a belief of genetic superiority. Racial discrimination means 'any distinction, exclusion, restriction or preference based on race, colour, or national or ethnic origin which has the purpose or effect of nullifying or impairing the recognition, enjoyment or exercise, on an equal footing, of human rights and fundamental freedoms in the political, economic, social, cultural or any other field of public life' (UN General Assembly, 1965, p. 2). It 'occurs if a person is, or a group of people are: treated less favourably because of their race, their colour, their descent, their national origin or their ethnic origin; and because of this less favourable treatment they are stopped from fully enjoying their human rights and their fundamental and basic freedoms' (HREOC, 2006, p. 2).

Racism is manifested as prejudice against particular people because of their race, beliefs, ethnic origin or nationality. Racism is often discriminatory action taken by the dominant group against a minority or subordinate group. Racism can be prevalent in societal institutions. Institutional racism is characterised by systems and processes that disadvantage or exclude people on the basis of their race. Cultural racism involves the imposition of a dominant frame of reference and the exclusion of all other viewpoints. For example, the frame of reference of White Australia is based on cultural racism (see Chapter 4).

Examples of racism include:

- name-calling or teasing on the basis of race;
- racist jokes;
- racial comments to or about strangers in the street, or a mocking imitation of someone who speaks differently;
- the deliberate exclusion of someone simply because they are of a different race or culture. This might take the form of excluding someone from a job, or refusing to serve them in a shop;
- the exclusion of Aboriginal people from venues and facilities: hairdressers, hotels, cafes, picture theatres, swimming pools, RSL clubs, Girl Guides, Boy Scouts, etc;
- the segregation of every aspect of life in South Africa prior to 1992;
- the segregation of black Americans in the 'Deep South' up to the 1960s;

> The impact of racism and unfair discrimination on individuals can include low levels of self-esteem, motivation, productivity or quality of work and increased levels of anxiety, depression and frustration. Racism and unfair discrimination in the workplace jeopardises productivity [and] limits creative thinking, innovation and problem solving. Racism and unfair discrimination in the community increase alienation, particularly among young people, and can lead to increased anti-social behaviour and disruption to normal family relationships. Racism can be compounded further by other forms of discrimination such as sex and class discrimination.
> —Multicultural & Community Affairs Group (2004, p. 4)

- the exclusion of Aboriginal people from state schools in Australia;
- the exclusion of Aboriginal people from wards in 'our' public hospitals up to the 1970s;
- the exclusion of Aboriginal and Torres Strait Islander perspectives from culture, history, heritage and education; and
- White Australia—by definition.

Racists tend to ignore the shared characteristics of humanity and focus on the perceived differences of other groups. Such differences are attributed to genetic inferiority, which also serves to justify further discrimination. Such a rationalisation has been used to oppress groups—often violently—and to deny basic human rights to groups considered genetically and/or culturally inferior.

What causes racism?

Racism has a multiplicity of causes. Given that societies are complex, so are the antecedents of racism. When a dominant group chooses to subordinate another group, this leads to disempowerment of the subordinate group—politically, economically and socially. The dominant group often utilises racism to support its vested interests and to justify the need to dominate a different group of people.

Ethnocentrism historically has contributed to racism in a number of countries throughout the world. Ethnocentrism involves considering one culture superior to others. It is also associated with behaviours that involve imposing a dominant culture on a culture that is considered to be of lesser value. Ethnocentrism is based on a

Abo Brand Sanitary White. *1921 advertisement for white paint (note that 'sanitary' in those days meant really clean). This ad illustrates CD Rowley's comment in 1971 that Aboriginal people were 'constantly exposed to deliberate or unthinking insult'* (Outcasts in White Australia). *Advertisers have often used Aboriginal people, culture and symbols to sell products; the boomerang is still the most popular Australian logo (for example: 'Buy Australian'). Courtesy Cozzolino Enterprises.*

pervasive and rigid ingroup–outgroup distinction: it involves stereotyped negative imagery and hostile attitudes to outgroups; stereotyped positive imagery and compliant attitudes regarding ingroups; and a hierarchical, authoritarian view of group interaction in which ingroups are rightly dominant and outgroups naturally subordinate (Adorno et al. 1950, p. 150).

Stevens (1980), in his classic work *The Politics of Prejudice*, notes that the patterns of control exercised by ingroups are classified as liquidation, subordination and segregation. He also notes that control can be characterised by such actions as the 'removal of private property, the imposition of a standard form of clothing or even address, indignities of speech and actions of those in control, and the application of physical violence' (1980, p. 15). All these types of actions are reflected clearly in Australian history—and in the paternalistic government policies of segregation, protection and assimilation (see Chapter 5).

The impact of institutionalised and cultural racism in Australia has been so pervasive that Australian education systems have failed to address fundamental issues to do with recognising the validity of Aboriginal history and culture and their rightful place in Australian society. This has resulted in the persistence of myths about Aboriginal people and their history that have been generated by a lack of knowledge, and in Australians not being empowered to challenge and overcome racism in their society.

Racism in Australian society has been supported by the lack of challenges to the 'knowledge base' on which institutionalised racism has been formed and on which it has been perpetuated. It has also led to the fostering of misconceptions and stereotypes about Aboriginal people and their history and cultures which have been generated by a lack of knowledge and understanding of Aboriginal people's experiences of Australian history. Many Australians still do not know the truth about their country's history.

Historical events and experiences are often the beginnings of racism. Many such events serve to reinforce Eurocentric attitudes and White Australia frames of reference. The attitudes towards subordinate groups in history

> **No way walk away**
>
> In June 2010, dual rugby international Timana Tahu walked out of the New South Wales Blues' State of Origin camp in protest at assistant coach league legend Andrew 'Joey' Johns referring to Queensland Aboriginal superstar Greg Inglis as a 'black c . . .' in a team bonding session.
>
> Johns quit the camp in disgrace, resigning as assistant coach of the Blues. His column in the *Daily Telegraph* was axed and his coaching consultancy with Tahu's Parramatta club cancelled, though main employer Channel Nine and radio network Austereo pledged to stand by him. Many schools were reported to be planning class activities on racism based on this incident and the slogan, *No way walk away*. Jeff McMullen, of Ian Thorpe's Fountain for Youth, published an open letter:
>
>> All of our football codes draw so much of their magic from Aborigines, Torres Strait Islanders, Maoris and others who must endure for most of their lives the disgusting slurs, on and off the field. Timana Tahu has demonstrated courage and principle. His example is what I want my own boy and girl to follow, not the cowardly behaviour of so many players, team officials and administrators who remain silent. Aboriginal players know the truth. Particularly in NSW, racism is an ugly part of the game, on and off the field. When are other sportsmen going to follow Timana Tahu, behave like real men and end racial vilification?
>
> Analysts identified a continuing culture of racist remarks being OK 'among mates' for a minority of the 'old-guard' in the National Rugby League. There were suggestions that it was far easier for Aboriginal players to be selected in Queensland—nearly 30 per cent of Queensland Origin players have been Indigenous.
>
> In a video statement, Tahu said similar remarks were made about Polynesian players in the Queensland team, and he had heard a number of racial slurs in his years playing alongside Johns for the Newcastle Knights.
>
> He said his hardline action was to set a standard for his children:
>
>> I believe I am a role model for children and I did this to show my kids this type of behaviour is wrong. This isn't about me or Andrew Johns, it's about arresting racism and standing up for my beliefs.
>>
>> Leaving Origin was a big decision for me and I'd like to clarify that it was not just one racial comment directed at one individual that offended me. The remarks were directed at various races and the situation was totally unacceptable.
>>
>> I want to move on now and hope something positive comes from it.
>
> Tahu's action makes me proud to be an Australian—proud that a senior Indigenous player can stand up and be counted and serve as a role model for all Australian children and in doing so sacrifice his own ambitions for the principle of zero tolerance of racism in one of Australia's favourite sports. What is also encouraging is the number of people, Indigenous and non-Indigenous, within sport, the media, and in the general community who support Tahu's stand.
>
> However, that Tahu has had to do this also should make all fair-minded Australians ashamed of senior sporting officials in New South Wales who continue to allow racism to flourish in the teeth of the magic and integrity that our Indigenous players bring to the code. To support Tahu's stance of *No way walk away* my family's Blues flag was taken down off our car and much to the delight of our friends in Queensland we cheered for the Maroons. Especially when Greg Inglis scored the first try!
>
> What needs to be very clear is that there is no place for racism anywhere in Australia and no excuses! The future for all Australian children depends on it. It's time for New South Wales to put a stop to racism for good and promote the sheer talent and admirable integrity of our Indigenous Australian sporting heroes. Thank you Timana Tahu for showing the way to a better Australia for all Australians.
>
> —Rhonda Craven

can continue in today's society, transmitted from one generation to the next. Often these inherited views go unchallenged generation after generation, as the historical basis for such views is not examined. Therefore, continued ignorance about the real history of a country can lead to racism being perpetuated. Oodgeroo Noonuccal (one of Australia's leading poets and an educator all her life) defined this phenomenon as 'racism is ignorance born of fear'. It is a state of mind that goes unchallenged until people are exposed to the facts and learn to question the basis of the attitudes they hold. This situation is often hampered by a lack of educational opportunities to address ignorance in the wider community. For example, not all pre-service or practising teachers have been educated to teach all Australians about Aboriginal Australia.

In 2008, the Director-General of the New South Wales Department of Education and Training told the Legislative Council inquiry into overcoming Indigenous disadvantage:

> If a culture's accumulated multiple knowledge, languages, histories, traditions and practices are accepted, respected and valued by those both within and outside that culture, then the likelihood is that that culture will be strong and resilient. If, however, a culture is subject to disrespect, disregard, vilification or violence, then it is very likely that culture will not be resilient. The measure of a socially just society is how well it allows all of its members to live equally and equitably and how well it respects diversity. Social justice is underpinned by the fundamental belief that all peoples have a right to be and to flourish, and this is only possible if the intrinsic value of individual cultures is recognised and protected. If we do not respect and value the cultures and histories of our Aboriginal children, young people, their families and communities, then we will be instrumental in undermining their capacity to maintain their cultural resilience. (NSW Legislative Council Standing Committee on Social Issues, 2009, 5.52)

> We just lived in a shack... My father is white. What I know now is that my father had a lot of trouble finding accommodation because he had an Aboriginal wife. He used to be refused accommodation. We ended up living in a tent for a long time in this isolated place at San Remo and had to carry our water in buckets. He used to cut down kerosene tins and we used to carry buckets of water a mile...
>
> I think my father must have loved my mother a lot to put up with it. After she died in particular. Yeah, I think so because he certainly had to suffer a lot of pain and torment and real taunts and racist abuse himself from rednecks.
>
> —Pat O'Shane, in Rintoul (1993, p. 41)

The evolution of Munyarl mythology

Over the past two centuries, the history of Australia has had adverse consequences for Aboriginal Australians (see Chapters 4–7). The impact has been in terms of socio-economic, cultural and political dispossession and disadvantage, and of the development of 'other Australian' attitudes towards Aboriginal Australians.

The development of such attitudes as racism, lack of understanding, discrimination, prejudice, apathy and exclusion has been facilitated through a number of factors, which have included:

- government policies that have discriminated against Aboriginal people by denying them basic human and citizen rights;
- a failure to acknowledge that White Australia has a black history;
- misinformation about Aboriginal cultures and peoples through social Darwinist arguments, maintained through education and other mainstream Australian institutions;
- the denial of adequate or appropriate education for Aboriginal people;
- genocidal attacks on Aboriginal people (e.g. massacres, forcible removal from homelands to missions, removal of children from families); and
- the history of racist media representation of Aboriginal people as being inferior to non-Aboriginal people, and their exclusion from mainstream media.

Aboriginal Studies is aimed at redressing these issues and fostering positive attitudes among other Australians. Misinformation can cause a number of sensitive issues to arise when teaching Aboriginal Studies—for example, myths about Aboriginal people, denial of actions directed against Aboriginal people and a lack of understanding of the consequences of cultural dominance and cultural dispossession. Misconceptions and stereotypes in the classroom also impact adversely on Aboriginal students' self-concepts, psycho-social well-being, academic achievement and ultimately their human potential.

The history of modern Australia began with a lie so terrible it resulted in the entire

Aboriginal population of Australia being dispossessed of their lands. This was the legal fiction of *terra nullius*—Latin words meaning 'a land belonging to no one'—the basis on which Captain James Cook claimed Eastern Australia for King George III (see Chapter 4). This claim meant that Cook did not recognise the existence of Aboriginal people, even though he had encountered resistance at landing places and had seen Aboriginal people's fires all the way up the coast. *Terra nullius* failed to recognise the validity of Aboriginal cultures, and even denied Aboriginal existence. It established the framework for historians and education authorities to ignore Australian history prior to 1770 and to fail to include the history of Aboriginal Australians from 1788. This was the beginning of the Aboriginal nightmare.

The initial relationship between Aboriginal Australians and the invading 'settlers' was based on Eurocentric assumptions. The British believed their culture and race to be superior. This view resulted in the generation of misconceptions and stereotypes—for example, seeing no churches, the British assumed that Aboriginal people had no religion. They did not realise that Aboriginal spirituality was part of their daily lives. Seeing no houses or farms, they assumed that Aboriginal people did not own the land. They did not realise that Aboriginal people had special rules as custodians of the land for future generations and a special relationship to it.

Many of Australia's past government policies were informed by the discipline of anthropology, the 'science of man'—the study of social evolution and functioning. Its starting point was the assumption that Europeans were at the top of the ladder of social evolution. Anthropology developed a discourse and a subject-matter that few Aboriginal people understood, and hence it excluded Aboriginal people. For example, R.M. and C.H. Berndt's (1964) book *The World of the First Australians* includes the topics of origins, archaeology, kinship, economic life, ritual, law and order, death and the afterlife. What is dramatically missing from this non-Aboriginal picture of traditional Aboriginal society is reference to the realities of life in the communities in which the research was conducted—invasion, dispossession, racism, 'protection' and assimilation.

This has resulted in history being written as the discourse of the conqueror, which in itself is Eurocentric and therefore biased. As noted Aboriginal historian James Wilson-Miller (personal communication) emphasises:

> Since the British invasion of the Hunter Valley in 1801, much has been written about my people, the Wonnarua and other Indigenous groups, Australia wide. In fact, collectively and over time, we became the most studied race of people in Australia. Academics have dealt with just about every aspect of Indigenous life. Archaeologists have dug, measured, recorded and drawn. Anthropologists have listened, tape-recorded, structured and transcribed. There seems to be a never-ending supply of information on Indigenous people, researched by countless people throughout Australia. Most documentation has been written by non-Indigenous people and interpreted in non-Indigenous ways. More recently, however—and especially from around the 1980s—there have been countless numbers of Indigenous writers, writing about our own people. We are now interpreting our own life-styles, both past and present, through our own eyes, thus, giving a truer perspective on our many contact histories.

Wilson-Miller specifically raises issues about non-Aboriginal research and documentation, and the ways in which misinterpretations have affected societal perceptions. Most writings about Aboriginal Australians from the late eighteenth century to the mid-twentieth century have been Eurocentric. These writings reflect the attitudes of the time and have helped to convey misconceptions and stereotypes to the wider Australian community.

Many people are aware that the 'White Australia' policy was finally abolished in December 1972—one of the first and most symbolic acts of the Whitlam government. Most people fail to see the connection between the 'White Australia' policy and Aboriginal Studies; this was, after all, an immigration policy and as such nothing to do with Aboriginal people nor relevant today. But White Australia was racist *by definition*—and, where it survives (and it does), it still is.

Australia's assimilation policies were linked directly to the 'White Australia' policy, which defined Australia as *White*—at the highest official level. This meant that Aboriginal people did not even exist, even after the 1967 Referendum. Also, the 'White Australia' policy was not abolished until less than 40 years ago—only two generations. The implications of this need to be understood: Every person in a position of power or influence or authority in Australia now who grew up in Australia grew up in 'White Australia'—potentially with all the attitudes and values and prejudices, and the frame of reference, of 'White Australia'. That includes most teachers in Australian schools (the average age of our teachers in 2005 was 44.96 and continues to rise (see <www.parliament.nsw.gov.au/prod/la/qala.nsf>).

What also needs to be understood is that, as a result of the Eurocentric frame of reference of White Australia, all the public institutions, all the mainstream history, all the 'heritage' and all education systems in Australia have been White European by definition. Decision-makers can change a policy with the stroke of a pen, but entrenched attitudes and values that have for generations been the staple of socialisation are not so easily changed. This applies especially to education systems—and it is why education has such a critical part to play in rectifying the misconceptions and stereotypes of 'White Australia'.

Rebutting common myths

Myths affect Aboriginal Australians every day. Some examples of discrimination and prejudice have been highlighted by the media, but many have not. Far too many Aboriginal people still experience overt discrimination—being refused service in hotels and shops, being physically and verbally abused, being passed over for work—even being killed for being Aboriginal. For example, Indigenous people are more likely than non-Indigenous people to die in custody. From 1990 to 1999, 51 Indigenous people died in police custody and 95 in prison custody. From 2000 to 2005, 44 Indigenous people died in police custody and 57 in prison custody (Williams, 2001; also see Johnston, 1991). Hence discrimination impacts on life itself. It also dramatically impacts on all aspects of life, including employment, education, housing, self-concept and psycho-social well-being. As such, discrimination limits life opportunities and ultimately blocks individuals from reaching their full potential.

"Oh! Mummy! Here's a man with a negative for a face!"

1938 cartoon by Stan Cross which appeared in Smith's Weekly. *By 1938—Sydney's Sesquicentenary—so few Australians had met any Aboriginal people that the little boy thinks a black man cannot exist. Courtesy State Library of NSW.*

> I think it's very hard to be an Aboriginal in Australia, especially if you are fair dinkum, because what you forgo is a lot of what other people take for granted. You have to contend with abuse, tension, conflict, poor relationships with people where otherwise you would have been friends, things you have to say to communities and groups, which you know are embarrassing and uncomfortable, but they've got to be said, otherwise who is going to say them and how will change come about?
> —Charles Perkins, in Rintoul (1993, p. 290)

Myths seem to have an enduring quality and spread rapidly once begun, even though they have no basis in fact. Myths about Aboriginal Australians are so pervasive that in 1992 the federal office of the then Minister for Aboriginal and Torres Strait Islander Affairs produced a booklet, *Rebutting the Myths: Some Facts about Aboriginal and Torres Strait Islander Affairs*, to counter some common distorted views and to set the record straight. This was revised by the new Liberal federal Minister (Commonwealth of Australia, 1997, <www.austlii.edu.au>). Craven (1996) also developed with the Teaching the Teachers Steering Committee the booklet *Using the Right Words in the Indigenous Australian Studies Classroom* to provide teachers with information on appropriate terminology to use in classrooms to avoid conveying misconceptions and stereotypes. The Australian Human Rights Commission (2008) has also produced *Face the Facts: Questions and Answers About Aboriginal and Torres Strait Islander Peoples* which is updated regularly. *Face the Facts* draws on primary research information including laws made by the Australian Parliament, government policies, academic research and statistics gathered by the Australian Bureau of Statistics to provide a snapshot of aspects of the social realities of Australia for Indigenous Australians. For teachers, *Face the Facts* is also produced as an educational resource that complies with national curriculum standards. Resources such as these are powerful tools for rebutting Munyarl mythology using facts.

Aboriginal people and alcohol

A common myth is that all Aboriginal people are alcoholics. When the facts are examined, this simply is not the case. In 2004–05, Indigenous people aged 18 years and over were more likely than non-Indigenous people to abstain from drinking alcohol altogether (ABS, 2008a). Furthermore, the rates of chronic risky/high-risk drinking were similar for both Indigenous and non-Indigenous Australians in 2004–05 (ABS, 2008a). This is not to deny the obvious problems caused by the comparatively higher proportion of Indigenous problem drinkers. For example, over 2004–05, rates of binge drinking were higher for Indigenous than non-Indigenous people—Indigenous Australians were twice as likely as non-Indigenous Australians to drink at short-term risky/high-risk levels at least once a week (ABS, 2008a). However, the myth that all Aboriginal people, or even the great majority, are alcoholics clearly is untrue given that more Indigenous Australians in comparison to other Australians do not drink at all.

Cartoon by Bronwyn Halls showing how stereotypes can affect our views of people from other cultures. Courtesy Bronwyn Halls.

Face the Facts education resource

Activity 5: The Facts—Aboriginal and Torres Strait Islander Peoples

This activity is designed to assist students in accessing the information included in *Face the Facts: Questions and Answers About Aboriginal and Torres Strait Islander Peoples* to identify some of the important issues facing Indigenous peoples today, and to identify how statistical information can be used to support an argument or proposal. This activity can be used in the classroom when adequate computer resources are available or alternatively set as a homework or individual assignment where more appropriate.

Step 1: Before/During/After Reading Activity

This B-D-A Activity is designed to assist students in accessing information in *Face the Facts: Questions and Answers About Aboriginal and Torres Strait Islander Peoples*. The Before/During/After Reading Activity is based on the K-W-L (what I know, what I want to know, and what I learned) strategy.

1. Students begin by brainstorming and listing in the 'before column' everything they know about Aboriginal and Torres Strait Islander peoples. A series of headings have been included to assist students with their responses. This step can be done individually, with partners, in small groups or the whole class can participate at once. However, it is important to always have students share and debate this information as a group before moving to the next step.
2. After brainstorming, students read *Face the Facts: Questions and Answers About Aboriginal and Torres Strait Islander Peoples*, writing brief notes on the new information they find in the 'during' column. This can also be done individually, with partners, or in small groups—depending on classroom dynamics and objectives. When students locate information in the text that agrees with statements they wrote in their 'before' column, they place a tick next to those statements to indicate that their background knowledge was correct.
3. In the next step (after reading), students briefly summarise the new information they have learned in the 'after' column.
4. Next, group or whole-class discussion should take place to revisit the 'before reading' statements that were listed on the worksheet and to share the information they have discovered and clarify any areas of confusion that may have arisen. The aim of this discussion is to establish what students already know about Aboriginal and Torres Strait Islander peoples.
5. Each student must then identify three questions or issues they have identified during the B-D-A activity for further research.

Additional resources

Further information about the K-W-L strategy is available via: MyRead Website—developed by the Australian Association for the Teaching of English (AATE) and the Australian Literacy Educators Association (ALEA) and published by the Department of Education, Science and Training (DEST), 2003, <www.myread.org/guide_frontloading.htm#kwl>, and the Teaching English Website—developed by Office for Curriculum, Leadership and Learning, Department of Education, Tasmania, <www.discover.tased.edu.au/english/choosing.htm#kwl>.

Step 2: Identifying the Facts About Aboriginal and Torres Strait Islander peoples

Using the questions they identified during the B-D-A activity, students must locate the facts. The focus of this investigation should be on statistical information that supports or challenges each student's assumptions about Indigenous issues.

Useful statistics are available in *Face the Facts: Questions and Answers About Aboriginal and Torres Strait Islander Peoples*. However, students should also be encouraged to use their research skills to discover additional facts. The following website may be useful: Australian Bureau of Statistics, <www.abs.gov.au>.

A table has been included in the worksheet to assist students in recording information discovered during their research.

> *Step 3: Using Statistics to Develop a Report, Proposal or Argument*
>
> During this step, students must reflect on the information they have discovered and evaluate whether the data they have discovered [is] sufficient to construct a report, proposal or argument. At this stage, teachers should work with students to finalise their report topics and assess the information they have gathered. The following instructions have been included in the worksheet.
>
> *Student instructions*
>
> Statistics are a powerful tool and can be used to provide the basis of strong arguments for change. Governments, community groups and individuals can all use statistics to make decisions about how to best allocate resources; identify those groups most in need and provide effective services in the community; propose change or development to address social issues—or simply satisfy one's curiosity.
>
> Now that you have located some statistical information about each of the questions/issues you have identified, select one area to investigate further. There are many issues/questions you could explore, including:
>
> **Indigenous population**
> How many Aboriginal and Torres Strait Islander people are there in Australia? Where do they live?
>
> **Indigenous health**
> Compare statistics on the health of Indigenous and non-Indigenous peoples.
>
> **Housing**
> Compare statistics on home ownership for Indigenous and non-Indigenous peoples.
>
> **Employment**
> Compare statistics on the levels of unemployment of Indigenous and non-Indigenous people.
>
> There are many other areas you could investigate. Use *Face the Facts: Questions and Answers About Aboriginal and Torres Strait Islander Peoples* to identify other areas which interest you.
>
> *Step 4: Presenting Your Report*
>
> To complete this activity, students must report on their findings, using statistics and other facts to support their argument. Students should be encouraged to share their reports with classmates. This could include publication of the reports in hard copy or on a website.
>
> *Source:* Australian Human Rights Commission (2008)

Another myth in relation to alcohol is what is known as the 'fire-water theory'; this maintains that Aboriginal people have a gene that causes them to be less tolerant of alcohol than other Australians (Brady, 2008). Historically, Aboriginal people may have seemed less tolerant to alcohol, simply because they had not been exposed to it—or, importantly, educated about it—prior to the British introducing alcohol to them. Therefore, the combined effects of alcohol, dispossession, and the consequent adverse and enduring impacts of these on Indigenous mental health, have likely created this myth. Furthermore, research undertaken by Hunter, Hall and Spargo (1991) found no evidence that Aboriginal people are biologically less able than Westerners to handle alcohol. Our student teachers are often astounded when they learn of these facts, and question why they have not been given this information previously.

Aboriginal people are lazy and don't want to work

The myth that Aboriginal people do not want to work has clearly contributed to today's unemployment rates (e.g. deterring employers from hiring Aboriginal employees), given that the unemployment rate for Indigenous people in 2006 was three times the rate for non-Indigenous

Rebutting the Myths. *A housewife rests on her broom and imagines white man 'working like a black'. She sees a black man asleep outdoors. But this idea is countered by a procession of Aboriginals carrying Aboriginal-enterprise placards in the blazing sun: CDEP, pearls, fishing, tourism, art, etc. Published by the office of the Minister for Aboriginal Affairs (1994, revised 1997). Courtesy Bruce Petty.*

people (16 per cent compared with 5 per cent) (ABS, 2008a). When the facts are examined, it can clearly be seen that most Aboriginal Australians prefer to work rather than receive unemployment entitlements. In fact, 57 per cent of Indigenous people aged 15–64 years work compared with 76 per cent of the non-Indigenous population (ABS, 2008 pp. 50–1; AHRC, 2008).

It also needs to be appreciated that Aboriginal Australians are incredibly talented at generating new businesses that add materially to national well-being. For example, in the arts field there are self-employed commercial artists, writers, book illustrators, fabric and rug designers, restaurant owners, comedians, musicians, cartoonists, actors, dancers, film-directors and filmmakers. Results from the 2006 Census showed that 33 per cent of self-employed Indigenous people were aged 35–44 years and 27 per cent were aged 45–54 years, and that employment patterns for these age groups were similar in the non-Indigenous population (ABS, 2006). Clearly, Aboriginal Australians and non-Aboriginal Australians are similarly enterprising.

The Community Development Employment Projects program (CDEP) is an Australian government-funded initiative for unemployed Indigenous peoples. It has been in operation since 1977. It enables local Indigenous organisations to provide employment and training in lieu of social security payments—'work for the dole'. In 2006, 14 200 Indigenous people reported their participation in CDEP (ABS, 2008a). However, the program has largely been abolished, except in some remote areas, though a replacement is being considered.

Another related myth about work is that Aboriginal people are unreliable workers—that is, they go off on 'walkabout'. This myth obviously has Eurocentric beginnings, and is clearly untrue given the large numbers of Aboriginal Australians who hold responsible and leadership positions in the workforce. The term 'walkabout' arose when Aboriginal people on stations needed to attend ceremonies, and with limited English explained to the station owners that they needed to 'go walk about'. Station owners and others then applied the term in a derogatory way to any absences from the station, and the term is now used worldwide.

We have been in many schools where Aboriginal visiting speakers are working. We have observed young schoolchildren ask visiting speakers questions like 'How come you have a car?' and 'Why don't you work?' Young children obviously were not born with these misconceptions and stereotypes, yet some children seem to assume Aboriginal people do not work or own material possessions. These types of issues show the enduring nature of myths and stereotypes about Aboriginal Australia that continue today.

Native title is just special treatment

Since the High Court recognised the existence of native title, a new category of myths about this decision has emerged. In fact, so widespread were these myths that in June 1993 the then Minister for Aboriginal and Torres Strait Islander Affairs, Robert Tickner, issued a paper called *Rebutting Mabo Myths*. At the time, Tickner (1993, p. 1) noted that:

> There is nothing radical about the High Court decision in the *Mabo* case. The *Mabo* decision broadly recognises that, in those remaining parts of Australia where Aboriginal people still occupy their traditional country on which their families

have lived for tens of thousands of years, they may be recognised as the owners of that land by the High Court of Australia.

Rebutting Mabo Myths went on to look at ten common myths about the *Mabo* decision. For example, some sections of the media promoted the myth that the native title case meant people's backyards were not safe from Aboriginal land claims. Given the High Court's stipulation that native title was extinguished on freehold land, this is simply not a threat. Further, to be successful, claimants must have continuously maintained their traditional association with the land. Hence the *Native Title Act* has thus far been of direct application only to a small percentage of Aboriginal Australians, mainly in remote areas.

Another common myth has been that the *Mabo* decision means that Aboriginal people will be given land for nothing while other Australians have to buy it. But the *Mabo* decision does not mean that Aboriginal people are given any land; rather, it means that they can keep the land they already have and where their families have lived for thousands of years. (After all, all Australians have the right to inherit property from their families.) The High Court decision also has nothing to do with special treatment or some sort of compensation for guilt: it is about justice. As Australia's Governor-General, the Hon. Bill Hayden AC, said in May 1993, at the official opening of the Australian Parliament:

> The *Mabo* judgment is, in the government's view, recognition of an historic truth and creates the best chance we have ever had for a nationally agreed and durable settlement. The government considers that this decision must, therefore, lead to us entering the twenty-first century with the fundamental relationship between the nation and its Aboriginal people rebuilt on fair and just foundations.

Some misconceptions and stereotypes

Eurocentric frames of reference

One of the most fundamental misconceptions is Aboriginal people not being recognised as

James Wilson-Miller, author of Koori: A Will to Win *and Head Curator of Koori History and Culture at the Powerhouse Museum, Sydney, holding a photo of his forebears taken at the St Clair Mission at Singleton in 1907. Photo: Peter Morris. Courtesy Fairfax Photo Library.*

Aboriginal—even when, for anyone who knows anything about Aboriginal Australia, it is quite obvious that they are. For example, James Wilson-Miller is a Koori. He was out with a group of friends at a Thai restaurant. Seeing his dark skin, the waitress asked him where he was from. James replied, 'Australia', and the waitress said, 'Yes, but what country were you born in?' Again James said, 'Australia.' 'Oh I see,' she said, 'but where were your parents born?' Again James told her, 'Australia.' 'Oh,' she said, and walked away looking rather puzzled. It had not even occurred to her that James could be Aboriginal. You might think this was just an isolated incident. But two weeks later, in a Mexican restaurant, exactly the same thing happened. Then it happened again at a cocktail party in the affluent Sydney suburb of Mosman. One of the guests spent some time trying to guess James's nationality: Tongan, Maori, Polynesian, even Balinese or Caribbean.

The Stereotyping of Aboriginal Women Artists

Aboriginal people in Australia have been under scrutiny since French, Dutch, Macassans, and English people sailed to this country. From the beginning of other people entering homelands, there was a prevailing thinking that the colonisers were superior to the 'primitive peoples' of this large land mass. This concept or way of thinking has prevailed in Australia, which can be indicated by the victory in becoming citizens of our country. While this moral victory cannot be diminished for the work done by many Aboriginal and non-Aboriginal people, it is ludicrous to consider that 190 years after the English arrived, this gave us the right to vote and equality in 1967. This one example helps to assist in some understanding of why people who are ignorant of Aboriginal issues consider it their automatic reflex to stereotype people.

This brings me to the substance of my writing, *The Stereotyping of Aboriginal Women Artists*. I write from the Djanbun clan member's perspective (Bundjalung Nation). It is an honour to be Aboriginal and the great pride I take in my relatives and past relatives is overwhelming. My life is saturated with art and my family. My father was Aboriginal, Bill Bancroft, and my mother is Polish and Scottish. I have witnessed when non-Aboriginal people question the identity of Aboriginal people, such as:

Don't you wish you were really Black?
I know Aboriginal people and you're not like them.

These comments, sometimes issued from the mouths of 'educated' people, equate to differential racism. The perpetrator has no concept of the individual Aboriginal person's life, history, what they have experienced, and family.

When an Aboriginal woman wants to paint or create, it is to evolve the artistic journey and be connected to the serpentine DNA of this country. All elements of cultural awareness accelerate the artistic hunger and this creates a response to society from the artist. This is a valuable national asset. Consider what it might be like to be quizzed about your identity or race when you are in a gallery with your own exhibition. To be interrogated about your lineage is not the appropriate way. People should be more patient and the individual's life will unfold over time and the art will be the visual history of that life and will not be vilification. What a great framework to forge an equitable society!

I am proudly an Aboriginal woman. The link to my past is not intangible, but real as I am a real human being and my art is a real product of my life's journey, and so is the art of many aspiring Aboriginal women artists in NSW, whose work has been largely ignored by the galleries, curators, and intellectuals.

Bronwyn Bancroft's art and designs have been exhibited around the world. A strong Bundjalung woman, she grew up in Tenterfield, northern New South Wales. She graduated from Canberra School of Arts in 1980, then set up her design company and shop Designer Aboriginals in 1985 and was the first Australian fashion designer to be invited to exhibit in Paris in 1987. One of the founders of Boomalli Aboriginal Artists' Cooperative in 1985, she turned her hand to painting and book illustration and has illustrated over twenty books, including books by Oodgeroo and Sally Morgan. For the Centenary of Federation in 2001, she was commissioned to plan and design a section of the Parade of Nations. Her latest book Why I Love Australia *celebrates our diverse landscape forms. She has a passion for equity in education.*

When he finally gave up, he was told James was Aboriginal. His response was, 'How quaint!' These incidents are not isolated to one person nor in time and space—they occur regularly to the majority of Indigenous Australians. This tells us that misconceptions and stereotypes continue to be rife in Australia.

It is also seriously worth thinking about how disturbing it must be to continually have your identity as an Australian not even acknowledged by fellow Australians, nor your status as Aboriginal (our first Australians) even considered. In the land down under, which is the one of the most egalitarian and successful multicultural nations in the world, clearly Aboriginal Australians are not even part of the frame of reference—and that is because of the most fundamental misconceptions: 'White Australia'. How this works in practice is that the 'real' Australia is still assumed to be 'white', so anyone with dark skin must by definition come from somewhere else and certainly is not born here. This misconception goes hand in glove with another fundamental stereotype: that 'real' Aboriginal people live only in the desert or Arnhem Land in the Northern Territory, wear lap-laps, carry spears and stand on one leg—and certainly do not go to restaurants or cocktail parties.

The 'real Aborigine' stereotype

The 'real Aborigine' stereotype has done enormous damage to Aboriginal people of all the so-called 'long-settled' areas of Australia. For Aboriginal Tasmanians, the denial is even worse. Generations of Australian children learnt that Truganini was the 'last Tasmanian Aboriginal' when she died in 1876. This is absolutely false, given there are more than 9000 Aboriginal people living in Tasmania now, yet many Australians still think there are no Aboriginal people left in the island state.

Another racist stereotype is that 'real' Aboriginal people only live in the Northern Territory. This denies the reality and historical cultural diversity of Aboriginal Australia. Also, given that most Indigenous Australians live in New South Wales, this is clearly incorrect (see Table 3.1).

Much anguish is caused to Aboriginal Australians when other Australians fail to comprehend or accept the Aboriginal identity of fair-skinned Aboriginal people. Such misconceptions ignore the reality of Australia's history. Many Aboriginal people are not dark-skinned and are—just like the rest of the nation— diverse in physical appearance. Many of our Aboriginal relations, friends and colleagues are fair-skinned, blond or blue-eyed. We have heard many anguished parents describe how school staff members have refused to appropriately acknowledge fair-skinned Aboriginal children's identity and culture. We have also comforted young children who have been told by their teachers that they are not Aboriginal because they are not dark-skinned. It is even worse when the fair-skinned child (whose younger brother

Table 3.1 Estimated state or territory of residence of Indigenous Australians, 2006

State/territory	Indigenous population	% of national total Indigenous population*	Total population	Indigenous people as % of State/territory population
New South Wales	148 178	28.7	6 817 182	2.2
Queensland	146 429	28.3	4 091 546	3.6
Western Australia	77 928	15.1	2 059 045	3.8
Northern Territory	66 582	12.9	210 674	31.6
Victoria	30 839	6.0	5 128 310	0.6
South Australia	26 044	5.0	1 568 204	1.7
Tasmania	16 900	3.3	489 922	3.4
ACT	4 043	0.8	334 225	1.2
Other territories	231	0.1	2 380	9.7
Australia	**517 174**	**100**	**20 701 488**	**2.5**

Source: Australian Bureau of Statistics, *Population Characteristics: Aboriginal and Torres Strait Islander Australians*, Catalogue No. 4713, Table 2.1 *Estimated Resident Population*, (27 March 2008), p. 16.

Kooris come in all colours. Aboriginal people, some originally from other parts of Australia, on the film set of the Teaching the Teachers video Munyarl Mythology. *Courtesy University of NSW.*

had darker skin) is told 'You're not Aboriginal, but your brother is'. The personal distress such stereotypes generate is rarely taken into account. The poem 'Fair Skin—Black Soul' by Burraga Gutya explains how this stereotype is based on fundamental misconceptions. This is also why it is important for all school staff, not just teachers, to understand and address misconceptions and stereotypes in schools.

Fair Skin—Black Soul

Whitefella, you're not listening,
I am not like you
we are worlds apart
with little in common.
You look in wonder
at my fair skin
and think, Ah he's one of us.
Wrong again.
You judge me on pigmentation
and not my inner being.
For despite my fairness
I am black,
I am a Murri
from the Kunja Nation.
I am proud—spiritual
and I resent the fact
you think I am white.
I didn't rape the land,
the women.
I didn't ask
to be left pale of skin
But now I DEMAND
my cultural respect.
Whitefella, this is your doing,
not mine.
You can only think
in one-dimensional terms.
You see but don't feel,
and whitefella you're wrong.
I am black.
I am a Murri
from the Kunja Nation.
And I stand proud.

—Burraga Gutya, in Canning (1990, p. 5).
Reproduced with permission.

Some people may think that misconceptions and stereotypes are merely name-calling—'Sticks and stones may break my bones but names will never hurt me'. This fails to recognise the pervasive nature of misconceptions and stereotypes, and the influence to which a dominant society can subject a minority. It also denies the reality of Australia's history and the dire consequences of this history. Furthermore, the application of misconceptions and stereotypes fundamentally impacts adversely on self-concepts and other psycho-social drivers of life potential (see Chapter 11).

The legacy of history

The tragedy facing Aboriginal Australians today is a legacy of our history. A hallmark of this history is the poor relationship between Aboriginal Australians and the wider Australian community. The impact such a relationship can have on Aboriginal Australians is tragic as well as pervasive. Patrick Dodson, Chairperson of the Council for Aboriginal Reconciliation until 1998, considers that 'there is no greater documented indicator of this failed relationship than the reports of the Royal Commission into Aboriginal Deaths in Custody into individual deaths'. He then goes on to describe the death of 22-year-old Mark Quayle as a tragic example of what can result from relationships based on misunderstanding and prejudice (Council for Aboriginal Reconciliation, 1994, pp. 5–8):

Attempting to kick alcohol abuse, which had had a major influence on the life of his peers, Mark had gone into withdrawal. Concerned for his health, Mark's brother and cousin drove him to hospital, where the Sister accepted him as a patient. His relatives asked if it was all right to leave, as one of them had to start work early that morning. The Sister said yes. Mark was disoriented, but quiet and well behaved. When offered coffee, he went outside to get firewood. Concerned for his welfare, the Sister rang the police to bring him back to the hospital. (Only three minutes had elapsed since Mark's relatives had left.) She also rang the Matron, who approved what she had done. When Mark returned with firewood 'to boil the billy for coffee', the Sister rang the police to cancel the call, but they had already left. Mark asked where the toilet was and went outside again.

Two constables arrived and found Mark in the street outside the hospital. They locked him in the police van. Commissioner Wootten reported: 'They had no justification whatever for doing this. They had only been asked to return him to the hospital, and he had done nothing to justify detention.'

The Sister had not attempted to obtain any medical history from Mark's relatives, nor had she made any physical examination. While Mark remained locked in the police van, the Sister rang the Royal Flying Doctor Service in Broken Hill and spoke to a doctor. Commissioner Wootten reported: 'She told the doctor only that the patient was called Mark Quayle and had been brought in by friends who said that he was "in the dings" [a colloquial term for alcohol withdrawal].' The doctor did not understand, and asked what was wrong with him. She said that he was hearing things and seeing things and acting strangely and had escaped twice. Without giving any more history or waiting for the doctor to ask any further questions, she went on to say that the police were there and had Mark in the paddy wagon and that he would probably spend the night in the police station. She asked if it was all right to 'just leave him as he is'. Unbelievably, the doctor immediately answered that that was 'fine'. He commented that it sounded as though the patient had had something or taken something, to which the Sister replied that she just did not know. The doctor then told her to take the patient's blood sugar 'before he heads off to the police station' just to make sure it was normal, and to 'wish him well as he goes away'.

> I had another daughter after that, Colleen, and those two were born in that era just before the referendum came in. They were graded, Colleen and Margaret. We got a letter stating that Margaret was one-sixteenth of an Aboriginal, Colleen was one-fourteenth of an Aboriginal. I don't know how they worked it out: same mother, same father. It was their shades of Aboriginality.
> —Veronica Brodie, Ngarrindjeri, in Rintoul (1993, p. 316)
>
> You'll hear: 'You're not Aboriginal, you don't look like an Aboriginal person, you haven't got a black skin.' What answer could you give them? Now when someone says you're part-Aboriginal, the answer is: 'What part of me is Aboriginal? Do I have a black leg or a black arm? What do you mean by part?'
> —Furley Gardner, in Rintoul (1993, p. 220)

The Sister asked the senior police officer whether he could have Mark at the police station and the constable replied 'if there is no other alternative, yes'. Commissioner Wootten said in his report that there were a number of sensible alternatives to locking Mark in a police cell (including sedation, which was the standard treatment for a patient with withdrawal symptoms). The Royal Commission describes what happened next:

'The police took Mark to the police station. Except that they did not fingerprint him, they treated him like a prisoner, removing his property including his watch, and checking whether there were any outstanding warrants on him, which there were not. Instead of placing him in a cell with access to a light switch, as they could have done, they locked him in a cell with no switch and left him in the dark. They then went away for over five hours.

When another constable came on duty at about 8.30 am he found Mark hanging from a flap on the cell door by a noose made of a strip from a blanket. Given Mark's disturbed and hallucinating condition and the effects of alcohol withdrawal, there is nothing surprising in his having hanged himself in the conditions in which he was left. There is not the slightest reason to believe that any other was directly involved in his death.'

Commissioner Wootten goes on to state that, indirectly, the responsibility for Mark's death

> The consequence of this history is the partial destruction of Aboriginal culture and a large part of the Aboriginal population and also disadvantage and inequality of Aboriginal people in all areas of social life where comparison is possible between Aboriginal and non-Aboriginal people. The other consequence is the considerable degree of breakdown of many Aboriginal communities and consequence of that and of many other factors, the losing of their way by many Aboriginal people and with it the resort to excessive drinking and with that violence and other evidence of breakdown of society. As this report shows, this legacy of history goes far to explain the over-representation of Aboriginal people in custody, and thereby the death of some of them.
> —Commissioner Elliott Johnston, Royal Commission into Aboriginal Deaths in Custody (1991)

lies with the Sister, the doctor and the two constables, 'all of whom acted in breach of their legal, professional and moral duties towards a person who was in their care and dependent on their proper attention. But while their conduct has to be examined and assessed, it would be wrong to smugly scapegoat them as monstrous individuals. *Underlying their uncaring conduct, which treated Mark as less than an equal human being, are attitudes to Aboriginals which are widespread, not only amongst police and in hospitals, but in the wider community. His death is a challenge to the conscience of all Australians.*' [our emphasis].

The members of Mark Quayle's family live with the knowledge that they placed Mark in the care of a hospital—an institution that all Australians should confidently regard as a place of care and protection. But their trust was shattered when they were stopped in the street with the news that Mark had been hanging in a police cell that morning. Commissioner Wootten goes on to make many other comments about the unsatisfactory nature of the internal police inquiry which followed Mark's death, and the way the white community closed ranks to attempt to unfairly 'blame the victim'. Kerry Carrington (1991) goes a little further, saying that:

> From a sociological perspective every white in Wilcannia could be regarded in some sense culpable creating the context in which Mark died, although some more consciously than others, by participating in the daily racial divisions in the town which normalize the mistreatment of Aboriginal people as natural, justifiable or inevitable. (Carrington, 1991, p. 184)

Mark Quayle's treatment was a result of a long history in the Wilcannia area of dispossession of Aboriginal people, economic pressures, rejection in the townships, and the resultant devastating effects on the Aboriginal community. Commissioner Wootten's report into Mark Quayle's death uses the word 'inhumanity' on numerous occasions when referring to Mark's treatment. From Dampier at Roebuck Bay in the 1600s, to Wilcannia in 1987, to the 101 deaths in custody in 2005 (Williams, 2001), the tragic legacy of *terra nullius* lives on.

This legacy is seen in many different areas of Australia every day now: in further deaths in custody across the nation, poor health, substandard housing, poor educational outcomes and low levels of employment. If it was ever in doubt that relationships and understanding between black and white in Australia needed mending, the Royal Commission into Aboriginal Deaths in Custody settled the question. What remains to be seen is whether and when the continuance of all these issues over two decades after the Royal Commission will be addressed.

> I believe that education, alongside legislation and policy, [is] central tools to break down barriers and promote community harmony and inclusion.
> —Tom Calma, Race Discrimination Commissioner, in Australian Human Rights Commission (2008, p. iii)

Using the right words

Much has been written on the pivotal role of language and the need for language to be investigated in the re-evaluation of social values. Rather than just memorising lists of politically correct words, teachers need to explore why some terms may be considered preferable to others. Important insight can be gained by exploring images created by terms such as 'tribe', or working out what can be learnt about legislators and bureaucrats who defined Aboriginal people as 'half-castes', and even 'quadroons' and 'octoroons'. Using the right words is not about imposing on teachers a language of politically correct words to be used in the classroom that has to be strictly adhered to. Rather, it involves thinking carefully about the terminology we use as educators to ensure that our terminology avoids conveying outdated misconceptions and stereotypes.

As teachers can easily and inadvertently convey or reinforce stereotypical attitudes and inaccurate information about Aboriginal Australia by using inappropriate terminology, it is important that we as teachers learn what is likely to be acceptable terminology. It is just as important that we learn the importance of consulting at the local level to determine what will be appropriate and acceptable. This can be done by consulting the local Aboriginal community or by asking the advice of Aboriginal Education resource people. It may be preferable to consult the community through an Aboriginal Education resource person. Also, the opinion of one Aboriginal person should not be taken as representing the views of the whole local community. If in doubt, the nearest Aboriginal Education Consultative Group (AECG) or Indigenous Education Consultative Body should be contacted for advice on how to proceed.

The Teaching the Teachers Steering Committee developed guidelines for teachers that suggest appropriate and inappropriate terminology to employ in Aboriginal Australian Studies courses (see Craven, 1996). These guidelines are designed to inform teachers of appropriate terminology and to serve as a starting point for discussions with local Aboriginal communities regarding the terminology they would prefer to be used in courses. They are also useful as a basis for discussion of less and more appropriate terminology. The guidelines were endorsed by the National Federation of AECGs.

The idea for this terminology list came from repeated corrections of stereotypical expressions used by student teachers when writing teaching units and in class discussions. The persistence of these stereotypes in the university classroom clearly demonstrated the need for this resource. The list is principally designed to help teachers by pointing out potential pitfalls of some terminology. It is designed to be educational by explaining why certain words may be preferable, while others may be offensive.

The tables list, in the first column, commonly used expressions that are often not appropriate. The second column lists more appropriate terminology. Across the page, underneath both columns, a rationale is provided of why some

> It is a fact that most Australians have little contact with Aboriginal and Torres Strait Islander people and base their views on stereotypes and a lack of understanding of Aboriginal values and cultures.
> —Patrick Dodson (1992, p. 1)

terms may be offensive and others are likely to be more acceptable to Aboriginal Australians. This resource is a useful guide for teachers.

In the wider community, debates have raged on the use of some terms. For example, the term 'invasion' as opposed to 'settlement' in curriculum documents has attracted community debate in several Australian states. Like the debate over native title and *Wik*, elements of community response have largely been reactionary and based on ignorance. Australia was not settled peacefully, therefore it was invaded. Describing the arrival of the Europeans as a 'settlement' attempts to view Australian history from the ships of England rather than the shores of Australia. Some teachers feel compelled either to strongly advocate the use of the word 'invasion' or to adamantly refuse to refer to such a word in the classroom. Others will use the word 'invasion' when referring to Aboriginal perspectives and 'settlement' when referring to non-Aboriginal perspectives. We would advocate educating students about the real history, to encourage them to debate the issues (e.g. ask children what they think about the invasion debate) and draw their own conclusions.

Telling the right stories

Ignorance about Aboriginal Australians has been rife in Australia since 1770. Due to the conspiracy of silence in past education, Australians have not experienced the benefit—or, more accurately, their *right*—of being taught the real history of Australia. This has meant that most Australians have been socialised to a British view of our history rather than being informed that 'White Australia has a black history'. Australians have been taught to view our history from the ships of England rather than the shores of Australia. Education institutions in the past have contributed to perpetuating this Eurocentric version and have failed to extinguish common myths about Australian history and Aboriginal cultures.

Teachers without experience in Aboriginal Studies can inadvertently perpetuate myths about Australian history. This is really not the fault of teachers, as they have not experienced appropriate education in this area. Many myths are perpetuated based on a White Australia frame of reference, therefore denying the existence of Aboriginal Australians. For example, 'Australia was discovered by Captain Cook' in terms of real history is impossible, as Aboriginal and Torres Strait Islander people were already here. 'The first settlement' is clearly incorrect when Aboriginal and Torres Strait Islander people had lived with this land since the beginning of the Dreaming. 'Blaxland, Lawson, and Wentworth were the first men to cross the Blue Mountains' cannot be true as Aboriginal men, women and children had crossed the Blue Mountains for thousands of years before these European explorers arrived. 'Australia was settled peacefully' is completely erroneous—in fact, sheer nonsense—when Australian history has documented the fact that war took place on the moving frontier as early as 1789 (see Reynolds, 1987, 1989). Yet these myths and others permeate Australian society.

Using the right names

The pervasive level of ignorance can be seen by examining some of the misconceptions and stereotypes perpetuated by not using the right names to refer to Aboriginal Australians. We have had to teach senior academics and colleagues to write 'Aboriginal' with a capital 'A'. The term 'aboriginal people' is used to describe Aboriginal people all over the world, whereas the term 'Aboriginal' denotes the Aboriginal people of Australia. Lower case is not used to identify other races of people (e.g. no-one would write 'australians', 'greeks' or 'italians'). Using upper case to denote a racial group also shows respect, but the lower case 'a' for Aboriginal is still used in some newspapers and magazines—also even in the writings of some leading Australians.

The use of common terms such as 'the Aborigines' or 'the Aboriginal people' tends to suggest that Aboriginal people/s are all the same and thus to stereotype Aboriginal Australians. The fact is that Aboriginal Australia was and is multicultural. Australia before the invasion comprised between 200 and 300 autonomous language groups. It can be said that the nations of Aboriginal Australia were, and are, as separate as the nations of Europe or Africa. Aboriginal identity is still based on belonging to the land in a local sense. The Dreaming is essentially local, belonging to places. Terms such as 'the Aborigines' imply that Aboriginal society is monocultural rather than diverse.

'Aboriginal people' and 'Torres Strait Islander people' or 'Aboriginal Australian people' are more appropriate terms, as they stress the humanity of Aboriginal and Torres Strait Islander people, which has in the past been widely denied or disregarded. 'Aboriginal' (in Latin, 'from the beginning') and other such European words have to be used because there is no Aboriginal word that can be used to refer to all Aboriginal people in Australia. Aboriginal-language generic people terms such as 'Koori', 'Murri', 'Nyoongah', and so on are even more appropriate to the areas where they apply. Aboriginal language group names are preferred—for example, Gamilaroi (a group in New South Wales) or Pitjantjatjara (a group in the Northern Territory and South Australia).

No more classifying people

Misconceptions and stereotypes are also conveyed by terms based on scientific racism that derive from a Eurocentric world-view. Some teachers and administrative school staff inadvertently use some of these terms. Offensive terms, including 'part-aborigine', 'full-blood', 'quarter-caste' and 'octoroon', were used by governments to classify Aboriginal and Torres Strait Islander people according to 'blood', skin colour and parentage. Exemption Certificates were issued to Aboriginal people with lighter skins (or a presumed high degree of 'civilisation') to allow them the same basic freedoms that other Australians were able to take for granted as citizens. These certificates classified people according to skin colour and tended to divide Aboriginal society. The terms are also Eurocentric in origin, and Aboriginal people may feel very offended when they are categorised by the colour of their skin. Aboriginal and Torres Strait Islander people understand their own history and identity, and recognise that

Guidelines for Appropriate Terminology for Indigenous Australian Studies

Dreaming and spirituality

Less appropriate	More appropriate
Dreamtime	The Dreaming The Dreamings

'Dreaming' or 'Dreamings' are mostly more appropriate as they describe Indigenous beliefs as ongoing today.

'Dreamtime' is used by many people to refer to the period of creation. The word 'Dreamtime' tends to indicate a time period which has finished. But the reality is that the Dreamings all over Australia are ongoing today. However many Aboriginal people still use the word 'Dreamtime' and this usage must be respected.

'Dreamtime' has been widely appropriated and trivialised, whereas 'Dreaming' has more serious connotations in terms of Aboriginal spirituality. The Dreaming/s establish/es the rules governing inter-relationships between people, land and spiritual beliefs.

Different Aboriginal groups have different 'Dreamings'. When referring to more than one group, 'The Dreamings' can be used to denote the plurality of Dreamings and stress cultural diversity. 'The Dreaming' can also be used as a generic term to express the commonality of Indigenous cultures. A capital letter is used when referring to the Dreaming/s to denote respect for Aboriginal people's beliefs. Some Aboriginal groups will also have a specific word in their own language that they use to refer to the Dreaming (e.g. Tjukurpa).

Religion	Spirituality

In terms of Indigenous belief systems, 'spirituality' or 'spiritual beliefs' are more appropriate for two reasons. Firstly, the word 'religion' has Western connotations and tends to refer mainly to established, organised, 'world' religions, such as the forms of Christianity, that seek to convert other peoples and cultures. Indigenous Australian spirituality is localised by definition, it is more a way of life, of connectedness and belonging. Secondly, many Indigenous people are offended by any in-depth study of Indigenous belief systems as such because of the secret–sacred nature of Indigenous beliefs.

However, it is important to also recognise that many Indigenous people are religious in terms of mainstream religions and as such hold religious beliefs in the usual sense of the word. These beliefs are often combined with Aboriginal spirituality.

Myths/Legends	Creation/Dreaming Stories
Story/Stories	Teachings from the Dreaming/s

Note: It is appropriate to use 'The Legends' when referring to Torres Strait Islander culture.

'Creation Stories' or 'Dreaming Stories' will be more appropriate as these expressions convey more respect for Aboriginal beliefs. Even more respect will be conveyed if these words are capitalised.

Using words such as 'myth' or 'legend' conveys the impression that information from the Dreaming is not true or trivial or only happened in the distant past. Such terms can convey the impression that Dreaming Stories are fairytales rather than Creation Stories.

In general, using the words 'story' or 'stories' alone should be avoided as such usage can convey the impression that Creation/Dreaming Stories are only stories, not even true. However, many Indigenous people will use expressions such as 'Emu story' to refer to a particular Dreaming Story.

Local community consultation wherever possible is critical to determine what usages are acceptable at the local level.

Source: Extracted from Craven (1996b)

Cartoon by Jolliffe, 1954. Eric Jolliffe was a prolific cartoonist, his work appearing in The Bulletin *and* Pix *for 50 years. He was famous for his* Witchetty's Tribe *cartoons featuring Aboriginal characters—athletic, joking men and hourglass-figure women. Aboriginal people claim to be the most studied people on earth, at the mercy of anthropologists' theories. Courtesy South Australian Museum.*

Our mission

A community where every person is able to participate fully without the fear of racism and discrimination. This mission links with the overarching *Canberra Social Plan*'s vision that we become a place where *all people reach their potential, make a contribution and share the benefits of our community.*

We value a community:

- committed to living in harmony with its natural environment;
- representing the best in Australian creativity;
- promoting lifelong learning and celebrating participation in community activities, culture, sport, recreation and work life;
- recognised for the way tolerance, fairness and equity shape the way we live; and
- where all people reach their potential, make a contribution and share the benefits of our community

(Multicultural and Community Affairs Group, 2004, p. 1)

---

physical features do not determine Aboriginal and Torres Strait Islander ancestry. Aboriginality is a spiritual feeling, an identity you know in your heart—it is not based on whether you are dark- or fair-skinned.

No more classifying cultures

Terms that have been used to classify Aboriginal cultures, such as 'primitive', 'simple', 'native', 'prehistoric' and 'stone-age', reflect Eurocentric world-views that are inaccurate, outdated and racist. These terms are offensive in that they imply Aboriginal and Torres Strait Islander societies were not as 'advanced' as European societies. They are based on the 'progress' model of history, which many people now question, and on the idea of evolution from 'lower' to 'higher' (Western) forms of social organisation. There is now more recognition of the effectiveness and sophistication of Aboriginal resource management, as well as of the complexity and balance of Aboriginal and Torres Strait Islander social organisation.

Combatting racism

Aboriginal Australian communities and educators have long been aware of the impact of the various forms of racism on their children's education, and have long called for action. The impact of all forms of racism on school education has been more widely recognised in recent years. Anti-racism policies are often mandatory across the system.

In the wider community, there is also more recognition of the impact of racism. There is anti-discrimination legislation at both the state and federal levels. There is wide awareness of attitudinal or overt racism and to a lesser extent of institutional or systemic racism—the way regulations, practices and whole systems can operate to disadvantage people from different language and cultural backgrounds. There is less awareness of cultural racism—the way the frame of reference in Australian institutions, including education, has always been white European by definition. This is why curriculum reform is so important in terms of the participation and outcomes of Aboriginal students. Now that there is more general awareness of racism and its impact, a growing whole-school curriculum area is anti-racist teaching and anti-racist strategies.

The Whole School Anti-Racism Project

Between 1991 and 1993, the Commonwealth Office of Multicultural Affairs, the New South Wales Ethnic Affairs Commission and the New South Wales Department of School Education co-funded the Whole School Anti-Racism Project. The project employed anti-racism coordinators in two schools, one with high Aboriginal enrolments, the other with majority non-English-speaking background enrolments, to develop and document whole-school community involvement in anti-racism strategies. Project materials were published in 1995, with a foreword by the then Prime Minister, Paul Keating:

> I particularly commend those who had the courage to look at what was really happening in school communities, to recognise and articulate negative attitudes in themselves and then to work, stretching their own capacities, on strategies to help themselves and their peers to address these most sensitive issues.

The Whole School Anti-Racism Project marked a very significant step forward in moves to eradicate racism in this country. Although the kit originated in New South Wales, all of Australia stands to gain. At the launch of the materials, the then Minister for Education, the Hon. John Aquilina, said the Whole School Anti-Racism Project was the only one of its kind in the world by which school communities can evaluate how well their school provides a racism-free environment: 'resource materials are designed to equip students, parents, teachers, administrators and local communities to actively speak out and challenge racism'. The aim of the package is to help school communities:

- to evaluate how well their school provides a racism-free environment; and
- to identify areas for action to develop and/or maintain a racism-free environment.

School communities are encouraged to use the materials as a working tool: they can photocopy sections as needed; let it support them in discovering where they are now; and use it to explore where they want to be, and how to get there.

The Whole School Anti-Racism Project comprises four documents in a box package:

- *School Communities Investigating Racism*—an overview of the project and the schools involved, with goals and intended outcomes;
- *Anti-Racism Planning Guide*—an evaluation and planning tool;
- *Strategies for Change*—a model for change and a range of 'how tos'; and
- *Understanding the Issues*—a collection of articles on racism and anti-racism education.

School Communities Investigating Racism outlines the project and the schools involved. It also provides background information, and identifies the project's goals and intended outcomes. It gives an overview of the activities undertaken by the selected school communities and identifies general issues to be considered by other schools when working towards a racism-free school community.

The *Anti-Racism Planning Guide* is an evaluation and planning tool. It is designed to assist schools to determine where they are—what their goals are in providing an educational and working environment that is free from racism.

Strategies for Change provides a model for change and a range of examples of how to collect information, set up workshops, conferences and meetings, get people involved, and improve school community participation. This document also provides examples of curriculum materials that can be used as strategies for change and how anti-racism education can be incorporated into teaching and learning programs.

Understanding the Issues is a collection of articles providing in-depth background and developmental reading on racism, anti-racism education, the effects of racism and why it must be addressed in school communities and Australian society.

The project materials are a way to empower Aboriginal communities and students to tackle racism in schools. Several aspects need to be recognised:

- Racism is not just an individual problem; it is systemic and involves the attitudes of the

Challenging racism in schools

Many issues and pitfalls confront schools as they commence to address the overt and covert causes of racism. Many schools have, in good faith, sought not only to implement mandatory Department policies, but also develop their own in-school strategies, looking at long-term changes to school policies and pedagogical practices. Yet even with the best of intentions and efforts, there appears to be little evidence of substantial attitudinal change or improved student outcomes for Aboriginal and many ethnic minority students.

The Whole School Anti-Racism Project, a training and development and curriculum handbook, developed out of earlier research in 1992. Some factors that impacted on the capacity of the schools involved in this research project to challenge long-held and deeply seated attitudes about students from non-dominant ethnic backgrounds raised issues that were seen as problematic matters for schools to consider. The Whole School Anti-Racism project material was meant to provide schools with an in-school model to implement whole school action and to complement the mandatory Anti-Racism Policy (1992). However, structural changes to the New South Wales Department of Education and Training, non-existent professional development and minimal support at a regional level saw the uptake of the material in schools languish.

What is of ongoing concern is how schools have seen their responsibilities in this area and how effective they have been in challenging racism. The context has been the political imperatives faced by schools and communities across Australia since the 1996 election, through the rise of Pauline Hanson and her One Nation party and the Howard government's practice of not recognising the issue of racism and papering over problems. One concern has been the simplistic and stereotyped conceptions that schools and the community have of racism, the individual and systemic role that schools have in circulating it, and their responsibility, and how this is the single most significant impediment to the development of school strategies to address it.

Where once invasion and colonisation was the heart of our problem, racism today has taken a subtler effect on the lives of Aboriginal people. Under the Howard government we witnessed an escalation of racism in our society, manifestations of the kind of deeper, ingrained control which can only occur where a society's institutions are geared to perpetuate the inequalities of racism. Not least in formal education. The media play an integral role with the way they represent Aboriginal issues compared to wider society, e.g. the Redfern Riot, the Cronulla riot, law and order issues etc.

The rise of new racism in countries like Australia occurred concurrently with the social dislocation caused by economic restructuring. The smaller the government, the greater the influence of big business and the lesser the effect that democratic institutions can have on the global economy. This may impede a government's ability, or even desire, to control national economies, social welfare, education and health.

The 'multicultural' approach to combating racism is a weak theory which is seen as being predicated on an assumption that racism is primarily an individual experience as opposed to a strong theory which positions racism as endemic to institutions. Multicultural strategies are based on an assumption that racism is the consequence of irrational or mistaken beliefs, and that targeted programs focusing on these can bring about changes to behaviour and attitudes.

An approach based on challenging endemic racism sees it as so entrenched and pervasive that educators cannot be expected to combat it adequately just by encouraging cultural tolerance. Racism cannot be fought without changes to the social, political and economic structures, which are both causes and effects of it. A 'strong' view does not accept weak excuses for the failure to overcome racism. Short of developing separate education systems, the main agents of change in schools will come from white administrators and teachers. Further, schools need to actively engage white students in the process of finding and implementing successful anti-racism strategies. I believe that it is to this area that we must turn our attention if we are to ever meet the challenges of this most pressing of social problems.

Darryl French was born in Moree, in northwest New South Wales, and was one of eleven children. He got back into education as a mature-age single parent raising three children. He worked with the New South Wales Department of School Education for six years, first as Home School Liaison Officer, then as Senior Education Officer when he co-wrote the Whole School Anti-Racism Project with Shirley Coyle. He was Field Officer with the New South Wales AECG for seven years, 1993 to 2000, then taught in the Bachelor of Community Management program at Macquarie University. At Australian Catholic University in the early 1990s he completed a Bachelor of Teaching and an Associate Diploma in Aboriginal Education. In 2000 he completed a Masters in Business Law at Macquarie University. Since 2005 he has been Aboriginal Programs Manager at Tranby College, teaching in the Diploma of Community Development and the Diploma of Aboriginal Studies.

whole community, and of the whole school community.
- Community involvement is important in all education. We need to recognise the importance of community involvement in addressing racism.
- Aboriginal people can make a significant contribution to schools and their communities.
- The views of students and the contributions they can make are valuable.
- Built on the strong foundations of experience in school communities, the Whole School Anti-Racism Project resource materials offer ideas about how to identify places where prejudice, discrimination or racism are affecting what happens in the school and how to develop new ways of doing things that give everyone a chance.

Anti-racism strategies

It is important to avoid perpetuating racism by omitting references to Aboriginal Australians. For example, if we teach about the gold rush without examining the impact of this era on the lives of Aboriginal Australians, we are denying their experience and their history. Likewise, if we teach about the early European 'settlement' of Australia without referring to the impact that such an invasion had on Aboriginal people, then we are falsifying Australian history by providing a Eurocentric version of history. Excluding the contributions of other cultures results in students not being aware that they exist or assuming that they are not worth mentioning.

Teachers should take a whole-school approach to combating racism, rather than attempting to combat racism in only one classroom. Likewise, it is important to seek the support and assistance of colleagues. Establish a committee to develop an anti-racist school policy: other teachers, students, parents (through the P&C) and community groups could be invited to participate in such a committee.

Promoting cultural diversity and individual differences in the school can enhance students' self-concepts and contribute to developing mutual respect and understanding. This involves acknowledging and valuing the individual cultural experiences of your students. It also helps to avoid racial stereotyping, as every culture is diverse and continually changing.

Furthering our own knowledge as teachers helps us to counter racist comments and stereotypes with factual information. Read Aboriginal and Torres Strait Islander Australian literature and history. Become familiar with local Aboriginal history by working closely with your local community or district consultants. Include works by Aboriginal authors as teaching resources and as references for the class library.

Much resource material in schools still contains information that is now recognised as racist and offensive. It can inadvertently be used by busy teachers and uncritical students. Try to review all resources in your school to check whether they acknowledge and value cultural diversity. Consider teaching your students how to evaluate the resources they use so they can detect cultural bias. This does not necessarily mean throwing out every resource that is blatantly racist, as such materials, when used

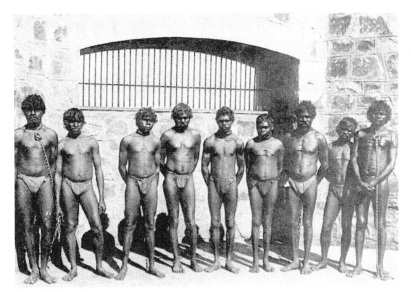

Aboriginal prisoners in neck chains, Roebourne Gaol, 1897. Using neck chains to secure groups of Aboriginal prisoners was still being defended as 'humane' in the 1940s. Police parties regularly chained together and brought back not only those Aboriginal people they thought were responsible for 'outrages', but also any who were witnesses. They also recruited 'trackers' from the gaols. The fitness and physiques of these men prove the health of traditional life. In contrast to the 'beaten' look of many Aboriginal photos of the day, these men are proud, confident in who they are, and defiant. Photo: Charles Henry Powell MIME. Courtesy Battye Library 3040P.

sensitively, can be useful in teaching students how to evaluate the resources they use, and allow them to analyse racist attitudes of the era (see Chapter 14).

Useful teaching strategies

Any effective Studies of Society-based program will not rely on any one discipline for its methodology. Studies of Society are concerned with the development of understandings that lead to the ability to 'read' society. It is an active area that should generate attitudes and values which lead to participation in debate, and action based on an ethical framework. Thus studies of society should reflect, as accurately as possible, historical and contemporary events that shape, or have shaped, our understanding of the world. In the context of Aboriginal Studies, children will be presented with points of view that may not be found in standard texts or commercially developed resources. Some strategies teachers may consider to counteract misconceptions include the following.

- *Teaching the truth.* In the past, Australian education systems have not taught our country's history fully and accurately. It is important for teachers to develop activities that allow students to learn the truth about Australia's history. Any unit of work that deals with history must surely incorporate Aboriginal perspectives to be accurate.
- *Beginning with the present.* In Australian classrooms, there are still some teachers focusing their Aboriginal Studies units solely on past Aboriginal societies. Aboriginal communities prefer teachers to focus units of work on present-day society and relate historical events to today's society.
- *Relating historical events to contemporary ones.* To make information more relevant to the learner, relate historical events back to today's society. Understanding how today's society was shaped by history enables students to plan and map a better future together. Teachers need to relate history lessons to more recent events.
- *Standing on the shore rather than the ship.* When engaging with Aboriginal and Torres Strait Islander issues, both historical and contemporary, students need to be provided with experiences that allow them to step into the place of people and events and view them from a variety of perspectives. This has been called 'moving from the ship to the shore'—a useful image when thinking about historical events to do with first contact and the following European colonisation.
- *Developing knowledge and appreciation of local Aboriginal culture/s.* While it is important to teach students about Aboriginal Studies from a national perspective, units of work should have a key focus on developing knowledge and appreciation of local

---

Aboriginal Education is not only the appropriate education of Aboriginal students but also involves the education or all Australian students about Aboriginal Australia.

Participation and outcomes of Aboriginal students will improve when Aboriginal history, cultures and contemporary issues are integrated to the curriculum for all students.

—New South Wales AECG Inc. pamphlet

Indigenous culture, history and initiatives. This is best started by consulting members of the local community.
- *Incorporating Aboriginal knowledge across the key learning areas.* 'I did Aboriginal Studies last term. I'm doing Convicts this term' is a view still expressed by some teachers. Such views compartmentalise and isolate Aboriginal Studies instead of articulating Aboriginal content and perspectives across the curriculum. Aboriginal Studies needs to be taught in a holistic approach that stretches across and throughout all the key learning areas.

The perpetuation of Munyarl mythology can be overcome in Australian society. All Australians can walk side by side to create a better future for our country. The objective is not to create guilt but to create an understanding of an important part of the history of Australia and the place of Aboriginal and Torres Strait Islander people in that history. Every informed Australian has a responsibility to stop the cycle of misinformation that is presented over family dinners, in restaurants, on public transport, in the workplace, in the media, and on the internet. The greatest contribution can be made by teachers, who can ensure that misconceptions, stereotypes and racism are addressed so that students who are our future are better informed to create an Australian society of which we can all be proud.

Right to be

Don't stereotype an image of what you want me to be
I'm a Woman and I'm Black and I need to be free
I'll give back your sense of values you bestowed upon me
And regain my pride, my culture, and true identity.
To the future I will strive and there's no looking back
I'll look to the women to support me on my track
I'll fight as a Woman for the right just to be
The most important contribution to this society.
Yes, I'm a Woman and I know that there's nothing that I lack
I'll progress with my learning till I finally get the knack
It's my independent thinking that makes me feel so strong
Our trust in solidarity, simply means we can't go wrong.
I don't want to be no second hand rose
I don't want to be on your centrefold pose
I'm a Woman and I'm Black and I need to be free
Being up front and powerful is the only way to be.

—Eva Johnson, in Gilbert (1988, p. 23–4)

Terra nullius: Invasion and colonisation

Nigel Parbury

Robbery under Arms, *cartoon by Bruce Petty uses the celebrated colonial bushranging novel to comment on the 'daylight robbery' of* terra nullius *as a judge signs a document under the arms of England. Courtesy Bruce Petty.*

Aboriginal Australia—To the Others

You once smiled a friendly smile,
Said we were kin to one another,
Thus with guile for a short while
Became to me a brother.
Then you swamped my way of gladness,
Took my children from my side,
Snapped shut the lawbook, oh my sadness
At Yirrkala's plea denied.
So, I remember Lake George hills,
The thin stick bones of people.
Sudden death and greed that kills,
That gave you church and steeple.
I cry again for Worrarra men,
Gone from kith and kind,
And I wondered when I would find a pen
To probe your freckled mind.
I mourned again for the Murray Tribe,
Gone too without a trace,
I thought of the Soldier's diatribe
The smile on the Governor's face.
You murdered me with rope with gun,
The massacre my enclave,
You buried me deep on McLarty's run
Flung into a common grave.
You propped me up with Christ, red tape,
Tobacco, grog and fears,
Then disease and lordly rape
Through the brutish years.
And now you primly say you're justified,
And sing of a nation's glory,
But I think of a people crucified—
The real Australian story.

—Jack Davis (1978 in Gilbert (1988) p. 58)

Terra Nullius

Terra nullius is Latin for 'land belonging to no one', a concept in (European) international law in the age of (European) colonisation. Using this legal fiction, Captain James Cook claimed eastern Australia for the Crown, against his instructions to 'negotiate with the native inhabitants'. He justified this by noting: 'We are to consider that we see this Country in the pure state of Nature, the Industry of Man has had nothing to do with any part of it. They seem to have no fix'd habitation but move about from place to place like wild Beasts in search of food.' (James Cook, quoted in Yarwood and Knowling, 1991, p. 31). There was resistance to Cook's first landing at Botany Bay. When the *Endeavour* ran into the Barrier Reef and had to put into what is now Cooktown for repairs, his camp was burned when the English refused to share turtle they had caught. Cook did not land on the coast again, but planted the British flag on Possession Island, off the tip of Cape York, to claim eastern Australia in the name of the King.

The Crown takeover of all the lands of Aboriginal Australia as *terra nullius* has affected Aboriginal lives ever since. *Terra nullius*, by definition, denied Aboriginal humanity and can be seen as a root cause of all the inhumanity. Most importantly, it meant there could be no treaty or agreement—all land belonged to the Crown. *Terra nullius* logically led to White Australia; to 'out-of-sight-out-of-mind' protection and segregation; to assimilation policies; to racist violence; and to deaths in custody.

The legacy of *terra nullius* survives. The 'White Australia' policy was not abolished until December 1972. Until then, Australia was still officially white. This meant that, until very recently, people in positions of power, influence or authority grew up to a greater or lesser extent with that frame of reference. Australian public institutions and traditions, mainstream history and 'heritage', education curricula and systems were European based and usually Eurocentric. Hence the uphill battle to include Aboriginal perspectives and Aboriginal issues constantly marginalised.

O.H.M.S. *Line drawing by Darren Kemp, visual arts student, Eora Centre Redfern Sydney, 1985. It shows the devastation of invasion. A line drawing does not look like 'Aboriginal art', but what is totally Aboriginal is the subtle and powerful use of symbols. Courtesy the artist.*

70 • TEACHING ABORIGINAL STUDIES

Governor Davey made his 'Proclamation to the Aborigines' in 1816 in an attempt to stop conflict between white settlers and local Aboriginal people. It uses illustrations to inform illiterate people—black and white—how they were expected to behave if they were to avoid punishment. It was an attempt to send a message of an intention of equality before the law. Courtesy Mitchell Library, State Library of NSW.

'Teaching the blacks a lesson'

Governor Phillip's instructions were:

> You are to endeavour by every possible means to open an intercourse with the natives, and to conciliate their affections, enjoining our subjects to live in amity and kindness with them. And if any of our subjects shall wantonly destroy them or give them any unnecessary interruption in the exercise of their several occupations, it is our will and pleasure that you do cause such offenders to be brought to punishment according to the degree of the offence. You will endeavour to procure an account of the numbers inhabiting the neighbourhood of the intended settlement, and report your opinion to one of our Secretaries of State in what manner our intercourse with these people may be turned to the advantage of this colony.
>
> —Instructions to Governor Phillip, 25 April 1787, *Historical Records of Australia* (1787, p. 15).

Martial law was declared time and again; however, what martial law meant on the ground is not always realised. On the Hawkesbury in 1805, Aboriginal people could be shot on sight if they approached the property of any settler; any settler 'harbouring' Aboriginals could be prosecuted. At Appin, southwest of Sydney, in 1816, Aboriginals carrying 'weapons' (including hunting implements) within a mile of any house or settlement, or gathering in groups of more than six—even unarmed—could be shot on sight.

The missionary Lancelot Threlkeld protested for years about the treatment of Aboriginal people. He describes the mood at Bathurst when martial law was declared in 1823:

> One of the largest holders of sheep in the Colony maintained at a public meeting at Bathurst, that the best thing that could be done, would be to shoot all the Blacks and manure the ground with their carcasses, which was all the good they were fit for! It was recommended likewise that the women and children should especially be shot as the most certain method of getting rid of the race... Sad was the havoc made upon the tribes at Bathurst. (quoted in Poad et al., 1990, p. 16).

As frontiers advanced, Aboriginals were often 'taught a lesson' in advance. Frontier 'wisdom' was that they were naturally treacherous and only waiting for a chance to attack the unguarded—best 'teach them a lesson' first. The inhumanity of frontier attitudes can only be explained in terms of the dehumanising effects of *terra nullius*—plus the fear and guilt of people who lived in an alien environment that they knew was stolen ground. Settlers were always aware that 'the natives' knew the land in a way they could never hope to—and could blend into the bush to be almost invisible. Pioneers could never be sure they were safe. This is why the carrying of weapons was standard practice on the frontiers for so long, why it was so often decided to 'teach the blacks a lesson' even before hostilities started—and why the bush itself was so suspect and so ruthlessly cleared.

Genocidal tendencies

Private retaliation was standard practice, not only quietly condoned but even encouraged. In 1796, Governor Hunter told settlers to combine against Aboriginal attacks, though he warned that random killing was murder. Later, Governor Darling refused to declare martial law—settlers should look after their own. Rev. W. Yate told an inquiry in 1835: 'I have heard again and again people say that they were nothing better than dogs and that it was no more harm to shoot them than it would be to shoot a dog.' (quoted in Parbury, 2005, p. 54)

In the Kimberley, Mary Durack recorded an Aboriginal man telling how he survived a massacre:

> 'Better shoot 'em,' one of the whitemen said. 'This little boy only gonna grow up to put a spear into some poor whitefella, and this little girl—well she gonna breed more blackfellas.' Then big Duncan McCaully come up. 'I can do with a boy,' he says, and he put me up on his saddle and someone else take Maggie. (Durack, 1959, pp. 314–15)

It is ironic that 'genocide' has usually been associated with Tasmania, where the 'final solution' was an attempt to save the people—and make the land safe for pastoral enterprise. At the height of the 'Black War', the Executive Council was told that the policy of extermination had been 'very successful' in New South Wales. But Tasmania has been the scapegoat of Australian race relations for generations. What happened in Victoria was actually worse. A Werribee squatter wrote that Aboriginals were one link from the 'orang-outang' and should be exterminated. The Aboriginal population of Gippsland, 'opened up' in 1840, has been estimated at 4000—by 1857, when the 'pioneers' held a celebratory dinner, there were about 100 left alive:

> The blacks are very quiet here now, poor wretches. No wild beast of the forest was ever hunted down with such unsparing perseverance as they are. Men, women and children are shot down wherever they can be met with. Some

Trucaninni's Dream of Childhood, David Boyd, c. 1960. A powerful image of Aboriginal suffering, the painting was part of Boyd's exhibition on Tasmanian Aboriginal history, which was savaged by critics as 'ugly' and 'un-Australian'. In colour, the flowers and the brilliant blue of the butterfly make the death masks even more tragic; in the background a little girl runs from a figure in top hat and tails. Courtesy David Boyd and the National Gallery of Australia.

excuse might be found for shooting the men by those who are daily getting their cattle speared, but what they can urge in their excuse who shoot the women and children I cannot conceive. I have protested against it at every station I have been in Gippsland, in the strongest language, but these things are kept very secret as the penalty would certainly be hanging.

—Letter from Henry Meyrick, Gippsland, April 1846, quoted in Poad, et al., (1990, p. 17).

Not only did this occur in Gippsland. Dame Mary Gilmore recorded:

Besides the poisoning, great hunting parties were formed by land-owners. With dogs the blacks were rounded up, and either shot where they stood, or driven into the swamps and rivers and drowned. The last method was pursued in Victoria and within my own memory in the Riverina. The value of this method was that it disposed of the bodies, for they floated out to sea. If there were no sea, the bones sank in the mud and were buried. Yet in at least one case in Western Victoria, floods, long after, washed up scores of broken skeletons and scattered them on farms. Only as late as 1924 a woman wrote me from a Victorian locality saying her people still found skulls washed up there after a rise in the river. (Gilmore, 1935, p. 244)

The Ipswich Coroner told an inquiry into the Native Police in 1861 that if the purpose of a protective force was to pursue the natives into the scrub and slaughter them, no force could be better suited (Rowley, 1972, p. 166). In the Northern Territory, official killing parties were referred to in official records as 'a picnic with the natives'. In Queensland in 1881, a Catholic priest said guests at a Christmas banquet at Government House had agreed extermination was the only solution to the 'Aboriginal problem'. In 1883, Sir Arthur Gordon, British High Commissioner in Queensland, wrote to his friend William Gladstone, Prime Minister of England:

The habit of regarding the natives as vermin, to be cleared off the face of the earth has given to the average Queenslander a tone of brutality and cruelty . . . I have heard men of culture and refinement, of the greatest kindness to their fellow whites . . . talk not only of the wholesale butchery . . . but of the individual murder of natives, exactly as they would talk of a day's sport or of having to kill some troublesome animal. (quoted in Parbury, 2005, p. 73)

Myall Creek shows how squatters operated beyond the reach of the law and outside its protection—the manager rode 250 miles to report the massacre. In 1829 Governor Darling had set 'Limits of Location' to restrict pastoral expansion. Economics meant these were widely ignored—any man could hope to make his fortune by taking stock outside the limits and squatting on Aboriginal land (to say nothing of big companies in London). Most squatters were men of influence, so their appeals for 'protection' were heard. As Governor Gipps wrote to the Secretary of State:

If Proprietors for the sake of obtaining better pasturage for their increasing flocks will venture with them to such a distance from protection they must be considered to run the same risk as man would do were they to drive their sheep into a Country infested with wolves, with this difference however that if they were really wolves the Government would urge the shepherds to combine and destroy them, *whilst now all we can do is to raise in the name of justice and humanity, a voice in favour of our poor savage fellow creatures, too feeble to be heard at such a distance.* (quoted in Parbury, 2005, p. 77, my emphasis).

Mounted Police and Blacks, *sketch by Governor Fitzroy's cousin Colonel Godfrey Mundy published in his* Our Antipodes, *London, 1852. Mundy was a professional soldier but was appalled at the 'blood-sport' slaughter of Aboriginals in northern NSW. He wrote that massacres were widely known about in the districts and pregnant women a special target, but justice seemed to be deaf as well as blind. Courtesy Mitchell Library, State Library of NSW.*

British Justice: Myall Creek

One evening in June 1838, a gang of stockmen rode on to Myall Creek station in northwest New South Wales, roped together at gunpoint 28 'friendly' Aboriginals, old men, women and children (the men were away working with the manager on another part of the run), took them into the bush and butchered them, returning next morning to burn the bodies. This was part of what one newspaper described as a drive to 'exterminate all the race of blacks in that quarter', including a massacre of 200 at Slaughterhouse Creek. That followed a three-month campaign by Major Nunn and the redcoats in response to the squatters' appeal for government protection against an Aboriginal 'uprising'. Nunn's orders amounted to open slather—'use your own judgement and do your utmost to suppress these outrages'. Nunn claimed to have shot every Aboriginal he saw—and encouraged local stockmen to carry on with the job when he left the district.

Eleven stockmen (convicts and ex-convicts, minus their leader, a free settler who was helped to escape) were arrested and brought to trial in Sydney. They were acquitted, to cheering in the court, on the technicality that no one could identify any victim (Aboriginal evidence was inadmissible). Then the Attorney-General ordered a retrial; seven of the stockmen were found guilty and hanged by Christmas (four had turned Queen's Evidence). This caused outrage. The trials were widely seen as a waste of time and money and an exercise in hypocrisy, the stockmen as victims of policy made in London by people who knew nothing of life on the Australian frontier. In fact, policy in London had changed. A Select Committee of the House of Commons had proclaimed in 1837 that the right of indigenous people to their land was a 'plain and sacred right'; the governor had new orders: no more treating Aboriginal people as 'open enemy', whatever had been the practice in the past. The squatters had been warned, explicitly.

Myall Creek was the tip of the iceberg of frontier violence. It is history because the manager insisted on reporting it (and was sacked), because policy in London had changed, and because white men were hanged for the murder of Aboriginals. This was the first time that had

Natives Driven to the Police Courts for Trespassing, *watercolour by South Australian artist W.A. Cawthorne, 1840s. Aboriginal people could be arrested for 'trespass' on their own land. Colonists thought they owned the land because it had been granted or sold to them, while squatters believed they had taken Crown land. Courtesy Mitchell Library, State Library of NSW.*

happened (apart from convicts). And the last. The men said they had no idea they had broken the law—such killing parties were so common, they said, and so often led by landowners who were also magistrates; they were only acting in defence of their masters' property. There was talk of poison at the hanging. The next year a squatter in Victoria was told: 'You touch me, the gubbna will hang you.'

Land rights in the colonies

Land rights is usually regarded as a modern idea. But the work of Henry Reynolds and others, shown in the 1997 ABC TV series *Frontier*, proves that land rights was a live issue in the colonies. From the start, there was an awareness of Aboriginal rights. In 1804, Governor King reported to London on his negotiations with Dharug people on the banks of the Hawkesbury, though the deal did not last (see Grenville, 2006); in 1806 he noted to his successor, Governor Bligh, that he had always regarded Aboriginals as the 'rightful possessors of the country'.

Tasmania's Governor Arthur wrote to London in 1835 that the failure to conclude a treaty had been a great mistake:

> **'This whispering in our hearts'**
>
> Are these unhappy people, the subjects of our King, in a state of rebellion or are they an injured people, whom we have invaded and with whom we are at war? Are they within the reach of our laws; or are they to be judged by the law of nations? Are they to be viewed in the light of murderers, or as prisoners of war? Are they British subjects at all, or a foreign enemy who has never yet been subdued and which resists our usurped authority and domination . . . We are at war with them: they look upon us as enemies—as invaders—as oppressors and persecutors—they resist our invasion. They have never been subdued, therefore they are not rebellious subjects, but an injured nation defending in their own way their rightful possessions which have been torn from them by force. (Letter to Launceston newspaper, quoted in Reynolds, 1998, p. 9).
>
> The title of Henry Reynolds' book, *This Whispering in Our Hearts* (1998)—which is about the people who stood up for Aboriginal rights in colonial times—comes from a speech by leading Sydney barrister Richard Windeyer, who listed all the arguments for the status quo based on *terra nullius*, then asked, 'Whence comes this whispering in our hearts?'

> On the first occupation of the colony it was a great oversight that a treaty was not, at that time, made with the natives, and such compensation given to the chiefs as would have been deemed a fair equivalent for what they surrendered . . . that feeling of injustice which I am persuaded they have always entertained would have had no existence. (quoted in McGrath, 1995, p. 13)

There is evidence that London recognised the injustice of *terra nullius*, but once done it was not easy to undo. Batman's famous treaty with the 'Chiefs' of the Yarra is usually dismissed as a swindle, but it stipulated a down-payment, then a yearly rent or tribute. Batman was from Tasmania, where the Black War had raged for a generation—and property values doubled after the 'Aboriginal problem' was solved. But *terra nullius* was the basis of the colony; no treaty could be allowed. In London, the Secretary of State for the Colonies noted that conceding Aboriginal rights to land would '*subvert the foundation on which all proprietary rights in New South Wales rest* and defeat a large part of the most important regulations of the local government' (my emphasis). It is highly likely that the 1840 Treaty of Waitangi came about because London realised what a mistake had been made in Australia.

In South Australia, the charter for the 'model' colony included provision for Aboriginal rights to their land, but the Act was about 'waste land'. Research carried out by Noel Pearson when he was a law student suggests that the Torrens Title system of land title registration was invented specifically to prevent Aboriginal claims in the new colony: Robert Torrens was the son of a main promoter of the colony and was sent to Australia for this purpose. His Torrens Title system of land registration provided indefeasible title—the name registered on the title cannot be challenged (Pearson, 1991).

From the time of the first annual blanket distributions by Governor Macquarie in 1816, settlers saw the blankets as colonial charity—pure benevolence. Aboriginals saw them as (inadequate) compensation for their land. In 1830s Sydney, the habit of making sarcastic reference to Aboriginals as 'Lords of the Soil' (because they walked around as if they owned the place) was also an implicit acknowledgement of their rights to land. Victoria's Aborigines Protection Board stated in 1862:

> How hopeless soever may be their condition, the people of this country must still perform their duty, nor grumble at a charge of six or seven thousand pounds a year for nearly fifty-six million acres of the richest lands in the world. (Aborigines Protection Board, quoted in Yarwood and Knowling, 1991, p. 160).

In 1888, New South Wales Premier Henry Parkes ridiculed a suggestion that Aboriginals be invited to a community banquet as part of the Centennial celebrations—'And remind them that we have robbed them?'.

Heather Goodall (1996) found that 45 per cent of the 114 Aboriginal reserves created in New South Wales up to 1910 were not government benevolence, as has usually been supposed, but local Aboriginals around the state reoccupying patches of their own land that were vacant, then demanding tenure. Some were able to gain permissive occupancy, a few bought freehold, some got local whites to raise funds or pass on their requests for title.

The Aboriginal enterprises described in *Survival* (Parbury, 2005, pp. 67–71) can also be seen as examples of self-determination in colonial times, and as a form of adaptation. The high numbers of Aboriginals living away from government reserves might be viewed in the same way. From the time Balloderree traded fish at Parramatta, Aboriginals carried on a range of barter-trade enterprises, as well as working in a range of seasonal and casual occupations in rural areas, mostly on their own terms. The decline of most of these occupations due to economic rationalism and recession has been a major reason for Aboriginal migration to the cities and big towns over recent generations.

The Myth of the Dying Race

No one knows how many people lived in pre-invasion Aboriginal Australia. Sir Joseph Banks thought the inland must be totally uninhabited—because there was no agriculture. Governor Phillip soon realised that there were far more 'Indians' than he had been led to believe. Later nineteenth century semi-official estimates put the pre-contact population at about 150 000. There were good reasons to under-estimate—the smaller the population of Aboriginal Australia, the easier to justify taking the land as not being used productively, and the less the guilt.

In 1838, the Aborigines Protection Society in London, on the basis of population figures collected in Australia, calculated that the population of Indigenous Australia could not possibly have been less than 1 400 000—and could have been as high as five million. Pre-invasion estimates were based on European views of what populations various areas of Australia could support—but land had been changed, indeed often ravaged, by 'settlement'. In 1930, the Commonwealth produced a figure of 300 000, which stood for several decades, then was 'at least 300 000'. In 1987, just in time for the Bicentennial, Peter White of Sydney University and John Mulvaney of the Australian National University published a revised official estimate—at least 750 000 and up to 900 000. Then the figure was revised up again to 1 million people.

The decline of Aboriginal populations was dramatic. Smallpox decimated Sydney Aboriginal peoples—by 1791, just three Gadigal people were counted—then spread through river systems. A census in 1837 found only 500 Aboriginals in the Nineteen Counties close to Sydney. Aboriginal extinction was predicted in 1817, said to be 'mathematically inevitable' by 1843. In the squatting districts of southeast Australia, populations fell *60 to 75* per cent in *ten to fifteen* years. Around Melbourne, birth rates dropped almost to zero. All of this created a climate for belief in Aboriginal extinction.

In 1859, Charles Darwin published *On the Origin of Species*. His ideas were based to some extent on earlier theories such as the Chain of Being (with European man at the top—see Chapter 5 for a description). Evolution by natural selection and the 'Law of the Survival of the Fittest' were irresistibly convenient explanations for the decline of Aboriginal populations, and gave the imprimatur of science to popular ideas. 'Proof' that Aboriginal extinction was 'scientifically inevitable' absolved colonists of guilt, while 'Survival of the Fittest' could justify anything.

When Truganini died in 1876 she was immediately said to be the 'last Tasmanian Aborigine'. In fact she was the last survivor of the Aboriginal Tasmanians who were exiled to Flinders Island in the 1830s. So fearful was Truganini of what happened to the body of her husband William Lanne that on her deathbed she cried for her body not to be desecrated, 'Don't let them cut me up, bury me behind the mountains.' But her body was dug up and her skeleton on display at the Tasmanian Museum and Art Gallery from 1904 to 1947. After many campaigns by the Tasmanian Aboriginal community, Truganini's remains were returned in 1976, cremated and the ashes scattered in the D'Entrecasteaux Channel near her Bruny Island home. Photo: Charles Woolley, courtesy Tasmanian Museum and Art Gallery.

Darwin's theories were popular in Australia—the capital of the Northern Territory was renamed in his honour. When Truganini died in 1876, she was immediately the 'Last Tasmanian Aborigine'; the Tasmanian Aboriginal race was extinct. If the Tasmanians had died out, it could be expected that Aboriginal peoples on the mainland would also solve the 'Aboriginal problem' by dying out. Tasmania became the scapegoat for Australian race relations.

In 1865, the *Brisbane Courier* predicted: 'The native race will perish before our advance as does the autumnal grass before a bush fire.' *Victoria and Its Metropolis* was published in 1888, the Centennial year. The Aboriginal race, it said, was 'wearing away very fast' but a 'careful retrospect' of colonial history did not suggest that Europeans were the 'active agents of their destruction'. For 'practical' people, colonisation was 'a distinct step in human progress, involving the sacrifice of a few thousands of an inferior race'. Frontier violence was only a minor factor in the 'passing of the Aborigines'; the real cause was the 'all ruling influence of the law of the survival of the strongest'.

The 'Myth of the Dying Race' was an article of faith for generations. By the late nineteenth century, most Australians lived in the cities and could live their whole lives and never see an Aboriginal. Meanwhile, as Aboriginal extinction was 'inevitable', there was nothing anyone could do about it. The most a concerned Christian could or even should do was to 'smooth the dying pillow'.

Fringe Dwelling Man

I stood there on the foreshores and watched the tall ships sail
I did not know or understand why their skins were pale
Different men from different shores they stood upon my shores
And did strange things to this land I've never seen before

They moved me onto stations droving cattle on the plains
The still and quiet of starry nights just took me home again
I always kept my dreamings and stories I was told
Round campfire nights and fishing days before the white man's hold

But I know winds they will bring with them all the things of change
Where the people and the places they never stay the same
But will they ever know or understand I was the chosen man
To be the father of this country and the keeper of the land

I stood there with my family and watched the men in cars
As they drove onto my reserve and took away my past
They took away my Mum and Dad and gave me to a stranger
I did not know or understand it just left me full of anger

I fought upon the battle fields and jungles of Vietnam
A self respected soldier there but home was just a black man
Where race discrimination I rose to fight each day
And crime, drugs and alcohol the price I had to pay

But I know winds they will bring with them all the things of change
Where the people and the places they never stay the same
But will they ever know or understand I was the chosen man
To be the father of this country and the keeper of the land

I stood there on the grasslands outside that great white house
I pitched my tent and stood my ground they could not move me out
I spread the word and told the world of hidden facts and lies
Of men, women and children with life drained from their eyes

Through years of false convictions I was in and out of gaol
The laws of white man's system was enough to turn you pale
The life they had before me behind those big steel doors

Where life and death between them I thought
   the latter was worth more

*But we know winds they will bring with them
   all the things of change*
*Where the people and the places they never
   stay the same*
*But will they ever know or understand I was
   the chosen man*
*To be the father of this country and the
   keeper of the land*
*The father of this country a fringe dwelling
   man.*

© Charles Trindall

Advance Australia Fair

As the Centenary approached, Australian society became more and more obsessed with racial purity. 'Advance Australia Fair' became the unofficial anthem. Henry Lawson refused to write about Aboriginals for fear of ridicule. William Lane, a founder of the Labor Party, said in 1888 that he would rather see his daughter dead than kissing a black man or 'nursing a coffee coloured brat that she was mother to' (Parbury, 2005, pp. 74–5). The 'White Australia' policy developed from unionists' fears of cheap labour and was written into the Labor Party platform. The policy was developed to keep coloured races—in particular Chinese and Pacific Islander labourers—out of Australia. But it also excluded the 'coloured people' inside Australia. We need to recognise now that White Australia was racist *by definition*, and still is where it survives. We cannot even say 'White Australia' without talking about racism in the same breath. Just like *terra nullius*, White Australia was a white lie—especially when, in the same breath, Australia also defined itself by symbols like the boomerang and nice-sounding place names.

(White) Australian art and literature as such developed at this time, and played a major role in defining and imaging Australia as white—ladies in landscapes. Much of the 'Australian' or 'Heidelberg' school of painters (Streeton, Roberts, etc.) can be seen as land-claim art. Literature, particularly bush ballads and stories, created the image of the (white) Australian bushman. History continued the process of writing Aboriginal Australia out. Children in school learnt the legends of heroic achievement in a hostile environment—'hardship-flies-and-blacks'. At the same time, Aboriginal people, symbols and culture were increasingly used to define Australia. Even the *Bulletin*, which until 1960 proclaimed 'AUSTRALIA FOR THE WHITE MAN' on its masthead, ran an 'Aboriginalities Page'. Nothing to do with Aboriginals as such, it contained outback yarns and jokes, bush lore and local gossip from the backblocks—putting down white roots in the land but using Aboriginality to do so.

Aboriginals were not considered for the constitutional conventions, mentioned just twice in the Commonwealth Constitution, both times in terms of their exclusion—from the Census and from the law-making powers of the Commonwealth. They were then excluded from pensions, banned from employment in post offices (and the rest of the Commonwealth public service) and barred from the armed services—until 1951.

In 1901, the *Bulletin*, the mouthpiece of Australian nationalism, wrote:

> If Australia is to be a country fit for our children and their children to live in we must KEEP THE BREED PURE. The half caste usually inherits the vices of both races and the virtues of neither. Do you want Australia to be a community of mongrels? (quoted in Parbury, 2005, p. 75)

The Commonwealth's first law, the *Immigration Restriction Act*, enshrined White Australia in law.

A 1937 report on development in the Northern Territory stressed the 'inviolability of the national policy of a White Australia. This is something that the Australian people regard as sacrosanct ... all sections of the people are united in ardent desire to maintain racial purity.' (Rowley, 1972, p. 286) 'White Australia' explains what Bill Stanner, in his 1968 ABC Boyer Lectures, called the 'great Australian silence'—historians not dealing with Aboriginal history and Aboriginal issues excluded from debate.

The frequent repetition of 1788 has tended to encourage people to think that the invasion was long ago; however, some massacres are within living memory, many more in folk memory. Aboriginal people should 'forget about all that' and 'get on with it now', we are still being told.

But, as Henry Reynolds wrote nearly 30 years ago, this is unlikely:

> White Australians frequently say 'all that' should be forgotten. But it will not be. It cannot be. Black memories are too deeply, too recently scarred. And forgetfulness is a strange prescription coming from a community which has revered the fallen warrior and emblazoned the phrase 'Lest We Forget' on monuments throughout the land. If the Aborigines are to enter our history 'on terms of most perfect equality', as Thomas Mitchell termed it, they will bring their dead with them and expect an honoured burial. (Reynolds, 1981, pp. 201–2)

A CURIOSITY IN HER OWN COUNTRY

A curiosity in her own Country. *Phil May, Bulletin, 1888. Courtesy State Library of NSW.*

Assimilation: The 'White Australia' policy

During the 1920s and 1930s, it became obvious that Aboriginals were not dying out as had been predicted for so many years. The so-called 'part-Aboriginal' population was actually increasing. The 1937 Commonwealth Native Affairs conference of federal and state ministers responsible for Aboriginal affairs agreed on a policy of assimilation. Like previous policies, assimilation was about White Australia. A.O. Neville, Chief Protector of Aborigines in Western Australia, told the conference:

> We have power under the act to take any child from its mother at any stage of its life ... Are we going to have a population of one million blacks in the Commonwealth or are we going to merge them into our white community and eventually forget that there were ever any Aborigines in Australia? (Native Welfare Conference, 1937)

The conference resolved that 'the destiny of the natives of Aboriginal origin, but not of the full blood lies in their ultimate absorption by the people of the Commonwealth, and it therefore recommends that all efforts be directed to that end' (quoted in Thompson & McMahon, 1996). Outlining the new policy in 1939, the Commonwealth minister explained it was to raise Aboriginal status 'so as to entitle them by right and qualification to the ordinary rights of citizenship, and enable them and help them to share in the opportunities that are available in their native land' (McEwen, 1939). The policy was framed towards a distant objective and should not in its details be condemned as being too ambitious or impracticable: 'In considering our obligations to raise the status of these people, one must not think in terms of years but of generations'.

Given the reputation of assimilation these days, it is worth noting that Rowley (1972) described it as the first really humane statement of Aboriginal policy since the end of the colonial administrations. In New South Wales, once assimilation became policy, the Protection Board and its successor from 1940, the Aborigines Welfare Board, pressured the Department of Education to enrol Aboriginal children in public schools and to promote an 'equal with white' policy in education. But opposition to Aboriginal children in public schools was so strong that this took a generation to implement. The regulation authorising principals to exclude Aboriginal children stayed on the books until 1972—the same year the 'White Australia' policy was formally abolished.

Changing White Australia: Struggling for justice

Through the 1950s and 1960s, Australian society changed. European immigration made a nonsense of Anglo Australia. People were shamed by media exposés of Third World Aboriginal living conditions in the 'Lucky Country', and shocked at restrictions on them in the 'land of the fair go'. Many diggers had come into contact with Aboriginals in northern Australia. In 1961, a Senate Select Committee touring Australia to look at the issue of Aboriginal voting rights was shocked to find men in Arnhem Land who had fought in World War II but had no vote. It decided to grant voting rights rather than wait until the people were 'ready'. Through the 1960s, restrictions—which differed from state to state—were abolished, and most protection and welfare laws were repealed by the end of the decade.

The meaning of assimilation softened, and in 1965 it changed to integration: a policy of Aboriginals entering Australian society on their own terms, preserving as much of their culture as they chose. Integration is often bracketed with assimilation, but the real difference was its recognition of Aboriginal identity, the element of choice and a recognition of value in Aboriginal culture. In allowing Aboriginal choice, integration looked forward to the policy of self-determination introduced by the 'It's Time' Labor government in 1972: 'Aboriginal communities determining the pace and the nature of their future development as significant components within a diverse Australia'.

Aboriginal action

Aboriginal political organisation began in the 1920s. In New South Wales, people started moving to Sydney as Aboriginal reserves on the

"OLD WHITE MAN CEREMONY CALLED ASSIMILATION."

Cartoon by Neil, Sun News Pictorial, *February 1985. Courtesy Neil Matterson.*

north coast were 'rationalised' by the Aborigines Protection Board. They camped at Salt Pan Creek, spoke at the Domain on Sundays and formed the Australian Aborigines Progressive Association. Also in the 1920s, the Native Union was formed in Western Australia with a deputation to the Premier. In the early 1930s, action began again; the Australian Aborigines League was set up in Melbourne in 1932, then the Aborigines Progressive Association in Dubbo in 1937.

The 150th anniversary of British settlement in Australia occurred in 1938, and was celebrated as the Sesquicentenary—'150 Years of Progress'. A focal point of the celebrations was a re-enactment of the first landing at Farm Cove in Sydney's Botanic Gardens. Aboriginal men were brought from Menindee and Brewarrina to participate, on pain of having

Day of Mourning. 'Aborigines Only' conference delegates outside the Australian Hall, Sydney, 26 January 1938. Left to right: William (Bill) Ferguson, Jack Kinchela, Helen Grosvenor, Selina Patten with baby, Jack Patten. Children in front: Abe Ingram, Esther (Ingram) Carrol, Neno Williams, Philip Ingram. Reported only by Man *magazine. A permanent conservation order was placed on the building in 1997, a first for Aboriginal history. Courtesy AIATSIS.*

their rations cut—local Aboriginals were seen as 'not Aboriginal enough', and too political. The Australian Aborigines League and the Aborigines Progressive Association hired the Australian Hall in Sydney and held a Day of Mourning 'For Aborigines Only'. One policeman and one photographer were allowed in. The APA and the AAL published a manifesto, *Aborigines Claim Citizen Rights*, and secured a meeting with the Prime Minister.

Land rights now

In 1963, the Commonwealth leased almost all of the Yirrkala reserve in Arnhem Land to the international mining company Nabalco for aluminium mining. Yirrkala people protested, sent the famous Bark Petition to Canberra, then sued the Commonwealth and Nabalco in the Supreme Court. They lost the *Gove case*, on the grounds that they did not own the land because it had not been granted to them by the Crown—though the judge recognised that the clan belonged to the land. This was one of the triggers for the famous Tent Embassy (initially a borrowed beach umbrella) in Canberra, set up on the lawns in front of Parliament House on Australia Day 1972, a symbol of Aboriginal people's living conditions and alienation in their own country.

Aboriginal men and women, paid little or nothing, had been the backbone of the outback pastoral industry from the beginning. In a 1966 test case, the Arbitration Commission decided there should be equal pay for all, black or white, but deferred the decision for three years to save employers hardship. The Gurindji people on Wave Hill station in the Northern Territory, owned by the English multinational pastoral company Vesteys, walked off the job in protest. They camped at their Dreaming place, Dagaragu (Wattie Creek), then demanded this land in a 1967 petition to the Governor-General as theirs by right. Led by Kadidjeri (Clever Man) Vincent Lingiari, they rejected all offers. Vesteys was embarrassed by the publicity and wanted to give the land back—but giving land to Aboriginals was such a radical idea that it took nine years and a change of government. The Gurindji stayed out on strike until 1975, when Prime Minister Whitlam formally handed back the deeds to the land.

In 1973, the Whitlam government set up the Woodward Royal Commission to work out how to return Aboriginal land to Indigenous people. In the words of the Prime Minister: 'We will legislate to give Aborigines land rights—not just because their case is beyond argument, but because all of us as Australians are diminished

---

To compensate for the dispossession of their land

On 20 February 1975, the Senate passed unanimously a motion moved by Senator Neville Bonner, Liberal Senator for Queensland (1971-83):

That the Senate accepts the fact that the indigenous people of Australia, now known as Aborigines and Torres Strait Islanders, were in possession of this entire nation prior to the 1788 First Fleet landing at Botany Bay, [and] urges the Australian Government to admit prior ownership by the said indigenous people, and introduce legislation to compensate the people now known as Aborigines and Torres Strait Islanders for the dispossession of their land.

The 1967 Referendum

Years of campaigning by Aboriginal and other Australians, led by the Federal Council for the Advancement of Aborigines and Torres Strait Islanders (FCAATSI), finally resulted in a Referendum on 27 May 1967, to count Aboriginals in the Census and allow the Commonwealth to pass laws for them. The 'Yes' vote was the highest for any referendum, 90.77 per cent, ranging from 95 per cent (Victoria) to 81 per cent (Western Australia). The lowest electorate approval was 71 per cent.

A major factor in this high vote was the national shame generated by the 1965 Freedom Rides, when Ted Noffs of the Wayside Chapel, with Sydney University students Charles Perkins, Jim Spigelman (now Chief Justice of New South Wales) and others chartered a bus to expose grassroots racism in New South Wales country towns, and this was picked up by national media. Charles Perkins remembered:

> I think it was a major turning point, a catalyst in black–white relations in the country, although it is not given that sort of status. It was the major turning point, I think, and more and more am I convinced of that. The time was right and I happened to be there.
>
> I think it changed the psychology of Aboriginal people. They realised, Hey, we don't have to cop this shit. That was the biggest thing. It was like the woman on the bus in America who refused to sit down the back, she wanted to sit in the front and said, 'That's it, the time has come, I'm going to sit in the front.' It was the same with me and all the mob there. It was badly organised, but it was something that had to happen and I think most great events happen by not too much design, but because they have to happen and, badly organised or otherwise, it happened. (Charles Perkins, quoted in Rintoul, 1993, pp. 287–8)

Charles Perkins with Aboriginal boys in Moree Baths during the 1965 Freedom Rides. Sydney University students formed the group 'Student Action For Aborigines' and toured country towns to expose racism, led by Charles Perkins, one of the first three Aboriginal graduates in Australia, and Jim Spigelman, now Chief Justice of the Supreme Court of NSW. The bus being run off the road outside Moree made headlines across the country—the shame of the Freedom Rides was a big factor in the 91 per cent 'Yes' vote in the referendum two years later. Courtesy News Limited.

while the Aborigines are denied their rightful place in the nation.' (Gough Whitlam, quoted in Parbury, 2005, p. 120)

As the states controlled land, the Commonwealth could legislate only for the Northern Territory. The *Aboriginal Land Rights (Northern Territory) Act* was passed by the Liberal Government in 1976—largely due to the personal conviction of Prime Minister Malcolm Fraser. It provided for claiming of reserve lands, pastoral leases and vacant Crown land on the basis of traditional ownership and continuous occupation. It also set up the Northern and Central Land Councils to advise on land claims. However, many Aboriginal peoples had been evicted from pastoral stations after the 1966 equal pay decision and thus lost their essential link with their land.

In 1983, the Hawke government was elected on a platform of national land rights. This was quietly dropped when the (Labor) government of Western Australia told Canberra that national land rights would cost Labor five or six seats in that state in the 1984 election. The Seaman Inquiry had recommended land rights in Western Australia, but the government buried the report. The same thing happened in Tasmania. In South Australia, the Pitjantjatjara lands were handed back in 1981 and the Maralinga Tjaruta lands in 1984.

In New South Wales, a Parliament Select Committee recognised the destruction and fragmentation of Aboriginal societies, and recommended land rights not only on the basis of prior ownership and tradition, but also of need and compensation. The 1983 *Land Rights*

'We Want Land Not Handouts', poster at the Tent Embassy in 1972. A badge designed for the Embassy read 'Ningla-A-Na'—We are hungry for our land. Originally a borrowed beach umbrella, the Tent Embassy was a headline symbol of Aboriginals being alien in their own land, the living conditions of most, and how often they were moved on, their homes bulldozed. Courtesy Canberra Times.

Act set up local, regional, and state Aboriginal Land Councils, and allocated 7.5 per cent of annual land tax revenues—half to be invested, for fifteen years until 1998—to fund land acquisition and provide an economic base. Until the Indigenous Land Fund Bill, this was the only land rights legislation that addressed the issues of dispossession and compensation.

In 1985, the Department of Aboriginal Affairs (replaced in 1990 by ATSIC) commissioned a report on attitudes to land rights. Australian National Opinion Polls found that support for land rights was 21 per cent across the country and as low as 6 per cent in Western Australia. The Commonwealth published the figures, used them to back off national land rights, suppressed the report and made a symbolic handback of Uluru (Ayers Rock)—boycotted by the Northern Territory government. In April 1986, the *National Times* got hold of the report—under the Freedom of Information Act—and published extracts. The 'scoop' sank like a stone—there was no media reaction anywhere. It makes for appalling reading:

> It would be easy to despair at the extent of ignorance, intolerance and misunderstanding uncovered by our research towards Aborigines generally and land rights more specifically...

A campaign is definitely, if not desperately, needed and ANOP recommends that to have any real and lasting impact, the campaign should be like no government has ever attempted.

Black rights generally, and land rights in particular, represent the most divisive and explosive issues we have ever dealt with—and, we suspect, that this country has faced in the post war period... We have never before so strongly recommended that a government campaign is needed in any area. (*National Times*, 18–24 April, 1986)

Ironically, what started to change attitudes was the approach of the Bicentennial. A flood of publications encouraged people to focus not only on Australian history, but also on issues of history—especially Aboriginal issues. At the same time, Aboriginal deaths in custody and the Royal Commission encouraged people to question Australian history and community attitudes.

Deaths in custody to reconciliation

In 1982, a 16-year-old Aboriginal boy, John Pat, was allegedly kicked to death by off-duty police (who were later acquitted) at Roebourne in Western Australia. This became a focus for growing outrage about Aboriginal deaths in police and prison custody, and inspired the formation of the National Committee to Defend Black Rights (CDBR). A spate of deaths in 1987, at the height of the Bicentennial build-up, forced the Commonwealth to set up a Royal Commission. The Commission sat through 1988 and beyond, generating headlines and horror stories almost daily.

The Commission decided very early that it needed to consider not only the facts of the deaths, but what it called the 'underlying circumstances'—the social forces that led to so many Aboriginals being in custody in the first place, and to them being treated as they were. This is why the Commission's report made 339 recommendations which essentially aimed to change mainstream Australian society at every point of contact—and change all systems.

Recommendation 339 was for a process of reconciliation. The Council for Aboriginal Reconciliation was set up by Act of Parliament (unanimously) to operate for ten years. Its first meeting produced a Vision Statement:

> A united Australia which respects this land of ours, values the Aboriginal and Torres Strait Islander heritage, and provides justice and equity for all.

With substantial resources, the Council ran a massive community education campaign through the 1990s, publishing issues papers, arresting posters and a full-colour quarterly magazine—all free—and setting up local reconciliation groups. Reconciliation Week, from 27 May (the Referendum) to 2 June (the *Mabo* judgment) began to be celebrated in 1996.

The end of *terra nullius*

In June 1992, in the *Mabo* case, the High Court finally overturned *terra nullius*—ruling it 'a travesty of fact and a fallacy of law'. Justices Deane and Gaudron recognised that 'Aborigines came to be treated as a different and inferior people, whose very existence could be ignored in determining the legal right to occupy and use their traditional homelands' (quoted in ATSIC, 1998, p. 9). Justice (later Chief Justice) Brennan ruled that Aboriginal dispossession had underwritten the development of Australia. (ATSIC, 1998, p. 51) The judgment referred specifically to the Murray Islands of the Torres Strait, but clearly had implications all over Australia.

The Redfern Park Statement

On 10 December 1992—International Human Rights Day—at Redfern Park, Prime Minister Paul Keating launched the United Nations International Year of the World's Indigenous Peoples. His speech was hailed for its straight-out admission of the black history of White Australia. Speaking of the *Mabo* judgment, the Prime Minister said: '*Mabo* is an historic decision—we can make it an historic turning point, the basis of a new relationship between Indigenous and non-Aboriginal Australians'.

He went on to say that the problem started with non-Aboriginal Australians who, 'with a few noble exceptions', failed to ask:

Expo '88. *Cartoon by Patrick Cook. An Aboriginal man in a cell in a party hat, party whistle drooping from his lips, Expo '88 poster on the wall, a noose hanging down above. Brisbane hosted 1988's World Expo, and while the country was celebrating 200 years since white colonisation, Aboriginal people were reluctant to participate as the anniversary was seen as a celebration of invasion. At the same time as these celebrations were occurring, the Royal Commission into Aboriginal Deaths in Custody was investigating high levels of deaths of Aboriginal people in gaol by suicide and other means. Many Aboriginals and a fair few whitefellas found the Bicentennial mantra, 'Celebration of a Nation', hard to take. Courtesy the artist.*

how would I feel if this were done to me?

As I said, it might help us if we non-Aboriginal Australians imagined ourselves dispossessed of land we had lived on for fifty thousand years—and then imagined ourselves told it had never been ours.

Imagine if ours was the oldest culture in the world and we were told it was worthless.

Imagine if we had resisted this settlement, suffered and died in the defence of our land, and then were told in history books that we had given up without a fight.

Imagine if non-Aboriginal Australians had served their country in peace and war and were then ignored in history books.

Imagine if our feats on the sporting field had inspired admiration and patriotism and yet did nothing to diminish prejudice.

Imagine if our spiritual life was denied and ridiculed.

Imagine if we had suffered the injustice and then were blamed for it.

(Keating, 1992)

> I include in this report a chapter on that history. I make no apology for doing so. I do so not because the chapter adds to what is known but because what is known is known to historians and Aboriginal people; it is little known to non-Aboriginal people and it is a principal thesis of this report that it must become more known.
>
> That Aboriginal people were dispossessed of their land without benefit of treaty, agreement or compensation is generally known. But I think little known is the extent of brutality and bloodshed that was involved in enforcing on the ground what was pronounced by the law . . .
>
> Aboriginal people were swept up into reserves where they were supervised as to every detail of their lives and there was a deliberate policy of destroying their spiritual and cultural beliefs . . . The extent of control seems incredible today . . .
>
> . . . the deliberate and systematic disempowerment of Aboriginal people starting with dispossession from their land and proceeding to almost every aspect of their life . . . Decisions were made abut them and for them and imposed on them . . . With loss of independence goes a loss of self-esteem . . .
>
> The damage to Aboriginal society was devastating. In some places it totally destroyed [the] population. In others, dependency, despair, alcohol, total loss of heart wrought decimation of culture . . .
>
> Every turn in the policy of government and the practice of the non-Aboriginal community was postulated on the inferiority of the Aboriginal people; the original expropriation of their land was based on the idea that the land was not occupied and the people uncivilised; the protection policy was based on the view that Aboriginal people could not achieve a place in the non-Aboriginal society and that they must be protected against themselves while the race died out; the assimilationist policy assumed that their culture and way of life is without value and that we confer a favour on them by assimilating them into our ways; even to the point of taking their children and removing them from family.
>
> —Commissioner Elliott Johnston, Royal Commission into Aboriginal Deaths in Custody (1991, pp. 7–9).

> It has given Aboriginal and Torres Strait Islander people—the victims of much of Australia's history since 1788—a measure of dignity and justice, and once again made land rights an important national issue. It has set a new agenda for debate on relations between Indigenous and Non-Indigenous Australians . . .
>
> For Aboriginal and Torres Strait Islander people, native title may provide less security and fewer rights than a statutory title—such as the inalienable freehold title available to traditional owners under the provisions of the *Aboriginal Land Rights (Northern Territory) Act* 1976. Nevertheless, the confirmation of native title has great symbolic importance for Australia's Indigenous people: it is a title not granted or given by the Crown; it preceded colonisation; and has survived the assertion of sovereignty by foreigners.
>
> —ATSIC (1993).

After *Mabo*

In response to the *Mabo* judgment, the Keating government, after prolonged negotiations with Indigenous leaders and pastoralists and miners, passed the *Native Title Act* in December 1993, establishing the National Native Title Tribunal to determine native title claims. In 1994, the *Indigenous Land Fund Act* was passed to address land needs of the majority of Aboriginal and Torres Strait Islander people, who as a result of dispossession cannot claim native title. The third element of the government's response was to be a social justice package. There were consultations with communities across Australia conducted by ATSIC, the Council for Aboriginal Reconciliation and the Office of the Aboriginal and Torres Strait Islander Social Justice Commissioner. Mick Dodson, the first Social Justice Commissioner, gave an Aboriginal view of social justice in his first annual report:

> Social Justice must always be considered from a perspective which is grounded in the daily lives of Indigenous Australians. Social justice is what faces you in the morning. It is awakening in a house with an adequate water supply, cooking facilities and sanitation. It is the ability to nourish your children and send them to a school where their education not only equips them for employment but reinforces their knowledge and appreciation of their cultural inheritance. It is the prospect of genuine employment and good health: a life of choices and opportunity, free from discrimination. (Dodson, 1993, p. 8)

The Aboriginal and Torres Strait Islander flags were recognised as flags of Australia, and the Council of Australian Governments made a Statement of Commitment to equity for Aboriginal people in government services. However, no further actions on the social justice recommendations eventuated. Following the election of the Howard government in 1996, the minister advised the Reconciliation Council that the government would be taking no further steps to implement the social justice package.

The empire strikes back

The election of the Howard Coalition government in March 1996 was partly the result of a backlash against Aboriginal rights and so-called 'special treatment'. Robert Tickner, Minister for Aboriginal Affairs, was the first to lose his seat, called as 'gone' by 7.00 p.m., an hour after counting started. The new government was widely perceived as hostile to Aboriginal aspirations, and to reconciliation. One of its first acts was to announce an audit of ATSIC programs, later found to be illegal. It announced that its focus would be on 'practical reconciliation'—real progress in health, housing and education—rather than symbolic gestures and abstract rights.

Pauline Hanson, Liberal candidate for the seat of Ipswich, disendorsed before the 1996 election for racist comments, ran as an independent and won the seat. Her maiden speech attacked 'special treatment' for Aboriginals and warned that Australia was in danger of being 'swamped by Asians'. Her attacks on what she called 'political correctness' struck a chord in the wider community—people who felt shut out of debates among 'elites'—and she proceeded to form Pauline Hanson's One Nation Party. This grew to be a rival people's movement. In the Queensland election in 1998, One Nation won thirteen seats. Eventually the Coalition and Labor both put One Nation last on their ballot papers, and it faded away—but not before demonstrating that the wider community had a way to go in achieving racial harmony, not to mention embarrassing Australia abroad, especially in Asia.

The *Wik* debate

In December 1996, the High Court delivered its judgment in the *Wik case*. The Wik and Thayorre peoples argued that their native title rights had survived the granting of pastoral leases in the past, and could coexist with pastoral and mining leases. The High Court ruled that native title rights were not necessarily extinguished by a valid pastoral lease, and could coexist with pastoral leases—depending on the terms of the lease and the legislation on which it was

Anyone for a bit of reconciliation? *Bill Leak,* Weekend Australian, *27–28 April 1996. Then National Party Premier of Queensland Rob Borbidge holding a piece of paper marked 'Mabo', invites an Aboriginal man at the bar to step outside, where a mob with clubs can be seen through the window, and sort out their 'problem with this legislation'. The* Native Title Act *was not popular in Queensland, as the rise of Pauline Hanson and the success of One Nation there showed. Courtesy Bill Leak and News Limited.*

Cartoon by Nicholson, The Australian *24 January 1997. Published not long after the Wik Case in December 1996, where the High Court ruled that a valid pastoral lease did not necessarily extinguish native title. It comments on the irony of city-dwellers being seen to force their views in favour of native title, and about other issues relating to Aboriginal rights, on country landowners while not acknowledging their own culpabilities. Courtesy Nicholson and News Limited.*

Telling the truth about what happened when the First Fleet arrived

G'day, I am Troy Cassar-Daley, country music singer-songwriter.

I think the most important thing to teach about Aboriginal Australia is that in this day and age it's not about skin colour, hair colour and facial features; it's about the way you feel in your heart about your culture and the spirit you carry with you in this life. I was fortunate enough to hunt and fish in and around this beautiful river on the north coast of New South Wales with my grandparents, uncles, aunties, and cousins speaking many Bundjalun words and phrases, feeling what it was like to grow up in a loving supporting extended Aboriginal family.

I think telling the absolute truth about what happened when the First Fleet arrived is imperative! And covering that truth in some detail, e.g. the fact that there were massacres that are now documented throughout Australia and the many struggles that Indigenous people faced through many generations of persecution on our road to being able to vote, to own our own land and to walk down the street and be accepted as Australians, then to the Apology for the Stolen Generations. There should be a section put in about the Stolen Generations because it was an actual policy of the governments of the day to breed out Aboriginal blood and make them whiter! Hence the name 'the White Australia Policy'.

Kids these days have a right to know about this dark side of Australian history and the effect it had on thousands of Aboriginal families across this land. This will in turn help young Australians of today to fully understand the social issues that face the modern-day Aboriginal person. If the kids of today are to be taught about Aboriginal Australia, we must not sugar-coat the truth!

In closing, I was driving with my band from Armidale to Grafton on tour one time just after the Olympics in Sydney and two of my band asked me why Peter Garrett wore a shirt at the ceremony that said SORRY . . . Two hours later after saying 'What!! You don't know why??' I had explained the whole story about the Stolen Generations. I think all Australians should know this story as part of their schooling. And many other stories of triumph and tragedy. And then we can all walk together as one mob and equality will be ours . . .

Troy Cassar-Daley is a country music singer-songwriter. Born in Sydney and raised in Grafton, Troy has released seven studio albums, won 20 Golden Guitars and four ARIA awards, and made countless tours across our wide brown land. When Troy came up with the title for his new album, I Love This Place, *he was thinking of a state of mind more than any place you can find on a map. Much as he loves hanging out with his wife and kids or throwing in a line on his farm an hour out of Brisbane, the much loved and respected Aussie country musician more wanted to share a blissful time and place in his life. Having won six Golden Guitars at the 2010 Tamworth Country Music Festival, he is giving back to his community by setting up an Indigenous scholarship to the new course at the Country Music Academy of Australia.*

---

based. This sparked outrage, including calls to reform the High Court. It also torpedoed the deal that got the *Native Title Act* through the Senate—agreement that a valid pastoral lease extinguished native title. Up to 80 per cent of Australia was now a grey area.

The High Court made it clear that in any case of conflict of rights, the rights of the leaseholder would prevail. The Prime Minister rejected calls for blanket extinguishment, called summit meetings of stakeholders, and promised a resolution of the issues by Easter. His solution was the so-called 'Ten-Point Plan'.

The *Wik* issue was hotly debated through 1997, and was a main focus of the Australian Reconciliation Convention in Melbourne in May, where reconciliation was explicitly tied to native title rights. Later in 1997 and again in March 1998, the government's proposed *Native Title Amendment Act* was rejected by the Senate, though most of the government's proposed amendments were accepted, thus providing a trigger for a double-dissolution election.

At the same time, *Bringing Them Home*, the Human Rights Commission's report on the removal of Aboriginal children, and the Prime Minister's continuing refusal to apologise both increased the focus on Aboriginal rights and unleashed a wave of grassroots action called the 'people's movement' after Patrick Dodson's call at the end of the Reconciliation Convention. Groups such as Women for Wik and Australians for Native Title and Reconciliation (ANTaR) overflowed suburban halls in blue-ribbon suburbs—even in the Prime Minister's electorate. The Governor-General, Sir William Deane, warned that he would 'weep for my country' if hopes for true reconciliation were not kept alive, that Australia would be diminished if 'we allow the most disadvantaged people in the country to be dispossessed'.

The movement reached a climax on 26 May 1998 when the first national Sorry Day was marked by ceremonies, rallies and public meetings across Australia. More than a million signatures were collected in thousands of Sorry Books. By this time, there were more than 260 local reconciliation groups.

> Yesterday's National Sorry Day saw the Australian public take into their own hands the issue of an apology to Indigenous people. This was a massive and inspiring expression of people's desire to heal the wounds of our past and walk forward together towards a true reconciliation which will allow this nation to really celebrate the centenary of our Federation in 2001...
>
> We have always said that reconciliation can only occur if the people make it their concern and actively work for it and support it.
>
> —Evelyn Scott, Chair, Reconciliation Council, media release, 27 May 1998

But there was widespread alarm at the prospect of a race-based election, particularly with the rise of One Nation, which had won a swag of seats in the Queensland election. Independent senator Brian Harradine, who had held up the government both times, 'blinked' and agreed to an amended *Native Title Act*—albeit with a number of key concessions. The Act was duly passed and native title dropped off the agenda.

Then Prime Minister, John Howard, still refused to apologise on behalf of the nation for the Stolen Generations, claiming that Australians now could not be held responsible for the past. A Statement of Regret negotiated with newly elected Indigenous Democrats Senator Aden Ridgeway in 1998 and passed by Parliament did not end the issue, and Senator Ridgeway was attacked for failing to consult.

As the Centenary of Federation approached and the Reconciliation Council prepared its final report, there were hopes that something could be achieved. But the Prime Minister refused to sign up to the Declaration for Reconciliation, and there was little hope for the Council's Roadmap for Reconciliation. On 27 May 2000, Corroboree 2000 was staged in the Sydney Opera House, but the nation's leaders could only put ochre handprints on the Reconciliation Council's Vision Statement—all that could be agreed. Next day, Sydney Harbour Bridge was closed while hundreds of thousands walked into the city for reconciliation, with packed trains carrying thousands more, followed by a festival in Darling Harbour. Through the rest of the year, there were similar bridge walks in cities and towns across the country.

The Reconciliation Council handed its final report to the Prime Minister in December and disbanded, replaced by Reconciliation Australia, with far fewer resources and focused on building relationships rather than the Council's community education. The Centenary of Federation was celebrated with every effort to include Aboriginal perspectives. John Howard won further elections in 2001 and 2004, and with leadership troubles in the Labor Party, looked set for life. ATSIC was abolished in 2004, though Labor had proposed this first, and the future looked grim for Aboriginal aspirations, as native title claims dragged on, fought tooth and nail by governments, and the High Court ruled that the Yorta Yorta people's essential link with their country had been 'washed away by history'.

Then it all changed. Kevin Rudd won the leadership of the Labor Party and took on John Howard, promising an apology to the Stolen Generations. In June 2007, reacting to the

Little Children are Sacred report on Aboriginal child sexual abuse in the Territory (Wild and Anderson, 2007), the Howard government pre-emptively announced the Northern Territory Intervention, sending in the army, taking over prescribed communities, disbanding CDEPs, and imposing income management on all Aboriginal welfare recipients, regardless of how well they cared for their families. This was greeted with some cynicism, and seen as a ploy for the coming election.

In November 2007, Labor won the federal election decisively. John Howard's loss of his own seat of Bennelong to former ABC TV presenter Maxine McKew was the icing on the cake for many people. On election night, there was euphoria such as had not been seen for years, a feeling of hope for the future—the long night of the soul was over. The first act of the Rudd government was an Aboriginal Welcome to Country at the opening of Parliament, followed by a formal Apology to Aboriginal people for the Stolen Generations and everything else that had been done to them. Stolen Generations survivors in the chamber, more in the Great Hall, thousands gathered outside, millions more watching on big screens in schools, colleges and workplaces, a video distributed across the country, this was celebrated as history and a new beginning.

Which Way Australia?

Labor has maintained the Northern Territory Intervention, in the face of an adverse report—though with promises that it will be modified and the *Racial Discrimination Act* reinstated. Consultations proceeded on a new representative body to replace ATSIC and the National Congress of Australia's First Peoples was set up. But compensation for the Stolen Generations was ruled out. Mick Dodson was named Australian of the Year for 2009, ahead of two other Aboriginal state finalists, and Prime Minister Rudd pledged to close the gap in life

'Sorry about that too'. *The first act of the Kevin Rudd Labor Government was the National Apology in 2008. It was a watershed moment, but there were always questions about compensation, which the Prime Minister ruled out. The cartoon by Brett Lethbridge appeared in Brisbane's* Courier Mail. *Courtesy the artist.*

expectancy, health, education and employment with record-level funding allocated. In November 2010, new Prime Minister Julia Gillard committed the Commonwealth to appoint an Expert Panel to consult and advise on constitutional recognition of Indigenous Australians by the end of 2011. However, some people feel that not enough has changed—nowhere near as much as they were led to expect.

Over the last generation, Australians have been forced to come to grips with the real story of Australian history and the nature of Australian identity. More than at any other time in Australian history, the whole issue of Aboriginal rights, the place of Aboriginal citizens in Australia and the nature of Australia are defining issues. The legacy of *terra nullius* is challenged. What is Australia?

A history of special treatment: The impact of government policies

James Wilson-Miller

To the memory of my grandmother Jean Miller and the original people of the Sydney area, the Eora.

Albert Namatjira. *Linocut by social realist artist Noel Counihan, 1959, created after Namatjira's death. With sell-out exhibitions, Aboriginal watercolourist Albert Namatjira was a celebrity and many suburban homes had a print of his paintings of the Centre. He was presented to the Queen but not allowed to build a house in Alice Springs. He began to drink, which as an 'exempted' Aboriginal he was allowed to do, but in 1959 he was convicted of supplying liquor to a relative who was not exempt—even though Aboriginal custom made sharing compulsory. Despite a public outcry he was sent to gaol, but died shortly after his release—many said of a broken heart. Courtesy Art Gallery of South Australia.*

Six O'clock . . . Outa Bed

She entered Coota a young girl
about eleven/twelve but already
mature for her years.
She knew how to look after her
younger brothers and sister, keep house
and herself, her mother made sure of that.
Her life was forcefully changed.
She was parted from her brothers
White washed into a 'new alien' white
way of thinking.
She never really had a childhood,
she went from baby clothes to
Government uniforms, controlled by the
times of day.
Six o'clock, outa bed, wash, dress, work,
　breakfast,
work, inferior schooling, home, change,
　clothes, work,
wash, tea, bed, nightmares, worry, little sleep,
cry.
Six o'clock, outa bed, wash . . .
Talk like whites, behave like whites,
pray like whites. Be white.
She knew her family for she was part of one,
where she grew up, the things she did,
the strong family ties she had, the old people,
the stories of long ago, her own
identity. Her mother.

She was a daughter, sister, granddaughter,
    great granddaughter, niece, aunty, cousin,
    friend.
She stood in many relationships with her
family, she was loved.
She was rebellious, she never
conformed, they never broke her spirit,
her family background made sure of that
and they were always in her thoughts.
Six o'clock, outa bed, wash . . .
she endured many years of this spirit
breaking torture, punished, bashed,
    humiliated, starved.
They serviced her out to white middle class
lazy white women's homes, Vaucluse, Rose
    Bay.
The North Shore.
She became a slave,
Six o'clock, outa bed, wash, work,
and all for a lousy little sixpence.
She was now in the 'White way of thinking'
of age, free, but not really!
She knew where her family was and found
them, her mother, grandmother, aunts, uncles,
    cousins, sister and brothers.
She came home.
My Mother.

—James Miller, in Human Rights and Equal Opportunity
Commission (1997, p. 56)

On 27 May 2009, Indigenous people across Australia attended and celebrated National Reconciliation Week. It had been on this date 42 years before, in 1967, that over 90 per cent of non-Indigenous Australians voted 'Yes' in a referendum that resulted in two things for Indigenous Australians: the right to be counted in the national Census, and the right of the Commonwealth government to legislate on behalf of Indigenous people.

No doubt the 1967 Referendum was a significant event, a milestone in Koori affairs from which 'certain benefits' did evolve, which were fought for by Koori political activists of the time. [I use Koori because I am a Koori. Other mobs have other generic names all over Australia (see next page)] However, Koori people were way behind then in all the basic needs that non-Indigenous Australians took for granted. The rights to quality housing, education, health services and legal representation are still the biggest obstacles for Kooris now, just as they were 43 years ago.

Since then, there have been so many state and Commonwealth government programs out of policies developed to address these dire social needs, and with them all has come the ranting and raving of over four decades of talkback radio, media commentators, some state and Commonwealth politicians (who should know better), that Kooris were getting so-called 'special treatment' over the wider Australian community. The main rant then was 'all Australians should be treated equally', and nothing much has changed since then. More recently, many have flouted policies established specifically to ban racial discrimination and vilification,

King Mickey Johnson, Illawarra, c. 1896. Squatters and authorities gave out king and queen breastplates to leading Aboriginal men and women in the hope of being able to deal with individuals rather than communities, but of course there were no kings or queens in Aboriginal Australia, only Elders and the rule of the law. This photo is unusual in the dignity and poise of the subject. Mickey Johnson was also an artist, one of the very few from those days whose work has survived. Courtesy Wadi Wadi people per Barbara Nicholson and National Library of Australia.

seemingly protected by powerful media influences or parliamentary privilege. However, what these people choose to forget—or just do not want to know—is that Kooris Australia wide have suffered and are still suffering from the effects of the colonialist policies of 'protection', segregation, separation, forced assimilation, institutionalisation and so-called integration. All these policies, one way or another, have socially engineered the lives and destinies of most Kooris today.

Special use of the term Koori

Throughout this chapter, I will continue to use the terms Koori, Indigenous Australians and other Indigenous terms to describe me and my people, rather than the more common terms 'Aboriginal' and 'Aborigine/s'. 'Aboriginal' and 'Aborigine' are Latin-derived English terms. When written with a lower-case 'a', they refer to any native inhabitants throughout the world before the advent of (mainly) European colonisation. They do not give me or my people a separate identity. Furthermore, they have mostly been used in a derogatory sense, to portray my people as 'simple', 'savage', 'pagan', 'cannibalistic' or 'barbaric'. Twentieth century school textbooks and some historians portrayed Kooris as simple-minded creatures who did not meet the 'proper' standards of British civilisation. Thus white propaganda caused many Anglo-Australians to associate Aboriginal Australian with inferiority.

In my use of the term Koori, I do not wish—nor is it my intention—to offend any Indigenous individuals or groups who do not identify with it. Koori is the traditional term that was used by my ancestors in the Hunter Valley and many other groups of what was to become New South Wales to identify themselves. It is probably the most significant Indigenous language identity term used in Australia today, with university centres, media commentators, politicians, publications—both recent and historic—and a national newspaper all using the term at various times, not to mention an Indigenous radio station. But this term is not used Australia-wide. 'Murri' is a term often used in western New South Wales and many parts of Queensland (and on my mother's father's side, I too can identify as a Murri). In southwest Western Australia, 'Nyoongah' is used, along with 'Yamatji' in the north. In South Australia, 'Nunga' is commonly used. In Victoria and Tasmania, 'Koori' again is most favoured (as Koorie in Victoria), although many Aboriginal Tasmanians use the term 'Palawa'. In some parts of the Northern Territory, 'Anangu-Mara' and 'Yolgnu' are used. There are many more Indigenous terms for our people throughout this country that are equally valid. They mean much more to our people than the forcefully imposed introduced terms.

The original inhabitants from the Sydney area were the first Indigenous people to feel the full impact of the British invasion, losing their homelands and succumbing to the many introduced diseases. I will always fully identify as a Koori out of respect for the memory of my ancestors and the original inhabitants of the Sydney area.

This chapter discusses aspects of the lived history of Koori people in New South Wales as an example of the policies of the New South Wales Aborigines Protection and Welfare Boards, which affected Koori people from 1883 to 1969,

Must This Be Their Fate. *Painting by social realist artist Jack Kilgour, 1971. Showing two pictures—traditional life in the desert or city life in the shadow of gaol with piles of grog bottles, with a mother and child standing next to a crucifix, looking down on the scene under the gaol walls. The artist asks, is this the only way for Aboriginal people? Courtesy Fred and Elinor Wrobel.*

and political events into the 1970s. These boards affected just about every Koori in New South Wales. The story might provide a deeper insight into the kinds of 'special treatment' imposed on Kooris by governments, bureaucratic ignorance and the paralysing apathy and deafening silence of the wider Australian society. I will also be using my immediate and extended families as much as possible, as unifying links to illustrate my story, within the context of and the delivery of special treatment policies.

The beginnings of special treatment

Let's go back a bit in time and look at what those early years of post-invasion meant for Kooris and the invaders. The history of 'special treatment' for Koori people started at the dawn of British invasion in 1770. Eighteen years after James Cook 'found' what was to become Botany Bay, Captain-General Arthur Phillip invaded the lands of the Cadigal Clan of the Eora Nation just north of Cook's Botany Bay. The flotsam and jetsam of British society disgorged itself: the 'illiterate, irreligious, immoral and corrupt denizens of London's East End' (Miller 1985, p. 7). These people were presided over by a military and a governing elite. The new people brought with them their physical luggage of animals, tools, knowledge of crops, building, and so on, and their invisible luggage: their religion, their social order, their notions of property and, worst of all, their racial prejudice. These were to affect Kooris in what was to become 'special treatment'—the desired way of treating Kooris by a boundless aggression of claimants of supposedly undiscovered lands, *terra nullius*. It was an inauspicious beginning, but the colony continued to push its way forward, imposing economic, social and political systems on Kooris. The land created by Koori Dreamings now became, clan by clan, the lands of Koori nightmares.

To be fair to the invaders, their society had not equipped them for what they were about to experience. The majority of British people then did not even know the Great South Land (Terra Australis, or New Holland) even existed. They certainly experienced problems when they set sail for this part of the world. Some said the 'lucky ones' died on the voyage here. Their

AN ABORIGINAL VIEW OF COOK'S STATUE

Cartoon in Sydney Punch, *1866. The statue of Captain Cook in Hyde Park south, with Cook shown as standing on the shoulders of Aboriginal men to 'discover' Australia. Note that Cook's 'plinth' includes not only the kangaroo and emu but also a grasstree, formerly known as a 'blackboy'. Courtesy Geoff Eagar.*

problems on arrival were what to do about practising their religions, what to do about food, what to do about their women, but most importantly what to do about the Kooris—those people who were claimed not to have existed eighteen years earlier. On the other hand, the Kooris were to experience problems unlike any ever before faced in this part of their world: their lands being invaded and flattened, sacred and significant sites being desecrated, the over-use of their fishing waters and hunting and gathering grounds, their women being taken at will, the new sicknesses that killed so many. Most of all, they had to work out what to do about the people they were to refer to as Gubbas (ghosts). You now had two very stressed human groups living in close proximity to each other—seemingly with nothing to offer one another.

British society was to introduce the real pacifier to the lands of the newcomers' dreams: the gun. Kooris soon knew the power of this funny-shaped spear which killed animals two or three spear throws away, without even leaving the hand. They felt the impact when their men fell down with great holes in their bodies after trying to protect what was theirs. It was magic, the Kooris thought, something to stay clear of. They avoided the 'settlement'.

> We watched the ships sail into
> the bay
> The white people who looked
> like dead clay
> Asked us to trust them in their
> strange ways
> As they claimed our rivers
> and streams
> And knocked down our trees.
> All we wanted was to be friends.
> They stole our land and ripped it
> apart,
> Polluted our streams, forests and hills.
> For when they wanted our lands,
> they just moved us on with guns.
> —Barry McGree, *Koori Mail*, 11 January 1996

The invaders disrupted and imposed their alien lifestyles on Kooris with no real intention of seeking conciliation or asking for permission, and no negotiations. Only Governor Phillip took the instructions of George III seriously by punishing convicts for offences committed against Kooris. These were 'to endeavour by every possible means to offer an intercourse with the natives and to conciliate their affections, encouraging all our subjects to live in amity and kindness with them' (Lippman, 1981, p. 15).

Eighteen years earlier, James Cook had been given similar orders but did not act on them, even though he displayed a positive attitude towards the Kooris he saw on his mapping of the east coast in 1770:

> From what I have seen of the natives of New South Wales, they may appear to be the most wretched people upon the earth, but in reality they are more happier than we Europeans, being wholly unacquainted not only with the superfluous, but the necessary conveniences so much sought after in Europe; they are happy in not knowing the use of them. They live in a tranquility that is not disturbed by the Inequality of Condition. The earth and sea of their own accord, furnishes them with all things necessary for life. (quoted in Woolmington, 1973, p. 13)

Cook, like many other men of the Enlightenment, saw Kooris as 'noble savages', whose total relationship with the land and nature was poles apart from European civilisation. However, even with this attitude, he refused to acknowledge officially that a human group existed, and went on to claim a little island that he called Possession Island in the name of the Crown, thus annexing the whole of the east coast. Cook's failure to recognise Koori people engineered the legal fiction of Australia being *terra nullius*, which in practice alienated Koori people according to British law from their lands. Cook became the symbol of total land loss for Aboriginal and Torres Strait Islander people. His expedition had been backed by the Royal Society of England, whose scientists would have been very much aware of Rousseau's noble savage concept: these people expected Cook to see noble savages and he did not disappoint them: 'He was a man of his times who took home the expectations of his times.' (Miller, 1985, p. 22)

Cook's vision of the noble savage was not to remain a popular belief among the first invaders of Australia. It was a radical French intellectual idea—the sort of idea that underscored the French Revolution. Rousseau's ideas became unpopular throughout Europe after 1789, especially among the aristocracy and the landed classes. In the newly invaded region of New South Wales, the idea of the noble savage was attacked by the colonists because the Kooris did not fit the fanciful ideal that European armchair philosophers held. Marine Captain Watkin Tench, who came with Arthur Phillip in the First Fleet, wrote of the Kooris with whom he came in contact:

> A thousand times... have I wished, that those European philosophers whose closest speculations exalt a state of nature above a state of civilisation, could survey the phantom which their heated imaginations have raised; a savage roaming for prey amidst his native deserts, a creature deformed by all those passions which afflict and degrade our nature unsoftened by the influence of religion, philosophy and legal instruction. (Tench, quoted in Horner 1974, p. 45)

Tench was experiencing what modern psychologists call cognitive dissonance. He expected to see a bronzed, neatly groomed denizen of an Arcadian paradise. He expected to see men and women who resembled Greek gods and goddesses. He expected the 'savages' to have a simple morality and a harmonious society. Instead, he saw a dust-covered people who on occasions fought with their partners. He saw natives who lived simply, but in Tench's mind primitively, and whose bodies—he thought—were scarred from violent conflicts with each other and from the harsh lifestyle they followed. He also noticed body deformities, such as a leg which had not set properly after a bad break. Tench condemned the Kooris for the way they interacted with each other, but he and many other early commentators forgot that violence, conflict and brutality were far more common in England at the time.

The people most vociferously opposed to the noble savage ideal were the early evangelical Christians. They saw nothing noble about living in a state of nature cut off from the knowledge of Christ, and they portrayed the Koori people of the various colonies as degraded, miserable, brutal and barbaric heathens. The gut feeling among most Englishmen at the time of first settlement was one of contempt for the Kooris. This was probably best expressed in the philosophy of the 'Great Chain of Being' (Lovejoy, 1976).

The Great Chain of Being was an ancient hierarchical order devised by the Greeks. It was redefined in the seventeenth century by English philosopher John Locke, who described all visible and invisible creation as a vertical chain of living or spiritual beings either superior or inferior to the links above and below. At the top of the chain sat God, the Creator. From God descended every other being. The Kooris were often described as only one link removed from the most intelligent animal, which was the ape. Needless to say, 'the "civilised" Englishman was at the top of the human scale—far closer to the angels than he was to the apes'. (Lovejoy, 1976).

Englishmen of the time used this belief to justify their supposed superiority over the aborigines of their colonies in Africa, Australia, Canada, the South Seas and the West Indies. Tench reverted to the theory of the Great Chain of Being when he wrote of the Kooris, making unfavourable comparisons between them and other Indigenous peoples of the world:

> They certainly rank very low, even in the scale of savages. They may perhaps dispute the right of precedency with the Hottentots, or even the shivering tribes who inhabit the shores of Magellan. But how inferior do they show themselves when compared to the subtle African, the patient watchful American ... or to the elegant timid Islanders of the South Seas. (quoted in Smith, 1960, p. 24)

The belief in the Great Chain of Being was racism in its crudest form. One of the earliest forms of prejudice directed at the Kooris of New Holland came from William Dampier, the English pirate who landed on New Holland's west coast in 1688. He wrote of the Yamatji he saw: 'The inhabitants of this country were the miserablest people in the world. The Hodmadads of Manonatopa, though a nasty people, yet for wealth are gentlemen to these.' (quoted in Mulvaney 1958, p. 135) They had refused to do work for him.

A similar view was being put forward by Englishmen who settled the east coast of New Holland 100 years later. In 1799 the missionary William Henry said of the Kooris:

> They are truely the most writched [sic] and deplorable beings my eyes have ever yet beheld. I think the Greenlanders and Labradorians or the inhabitants of Terra da Fuega, can not be more sunk to a level of brute creation than they. O Jesu, when will thy kingdom come with power amongst them? When shall the rays of thine Eternal gospel penetrate the gross darkness of their minds (well represented by their faces) and illumine their benighted souls. (quoted in Reece, 1974, p. 76)

Most missionaries of this era held similar views towards the Kooris they were trying to convert. These missionaries, and many other people, were influenced by the way the colour black was projected in the Bible. The Bible represented black as having evil connotations. Black meant death. It was the colour attributed to the Devil. Superstition portrayed black night as being the time when all evil took place. Europeans feared black magic. When the black faces of the natives of New South Wales were first seen by missionaries, these men of God assumed the Kooris to be an evil

Missions

'Mission' is a term loosely used for various Aboriginal and Torres Strait Islander reserves and government stations as well as Christian institutions. This map includes those places known to have been in the last category.

race of degenerates. If missionary views were negative, many settlers held even worse views. Peter Cunningham, one of the first white men to receive a land grant in the Hunter Valley, supported the belief that the Kooris were not far removed from the ape. He wrote:

> How is it that the abject animal state in which the [Aborigines] live should place them at the very zero of civilisation, constituting in a measure the connecting link between man and the monkey tribe—for really some of the old women only seem to require a tail to complete the identity. (Cunningham, 1996 [1834], p. 39)

Such racist statements from supposedly civilised people who prided themselves on their Christian brotherhood show that my people had to deal not only with the alien culture and land-grabbing habits of the invader but with the invisible forces of racist thinking. I feel this even more strongly when I realise that Peter Cunningham was writing about my ancestors, the Wonnarua people of the Hunter Valley.

Descriptions of Koori culture fared no better in the writings of the invaders, because if the Koori was among the lowest on the human scale, then Koori culture was seen as being primitive and animal like. A number of English writers portrayed Koori culture in this way. Cook wrote that:

> men and women and children go wholly naked; it is said of our first parents that after they had eaten the forbidden fruit they saw themselves naked and were ashamed; these people are naked and not ashamed; they live on fish and wild fowl, for they do not cultivate. (quoted in Beaglehole, 1955, p. 514)

Cook believed that the Kooris had not yet reached the stage of Adam and Eve. David Mann, a convict transported around 1800, believed that the culture of the Kooris was so barbarous that they could never be changed: 'They are a filthy disagreeable race of people; nor is it my opinion that any measures that could be adopted would ever make them otherwise.' (Mann, 1811, p. 46)

The missionary W. Pascoe Crook judged the Koori by his own quaint standards. In a letter to Joseph Hardcastle, he wrote of the Kooris as uncultured imbeciles:

> We saw natives in several places, they knew not how to put a cup to their mouth, but when presented with anything to drink would put their chin in the vessel and when anything was given them to eat they would open their mouths to receive it. (quoted in Woolmington, 1973, p. 13)

Pascoe Crook must have thought that the ability to use an English teacup was a sure sign of civilisation. Kooris at the time seem to have been judged by the Englishman's inflated opinions of his own society. Some Englishmen believed that the Kooris could be civilised, but even when they were hopeful of this their writings were still very unflattering. The Rev. Robert Cartwright wrote of Kooris in 1819:

> I think it will now be admitted by every candid person, that the materials we have to work upon, although extremely crude, are nevertheless good. Buried as is the intellect of these savages in Augean filth, we may yet find gems of the first magnitude and brilliance. (quoted in Woolmington, 1973, p. 23)

Some missionaries and a few settlers believed that Kooris were equal to the white man in the eyes of God and made positive statements about them. The Rev. Shelley, who founded the Parramatta Native Institutions, said in 1814:

> They have a peculiar aptness in learning the English language and pronounce it with much propriety. From the rambling naked state of these poor Natives they have generally been supposed as incapable of improvement, but I am persuaded that under the blessings of God, they are as capable of instruction as any other untutored savage. (quoted in Woolmington, 1973, p. 23)

Such missionaries hoped to produce a class of black Christian peasants. They wanted to change the Koori. They would not accept Kooris as they were, and this remained the case for at least 150 years. However, around the time the Hunter Valley was opened up for settlement, a new point of view—the humanitarian philosophy—was becoming faintly evident in white society. By the 1820s, a number of Englishmen believed that the settlement of Koori land was more harmful than beneficial to the Aborigines. These men were beginning to lobby the British government to stop the adverse effect that white settlement was having on the natives of the Empire.

One example of the new breed of humanitarian was Saxe Bannister, the Attorney-General

Blanket Day, NSW, early 1900s. Once a year, the government distributed blankets to communities. Aboriginal people saw these, and substandard rations, as inadequate compensation for their land. Kerry King Collection, AIATSIS Pictorial Archive.

of New South Wales during the time of Governors Brisbane and Darling in the 1820s. He was appalled by what he saw in New South Wales, particularly in the Hunter Valley. After leaving Australia, he wrote a pamphlet in which he said:

> In modern times with little advantage of tuition of any kind, all the uncivilised races have met with insult and injury at the hand of the professors of the new religion. They have found a large majority of white men their unvarying oppressors and even hostile to the missionaries, so generally their only friends. (Bannister, 1830, pp. 3–4)

Saxe Bannister was probably the first white law officer to talk of the rights of the Kooris in Australia. Thus, on the eve of the invasion of Koori lands, we find an English people confident and arrogant in the superiority of their race, culture and religion. They held few positive attitudes towards the Kooris, and could accept Kooris only for what they hoped they would become—black Christian peasants. Throughout the whole of this country, many Indigenous groups were socialised into the belief that this was the only way they were ever going to be recognised as having 'some worth'. This enforced socialisation evolved with the introduction of established reserves and evangelical missions. It was in these confines that Indigenous people were transformed into 'Aborigines'. The humanitarian attitude of the times held the view that 'all men are created equal in the eyes of God', but in order to gain this equality Indigenous people had to change. They would not be accepted as they were, only as what they might become.

By the beginning of the twentieth century, Indigenous people Australia wide were, at least by British law standards, landless. The laws of trespass and property rights meant that the public roads, designated reserves and established missions were the only 'safe havens' for Indigenous peoples. With all Indigenous land now 'stolen' and the laws of trespass policed, Indigenous people were forced to move to reserves and missions. They had no choice. If they persisted as Kooris, they were at the mercy of every gun-toting, redneck, racist landowner—and thus, at risk of becoming 'Aborigines'.

From the inception of trespass and control, segregated reserves and government stations, Kooris were socially engineered to the new social order of the times, becoming 'Aborigines'. Attwood (1989) highlights this in his book *The Making of the Aborigines*. By the turn of the century, most colonies had developed and, on the basis of government reports, were implementing policies of segregation, separation, assimilation, land, rations, controlled movement, 'half-castes', power over children, institutionalisation, and discrimination in education, health, housing, employment and especially the law. At last a growing tide of books published from the 1970s onwards has seen to it that most Indigenous people around this country know only too well their history of 'special treatment'.

My late grandmother's experiences of 'special treatment'

One of the most draconian of 'special treatment' policies was the taking away of our children. This was the main mechanism that all governments around this country used to force Indigenous peoples to conform to the so-called right and proper social standards by which white people wanted us to live.

My own family and ancestors have experienced everything that the invaders have handed

Mealtime at Kinchela Boys Home, north coast NSW, notorious as the place where generations of Aboriginal boys stayed after being taken from their families. Courtesy AIATSIS.

them—the initial contact, the frontier slaughters, the spread of disease after contact, the forcible removal of Kooris to segregated reserves, the later dispersal of Kooris from many of these reserves, the network of discriminatory legislation, the exclusion of Koori children from state schools, and the kidnapping of Koori children and their incarceration in government and religious institutions. It forms a story of racial history as ignominious as that anywhere else in the world. Behind it all lies the destruction of Koori identity and separateness.

In 1910, my late grandmother, Jean Miller, was born at St Clair mission, outside Singleton in New South Wales. She spent her childhood growing up on the St Clair mission, where she 'spent many happy years'. Years later, as a young girl living in La Perouse, she was to feel the effects of the Board's new policy towards Koori children. She was separated from her mother. Two white people came to where she was living at La Perouse and asked her mother whether they could have her. My great-grandmother Harriet agreed, and Jean was taken to live and work at Mosman. Nan felt like she was just given away as you would give away a puppy. The year was 1924 and at 14 she was too young to understand why her mother had agreed that she could go. But her mother did not really have a choice. The 1916 regulations of the Aborigines Protection Board stated:

> All girls reaching the age of 14 years, shall leave the reserve. In order to effect this result, the mothers shall be given the option and opportunity of themselves placing their girls out in situations of the Board's officers. If they fail to do this within a period of one month, after being notified, the Board's Inspectors shall have the power to dispatch such girls to Sydney or to Cootamundra Home for a period of training as arranged by the Secretary. (Aborigines Protection Board Minutes, 4/7124, p. 2, cl. 2, 1916)

For four years, my grandmother was a domestic servant at Mosman. She earned one shilling and sixpence per week, of which one shilling and threepence was banked by the Board, leaving her with threepence—not even a 'lousy little sixpence'. When she left the services of the Board, she went back to the tribal homelands of her people, the lands of the Wonnarua.

My mother, Kathleen, was born in 1929, the year of the Great Depression. It was during the 1920s and 1930s that Koori people in New South Wales suffered the greatest oppression at the hands of the Board. Koori children were 'legally kidnapped' and transported to the infamous 'white-out' institutions of Kinchela, Cootamundra and Bomaderry. In these centres, Koori children were deliberately and systematically socially engineered into the ways white society deemed most 'proper'.

After staying in Singleton for a number of years, my grandmother and her young family moved to Redfern, where most of her relatives were living at the time. She rented accommodation in Hugo Street and proceeded to make a life for herself and five young children. Jean was also a single mother. Her immediate surroundings were hostile. After an altercation with a neighbour, also a close relative, she was reported. My grandmother and her young family were now under the close scrutiny of the Aborigines Protection Board. At 4.00 a.m. on 5 December 1940, the horror which so many New South Wales Kooris dreaded descended on my family. As my grandmother stated:

> The Welfare come the next morning about four o'clock they come, two Ds and the Welfare. Four o'clock in the morning, and we was all asleep—poor little kids all asleep—your mother, Dotty, Ernie, Raymond and Leslie. Five kids they took away from me that morning. (Miller, 1985, p. 158)

In reality, the authorities pulled up in black cars, banged heavily on the door and when my Nan opened it they barged straight in, nearly knocking her over, and started grabbing my uncles and aunty. My mother acted very quickly and rolled off her bed in the front room between the bed and wall, pulled her quilt over her and hid under a bed unnoticed—witnessing the full brutality of the child-grabbing antics of the authorities. She was terrified as she heard her brothers and sister struggling, screaming and crying out for their mother, but Nan was helpless—what could she do? She was completely powerless. My mother later gave herself up during the morning to be with her younger brothers and sister. The whole operation was planned and calculated. It is interesting to remember that this was December 1940 and

Koori soldiers were fighting the Germans in Europe. One of the most notorious tactics of the Nazis was the dawn raids by their Gestapo to take away people when they were most vulnerable and least able to resist or escape. Yet these tactics were being used against defenceless Koori people in a supposedly democratic country. It was early 1941 when my mother and her sister Dorothy were sent to Cootamundra. My three uncles ended up in Bomaderry Infants' Home until they were of age to be sent to Kinchela Boys' Home near Kempsey.

It is hard to fathom just what was going through the minds of my mother, her sister and brothers then. The only person on this earth they loved and trusted could do nothing to help them. And how bad would my Nan have felt seeing this happen to her children?

My grandmother had a further four children, two of whom she was also forced to hand over. Seven children of my grandmother were to feel and live the nightmare years of the 'Stolen Generations'. Many Kooris still bear the emotional scars of this inhuman treatment of Koori children, which lasted legally in New South Wales from 1909 to 1969.

From the Aborigines Protection Board's inception in 1883 until it was abolished and replaced by the Aborigines Welfare Board in 1940, policies of special treatment were based primarily on changing the overall structure of Koori lifestyles to suit the ideals the Board believed Kooris could attain. In 1909, a year before my grandmother was born, an official of the Aborigines Protection Board told the Australasian Catholic Congress:

> We have today 3200 children growing up in our midst, three fourths of whom range from half-castes to almost white, with no prospects ahead of the great majority, under the present system, but lives of idleness and vice... For adults we can only make their track as smooth as possible, they will soon pass away; but the children require our gravest consideration... Amongst all those who have had large experience with the Aborigines, and who take a deep interest in their welfare, there is no difference of opinion as to the only solution of this great problem: the removal of the children and their complete isolation from the influences of the camps... In the course of a few years there will be no need for the camps and stations; the old people will have passed away and their progeny will be absorbed into the industrial classes of the country. (quoted in Edwards and Read, 1989, p. 397)

What? Waiting for a whole race of human beings to die out, so white society could be free of the 'aborigine problem'!

Special treatment: A national policy

Similar policies were implemented in other states, as the quote below, referring to Victoria, shows:

> A Gunditjmara Elder reported seeing little children screaming in the motor cars, welfare officers and police pulling them back in the car.
>
> It must have been terrifying for little children, seeing white people come and forcibly put them in the car and slam the door and take them away and no parents were there at the time to come to their rescue and they were screaming. You can imagine the terror that went through them little children's hearts. It must have been horrifying for them, getting plucked away from their tribal environment to be chucked in the institution somewhere, with walls and stern people, with all the kindness they left behind with the old people. (Henry 'Banjo' Clarke, Gunditjmara Elder, in Rintoul, 1993, p. 232)

These policies were inhuman. They undermined the whole fabric of Koori society. If this had happened to the wider Australian community in the way it was enacted towards Indigenous Australians, I believe worldwide condemnation would have stepped in to prevent it.

One of this country's most recognised and recorded Indigenous musicians, Archie Roach, tells of his experiences when he was taken away from Framlingham, and the deceitful way the welfare authorities went about it:

> I remember them coming in the big van—the Welfare rep and the police. The police mainly is what I remember. I didn't know what a Welfare rep was. I just thought they were police uniforms. When they came, they had things like balloons and party hats. We thought we were going on a big picnic, some sort of a party. They told us that we were going on a big party, all the

kids. All the families of the mission were sort of standing around and yelling at these people. It was a bit confusing at first, I didn't realise what was happening. They went to the school and took some of my cousins out of school, and then they put us in the van. I could see Mum was crying. I couldn't understand that. That's when I got frightened then, when Mum started to cry. I knew something was wrong. And Dad was running through, and he was like a madman. He wanted to fight everybody and they had to restrain him... I was confused, I remember asking my sisters when we were going back home. I thought we were sent away for a holiday or something. I don't know if they knew much more themselves. They were only young, but they were older than me. Life in the homes wasn't too good. I just wanted to leave, I wanted to get back home. But after a year or so in the home, I don't know, I just sort of got used to that way of living. (quoted in Rintoul, 1993, p. 141)

A Doomadgee woman told what had happened to her for merely speaking her own homeland language:

My sister and I had our mouths washed out with soap for speaking our language. The face-washer, they rubbed soap on it and they got us and put it in our mouths. Terrible, you know to have soap up your nose and your mouth just because you're talking: we couldn't speak a word of English, you know. We had to learn English and we had to live like white people because your mother and father's way is heathenism. I didn't understand what heathenism was until a lot later on, when I left that reserve and I got hold of a dictionary, but I knew it must have been bad because of the tone of their voice. (quoted in Rintoul, 1993, p. 141)

These institutions were nothing more than child slave labour camps. It was the way that government and religious authorities inducted Indigenous children into white Anglo-Saxon and Protestant work ethics, as Henry Fourmile from Queensland states:

There was a dormitory set up—one for girls, one for boys, when we were ten years of age. I remember going there, till we were sixteen. We had to do that. We were taken off our parents, forcibly. It was a very sad day. I cried for about a week after. No one actually came to get me.

'Home is a heap of iron for Patricia Shane at the Wilcannia Aboriginal Settlement. Her garden is the desert dust.' Sunday Australian, *14 March 1971. A powerful image of Aboriginal living conditions, one of a long line of media exposés that shocked people over breakfast, but rarely made any difference on the ground. Courtesy News Limited.*

Fence line of the Kahlin Home for Aboriginal children, Darwin, Northern Territory, 1930s. Missions always aimed to keep Aboriginal children as far away as possible from their families. Photo: E.H. Wilson. Courtesy AIATSIS.

It was a known thing that as soon as your sons or daughters reached the age of ten you were to take them up to the dormitory and place them in the dormitory...

We were allowed to come home on Saturdays... We had our little jobs to do, like sweeping the premises, sometimes with a broom but mainly with our fingers. We all used to line up regimentally and bend down and start raking up the leaves and sticks with our fingers, down on our hands and knees. (quoted in Rintoul, 1993, p. 114)

Brian Champion of Western Australia tells of the harshness at the Norseman Mission:

We had to go. Mum and Dad had no authority. We went from Kalgoorlie to Norseman to be put into the mission. It was Church of Christ Norseman Mission. It was all the children there. I was the smallest out of the three.

You cried yourself to sleep, of course... because you've got no parent, you've got no one to back you up and cuddle you or anything else. And after months and months of that... well, you just hardened to it. I know what it's like to cry yourself to sleep at night when you haven't got your parents around you...

I was put in bags, me and another bloke... put in bags and hung up on the line for doing wrong.

My brother, Ben, was flogged that much he could barely crawl. He was flogged by a superintendent. My mother complained and she took the case into Norseman and went to a JP and reported these things.

Well, naturally... you were an Aboriginal, and Aboriginals didn't stand for much. The police were the bosses, the Native Affairs were the bosses, and whoever was put in control, them were the bosses too. An Aboriginal wasn't given any say. Don't care how much you was half killed. If the evidence was all there it still didn't make any difference. You was an Aboriginal and that was it. Aboriginals didn't have any say. Aboriginals weren't really treated as humans. (quoted in Rintoul, 1993, pp. 343–4)

These sample experiences of Indigenous people show how many individuals and groups throughout this country have suffered under the policy of forced systematic socialisation practices. These policies were deliberately enacted to force total conformity to the laws and the mores of White Australian society. Indigenous people were never going to be recognised for what they were, only what they might become. Very little has changed: Indigenous people are still being expected to change.

My uncles' experiences of 'special treatment'

I was never taken away, but I grew up living for only a short time with my mother. My grandmother reared me along with two older aunts, Valery and Rhoda. Redbourneberry Hill became my home in the land of my ancestors, the Gringai Clan of the Wonnarua Nation. We lived in poverty, but it was a happy poverty. There were always chores for me to do. Fetching water from the Hunter River, rabbit trapping, getting firewood and getting offal from the slaughterhouse were just some of the things I had to do. However, we were always reminded by my Nan about what had happened to her and her experiences with the Protection and Welfare Authorities. It was Nan who protected me from the authorities. Had it not been for her, I would have been sent to Kinchela Boys' home, like my mother's brothers.

My uncles Ernie, Leslie and my late Uncle Ray were sent there in the mid-1940s. Kinchela had once been the Board's most horrendous institution. For example, the manager of Kinchela in 1933 was warned by the Board that he must not use a stockwhip on the boys, or tie them up. He was not to send them out as labourers (probably slave labour) on local farms. All of this led to an inquiry into the manager's actions, but the outcome was that he was merely told to keep a punishment book. A Koori man questioned some years later told how he was locked in a shed for several days, and another questioned in 1981 said the scars on his feet were caused from frostbite he got 40 years earlier at Kinchela, bringing in the cows on frosty mornings without shoes. It was reported that the boys did two hours' work after school each day, but an inspecting welfare official who visited the home in 1939 thought that the boys probably had to work more like four hours a day, with no time at all for leisure in winter.

Breaking the colour bar in rugby league in the bush

In 1929, Boomerangs Rugby League Football Club, from the Condobolin Aboriginal reserve, challenged Canowindra Club to a match. Canowindra refused because the Boomerangs were an all-Aboriginal team. The Condobolin town team also refused to play the Boomerangs, and wanted to bar them, but the Rugby League Group XI (based in Parkes) refused, as reported in the *Sydney Morning Herald*. The Boomerangs were then deluged with invitations from Riverina clubs offering 75 per cent of gate takings and help with transport and accommodation. The Boomerangs tour of the Riverina lasted seven weeks; they lost only one game—and blamed partying too hard the night before.

In a time when racial theories and the White Australia policy were largely unchallenged, when Aboriginals and South Sea Islanders were denied the pension and a few years previous Coolangatta's Capitol Theatre, for example, opened with strictly segregated seating, the working class 'leaguies' of the Riverina showed they saw no place for racial superiority in their sport.

Also in 1929 the Tweed Heads Football Club voted to bar 'dark' players. Local Aboriginals and the sons of South Sea Islanders who had escaped the deportations of the early Commonwealth years were keen players, and so they formed their own club, and by 1935 the Tweed Heads All Blacks dominated their competition. In August 1930, the *Beaudesert Times* reported a match between a combined Tweed–Currumbin side and the Beaudesert All Blacks: Beaudesert players, it said, 'displayed exceptional speed', but the combined side won 15–6. At the start of the 1934 season the Queensland Rugby League admitted the thirteen clubs of the Lower South Burnett Rugby League to the Wide Bay competition, so that Frank Fisher (Cathy Freeman's grandfather), the spectacular five-eighth from Barambah Mission, could be selected in the Wide Bay side to play the Great Britain touring side in 1936. Great Britain won 35–8, but Frank Fisher scored one of Wide Bay's two tries.

The sheer ability of the dark players and the discrediting of so-called racial supremacy after World War II saw more Aboriginal and Islander players selected in representative teams. It is important for today's players and followers of the game to understand the struggle of the early dark players to gain acceptance and recognition.

Unfortunately, no photos of the Boomerangs tour have yet been found. Any information about early Aboriginal and Islander teams will be gratefully acknowledged. Contact David Huggonson 02 6288 2722.

Barambah Aboriginal rugby league team, 1930s. One of the team is Cathy Freeman's grandfather Frank 'Big Shot' Fisher, the champion five-eighth who played against the touring Great Britain side. Barambah was renamed Cherbourg. Courtesy David Huggonson.

The behaviour of the inmates was similar to that of prisoners in a concentration camp—the same welfare official reported that 'there is a noticeable tendency for the boys to sit on their haunches motionless and almost silent'. (Read 1982, p. 11)

However, by the time my uncles went to Kinchela, some situations had improved considerably. Uncle Ernie said that in his opinion the home was run 'spot on'. In his own words:

> The bloke running the home in those days was a bloke by the name of Rossiter. He treated all the boys at the home as though they were his sons. He spent that much money on the home. We lived right on the banks of the river and had a swimming pool there—a netted thing it was—but that wasn't good enough. Mr Rossiter got a big swimming pool put in the ground at the home, because he was worried that sharks would get us in the old pool with its torn net. This was government money he spent. We even had pictures in the hall on Saturday nights and he run it. He run that home perfectly. In the end this bloke got the sack. I think it was because he did too much for us boys. (Quoted in Miller, 1985, p. 167)

Although my Uncle Ernie states that he was treated alright—and there are many of the Stolen Generations who will also attest to this—the fact remains that these institutions were established to supposedly give Indigenous children the 'opportunity' to merge into the wider community and to coexist amicably, using their 'new-found' experiences to better themselves. However, a great many came out of the homes far less educated, far less healthy (both physically and emotionally), with fewer employment opportunities and still economically deprived. For the so-called 'benefits', Indigenous Australians had to bear being ripped from their mothers' and fathers' arms and isolated from their communities, culture and land—an experience that would shatter anyone's life.

The political fightback

After decades of being treated as sub-human by the colonists and settlers, suffering under inferior government policies of 'special treatment' and ignorant bureaucrats, Kooris began to assert themselves politically, to demand equality in the basic services which the wider Australian community took for granted. It is difficult to say just where and when this political upsurge in Koori determination occurred, because Kooris have largely been written out of Australia's history until quite recent times.

Many historians, both black and white, have researched and brought to light Koori individuals, organisations and events that reflect Koori dissatisfaction, and highlighted the political action that arose out of the treatment that had been experienced by Kooris since white colonisation. Many of these writings encompass the truly resilient nature of Kooris by showing that Kooris did fight for their country. Australia was never given to the invaders.

To fight for one's country is considered a great honour—to fight for freedom, for democracy against external forces, to protect the social, economic and political fabric of one's heritage and culture was and still is a mark of distinction by anyone's standards. Especially in the land of 'Lest We Forget'. Kooris fought for their country too. Kooris have been involved in every Australian war since World War I. Yet 'mateship' that developed in the trenches of Gallipoli, the deserts of the Middle East, the jungles of New Guinea, and then Borneo and Vietnam was very much forgotten when the Diggers returned to Australia. Koori ex-servicemen returned to live a totalitarian existence under unequal oppressive government policies that controlled every facet of their lives. They couldn't even drink with their mates. The freedom they experienced while fighting to free this country overseas was lost when they returned. Not only did Koori ex-servicemen fight and die overseas for this country—they had to come back to fight for their basic rights in this country. Their war service has only recently been recognised.

The political fightback that has been best documented was the fightback of the 1930s. Koori men and women formed the Aborigines Progressive Association, and utilised political mechanisms similar to those used by the wider community. They were outspoken and voiced their opinions effectively. They formed pressure groups, lobbied government officials, and used the media and the trade unions to publicise their cause. People like Bill Ferguson, Pearl Gibbs, Margaret Tucker, Jack Patten, Doug Nicholls and Bert Groves fought for the abolition of the Aborigines Protection Board. They organised the first Koori Day of Mourning on 28 January 1938, which commemorated the Sesquicentenary ('150 Years of Progress') of white occupation of Australia. These people set the scene for later Koori political activism.

In the 1950s, the Australian Aboriginal Fellowship (AAF) was established by a small group of black and white Australians. This organisation had a much wider involvement in Koori affairs throughout Australia, and was seen as the starting point for Kooris politically asserting themselves on the federal front. The Foundation for Aboriginal Affairs was set up in the mid-1960s, and members worked tirelessly for Koori affairs right up to 1970. It was due to AAF involvement that many similar organisations were establishing themselves in towns throughout New South Wales, Queensland and Victoria to fight for Koori issues. Pretty soon, Australia's Koori population was being represented by many organisations on a local and state basis, but with no federal voice.

The Federal Council for Advancement of Aboriginal and Torres Strait Islanders (FCAATSI) was formed in the late 1950s. It gave Kooris their federal voice, the last non-Koori president being Don Dunstan. At last the plight of Kooris was infiltrating federal politics, but reform for Kooris on a federal basis was yet to come. However, FCAATSI was instrumental in determining the attitude dissonance in white Australians that led to Kooris being given 'first-class citizenship' status in the 1967 Referendum.

It was pressure from FCAATSI that led to the setting up of the Office of Aboriginal Affairs, with Prime Minister John Gorton giving Billy Wentworth that post. It was not a government department, and was later downgraded by Prime Minister William McMahon. During the late 1960s and early 1970s, a new wave of Koori political activists began to assert themselves. People like the late Charles Perkins—who at the time was a student at the University of Sydney—along with his fellow students and many other non-Indigenous sympathisers, began prodding and then systematically breaking down the white racist attitudes in towns throughout New South Wales by confronting their racism at their own doorsteps in Walgett, Moree and Kempsey. The Freedom Rides was one of the most significant turning points for Indigenous Australians then. In my opinion, the late Charles Perkins did more for Indigenous Australians, Australia wide, than any other Koori, alive or dead. He was our Ghandi, our Martin Luther King Jnr and Nelson Mandela all rolled into one.

During the 1960s and 1970s, worldwide events influenced these new Koori activists. Martin Luther King's civil rights movement, as well as the treatment of blacks in South Africa and England played major roles in determining strategies for the Koori struggle. Kooris read Malcolm X, Angela Davis, Stokeley Carmichael, Steve Biko and Nelson Mandela. In those days, it was all about black civil rights. But in the early 1970s, land rights became the basis for Kooris' own political struggle. In order to know what the land meant to Kooris, Elders were consulted to tell of the sacred and significant traditional land values, and the impact of the American civil rights movement subsided somewhat.

Judgement by his Peers *by Gordon Syron. This is Syron's own story: his request for trial by Aboriginal people, his peers, was denied on the grounds he wasn't 'black enough'. Fronting a calendar and made into a poster and a postcard,* Judgement by his Peers *is an icon of the Aboriginal struggle. Self-taught in gaol and known as the 'Father of urban Aboriginal art', Gordon Syron's first exhibition was on 'the Block' at Redfern, while on day release. He has painted on the 'redcoat' invasion and deaths in custody and his painting* Where the Wildflowers Once Grew *mourns the beauty that was lost when sandminers ripped a foot of topsoil off thousands of acres up the coast.* Judgement By His Peers *has hung in the Aboriginal Legal Service, Sydney Town Hall and at the Independent Commission Against Corruption. Courtesy Gordon Syron.*

Australia Day 1972 saw the establishment of the Koori Tent Embassy on the lawns of Parliament House, Canberra—a powerful symbol during the lead-up to the federal election of 1972. It gave rise to the struggle for basic equality for Kooris throughout Australia, and in some ways contributed to the demise of the McMahon government. This most significant event captured national and international media. The Labor Party promised land rights legislation because it was, in Gough Whitlam's words, unarguable. Labor also sensed that many voters would support the Koori protest. The McMahon government at the time helped the land rights cause by declaring the Tent Embassy illegal; it was just what we wanted. Police moved in and began dismantling the embassy and arresting demonstrators. The media captured this, and the McMahon government survived only another two months. The new Whitlam government set up the Woodward Commission, and subsequently land rights policies were established in Northern and Central Australia.

But before this, the policies of the Aborigines Boards had already come to an end. On 20 March 1969 the Aborigines Welfare Board ceased to exist, and with it went the legally sanctioned powers of total oppression of Kooris and the draconian policies of segregation, separation, assimilation, land, rations, 'half-castes', controlled movement, power over children, institutionalisation and discrimination in health, education and employment. These past policies dehumanised the majority of Kooris, who lived and died not knowing a life outside of them. Many Kooris who can remember those years have been irreparably damaged.

Cynical song

Moments of madness drives me crazy now and then
Death through self conviction I can't comprehend
Dreaming of things that make no sense in the end
Sometime think I'm really going crazy

Silhouettes of Sydney in the early morning light
Is a scene I'm getting used to
That sends shivers down my spine

Cartoon by Cathy Wilcox, Sydney Morning Herald, *30 May 1998, just after the first Sorry Day. Then prime minister John Howard was under fire all over Australia for his dogged refusal to apologise to Aboriginal people for the pain of the Stolen Generations. Here he finds he has no heart and is comforted by an Aboriginal woman patting his arm. Courtesy Cathy Wilcox.*

Reflection without action just seems a waste of time
Thinking bout things that might have been

Maybe maybe maybe it's just me
Maybe just maybe I just never seen
That happiness was never really far from where I've been
Just couldn't tell the forest from the trees

Sisters biting loose change down at Central once again
Brothers in the park there drinking moselle in the rain
While just along the road way they got their red wine and champagne
Talking 'bout the ways to fix his problem

There's people all around me but I'm always on my own
The art of conversation seems best when I'm alone
And one-way consultations they're so common on the phone
Maybe that's the way it's always been

Maybe maybe maybe it's just me
Maybe just maybe I just never seen
That happiness was never really far from where I've been

Just couldn't tell the forest from the trees

The visitors are teaching tourists about our country's ancient ways
The Blackman's in the corner and they make sure there he stays
And in the shop front window my culture's just a game
They can sell it but they'll never understand it

You work your fingers to the bone but never toughen up your heart
You get an education but never get real smart
Cause in the lucky country success isn't all that hard
If you got the right biological credentials

© Charles Trindall

The National Inquiry into the Separation of Aboriginal and Torres Strait Islander Children from Their Families

In 1996, I gave evidence to the National Inquiry into the separation of Aboriginal and Torres Strait Islander children from their families. Many individuals and organisations were consulted Australia wide. It was from my evidence that I can proudly say the report *Bringing Them Home* was named. This report was the most compelling document ever written on the Stolen Generations. A report such as this could not have the impact it has had without recording the life experiences of institutionalised children, and rebutting the myth that 'it was in their best interest'.

The Inquiry found that 'entrenched disadvantage and dispossession mean the removal of Indigenous children continues today. Indigenous children are six times more likely to be removed for child welfare reasons and 21 times more likely for juvenile justice detention, than non-Indigenous children'. It also found that:

> in child welfare, Indigenous children are more likely than non-Indigenous children to be removed on the ground of 'neglect' rather than 'abuse'. Often Indigenous parenting styles are wrongly seen as the cause.
>
> Aboriginal families continue to be seen as the 'problem', and Aboriginal children continue to

> We may go home, but we cannot relive our childhoods. We may reunite with our mothers, fathers, sisters, brothers, aunties, uncles, communities, but we cannot relive the 20, 30, 40 years that we spent without their love and care, and they cannot undo the grief and mourning they felt when we were separated from them. We can go home to ourselves as Aboriginals, but this does not erase the attacks inflicted on our hearts, minds, bodies and souls, by caretakers who thought their mission was to eliminate us as Aboriginals.
>
> —Link Up (NSW), quoted in Human Rights and Equal Opportunity Commission (1997, p. 3)

> The Inquiry has not been 'raking over the past' for its own sake. The truth is the past is very much with us today, in the continuing devastation of the lives of Indigenous Australians.
>
> That devastation cannot be addressed unless the whole community listens with an open heart and mind to the stories of what happened and, having listened and understood, commits itself to reconciliation.
>
> —Human Rights and Equal Opportunity Commission (1997, p. 4)

> be seen as potentially 'saveable' if they can be separated from the 'dysfunctional' or 'culturally deprived' environments of their families and communities. Non-Aboriginals continue to feel that Aboriginal adults are 'hopeless' and cannot be changed, but Aboriginal children 'have a chance'.
>
> —Link Up (NSW), in Human Rights and Equal Opportunity Commission (1997, p. 31)

The report recommended that:

> Governments have a responsibility to respond with 'reparation' to those affected. 'Reparation' is the appropriate response to gross violations of human rights. According to international legal principles, reparation has five parts:
>
> 1. acknowledgement of the truth and an apology;
> 2. guarantees that these human rights won't be breached again;
> 3. returning what has been lost as much as possible (known as restitution);
> 4. rehabilitation; and
> 5. compensation.
>
> —Human Rights and Equal Opportunity Commission (1997, p. 28)

The report emphasised that: 'Everybody—including primary and secondary school

> The Inquiry found that experiences of forcibly removed children overwhelmingly contradict the view that it was in their 'best interests' at the time. A 1994 Australian Bureau of Statistics (ABS) survey found people who were forcibly removed in childhood are twice as likely to assess their health stats as poor or only fair (29%) compared with people who were not removed (15.4%).
>
> The ABS found forcibly removed people are not better educated, not more likely to be employed and not receiving significantly higher incomes than people who were raised in their communities. However, they are twice as likely to have been arrested more than once in the past five years, with one in five removed people having this experience.
>
> —Human Rights and Equal Opportunity Commission (1997, p. 19)

> Justice requires that the wider Australia [sic] community be informed about these policies and practices, and be informed about the resolute resistance Aboriginal people have continuously maintained. We want the wider community, Aboriginal and non-Aboriginal alike, to be informed about and recognise not only the courage and strength we have in surviving as a people and in seeking to reunite with our people despite years of retention in non-Aboriginal environments. It is equally important for it to be recognised that separation policy and practice is not something that happened a long time ago, it is not ancient history. Rather it has continued in various forms and guises up to the present and for the future of many Aboriginals.
>
> —Link-Up (New South Wales) Submission to Human Rights and Equal Opportunity Commission (1997b, p. 294)

> As a child I had no mother's arms to hold me. No father to lead me into the world. Us taken-away kids only had each other. All of us damaged and too young to know what to do. We had strangers standing over us. Some were nice and did the best they could. But many were just cruel, nasty types. We were flogged often. We learnt to shut up and keep our eyes to the ground, for fear of being singled out and punished. We lived in dread of being sent away again where we could be even worse off. Many of us grew up hard and tough. Others were explosive and angry. A lot grew up just struggling to cope at all. They found their peace in other institutions or alcohol. Most of us learnt how to occupy a small space and avoid anything that looked like trouble. We had few ideas about relationships. No one showed us how to be lovers or parents. How to feel safe loving someone when that risked them being taken away and leaving us alone again. Everyone and everything we loved was taken away from us kids.
>
> —Alex Kruger

children, judges, doctors, police and other decision-makers—should be told about the history of forcible removal and the continuing effects on families, communities and the next generation.' (1997, p. 30) The report also recommended that: 'Australian parliaments, police forces and churches should acknowledge their responsibility and apologise to everyone affected by forcible removal.' (1997, p. 30). It called for a National Sorry Day for the Stolen Generations and their families.

This event was first held on 26 May 1998, and was supported by many individuals and organisations signing Sorry Books. It received a great deal of positive support, although some thought otherwise and expressed their views in letters to the editor:

> Tuesday's Sorry Day did not exactly divide the nation but it did provoke widely diverging points of view. Many saw it as a symbolic gesture, a necessary purgative, that would help bring understanding, a fresh start and happier relations between white and black Australians. Others saw it as divisive, believing that because they had nothing to do with removing the children, they had nothing for which to apologise. (*Sydney Morning Herald*, 30 May 1998, p. 31)

These Australians, as well as the Prime Minister of the day, John Howard, seemed to fail to understand what Sorry Day was all about, although Indigenous people had repeatedly explained that it was not about guilt but rather respecting and acknowledging fellow Australians' pain.

Even today, there are still bleatings from some non-Indigenous individuals and groups about so-called 'special treatment' that Indigenous Australians are supposed to get. Nothing can be further from the truth. These people are crying out about the rights of other Australians as if they never had any rights at all. But the rights to land, education, housing, health, employment and the protection of the legal system since invasion times have been developed for and by non-Indigenous Australians, who have always had these rights afforded them because they were Australians. Indigenous people are also Australians. How could they achieve when the whole social system in this country excluded them? When the racist attitudes that dominated and suppressed Indigenous people in the past are still manifested today in the speeches of ignorant parliamentarians, oppressive government policies and the out-of-touch print, radio and television media—how can Indigenous people be expected to achieve even now?

The levels of achievement that Indigenous people are experiencing today have come about through the resilient spirit of Indigenous people as a whole. We want equality with the wider Australian community—equality that guarantees access to the basic necessities that other Australians take for granted. Indigenous people want to be Indigenous people in their own country and not be penalised because they are Indigenous. I believe Australia is far better than it once was for its Indigenous people, but not as good as it might become. As the Human Rights and Equal Opportunity Commission noted: 'It is for all of us to make the journey of reconciliation, and with open hearts and minds it is possible for us to begin "bringing them home".' (1997, p. 32)

Undated 1930s newspaper clipping, 'Homes are Sought for these Children'. Clearly Aboriginal children were expected to be strong to do work round the house. The handwritten note below the article clearly comes from a prospective parent and says: 'I like the little girl in centre of group, but if taken by anyone else, any of the others would do, as long as they are strong.' Courtesy National Archives.

An example of what Aboriginal people mean by 'special treatment'. Cartoonist Geoff Pryor makes the point that deaths in custody may be suicides, but society is really responsible. The daggers are labelled 'disease', 'boredom', 'poverty' and 'neglect'. Courtesy Geoff Pryor and Canberra Times.

> The distinction has been made before but I'll say it again—not sorry in the commonly accepted sense of the word, where guilt and blame are appropriated. But sorry in the sorry business sense of the word, where grief is met with respect and comfort.
> —Wendy Hermeston, Senior Caseworker, Link Up, Sorry Day ceremony, Government House, Sydney, 26 May 1998
>
> Sorry Day is not about guilt. It is about understanding. For our people, saying sorry is simply a way of recognising another person's suffering.
> I feel sorry for those that can't say sorry. It's all to do with providing leadership and I feel sorry that we can't unite on an occasion like this that acknowledges a part of our history.
> —Gatjil Djerkurra, ATSIC chairman, at the Honour the Grief ceremony, Parliament House, Canberra, quoted in Sydney Morning Herald, 30 May 1998, p. 41
>
> I would like to apologise for those Australians who did not have the compassion in their hearts to join in, particularly the Prime Minister.
> —Mick Dodson, at the Honour the Grief ceremony, Parliament House, Canberra, quoted in Sydney Morning Herald, 30 May 1998, p. 41

Discovering shared history: Moving towards new understanding in Australian schools

6

Paddy Cavanagh

The starting point for reconciliation, must be a reflection on history and the present situation of Indigenous Australians. (Pearson, 2007)

Privates G. Leonard and H. West of the 2/1st Battalion AIF, pictured in Sydney before leaving for active service in 1941. Both were killed in action in 1942. Many Aboriginal men and women served in Australia's wars, even though they were officially barred from recruitment until 1951. An Aboriginal researcher at Griffith University has found that Aboriginal trackers were sent to the Boer War, but found no evidence they ever made it back. Courtesy Australian War Memorial (Neg. No 010375).

The teaching of Australian history prior to 1980

Until the 1980s, the teaching of history in Australian schools almost always represented the nation's past from a very narrow perspective. Through more than 100 years of compulsory universal education, Australian children had been taught little about Aboriginal people and culture and even less about the history of the relationship between Aboriginal and non-Aboriginal people. This was particularly evident in the teaching of Social Studies in primary schools and History in the junior years of secondary schools. The themes that pervaded these curricula prior to the 1980s are familiar to anyone whose school education was completed before that time. The country's short history, particularly its humble convict origins, was the source of some embarrassment, so schools focused instead on teaching children their long British heritage. Generally, the *real* history of Australia was only seen as beginning with Cook's *discovery* of the country in 1770 and this, along with the establishment of the first British *settlement* by Governor Phillip in 1788, was represented as the beginning of *civilisation* in Australia.

This colonial deference to Australia's British past ebbed only slowly, but by the 1960s the taint of convictism had largely disappeared and the convict era had become an acceptable part of the nation's story. By then the convicts were typically represented in school history courses as the oppressed victims of Britain's Industrial Revolution and stories of the successfully emancipated few were promoted as examples of the individual redemption possible in a land of opportunity. Another prominent theme was the successful economic development of the country. Governor Macquarie's insight and initiative in establishing a currency and the Bank of New South Wales were highlighted, as was the story of the squatters *taking up land* and establishing the pastoral industry. Macquarie was also feted as the most successful of the Governors for embedding the ideals of egalitarianism and the *fair go* in the Australian ethos. As students inked their initials into shared wooden desks, other aspects of the Australian identity were drummed into them through tales of the heroism of pioneering settlers and the *mateship* that was engendered as they endured the extremes of flood, fire and drought to tame the wild bush. The discovery of gold returned the students' attention to the theme of progress and development. Before the students snoozed off completely, teachers would wind up their courses on colonial history with an account of late nineteenth century industrialisation and urbanisation. The improvements in transport that opened up markets for the country's agricultural produce and the good economic sense that was Federation concluded the course as the bell rang and the kids rushed out in search of something interesting.

Much of this optimistic story of economic progress and development in an *Australia Unlimited* was repeated in the secondary curriculum. But considerable attention was also given there to the creation of the Anzac Legend in World War I and its consolidation in World War II. In the post-1960s era, senior history courses also began to include aspects of Australian social and political developments in the twentieth century, such as the trade union movement, the Great Depression and the Women's Movement. This was a view of the past that the conservative historian Geoffrey Blainey described as the *Three Cheers view of history*—an optimistic and patriotic view of a successful past which Blainey himself admitted had a long run in Australian universities and schools (Blainey, 1993a). By the

Lest We Forget: 20,000 Blacks Killed by 1900. *Photomontage by Ann Stephen, 1981, made into a postcard. A hugely subversive image: a parody of Anzac Day celebrations, featuring the war memorial in Melbourne, a military band of 'redcoats' and the sacred phrase 'Lest We Forget'. The reverse of the postcard featured quotes from Aboriginal history, such as: 'Blackfellow by and by all gone, plenty shoot 'em white fellow long time, plenty, plenty.'—James Dredge, Victorian Aboriginal, 1840. And '... at least 20,000 Aborigines were killed as a direct result of conflict with the settlers.'—Henry Reynolds,* The Other Side of the Frontier, *1981. Courtesy Ann Stephen.*

1960s, some critics had begun to question this extremely narrow view of the past for promoting a *Great Australian Silence* through its omission of meaningful references to Aboriginal people and the history of dispossession that began in 1788 (Stanner, 1968) but it took more than a decade for these criticisms to begin to impact on the curriculum and resources in schools.

A flawed historiography

The nature of dispossession and its impact on Aboriginal people had not always been ignored by Australian historians. Indeed, in the second half of the nineteenth century and the early years of the twentieth, several early histories had been quite sympathetic to the plight of Aboriginal people. These were written by first-hand observers of dispossession and they were often forthright in describing its devastating impact on Aboriginal people. These early histories included works on Tasmania (West, 1852; Bonwick, 1869; Calder, 1875) and on New South Wales by Barton (1889).

Bonwick described the colonial relationship between Aboriginal and non-Aboriginal people as 'a war of the races... [in which] no one could justify the many murderous acts by which it was sought to hold (the Aborigines) in check when their numbers made them formidable' (in Barton, 1889, p. 133). This forthright approach began to disappear as the colonial experience lost its immediacy for historians. This was accentuated by the segregation of Aboriginal people that accompanied the protection policies. The lack of documented Aboriginal viewpoints also hampered historians, and after World War I history was almost exclusively written from the viewpoint of the colonisers as the Great Australian Silence took effect.

A new generation of historians was more interested in the transplanted British heritage of Australia than in its displaced Aboriginal heritage. These writers were convinced that:

> British political institutions and the Protestant religion were the creators of political liberty and material progress. It was because Macaulay persuaded teachers that the seventeenth century was the decisive period in the moulding of both British political institutions and the Protestant religion that... men and women studied that era not as a discipline or diversion for the mind, but because such a study would reveal to them the secrets of political liberty and material progress.
> (Clark, 1980b, p. 3)

The effect of these Anglocentric assumptions was starkly evident in the first academic national history, W.K. Hancock's *Australia* (first published in 1930). Hancock showed similar sympathetic insight to earlier historians in entitling his first chapter *The Invasion of Australia*. In the first of only two references to Aboriginal people, he wrote critically of the brutality of colonisation and the ineffectual policies that had attempted to ameliorate this:

> In truth, a hunting and a pastoral economy cannot co-exist within the same bounds. Yet sometimes the invading British did their wreckers' work with the unnecessary brutality of stupid children. The

Illustration by George Lambert for The Child's Book of Wonder, 1920. *An example of the lies fed to students by school books of the past. Compare this with the next image.*

Engraving by Thomas Chambers from expedition artist Sydney Parkinson's drawing of resistance to Cook's first landing at Botany Bay, with the two Aboriginal men drawn as antique Greek heroes. The 'sword' held by the foreground figure is actually a woomera. Botany Council's logo for many years, until replaced in the 1990s by a stylised banksia. Courtesy Mortlock Library of South Australiana, State Library of South Australia.

aboriginal race had always possessed enthusiastic friends, but these friends have never agreed upon a consistent and practical policy for the black man's preservation. It might still be possible to save a remnant of the race upon well-policed local reserves in Central and Northern Australia. This would cost hard thought and hard cash. Australian democracy is genuinely benevolent but is preoccupied with its own affairs. From time to time it remembers the primitive people whom it dispossessed, and sheds over their predestined passing an economical tear. (Hancock, 1961 [1930], p. 21)

Hancock's acceptance of Darwinian assumptions about the inevitable extinction of Aboriginal society and the paternalistic tone he adopted were typical of the era. This was evident when he completed his consideration of cross-cultural relationships with the second of the two paragraphs he devoted to the subject. Like a battered woman drawing a discreet blind on the brutal history of a relationship, he concluded with an optimistic expression of hope that the tragedy of dispossession might bring the material benefits of civilisation:

> From the flame and ruin of dreary scrub arise fertile corn lands and a rich permanence, and the wounds which the violence of the British inflicted upon Australia are healed as impatience to possess slackens into a true partnership. (Hancock, 1961, p. 23)

Historians who followed Hancock in the post-World War II era failed to move behind the discreet curtain that had been drawn across the brutality of dispossession and the Great Australian Silence was confirmed. This reticence was evident in the work of even the most prominent of historians, Manning Clark, who only began to address this in his later work. Clark attempted to explain his profession's failure by noting the cultural blinkers that affected them all:

> On that question I began with my mind filled with the prejudices of my generation... My prejudice, shared with other members of my generation, was that there was only one culture in Australia—European culture; only one way of life—the transplanted European way of life. (Clark, 1980a, p. 47)

That Clark was not alone in overlooking Aboriginal issues is immediately obvious when thumbing through the index of almost any academic history published during the 1950s, 1960s and early 1970s:

- R.M Crawford's *Australia*, first published in 1952 and reprinted seven times up to 1963, contained only two references to Aboriginal people.
- Manning Clark's *Short History of Australia* was a slight improvement. First published in 1963 and reissued in 1969, 1980 and 1981, it ultimately contained seventeen short references.
- Humphrey McQueen's *A New Britannia*, published in 1970 with reprints in 1971, 1976 and 1978, contained only four short references.

The Expulsion. *Gouache stencil by Margaret Preston, 1952. Aboriginal people being driven out of the Garden of Eden by a white angel with a flaming sword. This represents both the exclusion of Aboriginal people from white society (and the role of churches in this) and refers to colonial times when Australia was so often labelled a 'Garden of Eden' (or 'the Promised Land'). Courtesy Art Gallery of NSW.*

Dame Mary Gilmore with Aboriginal children at her 91st birthday party at Paddington Town Hall, Sydney, 1956. Mary Gilmore grew up with Aboriginal people in the bush and fought for Aboriginal rights all her life. Her father had been run out of the Hunter Valley for refusing to be involved in 'killing times'. Old Days, Old Ways *(1934), about growing up in the bush, includes glimpses of Aboriginal life in the mid-to-late 19th century. Photo: Harry Gordon. Courtesy Fairfax Photo Library.*

- Frank Crowley's *A New History of Australia*, first published in 1974, provided a more extensive coverage, but the contributors to this collection of essays still clearly regarded other issues—wars and conscription; agriculture and pastoralism; mining and economic development; class conflict, trade unions and the Labor Party—as central to Australian history.

This approach to the writing of history was by no means unique to Australia. It was an era when it was accepted that history was written by the *winners* and inevitably represented 'the story of the survivors and victors in the human ant heap' (Clark, 1980c, p. 30). We were conditioned to view the Peloponnesian Wars through the eyes of the Greeks rather than the Persians, and the American Civil War through the eyes of the industrial North rather than the agricultural South. It was as difficult to view the colonial past through the eyes of Aboriginal people as it was to consider the possibility of Allied war crimes in Dresden and Hiroshima.

It is therefore difficult to blame teachers for their promotion of the *Three Cheers Approach* in Australian school history courses prior to 1980. They were merely echoing the silence and repeating the methodology of the academics who had taught them in universities and teacher training colleges since early in the twentieth century.

Sowing the seeds of a new historiography

Influenced by events in other parts of the world since the end of World War II, social and political change in Australia were creating fertile ground for challenges to the *settlers' histories* that had dominated Australian historiography for the previous two generations. The *winds of change* that swept through the colonial world of the old imperial powers after World War II also blew across Australia. By the 1950s and 1960s, the whole world was being influenced by the Civil Rights and Black Power movements in America and then by the liberation struggles of formerly colonised peoples in Vietnam and elsewhere. In Australia, the old policies of protection finally gave way to the new assimilation policy. Not surprisingly, the post-colonial paternalism of this policy was quickly challenged by a new generation of young Aboriginal activists, including Charles Perkins.

There was a mood for change and some cause for optimism in the result of the 1967 Referendum. Aboriginal issues had become much more prominent in the nation's political landscape and, following the 1972 election of the Whitlam Labor government, changes proceeded apace. Land rights calls began and were maintained with considerable bipartisan support, even after the Fraser Coalition government replaced that of Whitlam. The dramatic increase that had occurred in federal government spending on Aboriginal affairs was also maintained, and successive federal governments moved away from the degrading paternalism of the assimilation policy to the more empowering policies of self-determination and self-management. Even the Catholic Bishops of Australia, largely silent on Aboriginal issues since their first Archbishop, Bede Polding, had criticised aspects of dispossession, embraced the mood for a changed relationship with Aboriginal Australians. Many a Catholic must have been jolted from slumber when hearing extracts from the Bishops' statement read from the pulpit on Social Justice Sunday in 1978. This left no doubt that the current conditions of Aboriginal people were directly linked to their experience of colonisation:

> The root cause is found in the fact and methods of the European colonisation of our country. To ignore the reality, to feel no sense of shame, to deny that we still share the same underlying racism and values, would be a denial of human and Christian responsibility. (Catholic Commission for Justice and Peace, 1978, p. 6)

The Bishops even offered encouragement to those historians, beginning to challenge the Great Australian Silence on the nation's colonial past:

> It is only in recent years that attempts have been made to write a history of the Aboriginal people of Australia, and to place the history of white settlement within that framework. It is only when placed there that the nature and impact of colonial settlement can be appreciated. Regrettably little use has been made of such material in schools. (Catholic Commission for Justice and Peace, 1978, p. 6).

The slow pace of change in schools

The Bishops' regret that the new histories were still rare in schools was justified. The rapidity of social change had left schools lagging behind, and curriculum, resources and pedagogy still reflected the paternalism of the assimilation and earlier eras (Cavanagh, 2005). School history texts of the 1960s and 1970s had begun to make reference to Aboriginal people and issues. Typically, however, Aboriginal content was consigned to the first chapter, where it was often labelled 'pre-history'—a term that seemed to confirm the conventional view that *real* Australian history began with the arrival of the British at the end of the eighteenth century.

This message was often reinforced by the refusal of authors or editors to provide the respect inherent in the use of the upper case in the word *Aboriginal,* almost invariably writing the lower case *aboriginal*. Aboriginal people found this demeaning (also see Chapter 3) and the extent to which this offensive usage has continued remains surprising.

The typical texts of this time adopted a patronising and paternalistic tone towards Aboriginal people. They emphasised the exotic and esoteric aspects of traditional culture and failed to recognise the many adaptations since 1788. Their emphasis was on the esoteric reinforced stereotypes of Aboriginal people as *strange, primitive* and even *foreign*, and there was little understanding of the knowledge of Aboriginal spirituality that anthropologists and archaeologists had begun to document. Furthermore, once the opening chapter concluded, Aboriginal people, culture and issues disappeared from the remainder of the story. There was no concept of a *shared history* after 1788, but instead an almost exclusive focus on the story of White Australia. Any reference to Aboriginal individuals was normally reserved for the tragic or flawed, like Bennelong and Albert Namatjira, or those who cooperated with the invaders, like Wylie and Jacky Jacky. Mostly, however, Aboriginal people and their concerns were kept very firmly in the background—as shadowy figures that were never in focus.

Conspicuously absent was any reference to the complex and controversial issues that confronted both European and Aboriginal cultures in their *shared history* after 1788. Little mention was made of dispossession, and even less of any accompanying violence. Positive terms like 'exploration' and 'settlement' were invariably

IMPORTANT: Each year more and more aborigines are learning to live the way we do. They find it easier to live that way. They are being helped by the white people to find good jobs and live in clean homes. We should remember that these people lived in Australia long before the white men came and we should do all we can to help them.

Illustration from New Effective Social Studies Grade 3 *by J.B. Gregory and J.M.C. Wicks, Horwitz Martin, 1969. This book was still in circulation at a Sydney high school in the early 1980s. Courtesy Mitchell Library, State Library of NSW.*

used in preference to negative terms like 'invasion', 'colonisation', or 'conquest'. Blindness to white Australia's black history was encouraged also by suggestions that Aboriginal people had either died out or simply drifted away from the coastal areas and into the interior.

Even when well intentioned, these texts reflected the Great Australian Silence of the country's historians and the degrading paternalism of the government's assimilation policy. A striking example of this was in a popular text still being used by schools in the 1980s:

Community reaction to institutionalised racism

There was some cause for optimism in education when, in 1982, the New South Wales Department of Education introduced the first Aboriginal Education Policy (AEP). This policy precedent was soon followed by South Australia and other states, and later by various Catholic Education Offices. A common feature of these AEPs was curriculum change through the introduction of Aboriginal Studies programs and Aboriginal Studies Perspectives in other Key Learning Areas, particularly History. However, progress was slow. For some time, many principals and schools did not see the relevance of AEPs, and even senior officers in the Department had difficulty in adjusting to the more inclusive view of the past that the AEP required. Resources prepared by the Department's Aboriginal Education Unit were carefully scrutinised to ensure that they did not depart from the conventional interpretations of Australian history. On at least one occasion, a document was recalled, pulped and rewritten before distribution. Furthermore, the acclaimed documentary *Lousy Little Sixpence* was initially rejected by the Department after advice from senior officers that it was inaccurate.

Not surprisingly, Aboriginal parents and community members began losing patience. The slow pace of change did not meet the expectations that had been raised by the social and political changes of the previous decade or the promise of the AEPs and they were angered by the continuation of outmoded curriculum and resources. Articulate Aboriginal spokespeople began voicing concern at the institutionalised racism they had experienced, particularly in their school history classes, and the continued manifestation of this in outmoded curriculum and resources.

Linda Burney, who was then Secretary of the New South Wales Aboriginal Education Consultative Group (AECG) but would later become both the first Aboriginal Member of the New South Wales Parliament and its first Aboriginal minister, criticised the Department of Education's AEP as being little more than words on paper. She often recalled her feelings of humiliation as a young school student when taught that Aboriginal people were one of the *pests* that squatters had to contend with. Similar memories of the experience of Australian history at school were recounted in the autobiography of the popular tennis player, Evonne Goolagong-Cawley (Cawley and Jarrett, 1993). Lynette Riley, a prominent Indigenous educator, often expressed her dismay at being taught that Captain Cook had discovered Australia, a concept that curtailed the affirmation of Aboriginal achievements in Indigenous peoples' long occupation of Australia prior to European settlement. These successful Aboriginal women had all managed to rise above the humiliations of their schooling. However, all realised that their success was atypical and their complaints reflected community frustration that schools still failed to teach what Burney called 'real Australian history'. They also realised that the institutionalised racism they had experienced was still present in schools. Their concern was that many Aboriginal students were still being denied positive reinforcement of their own culture, history and identity and learning nothing that could make them proud of being Aboriginal Australians.

That some members of the community were even more frustrated and desperate in their demands for curriculum and pedagogical change was dramatically demonstrated in 1983 when a group of parents, including Jenny Munro and Kaye Bellear, objected to the way their children were being taught history. They formed a committee to lobby for change but, frustrated by a lack of response from the school, eventually took the matter into their own hands and forcibly removed some outmoded texts from the school's book-room. Confronting the school's principal, one of the parents demanded: 'Are you going to burn these bastards, or am I?' When the principal then threatened to call the police she responded: 'Go ahead! I would love to go to Redfern court and be charged with stealing racist books!'

The matter was not taken any further, but fortunately changes in historiography that were already brewing in universities soon began to percolate through the curriculum and resources of Australian schools.

New approaches in historiography

In academic circles, the seminal work in the new historiography was Charles Rowley's (1972) *The Destruction of Aboriginal Society*. This was followed nine years later by Henry Reynolds' (1981) more popular *The Other Side of the Frontier*; coincidentally, this was the same year that the first AEP was launched in New South Wales. Reynolds was a prolific writer, and this first book was followed by many others. Though populist in some ways, he established a framework for writing the history of cross-cultural contact in Australia through Aboriginal eyes.

Other very important works to emerge from the academic world at this time were those of Diane Barwick on Victoria (1972), Peter Biskup on Western Australia (1973), Lyndall Ryan on Tasmania (1981), Peter Read on New South Wales (1982), Noel Loos on Queensland (1982) and another national history by Richard Broome (1982). Also important in this new history was the art historian Bernard Smith, whose *European Vision and the South Pacific* (1960) was reissued in 1985. Alan Moorehead's (1966) *The Fatal Impact* and Keith Willey's (1979) *When the Sky Fell Down*, though less academic in their approach, also had some impact in changing attitudes at the time, particularly among teachers. So did Geoffrey Blainey's (1976) *The Triumph of the Nomads*, which—even though Blainey himself would come to be regarded as a vocal opponent of the new historiography—was important at the time in changing some stereotyped views of Aboriginal culture. Less influential, but equally important to note, was Hanna Middleton's (1977) Marxist analysis of contact history that attempted to define the Aboriginal struggle as 'a manifestation in Australia of the world-wide national liberation movement' (1977, pp. 175–6).

Initially, Aboriginal voices in the *new history* remained rare. There was naturally some suspicion of any *white* versions of Australian history which Aboriginal academic activists like Wayne Atkinson, Marcia Langton and others dismissed as *colonialist propaganda*. They suggested that Aboriginal people should be the 'guardians and custodians of [their] history and culture' because of their mistrust of the cultural theft of white historians and others (Atkinson et al., 1983). However, Aboriginal interpretations of history soon began appearing in other media, particularly in the visual and performing arts and in film through documentaries like *Lousy Little Sixpence* (Morgan, 1982) and the award-winning doco-drama series *Women of the Sun*. In addition, numerous autobiographical and family histories were soon being published, though some of these had only limited appeal to wider audiences. James Miller's (1985) history, *Koori: A Will to Win: The Heroic Resistance, Survival and Triumph of Black Australia*, probably appealed most widely because of its contextualisation of family history within state and national developments.

Suddenly, it seemed, the Great Australian Silence had broken and been replaced by a clamouring of many voices demanding more inclusive perspectives in the story of Australia's past. The

Aboriginal women at Cummeragunja (southwest NSW) knitting woollens for the troops in World War II. Like Aboriginal war service, contributions by Aboriginal people on the home front tended to be ignored, or were simply not known about. Photo: Merle Jackomos. Courtesy Alick Jackomos Collection, AIATSIS.

demand for such perspectives was stoked by the AEP strategy of encouraging both discrete Aboriginal Studies programs and Aboriginal perspectives in all curriculum areas. Demand for resources providing Aboriginal perspectives received a further boost in 1983 when the New South Wales Board of Secondary School Studies introduced its HSC Option D Australian History course in which up to 33 per cent of the content could be devoted to Aboriginal history. Another significant development took place in 1986 when the then Minister for Education in New South Wales, Rodney Cavalier, approved a submission from the AECG and authorized the development of a Two-Unit Higher School Certificate (HSC) course in Aboriginal Studies. It seemed that the new history had triumphed and that the dominance of settlers' history and the white triumphalism of the Three Cheers Approach were doomed to extinction.

The reaction: Criticisms of *black armband* history

Indications that this was not the case, and that there would be a significant reaction to the new history, came in the lead-up to the 1988 Bicentennial celebrations. From the mid-1980s, the conservative historian Geoffrey Blainey had begun vocal opposition to the *new histories*, claiming that the pendulum had swung too far away from the celebration of national achievement. In 1985 he claimed that a richly subsidised multicultural lobby had little respect for the history of Australia and that schools and universities were promoting a view of Australian history as 'violent exploitation, repression, racism, sexism, capitalism, colonialism and a few other isms' (Blainey, 1991, pp. 45–51; McKenna, 1997). By 1987, such views were part of the context of the preparations for the 1988 Bicentennial celebrations, which to many appeared to be in danger of becoming a whites-only party—an orgy of self-congratulation that would return to the triumphalism of settlers' history.

Sensing a retreat from the new history, the National Aboriginal and Islanders Day Observance Committee (NAIDOC) adopted the slogan 'White Australia has a Black History' as the theme for the NAIDOC Week celebrations of 1987. The dramatic slogan was emblazoned across a poster publicising that year's NAIDOC celebrations—a seemingly blunt affirmation of the reality of the many metaphorically black pages of Australia's past that the writers of the new history were only just beginning to recover and document.

Essentially, the poster was only a gentle reminder to non-Aboriginal Australians of both the long history of Aboriginal people in Australia before colonisation and their contributions to the social, cultural, and economic development of the country since 1788. Underneath the bold statement, embedded in illustrations of traditional culture, were illustrations representing Aboriginal involvement in the development of the pastoral industry and their participation in

White Australia Has a Black History. *Poster by Queensland Aboriginal artist Laurie Nilsen for NAIDOC Week 1987. A positive view of history and Aboriginal contributions: war service, stock work, cane cutting and sporting success. The central images are of Evonne Goolagong, twice Wimbledon champion and 1971 Australian of the Year, and Mark Ella, captain of the Wallabies and Young Australian of the Year 1982. Courtesy Laurie Nilsen.*

the army during the two World Wars. The poster also highlighted Aboriginal contributions to Australian sporting culture, with representations of the Rugby Union player Mark Ella and the Wimbledon tennis champion Evonne Goolagong.

Tensions over the nature of Australian history continued in the lead-up to the Bicentenary and culminated in the huge protests of 26 January 1988. Five days earlier, Aboriginal protesters demonstrated their specific rejection of any return to white triumphalism in Australian history when they hurled a copy of Professor John Molony's (1988) *Bicentennial History of Australia* into the waters of Sydney Harbour because of its inadequacies in addressing Aboriginal issues (McKenna, 1997–98).

The tensions continued throughout 1988, when they became part of political debate. In his *Future Directions* statement, John Howard—then leader of the Liberal Party in Opposition for the first time—expressed his dismay that 'people's confidence in the past had come under attack by professional purveyors of guilt'. He criticised a 'guilt industry' that he claimed was teaching Australians 'to be ashamed of their past' (Howard, 1988). Howard was supported by conservative historian John Hirst (1989, 1993), who was highly critical of a 'black school of history'. Prominent mining industry spokesperson and Liberal Party official Hugh Morgan also criticised the development of a 'guilt industry' in Australian universities and worried about the influence of this on mining development.

Initial consolidation: The Redfern Park Speech

Howard only survived as opposition leader until May 1989, when he was deposed by Andrew Peacock. Benefiting from Liberal Party disunity, the Hawke–Keating governments easily rode out any controversy and continued to promote more inclusive policies in Aboriginal affairs, including education. After the interruption of the Bicentennial there was once again optimism that the shutters which had been almost completely drawn on much of Australia's history would finally be thrown open to the light. It was during the Hawke–Keating era that inquiries were launched into Aboriginal Deaths in Custody and into the past removal of Aboriginal children from their families. In September 1991, a new policy of reconciliation was adopted with bipartisan support when the Council for Aboriginal Reconciliation was established with the unanimous approval of both Houses of Parliament. The eventual reports from the two inquiries and the Reconciliation Council advocated the education of all Australians about Aboriginal history as a strategy for improving relations between Aboriginal and non-Aboriginal Australians.

A high-water mark for optimism that a more inclusive Australian history would be accepted was the Redfern Park Speech given by the Prime Minister, Paul Keating, on 10 December 1992. In this remarkable speech, Keating acknowledged the violence and pain that Europeans had used to dispossess Aboriginal people:

> it was we who did the dispossessing. We took the traditional lands and smashed the traditional way of life. We brought the diseases. The alcohol. We committed the murders. We took the children from their mothers. We practised discrimination and exclusion. (Keating, 1993)

The speech marked the opening of the United Nations' International Year of the World's Indigenous Peoples in 1993. However, it must also be seen in the context of the High Court's decision in the *Mabo case* only six months earlier, in June 1992. After 204 years of British settlement, this legal ruling overturned the notion of *terra nullius* on which land title was based and recognised the existence of *native title* throughout Australia at the time of colonisation. The High Court's *Mabo* decision had made use of the new interpretations of Australia history (McKenna, 1997–98, p. 3), particularly the work of Reynolds, and Keating's speech was a further endorsement of the new historiography. During the speech, he noted that an 'isolated outbreak of hysteria and hostility' had accompanied the court's overturning of what he called the 'bizarre conceit' of *terra nullius*. He could not then have anticipated how these 'isolated outbreaks' would escalate into a full-blown cultural war that would rage for more than a decade.

The initial reaction: The storm over native title

Somewhat surprisingly, Keating won the federal election held in March 1993. This was the unwinnable election that Keating would also describe as the 'sweetest victory of all' for his 'true believers'. It was an election dominated by dry economic issues, and the development of a new Australian identity and a new historiography were not prominent in the campaign. However, the fierce reaction against the new historiography and its impact on the Australian identity soon re-emerged. This was initially led by conservative politicians who saw threats to their constituencies in the *Mabo* decision and the development of native title legislation that was part of the new Keating government's agenda. Soon after the election, opposition politicians began making quite irresponsible comments on Aboriginal culture and launching bitter attacks on the new history.

Ray Groom, Liberal Premier of Tasmania, accused Keating of being *hell-bent* on using the *Mabo* decision to rewrite Australia's history, and denied that there was ever any genocide in Tasmania. His party colleague Marshal Perron, the Country–Liberal Party Chief Minister of the Northern Territory, was even more derogatory, arguing that Aborigines were centuries behind other Australians in their cultural attitudes and aspirations and had 'appalling hygiene'. This irresponsible hysteria was not confined to provincial party hacks but also spewed out of the mouths of federal political leaders. For example, Tim Fischer, the federal leader of the National Party, claimed that Aboriginal dispossession had been *inevitable*, and was not something of which white Australians should be ashamed. Their culture had been *relatively stationary* and they had not even developed a wheeled cart. Moreover, they had no more affinity to the land than did farmers, and the *Mabo* debate had been hijacked by 'politically correct agenda setters'. John Hewson, then leader of the federal parliamentary Liberal Party and alternative prime minister, wrung his hands and issued cautionary statements about 'a guilt industry falsifying the past' and causing the teaching of Australian history to be divisive. The politicians were supported by their officials and leading business supporters. Hugh Morgan—long a prominent figure in the Liberal Party, Australian business and mining—complained on several occasions of a 'guilt industry' and dismissed claims of massacres as a 'nonsense'.

Historians also joined in the debate, with some challenging the methods and emotionalism of the writers of the new histories. Geoffrey Blainey warned of the dangers of creating two Australias, and accused the High Court judges of being *noteworthy in their ignorance* of Australian history (Blainey, 1993a, 1993b). John Hirst (1993) of Melbourne University warned of the dangers of presenting a 'rose-coloured view

Too Dark for the Light Horse, poster for Aboriginal war service exhibition at the Australian War Memorial, 1993. The title comes from a 1916 cartoon by B.E. Minns (who also painted Aboriginal portraits). A squatter asks Jacky why he is not fighting for his country. The answer: 'Plurry recruiting sergeant, him say me too dark for the Light Horse!' Heather Goodall (*Invasion to Embassy*) was told of a story that went round the reserves in World War II: the squatter asking why Jacky is not fighting for his country and Jacky saying, 'All right then. Come down on the flat and we'll have it out now!' The 'Jacky Jacky' stories are well-known bush yarns and feature an Aboriginal character known for his cheekiness. Courtesy Australian War Memorial.

of Aboriginal society' and of 'a reluctance to offend contemporary sensibilities'. He warned of a *sanitising* process in the new versions of Australian history and of a resurrection of the noble savage concept. Henry Reynolds responded that whatever the distortions found in the newer histories, they generally presented 'a much truer story than in the past' (Reynolds, 1994). For the next three years, debate over historiography and national identity simmered in the background while the High Court considered the *Wik case* to determine whether native title was extinguished by pastoral leases or could coexist with them.

The major reaction: The conservative reclaiming of history in the Howard years

The resurrection of John Howard as leader of the Liberal Party in December 1995 saw the debate re-ignited. Almost immediately, he began promoting the same views on Australian history and identity he had first aired in 1988—an indication that the views were deeply held. But Howard was also an astute politician. His active and immediate re-engagement in the debate suggests that he detected in it the opportunity for political advantage—a strategy of wedge politics, which involved tapping into the sense of grievance felt by 'the Aussie battlers' to whom he appealed about the perceived political correctness of the Keating government. This also provided Howard with a strategy for reclaiming the support of the significant disaffected minority who began flirting with the extreme xenophobic policies of Pauline Hanson. Hanson had been disendorsed by the Liberal Party because of her racist speeches in the 1996 election but still won her seat at the election as an independent candidate. The support that flowed to the One Nation Party she subsequently established was seen as a threat to the continued success of the Liberal Party; however, Howard's very public criticisms of political correctness and 'black armband history' helped defuse this. That this strategy had political benefits was evident on the night of Howard's landslide election victory. The very first ALP seat to fall that election night was the formerly extremely safe ALP seat of Robert Tickner, Keating's fearless Minister for Aboriginal Affairs and Minister Assisting the Prime Minister on Aboriginal Reconciliation.

Soon after the election, Howard was publicly rejecting what he termed the 'black armband' approach to history. In a speech in Parliament in October, he spoke of a 'remarkably positive history' and his belief that most Australians wanted their leaders to express more pride in this past for which others had been too apologetic. In a blatant return to the Three Cheers school, he concluded that 'the Australian achievement has been a heroic one, a courageous one and a humanitarian one' (Howard, 1996a).

On other occasions, Howard criticised the teaching of Australian history in schools and universities:

> *I sympathise fundamentally with Australians who are insulted when they are told that we have a racist bigoted past... Australians are told that quite regularly... Our children are taught that... some of the school curricula go close to teaching children that we have a racist bigoted past.* (Howard, 1996b)

Here was a quite different view of the past than the one enunciated by Keating in Redfern Park just four years earlier. For some, this radical shift represented a counter-revolution against the national sensibility concerning Aboriginal dispossession that had been developing in Australia since the 1960s (Manne, 2003, p. 5). However, Howard again found academic support, with retired academic economist Keith Windschuttle replacing Blainey as the most vocal critic of black armband history.

The views of Windschuttle and Howard were widely publicised and supported by conservative commentators in the media, including Paddy McGuiness, Frank and Miranda Devine, Gerard Henderson, Piers Akerman, Michael Duffy, Christopher Pearson and Andrew Bolt. The lengthy debate that ensued in academic and political circles throughout Australia became so acrimonious that it came to be termed the *History Wars* (or *Culture Wars*). Windschuttle's thesis first went public as a lengthy three-part article in the magazine *Quadrant* in 2000 and was later developed in more detail in his book *The Fabrication of Aboriginal History,* an analysis of race relations in colonial Tasmania. His views were also widely publicised through arti-

Stolen History. *Cartoon by Bruce Petty from 2000 when the Commonwealth submission to the Senate Stolen Generations inquiry claimed there had never been a generation of Aboriginal children taken away. Then Prime Minister Howard and Aboriginal Affairs Minister Philip Ruddock rip pages out of history books saying, 'It's for your own good.' Courtesy Bruce Petty.*

cles in the media, particularly in *The Australian* and other news outlets.

Essentially, Windschuttle argued that claims of violence against Aboriginal people in colonial Australia were exaggerated, highly suspect and unsupported by the conventional primary sources, which he argued should be the basis of all historical research. He claimed that historians were *fabricating* incidents and *doctoring* evidence to suit contemporary political agendas. He was also dismissive of Aboriginal oral histories, which he suggested were 'worthless as historical evidence unless corroborated by original documents' (Windschuttle, 2003, p. 110). He was particularly critical of the work of Henry Reynolds and Lyndall Ryan, both of whom he accused of shoddy research and documentation. Two other prime targets were the former Governor-General, Sir William Deane, for his public apology to the Kija people of the Kimberleys for an alleged massacre at Mistake Creek in the 1930s, and Dawn Casey, the then Aboriginal Director of the National Museum in Canberra, for the museum's representation of Australian history. Windschuttle's ideas appeared to be endorsed by the government when he was appointed to the boards of both the National Museum and the Australian Broadcasting Corporation.

In turn, academic critics of Windschuttle attacked his revisionism for 'primarily reflecting the pre-determined national political agenda' of the government (Boyce, 2003, p. 17) and of attempting to revive the concept of *terra nullius* (Reynolds, 2003, p. 109). Other critics see his work in the context of a conservative reaction against the perceived dominance of liberal academics in universities throughout the Western world (Moses, 2003). His methods have also been criticised for being highly selective and for using incomplete and out-of-date sources (Ryan, 2003, p. 255), and for failing to appreciate the multidisciplinary approach of contemporary historiography. His highly personal and vitriolic attacks on individuals have been highly criticised. So too have his callous portrayals of Aboriginal people as a doomed, inferior race—portrayals seen as a reinvention of the theory of social evolution (Breen, 2003, p. 139). Others have suggested that he overstates the influence of Reynolds and largely ignores the more detailed earlier work of Charles Rowley and others. They also point out that, since 1981, the literature is much more diverse than Windschuttle admits and that it has long moved on from a simplistic focus on frontier violence (Attwood, 2003, p. 170).

Examples of this new literature abound. They include works like Ann McGrath's (1987) *Born in the Cattle*, which challenged the notion of frontier conflict being overwhelmingly important. Instead, McGrath highlights Aboriginal accommodation through their involvement in the pastoral industry and the role of women in cross-cultural relationships. *Contested Ground* (1995), edited by McGrath, also explores a range of influences in cross-cultural relations. More recently, Inga Clendinnen (1999, 2005) explored initial contact from the different perspectives of Governor Phillip as well as of Aboriginal people like Bennelong. The relationship of Aboriginal people to the land is another significant theme developed in historiography. Heather Goodall's *Invasion to Embassy* (Goodall, 1996) provides a detailed analysis of this relationship in New South Wales and of the struggle since 1788 to regain land. Mark McKenna's *Looking for Blackfellas' Point* (McKenna, 2002) developed this theme by exploring the longing for a sense of place of both Aboriginal and non-Aboriginal people. Bain Attwood takes a different approach to the history of cross-cultural relationships. In *The Making of the Aborigines* (Attwood, 1989), he provides an extremely detailed analysis of life on missions and reserves in Victoria and New South Wales in the late nineteenth and early twentieth centuries. In *A Life Together, a Life Apart* (Attwood, 1994), he reverses the historical camera so that this experience is viewed through the eyes of the missionaries themselves. More recently, Attwood (1999, 2003) has focused on the Aboriginal struggle for political and civil rights.

Windschuttle's dismissal of the value of oral records also ignores newly emerging work by the Aboriginal historian John Maynard, who is also exploring the Aboriginal political struggle, focusing in particular on the 1920s and 1930s when his grandfather, Fred Maynard, was an influential figure. Like James Miller 20 years earlier, Maynard has not confined his work within a local or family context. Indeed, he has broken new ground by exploring international influences through the links his grandfather and others had with an organisation called the Coloured Progressive Association, as well as with the Afro-American world boxing champion Jack Johnson, and the Afro-American activist Marcus Garvey and his Universal Negro Improvement Association (Maynard, 2004, 2007).

Windschuttle's critique has also failed to take into account the more recent general works in Australian history. Two of the most prominent contemporary historians, Alan Atkinson (1997, 2004) and Stuart McIntyre (2004), demonstrate that it is now the norm for professional historians to seamlessly incorporate Aboriginal perspectives throughout mainstream histories.

Acceptance of a shared history: Encouraging signs

By 2007, despite the confusion caused by 25 years of controversy over the nation's history, there had been some shift in community opinion and an acceptance of a more inclusive view of the past—even, it seems, from those at the centre of the fierce public debate. This became strikingly evident on 11 October 2007 when, in one of his final acts as Prime Minister before his government went into caretaker mode prior to the federal election, John Howard launched a *Guide to the Teaching of Australian History in Years 9 and 10* in Australian schools (Department of Education, Science and Training (DEST), 2007). In introducing this resource, Howard described it as the culmination of the 'root and branch renewal of the teaching of Australian History in our schools' that he had been so strongly advocating for the previous 20 years. However, the *Guide* was certainly not a whitewash of the nation's past nor a return to the triumphalist settlers' histories that many had anticipated. Indeed, it affirmed the interpretation and evaluation of diverse forms of evidence and the appreciation of conflicting accounts of the past and differences in historical interpretation as key elements of history. It also acknowledged that history was important in helping all students, including Indigenous students, develop an understanding of their identity and the contribution of their forebears to Australia's history. The application of Indigenous and other perspectives was listed as one of seven historical literacy skills to be developed (DEST, 2007, pp. 5–8).

Considering the relatively minor position of Australian history in the curriculum in states other than New South Wales, the proposed topics were also encouraging. The *Guide* was specific in stating that an 'understanding of Australia's first peoples is vital and that there must be a consideration of Indigenous responses to dispossession'. Events like the Myall Creek Massacre of 1838, the 1938 *Day of Mourning*, the 1967 Referendum, and the 1992 *Mabo* judgment were all listed as 'Milestone Events' in the narrative of Australian History (DEST, 2007, pp. 11–15). The *Guide* also noted that the 'Indigenous experience defines Australian history' prior to 1788 and that, since then, 'Aboriginal and Torres Strait Islander perspectives inform central aspects of Australian history'. This acceptance of Aboriginal perspectives is evident in the Explanatory Notes that accompany the list of Milestone Events. These encouraged teachers and students to consider such issues as 'Indigenous encounters with explorers; Indigenous responses to dispossession'; the policies of 'protection' and 'missionary activity'; changing attitudes 'towards the conditions and heritage of Indigenous Australians';

> **For me political art and education always go hand in hand**
>
> There are vital issues that must be addressed in our education systems. First, we must teach all our kids this nation's real history—that is, two-way histories of what happened in each place around the country. This must include the histories of the struggle for Indigenous rights. *Proof* will continue to be a valuable resource for this larger aspiration—the website will be maintained for this purpose. Go to <http://www.junogemes.com>.
>
> Australians being taught the real history of this country in every school—the two-way story, the tragedies and the triumphs—is the way forward to cross-cultural understanding, respect and reconciliation. Learning from our mistakes—starting with taking responsibility for them—is the great lesson in life for all of us.
>
> Looking back at 30-plus years of my working life, I have seen Indigenous and non-Indigenous kids filled with pride at the courage and resourcefulness of the many great visionary leaders in the struggle for justice and what they contributed to Indigenous rights, and Australian society.
>
> Second, we must continue to honour the great Indigenous leaders of the past 30 years. Through these portraits we can remember their great important work, their courage and sacrifice. None of us would be where we are now without their contribution to our lives and our culture. It's very important for Indigenous kids to have heroes and heroines from their own culture. In a subtle way it can inspire them towards a direction in their lives that is right for them.
>
>
>
> On *Lois at Nielsen Park*, 1979: 'Lois Cook was a dancer at the Aboriginal Islander Dance Theatre and a friend of mine when I was photographing there. She was such a beautiful woman; she wanted to try a career as a model. We talked about ways to make this happen. I borrowed some clothes and jewellery from friends of mine who were designers, Rosie Nice and Jenny Kee. Lois and I went to Nielsen Park for a photo shoot. All the shots were just stunning. Lois was only five-two but I thought her face was so beautiful we could get past that. What we hoped for was the cover of Vogue.' Christine Anu got there twenty years later. © Juno Gemes Archive.
>
> *Juno Gemes: Born in Hungary, educated in Australia where schoolmates told her, 'Because we were here first' to explain their put-downs of her, Juno Gemes is one of Australia's most celebrated contemporary photographers. In words and images she has spent 40 years documenting the changing social landscapes of Australia. In particular she has focused on lives and 'the struggle'—the political campaigns of Aboriginal people. Her lifetime exhibition* Proof: Portraits from the Movement 1978–2003 *opened at the National Portrait Gallery in 2003, then toured until 2008. Juno was one of only ten photographers invited to document the National Apology in Canberra in 2008. She is married to leading poet Robert Adamson, and they live on the Hawkesbury River north of Sydney.*

assimilation, integration and multiculturalism; and social protest movements, as well as 'Indigenous land rights and reconciliation' (DEST, 2007, pp. 10–16). This was certainly an enormous change from the history that the Prime Minister's generation had been taught when they attended school in the 1950s and 1960s. This proposed new approach, despite (or perhaps because of) the long and acrimonious debate that had preceded it, suggested that very positive changes had occurred in Australian society since the 1970s. Like Keating's Redfern Park Speech, Howard's new *Guide to the Teaching of Australian History* could have come to be seen as a second high-water mark in the search for a shared history.

On the same day that he released the *Guide,* John Howard also promised that, if re-elected, he would hold a referendum to formally recognise Indigenous Australians and incorporate a statement of reconciliation in the Australian Constitution. While still rejecting the appropriateness of an apology, he admitted that coming to terms with reconciliation had been a struggle for him personally as he felt uncomfortable with the idea of guilt and shame and 'a repudiation of the Australia I grew up in'. At the same time he also accepted the blame for the 'dwindling of relationships' between himself and Aboriginal leaders and for a failure to fulfil a 1998 election promise to achieve reconciliation by 2001 (Shanahan, 2007). These remarkable admissions and promises brought a mixed response from political and Aboriginal leaders around the country. Paul Keating said the sentiments were admirable enough but dismissed the proposal for a referendum as a form of deathbed repentance that had come eleven years too late and only because the government was facing defeat in the imminent election (Norrington, 2007). However, the leader of the opposition, Kevin Rudd, offered bipartisan support for the referendum proposal (Shanahan, 2007). The reaction of Aboriginal leaders was also mixed. Former Aboriginal and Torres Strait Islander Commission (ATSIC) Chair Lowitja O'Donoghue saw the Prime Minister's suggestions as cynical politics, dismissing his proposals as 'another bloody election promise—not before time, it's what we've fought for, but who believes him? I don't.' (quoted in Shanahan, 2007)

Other Aboriginal leaders were more supportive. The West Australian activist Dennis Eggington thought Howard's proposal would 'refocus the reconciliation process' and that 'it was a good sign in the sense that those Australians who support and follow John Howard can see the shift and shift their own thinking towards first nations peoples in this country' (quoted in Pearson, 2007). The most pertinent comment was probably that of Noel Pearson, who highlighted the link between policy developments and a genuine appreciation of the Aboriginal position in Australian history: 'The starting point for reconciliation must be a reflection on history and the present situation of Indigenous Australians.' The approach being adopted by Howard suggested that he had committed to this reflection and so represented a 'momentous symbolic moment in time' (Pearson, 2007).

Developing awareness of the benefits of *shared history*

Clearly, even before the November 2007 election, there was considerable cause for optimism that there would be an end to the worst extremes of the culture wars and an acceptance of new approaches to the relationship between Aboriginal and non-Aboriginal people in Australian history. The demands of political conservatives that all Australian children be taught the narrative of Australian history should never have been unwelcome, as there is too little Australian history taught in our schools. Unfortunately, what was not recognised in many of their demands was that good history is always inclusive and that historical evidence can be interpreted in a variety of ways and lead to different conclusions. However, the History Wars that were engendered by this social and political debate ultimately led to a greater appreciation of history as more than a simple narrative, and to the realisation that new interpretations of the past will continue to evolve. There are now fewer people who think there is a simple, standard interpretation of the past. Those who still hold this view do not understand the discipline and will continue to be unnerved as new insights into the past are produced and revised by historians. Despite arousing some controversy, the *Guide to the Teaching of Australian History* that Howard released just prior to the November election seemed to acknowledge this and, to some extent, incorporated the concept of a shared history. Though presented as a Commonwealth initiative that needed to be adopted by the states, it was in fact an endorsement of the approach of those curriculum writers in the states (particularly in New South Wales) that had long recognised the benefits of an inclusive curriculum and the teaching of shared history.

The Labor government committed itself to a national History curriculum, and it has been anticipated that this will endorse and further develop the concept of a shared history that makes the past far more interesting and intelligible. Unlike the monochrome ethnocentric paradigms of triumphalist settlers' history, shared history encourages students to develop valuable skills in research and evaluation by exploring the past from a range of different viewpoints rather than just those of settlers or governors. Shared history also allows students to develop insights into the human condition and explore the moral lessons that Manning Clark saw in history. The shared history of Australia should encourage students to investigate the capacity of all people, regardless of race, to act with good sense and moral virtue and their equal capacity for wickedness through ignorance and greed. Though complex, problematic and at times painful, shared history facilitates genuine reconciliation and understanding between Aboriginal and non-Aboriginal peoples.

Developments under 'new' Labor

Shortly after the 2007 federal election, there were positive indications that the new Labor government was prepared to meet the painful challenges of our shared history. In particular, the incorporation of an Aboriginal smoking ceremony and formal welcome into the ceremonial opening of the new Parliament, followed a day later by a dramatic formal apology to the Stolen Generations, suggested a new approach to reconciliation and, significantly, to our interpretation of the past. Unfortunately, the early promise of Labor was not fulfilled. In the time since the Apology there has been evidence of growing disillusion within the Aboriginal community regarding its policies and approaches to Aboriginal issues. Much of this unease stems from its continuation of the Northern Territory Emergency Response (the Intervention) and the suspension of the *Racial Discrimination Act*, seemingly without regard to its implications for human rights. Moreover, there are concerns that the intervention is not delivering the improvements that were promised in health, housing and infrastructure (Australian Medical Association, 2007; Australians for Native Title and Reconciliation, 2008; European Network for Indigenous Australian Rights, 2008; Toohey, 2009; Anderson, 2009).

There was also a growing realisation that Rudd as Prime Minister shared the determination of his immediate predecessor to placate any mainstream Australian unease at concessions to Aboriginal demands. Thus he immediately rejected the suggestion of the 2009 Australian of the Year, Professor Mick Dodson, that consideration be given to the celebration of Australia Day on a more inclusive date than 26 January:

> Mr Rudd stared down Prof. Dodson, who was sitting just metres away from the lectern, and said 'No. To our indigenous leaders, and those who call for a change to our national day, let me say a simple, respectful but straightforward no'. (Peating, 2009)

Prime Minister Rudd also quickly intervened to reject a proposal that recommended banning the climbing of Uluru by tourists out of respect for the beliefs of the local Aboriginal people. When the proposal, part of a ten-year draft plan for the Uluru–Kata Tjuta National Park, was released early in July 2009, the Prime Minister's response was once again an immediate and unequivocal 'No!'

Mr Rudd told Fairfax Radio that, while it is important the landscape is properly protected, this does not mean keeping people out.

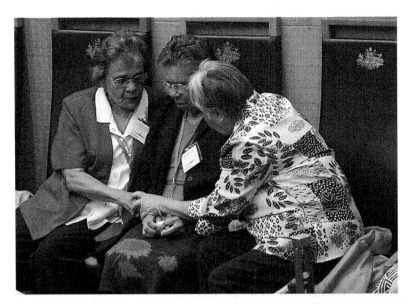

At the National Apology in Parliament House Canberra, February 2008. Aboriginal women comfort each other. © Juno Gemes Archive.

As a matter of general principle my view has always been that people should be able to have appropriate access to Uluru. It's a bit like managing the Great Barrier Reef. I think it would be very sad if we got to the stage where Australians, and, frankly, our guests from abroad weren't able to enjoy that experience.

Asked specifically whether he meant climbing Uluru, Mr Rudd responded: 'Yeah, to climb it.' (ABC Radio News, 2009)

Hopes that the historic Apology would mark an end to the tensions between Aboriginal and non-Aboriginal Australians were perhaps always unrealistic, as those tensions are very deep seated and ultimately rooted in our colonial past rather than in the misguided protection and welfare policies of the first half of the twentieth century. Tensions will remain until the vast majority of the Australian population, both Indigenous and non-Indigenous, understand and are capable of addressing the history of colonisation and the nature of dispossession.

Recent curriculum developments

The development of this understanding will be a long-term process, in which the development of a national History curriculum plays a crucial part. The development of this national curriculum has been restarted by the new government, and a National History Curriculum Advisory Group chaired by Professor Stuart Macintyre released a draft document in October 2008 (National Curriculum Board, 2008). This draft, the *National History Curriculum Framing Paper*, notes the usefulness of the *Guide to the Teaching of Australian History in Years 9 and 10* previously developed by the Australian History Reference Group and released by Prime Minister Howard at the end of 2007. Surprisingly, however, it appears to contain less detail on Aboriginal history and the history of contact than did the earlier document. Hopes that this shortcoming will be addressed in the final document might be fragile in view of the remarkably conservative response of the influential History Teachers Association of New South Wales. They expressed not only alarm that the development of a national curriculum and the expansion of history courses would 'mean that more history will be taught, in many cases by teachers with no history background', but also that the new curriculum might be overstating the importance of Australian history.

On 1 March 2010 the then Commonwealth Minister for Education, Julia Gillard, released a draft national curriculum in History and announced that, following a consultation period up to 23 May 2010, a new syllabus would be released for implementation in all Australian schools.

Despite the fears of some conservatives that the new syllabus would represent a return to some form of *political correctness* in teaching the nation's history in Australian schools, the proposed new History syllabus suggested that the Rudd Government was as adventurous as its predecessor in its determination to *return to the basics* in Australian education. The history of the relationship between Aboriginal and non-Aboriginal people in Australian history is largely glossed over. Indeed, the proposed new syllabus is so cautious about teaching Indigenous history that conservatives should welcome it with open arms.

The proposed new syllabus completely fails to integrate the history of Aboriginal and Torres Strait Islander people into the national story. Instead, it allocates a few discrete topics to the Indigenous story, but the syllabus is so content-heavy that these will be swamped and overlooked by teachers whose pre-service training still leaves most unprepared to teach this particular aspect of Australia's story.

The draft document pays lip service to this key component of our history with its uncontroversial, indeed irrefutable, assertion that history is *interpretive by nature*, *promotes debates and encourages thinking about human values* and *contributes to an understanding of Aboriginal and Torres Strait Islander cultures* and the ongoing role of Indigenous people in Australian life. The draft also highlights the cross-cultural dimensions of history and suggests that it is appropriate to include Indigenous perspectives in the teaching of history in Australian schools.

Unfortunately however, the little progress in curriculum development in this area will be set back at least 30 years by this new syllabus which is far less explicit and specific in addressing contact history than are the Stages 1–3 Human

Society and Its Environment Syllabus or the Stages 4–5 History Syllabus that already exist in New South Wales. For example, in the primary syllabus there is an overall emphasis on developing knowledge and understanding of colonial lives, colonial development, stories of federation and nationhood and the growth of democratic government. There is also a remarkably retrospective focus on the *character of the British Empire, Australia's place in it and the significance of Australia's British heritage*, with a few concessions to our links with the Asia–Pacific region and the contributions of migrants.

If proof were needed that the government is as determined as its predecessor to return education to what it perceives as *the basics* then this sanitised version of the history of contact between Aboriginal and non-Aboriginal people is it. Schools that still have their old imperial maps with so much of the world coloured in red should dig them out of their storerooms, dust them off and prepare them for a new hanging when Ms Gillard dispatches this part of her 'education revolution' into the nation's classrooms.

The secondary curriculum is no better. The curriculum industry has come up with a syllabus that is barely different from what was offered by schools in the 1960s. For example, Year 7 begins with the nature of history, then goes on to depth studies on the ancient world focusing on Egypt or Greece or Rome. Of 23 depth studies proposed—a remarkably high number for a Year 7 course—seven offer the option of studying *the ancient world* in China, or India, or Australia. As the vast majority of teachers know so little about local history, and given that our neo-liberal world is enthralled by the boom economies of India and China, there seems little doubt as to which will prove to be the least popular of these options.

In Year 9, the main study for the year is *The Making of the Modern World and Australia*—a theme that evokes all those school history texts of the 1950s and 1960s. Three broad inquiry questions are to be pursued in Year 9:

1. What is progress?
2. How are societies influenced by global change?
3. How do societies understand their indigenous past?

The third of these questions would appear to give some hope that teachers and students might at last come to grips with the central importance of the relationship between Aboriginal and non-Aboriginal peoples in the nation's history. However, of 21 areas of study suggested only one (topic 14) actually specifies *the consequences of contact, intended and unintended, between ATSI people and Europeans in Australia*. However, this study of the impact of colonisation in Australia is a comparative study with ONE other part of the Asia-Pacific.

Of the 20 topics for Year 10, only one (topic 16) specifies Aboriginal content: study of *the civil rights struggles of ATSI people with reference to government policies (including protection, assimilation, integration, reconciliation and self-determination), the 1967 Referendum, the Mabo decision and the Apology to the Stolen Generations*.

Overall the draft syllabus is almost reactionary. It has diminished rather than increased the focus on the shared history of Aboriginal and non-Aboriginal peoples in Australia and it has swamped Aboriginal content by compressing what should be a twelve-year program into ten. For a government that came to power emphasising a dramatically different approach to Indigenous affairs from that offered by its predecessor, the proposed new National Curriculum in history looks like a depressing return to the past.

The challenges ahead

Clearly, whatever the fate of the proposed Australian curriculum, there remain many challenges ahead for those wanting to see a more inclusive approach to Australian history implemented in our schools. The first challenge for history educators is to ensure that teachers have an understanding of the necessary content for teaching a shared history. This will require a revival of Australian history at universities and in teacher training courses—a development that may be stimulated by the push for a national History curriculum.

To develop an appropriate pedagogy for a shared history may be more difficult, for academics and teachers will need to cast aside their own prejudices and honestly address some of the issues that have been raised by critics like Howard and Windschuttle in the course of the History Wars. In the first place, teaching that fosters guilt must be avoided. No one appreciates having their own culture and identity denigrated, even if the intention is to develop a better appreciation of the culture and identity of another. Even Keating agreed with Howard on this when, in his Redfern Park speech, he clearly rejected guilt as unproductive: 'Down the years, there has been no shortage of guilt, but it has not produced the responses we need. Guilt is not a very constructive emotion.' (Keating, 1993)

The teaching of a genuine shared history must also embrace the diversity of the Aboriginal experience, and this must not be obscured by the push for a national curriculum. For instance, the experience of contact around Sydney and elsewhere in southeastern Australia has been different in many significant ways from the much more recent experience of Aboriginal peoples in the northwest of the country. Since the advent of Aboriginal education policies, Aboriginal people have insisted that the diversity of these experiences be recognised. As well, teachers must be prepared to give equal emphasis to Aboriginal and non-Aboriginal perspectives. All must be recognised, for to prefer one is to make others feel marginalised, excluded or undervalued. While recognising that White Australia does indeed have a black history, we must also recognise its achievements. Similarly, a genuine shared history will also recognise that it is as unproductive to romanticise our Aboriginal heritage as it is to ignore or denigrate it.

A shared history must also develop and maintain respect for historical argument based on carefully documented evidence. Windschuttle's critique has exposed some histories that were less than rigorous in doing this. The emotional populism of John Pilger (1986) and even of some of Reynolds' work were easy targets. Significantly, Windschuttle is yet to publish his long-promised critique of the work of Rowley, whose carefully structured and meticulously documented arguments about the nature of dispossession will always defy the superficial analysis of amateur and partisan historians like Windschuttle. Even Howard's *Guide to the Teaching of Australian History* recognised that evidence can come from many sources—including the oral histories that Windschuttle and others reject far too easily. As well as oral histories, Aboriginal visual and performing arts since the eighteenth century, as well as music and song, represent alternative sources of Aboriginal views that are yet to be fully mined by historians (Cavanagh, 2002; Marett et al., 2007).

In teaching shared history, we must continue to develop our students' skills in recognising, analysing and evaluating different forms of evidence. Once students can do this, they can be taught the more advanced skills required to construct and support their own historical arguments and form their own opinions. Finally, a shared history must recognise that the best pictures of the past are those recreated from many viewpoints, not just from one. In a genuinely shared history, the defensive insularity advocated by some academics—Aboriginal and non-Aboriginal (Atkinson et al. 1983)—is unhelpful, merely replacing one form of narrow ethnocentric history with another.

To understand the evolution of contemporary Australia, we need to look at the events surrounding the establishment of European Australia since the eighteenth century not just through the apprehensive eyes of those on the boats looking in but also through the equally apprehensive eyes of those on the shore looking out. Similarly, to understand the failings of the missions and the protection and assimilation policies that created the Stolen Generations, we must evaluate them through at least two sets of eyes: the white, often idealistic, eyes of those who established and implemented these policies, and the black eyes of those who suffered under them. Additionally, we must be able to view such events through a diversity of Aboriginal eyes. From the time of the first settlement, for instance, there were Aboriginal people—like Bennelong—who collaborated as well as those—like Pemulwuy—who resisted and those who made do as best they could, like Colbee. Such diversity is the essence of humanity. To pretend that there was a single, united or heroic response to contact, or that all Aboriginal people were the unwitting victims of the events happening around them, is to deny them their humanity. If history is approached in this way, then a genuine shared history is possible. This is the real history of Australia that people like Linda Burney have longed for—a history that does not belong on one side of the racial divide or the other, but is shared between us. It is a history, in other words, that can promote genuine reconciliation while giving us all a fuller understanding of our national identity.

The longer timelines of history

More than half a century of wandering the world has shaped my view of the human story and deepened my appreciation of the oldest continuous culture.

The Children of the Sunrise have much to teach us about the true timelines of history. I am not romanticising the past; however, to understand what it is to be Australian, we need to know the longer timelines.

In my family we make a constant effort to educate our boy and girl in what we call Indigenous Studies and the earth sciences.

You see, Indigenous people and earth scientists have taught me to look at our world and history with a fresh sense of wonder, with insights that bring an appreciation of what is happening around us. Awaken this sense of discovery in students and their curiosity will ensure that they find out more. They will embrace that lifelong love of learning.

Every good storyteller understands, of course, that how you start is critical. So share with young children the way the human story really begins.

The truth is, long before human wandering, our great southern continent was on a journey every bit as fascinating as our own. When I was camped in Antarctica and contemplating the super-continents of the past, our land joined to others, so much of what followed began to make far more sense. Fossil evidence along the 'dinosaur coast' of Victoria, a platypus find in what is now South America and Aboriginal rock paintings of large diprododons fill in important parts of the story.

If children understand that this world existed before humans, that many other species—including some with us today—were here long ago, they develop very early a profound respect for the beauty of life itself. If you think about it, this is an Aboriginal way of seeing the world. The animist and earth scientist have much in common, as the best minds discover.

In this way, Indigenous studies taught with imagination can enrich education from the youngest age. We gain a deep respect for Aboriginal wandering, the coming and the going, the adaptability to climate change, an Ice Age, species extinction and massive changes to the forests and animals. So many crucial aspects of contemporary life, including our water shortages, soil erosion, global warming and over-population, are better understood once the longer timelines of history are there as a holistic framework.

In *My Land, My Tracks*, Ernie Grant, a distinguished Aboriginal educator, introduces teachers to this perspective. Land, language, culture, time, place and relationships form a teaching framework. Together, Ernie Grant and I walked through his Jirrball country, the rainforest and canefields near Tully in far north Queensland. As this gifted man described the changes to the natural world over almost eight decades of his lifetime, he gave me a most valuable lesson that became part of a DVD teaching tool for Indigenous Studies. By mapping the past carefully in an Indigenous sense, any student—black or white—is better prepared for the journey through contemporary history. By overlaying these different maps of present and past we can see what is changing. Teachers who understand the transitions experienced by Indigenous students find themselves on the same wavelength, learning together.

We need to appreciate a multiplicity of Indigenous perspectives on vital parts of our shared history. We must explore the truth and grasp why it is important.

'So many of our problems,' Ernie Grant told me, 'come down to these few words. *It didn't happen.*'

Aboriginal historians, including Dr Gary Foley and Dr John Maynard, have pointed out that most Australian students are missing out on large swathes of important history. The so-called Culture Wars have inhibited, or at least distracted, high school teachers and students from examining a bolder and more informative narrative. We should not be trapped by a syllabus but challenged by it. Draw on contemporary events like the Apology over the Stolen Generations to investigate how the removal of Aboriginal children and Aboriginal displacement from country are deep-set historical patterns shaping attitudes and events today.

While most students discuss the original dispossession of Aboriginal people, few learn that there was a second dispossession after World War I when land being farmed by Aboriginal people was taken to distribute to soldier settlers. Students need to understand the common experience of Aboriginal soldiers who came home decorated with medals for helping defend the country but then got so little, with too many ending up broke or abandoned in asylums.

Injustice glares at us throughout this story. Students of this history begin to understand the alienation, dysfunction and despair. They walk in the other person's shoes, realising why some Australians, black and white, stood together to strike at the heart of this country's most dangerous big lie: *It didn't happen.*

So many of the important figures of Aboriginal history—Fred Maynard, William Ferguson, Jack Patton, Vincent Lingiari and Eddie Mabo—died before the seeds that they planted flowered into the freedom and equality that they ached to see. It is the responsibility of history, of thoughtful teaching, to honour their memory and their extraordinary contribution to Australia.

Indigenous studies should also embrace the hope created by the wonderful accomplishments of gifted Indigenous people. David Unaipon is on a bank note but how many students know his story? Will we explain the contribution of Sally Goold, the first Aboriginal nurse, or Dr Kelvin Kong, the first Aboriginal surgeon? If we mention Boyd or Nolan in art classes, will we know enough about Rover Thomas or Emily Kame Kngwarreye? Have we read the plays of Richard Frankland or seen Tom Lewis perform in *Othello*? Is the poetry of Odgeroo Noonuccal on our bookshelves along with Shakespeare?

There is a moral imperative also to see that Indigenous Studies becomes one of the foundation stones of Australian learning. Surely our greatest civil rights challenge today is closing the gap in Indigenous education, as this is one of the most important steps to close the gap in life expectancy. To create equality in education and health, all Australian children need to understand the paths that brought them together. We must close this space between our children.

By educating our own boy and girl about the strength, beauty and resilience of Indigenous culture, we have seen them develop very naturally a sense of time that makes each day a precious opportunity to learn more.

Dr Jeff McMullen AM is a journalist, film-maker and author. He contributes to Indigenous education as CEO (gratis) of Ian Thorpe's Fountain for Youth, Trustee of the Jimmy Little Foundation and as a Director of the Australian Indigenous Mentoring Experience (AIME). He is pictured here with Dr Ernie Grant of Echo Creek community, Tully, Queensland.

A history of Aboriginal education

Nigel Parbury

The Teachers

(For mother, who was never taught to read and write)
Holy men, you came to preach:
Poor black heathen, we will teach
Sense of sin and fear of hell
Fear of God and boss as well;
We will teach you work for pay,
We will teach you to obey
Laws of God and laws of mammon...
And we answer, 'No more gammon,
If you have to teach the light
Teach us first to read and write.'
—Oodgeroo Noonuccal (2008, p. 23)

Introduction

The history of Aboriginal education cannot be separated from prevailing attitudes of the Australian community since the invasion. It is easy to be outraged, and to blame Education Departments, Protection Boards or governments. It is just as easy to forget that none of this could have happened without the consent or connivance—tacit or open—of the community in general. As one New South Wales school principal wrote in 1902 to justify his exclusion of Aboriginal children: 'It is the will of the people with the Minister's sanction.'

Aboriginal boys with their teacher/manager, Carowra Tank Aboriginal School, NSW, Christmas 1929. By permission of Aboriginal Affairs NSW. Courtesy Archives NSW.

Everyone knows education affects life chances. Over 20 years ago, the Royal Commission into Aboriginal Deaths in Custody provided shocking proof. Of the 99 Aboriginal lives investigated:

- 40 people had not got past primary school;
- 20 had not finished primary school;
- eight had no primary schooling at all;
- only two had finished secondary school;
- only three had gone to TAFE, and only one of them had completed a course; and
- not one had attended university.

Missionary endeavours

In 1814, Governor Macquarie set up the Native Institution, a dormitory (lock-in) school at Parramatta. In 1819, Maria Lock, an Aboriginal girl from this school, topped the colony in the Anniversary Schools Examination—clear proof that Aboriginal students could perform academically, but soon forgotten. The school was moved to Blacktown in 1821 and closed by 1830. The Native Institution was the first in a long line of Christian missions with government support that targeted children. Adelaide's Protector of Aborigines wrote in 1840: 'Our chief hope now is decidedly in the children; and the complete success as far as regards their education and civilisation would be before us if it were possible to remove them from the influence of their parents.' (quoted in Rowley, 1972, p. 103) One suggestion was that all Aboriginal children from the earliest possible age be removed to some remote part of the colony to prevent any contact.

These attitudes survived. In the late 1940s, the New South Wales Aborigines Welfare Board planned Aboriginal hostels in Sydney—to remove the children from the environment of the station or reserve, which was 'not conducive to ambition or enterprise on the part of the children to raise themselves beyond the standards of their parents'. (quoted in Fletcher, 1989b, p. 241)

Missions were based on the unassailable conviction that Christianity was the one true civilised religion. The 1837 House of Commons Select Committee inquiry into the treatment of Indigenous peoples in the Empire was told that the best possible restitution would be the gift of Christianity. There was always a strong protective element in missionary education. Governor Gipps wrote in 1841: 'Missionary and other establishments for the Education of the Aborigines should be placed as far as possible from the resort of ordinary settlers.' (quoted in McGrath, 1995, p. 135)

In 1848, the Board of National Education in New South Wales decided it was 'impracticable to provide any form of educational facilities for the children of the Blacks'. A Legislative Council Select Committee noted the total failure of reformist plans which had cost £61 000 over thirteen years. Far more real good, it said, would be done by promoting the religious and educational interests of the white settlers in the interior—this would 'doubtless tend to the benefit of the Aborigine'.

The failure of missions was said to be because children had remained under the influence of their tribes. Rejection of Christianity was 'proof' of Aboriginal degradation. All missions in southeast Australia were closed by 1850. The 1856 New South Wales Select Committee on the (Queensland) Native Police concluded that there was 'very little hope of ever civilising the Aborigine'.

In the second half of the nineteenth century, there was another wave of missions. As before, the agenda was to replace Aboriginal culture with an Anglo-European work and faith ethic.

Boys at physical training, Finniss Springs Mission, South Australia, 1945. Photo: Robert Pearce. Courtesy AIATSIS Pictorial Archive.

> The first step was to have them all well washed with warm soap and water, have their hair cut and put on clean clothes. Their parents were very averse to the hair-cutting process for the bigger boys. It is the custom of the natives to let a youth's hair grow from the time he is ten years old until he is sixteen or seventeen—that is until he is made a young man, or *narumbe*... But I insisted that my pupils must have their hair cut, and after some scolding from their mothers I carried the point...
>
> The schoolboys are glorying in the fact that they have done several things in defiance of native customs, and have received no harm. They have eaten wallaby, and yet have not turned grey. They have eaten *tyere* (fish), and have no sore legs. They have cooked *ngaikunde* (fish) with *palye*, and yet there are plenty more.
>
> —Rev. George Taplin in Mattingley and Hampton (1988, p. 101)

Denigration of black people was constant. 'Maydinna', the second story of the 1982 TV series *Women of the Sun*, features a missionary showing Aboriginal children pictures of white angels and black devils. Well within living memory, Aboriginal girls from mission homes would cross the street to avoid Aboriginal men because they had been trained to believe they were bad.

The dying race

Almost from the beginning, there were expectations of Aboriginal extinction, fuelled by dramatic population declines due to massacre, disease and despair. The 'Myth of the Dying Race' developed from Darwin's theories of natural selection and 'survival of the fittest'. The decline of Aboriginal populations was now ratified by science and regarded as 'inevitable'. The dying race ideology was a major rationale for the segregation of Aboriginal people on reserves ('smoothing the dying pillow'), and for establishing separate Aboriginal schools. As Rowley (1972) pointed out, well before 1900 ideas of white superiority had been reinforced by popular education. Stories and pictures of lone white men—even boys—controlling any number of coloured men (with guns) were part of every schoolboy's education.

Exclusion on demand

In New South Wales, the *Public Instruction Act* of 1880 prescribed 'free, secular and compulsory' education for all children. But in 1883 the board of management of Yass Public School threatened to withdraw all white children if fifteen Aboriginal students were not expelled—the Aboriginal children were ordered out of the school. The Minister for Education stated government policy:

> As a general rule . . . no child whatever its creed or colour or circumstances ought to be excluded from a public school. But cases may arise, especially amongst the Aboriginal tribes, where the admission of a child or children may be prejudicial to the whole school. At the same time I cannot regard with any satisfaction the excluding of children from the means of instruction because of the errors of neglect of their parents and I think some steps ought to be taken by the department to meet such a case as that of the Aboriginal children at Yass by offering facilities for the instruction of children whom it may be necessary on sanitary grounds to keep out of the ordinary schools. (George Reid, Minister for Education, 1883)

Protection Board policy was that if a sufficient number of Aboriginal children were excluded—and if funds were available—a separate school would be built. By 1900 there were thirteen 'Aboriginal' schools in New South Wales. Where there were 'Aboriginal' schools, Aboriginal children had even less chance of admission to public schools. Exclusions increased, and by the early twentieth century most Aboriginal children were in 'Aboriginal' schools.

This was paralleled in other states. In Western Australia in the first years of the twentieth century, the Minister for Education authorised the wholesale expulsion of Aboriginal children from most government schools. An Aboriginal parent, John Kickett, wrote to the minister in 1916:

> Sir, I wish you would let me Know if there would be any Objection my children attending the State School at Quairading. Some time ago there were a few of them going Native Children and Some were not Clean so the Schools Board put a stop to them . . . I was thinking to Write first to you to

Kinchela School classroom. Note the desks in rows, plenty of writing on the blackboard, a boy out front reading and being checked by the teacher—little sign of preferred Aboriginal learning styles. Courtesy AIATSIS.

see what you got to Say am living on My Block My Children wants to learn something I have been to School... this is my own handwriting... Probbley this is the first letter you ever got from an Half-Cast... I want to Bring My Children up to the Best away... Sir do what you can for me. (quoted in McGrath, 1995, p. 253)

Second-class schooling

Across Australia, reserve schools had untrained teachers and sub-standard facilities; their 'syllabus' was manual chores for boys and domestic work for girls. Many people now see these schools as a deliberate attempt to create an Aboriginal 'under-class' for the economic benefit of whites. But it can equally be argued that the lower curriculum in Aboriginal schools, and the emphasis on manual and domestic work, were just as much due to two firm convictions: first, that this was all Aboriginal children were capable of; and second, that the level of prejudice in the white community was such that it would be a waste of time to train Aboriginal students for any higher occupations. In 1901, Archibald Meston, architect of the Queensland Act, told Parliament that 'no practically useful results can possibly accrue by teaching our mainland blacks composition, fractions, decimals or any other subjects that will in any way enable them to come into competition with Europeans'. (quoted in Fesl, 1993, p. 107)

Assimilation: The 'White Australia' policy

In 1937, the first Commonwealth Native Welfare Conference resolved that 'the destiny of the natives of Aboriginal origin but not of the full blood lies in their ultimate absorption by the people of the Commonwealth, and... all efforts should be directed to that end'. Accordingly, all state authorities 'should [work] towards the education of children of mixed Aboriginal blood at white standards, and their subsequent employment under the same conditions as whites with a view to their taking their place in the white community'. Policy was to provide for physical needs, health, and, 'within the limits of their ability', education and training 'to perform some useful service'. So education authorities began to include Aboriginal children in schools.

In the 1940s, Exemption Certificates were introduced for Aboriginal people who were sufficiently 'developed' in their lifestyle to warrant being exempted from the restrictions of the Act—those who qualified were 'deemed not to be an Aborigine or person apparently having an admixture of Aboriginal blood'. South Australian certificates read 'ceases to be an Aborigine for the purposes of the Act'.

Children of 'exempted' parents were automatically admitted to public schools. But even with government support, admission for all Aboriginal children took over a generation. A 1940s Lismore RSL protest against the exclusion of Aboriginal children was really a dispute between local public schools as to which of them should be forced to admit Aboriginal children—one principal said his school should 'enjoy the same right to exclude Aboriginal children as other public schools in Lismore'.

Deficit theory

Scientists labelled Aborigines a 'child race'. In 1926, the anthropologist Sir Baldwin Spencer wrote that the structural simplicity of the Aboriginal brain meant that 'he is like an overgrown child in matters of character and emotional expression', and 'ill-suited to higher forms of education'. In 1941, the revised New South Wales Aboriginal Syllabus stated that 'full-blood' pupils would be unable to proceed beyond Grade 3, but those with 'white blood' would often be 'intelligent enough for the ordinary Public School syllabus'; Aboriginal pupils came from 'culturally restricted environments'; and schools should teach 'socially desirable personal habits and qualities'. The new Course of Studies for Primary Schools was 380 pages, but the Aboriginal syllabus was just fourteen pages, up from five. Aboriginal students were not expected to reach secondary school.

Social scientists using Western testing models 'proved' the intellectual inferiority of Aboriginal students. These results confirmed official and popular assumptions, and were used both to justify lower levels of support and excuse lower levels of achievement. In its 1961 report, the

> When you reached the age of thirteen, that was the age for people to leave school. You went as far as seventh class. I was in seventh class from the time I was about six. That was it. You just didn't advance any further. I was in seventh class for about six or seven years. The just didn't learn you any more, you couldn't go up the ladder any further. You could read and write. I could do just about anything that needed to be done in the school in those days. When kids became of age to leave school, round about thirteen, you had to work on the mission, work for rations, or you had to get off. I walked off the day I left school. The mission manager came and asked me what I wanted to do, whether I wanted to stay there and work for rations or if I didn't I'd have to get off, so I came out of school, packed my swag and walked off the place.
> —Tombo Winters, Brewarrina, in Rintoul (1993, p. 9)
>
> I never went to school. Everything I know is from when I worked for white people and lived with my old Aboriginal friends. I learnt to read and write from a white girl, when I was working for her father. I couldn't even read and write until I was about seventeen. I had about two days, I think, my record of school. I went to school two days and I seen this wild schoolteacher fella belting kids with rulers and that finished me mate. I headed for the bush and back to my old people. As long as I could work and knew what money was, that's all . . .
> —Henry 'Banjo' Clarke, Framlingham, in Rintoul (1993, pp. 230–1)
>
> We weren't allowed to go to school. Any other nationality in Colli could go to school, but not Aboriginals when I was growing up. So, I guess I got about three days' education at the Presbyterian minister's house—three half days—in my lifetime. My two older brothers used to go. I suppose if you counted up the times that they went in their lifetime it would be about six. This minister's wife was very concerned about that aspect. She really wanted to try and get support to get Aboriginal children some kind of schooling, but it wasn't until the mid-forties that Aboriginal kids were finally enrolled in some kind of school, which was segregated . . . the Education Department funded one position to teach the Aboriginal kids by themselves.
> —Isabel Flick, Collarenebri, in Rintoul (1993, p. 55)
>
> My first formal education was with correspondence schools, which I used to enjoy. Then when I was seven we moved to Brisbane, for the sake of our education, because both my mother and my father had been forced at gunpoint off our lands on to what I call concentration camps—a concentration camp called Cherbourg—where education for everyone was limited to a very low level because people were not allowed to learn above a limited vocabulary of English for males and no literacy, and a little bit of literacy—enough to understand orders—for girls. My parents were the slave labour force at that time and my mother saw education as a way of overcoming some of this, mainly because it was restricted and she saw that if they were restricting something and limiting us and allowing themselves to get more education then the way up was to get education and break through that barrier.
> —Dr Eve Fesl, Gabi Gabi, Director of Koori Research Centre, Monash University, in Rintoul (1993, p. 340)

New South Wales Aborigines Welfare Board said low retention rates of Aboriginal students were due to the fact that 'Aboriginal children, as a whole, do not possess an intelligence quotient comparable to their white counterparts' (quoted in McGrath, 1995, p. 97). This statement was then retracted and parents were blamed instead.

A case study in segregation

Housing in Gulargambone was segregated—most Aboriginal people lived across the river and whites would neither sell town lots nor rent houses to Aboriginal people. The cinema and the hospital were segregated; cafes would not serve meals to Aboriginal people; men with Exemption Certificates were refused service at the hotel. Even religion was segregated—the body of an Aboriginal person had to be moved to the reserve to wait for the clergyman to come from Gilgandra. Aboriginal men were needed for football teams, but Aboriginal supporters were not allowed to travel in the 'followers' bus. Aboriginal children from the reserve had to walk past the public school to get to their school. Even children of parents with Exemption Certificates were barred from the public school.

In 1955 the Governor General visited Gulargambone, and was clearly displeased at the obvious segregation of Aboriginal students in the line-up to welcome him to the town. In 1958, the Department of Education closed the Aboriginal school and enrolled the students in the public school. The principal Doug Swan's handling of the community reaction started his rise to the top. But even after this an invitation for learn-to-swim classes in the Bowling Club's new pool was for white students only. When the principal insisted on the school's right to decide which children should participate, a vigilante group threatened to enforce the ban with shotguns.

Source: Adapted from Fletcher (1989a, pp. 229–34).

Meanwhile in remote Australia

From early in the twentieth century, there were more missions in remote Australia. In 1950, the Commonwealth Department of Education created special Aboriginal schools in the Northern Territory. More government money was made available to missions to become government agents in education. For the same reasons, some pastoralists also established Aboriginal schools. Schooling was to be in English on the grounds that the students needed to adopt English, and that English words and concepts could not be translated into Aboriginal languages.

A 1929 report on Aboriginal affairs in the Northern Territory by the Queensland 'expert' J.W. Bleakley noted that pastoralists were absolutely dependent on Aboriginal labour. It attacked their contemptuous attitude to Aboriginal children, the idea that education would only make them cunning and 'cheeky', and the lack of facilities for training (Rowley, 1972, p. 259). The same attitudes show up in a 1948 Western Australian report:

> In regard to the pastoral districts generally, in my view, it is most undesirable to remove the native children from the stations to the towns for schooling. The influence of the towns spoils the native for future employment on the stations and they should not be encouraged to enter the towns at all if it is at all possible to educate them otherwise. The pastoral industry is an important one to the economy of the State and it is almost entirely dependent on native labour. So long as the natives receive fair treatment on the stations it is in their best interests, as well as the State's, that they be employed in the pastoral industry. (Bateman Report on Survey of Native Affairs Western Australia, 1948, quoted in Yarwood and Knowling, 1991, p. 264)

From 1965, assimilation was replaced by integration—Aboriginal people entering Australian society on their own terms, preserving as much of their culture as they chose. Integration is often regarded as equivalent to assimilation, but the critical difference is that assimilation saw Aboriginal culture as entirely worthless, to be completely discarded, whereas integration was about the blending of cultures, and seeing value in Aboriginal culture. However, ignorance of the cultural differences of Aboriginal students combined with deficit assumptions about their culture and background to poison Aboriginal education.

The station owners in that area... spoke fairly fluently the language in that area, and the white children, whenever we could get to them, they also spoke the language fluently—the Alyawarra-Anmatjira language—so we didn't have to speak English at all. I still feel that this is probably why it took me a long time to realise that Australia is a racist country, because I came from that background. When I asked one of the station owner's daughters what school was, she said, 'School is a place you go and learn'. But she told me in my own language. And then she looked at me and she said, 'But only white kids go there.'
—Rosalie Kunoth-Monks, Alice Springs, quoted in Rintoul (1993, p. 333)

Going to school was hard. We had to put up with being called 'black bastards'. There was one teacher there that I got a caning off for something I done out of school. He said I rode his son's bike. He caned me nine times. The education system here hasn't changed. We've only had one Aboriginal student pass Year 12 in a population of about 700 Aborigines. I got up to Year 10. I couldn't survive in the school, and you could get a job in the meatworks and that.
—Joe Burgoyne, Port Lincoln, South Australia, quoted in Rintoul (1993, p. 345).

I was a terrible student, always playing up, and I was always outside the headmaster's office, especially on a Friday. But come one o'clock on a Friday when the bus had to go for a sport, it always came over the loudspeaker: 'Annette Peardon, please report to the bus.' I went through the school years of being asked, 'How come you're black?' and being called 'Abo' and everything else, but because of my sporting ability I managed to cope with that. That was my kick-back, my way of getting revenge, I suppose, on white kids, bragging about the sporting ability that me and a lot of the Aboriginal children in those days had. When it came to the stage of talking about Aboriginals in school, I would try and raise my hand, but I was constantly told there weren't any Aboriginals in Tasmania. It became a search for me, of why I was different, who I was and how come I ended up where I did.
—Annette Peardon, Tasmania, quoted in Rintoul (1993, pp. 338–9)

They just put us in the corner and belted the Jesus out of us if we even looked like trouble. One teacher made us sit on the verandah before class and go through each other's hair for lice. If we found any we were sent home, so if we didn't like coming to school we would tell her we found some and when she chucked us out of the school we went off into the bush all day. Most of my time at school was digging the teacher's garden and putting rocks around it.
—Aboriginal people of Warburton, Western Australia, quoted in Greene (1983, pp. 18–19)

Across Australia, social change challenged white attitudes. Post-war immigration eroded Anglo hegemony. Media exposés, plus the Freedom Rides, made more Australians ashamed of Aboriginal living conditions, and

> **Schooling at Turtle Point**
>
> Turtle Point was an Aboriginal Reserve near Tabulam on the Far North Coast of New South Wales. Tabulam is on the Bruxner Highway between Casino and Tenterfield.
>
> Our teacher lived up near the village of Tabulam, and he used to walk to Turtle Point, a distance of about 4 miles a day, to teach us to read and to write and do arithmetic. Just the basics. This teacher did not like to teach us kids, maybe because he did not understand Kooris' ways of life. This was the mid-'40s.
>
> If us kids did not understand what he tried to teach us, he would slap us on the side of the head and that would make our ears ring. Up in Tabulam things were totally different. This was a non-Aboriginal school. This school had a white fence around it and a field for kids to play on; also a playground; whereas Turtle Point did not have a fence around the school, no playground, only a bare patch of ground where the kids played marbles. We did not wear uniforms or shoes. These things were only used by non-Aboriginal schools. We were given a handout of a shirt and trousers twice a year, one for summer and one for winter. We were given slates to write on when first we went to school, then after a couple of months we were given books and pencils to use to write with . . . We were never given a pen to write with. We would never have qualified to get to high school because our classes only went to Grade 4. Our education on the mission was certainly limited.
>
> —Uncle Charles Moran, Bundjalung Elder
>
> And then at the school we didn't know any different, but now that I look back I know that it was wrong for the manager who taught us school to teach us all about England. At that time, there were lots of older people there who could have been teaching us our culture too, our language. It's sad that it has died. I remember the old people not being allowed to speak the dialect, and over and over again I heard the old people say, 'Don't tell them any secrets, don't tell the white man our secrets.' They started keeping things to themselves. And I heard the old people say too, 'No, you've got to forget about that now, you've got to go the white man's way.' That was wrong.
>
> —June Barker, Gongolgon, in Rintoul (1993, pp. 240–1)
>
> I went on to Cherbourg when I was quite young. At school, they used to always teach us about all the wild blacks that used to slaughter all the white settlers; that was always the trend I can remember about school. That's what they taught us and we had no option but to learn things like that.
>
> I stayed at school until I was 14, on Cherbourg. I went to eighth grade, which was equivalent to about fifth grade in a non-Aboriginal school. But growing up on Cherbourg was something you had to be part of to believe, because you learned all these bad things about the blacks and never any of the bad things about what the whites used to do to our ancestors, and it saddens me now when you think about it because that would instil in any person, especially from a young age, that the blacks were no good.
>
> —Noel Blair, Aboriginal Child Care Agency, Brisbane, in Rintoul (1993, p. 348)

their limited rights. The 1967 Referendum recognised Aboriginals as citizens in their own land. Control of missions began to pass from church and welfare agencies to communities; Education Departments took over reserve schools. Rural recession and rationalisation, plus 'pepperpot' housing policies, brought more Aboriginals to the cities and major towns; high birth rates meant more Aboriginal students in schools.

International organisations like the Van Leer Foundation brought a new understanding of the educational needs of minority and Aboriginal groups. However, this was based on cultural deficit and deprivation theories—failure was due to disadvantaged or deprived homes, which lacked stimulation of learning and language; thus children were unable to benefit from schooling to the same extent as children of enriched homes. Programs aimed to supply the development experiences children missed due to 'deficient' home backgrounds.

In 1971, a second New South Wales Teachers Federation survey identified 1608 Aboriginal secondary students, compared with 514 in 1964. Over half of Aboriginal students in Year 7 were classified as 'slow learners'. Only 0.8 per cent sat for the Higher School Certificate. The survey reported that education problems could not be isolated from the social and economic backgrounds of Aboriginal students. One response said: 'The biggest single cause of retardation . . . is the negative or hostile attitude to learning in the older generation from which this group develops most of its attitudes.' (Fletcher, 1989b, pp. 288–90)

Listening to Aboriginal people: The birth of AECGs

The National Aboriginal Education Committee (NAEC) was set up in 1975 to advise the Commonwealth. It promoted Aboriginal views on education through a series of publications and launched a campaign to train 1000 Aboriginal teachers by 1990. In the same year, the Commonwealth Schools Commission set up its Aboriginal Consultative Group, which recommended Aboriginal control of Indigenous education. Funds were then offered to state Departments of Education to enable them to form their own advisory groups, which were set

The Aboriginal Education Council (NSW)

In 1963 Alan Duncan formed the Consultative Committee on Aboriginal Education. A former teacher-manager at Moonacullah and Woodenbong reserves, Alan sat on the Teachers Federation Aboriginal Education Committee, was a leading ALP branch member, and worked on the Referendum campaign. The name said what it was about: working *with* blackfellas as opposed to doing it for them. Alan worked closely with Ken Brindle and Bert Groves, pioneers of Aboriginal action.

The committee, mainly whitefellas who wanted a fair go for Aboriginal kids, became the Aboriginal Education Council (AEC). The AEC relied on fundraising, donations and volunteers. Its philosophy was positive reinforcement to build self-concept; not *what* was taught, but *how*. Patrick White was a member and willed part of his estate to the AEC; other members also left bequests. Sydney University Chancellor Sir Hermann Black was a great supporter.

The AEC ran pilot projects based on action research, to be taken up by government when their effectiveness was demonstrated. In 1966 it set up incentive secondary scholarships for Aboriginal students. It organised coaching, and set up a study centre at La Perouse, managed by the community. When the Aboriginal Children's Advancement Society opened Kirinari Hostel at Sutherland for rural Aboriginal students in 1967, the AEC provided scholarships for them to attend local high schools. In 1973 the Labor government gave scholarships to all Aboriginal secondary students, so the AEC began funding scholarships for primary students in government schools.

Common problems included: schools with large Aboriginal populations rarely having, due to poverty, the equipment that P&Cs bought for schools; many Aboriginal students being placed in 'slow learner' classes; and a general view that school was bad news, causing poor attendance. So the AEC organised special assistance to selected schools. At Weilmoringle, the wife of a station owner near the school recalled:

'Alan Duncan and Ken Brindle, Aboriginal liaison officer of the Department of Adult Education, University of Sydney, arrived one day with a station wagon packed to the gunwales with goodies, games and a TV set, much to the excitement of the children.

'The AEC support allowed for the creation of a compensatory learning environment as an incentive for the children to come to school . . . *Women's Weekly*s, comics, toys, books, hobby activities and records . . . creating an environment in which to learn.'

Actions such as this inspired the Australian Schools Commission to start the Disadvantaged Schools Program and the Country Areas Program.

In 1974 the AEC employed Aboriginal Teacher Aides (ATAs) at Weilmoringle and Walhallow, partly to support better use of the modern aids. This pilot led the Department of Education to employ Aboriginal Teacher Aides, and Alan Duncan then set up the ATA Training Course at Sydney University. The AEC also piloted Aboriginal Home School Liaison Officers, and the success of this led the Department of Education to begin employing Aboriginal people in its Home School Liaison program—another AEC first changing the system.

When Ken Brindle died soon after finishing his work of collating Aboriginal family records in State Archives, the AEC set up the Ken Brindle Awards, scholarships for university study, in his memory. In 2003, it began to again fund secondary scholarships.

Recently, the AEC has set up primary and secondary Patrick White Awards for young Indigenous writers in schools and now leads a consortium with the Department of Education and Training and the Office of the Board of Studies developing a text for HSC Aboriginal Studies—a long-felt need—to be available in 2011.

---

up in the following years. In New South Wales, there was no response until the officer in charge of Aboriginal education pointed out that this would show the department was willing to listen to Aboriginal advice, and would cost nothing. The department then invited Aboriginal people to sit on its committee. Members decided that there needed to be a community-based Aboriginal Education Consultative Group, and this grew from 1978, with a local–regional–state structure.

Figure 5.1. The deficit model, illustrating the vicious circle of attitudes and expectations, experiences and practices that have affected and still affect the education of Aboriginal students in Australian schools. (Adapted from B. Cambourne & J. Turbill 1990)

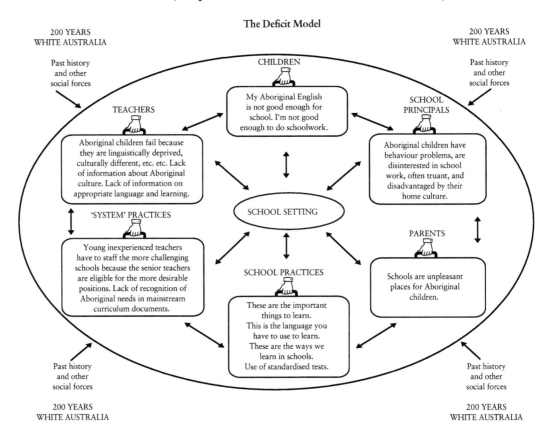

Aboriginal Studies

In February 1975, a Commonwealth press release announced compulsory lessons on race relations and Aboriginal society for all schools. No such agreement had been negotiated with the states, which controlled curriculum. Later in 1975, the Schools Commission's Aboriginal Consultative Group recommended funding for all states to develop an Aboriginal Studies curriculum. No funding was provided and again there was no action.

From 1986, New South Wales began to develop an HSC syllabus in Aboriginal Studies. This was taught in schools from 1991. A Years 7–10 Aboriginal Studies syllabus was launched in 1994, enabling New South Wales students to elect Aboriginal Studies through Years 7–12. Mandatory Aboriginal perspectives were included in the compulsory Australian content of Years 7–10 History and Geography, and into K–6 Human Society and Its Environment.

Aboriginal and Torres Strait Islander Studies and perspectives now exist in various forms in all education systems, as well as in teacher training, thanks to the Teaching the Teachers project (see Foreword). Knowledge of Aboriginal cultural heritage was included in the 1989 Common and Agreed National Goals of Schooling and in the National Statement and Profile of Studies of Society and Environment. The Royal Commission into Aboriginal Deaths in Custody and the 1994 Review of Education for Aboriginal and Torres Strait Islander Peoples called for compulsory Aboriginal Studies in all schooling (see Chapter 1).

'I believed in people, not racism'

In 1952, I started my career in Aboriginal education as Teacher-Supervisor at Moonahcullah Aboriginal Reserve. This was a one-teacher school in a very isolated community, 26 miles north west of Deniliquin. There was no electricity and no phone; water was pumped up from the river. The nearest phone was on the next property, a mile and a bit up the road, but the 'mission' was not popular with locals. In wet weather, I had to row across the river to drive the truck or have the truck driven into town when the roads were too muddy or my driver/handyman had too many and wasn't fit to drive.

I was paid my teacher salary by the Education Department. On top of that I received a full seventeen shillings and sixpence a week for being supervisor of the station, 24 hours a day, seven days a week! My wife got fifteen bob a week for teaching the girls home science and sewing (while I taught the boys woodwork skills) paid as an allowance to me.

In 1955 I was promoted to teacher-principal at Woodenbong Aboriginal School. The reserve was eight miles from Woodenbong and 90-odd miles across the border to Brisbane. Some families moved back to the mission when they heard I treated Aborigines as people, so I got a teacher to help me. I also had a handyman, paid by the Aborigines Welfare Board (AWB). Again, no electricity and no phone. Woodenbong was a very vibrant Aboriginal community who always let you know what they thought about anything. I was very pleased to be able to motivate a couple of the girls to go on with their education. My son remembers he was not allowed to go to my school, but had to travel miles on the 'horrible' bus to the 'horrible' white school in town.

Next, I was principal of Hillston Central School in the western Riverina from 1959 to 1962. This was a mainstream school with about 20 per cent Aboriginal enrolment. The community there was like the one at Moonahculla, inclined to be shy and reserved, not wanting to cause any fuss. Then in 1963 I started in the Department of Adult Education at Sydney University.

Although the Aborigines Welfare Board was supposed to be an improvement on the Aborigines Protection Board which it had replaced in 1940, and there was a new director, the change meant nothing on the ground—it was the same people top to bottom. I found the officials I had to work with were mainly nasty people who didn't like Aborigines and treated them like dirt. I never heard any of them refer to Aborigines as good; most of them were anti-Aboriginal. They were tough people, hard as nails and mean. There was also a hell of a lot of prejudice in the wider community, and among teachers. A lot of people wanted to believe that 'blacks' were inferior, intellectually and morally.

What I found hardest to take was the way Aborigines were treated. I was captivated by the Aboriginal people I met and worked with at Moonahcullah, Woodenbong and Hillston (and later all over when I worked in adult education and with the Aboriginal Education Council). I found them very decent people, salt of the earth. I liked them and they liked me. I treated them as equal and they responded—flaming terrific people. In school, I treated Aboriginal kids the same as any others—and got more from them that way. I believed in people, not racism.

I cannot remember ever meeting a nasty Aborigine (except Dick the football star at Moonahcullah when he was drunk after a game). As far as I'm concerned, they have never been given a fair go, especially in our schools. That's why we set up the Aboriginal Education Council, to give Aboriginal kids opportunities. Understandably, a lot of Aborigines don't like the way they've been treated, or the way governments always want to manage them and 'know best'. And why would they? They don't like being told what to do. They want to work with you.

Alan T Duncan OAM, BA, MEd, DipAnth Syd, Duine Urramach, Hon. Fellow UWS. Born in 1924, his fourth birthday was en route to Australia. He was educated at Regents Park Public School and Homebush Junior Boys High School, then night school and work with the Commonwealth Office of Education. In World War II he served with the Air Force in New Guinea as a radar operator, and after the war qualified as a teacher.

> *He was teacher/supervisor at Moonahcullah Aboriginal School and Reserve (1952–54); then principal of Woodenbong Aboriginal School (1955–57) and Hillston Central School (1958–62). In 1963 he was seconded to the Department of Adult Education at the University of Sydney to initiate adult education programs for Aboriginals, rising to head of the department.*
>
> *In 1963 he started the Consultative Committee on Aboriginal Education which became the Aboriginal Education Council (AEC), to improve opportunities for Aboriginal students in public schools. The AEC pioneered study grants, study centres, Aboriginal Teachers Aides (ATAs), Aboriginal home-school liaison and scholarships, including for rural students at Kirinari Hostel at Gymea. Alan worked closely with Bert Groves, Ken Brindle and Aboriginal communities.*
>
> *Alan Duncan started the ATA training course at the University of Sydney, instituted the JOBS (Job Opportunity through Better Skills) project, got Aboriginal discussion groups going in Surry Hills, Kempsey and Wreck Bay, and with Pastor Doug Nicholls and Kath Walker started Aboriginal leadership training schools and family education centres.*
>
> *He was involved in the Aboriginal interest group of the New South Wales Teachers Federation, was an Australian Labor Party branch member, policy committee chair and local campaign director, as well as New South Wales secretary of the 1967 referendum campaign, working with Kath Walker.*
>
> *Alan was a member of the Teaching the Teachers steering committee, and a founding member of the Aboriginal Studies Association, for whom he was treasurer for some years. He was a member of the Evening and Community Colleges Association and the Ethnic Communities Council, and a part-time commissioner of the Ethnic Affairs Commission of New South Wales. He is a life member of Adult Learning Australia.*
>
> *Alan Duncan was awarded the Medal of the Order of Australia (OAM) in 1982 for services to adult education. He was appointed to the Council of Milperra College of Advanced Education (now University of Western Sydney, Bankstown Campus) and in 1995 was elected Fellow of the University, receiving a Certificate of Appreciation in 2000.*
>
> *He is President Emeritus of the Aboriginal Education Council. In his private life he has been deeply involved in Scottish history and heritage, and his local Presbyterian church.*

A National Aboriginal Education Policy

In 1988 the 'Hughes Report' of the Aboriginal Education Policy Task Force, chaired by South Australian Aboriginal educator Dr Paul Hughes, made 57 specific recommendations to change education systems. From this, the National Aboriginal and Torres Strait Islander Education Policy (NATSIEP or AEP, now the Indigenous Education Policy, IEP) was developed. IEP provided extra funding for Aboriginal education in all sectors for guaranteed three-year periods—an improvement on the insecurity of having to make submissions every year. Funding for AECGs/IECBs was also made triennial. The policy was to be about strategic coordination across all sectors. But 'higher education' (universities) was on a different funding program and even a different triennium. Unlike the Hughes Report, the policy was widely seen as fitting Aboriginal education into existing systems—there was not a word on teacher education or racism.

The first Main Purpose of IEP is involving Aboriginal people in decision-making. However, agreements are signed by ministers and the most important decisions have always been made by Canberra—first DEET, then DEETYA, then DETYA, then DEST, now DEEWR. The Act was the *Aboriginal Education (Supplementary Assistance) Act*—to top up existing programs. However, some states and systems tended to use IEP funds to fund most or all Aboriginal programs, continuing the 'black money' syndrome whereby programs happen if there is Aboriginal funding.

Three funding programs were also introduced:

- ATAS (Aboriginal Tutorial Assistance Scheme, now ITAS)—which provided tutoring for Aboriginal students and Homework Centres;

> **'You don't stop muckin' up, I'm gunna send you to school'**
>
> In 2007 on a trip to the remote Kimberley region in Western Australia, I visited a store run by a local Indigenous community. As I stood there, I reminisced as to how different this success story had become for Indigenous people since more than four decades ago when I first became involved in aspects of research and Indigenous education.
>
> Yet to me the importance of still achieving successful outcomes in educational achievement is also evident from what also occurred in the store, when I overheard an Indigenous mother threatening her misbehaving school-age child that if he didn't behave she would make him go to school! This certainly may have been an isolated occurrence but is indicative of issues related to Indigenous studies.
>
> As a state primary school teacher in the early 1960s, I became increasingly aware and involved in Aboriginal education as the school [in which] I taught had a significant proportion of Indigenous students. These were the times of what I saw as the dawn of a new era in giving equal education and rights to all our students regardless of background. The school texts and government policies had till now reflected an attitude that Indigenous students were racially inferior and lacking intelligence. With the coming Referendum giving equal rights, this was to bring about change.
>
> When my own career moved into tertiary teacher education in the late 1960s, I became involved in developing and modifying courses for trainee teachers .Inspired by the work of Colin Tatz at Monash and Alan Duncan of Sydney University, and being appalled by the fact that only one or two Indigenous students attended university, I implemented courses that in the past were based on anthropological and ethnographic studies, to practical hands on with Indigenous speakers and field trips which involved both the students and the Aboriginal community in developing Aboriginal Studies.
>
> Since those days of the early 1970s, we now have a growing number of Indigenous students in both secondary and tertiary education. Nowadays universities have Indigenous departments staffed with Indigenous academics and there is a growing vibrancy of academic achievement as well. Aboriginal Studies is now also often a compulsory component of all Teacher Education courses.
>
> A major success in all this has been the seminal work of Rhonda Craven who, in consultation with Indigenous colleagues, has developed a large number of educational resources and appropriate teaching materials for the teaching of Aboriginal Studies in both schools and tertiary institutions.
>
> So there has been much success in education yet much still needs to be achieved, as was brought home to me by that mother in the store.
>
> Four decades ago it was seen that education was a major factor as it is today and that we still need to develop successful strategies in Aboriginal education.
>
>
>
> *Kurt Marder* became interested in Aboriginal education in the early 1960s when he taught at a school with a high proportion of Aboriginal students. Moving into teacher education in the late '60s, he was inspired by the work of Colin Tatz and Alan Duncan—and deeply shocked at how few Aboriginal students got as far as university. Finding courses based on anthropology and ethnographic studies, he changed them to hands-on experiences; Aboriginal speakers, field trips and involving communities in developing Aboriginal Studies. He is now attached to the Educational Excellence and Equity program in the Centre for Educational Research at the University of Western Sydney.

- ASSPA (Aboriginal Student Support and Parent Awareness)—direct funding to schools per Aboriginal student; and
- VEGAS (Vocational Education Guidance for Aboriginals Scheme)—vocational seminars for secondary students.

In 1996, the Commonwealth changed the system of allocating IESIP funds to a per capita basis. Providers were defined and funds allocated on the basis of how many Aboriginal and Torres Strait Islander students were educated in their systems or institutions. More recently,

> **'Only Aboriginal'**
> So many Aboriginal students in New South Wales schools were placed in 'low-ability' classes that in the 1980s when these classes were called OA ('Other Activities'), the AECG said OA really meant 'Only Aboriginal'. A 1986 AECG survey found that Aboriginal children were way over-represented in these classes. In 1989 a survey of three inner-Sydney schools found that up to 80 per cent of Aboriginal students suffered on and off from otitis media, and could not always hear in class. As AECG people said, 'Can't hear, can't learn'.

> **The First Aboriginal Education Policy**
> The 1982 New South Wales Aboriginal Education Policy was written in collaboration with the New South Wales AECG. It was the first such policy in Australia. Its focus was appropriate education for Aboriginal students and community involvement. The Aboriginal Education Unit wrote support documents on Aboriginal history and culture and teaching Aboriginal students. The policy was made mandatory for all schools in 1987; however, too many schools felt that the policy did not apply if they had no Aboriginal students. The policy was rewritten in 1995 by the New South Wales AECG and the Department of School Education to include all students, all staff and all schools, and to address educational achievement by Aboriginal students, as well as educating all students about Aboriginal Australia. A further rewrite of the policy in 2007–08, again with the AECG, focused on benchmarks and accountability.

> My vision for all young people going through the school system in this country is that Aboriginal Studies will be a mandatory part of every child's experience, and that it should be as normal as History or English. This needs to be a fundamental part of developing the Australian identity.
>   I remember as a student in Year 7 being made to feel ashamed that I was Aboriginal, because of what I was being taught. I would like to think that that no longer happens, although I'm not so sure of it.
> —Linda Burney, NSW Minister for Community Services and AECG President 1988–98, quoted in ATSIC (1998)

> There was a time when it was never acknowledged that there was a problem with black–white relations. Racism was 'never a problem' in this country until we put it on the agenda and now it's never off the agenda, for the very good reason that it still exists. That is a huge victory, in my opinion: for example, the fact that in schools we now teach Aboriginal studies so that kids are now learning that there was not a peaceful settlement by the British of this country in 1788. In my book those are the really big victories. Having people in positions like mine: sure, they're victories, but the really big one is the acknowledgment that, as they say, white Australia has a black history.
> —Pat O'Shane, quoted in Rintoul (1993, p. 53)

extra funds have been allocated for remote area students. Funding for AECGs, which had been automatic and indexed since 1990, is now negotiated as contracts based on performance on agreed criteria. More recently, funding has changed, with more funds allocated to remote areas to cope with high costs and target low levels of education provision and attainment.

Two-way schooling and Aboriginal languages

In the 1960s, an outstation movement began in isolated areas such as Elcho Island and Ernabella, but without government support these community initiatives had little success. The first bilingual programs were introduced in the 1960s. Before this, Aboriginal children who spoke only an Aboriginal language were taught in English. If they were taught at all, it was mainly by imported teachers with little knowledge of the local Aboriginal language or culture. The Whitlam government's self-determination policy included primary schooling in community languages: experimental programs in five Northern Territory communities in 1973; by 1977 there were 20 bilingual schools, and by 1992 there were 25. However, this was a small proportion of community schools, and some felt that bilingual schooling should be about cultural survival and maintaining languages rather than just education.

The 1991 Commonwealth languages policy, *Australia's Language: The Australian Language and Literacy Policy*, stressed the urgent need to preserve and maintain Aboriginal languages. In 1992, the House of Representatives Standing Committee on Aboriginal and Torres Strait Islander Affairs published *A Matter of Survival*, dealing with Aboriginal languages. They found that one in ten of an estimated 250 languages survived in a relatively healthy state, about a third were still spoken by some people and many were spoken only by a handful of older speakers and were likely to die with them. Not one Aboriginal or Torres Strait Islander language was taught to Year 12 level, and it was extremely rare to find any Indigenous language in high school.

Across Australia, there have been a number of projects to revive and teach Aboriginal languages in schools. The Federation of Aboriginal and Torres Strait Islander Languages (FATSIL) lobbies for languages; its *Voices of the Land* magazine promotes policies and programs. The Australian Indigenous Languages Framework is a federally funded national curriculum initiative to develop appropriate curriculum for the teaching of Aboriginal languages in schools. It takes account of the diversity of Aboriginal languages, and is flexible enough to accommodate the full range of languages and linguistic heritage, from languages that are still spoken by entire communities and passed on to children to those that are no longer spoken. It also aims to teach all Australians about the nature of Aboriginal languages. It recognises the loss of linguistic heritage, but its main focus is promoting Aboriginal and Torres Strait Islander languages and their importance in Australian society.

'Can't hear, can't learn'

In 1989, a survey of three inner-Sydney schools found over 80 per cent of Aboriginal students affected by otitis media (middle ear disease, or 'glue ear'), previously thought to be a remote-area problem. Otitis media comes and goes. It affects Aboriginal children from birth—ten times more it does than non-Aboriginal Australians. It is suggested to be caused by respiratory infections and living conditions, but no one really knows for sure. Otitis media is an obvious example of the interrelationship of health and education issues. Most health and educational professionals had been unaware of the problem—too many still are. An AECG research project reported on best practice across Australia to increase awareness, promote health and education networking, and involve Aboriginal communities. In August 1994, a national conference on Aboriginal otitis media was held in Alice Springs and in August 1995 a New South Wales conference took place with health and education agencies working together. But, as with so many programs, years down the track the links are being re-forged.

Other critical health–education issues are family violence and the impact of drug and alcohol abuse on education. Recently there has been a focus on child protection. Collaborative strategies with community involvement are more effective as they recognise the holistic nature of Aboriginal cultures and the fact that issues are interrelated, as shown by the comment, 'Can't hear, can't learn' made about otitis media.

The horror stories of the past in Aboriginal education can be used to raise awareness. So many Aboriginal adults who were failed by schooling have achieved in 'second-chance' education, particularly in TAFE. Many now work in universities or are writers and can pass on their experiences.

> **'I am passionate about education'**
>
> I trace my achievements to teachers in primary school in the 1940s who took an interest in me. I learnt that education was the key to my future as a young Aboriginal child, growing up in an institution, who could normally only expect to become a domestic for a white family.
>
> A teacher in high school mentored me and consequently I won a scholarship to business college, thus guaranteeing me another choice in life.
>
> I have had many mentors in my career. In 1984 I was mentored into the Mt Eliza Management Program for potential high flyers. I still had a wish to further my education and began a part-time law degree in 1994, which I completed eight years later. Travelling both in Australia and overseas has also broadened my education.
>
> I am passionate about education and encouraged my children through to university and am now encouraging my grandchildren.
>
>
>
> *Dr Sue Gordon AM*, born at Belele Station near Meekatharra, Western Australia, taken away at four and raised at Sister Kate's Home in Perth. She served with the Women's Royal Australian Army Corps 1961–64, then worked in administration, winning an Aboriginal Overseas Study Award in 1977. In 1986, she was appointed Commissioner of Aboriginal Planning, the first Aboriginal head of a government department in Western Australia, and in 1988 was the first full-time magistrate of the Perth Children's Court and first Aboriginal magistrate. In 1990, she was one of the five interim ATSIC Commissioners. In 2002, she headed the Gordon Inquiry into family violence and child abuse. In 2004 she was appointed chair of the National Indigenous Council which replaced ATSIC. She then chaired the Northern Territory Intervention steering committee. She was awarded the Order of Australia in 1993, and holds an honorary Doctorate of Letters (D.Litt) from the University of Western Australia. She is widowed with two sons, one a lawyer, one a civil engineer.

Two-way schooling: Garma theory

In 1989, Manduwuy Yunupingu was appointed principal of Yirrkala Community School. The school initiated a radical 'both-ways' curriculum—integrating the best aspects of both Yolngu (Arnhem Land) and Balanda (white) cultures.

Heavily backed by clan Elders and Aboriginal teachers of the Yirrkala Action Group, formed in 1984 to Aboriginalise curriculum, the school negotiated with the Northern Territory government to institute Garma education. Garma is a Yolngu metaphor to describe where a flow of water from the sea and a river of water from the land mutually engulf each other, flow into a lagoon and become one. A vortex is created and the strengths of the two rivers moving around together enable deeper understanding. Manduwuy says:

> In order to know about the unknown (Western knowledge) you have to go through an educational process, but with the two-way process the emphasis is made on traditional education more than contemporary education... I find it interesting that through learning your own traditional knowledge you can then learn more about the unknown knowledge.
>
> [Yolngu learning] is different in that it is centred on kinship... a system that is governed in a social sense—how we relate to each other and how things are run; everyday, normal sort of things. We learn and abide by the kinship system and it can be applied to Western areas where Yolngu people have traditionally had trouble grasping concepts, such as mathematics and the sciences. In mathematics you have recursive processes and even though it is an ongoing thing it keeps coming back—similar in that after 10 you keep on counting from one to the next 10.
>
> By applying the recurring themes of our kinship system, this is an area to which Aboriginal children can be linked. There are similarities which can help us grasp the concepts of mathematics and ultimately enable Yolngu people to function in a contemporary world.

Yirrkala Community School was at the forefront of the 'two-way' system of schooling, applied in many forms to smaller schools at homelands centres in the Top End, and filtering through to other parts of the Northern Territory.

In his own schooling experience, Manduwuy tells how he had to fight the old European approach to educating Aboriginal people:

> I had to fight, or resist, that whole assimilation approach and all the other indoctrination processes—doctrines which come in with the Balanda world. I tended to avoid all that and go a different way because I found there are alternatives within the Balanda society, alternatives which reflect on some of the things which I enjoy doing and correspond with my life. So why not join forces with those? That's what I have been able to do, particularly with my music—seek alternative things within the mainstream and do things which the whole of society accepts.

All along the way I found strength from within my Yolngu culture.

Source: Adapted from *Australian Educator*, Winter 1993.

Aboriginal education: Changing the system

Enormous progress has been made in Aboriginal education. Systems have changed and there is access to education in a way that could barely have been imagined a generation ago. For example, in 1996 there were almost 7000 Aboriginal and Torres Strait Islander students in higher education. When Commonwealth secondary assistance programs began in 1969, there were 115 recipients; by 1996 there were over 48 000. In 1999, there were 2206 Indigenous students in Year 12; in 2009, this had more than doubled to 4779. Retention has also improved from 32 per cent in 1998 to 42.9 per cent in 2007, closing the gap a bit. But for all these improvements, the critical issue is participation—real engagement of Aboriginal students.

The future of community involvement in Aboriginal schooling is in some doubt. Aboriginal advisory structures across the country differ; not all are directly linked to grassroots community. In much of Australia, the community-based AECG ideal has faded and most advisory bodies are within government. National-level Aboriginal advice on education is also an issue. Most of the most important decisions are taken at the central level by ministers or DEEWR officers. Following the demise of the National Federation of AECGs, there is no national advisory body. ATSIC was charged with advising on Aboriginal education, but had no programs and little expertise in the field. It was abolished in 2004. There are also issues with the regulation and administration of Abstudy benefits.

When the IEP was developed, the direct assistance programs, ASSPA, ATAS and VEGAS were introduced without consultation. Partly as a result, ASSPA tended to disempower local AECGs, where these existed (see below). This was seen as typical of the Commonwealth tendency to set up alternatives to Aboriginal structures. VEGAS was initially under-funded for what it aimed to achieve. ASSPA also caused fights as funding levels depended on whether the school was classed as 'non-remote' or 'remote' (double funding), and rigid application of criteria led to stupidities like Moree being 'remote', but Boggabilla 'non-remote' (closer to Brisbane).

There were also issues with inappropriate use of funds and committees being in practice run by school principals rather than communities. However, ASSPA was a most valuable program for its potential to bring Aboriginal culture and community into school education, as well as provide funds for resources. It was abolished in 2005 and replaced by the Parent–School Partnership Initiative. PSPI encourage partnerships of schools and communities to apply for funding for projects—but with a complex process that has taken time to work smoothly, and needs high-level skills just to apply. This has now been replaced by the Parents and Community Engagement (PaCE) program.

One issue is that no funding is provided for schools without Aboriginal students to educate all students about Aboriginal

---

The importance of relevance

During the 1970s Walgett was the principal centre for action research leading to successful teaching of Aboriginal students in New South Wales. The Walgett Aboriginal Education conferences of that period were the medium through which positive developments were disseminated. As principal of Walgett Public School I was very much involved in the numerous successful projects.

Early on I was impressed by our successes with experiential learning. From this I developed a theory of the more important concept, 'relevance'. Relevance, which is wider than experience, is the key. Relevance can be built into any teaching program—drawing from the psychology of the students, their everyday and extended environments, and the cultural factors in their lives. Linking to these is their acculturated learning modalities. In Walgett at that time most non-Aboriginal students were predominantly aural learners, whereas the Aboriginals were heavily visually oriented.

One of our early observations was that Aboriginal subject matter in the lesson did not ensure full participation by Aboriginal students. For example, I presented a couple of the legendary stories recorded by K.L. Parker to a group comprising 50 per cent of students from each group. For the first story the recall by the non-Aboriginal group was much better than the Aboriginal group. The Parker stories came with a visual representation of the story, called a 'dreaming'. As the second story was read, the students worked on a copy of its 'dreaming' in colour. The recall of the Aboriginal group then was the same as the non-Aboriginal group.

Work at Walgett High School at the same time confirmed a need also with secondary students to make sure the subject material was relevant to the Aboriginal students. Teachers have to *engage* students, otherwise valuable learning opportunities will be wasted.

Specific Aboriginal studies should not be the school's only Aboriginal focus. It's not difficult to introduce Aboriginal perspectives into a wide range of curriculum areas. And a caution: don't spoil a good Aboriginal Studies course by infringing on local cultural sensitivities. What is planned should first be run by a local Elder. The more parents and local community can be *engaged*, the greater the successes will be.

Laurie and Peg Craddock. Peg also taught at Walgett Public School. Photo: Vicki Barton.

Laurie Craddock was appointed deputy principal at Walgett Public School in 1967. With the principal of the high school, Ed Gaskell, he developed ways of starting from where Aboriginal students were at, which produced results equal to those of any school in the State. In 1971, he started what became known as the Walgett Aboriginal Education conferences, which ran through the '70s and were the most important of their time, surely an influence on the young Walgett men who helped start the AECG. Promoted to head office, he was Assistant Director of Special Programs, in charge of Aboriginal education, and worked closely with the Aboriginal Education Unit and the AECG to change education for Aboriginal kids. He was awarded Associate Life Membership of the AECG in 1989. Moving on to Sydney University, he continued to work on Aboriginal education. He was a long-time member of the Aboriginal Education Council, and a trustee of the Norman Catts Trust for 25 years. Laurie 'retired' in 1997.

> **Schooling—what schooling?**
>
> Norm Newlin is my name and I went to school in a two-room school at Tea Gardens, just north of Newcastle, from 1939 to 1949. When I left that school I had less than a primary school education. I believe that when my mother took me to enrol the teacher saw my mother's Aboriginality and placed me down the back of the room and ignored me. I was ignored for many years. I was 11 in third class when I was sort of discovered by a teacher and promoted to fourth class; by then it was too late to catch up on work I'd missed out on.
>
> Two very vivid memories of my school days stand out in my memory. The first one was when I put up my hand to answer a question about Holland. The teacher said to me: 'Put down your hand, you wouldn't know the answer.' From that time on I would never answer a question and if I was asked one, my reply was, 'I don't know.'
>
> The other incident was an essay about roses. We never had a flower garden, just a vegetable garden. I sat there for the full period and finally came up with, 'Big roses have big thorns and little roses have little thorns.'
>
> For this effort I was dragged out in front of the class and humiliated, hit around the head with the book. The book was thrown across the room. I was told to get the book and get back down the back where I belonged. Whenever a child in the class did something that displeased this teacher, they would be asked if they wanted to be 'stupid like Newlin'.
>
> These experiences left me with a feeling of very low self-esteem. This low self-esteem caused me to drink heavily, get myself tattooed on a large part of my body. For 40 years I believed I was stupid.
>
> In 1985 I began to get an education at the then Sydney CAE, going from there to the University of Technology to complete a degree in Communication.
>
> I wrote my first poem in 1985 and within a year, I was awarded a six-month grant from the Aboriginal Arts Board. In 1988 I had a book of poems published and in that year I was also awarded a two-month grant to go the US to meet and talk to Native Americans and Black Americans who were writers.
>
> I have lectured in universities in New South Wales and had my work included in a textbook for New South Wales high schools. I have since overcome my alcohol addiction and have been sober for 26 years.
>
> —Norm Newlin, Worimi Elder

Australia, as in AEP Goal 21. An element of the short-lived Reconciliation and Schooling Strategy of the 1990s was its Visiting Speakers Program—$1 million a year to fund Aboriginal speakers in schools across Australia, targeted at schools without Aboriginal students. However, the scheme was cancelled in 1995, leaving systems and schools responsible. Nothing has replaced it.

In 1999, an Indigenous Education Forum in Alice Springs brought together key players from all sectors across the country. Minister David Kemp flew in to open and launch Bob Collins' *Learning Lessons* report: most Aboriginal education in the Territory produced people who could not meet Year 3 standards, and Aboriginal corporations had to employ whitefellas. The secretary of his department (DETYA, at the time) was there for the whole three days, and wrote at the head of one group's butcher's-paper sheet: 'Let's stop talking high principle and just . . . do it!' The 'silo mentality' of most agencies was illustrated by Aboriginal education not knowing what Aboriginal health was doing on a school health issue.

Boys' education issues, particularly in secondary schooling, tend to be more acute for Aboriginal students. Partly due to low Aboriginal Education Worker (AEW) wages, Aboriginal women predominate in Aboriginal education and there is a shortage of male role models. In rural and remote areas, employment opportunities are few and largely non-existent for Aboriginals, so there may seem to be little point in education. Older Aboriginal boys, particularly in more traditional areas, may be regarded as men in their culture but are still treated as subordinate at school. The problem is compounded by racism, both attitudinal and institutional, as well as the cultural racism that still excludes Aboriginal Australia from the curriculum. Another core issue, particularly in remote areas, is that Aboriginal children are allowed to do what they like at home.

Aboriginal boys who react to racism often feel victimised by school authorities, while those who cause incidents get away with it. Anti-racism policies and resources such as the Whole School Anti-Racism Project (New South Wales Department of Education, 1995) exist, but school authorities still seem more concerned with 'discipline' issues such as uniforms and swearing than racism. School curricula are being reformed but often remain Eurocentric, with little or token recognition of Aboriginal culture. One reason why TAFE systems have been so successful in providing second-chance Aboriginal education is the failure of schooling—and because TAFE treats students as people.

Aboriginal stories are critical to changing attitudes to bring about the systemic change that needs to happen if Aboriginal students are to get a fair go in education, and be engaged.

'You are a repeat offender'. Cartoon by Tandberg, *The Age*, 23 December 1996. Inspired by outrage at the jailing of two Aboriginal boys for spitting at MP Pauline Hanson in her office, this cartoon won a Walkley Award. Courtesy Ron Tandberg.

As Sally Morgan wrote in her introduction to *The Lost Children* (Edwards and Read, 1989), stories of Stolen Generations survivors:

> In the telling we assert the validity of our own experience and we call the silence of two hundred years a lie. And it is important to you, the listener, because, like it or not, we are a part of you. We have to find a way of living together in this country, and that will only come when our hearts, minds and wills are set towards reconciliation. It will only come when thousands of stories have been spoken and listened to with understanding. (1989, p. vii)

One hopeful sign is the continuing proliferation of Aboriginal resources, to the point where it is difficult to keep up with what is available—most especially with new technology, CD-ROMs, websites, etc. (see Chapter 14). There is a growing demand for the input of Aboriginal people in schools.

When the New South Wales AECG conducted community consultations on rewriting the Aboriginal Education Policy, the major theme of the feedback was that 'Aboriginal kids must have the right to be Aboriginal!' This may seem obvious, but this is precisely what was denied them through the dark years of White Australia.

We need to remember that in many areas this is still the case. Where Aboriginal English

Lands of shame

In *Lands of Shame* (2007), ANU economist and Boyer lecturer Professor Helen Hughes laid bare decades of Indigenous affairs in law, health, education, economics . . . the whole of life. The book is laced with statistics (e.g. 56 000 doctors, 100 of them Indigenous with one surgeon), court and media horror stories, inaction by the Northern Territory and most states. Its cover image is a photo of a closed school door with handprints in paint, the image of 'homeland' communities locked out of mainstream-standard education—and from employment and the life to which they should be entitled as Australians. Hughes argues that decades of policy have shut Indigenous people out of Australian life—the total exclusion of White Australia, then 30 years of 'exceptionalist' ('special treatment') policies. At the core, she argues, is the ideal—based on the communalism of Marxist philosophy—of Indigenous people living on their own country in 'homelands' returned through land rights or native title.

She notes that Bob Collins' report on Territory education, *Learning Lessons*, found Indigenous organisations in the Northern Territory employing non-Indigenous workers because schools did not produce Grade 3 literacy—and sank like a stone. Indigenous statistics, she says, are bad enough across the country, but aggregating statistics masks appalling facts in 'homeland' Australia: about 90 000 people in 1200 'settlements', many in effect defunct or recreational camps, most with no schools, medical services or facilities, just five primary schools up to mainstream standards, a handful of secondary schools doing remedial primary work, students up to eight months behind for every year of schooling.

And it gets worse: enrolment and attendance records not available or not even kept, schools closed for weeks at a time, and when open not even a pencil to be found—nothing of the technology most schools take for granted. Many teaching nothing much any time—on the grounds that 'Western' (i.e. Australian) curriculum is 'inappropriate'. Much teaching based on post-modern education theory which, she says, does most damage to the already disadvantaged—like 'whole-language' literacy in a second language! Meanwhile, youth learn about life from the media or 'gangsta' movies, and graduate to 'sit-down money'—or worse, like petrol sniffing. Education, any sort of aspiration, is out of the question if no one anywhere has a job or much of a life. From Palm Island to Halls Creek, Nhulunbuy to Kalgoorlie, these Indigenous people are entitled to proper schooling, just like all of us. Australians must make it happen.

—Helen Hughes (2007).

is not respected, the culture and backgrounds of Aboriginal students are denigrated and rejected. Participation is critical in Aboriginal education. Remembering that just two of the 99 Aboriginal people investigated by the Royal Commission into Aboriginal Deaths in Custody had completed secondary schooling, we need to be aware that the cycle of custody too often

Croc Festival—'reconciliation in action'

The Croc Festival is an annual festival for school children in remote and regional areas. It focuses on building relationships between indigenous and non-indigenous Australian. Courtesy Indigenous Festivals of Australia.

In 1996, the Queensland Minister for Health asked Peter Sjoquist, executive producer of the Rock Eisteddfod, to do something to promote health and education for remote communities. Starting at Weipa in 1998 and ending in 2007, 57 Croc Festivals were staged across rural and remote Australia. Croc Festival was non-competitive, encouraging students to be the best they could be. Instead of bringing schools to the cities to compete, it took professional staging, sound and lighting to the bush. Performance was the hook to get schools in. Once there, students were targeted with interactive and fun health, education, sports and careers workshops, involving partnerships with the best programs in the country, such as Questacon, Luxottica I-care (OPSM), TAFE and BeyondBlue.

Everything about Croc Festival showed the importance of students—state-of-the-art stage, sound and lighting trucked across the country; framed gold CD trophies presented to performers; role models and Cabinet ministers flown in; professional photographers and video-makers; the best in careers and health expos and workshops; active sports with national stars, such as Evonne Goolagong-Cawley. A student said, 'I have never felt THIS important!'

Peter Sjoquist said Croc Festival was about celebrating the fantastic talents of remote-area youth and promoting the importance of school to get to meaningful work in the future. It was:

> a lot more than putting on a school performance—students learn about teamwork, respect for others, problem-solving and personal management skills. Performing on stage is something they will remember forever, but what is equally important is the skills they . . . build in the process. Improved self-esteem, team skills and a sense of self-worth are just some of the benefits . . . a practical example of proactive lifestyle decisions in action . . . an opportunity for people to be involved in an event that they would not otherwise be exposed to, and the best part is they love being involved in it.

Governor-General, Sir William Deane described Croc Festival as:

> reconciliation in action. It's coming together, talking together, walking together, living together, achieving together, playing, performing and having a good time together. It's trying to build, from the pain of the past, a future together.

Croc Festival celebrated youth and youth culture to inspire young people to 'have a go' and improve their education, health and career prospects, to be the best they could be in a 100 per cent-in-control, no-smokes, no-alcohol, no-drugs community setting. Its success was in engaging students, making them come alive. One said he wished he could live at the Croc Festival. Another said: 'Thanks for

> bringing us; it's the best day I've ever had at school.' A teacher wrote: 'Amazing . . . a highlight of my students' lives. They are still on a natural high.' Another wrote that one of the best things was 500 parents being on the school oval—'normally it's just so hard to get them to come through the gates'.
>
> Bringing together an amazing coalition of government, business, arts, sports and philanthropy, Croc Festival capitalised on the desire of many workers in service industries to do something for Indigenous youth. For example, Luxottica I-Care (formerly OPSM) said its staff were begging to be involved in more than one festival, but management had to share it around.
>
> From one event at Weipa in 1998, Croc Festival grew to seven a year—the biggest and best youth education and performing arts festival in Australia. But in 2008, with eight festivals in planning, the government cut its funding and imposed conditions which Indigenous Festivals of Australia found unacceptable, so it cancelled the 2008 events. DEEWR then reallocated the funds. Hopefully, Croc Festival will be back.

begins with alienation from school, frequently caused by inappropriate programs and discipline, often reacting to racism (see boys' issues above), and that Aboriginal youth are heavily over-represented both in school suspension statistics and in juvenile institutions across Australia.

Nearly 20 years ago, Merridy Malin observed a Reception class in an Adelaide school over a year. Three obviously Aboriginal students came into the school bright-eyed and eager; by the end of the year, they were traumatised, other students ostracised them, and the teacher saw them only as trouble. The teacher was not racist as such—simply just as ignorant of Aboriginal kids as most teachers. Many people still assume that Aboriginal kids in urban settings are assimilated, not really Aboriginal. This is simply not the case.

Teachers need to like Aboriginal students. Years ago, Aboriginal kids in a western Sydney school defined a good teacher as: 'Someone that likes us and is fair'. Knowing where they come from may help to appreciate their positive points. Racism and stereotyping of Aboriginal people must be addressed—issues that were particularly acute when Australians were forced to confront the real history and nature of Australia, and a White Australia backlash released 'free speech' from the constraints of so-called 'political correctness'.

Teacher education is critical. Teachers need to know about the culture, background and history of Aboriginal students, and this needs to be mandatory in teacher education programs. Aboriginal Studies also needs to be incorporated into in-service programs, remembering that the average teacher grew up learning little or nothing about Aboriginal Australia in school, and nothing again in training.

A cause for optimism was the extraordinary groundswell of support for the 1998 first National Sorry Day, particularly in schools—the more remarkable as this was no official commemoration, but a spontaneous response. The hearts and minds of Middle Australia were at last being touched. Kevin Rudd's national Apology of 2008 generated even more emotion across the country—thousands massed in Canberra, thousands more watched on big screens in schools, universities and workplaces across the country, millions more viewed the ceremony on ABC TV at home. From the Bicentennial to *Mabo* to *Wik* to Sorry Day to the Apology, the frame of reference of Australia is changing at last.

Problems remain. Statistics have improved, though national figures tend to mask appalling outcomes in some areas. There seems to be a new 'special treatment' culture—the idea that massive resources and huge structural change are needed. Some Aboriginal students have a feeling of entitlement because they are Aboriginal, while some reports suggest that others just want to be themselves and resent being singled out. There is evidence that Aboriginal students who are just themselves tend to do better. Meanwhile, no one knows why so many Aboriginal students have such problems with literacy, given that Aboriginals have always been linguists and given the expressive qualities and rich metaphors of Aboriginal English.

Education is fundamental. Aboriginal people say, 'Our kids are our future'. What happens in schools today not only determines the future down the track, it also has an immediate impact on students, their families and whole-school communities. Everyone can make a difference. The paradigm can be changed. Engagement is the answer—the question is how to make it happen. It is well said that 'Koori kids can do anything'. This should have been obvious from the time when Maria Lock topped the colony in a public exam in 1819. Much needs to be done to change Aboriginal education—but it *can* be done. The input of communities and the goodwill of all involved will be critical.

> **School in a war zone**
>
> Tennant Creek is on Warumungu land in the Northern Territory. The story goes that the town started when a beer truck broke down on the way to the telegraph station and the people moved to the beer. There was a gold rush in the 1930s, with lashings of grog. Few Aboriginal people lived in the town in the old days, then there was a huge influx from all around when equal wages came in and the pastoralists turfed off their Aboriginal workers and the workers' families.
>
> Alexis Wright's *Grog War* tells the story of the community's ten-year struggle, from 1986 to 1996, to get restrictions on grog sales in Tennant Creek to stem the horrific damage alcohol was doing to the community. Led by the Julalikari Council, the town's biggest employer, and the Indigenous health service Anyinginyi Congress (not one program of either organisation was unaffected by grog), this campaign born of self-determination transformed a them-and-us mentality to a whole-community responsibility. The struggle took so long because the Aboriginal community insisted it was not about special measures for Aboriginal people, but restrictions for all alike.
>
> In *Grog War*, Dave Curtis, one of the leaders of the struggle, recalls his experiences at school:
>
> 'When I was at school in the early sixties there were only a few Aboriginal families living in Tennant Creek then . . .' He always came top of his class but this did not help when there was trouble. He remembers a time when one of the kids in his class lost sixpence. The teacher ordered a search of the whole classroom. When the sixpence wasn't found the teacher blamed him. 'You took it didn't you?' (p. 65)
>
> '. . . when I was at school here in Tennant Creek. We weren't in separate classes. We were all the same. We were just kids at school. We'd get into fights with white kids and with other Aboriginal kids. The racism came from the teachers but not the kids. We believed we were just as good as anyone else . . .' (p. 78)
>
> Other vignettes through *Grog War* show how hard it could be just to get kids to school, and how marginal it was to some people's lives:
>
> Kids virtually never went to school. 'We too shame', the kids told John Havnen, while looking at each other's sore eyes, runny noses and dirty clothes. There was never any water for a bath. Or to wash clothes. Often kids were simply withdrawn from school. (p. 69)
>
> '. . . And this will go on all day and all night. Half the time we don't get sleep. Half the time my kids don't get rest, and the kids—they've got to go to school.' (p. 159)
>
> Primary school boys who hardly went to school and should have been starting high school. (p. 208)
>
> They [the kids] started winding each other up about all the items in their life that made them angry. It was a game of who could get the angriest. There was plenty of fuel. Family members. School. Friends. White people. Shop owners. Cops. Nothing to do. Having no money. Having nothing. Never having anything. It was like a competition . . . The sound of bottles breaking triggered the willy-nilly smashing of beer bottles because they hated grog. (p. 209)

8 Reconciliation matters

Nina Burridge

A united Australia which respects this land of ours, values Aboriginal and Torres Strait Islander heritage, and provides justice and equity for all.

—Vision Statement, Council for Aboriginal Reconciliation, 1991

Introduction

Learning to live and walk together in racial and cultural harmony with a shared sense of history, as equal members of the Australian nation: that was the aspiration of the Council for Aboriginal Reconciliation (CAR) created by the federal Labor government in 1991, in response to the Royal Commission into Aboriginal Deaths in Custody (Johnston, 1991). The Council was given ten years to accomplish its mission. The expectation was that in that time the nation would debate and work towards viable resolution of the issues affecting Indigenous and non-Indigenous Australians as we moved towards a new century.

Nearly two decades after the Council was created and almost one decade after its dissolution, the newly elected Prime Minister of Australia, Kevin Rudd, opened the 42nd Parliament on 13 February 2008 with a formal apology to Indigenous Australians on behalf of the nation. To most Aboriginal and Torres Strait Islander people, and to many other Australians, this was a momentous occasion. It had been a long time coming. Reconciliation had been placed on the backburner of policy reform by the previous Howard Coalition government, the media and much of the public since the great symbolic walk across the Sydney Harbour Bridge in May 2000.

This chapter provides a brief overview of the movement for reconciliation focusing on the work of the Council and its successor, Reconciliation Australia, in educating the community about the central issues of reconciliation. Further, the reasons why the reconciliation movement has been so slow in progressing its vision during the last 20 years will be discussed. Insights will also be provided into ways of rebuilding the road to genuine reconciliation while acknowledging the reality that such a process will encounter many obstacles. One underlying premise is that education is still the key to clarifying the misunderstandings surrounding reconciliation. Ultimately, education is still central to improving the life chances of Indigenous people and, on the wider national scale, in bringing the nation to a shared understanding of what reconciliation can mean for both Indigenous and non-Indigenous Australians.

Aboriginal Studies is vitally important

I make no claim to Aboriginal blood. My ancestors were Scottish highlanders—dispossessed and driven from their homelands. But I know I don't belong in Scotland either. I made it my quest to learn from Aboriginal people in this country so that I can share in a deeper belonging. And by and large that has happened. To me, being Indigenous is about that—really belonging to country and being an integral member of a family of living things and objects in that place. It has more to do with a state of mind and spirit rather than one's ancestry. Though people who have Aboriginal ancestry are blessed in that they inherit a ready made attunement—they shouldn't have to work too hard to find a connection.

Over the last decade or so I have returned to live in 'Tjapwurrung' country in western Victoria where I was born. These old tribal names, territories and boundaries are more meaningful to me than shire or state borders. If you learn about them you can often see how they make sound ecological, geographical and environmental sense.

One of the most satisfying things I have done is start an annual 'healing walk' with Indigenous people along various waterways in my region. This has been occurring since 2005 and involves an overland walk of about a week's duration.

The walk has allowed us to access and reconnect with ancestral country, interact with farmers and landholders, monitor the state of the environment and waterways, and promote reconciliation and cross-cultural understanding.

Aboriginal Studies is vitally important. Aboriginal people know this country the best. They belong to the land and know how to survive in it. You must respect that. Then you will be welcomed and shown how to live too. Don't be fooled by the computer age. There is wisdom in their cultural heritage relevant for all of us, and you will come to learn the true history of Australia.

Growing up seeing land degradation happen on a farm near Lake Bolac in western Victoria, **Neil Murray** *used to wonder what had happened to the people of the land. As a young man he went to Central Australia, working at Papunya and Kintore. Here he co-founded Warumpi Band and wrote many of their songs, most notably the anthem 'Blackfella, Whitefella' and 'My Island Home' (APRA song of the year 2005). As Neil Murray and the Rainmakers and as a solo artist he has released eight CDs, and performed several times at the Edinburgh Festival. As well as top songs like 'Eddie Mabo' and 'Myall Creek', his writing includes* Sing for Me, Countryman, *an 'autofictographical' novel of his years in Central Australia with Warumpi Band, a play* King for This Place, *and most recently,* One Man Tribe, *a book of poetry. He says: 'My artistic views, vision and creative output have been significantly shaped by the influence of Aboriginal people and their culture.'*

Left to right, legend Jimmy Little, Neil Murray and Brendan Gallagher singing Neil's Warumpi Band song 'Blackfella, Whitefella' at ANTaR's Sea of Hands tenth anniversary concert in Victoria Park, Sydney. Photo: Lou Weber, courtesy ANTaR.

The policy of reconciliation

In an historical sense, Aboriginal peoples' struggle for recognition in their own land had already been going on for many decades prior to the policy of reconciliation. Colonial, state and federal governments had been implementing myriad policies designed to 'protect', 'assimilate' and 'integrate' Aboriginal people into mainstream society since the early nineteenth century.

The idea of some formal agreement was another attempt, as the Bicentenary approached, at formulating solutions to non-Aboriginal Australia's troubled relationship with its Indigenous peoples. It emerged from a consultative process with Aboriginal people begun in the early 1980s to ascertain whether the Australian legal system might be able to incorporate a type of treaty (*makarrata*) or a 'compact' between Australia's Indigenous people and the Commonwealth government. The Aboriginal Treaty Committee and the National Aboriginal Conference (NAC)—an Aboriginal advisory body to the federal government—were charged with investigating the possibility of a treaty to be signed in time for the Bicentenary in 1988. However, the realities of state politics of the time, particularly in Western Australia with its mining interests, negated this option.

The treaty concept devolved into 'an understanding' or a 'compact' by June 1988; this was known as the Barunga Statement (Horton, 1994). It emphasised the need for extensive consultation with Aboriginal people in working towards 'a sense of reconciliation'. Two years later, the shocking findings of the Royal Commission into Aboriginal Deaths in Custody (Johnston, 1991) inspired the commissioners to strongly advocate the creation of a body to advance a process of reconciliation between Aboriginal and non-Aboriginal people. The final Recommendation, number 339, read:

> That all political leaders and their parties recognise that Reconciliation between the Aboriginal and non-Aboriginal communities in Australia must be achieved if community division, discord and injustice to Aboriginal people are to be avoided. To this end the Commission recommends that political leaders use their best endeavours to ensure bipartisan public support for the process of Reconciliation and that the urgency and necessity of the process be acknowledged. (Johnston, 1991, cited in Commonwealth of Australia, 1992, p. 10)

The creation of the Council for Aboriginal Reconciliation

The Council for Aboriginal Reconciliation was created in mid-1991 through an Act of federal Parliament that was passed with cross-party support—a rare achievement in the adversarial atmosphere of the nation's legislature. This 25-member body, representing government, Aboriginal organisations, community leaders and church groups, had a majority of Aboriginal representatives and an Aboriginal chair. It was given a ten-year mandate to consult widely with Aboriginal and non-Aboriginal people throughout the nation to discuss the process of reconciling a difficult history of inter-cultural conflict over the previous 200 years. One underlying function of the Council was the education of the Australian community on the key issues of reconciliation.

The Federal Minister for Aboriginal Affairs, Robert Tickner, enumerated the threefold purpose of the Council in the process of reconciliation:

- 'To raise awareness of Aboriginal and Torres Strait Islander issues among non-Aboriginal people in Australia, to create better appreciation of the Aboriginal and Torres Strait Islander cultures, history, dispossession, disadvantage and the need to address that disadvantage;
- To foster a national commitment from governments at all levels to cooperate to address Aboriginal and Torres Strait Islander disadvantage; and
- To consult the community and advise the Government on whether Reconciliation would be advanced by a formal document or documents and whether a document or documents would benefit the Australian community as a whole.' (Tickner, 1993, p. 37)

The first chairperson of the Council was Patrick Dodson, a highly respected Aboriginal leader who remained chairperson until 1998, when he resigned and was replaced by Evelyn Scott, a veteran of the 1967 Referendum.

Reclaiming Local History

Journey of the Spirit: The Woodford Bay Reconciliation Memorial Ceremony DVD and Study Guide

On 7 February 2004, over 500 Aboriginal and non-Aboriginal people, including local school students, gathered together at Woodford Bay, on Sydney's Lower North Shore, in Cameraygal Country.

They came to be part of the truth-telling of Australian history; to witness New South Wales Governor Professor Marie Bashir AC and Rob Welsh, Chairperson, Metropolitan Local Aboriginal Land Council (MLALC) jointly unveil a plaque acknowledging Aboriginal resistance to British invasion . . . and thus dispelling the long-promoted myth of a 'peaceful settlement'.

This historic event came to fruition through the initiative of Lane Cove Residents for Reconciliation (LCRR) in partnership with the Metropolitan Local Aboriginal Land Council (custodians of the area), Lane Cove Historical Society and Lane Cove Council and community.

Acknowledging the truths of our intertwined black/white history is fundamental to reconciliation, to social justice and to a truly mature and united Australia.

In 2008 LCRR and MLALC produced the *Journey of the Spirit* DVD (33 min) and Study Guide (12 pages) insert, endorsed by New South Wales Reconciliation Council, New South Wales Aboriginal Education Consultative Group and Tranby Aboriginal College. For more information, phone (02) 9427 2055.

This DVD, along with its Study Guide, is an educational resource to assist schools, local councils and communities, and business and faith groups in researching the truth of their own local black/white history.

As Rob Welsh stated: 'There is still potential to build a bridge between our peoples, and resources like this DVD/SG can help us cross that bridge together.'

—Kerrie McKenzie, Convenor, Lane Cove Residents for Reconciliation

Opening the Woodford Bay memorial, 7 February 2004. Left to right: Councillor John May, Mayor of Lane Cove; Charlene Davison, Lane Cove Residents for Reconciliation, joint MC; Her Excellency Governor Professor Marie Bashir, AC; Rob Welsh, Chair, Metropolitan Local Aboriginal Land Council; Uncle Charles Madden, Metropolitan Local Aboriginal Land Council; Ricky Lyons, Metropolitan Local Aboriginal Land Council, joint MC; Kerrie McKenzie, Convenor, Lane Cove Residents for Reconciliation. Courtesy Lane Cove Residents for Reconciliation.

Kerrie McKenzie *was educated at Sydney Girls High School, Bathurst Teachers College and Tranby Aboriginal College, where she was one of the first non-Aboriginal group to complete the Advanced Diploma in Applied Aboriginal Studies. She taught in New South Wales public schools for 35 years, rising to Acting Principal; from 1964 to 1966 she was a supply teacher in London schools. In 1998, she co-founded Lane Cove Residents for Reconciliation, one of the most successful local reconciliation groups in Australia, and in 2000 co-founded Northern Sydney Residents for Reconciliation Network, the first reconciliation network in Sydney; she serves as co-convenor of both. She received a* Sam Lewis Peace Award for Teachers *in 1986 and was nominated for a* Women '88 Award *in 1988; in 2003 she won Lane Cove Council's* Citizenship Award for Leadership; *she was co-recipient of a* National Reconciliation Award *in 2000 and of the* Northern Sydney Guringai Festival Award *in 2004. In 2010 she is featured in* Who's Who of Australian Women. *She co-produced* Children's Voices for Reconciliation *and* Journey of the Spirit, *the DVD story of the commemoration of Aboriginal resistance at Woodford Bay. Kerrie is a passionate advocate for reconciliation, Aboriginal rights and social justice.*

The work of the Council

During its ten-year term the Council undertook a comprehensive program of raising awareness of Indigenous history and issues through resources for educating the whole community—particularly through schools, community outreach programs and a public relations communication network that included journalists' camps. Resources included videos, a full-colour quarterly titled *Walking Together*, newsletters and education kits, all distributed widely. The Council commissioned research on the level of support for reconciliation and what the term meant for ordinary Australians. Just as importantly, it promoted and assisted the creation of grassroots reconciliation groups throughout Australia.

The Council's publications, covering all aspects of the reconciliation agenda, can be seen as an exercise in 'nation-building'. The newly formed Council was itself exploring meanings and key issues of reconciliation. One of its first publications was a set of monographs on eight key areas of reconciliation. Based on the premise of both cultures 'working together', these were designed to inform the public of the issues at hand. These eight key issues were (CAR, 1993):

1. *Understanding country*. The importance of land and sea in Aboriginal and Torres Strait Islander societies.
2. *Improving relationships*. Better relationships between Indigenous Australians and the wider community.
3. *Valuing cultures*. Recognising Indigenous cultures as a valued part of Australian heritage.
4. *Sharing histories*. A sense for all Australians of a shared ownership of their history.
5. *Addressing disadvantage*. A greater awareness of the causes of Indigenous Australians' disadvantage.
6. *Responding to custody levels*. A greater community response to addressing the underlying causes.
7. *Agreeing on a document*. Will the process of reconciliation be advanced by a document or documents of reconciliation?
8. *Controlling destinies*. Greater opportunities for Indigenous Australians to control their destinies.

The Council's education committee was responsible for the dissemination of information regarding education programs and literature. Apart from its efforts to raise awareness of reconciliation through the popular press, it produced the *Study Circles* kit, and the video resource kit *Around the Kitchen Table*, aimed at setting up reconciliation groups or circles throughout the Australian community to address the key issues. The Council's quarterly magazine, *Walking Together*, together with other resources such as the schools kit *Towards Reconciliation: Activities for Reconciliation Week* and the youth magazine *Streetwize*, was designed to educate students on the key areas for reconciliation and to provide teaching ideas for classroom use. Many of these resources ceased circulation with the end of the Council's term. A lack of dedicated resources towards reconciliation is one reason why Indigenous issues and reconciliation have not featured so prominently in mainstream education and community settings.

Council reports

In addition to its education resources and programs, the Council, as a government entity, produced annual and triennial reports, as well as strategic plans, all of which present the Council's work and provide an overview of its activities. These reports include *Together We Can't Lose* (CAR, 1994a), *Walking Together: The First Steps* (CAR, 1994b), *Weaving the Threads* (CAR, 1994c), and special reports on such issues as mining, *Exploring Common Ground* (CAR, 1993a) and *Native Title: Making Things Right* (CAR, 1993b). The Council's three strategic plans (for 1991–94, 1995–98 and 1998–2000) also provide insights into its work.

Reconciliation, Australia's Challenge was the Council's final report tabled in Federal Parliament in December 2000 (CAR, 2000e). In part, it documents the history of the Council's work since 1991, setting out its milestones and summarising social research into community attitudes to reconciliation (CAR, 2000c, pp. 31–3). It also sought to provide pointers for the future of reconciliation through a series of action-oriented recommendations, in the *Road Map for Reconciliation* (CAR 2000a).

> **A call to the nation**
>
> We, the participants at the convention, affirm to all the people of this nation: that reconciliation between Australia's Indigenous peoples and other Australians is central to the renewal of this national ethos of a fair go for all; and that until we achieve such reconciliation, this nation will remain diminished.
>
> We further declare that reconciliation and the renewal of the nation can be achieved only through a people's movement which obtains the commitment of Australians in all of their diversity to make reconciliation a living reality in their communities, workplaces, institutions, organisations and in all expressions of our common citizenship.
>
> This convention has been a profoundly moving experience for all of us privileged to take part, and has renewed the spirit and determination of all participants to carry on their work for reconciliation. The commitment and the spirit we have all witnessed here demonstrate that the principals and values of reconciliation have become embedded in the hearts and minds of many Australians.
>
> This convention has put reconciliation firmly in the centre of the national political agenda. Despite the airing of differences on the specific issues, the convention also witnesses some profoundly unifying statements from political and community leaders who all affirmed [their] support for reconciliation and found common ground in recognising some requirements of reconciliation. These included coming to terms with our intertwining histories, better human relationships, and the addressing of disadvantage.
>
> We note that leaders across the social spectrum expressed their own personal apologies and sorrow for the treatment of Indigenous peoples; this was itself an historical moment. We call on all parliaments, local governments, organisations and institutions to follow this lead with their own form of apology so that we can all move forward together to share responsibility for the future of this nation.
>
> We call on our fellow Australians to join together across this land to build a people's movement for reconciliation of sufficient breadth and power to guarantee that Australia can truly celebrate the centenary of its nationhood in 2001 confident that it has established a sound foundation for reconciliation.
>
> We commit ourselves to leave this gathering determined to work with all those prepared to join us in this movement. We call on all Australians not to stand on the sidelines but to demonstrate a commitment to reconciliation by becoming personally involved in reconciliation activities in their neighbourhood, their communities, and their workplace.
>
> This will ensure that Australia can walk together beyond the centenary of Federation into the next millennium towards this vision of:
>
> > A united Australia which respects this land of ours; values the Aboriginal and Torres Strait Islander heritage; and provides justice and equity for all.
> >
> > —National Reconciliation Convention, May 1997

The people's movement

From its inception, the Council understood the important role of communities at the grassroots level in the reconciliation process. In the words of Patrick Dodson:

> While I've spoken of reconciliation in national and sectoral terms, it's important not to lose sight of the fact that reconciliation is basically a grassroots process. It's about people living and working together, and solving problems in local communities. The Council has heard many stories about people working together to improve community relations. (Dodson, 1992, p. 3)

In the build-up to the Reconciliation Convention to be held in May 1997, the Council launched its *Renewal of the Nation* strategy to empower local communities to set up reconciliation networks. Over 100 meetings, involving more than 10 000 people, took place all around the country in the year prior to the Convention (CAR, 1997b, p. 2). A resource package was distributed to help facilitate the meetings. The aim was to discuss ways of advancing reconciliation in the local community. National surveys were conducted to ascertain what reconciliation meant to ordinary Australians.

The Reconciliation Convention

The Reconciliation Convention was held in May 1997. It was a gathering of almost two thousand people, including leaders of governments, prominent Indigenous and non-Indigenous leaders and supporters of reconciliation from all parts of Australia. One key event underlined the importance of the context of the gathering: the release of the Human Rights and Equal Opportunity Commission's *Bringing Them Home* report (HREOC, 1997) on the Stolen Generations. This was the trigger for the symbolic protest during the Prime Minister's opening address.

The silent protest organised by Aboriginal academic Pearl Wymarra was quickly taken up by many convention delegates, who turned their backs to Howard during his speech. His lectern-thumping performance in defence of his proposed native title legislation and his

Reconciliation Council Chair Patrick Dodson and then Prime Minister John Howard light candles for the first Reconciliation Week, 1996. In the Weekend Australian *that week, cartoonist Bill Leak showed Howard lighting Patrick Dodson's candle so that it blew up in his face; many people felt the Howard Government sabotaged reconciliation. Courtesy News Limited.*

refusal to make a public apology on behalf of the nation for past policies on the 'Stolen Generations' only heightened the tension of the debate (*Sydney Morning Herald*, 27 May 1997, p. 1). The Prime Minister's speech at the Convention further widened the gap between those who were passionate supporters of the reconciliation movement and those who sided with him on the nature of our history, native title and the 'Stolen Generations'.

Sustaining the movement for reconciliation

The people's movement intensified after the Reconciliation Convention in 1997. The Prime Minister's refusal to say sorry, the passions aroused by the High Court *Wik* native title decision, and the federal government's response proposing the ten-point Wik plan resulted in a polarisation of views. The ascent of Pauline Hanson's One Nation party added another divisive element, and reconciliation became much more adversarial. In this sense, reconciliation can be seen as not only a 'people's movement', but also as an 'instrument of struggle'—much like the South African struggle for justice. It is in this context that such terms as 'true', 'genuine' or 'substantive' reconciliation are used to denote the struggle for Indigenous rights.

Education is the key

Education is a vital part of achieving reconciliation in this country.

Many people think of education as schools and classrooms and formal instruction, but education for reconciliation needs to be much broader. It is about people and culture as much as it is about books and facts.

All Australians, from the oldest to the newest, need to know about Aboriginal Australia—for one simple, fundamental reason—*because this is Australia*. The nation needs to embrace its truth.

Lessons learnt by students percolate into the community. What we have to do is change the frame of reference of mainstream Australia, so that Indigenous people and Indigenous issues are no longer on the margins, or 'out of sight, out of mind', but part of the mainstream agenda, integral and intrinsic to public debate in this country. Teachers have a hugely important role in this. That is why teacher education is so critical. Teachers must be able to lead the way to a new understanding.

Born in Whitton, near Leeton in the Riverina, **Linda Burney** *was the first Aboriginal teacher graduate from Mitchell CAE. She began teaching at Mt Druitt, then worked with the Aboriginal Education Unit on the first Aboriginal Education Policy in Australia. She was President of the New South Wales AECG 1988–98, appointed to the Council for Aboriginal Reconciliation in 1994. She was Director General of the Department of Aboriginal Affairs, then was elected to Parliament in 2003, the first Aboriginal MP, then in 2007 first Aboriginal Minister. She is Minister for Community Services, lead Minister of Human Services portfolios and Minister for the State Plan. Among many honours, she was named as one of the 100 most influential Australians.*

'Linda Burney: A Decade of Change', cover of the 1998 farewell edition of the New South Wales AECG magazine Pemulwuy *edited by Dani Redmond. Photo: Sue Lindsay.*

Genocide is not the attempt to destroy an individual, genocide is the attempt to destroy a people, a culture. Listen to this, bear . . . in mind that the history of our laws and practices directed to assimilation testified to an intention to put an end to the Aboriginal race by removing their children in order to bring them up in white society. In many cases all knowledge of their Aboriginality was denied them, they were not allowed to have access to their family, or their language, or their land, or their culture, or their history.

—Sir Ronald Wilson, President, Human Rights Commission (Council for Aboriginal Reconciliation, 1997b, p. 36)

Although the activities of the reconciliation networks have been less widespread since 2000, the people's movement can be seen as the most successful aspect of the reconciliation process and the most durable, as it still operates with the assistance of the state-based reconciliation committees. The New South Wales Reconciliation Council is one example of a state government-funded body that is continuing to support local reconciliation activities. It is affiliated with over 100 groups throughout New South Wales from inner Sydney city groups and suburban networks to regional networks located as far west as Broken Hill, north to Coffs Harbour and the Tweed Valley and south to Albury and Bega. Their continued involvement in the reconciliation process is evidenced by the flurry of activity amongst local reconciliation groups after the announcement that the new Prime Minister, Kevin Rudd, was to say sorry at the opening of the new Parliament in February 2008. Many communities organised local events and commemorations for the historic national apology.

Reconciliation and the Stolen Generations

The tabling in Parliament in May 1997 of the *Bringing Them Home* report (HREOC, 1997) brought into focus the generations of Aboriginal children taken from their families as a result of deliberate government policies enacted during the protection and assimilationist eras. The report documented the personal stories of those removed and the history of the policies of Aboriginal child removal. The condemnation of this report by many on the conservative side of politics as factually flawed and not well researched inflamed the 'Culture Wars'. This is the name given to the great debates on aspects of Australia's history that pitched historians, politicians, media commentators, and academics against each other in heated debates about interpretations of our past; they have been occurring ever since 1993 when historian Geoffrey Blainey spoke of the 'black armband' view of Australian history (see Chapter 6).

One small but telling example of the emotional heat generated in the debate is the commentary by Paddy McGuinness in the *Herald* and as editor of *Quadrant*, the conservative literary magazine, who often wrote of the 'mawkish sentimentality' of 'politically correct' leftist views on Aboriginal issues and the 'myths' of the *Bringing Them Home* report, which he termed the 'Big Lie' (*Sydney Morning Herald*, 6 April 2000, p. 6). The attack on *Bringing Them Home*, according to Robert Manne (2001), was an example of how the right has sought to undermine key popular Indigenous issues in the community as part of the cultural wars on the meaning of Aboriginal dispossession and the nature of Australian history. The *Bringing Them Home* report presented Indigenous voices telling their own stories. Many conservative ears questioned its methodology and discredited it as unscholarly—yet it was the stories that caught the nation's imagination and influenced public opinion. These debates on the nature of Australia's past and how it is reflected in our history books in schools and universities have been ongoing ever since, with obvious ramifications for education at all levels.

Saying 'sorry'

The movement for saying 'sorry' was the follow-up to the tabling of the *Bringing them Home* report. Individuals could express this in thousands of 'Sorry Books', which were placed in libraries and other community spaces across the country in the lead-up to Reconciliation Week in 1998. Local government bodies and organisations held ceremonies and recorded expressions of sorrow on commemorative plaques or in documents. State governments documented their pledges of being 'sorry' on behalf of their states, though most were carefully worded to eliminate any hint of compensation.

There was heated and emotive debate between those who wanted the Prime Minister to make a collective apology on behalf of the nation and those who felt that there was no basis for an apology. In 1999, federal Parliament, at the instigation of newly elected Australian Democrats Senator Aden Ridgeway (who is Aboriginal), agreed to a motion which demonstrated the Parliament's commitment to the cause of reconciliation by expressing 'its deep and sincere regret that indigenous Australians suffered under the practices of past generations' (Ridgeway, cited in Grattan, 2000, p. 15). The concession made by Ridgeway in securing the motion was to allow the words 'sincere regret' rather than 'sorrow' in crucial parts of the motion.

The debate continued to be played out openly in the media. The concept of 'sorry' and 'sorry business' was often misunderstood and misrepresented by the popular press. Talkback radio relished the controversy, as did newspapers such as the *Sun-Herald* and *Daily Telegraph*, almost turning the debate into a farce. Mike Gibson of the *Daily Telegraph* wrote: 'I'm really sorry for so many things. Like chocolate double malteds ... I'm sorry that my uncles on my mother's side lost their hair.' (*Daily Telegraph*, 26 May 1998, p. 9). The same paper carried a Warren cartoon of Nazi-like 'thought police' waking you up in the middle of the night with a caption 'Wake Up—Time to Say Sorry' (*Daily Telegraph,* 26 May 1998, p. 10).

As a result of the backlash to the idea of saying 'sorry', the Sorry Day campaign was replaced with the 'Journey of Healing', and by mid-1999 the word 'sorry' had become so politicised and misunderstood that a change of heart by the Howard government was not possible. In contrast, the move to say sorry in 2008 was strongly supported by the print and visual media, though opposition was expressed in some online opinion columns and on talkback radio. This level of support was not forthcoming in 2000.

The declaration towards reconciliation

In the final year of the Council for Aboriginal Reconciliation's term, when the national reconciliation documents were handed to Prime Minister Howard in May 2000, the nation had not yet agreed on a formal document for reconciliation. What was handed to the Prime Minister was a 'Declaration *Towards* Reconciliation' (CAR, 2000c). Even that was not agreed. There had been much discussion and dispute about the wording of the Australian Declaration for Reconciliation. The words in dispute related to ownership of land and recognition of customary laws as well as any reference to an apology that the Prime Minister refused to make. The *Road Map for Reconciliation* document (CAR, 2000a) set out future national strategies towards reconciliation.

Reconciliation Australia

Reconciliation Australia was set up in 2000 to replace the Council for Aboriginal Reconciliation. It is an independent, not-for-profit organisation that was established with initial funding from the federal government. Its board is not government appointed and is made up of Indigenous and non-Indigenous people; however, its scale of operation is much reduced in comparison to the Council. It is reliant on community and corporate support for its programs. Its vision is similar to the body it replaced:

> An Australia that provides equal life chances for all, recognising and respecting the special place, culture and contribution of Aboriginal and Torres Strait Islander peoples as the First Australians (<http://www.reconciliation.org.au/home/about-ra>).

Its priority areas at its inception were to continue 'constructive discussion on all aspects of the Indigenous rights agenda and the approach to a treaty and/or agreements and providing leadership for the people's movement' (<www.reconciliation.org.au/home/about-ra>).

Reconciliation Australia has sought to foster the people's movement through initiatives to:

- foster good relations and work closely with the various State Reconciliation Committees;
- support the continuation of National Reconciliation Week;
- partner with education organisations in each state to: (a) support school curricula in their treatment of Indigenous issues and their contribution to a shared understanding of our history; and (b) empower communities to advance reconciliation in the areas of education and Indigenous employment by developing resources and role models to meet those needs; and
- develop a reconciliation awards scheme which both identifies best practice and ensures recognition of the efforts of communities and individuals who achieve real outcomes for reconciliation (Reconciliation Australia, 2001, p. 2).

Reconciliation Australia also offers a variety of resources online and provides web-based interactive discussions on reconciliation. It has introduced a number of innovative programs with schools and with the corporate sector. Corporate sponsorship of reconciliation was a key initiative for Reconciliation Australia. It has secured the support of major companies such as BHP Billiton in its Indigenous community capacity-building programs. The company has supported the Good Indigenous Governance program since 2002 (<www.reconciliation.org.au/igawards>). Other supporters of Reconciliation Australia's work include the Australian Football League (AFL), Qantas, the National Australia Bank, and other smaller organisations that provide pro bono work and in-kind support.

In 2006, Reconciliation Australia launched its Reconciliation Action Plan (RAP) program (<www.reconciliation.org.au/home/reconciliation-action-plans>), designed to help organisations build positive relationships between Indigenous and non-Indigenous people in their workplaces and beyond. The RAP should fit within an organisation's strategic plan to identify clear actions and targets to address Indigenous disadvantage in the community as part of a company's corporate governance responsibilities. Companies that have signed up to RAP include BHP Billiton, the ANZ Bank, Centrelink, Oxfam Australia, and major local government bodies such as the Melbourne City Council.

Developing a school RAP is one way to progress reconciliation within the education sector. Reconciliation Australia is supporting schools in their development of action plans by providing resources and a template for schools to design their own. Many schools have made a serious commitment to reconciliation and have reconciliation statements in place. The plan is a way of making that commitment a reality. It is meant to be a straightforward plan of activities based on 'building good relationships; respecting the special contribution of Aboriginal and Torres Strait Islander peoples to Australia; and working together to ensure Indigenous children have the same life opportunities as other children in this prosperous country' (Reconciliation Australia, <www.reconciliation.org.au>).

Defining reconciliation

Reconciliation is not easy to define. It is problematic because it is defined in very different terms by a variety of individuals and groups, as it is often linked to their social and political orientation. The Council's research (Sweeney and Associates, 1996; Newspoll, 2000) illustrated that, on the whole, Indigenous Australians were more united than the mainstream community regarding what reconciliation meant. Politicians, policy-makers, church groups, political lobbyists, the media, academics and many ordinary citizens have had different perspectives on what constitutes reconciliation. Terms such as 'practical' reconciliation; 'symbolic' reconciliation; 'genuine' reconciliation; 'true' reconciliation; 'substantive' reconciliation; 'soft' reconciliation; and 'hard' reconciliation were and are used to help in finding meanings for reconciliation. There has been a high level of rhetoric in much of what has been spoken and written about the reconciliation process. Many of the questions that arose related to the extent of support for the 'hard/substantive' issues of reconciliation, such as a 'treaty' and just compensation for past injustices as opposed to the 'soft', more symbolic type of reconciliation (see Table 8.1). Increasingly, the Howard government, with support from some Indigenous leaders and community members, gave credence to 'practical' reconciliation as a viable alternative.

'Hard', 'genuine', 'true' or 'substantive' reconciliation refers to the call by many Indigenous leaders for recognition of the unique rights Indigenous people possess that have to do with native title, customary law, the right to just compensation for past acts of dispossession and a 'treaty' between Indigenous and non-Indigenous Australians. 'Symbolic' reconciliation is the most popular amongst mainstream Australians. The symbols of reconciliation are seen as non-adversarial. At times, symbolic acts may be interpreted as superficial or tokenistic although they are seen as essential elements of the journey to a more substantive reconciliation. The rhetoric of reconciliation refers to all the political speeches and policies, the exaggerated claims and the heightened aspirations that are not followed up by authentic actions. At the more conservative end of the reconciliation spectrum can be found former Prime Minister Howard's 'practical' reconciliation—referring to the programs and strategies designed to correct the level of social and economic disadvantage in health, housing and education faced by Indigenous communities throughout the nation.

Table 8.1 Reconciliation Typologies

Hard	Soft	Assimilationist
Substantive, 'genuine' or 'true'	*Symbolic—Rhetorical*	*Normative—Practical*
• 'Treaty'/sovereignty	• Ceremonies	• Standard health
• Compensation	• Marches	• Housing
• Land/sea rights	• Gatherings, celebrations	• Education
• First nations people	• Aspirational	• All one nation

To the more conservative elements in mainstream Australia, reconciliation is about equality and assimilation rather than Aboriginal peoples possessing distinct political and cultural rights. In this mode, reconciliation affirms the status quo. Its aspiration is to see Aboriginal people adopt mainstream cultural values and lifestyles. This focus is seen as part of an assimilationist agenda that does not allow for the rights of Indigenous peoples to be recognised. In the words of Professor Mick Dodson, responding to Prime Minister Howard's speech espousing practical reconciliation at Corroboree 2000:

> Don't be distracted by notions of practical Reconciliation, because they mean practically nothing. Now although issues of health, housing and education of Indigenous Australians are of course of key concern to us as a nation, they are not issues that are at the very heart or the very soul of Reconciliation. But they are, to put it quite simply and plainly, the entitlements every Australian should enjoy... Reconciliation is about deeper things, to do with nation, soul and spirit. Reconciliation is about the blood and flesh of the lives we must lead together, and not the nuts and bolts of the entitlements as citizens we should enjoy. (Dodson, 2000)

At one end of the debate, it is said that 'hard' or 'substantive' reconciliation must involve the acceptance of a treaty, a bill of rights, just compensation and a social justice package that clearly addresses Indigenous disadvantage. 'Soft' reconciliation encompasses the 'feel good' symbolic elements such as the public events and ceremonies of reconciliation. Within the community, for example, symbolic victories by Indigenous athletes or Indigenous artists can help to publicise the cause of reconciliation in a lateral way—by heightening awareness of Indigenous people and Indigenous talent. When

Cartoon by Bruce Petty, The Age, *11 February 1985, the year of Victoria's 150-year celebrations. Crowds celebrate on the left and Aboriginal people sit down on the right. Courtesy Bruce Petty.*

Bridgewalk photo by slide-show storyteller William Yang. Whitefella walkers carrying a huge Aboriginal-hands banner onto the Harbour Bridge. One of a number of photos of the bridgewalk used in Yang's shows, and typical of the support of many artists for Aboriginal causes. Courtesy the artist.

Cathy Freeman lit the Olympic flame and won the 400 metres final at the Sydney Olympic Games in September 2000, it was a 'triumph' for reconciliation. Anne Summers claimed in the *Sydney Morning Herald* that the choice of Cathy Freeman to light the Olympic cauldron 'redefined Australia to the rest of the world' (Summers, 2000, p. 12).

The varying interpretations of meanings of reconciliation were evident in the Sydney Bridge Walk 2000, when well over 250 000 people walked across the Harbour Bridge. Again, it was hailed as a great triumph for reconciliation. Capitalising on the huge crowd, many Aboriginal leaders saw the walk as a mandate for a treaty. Interestingly, the mainstream media had a different perspective, as a subsequent editorial in *The Australian* stated: 'ATSIC Chairman Geoff Clark used the Sydney Harbour walk to claim a mandate for a treaty. He was wrong. People walked for reconciliation.' (Editorial, *The Australian*, 8 December 2000, p. 12) To many, walking for reconciliation was different from walking for a treaty. Herein lies the deep paradox of reconciliation. If reconciliation is not about a treaty—with all of its concomitant repercussions (compensation, social justice, a charter of rights, land rights)—then can it be called substantive or authentic? In essence, mainstream Australia needs to address the question of whether reconciliation is merely to be a symbolic expression of nationhood or whether there are more complex realities to be faced as a nation before Indigenous and non-Indigenous Australians are truly reconciled.

Inquiry into the progress towards reconciliation

In response to the lack of progress towards reconciliation after Corroboree 2000, in August 2002, the Senate initiated an inquiry into the 'progress towards national Reconciliation, including an examination of the adequacy and effectiveness of the Commonwealth Government's response to, and implementation of, the recommendations contained ... [in the Council's report]' (Parliament of Australia, 2002, p. 1). A significant proportion of the submissions to the inquiry highlighted lack of progress (ATSIC, 2003; Centre for Public Law, 2002; Cull, 2002; Edmund Rice Centre, 2002; National Assembly of the Uniting Church, 2002). The federal government defended its response by noting that it was committed to 'practical' reconciliation rather than a rights-based agenda:

> The Government's key objective is to provide Indigenous people with access to social and economic opportunities ... the challenge of ensuring that Indigenous peoples are able to effectively access their basic citizenship rights is one that faces all governments. It is the litmus test of reconciliation. (Ruddock, 2002, p. 2)

Yet research on the government's focus on 'practical' reconciliation illustrated that progress was slow. According to Altman and Hunter (2003), in a discussion paper from the Centre for Aboriginal Economic Policy Research discussing the socio-economic variables on which the assessments census data were based:

> In the period 1991–2001, there was relative improvement in five variables, and a relative decline in five variables. Of particular concern was relative decline over the period in educational and health status. In terms of reconciliation, if this is interpreted in relative and 'practical' socio-economic terms, there is less reconciliation in 2001 than in 1996. (Altman and Hunter, 2003, p. 11)

The frustration at the lack of progress and ambiguities of reconciliation are exemplified by the following quote from an Indigenous person to the Senate Committee:

> What is Reconciliation? Nothing much has changed in Gove where I live. Reconciliation is a big whitefella word. What does it mean? People ask me that and I don't know what to say. I was on Sydney Harbour Bridge when everybody walked across the bridge and they did that for 'reconciliation'. I been grown up in the bush and I know our law. Our law never changes ... I don't understand your law. It always changes. The only thing that stays the same for the white man is that he never listens to our law and our kids keep getting locked up with that mandatory sentencing. I don't understand your reconciliation. (Commonwealth of Australia, 2003, p. 14)

Animations from The Dreaming *series produced by Aboriginal Nations using Aboriginal animators were featured on Australia Post stamps in 1997. National Philatelic Collection. Courtesy Australia Post.*

In its submission to the Senate Inquiry, Reconciliation Australia (2002) expressed its concern about the redefinition of reconciliation, 'narrowing it to the delivery of citizenship rights' (2002, p. 2), and about the lack of progress on many issues. It further noted:

> The Committee will be aware that a statement often heard is that 'reconciliation is off the agenda'. At the heart of this comment is a recognition that reconciliation resources are no longer visible and a belief that the current federal government is not committed to the reconciliation process.
>
> It is certainly true that the federal government has abrogated its leadership role in the broader reconciliation agenda and substituted a focus on practical reconciliation. This emphasis on practical reconciliation has limited the reconciliation process developed by the Council for Aboriginal Reconciliation. It is also true that sufficient resources are no longer available to allow wide community communication and education. (Reconciliation Australia, 2002, p. 2)

In the years that followed the inquiry, the focus on reconciliation continued to wane, as did media interest—which was limited to reporting events such as Reconciliation and NAIDOC Weeks, mostly in local, community-based newspapers rather than established national media. Well-known activists within the reconciliation movement categorically state that the agenda for reconciliation was sidelined by the conservative Howard government from 1996 to 2007: 'Howard stopped the bi-partisanship model . . . and withdrew from Reconciliation. It showed a fundamental lack of understanding of the spiritual connections of Aboriginal lives . . . This is not an age of symbols and matters of the heart and spirit.' (Glendenning, 2006, personal communication)

Observational evidence through the work of Reconciliation Australia and the state Reconciliation Councils suggests that local community reconciliation groups are still active; however, without empirical research, it is impossible to gauge the extent of their activities or the extent of community engagement with reconciliation. As noted earlier, Reconciliation Australia is fostering discussion on reconciliation through its well-resourced online interactive website that details its activities and provides discussion boards and blog pages that allow for community views to be expressed.

Youth and reconciliation

Youth have been involved in the reconciliation movement, either through their local or school networks. One excellent example of this is Kormilda College in the Northern Territory, which instigated a Youth Reconciliation Convention that first met in June 1997, involving youth from Darwin. The impetus for this conference came from youth. As Year 11 student at Kormilda, Sonia Hunt, said: 'Young people should stand up and talk to adults, so that they can understand how we feel and what we think before deciding our future.' (Hunt, 1997, p. 4) The following year, the conference involved youth from around the nation. Titled 'Forum for the Future', this confrence produced a Youth Charter, which was presented to Indigenous leaders and the Governor-General. Church groups and state Reconciliation Councils have continued to support the involvement of youth in reconciliation.

Another youth organisation is the ReconciliACTION Network, a volunteer network started in 2002, which comprises Indigenous and non-Indigenous young people who have an interest in reconciliation and Indigenous rights issues and those who are active in their communities. It has branches in New South Wales, the Australian Capital Territory and Victoria. In 2005, it organised a re-enactment of the 1965 Freedom Ride and has been instrumental in organising forums and seminars on reconciliation.

May understanding and reconciliation grow with this tree

A eucalypt native to western Sydney was planted at Werrington North campus' Frogmore House on Sorry Day 26 May 1998 by the University of Western Sydney, with the plaque: 'May understanding and reconciliation grow with this tree'. In a special ceremony, UWS issued a Statement of Reconciliation:

> The University of Western Sydney embraces the vision statement of the Council for Aboriginal Reconciliation: 'A united Australia which respects this land of ours, values the Aboriginal and Torres Strait Islander heritage, and provides justice and equity for all'. The University of Western Sydney therefore seeks to respond and be part of the wish of the vast majority of Australians to participate in the creation of a confident and harmonious nation where:
> - we acknowledge Aboriginal and Torres Strait Islander people as the original inhabitants of this continent and we recognise their loss of land, children, languages, health, and kin;
> - we believe that Australia will only become a mature nation if the past is acknowledged, the present understood, and the future confidently based on the co-existence of rights.

Ten years later, on 13 February 2008, in common with education sites and many workplaces across the country, UWS held a special gathering at Frogmore House to celebrate the event so many people had wanted so long, the national Apology day. The apology was screened in all the university's libraries, and broadcast on radio and TV across all campuses.

Vice Chancellor Professor Janice Reid says the tree symbolises the strength of the UWS commitment to practical reconciliation and to a future built on a recognition of the immense suffering of many Indigenous people. She says the university's conviction is that we, as a nation, must do better:

> As others have said, we are diminished by the poverty and ill-health of Indigenous communities. We are now uplifted by the national bipartisan apology for the suffering of Indigenous families. The spirit the apology has engendered opens up at last the prospect of a fair and just future for Indigenous Australians.

The future for reconciliation

The journey to a resolution of non-Aboriginal Australia's troubled relationship with its Indigenous peoples and their rights has been convoluted and complex. After many years of neglect, the process of reconciling black and white Australians has been placed firmly on the federal government's agenda after the national apology of February 2008. However, the process still remains the 'unfinished business' of the Australian social and political landscape, and while much has been made of the symbolic gesture of a national apology, the test will be how governments, and communities at all levels, address the level of disadvantage faced by many Indigenous Australians on so many of our social indicators. For an example that pinpoints the complexities involved in addressing Indigenous disadvantage, one needs to look no further than the Howard federal government's intervention in the Northern Territory in June 2007, in response to the *Little Children are Sacred* report (Wild and Anderson, 2007) on the high levels of child sexual abuse in remote Indigenous communities. The methods employed in this landmark action again polarised black and white Australians. Aboriginal supporters of the government's actions, such as Dr Sue Gordon, head of the Australian government's National Indigenous Council (which replaced ATSIC in 2004) and Noel Pearson from Cape York, emphasised the need for emergency actions. Those who opposed the intervention highlighted the government's lack of consultation with Aboriginal leaders, the removal of the permit system restricting entry to Aboriginal lands and the suspension of the nation's anti-discrimination laws in order to carry out their actions. Suspicion at the motives behind the intervention occurred because of the lack of trust of government authorities—particularly in the Howard government years—and their intentions. How future governments consult Indigenous stakeholders, and incorporate them into the decision-making processes that impact on local communities, will be a testing point for the success of reconciliation in the future.

A change of heart? 'New' reconciliation

Former Prime Minister John Howard, in a move which surprised many, in October 2007 in the lead-up to the federal election made a commitment to a 'new' form of reconciliation with Indigenous peoples. He accepted the blame for the 'dwindling of relationships' between himself and Indigenous leaders, and promised a referendum on amending the preamble to the constitution to recognise Indigenous peoples. He described the new reconciliation as a topic of national importance 'that goes to the heart of our national and shared destiny' (quoted in Shanahan, 2007). However, Mr Howard ruled out a national apology for past acts of dispossession and a treaty, because this implied 'that in some way we are dealing with two separate nations'. He claimed that Australia was 'one great tribe; one Australia'. The reaction from the Aboriginal community varied from a high level of cynicism at the timing of the announcement to a welcomed change—at least reconciliation was back on the national agenda.

A national apology

The national apology to Australia's Aboriginal and Torres Strait Islander peoples was an event that captured the nation's imagination at the opening of the 42nd Parliament in Canberra on 13 February 2008. Members of the Stolen Generations were invited to the nation's capital to witness the event. Screens were erected outside the Parliament to accommodate the thousands of people who gathered to watch the proceedings. These gatherings of like-minded Indigenous and non-Indigenous Australians occurred in many communities throughout the nation. They took place in schools, parks, local government halls, lecture rooms and even corporate boardrooms. The apology had cross-party support from the Parliament, although five members of the Liberal-National opposition absented themselves from the chamber. The Prime Minister's words emphasised the hurt and sorrow of past policies:

> We apologise for the laws and policies of successive parliaments and governments that have inflicted profound grief, suffering and loss on these our fellow Australians.

> **Sincere reconciliation**
>
> Sincere reconciliation is more than just shaking hands with 2 per cent of the population and saying: 'Forget the past. We know it was wrong. Let's be friends, It won't happen again.' Sorry about that! Sincere reconciliation is acknowledging the past inferior social policies of special treatment and how they still affect Indigenous society today. It means addressing the levels of disadvantage still faced by so many Indigenous peoples. It means totally eradicating all forms of racism in Australia, so that people in this country who are supposedly different from the 'norm' can maintain their differences without being penalised for them. Sincere reconciliation is all Australian people sharing in all the positive social, economic, political and cultural arenas of this country and saying, 'We are all Australians' are we not? At the same time, sincere reconciliation must involve acceptance of the special place of Australia's Indigenous peoples as the real custodians of this land. Sincere reconciliation also means an appropriate social justice package negotiated with Indigenous peoples. It involves not tolerating the fourth world conditions in which some Indigenous people are forced to live.
>
> —James Wilson Miller

> We apologise especially for the removal of Aboriginal and Torres Strait Islander children from their families, their communities and their country. For the pain, suffering and hurt of these Stolen Generations, their descendants and for their families left behind, we say sorry. To the mothers and the fathers, the brothers and the sisters, for the breaking up of families and communities, we say sorry. And for the indignity and degradation thus inflicted on a proud people and a proud culture, we say sorry.

> We the parliament of Australia respectfully request that this apology be received in the spirit in which it is offered as part of the healing of the nation.

> For the future we take heart; resolving that this new page in the history of our great continent can now be written.

> We today take this first step by acknowledging the past and laying claim to a future that embraces all Australians. (<www.smh.com.au/news/national/kevin-rudds-sorry-speech/2008>, accessed 29 August 2009)

The apology resonated with a renewed spirit of unity amongst many Australians. While some disagreed and aired their disapproval on talk-back radio, the majority of people agreed that it was a positive action. In reality, however, the years following the national apology will be crucial in the reconciliation process. What many Aboriginal and Torres Strait Islander people call the 'unfinished business' of reconciliation (i.e. those 'hard' issues of treaty, compensation, self-determination, and first nations rights) still remains at the crux of the dispute about what constitutes reconciliation. Whether this 'unfinished business' is incorporated into the national discourse of reconciliation will depend on good leadership and campaigns to educate the nation about what this involves. Then, as in previous debates, it will be a case of what form of reconciliation the nation wants.

The role of education

The Council for Aboriginal Reconciliation placed great emphasis on education as the pivotal point of the campaigns for reconciliation. The premise that education is the key in managing the relationships between black and white Australians, and in securing a better future for Indigenous people, still has currency. Valuing Aboriginal history and culture and engaging in culturally appropriate ways of working with Indigenous communities and Indigenous students in schools are vital.

Education is an essential pathway to bridging the divide in educational attainment between Aboriginal and non-Aboriginal students. Research on best practice models (see Chapters 11 and 12) for teaching Indigenous students points to the level of teachers' commitment as the crucial link to student engagement in the classroom, improvement of students' self-concept and student retention rates at school. One other aspect of good practice is applying culturally appropriate methods of working with Aboriginal people (see Chapter 10). There is also a large body of research that points to the fact that good teachers and good teaching matter (Rowe, 2002; 2006; Craven, 2005; Hattie, 2003; also see Chapter 11). This is particularly important when teaching Indigenous students.

Research conducted in schools where reconciliation forms part of the school program (Burridge, 2003) has identified a set of characteristics common to schools which are supportive of reconciliation. Most schools display a combination of some of the following:

- a positive history—a sense of shared history between the Aboriginal community and the non-Aboriginal community within the locality of the school (in communities where there has been a history of divisiveness between Aboriginal and non-Aboriginal people and even between different Aboriginal groups, there is less of a spirit to come together);
- at least one key figure in the school who organises the program and has the leadership qualities to set up mechanisms (such as a committee) to follow through with a program of activities, to write curriculum programs and to initiate contact with Aboriginal communities;
- a supportive Aboriginal community, including leading Elders, who are willing to become involved in school activities and to urge the school executive into action;
- a supportive principal and school executive team—for funding assistance, for general support and morale, to encourage staff to get involved and to implement staff development policies;
- quality resources that focus on reconciliation as a theme;

Cathy Freeman featured in a Nike ad which was mounted on the side of the MSB building, Kent Street, Sydney, 2000. Cathy captured the public imagination while competing for Australia at the Sydney 2000 Olympics. A water policeman said the roar of sound coming across Homebush Bay when she won the 400 metres was like nothing he had ever heard. It was said that Cathy Freeman did more to bring all Australians together than any politician. Courtesy Nike Australia.

'Build bridges between you and us'

Reverend Roy Wotton is 96 not out. During World War II, he was an Army chaplain in New Guinea, serving on the Kokoda Track. Reverend Wotton was always up with the troops in the front line, and was one of the few chaplains to be awarded the Combat Medal.

Reverend Roy Wotton holding a photo of Stewart Murray in Army uniform in World War II. Photo: Larry McGrath.

In 2005, Reverend Wotton was one of eight veterans who spoke to camera for Larry McGrath's personal and powerful film *Remembrance: A Farewell to a Generation Now Passing into History* (available from New South Wales History Teachers Association). Among other memories, he spoke with feeling of a spiritual relationship with an Aboriginal digger:

> I had a wonderful experience during the war when I became friends with an Aboriginal named Stewart Murray. Stewart always insisted on helping me with the burial parties. You could say this was where religion comes into it, he was Church of Christ, but that wasn't it. Aboriginal instincts . . . the affinity he had with his dead mates, he had that spiritual power I didn't have. And the idea of 'the ground'—this was like putting them to bed with mother. This concept they had of the earth—'mother earth'.
>
> He always volunteered and didn't let me do the dirty work, and when a bloke was killed and had been out in the tropical sun for a week, you could imagine it wasn't very nice . . . and he always did that work for me.
>
> One day while we were burying a bloke I turned to him and said, 'Stewart, what are you going to do when this is all over?' And he said: 'I'm going to build bridges between you and us.'
>
> He was the best forward scout in the battalion. Any bloke who took on that job in the jungle was 'mad'. Imagine a patrol going through the jungle looking for the enemy and then bring back information about the enemy. He was far and away the best forward scout I ever saw.

Reverend Wotton also remembers Stewart Murray's platoon leader saying he had 'natural leadership skills'; other officers said the same. Stewart himself told Reverend Wotton the army was the first time he ever felt equal to anyone and part of society. Stewart Murray's leadership was demonstrated over and again through his life after the war. He was Aboriginal Father of the Year in 1969, the second Aboriginal JP after Sir Douglas Nicholls, and was honoured with an OAM. He died in 1989, survived by his wife Nora, daughter of Sir Doug Nicholls, and their children Diane, Stephen, Gary, Brian, Margaret (d.), Wayne, Beverly and Gregory.

Reverend Wotton and Stewart Murray remained in each other's thoughts, one in Sydney, as Rector of St Johns at Gordon, the other in Melbourne, working to build the bridges. In the early 1970s, Stewart had formed an Aboriginal tradesmen's company and won a contract for work on the Ballarat RSL. But when the men turned up for work with an Aboriginal flag, they were ordered off the job and the contract was cancelled. The story went public and Stewart rang Reverend Wotton in Sydney. Reverend Wotton intervened on their behalf, and the fight was won eventually. Later Reverend Wotton and Stewart Murray marched together for Anzac Day.

In 2007, in failing health, Reverend Wotton travelled to Melbourne to meet Stewart Murray's widow Nora and their family, and be with them at the historic unveiling of a bronze statue of Sir Douglas and Lady Gladys Nicholls at Parliament Gardens near the Victorian Parliament, the first ever statue of Aboriginal citizens in Victoria. Their meeting and the ceremony of unveiling the statue were filmed for Foxtel, and this was a TV story for the History Channel.

> *Stewart Murray JP, OAM* was born at Lake Boga, a member of the Wamba Wamba, Baraparapa, Wiradjeri, Yorta Yorta and Dhuhduroa Nations. He enlisted in December 1941, at the height of the Japanese invasion scare—which may have been why, as he recalled, the recruiting officer did not look to see who he was or what colour and didn't seem to care. He told his son that once he was in uniform he felt good, better than in civilian clothes; other soldiers couldn't believe that Aboriginal people had to live on reserves and missions and were not allowed to drink in hotels. But when he applied for soldier settler grants in New South Wales and Victoria, he was knocked back.
>
> He was a leader in the Aborigines Advancement League, the National Tribal Council, the Dandenong Aboriginal Cooperative and the Victorian Aboriginal Land Council, as well as helping to establish legal services and housing co-ops. He was one of the people who used to make sure there was legal representation for Aboriginal prisoners in the Fitzroy lock-up and for members of the Stolen Generations. In 1982 he was a leader in claiming the closed Collingwood tip, which was part of the 1830s Merri Creek Aboriginal reserve, and another 27 acres at Clifton Hill. In the same year, he was appointed a Justice of the Peace. He also claimed the MCG to publicise the dispossession of his people of their lands and waters.
>
> His son Gary Murray was inaugural Executive Officer of the Victorian Aboriginal Education Consultative Group, then ran the Lake Condah Aboriginal Cooperative. He was a founding member of Camp Jungai Co-op, and coordinated the operations of the Murray River Regional Aboriginal Land Council then the Moama Local Aboriginal Land Council. He was a leader in the movement for the return of Aboriginal remains and cultural materials from museums, involved directly in a range of Murray River Traditional Owner Groups' native title negotiations including the sign-off of agreements with explorers, miners and land proponents. He has facilitated an Aboriginal astronomy exhibition at the Melbourne Planetarium and is working on a book, exhibition and website on his parents' life and times.

- cooperative staff who are inclusive and who value cultural differences, foster those values amongst students and show willingness to utilise the symbols of reconciliation in the classroom;
- a supportive student body with a number of key student leaders who are willing to speak out for reconciliation and initiate and organise student involvement in projects;
- a generally supportive parent body, including a few key parents who have influence in the local school community and are committed to reconciliation as a policy; and
- a belief amongst a significant portion of the school community that the policy of reconciliation embodies the principles of a fair and just society for all Australians to enjoy.

Summary: Learning from the past, educating for the future

This chapter has provided insights into the nation's approach to reconciliation and education's role in raising awareness of it in schools and in the wider community. A key premise underpinning the content of this chapter is that in reflecting on the past we can construct a better way to negotiate the future. There are plentiful resources to assist teachers to be effective in the classroom (see Chapter 14). Australia as a nation would benefit from engaging in the dialogue of reconciliation and confronting the issues raised in a genuine negotiated reconciliation process with Indigenous Australians. Schools and teachers have a critical role to play in advancing this process.

United We Win

The glare of a thousand years is shed on the black man's wistful face,
Fringe-dwellers now on the edge of towns, one of a dying race;
But he has no bitterness in his heart for the white man just the same;
He knows he has white friends today, he knows they are not to blame.
Curse no more the nation's great, the glorious pioneers,
Murders honoured with fame and wealth, won of our blood and tears;
Brood no more on the bloody past that is gone without regret,
But look to the light of happier days that will shine for your children yet.
For in spite of public apathy and the segregation pack
There is mateship now, and the good white hand stretched out to grip the black.
He knows there are white friends here today who will help us fight the past,
Till a world of workers from shore to shore as equals live at last.

—Oodgeroo Noonuccal (2008, p. 72)

Educating for the future

Rhonda Craven

Photo: Vicki Barton

The theme of reconciliation permeates this text, as educating for a better future involves two critical elements: teaching all Australians to understand, respect and appreciate Indigenous history and culture; and effectively teaching Indigenous students so that they attain educational and life outcomes commensurate to their non-Indigenous peers. This chapter aims to assist teachers to educate for the future by presenting an overview of: (1) the Australian Reconciliation Barometer research project (Reconciliation Australia, 2009), which examined the nature of the relationship between Indigenous and other Australians and has identified areas for improvement which have important implications for education; (2) why the role of teachers in the reconciliation process is vital; (3) some useful teaching strategies; (4) some useful teaching resources from Reconciliation Australia; and (5) some example strategies for promoting reconciliation.

The Australian Reconciliation Barometer

The Barometer is a national research study that looks at the relationship between Indigenous people and other Australians conducted for Reconciliation Australia by Auspoll. The Barometer explores how we see each other, how we feel about each other, how our perceptions affect progress towards reconciliation and closing the gaps, and where we aspire to be as Australians. The first study was completed in September 2008. It involved 1007 Australians and is designed to be repeated every two years. To read the full Barometer and details of how the research was done, go to <www.reconciliation.org.au>.

The Barometer recognises that attitudes and behaviour towards reconciliation will require changes in four core areas:

No Excuses

Before they even come inside the school gate, teachers of Aboriginal children—and all children—must have a working knowledge of the true history of this country. They must know and appreciate this land is long settled—for tens of thousands of years—occupied very well and in harmony. Teachers need to have a knowledge of the map of Aboriginal Australia—not six states and two territories, but hundreds of countries. They need to appreciate how diverse Aboriginal Australia was, and still is.

New teachers, all teachers, need to be able to integrate Aboriginal perspectives in all their teaching. They need to know about the Stolen Generations and understand how this has affected Aboriginal families down the generations—because, as one woman says in the *Bringing Them Home* video, 'We're family people. We're family people.'

Teachers need to understand how traditional Aboriginal life was about looking after country and Koori people now still have a family connection with the land. They need to know and be able to teach that there was no such thing as a fence in Aboriginal Australia—only landmarks to read the country.

When teachers take students to the War Memorial in Canberra, they must be able to teach that Aboriginal men, and women, have fought for their country in Australia's wars—even when they were officially barred from the armed forces—but never got the benefit of soldier settlement land grants like others. High school teachers will need to be able to teach about social justice, deaths in custody and the Royal Commission and combating racism.

On Clean Up Australia Day, teachers must be able to teach children that there was no 'Clean Up Australia' in Aboriginal times—because there was no rubbish. People didn't rubbish Australia then, only now. Finally, teachers need to understand and teach how well Aboriginal land management worked. The Australia that the 'first settlers' found was a paradise, spoken of as a 'Garden of Eden'— you could see the yabbies on the bottom of the Hawkesbury River in the early days.

Aunty Ruth Simms grew up at La Perouse, being taught all about country by her family. A Yuin woman, she has been involved in education for over 30 years, and a member of the New South Wales AECG since its first South Coast meeting at Huskisson in 1978. She served many years as Regional Rep for Upper South Coast and served on the AECG executive. She represented the AECG on the Teaching the Teachers steering committee. She has attended all World Indigenous People's Conferences: Education (WIPCE) since 1987. Known across the state as Aunty Ruth, she is treasured as one of the rocks of the AECG, a grass-roots person who speaks her mind straight-out and lives by cultural principles. She has worked for Koori students, and all students, for more than a generation at Nowra Public School and now looks after the children of her former students.

---

1. *Awareness:* What do people know about the facts of Aboriginal and Torres Strait Islander life and history?
2. *Attitudes:* What are the opinions and beliefs that Indigenous and non-Indigenous people hold about each other and our relationship?
3. *Perceptions:* What are the cultural stereotypes and preconceptions the general public holds in relation to Indigenous people and vice versa?
4. *Action:* What are people prepared to do to bring about an improvement in the relationship between Indigenous and non-Indigenous Australians?

(Reconciliation Australia, 2009, p. 2)

Awareness

Figure 9.1 summarises the results of the Barometer in relation to awareness of the facts in 2008. There is a substantial gap in the perceived level of knowledge about Indigenous culture and history. A total of 88 per cent of the Indigenous respondents believed they had a good knowledge of their own history, while only 35 per cent of the non-Indigenous sample agreed. Similarly, 90 per cent of the Indigenous respondents compared with 43 per cent of the non-Indigenous respondents reported that they had a good knowledge of Indigenous

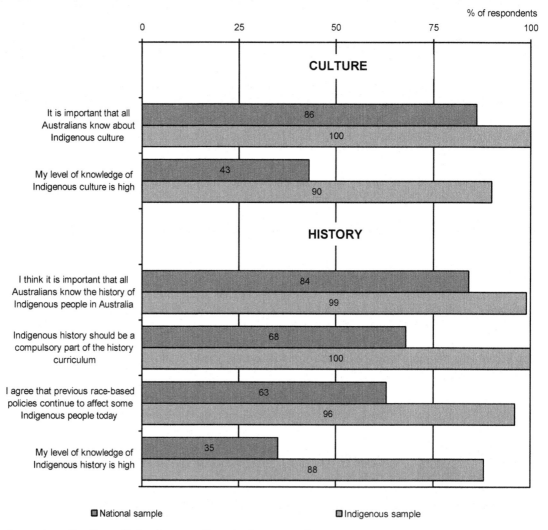

Figure 9.1 Awareness Indicators

Source: Australian Reconciliation Barometer Executive Summary p. 9

culture. This gap exists despite the fact that Indigenous and non-Indigenous respondents agree that it is important that all Australians know about Indigenous history and culture, and that Indigenous history should form part of the school curriculum. Clearly, we as teachers have a lot of work to do in classrooms to rectify these issues.

Attitudes

Figure 9.2 summarises the Barometer 2008 results in relation to attitudes. These results suggest that, although Indigenous and non-Indigenous respondents agree that the relationship between Indigenous and non-Indigenous Australians is important to Australia, 59 per cent of non-Indigenous respondents compared with 92 per cent of Indigenous respondents believe Indigenous people hold a special place as the first Australians. These results suggest that misconceptions and stereotypes about Indigenous Australia (see Chapter 3) need to be addressed.

Only about half of Indigenous and non-Indigenous respondents agree that either the relationship between Indigenous and other Australians today is good or that the relationship is improving (see Figure 9.2). The results relating to trust (see Figure 9.2) are of concern, with low agreement on items about trust of

EDUCATING FOR THE FUTURE • 175

Figure 9.2 Attitude indicators

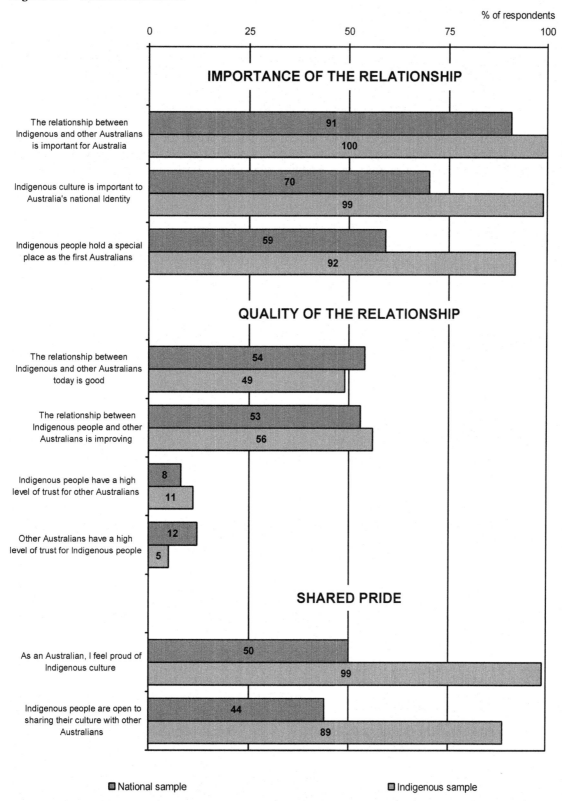

Source: Australian Reconciliation Barometer Executive Summary p. 10

> **Teachers have a unique opportunity**
>
> Teachers of Aboriginal and Torres Strait Islander students have a unique opportunity to be the architects of transformative learning. As I see it, the role of the teacher is to guide students to new insights about the world and, importantly, to work with children to develop their potential as citizens and contributors to society. Youth is the domain of optimism, and good teachers develop in children an understanding that all things are possible, and no horizon is too far to reach.
>
> The culture and the resourcing of school education in Australia bring some distinct challenges for Aboriginal and Torres Strait Islander children. Teachers must be mindful to the barriers that prevent our children from achieving their full potential. It is a complex but rewarding task to minimise these barriers, and lead young people in learning. I can't think of another profession that brings with it the potential for so much that is positive and possible. Finally, I urge all teachers to learn about, understand and celebrate the Indigenous people, culture and society they encounter wherever they work.
>
>
>
> *Tom Calma* *is a Kungarakan and Iwaidja Elder who has been involved in Indigenous affairs for over 30 years. He has been a senior diplomat in India and Vietnam, senior adviser to the federal Minister for Indigenous Affairs, and manager of the Community Education and Development Branch of Aboriginal and Torres Strait Islander Services (ATSIS). From 2004 to 2009 he was Aboriginal and Torres Strait Islander Social Justice Commissioner and Race Discrimination Commissioner. In 2009–10 he led the development of a national Indigenous advisory body. He is an ambassador for White Ribbon Day, the international Day for the Elimination of Violence Against Women, and national patron of Wakakirri National Story Festival.*

Indigenous people and other Australians. These results imply we have a lot of work to do to improve this relationship and trust between Indigenous people and other Australians.

The results in relation to shared pride are of concern. While 99 per cent of Indigenous respondents reported being proud of Indigenous culture, only 50 per cent of non-Indigenous respondents agreed. The results in relation to the item concerning how much the overall population feels that Indigenous people are prepared to share their culture with other Australians are regarded by Reconciliation Australia as amongst the most interesting of the entire study. Only 44 per cent of the non-Indigenous respondents believe that Indigenous people are open to sharing their culture with other Australians compared with 99 per cent of Indigenous respondents. Reconciliation Australia suggests 'one important way to close this gap is to support Indigenous Australians in finding ways to share their culture with non-Indigenous people, and to support non-Indigenous Australians in finding ways to learn about, experience and take pride in Indigenous culture' (Reconciliation Australia, 2009, p. 5).

Perceptions

The Barometer also shows we have lots in common in regard to national identity—being good at sport, good-humoured, easy-going and not so disciplined, hard-working, cooperative and respectful (see Figure 9.3). Interestingly, on every indicator, non-Indigenous respondents rated the overall Australian population more highly when it came to possessing each positive trait. In contrast, for almost every indicator the Indigenous respondents rated themselves ahead of the overall Australian population. Reconciliation Australia considers that these results imply 'that Indigenous people hold a more generous view towards the general population than is felt the other way around' (Reconciliation Australia, 2009, p. 6). Indigenous respondents rated Indigenous people behind the rest of the population on only one characteristic—hard-working—whereas

> **Promoting the education of Indigenous Australians**
>
> Ever since I started teaching, I have seen the lack of a decent education for Indigenous Australians as the single biggest educational issue in this country.
>
> Most of my school experience has been in boarding schools, and hence I saw the advantages they could offer Indigenous students, as Indigenous students should be receiving the best education possible. I also noticed that there were very few Indigenous students in independent schools, and yet these were some of the best schools in the country.
>
> One of the biggest issues was school fees and funding. There is very little assistance available for day students, but there is up to $17 000 available (through Abstudy) for boarders aged under 16 years. Most parents and schools were unaware of this money. In fact, the federal government Abstudy document has 101 chapters, and most Centrelink workers are not familiar with it!
>
> What worked at St Joseph's College was establishing a relationship between the school and an Indigenous community, so that a *dialogue* was possible. Families came to the school, had an extensive tour of all facilities, met staff and students, and eventually went home feeling that they had a good understanding of what the school was about. The school also visited the community, and became familiar with prospective boarding students' background. What also worked was having a few students coming from the same community; this lessened their sense of being homesick.
>
> Today in New South Wales, 75 per cent of boarding schools have Indigenous students, including the majority of GPS schools. Since the government apology in February 2008, many independent schools fly the Aboriginal flag, and most have 'Welcome to Country' as a standard feature of school gatherings.
>
> The future? A decent education will lead more Indigenous students into better employment possibilities, and we will also have a generation of non-Indigenous students who have been to school with Indigenous students, and hence have a stronger appreciation of the gifts that Indigenous people have brought to this country, Australia.
>
> —Brother Paul Hough, Indigenous Education Adviser, Association of Independent Schools
>
>
>
> ***Brother Paul Hough AM, FACE.*** *Educated at Marist Brothers Kogarah, Brother Paul Hough joined the Marist Brothers in 1964. He gained an honours degree in Physics at Sydney University in 1969, then taught at Grafton for five years. From 1975 to 1977, he taught senior Physics at St Joseph's College, Hunters Hill, as well as coaching and cadets, and worked with Mum Shirl and Father Ted Kennedy at Redfern. From 1978 to 1981 he worked with the Marist Retreat and Vocations team for New South Wales and Queensland schools. From 1982 to 1987 he was principal at St Augustine's College, Cairns, with about 200 boarders including boys from Aboriginal and Torres Strait communities. In 1988 and 1989 he was deputy headmaster at St Joseph's, Kieta, Bougainville. In 1990–91 he studied in the USA and Europe, taking a masters in Educational Administration. From 1992 he was principal at St Gregory's, Campbelltown, making links with Bourke and Yarrabah Aboriginal communities. In 2001 he was appointed principal a St Joseph's, Hunters Hill, being awarded FACE for his work there in 2006. In 2007 he was awarded AM for his work at Joey's, and asked to work full-time in Indigenous education. He was Indigenous Coordinator with the Association of Independent Schools and is now working in vocational education with Catholic Education, Cairns diocese, Queensland.*

non-Indigenous participants rated Indigenous Australians as not very similar to the rest of Australia in being cooperative, disciplined and hard-working. It seems that more needs to be done in Australian classrooms to address these specific misconceptions and stereotypes (see Chapter 3). Indigenous respondents also considered that other Australians were not very similar to Indigenous people in being respectful. This suggests that the relationship could be improved if non-Indigenous Australians were seen to be more respectful.

Figure 9.3 Perceptions of each other

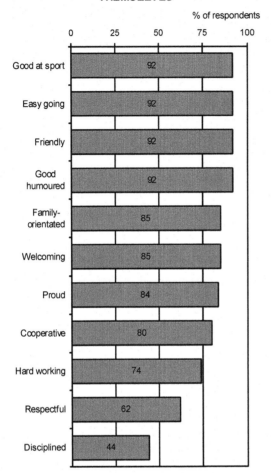
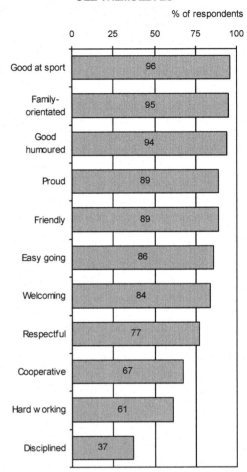

Source: Australian Reconciliation Barometer Executive Summary p. 11

Action

A total of 64 per cent of non-Indigenous respondents reported that they had taken steps to advance reconciliation or to help disadvantaged Indigenous people in the last twelve months (see Figure 9.4). This bodes well for reconciliation. Some 76 per cent of non-Indigenous respondents also reported that they would like to have contact with Indigenous people in the future. However, only 20 per cent of Australians said they knew what they could do to help disadvantaged Indigenous people. Reconciliation Australia suggests that 'a key objective for the reconciliation process is to improve the knowledge and understanding of Australians about how they can be involved and help to overcome Indigenous disadvantage' (Reconciliation Australia, 2009, p. 7). Teachers have an enormous role to play in helping to address this objective in Australian classrooms and school communities.

Implications for teaching

The results of this study have important implications for the classroom. Clearly we need to focus on increasing our students' and school communities' knowledge about Indigenous history and culture, and the special place of Indigenous people in our nation as the first Australians. We also need to improve the relationship and

Figure 9.4 How Australians, overall, see themselves and Indigenous people

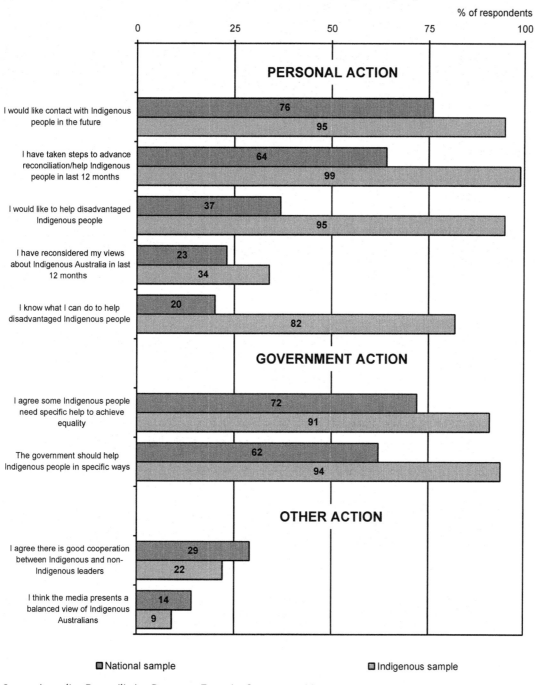

Source: Australian Reconciliation Barometer Executive Summary p. 14

trust between Indigenous and non-Indigenous Australians. We can also play a proactive role in increasing pride in Indigenous Australia based on the incredible wealth of achievements of one of the oldest cultures in the world and the extraordinary number of Indigenous Australians who are making invaluable contributions to Australia's future (see Chapter 2). Teachers can also readily provide opportunities for Indigenous people to share their culture with students and communities, which can make a critical contribution to firmly establishing and importantly enacting the

> ### The Yachad Accelerated Learning Project (YALP)
>
> The Yachad Accelerated Learning Project (YALP) is an innovative pilot project to improve the literacy and numeracy skills of academically low-achieving students, particularly Indigenous ones, in regional, rural and remote locations in Australia.
>
> This project draws on the expertise of a team of Israeli educators from the NCJW Institute for Innovation in Education at the Hebrew University of Jerusalem, gathered from a variety of educational settings, sharing basic underlying principles fundamental to learning in general and accelerated learning in particular.
>
> *Yachad* is a Hebrew word that means 'together', and it is used to express the commitment to work together: students, school educators, families and communities as well as state and federal governments, industry and philanthropic partners in Australia.
>
> *How does it work?*
>
> YALP is an inclusive project that complements and supports other programs conducted at the school. Rather than being one-size-fits-all, YALP has a flexible modular structure in order to cater to the unique needs of each learning setting and each individual student. Based on local culturally appropriate materials, YALP comprises four key components: tutoring; accelerated learning; professional development; and community engagement. These all come together in YALP's tutoring package—*The Ten Minute System* (10MS).
>
> *The Ten Minute System*
>
> YALP's tutoring package, The Ten Minute System, is a one-on-one tutoring model consisting of three to five ten-minute sessions a week. The brief sessions conducted in a non-threatening learning environment fully utilise the attention span of learners judged to be 'at risk' by tackling in a variety of ways the specific problem that needs to addressed. By pre/post testing and recycling chunks of learning in short, focused and regular tailor-made sessions, recurring opportunities for success are created.
>
> Through the introduction and implementation of YALP's tutoring package, the project brings to the school YALP's approach to accelerated learning, which is delivered through a variety of professional development sessions: one-on-one with tutors and teachers, team meetings and whole-of-school get-togethers. Since these principles of accelerated learning are applicable to whole-class heterogeneous settings as well, by engaging classroom teachers together with tutors working with the individual tutees, YALP becomes part of the school routine. The impact of this goes beyond the individual learners involved in the program and touches many more students.
>
> Furthermore, YALP encourages parents and other caregivers to be involved in the project. YALP educators establish warm and supportive relationships with the students' families and the community. YALP is expanding its tutoring package into the community in order to train parents and caregivers in the Ten Minute System so that they too can provide learning support to their children. This will also strengthen the ties between the schools and the community.
>
> Following the initial introduction to the project, YALP continues to offer professional support and guidance to the school and community in order to create the foundation for school and community ownership and sustainability.
>
> *Where is YALP?*
>
> YALP has been operating in primary, secondary and post-compulsory schools in four states and the Northern Territory. For more information, visit the YALP website at <www.yalp.org.au>

process of reconciliation. We can also readily teach students to comprehend the facts so that they are empowered to address enduring misconceptions and stereotypes (see Chapter 3). In these ways, we can make a vital contribution to driving reconciliation and creating a more equitable Australia for all Australians based on mutual trust, respect and understanding.

The role of teachers in the reconciliation process

The new generation of teachers will empower Australians to challenge and shape the very social fabric of our society. By teaching appropriate Indigenous Australian Studies, teachers can contribute to:

- ensuring that all Australian children experience their right to learn the true history of this country;
- equipping all Australians with the knowledge, skills and attitudes to understand and address contemporary Indigenous issues and be proactive agents in the reconciliation process;
- enhancing the educational participation, education outcomes, and identity and academic self-concepts of Indigenous students;
- challenging the frames of reference of 'White Australia' and creating a more socially just Australia that acknowledges and respects the validity of Indigenous Australian cultures;
- stopping the cycle of misinformation about Indigenous Australia and counteracting racism in Australian society that contributes to the appalling socio-economic disadvantages to which Indigenous Australians are subject; and
- proactively tackling critical social justice issues of our time.

Long-term reconciliation cannot be achieved and maintained without teaching all Australian students Indigenous Australian Studies. Clearly, the role of teachers is vital to the success of the reconciliation process. If teachers can teach their students the truth, help them debunk the myths, and empower them to identify and act upon addressing address social and economic disadvantage, it may be possible to change entrenched societal attitudes and thereby the very social fabric of Australian society.

The role of education in addressing disadvantage

The Royal Commission into Aboriginal Deaths in Custody (1991) made firm recommendations about the role of education in redressing the problems related to Aboriginal disadvantage. As the Commission stressed, Indigenous education includes both the overall education of Indigenous students and the education of all students about Indigenous people, cultures and history. From a practical perspective, this means that every Australian student at every level of education should be taught Indigenous Australian Studies.

The Commission (1991) recommended that 'curricula of all schools at all levels should reflect the fact that Australia has an Aboriginal history'. This means that Indigenous perspectives should be integral to the teaching of history in our schools. For generations, our history has glorified the pioneer and neglected to include Indigenous Australians' experiences of our history. What is needed in schools is to teach that 'Australia has a black history'. This involves teaching the truth about our history as well as incorporating Indigenous experiences and viewpoints.

The Commission also acknowledged that: 'A knowledge and understanding of Aboriginal people, culture and history is essential to a complete understanding of Australian society.' Committed teachers can see that the subject area is explored in appropriate depth by including a balance of present, past and future perspectives (see Chapter 15).

The critical nature of consultation (see Chapter 10) was acknowledged by the Commission in the following two recommendations:

- Consultation with Aboriginal communities is essential when developing curriculum materials for Aboriginal education.
- Participation of Aboriginal communities in schools should be an integral part of the teaching process when teaching Aboriginal history.

Consultation ensures that Indigenous perspectives permeate the curriculum, that subject-matter is taught accurately and is delivered in an appropriate manner, and that students can see they are learning about critical social issues that adversely affect Indigenous Australians today.

The Commission also recognised that teachers could address the educational disadvantage experienced by Indigenous students. It identified the need to:

Students on stage at Gosford Showground (New South Wales) in the schools–community production of 1788: The Great South Land *sponsored by Gosford City Council. An integrated school musical and resource kit developed with the New South Wales AECG, a 'reconciliation rock musical' and winner of a National Reconciliation Award. The video* Nothing's Going to Stop Our Dream, *of the Taree schools–community performance, can be viewed online. Courtesy Chris Robinson.*

- promote self-esteem and self-confidence in Aboriginal students through the valuing of their culture and history (and to promote the valuing of all cultures and all heritages by all students);
- achieve the participation of Aboriginal students at all levels of the education continuum; and
- promote knowledge and understanding of the educational needs of Aboriginal students within all sections of the education community.

When schools make a real effort to acknowledge the validity of Indigenous students' cultures and history, and promote their self-concept, educational participation and outcomes for Indigenous students improve considerably. Whether there is only one Indigenous student in the school or 100, such strategies need to be employed. For example, in one local primary school there are five Indigenous students. The school formed a 'Koori kids' group to enable these students to meet regularly and celebrate their identity with the rest of the student and school community population. This group participates in regular school assembly performances, flag-raising ceremonies and special community events. In other words, the school has acknowledged and promoted the Aboriginality of these students. This has also led to non-Indigenous students of the school being keen to learn more about Aboriginal culture and history.

Such important strategies are impossible to implement without appropriate teacher education courses in Indigenous Australian Studies. Recommendation 295 of the Royal Commission into Aboriginal Deaths in Custody (1991) clearly states the need for pre-service teacher training courses which include units on teaching Indigenous history and cultures from the perspective of Indigenous people. It also recommends that extensive in-service training be provided so that 'teachers may improve their skills, knowledge and understanding to teach curricula which incorporate Aboriginal viewpoints on social, cultural and historical matters and that Aboriginal people should be involved in the training courses both at student teacher and at in-service level' (see also recommendations 290 and 291). It is time that every teacher education institution requires student teachers to undertake a core subject in Indigenous Australian Studies so that they can be prepared with the knowledge, skills and attitudes to understand

Advance Australia Fair

Australia, celebrate as one, with peace and harmony.
Our precious water, soil and sun, grant life for you and me.
Our land abounds in nature's gifts to love, respect and share,
And honouring the Dreaming, advance Australia fair.
With joyful hearts then let us sing, advance Australia fair.

Australia, let us stand as one, upon this sacred land.
A new day dawns, we're moving on to trust and understand.
Combine our ancient history and cultures everywhere,
To bond together for all time, advance Australia fair.
With joyful hearts then let us sing, advance Australia fair.

Australia, let us strive as one, to work with willing hands.
Our Southern Cross will guide us on, as friends with other lands.
While we embrace tomorrow's world with courage, truth and care,
And all our actions prove the words, advance Australia fair,
With joyful hearts then let us sing, advance Australia fair.

And when this special land of ours is in our children's care,
For shore to shore forever more, advance Australia fair.
With joyful hearts then let us sing, advance... Australia... fair.

Words by Judith Durham OAM (2008), Peter Dodds McCormick (1878), Kutcha Edwards, Bill Hauritz OAM, Camilla Chance, Lou Bennett.

Resources available from Reconciliation Australia

It is critical that Australian students be given the opportunity to fully explore the historical basis of reconciliation, identify current strategies being implemented by a wide range of groups, and contribute to proactively shaping the process. The Council for Aboriginal Reconciliation (CAR) has produced a wealth of useful materials that can be adapted to create stimulating teaching activities. For example, *Addressing the Key Issues for Reconciliation* (CAR 1997a) is a series of nine books dealing with information on the key issues of: understanding country; improving relationships; valuing cultures; sharing histories; addressing disadvantage; responding to custody levels; agreeing on a document; and controlling destinies. The first book of the series is a useful summary of each of the eight key issues. These are available from Reconciliation Australia, which also has up-to-date information about reconciliation today. Both the Council for Aboriginal Reconciliation and Reconciliation Australia can be found at <www.austlii.edu.au/au/orgs/car/>. Reconciliation Australia also produces a quarterly newsletter, which provides regular updated information on the process of reconciliation, and includes articles on what schools around the country are doing to contribute to the process. Resources available from Reconciliation Australia include information about:

- current issues affecting Indigenous Australians and the reconciliation movement, in the form of Q&A fact sheets;
- the apology to the Stolen Generations, with a link to access a DVD copy of Reconciliation Australia's documentary *The Apology*, which is a must for all Australians to view as this defining moment of our nation's history moved a nation;
- cultural awareness training—Reconciliation Australia has a register where training providers can upload their details so that individuals and organisations looking for cultural awareness training can contact them;
- National Reconciliation Week (NRW)— each year Reconciliation Australia updates information on the NRW theme, so teachers can access materials to help promote NRW

Joey's

St Joseph's College Hunter's Hill in Sydney (Joey's), is one of the oldest (established 1881) and most prestigious boarding schools for boys in Australia. Joey's has an impressive track record in achieving high academic standards, and in education for rural and remote students. It also has a huge reputation in schoolboy Rugby Union.

For some decades, individual Indigenous boys had boarded at Joey's. In 1998 Joey's decided the key to real success with Indigenous students lay in a critical mass of Indigenous scholarships within each year group. The Indigenous Fund, established in 2005, aims to generate funding for more scholarships into the future, to sustain a mass of scholarships and assist with all costs of scholarship students and of family involvement in the school. Joey's vision is to create a model for other schools across Australia—financially sustainable opportunities for Indigenous students, and developing leaders from within Indigenous communities. As declared by Sir William Deane in his role as Patron, Joey's Indigenous program is:

> Reconciliation in action. Its whole basis lies in an acceptance of the truth that education is both the key and the hope in so far as the future of Indigenous Australians is concerned. And, perhaps most important . . . dramatically demonstrates the potential of young Indigenous Australians to overcome the circumstances and consequences of disadvantage, and even to excel, if only they are given a real chance of an effective secondary education in conditions favorable to development and learning.

Joey's Indigenous Fund is based on a belief that if Indigenous students receive a high-quality education, they can realise their real potential and real progress can be made in improving the situation of their communities. Indigenous students at Joey's come from more than 26 communities. This means broad potential to make a positive contribution to Indigenous communities across the state. The program is about Indigenous students achieving their real potential through holistic education with high expectations for every Indigenous student—and, just as importantly, culturally appropriate pastoral care.

Joey's program benefits not only the Indigenous boarders but also has long-term benefits for their schoolmates, who spend up to six years living with them, getting to know them as people and learning about Indigenous Australia. They learn by experience that Indigenous students can be 'one of the boys', and they learn to understand Indigenous issues. This lays strong foundations for the future of Australian society.

The Indigenous Program aims to have around 40 Indigenous student enrolments each year, making 5 per cent of the school's boarding population Indigenous. To make this happen, the school aims to raise approximately $5 million to allow an annual income to be generated to ensure this level of enrolment can be maintained.

Andrew Penfold comments that:

> The St Joseph's College Indigenous Fund was never about supporting a privileged Independent school, but about assisting disadvantaged Indigenous children . . . I have been overwhelmed by the values that the College stands for and its deep and genuine conviction to social justice and giving everyone a fair go. Any student that is fortunate enough to experience life as a Joey's boy will leave the school with a core set of values that will set them on a course to make the world a better place. I hope they all strive for better things not just in their own lives but in the world around them. I look forward with great optimism to the continued success.

What makes the program work? Some factors include:

- *critical mass*—to reduce isolation and culture shock;
- *leadership and commitment*—from the governing body down—together with a supportive school community and committed, experienced and qualified staff;
- *cultural awareness among staff*—familiarity with Indigenous cultural and social protocols;

- *family support, engagement and enthusiasm*—making sure a sound relationship is established with each student's family;
- *Indigenous person on staff*—cultural support and parent liaison;
- *community relations*—knowing the town and having support networks in the community;
- *Indigenous community and leaders support*—prominent Indigenous leaders help design the program and be role models;
- *initial educational skills and learning assessment*—individual and continuing support program; and tutoring;
- *continual evaluation and monitoring*—continuous learning by the College;
- *one set of rules*—firm and set rules;
- *supervised homework*—regular study hours, time to complete work, with reduced distractions and noise;
- *extra-curricular and other experiences*—development of talents and interests;
- *post-school support*—create networks and pathways to provide mentoring into tertiary and career opportunities.

Source: Lynette Riley in consultation with Andrew Penfold (2006).

in their school. Reconciliation Australia also puts together annual posters for use in promoting NRW—these are great teaching resources. Posters can be ordered from the website;
- NAIDOC Week—NAIDOC originally stood for 'National Aborigines and Islanders Day Observance Committee', which was once responsible for organising national activities during NAIDOC Week; now its acronym has become the name of the week itself. NAIDOC celebrations are held around Australia to celebrate the history, culture and achievements of Aboriginal and Torres Strait Islander people. The week is celebrated not just in the Indigenous community, but also in increasing numbers of government agencies, schools, local councils and workplaces. Each year, a poster is produced based on the theme for the year and following a national art competition. For more information on NAIDOC Week, and to order copies of current and past posters, visit <www.naidoc.org.au>;
- the latest editions of Reconciliation Australia's publications;
- speeches from Reconciliation Australia, made by staff and board members;
- links to other websites that provide further information;
- *ABS Social Trends* reports—Reconciliation Australia has collected some very interesting information on Indigenous Australians from the *Social Trends* report. The highlights from the report are featured in this section of the website;
- *Reconciliation News*. Reconciliation Australia's newsletter comes out three times a year—it is possible to download previous editions or join the mailing list to receive a copy;
- the 1967 Referendum—in 2007, Reconciliation Australia worked to commemorate the 40th Anniversary of the 1967 Referendum—all the materials developed are accessible in this section of the website;
- the history of reconciliation—this section provides a timeline of the reconciliation movement and is a great teaching resource;
- the 2020 Summit of 2008—In 2008, two staff members from Reconciliation Australia participated in the Prime Minister's 2020 Summit. Find out more information about the Summit and Reconciliation Australia's participants in this section of the website.

Reconciliation Australia has an online archive of CAR resources, which includes:

- booklets produced by the Council that provide important historical background information (e.g. *Exploring Common Ground: Aboriginal Reconciliation and the mining industry (1993a)*); *Making Things Right: Reconciliation after the High Court Decision on Mabo*;
- an extract from the *Royal Commission into Aboriginal Deaths in Custody Final*

Report (1991); Chapter 38, 'The Process of Reconciliation';
- the *Council for Aboriginal Reconciliation Act* 1991 and Council for Aboriginal Reconciliation Bill 1991—Second Reading Speech by the Minister assisting the Prime Minister for Aboriginal Reconciliation, the Hon. Robert Tickner, MP, both significant historical documents;
- the Study *Circle Kit* (n.d.), which can readily be adapted for a wealth of classroom activities. It is also a useful resource for teaching members of the school community about the reconciliation process;
- *Reconciliation: Australia's Challenge*—the Council's final report to Parliament (December 2000)—an important historical document;
- Council speeches containing a wealth of historical material;
- information on reconciliation walks in Sydney, Melbourne and Perth;
- the Vincent Lingiari Lectures, including the Vincent Lingiari Memorial Lecture by the Rt Hon. Malcolm Fraser on 24 August 2000; *Until the Chains are Broken*, the Fourth Vincent Lingiari Lecture by Pat Dodson on 27 August 1999; *We Know These Things to Be True*, the Third Vincent Lingiari Lecture by Galarrwuy Yunupingu AM on 20 August 1998; *Dragging the Chain 1887–1997*, the Second Vincent Lingiari Lecture by Gough Whitlam on 29 August 1997; and *Some Signposts from Daguragu*, the Inaugural Vincent Lingiari Lecture by Sir William Deane on 22 August 1996;
- videotapes produced by CAR, which are a valuable resource; many school libraries have copies of these. For example, the complete Redfern Park statement is on the video *Walking Together*; no Australian student should be deprived of the opportunity to see the delivery of and the audience reactions to this important historic statement.
- Australian Reconciliation Convention highlights:
  – *Walking Together: An Introduction to the Council for Aboriginal Reconciliation*;
  – *Talking Together: Women and Reconciliation*;
  – *Talkin' Businesss* explaining the Council's consultation program, vision and key issues;
  – *Making Things Right: Reconciliation After the High Court Decision on Native Title*;
  – *Working as One: Reconciliation in the Workplace*;
- posters, often a great discussion starter. They are also useful for promoting reconciliation in the classroom, school and wider community. Sources of posters include Reconciliation Australia, AnTAR and NAIDOC;
- the *Justice and Equity* CD-ROM. This resource is a must for every teacher, and most school libraries will have a copy. It contains a wealth of multimedia resources on the reconciliation process and social justice for all Australians.

Some teaching ideas

The following sample teaching ideas could be developed to explore the focus question: What is reconciliation and why is it important?

Present perspectives

- On a map of Australia, ask students to write down the names of different Indigenous cultural groups. Make a class table that displays the results. Ask students to clarify the number of students in the class that identified Aboriginal Australians and Torres Strait Islander Australians. Ask students to discuss what they think students in a school:
  – with no Indigenous Australians would list, and why;
  – with a high population of Indigenous Australians would list, and why;
  – with one Indigenous child in the school would list, and why; and
  – with half-Indigenous and half non-Indigenous students would list, and why.
- Ask students to look up the word 'reconciliation' in a dictionary and thesaurus and ask them whether they know what the word means. Ask students to discuss what they think the word might mean. Ask students in groups to act out a two-minute scene or draw a general scene that shows reconciliation in

action. Ask students to explain how their drawing or scene shows reconciliation.
- Play students the beginning of the video *Why Teach Aboriginal Studies?* by the University of New South Wales so they can hear Oodgeroo Noonuccal (Kath Walker) read her poem 'Aboriginal Charter of Rights' or read the poem to the class from the book *My People* (Noonuccal, 2008). Ask students in groups to discuss what a section of the poem means in relation to reconciliation and act out this section for the rest of the class. Put the group dramas together to create a class assembly item.
- Ask students to view the video *Kath Walker* by Equality Videos or *Oodgeroo—A Life* (ABC TV). Ask students to identify some key things Oodgeroo did in her life to promote reconciliation (e.g. a timeline). Ask a local community member to talk about Oodgeroo's achievements, and ask students to read about her other achievements (e.g. look at some of Oodgeroo's books, read extracts from the book *Oodgeroo—A Tribute* (Shoemaker, 1994).
- Ask students to choose one of Oodgeroo's poems. In groups, students could then discuss the meaning of their poems with local Indigenous community members. Students can be asked to read their poem on a class tape and explain on tape what they think the poem is about and how it helps to promote reconciliation.
- Ask Indigenous community members to explain what they think reconciliation is, and show you or tell you about some of the initiatives in your community to promote reconciliation. Make a 'big book' for younger children, profiling what members in your community are doing.
- Ask students to read a local newspaper article that shows an example of reconciliation. Ask children to highlight the key sentences in the article and discuss how the article shows an example of reconciliation. Start a collection of newspaper articles showing examples of reconciliation to put in a class book. Look at Reconciliation Australia newsletters as well.
- Identify and visit local organisations that are promoting reconciliation in your community (e.g. local Aboriginal Land Councils, the local AECG, church groups, the local council). Identify why each group promotes reconciliation and how it does this.
- Invite local Indigenous and non-Indigenous community members to explain to your class why they think reconciliation is important and what they are doing to promote it.
- Invite someone in the community who is contributing to reconciliation to visit your class and explain their role in the process. Students write an advertisement or newspaper article promoting their work.
- Watch the CAR videos *Walking Together* and *Talkin' Business*. Ask students to identify what the role of CAR was in the reconciliation process and the Council's vision. Ask students to find out about the role of Reconciliation Australia and identify its vision. Ask students to design a slogan or a poster to promote the work of Reconciliation Australia. Write a banner poem about reconciliation with each letter of the word 'reconciliation' representing a word or action that will help to achieve it.
- Get students to look at Reconciliation Australia newsletters. Ask them to identify what Reconciliation Australia and different groups in the Australian community are doing to promote reconciliation. Make a display of initiatives in the community for all students in the school to see.
- Watch the CAR video *Talking Together* to hear the views of four Australian women about the importance of healing the relationship between Indigenous and non-Indigenous Australians. Identify their reasons.
- Read and discuss other people's views about the reconciliation process (e.g. see CAR's *Study Circle* kit, newspaper articles and poems and read the results of The Australian Reconciliation Barometer (RA, 2009).
- Perform a play that shows the disadvantages for Indigenous Australia based on current statistics for Indigenous people. Discuss how these statistics demonstrate the urgent need for reconciliation.
- Invite an Indigenous community member to talk about how their life has been affected by socio-economic disadvantage, and why it is important to address disadvantage.
- Watch the video *Munyarl Mythology* (produced by the University of New South Wales). Discuss how misconceptions and myths adversely affect Indigenous peoples.

Ashfield Public School: Living in Harmony . . . a low-key approach to Indigenous education

Ashfield Public School in Sydney's inner west, under the dynamic leadership of principal Robyn Hutchinson, has generated a Partnership Program that links the school into its community, as well as connecting to the future and the world through its website. Ashfield Public School sees itself as a 0–12 Learning Community Hub in its local community, with a four-way partnership of the primary school (students, staff, parents, and the community and all its agencies), the local secondary high school, the Department of Education and Training and Wests Ashfield Sports Club, a particularly strong partner. The partnership is about developing the school's basic philosophy of inclusiveness, believing in the potential of every child, the importance of students engaging in learning and learning resilience, and building a school culture of inquiry and positive relationships.

The Ashfield Public School community is on a learning journey, where engagement with learning, through an Inquiry-based approach coupled with relationship-building restorative processes, underpins all dimensions of the school's operations.

A foundational aspect of the partnership program of Ashfield School is the year-round Transition to School Program, as part of the school's Early Learning Program. This focuses around a supported playgroup Play and Learn for 0–5s and their carers, run by Good Beginnings twice a week throughout the year. The 3- and 4-year-old children and their families link directly with the kindergarten and primary school children from Term 2 onwards, making for a good transition and an opportunity to assess needs prior to children's entry into school.

The school prides itself on being an inclusive school, celebrating its diversity and focusing on building relationships—all of which undergirds the development of lifelong learning processes in children. The school's student body plays an instrumental role in organising a number of key events throughout the year, including Harmony Day, Reconciliation and NAIDOC Week events, an Arts Festival and Talent Enrichment and Fun Days.

The school's success in building relationships with its community is recognised by a number of awards and sponsorships.

Ashfield Public School has won an Australian Government Living in Harmony grant of $50 000—one of only 40 across the country—for its strategies to develop children's social skills and positive relationships. The school also won an Australian Government Chaplaincy position. Ashfield's chaplain is known as a Community Liaison Coordinator (Connector), to connect students and families with services, be a mentor for all, be fun to be with, and build relationships and support where needed.

These two Support Staff positions, the Living in Harmony worker and the chaplain, totalling four days of teacher class-free time, enable student and family needs to be met more fully, through social skills programs, individual support, counselling, storytelling and parent workshops.

Wangal Garden at Ashfield Public School, Sydney. Photo: Vicki Barton.

A major milestone for Ashfield Public School was the opening of the Wangal garden and playground, with its Indigenous bush garden of native plants and selected rocks commemorating the original traditional owners of the land on which the school stands, the Wangal people. This was the culmination of a five-year dream, including eighteen months of the front of the school being a construction site, saving up grant monies and attracting sponsors. In 2006, the vision became a reality. With a large grant from Wests Ashfield for an Indigenous garden, an Investing in Schools grant from the Department of Education and Training, and a donation from the school's P&C group, work could proceed. The whole school community workshopped ideas with the design team from Urban Landscapes, who produced a fabulous design. The Wangal garden playground was opened in 2007 with a smoking ceremony by Uncle Max Eulo, with honoured guests being local state and federal Members of Parliament and the Chair of the Metropolitan Local Aboriginal Land Council.

With its Indigenous plants chosen under the guidance of John Lennis, Indigenous botanist, and carefully selected patterned rocks at the main entrance to the school, the Indigenous garden lets students and everyone in the school community learn about the land, experience, create, imagine or just be in a beautiful space. Celebrating the new garden says publicly that Ashfield Public School holds the traditional custodians of this land, the Wangal people, in the deepest respect. Ashfield Public School takes every opportunity to learn about its 60 000-plus year heritage, and to support the struggle for social justice for all Australia's citizens—needed to build the bridges for a true partnership of cultures into the future. The song says, 'From little things big things grow'. One teacher commented: 'What a wonderful legacy these children at this school are leaving to the future generations.'

It is in this context that the very small number of Indigenous students at Ashfield share their culture with pride, in very low-key ways, alongside the 40-plus other cultures represented within the school. The school is working on extending and deepening this deep respect and understanding within its multicultural community.

Principal Robyn Hutchinson in Wangal Garden
Photo: Vicki Barton.

Robyn Hutchinson has been involved in public education for over 40 years, with a long-term commitment to Indigenous education principles, including raising awareness among Aboriginal and non-Aboriginal families alike of the importance of the true history of Australia. She attended one of the first Tranby courses for non-Indigenous people, led by Jack Beetson. At Brighton le Sands PS, the whole school staged a mock Invasion Day in 1988, culminating in the performance of a play written for the occasion, 'Discovery or Invasion?', and students created a 50 000-year timeline. The school was part of the La Perouse inter-school Aboriginal Student Support and Parent Awareness program (ASSPA) group, and students enjoyed being a sister school with the Kirinari Hostel students from Gymea HS.

When she was principal at Lewisham PS ten years ago, the students called on the Prime Minister for an apology to the Stolen Generations, and made the Sydney Morning Herald. National Association for the Prevention of Child Abuse and Neglect (NAPCAN) invited the choir and the Indigenous dance group to Admiralty House to perform and to present a major Aboriginal artwork created by the students to Governor General Sir William Deane. A number of Artists in Residence working with students in various schools where Robyn has worked over the years, both in New South Wales and Western Australia, have contributed to raising Indigenous awareness through their artwork and storytelling. More recently at Ashfield Public School, the Wangal Indigenous bush-tucker playground, named for the Aboriginal traditional owners, has been developed with the support of local Aboriginal people, the local sports club and the Department of Education and Training. In three schools Robyn has led, Indigenous symbolism has been incorporated into the re-designing of the school logo. She has made sure that the schools where she has worked have always flown the Aboriginal, Torres Strait Island and Australian flags. In 2010, Ashfield Public School, believing in the power of symbols, was able to install a second school flagpole, flying the same three flags, in the Wangal playground at the front of the school, as a public sign of its commitment to the Indigenous custodians of the land.

Reconciliation Day at Penshurst West Public School. Parent James Wilson-Miller helps students paint the Georges River story on a giant boomerang. Photo: Lisa Car.

Students could draw a table to identify the myths explored in the video along with the facts that debunk these myths. Read the book *Face the Facts* (AHRC, 2008). Students identify the myths needing to be debunked then draw a cartoon to debunk one of these myths. Create a class book debunking myths with the facts.
- Invite an Indigenous community member to talk about how misconceptions and stereotypes have affected Indigenous people, and why it is important to rebut them.
- Students read one myth from the booklet *Face the Facts* (AHRC, 2008), then design a cartoon to rebut the myth they have examined and explain their cartoon to a group of students. Students display cartoons around the school and community to rebut the myths.

Past perspectives

- Students listen to a song from the *1788: The Great South Land* (now available as 'When the Sky Fell Down') musical resource kit, complete some of the activities that relate to the song and act out the song as a play. Better still, use the activities in the kit to develop a sequence of teaching activities for your students and perform the musical, as a class or school, for your local community. This kit is available in a number of libraries.
- Students watch a video providing an overview of Australia's history (e.g. *Discovering Australia's Aboriginal History*, ABC TV or *The First Australians* (SBS). List key events in Australia's history.
- Students read the poem 'Aboriginal Australia—To the Others' by Jack Davis (see Chapter 4). They discuss what they think the poem means and whether such views of history need to be addressed in the context of the reconciliation process.
- Students watch a video about invasion and resistance in the Sydney region (e.g. *Warriors*, Rainbow Serpent Series).
- Invite Indigenous community members to talk to the class about the historical experiences of their families. Based on the stories, make library books or a class play or musical about the experiences of local community members.
- Read an Indigenous person's life story (e.g. *My Place for Young Readers*, by Sally Morgan, 2005). Discuss how this person's life may have been different if reconciliation had taken place earlier. In a group, act out one event in the person's life and then act out how that event could have been if reconciliation had taken place at the time.
- Watch the video *Koori—A Will to Win* (New South Wales Film Corporation). Discuss how the policy of taking children away affected the family of James Miller.
- Watch the video *Bringing Them Home* (Human Rights and Equal Opportunity Commission). Ask students to discuss and summarise the main findings of the report in groups. Ask students to read extracts from the summary of the *Bringing Them Home* report and add to their own summary.
- Invite local Indigenous community members to describe how the policy of taking children away affected their lives.
- Watch the videos *Link-Up* and *Lousy Little Sixpence* (Ronin Films) to find out more about the policy of taking children away.

Students write a story about how they would feel if this happened to them.
- Listen to a song that describes the effects of taking Indigenous children away from their families (e.g., 'Brown Skin Baby' by Bob Randall, 'Took the Children Away' by Archie Roach or 'Real Name' in *1788: The Great South Land*). Discuss what the words mean. Create a drama play to re-enact a segment of the song. Perform your interpretation of the meaning of the song to a school assembly.
- In groups, students explore the causes and consequences of, and possible solutions to one of the key issues of reconciliation using booklets about each key issue produced by the Council for Aboriginal Reconciliation. Each group makes a class display or class DVD (e.g. news reporter segment) to teach the rest of the class about the issue explored. Students write some quiz questions for other groups to show they understand what the key issue is about. Conduct a class quiz game to see which group knows the most about all the key issues.
- Watch the video *Babakiuweria* (ABC TV). Discuss how this video shows that reconciliation is important because of historical events.
- Invite Indigenous members of the community to discuss what they think the video *Babakiuweria* teaches people to think about.
- Look at posters and newspaper articles that comment on Australia's history and reconciliation. Ask students to identify what aspects of history people need to understand to promote reconciliation. Write a letter to a newspaper editor to explain their views.
- Ask students to make a mobile timeline of Australia's history based on cartoons in the books *200 in the Shade* (Swain, 1988) and *Beyond a Joke* (Cooke, 1988). Display your cartoon timeline in a local bank or shop.

Futures perspectives

- Read the poem 'United We Win' by Oodgeroo Noonuccal. Discuss the reconciliation message Oodgeroo is conveying in the poem.
- Students discuss with local Indigenous community members what needs to be done so that the vision of Reconciliation Australia is achieved. Draw a picture or write a poem or story to show what Australian society could be like if reconciliation were achieved.
- Students brainstorm ways that each of the eight key issues of reconciliation could be addressed, then decide how they could contribute to tackling some of the key issues in their community (e.g. devising community information pamphlets, holding a reconciliation information day for the community, designing a badge or a t-shirt with a slogan).
- Students conduct a survey to ascertain what community members know about the reconciliation process. Collate the results of the survey and decide on a course of action to tell community members how they can contribute to reconciliation (e.g. posters in local shops, car bumper stickers, a class-developed pamphlet, articles in the local newspaper).

Teaching about reconciliation: Some more ideas

Fostering cooperation and collaboration in the classroom is one of the first steps in working towards a positive classroom climate and encouraging reconciliation. A classroom in which students feel valued, and where differences in cultures, languages and learning styles are appreciated rather than seen as barriers to learning, has to be one of the key aims of any teacher committed to reconciliation.

Some other activities may involve inviting children to:

- research and write a guide for local tourist operators, encouraging them to include information about local Aboriginal and Torres Strait Islander history, culture and enterprises in their brochures and tours;
- find out whether local governments consult Aboriginal and Torres Strait Islander groups before decisions are made affecting their land and resources, and whether they seek input into management decisions from these groups;
- find out whether a local history is written for their area, and how it covers Aboriginal

> **Girri Girri Sports Academy – 'Strong, Proud, Active'**
>
> The Girri Girri Sports Academy for Indigenous Students caters for Aboriginal secondary students who are gifted at sports in western New South Wales. It involves Aboriginal students at Denison Secondary College (Bathurst High and Kelso High campuses), Canobolas Rural Technology High School, Cowra High School, Orange High School, Forbes High School, Bourke High School, Condobolin High School and Brewarrina Central School.
>
>
>
> *Girri Girri Sports Academy students on the sports field. Photos courtesy Doreen Conroy.*
>
> The name 'Girri Girri'—Wiradjuri for happy, joyful, cheerful and glad—was chosen by Aboriginal students at the Kelso Campus of Denison Secondary Education College, who were enrolled in the College's Wiradjuri Language Program (for both Aboriginal and non-Aboriginal students). The motto 'Strong, Proud, Active' came out of student–staff workshops at the first 'getting to know you' camp at Lake Burrendong Sport and Recreation Centre in May 2007, and was agreed as best expressing the goals of students and the program. There is also a 'Girri Girri Ballad' by Ron Simpson.
>
> As well as developing excellence in sports, Girri Girri aims to improve attendance and retention rates and provide opportunities to improve literacy and numeracy skills. Students are required to participate in school sports, represent the school in sports, culture and leadership, and be a member of a sporting team or coach a team in a community competition. Each student has a personalised learning plan incorporating their chosen sport's fitness program and they are linked to a buddy/mentor in his or her chosen sport.
>
> The Academy offers a differentiated curriculum, including vocational qualifications, outdoor recreation skills, leadership skills, work experience and sporting clinics. Students are expected to gain a set of qualifications in each calendar year, for example a first aid certificate, a Level 1 coaching qualification, be able to swim 50 metres and another qualification in their area of interest.
>
> Students participate two periods per week in the Academy program at their own school, and all Academy members from all schools meet three times a year for two-to-three-day camps. The camps include guest speakers and role models speaking on their success, opportunities to develop leadership and sporting skills, career education, and pathways to success programs. Academy students at each school may also meet before school once or twice a week for fitness sessions. Students' attendance and engagement in learning are monitored by the teacher in charge of the program at each school.
>
> Fifteen to 20 students from each of the nine Girri Girri schools are involved in the Academy program, with dedicated teacher co-ordinators running the program at each school. Among many highlights, seven Girri Girri students were selected in the Lloyd McDermott Rugby Country NSW Under 16 Aboriginal Rugby Union Representative team.
>
> The Girri Girri Academy program is run by the New South Wales Department of Education and Training (DET) and supported by the federal Department of Education, Employment and Workplace Relations (DEEWR).

and Torres Strait Islander history. Are there any oral histories?;
- invite Aboriginal and Torres Strait Islander people to talk to your group about the local history of your area and any local historical sites;
- visit the local historical society or museum to see how Aboriginal and Torres Strait Islander history is presented;
- research their own family histories, and compare their stories of a particular time

- with an Indigenous family's story from the same time;
- examine the programs and textbooks in your library or local schools to see how history is being presented;
- invite a representative of a local Indigenous organisation to speak to the group about their work;
- try to organise a visit to a local Indigenous organisation;
- find out whether their local government and chamber of commerce have policies to assist in overcoming Aboriginal and Torres Strait Islander unemployment locally;
- consider putting forth their views on reconciliation by writing a letter to the local paper;
- read Aboriginal and Torres Strait Islander literature;
- consider a class subscription to *Koori Mail* or *Land Rights News*;
- watch/listen to expanding Indigenous media (e.g. ABC's *Blackout*, *Speaking Out*, Koori Radio, CAAMA Radio, Imparja TV in the Northern Territory, National Indigenous TV);
- contact the Australian Press Council if racist or inaccurate comments appear in the local media;
- write to the Human Rights Commission office in your state or territory for information on the *Racial Discrimination Act* and the work the Commission does;
- research the effects of changes in government policy in the past on Indigenous people in your area;
- invite an Aboriginal or Torres Strait Islander organisation to provide a speaker to your class;
- find out what, if any, legislation operates in your area to deal with land claims and the protection of sacred sites;
- look up some of the recommendations of the Royal Commission into Aboriginal Deaths in Custody to find out what is being done about them;
- collect information for a timeline to reconciliation;
- collect press reports;
- contact the United Nations for more information on its role in Indigenous issues;
- visit your local MP to discuss the options for reconciliation, and what is being done to consider them in your local community; or approach your local council on the same issue;
- participate in creating a sister school with which to discuss your views;
- design a classroom or school mural on the theme of reconciliation in which all students participate; and
- write a story on their vision of society in the new century.

Stand up and be counted

As Patrick Dodson says, we have been asked to stand up and be counted. This one chance to achieve social justice for all Australians can be achieved if we as teachers are willing to stand up and be counted. Teachers have a vital role to play in contributing to the reconciliation process. The role involves teaching for reconciliation and educating for the future rather than just teaching the current state of play. It also involves ensuring that Indigenous students are receiving and gaining the benefits of excellence in educational practice. Teachers can provide the impetus for addressing critical social justice issues of our time and thereby contribute to creating a more socially just Australia for all Australians.

Menindee Central School students on stage with Indigenous NRL star David Peachey at the Swan Hill Croc Festival, 2004. Courtesy Indigenous Festivals of Australia.

Community involvement

Bev Smith

Gavin Andrews of Tharawal Local Aboriginal Land Council explaining Aboriginal culture to schoolchildren from The Oaks Public School (NSW) in 1994.

> Because so many teachers know so little about Aboriginal culture and about Aboriginal education history, there is very little understanding of the reasons why Aboriginal people might be reluctant to have much to do with schools, and often even less understanding of what might be the appropriate ways to invite Aboriginal community involvement.
> —Linda Burney

> Most teachers have never even met or spoken to an Aboriginal person, and that has its own effect, but when an Aboriginal person speaks to them about their history, it ceases to be just a history lesson. People are confronted with a new way of looking at the world, and must decide what they are going to do about that.
> —Damien Coghlan

In the words of the Department of Education, Employment and Workplace Relations:

> Research shows that high levels of parental and community involvement is strongly related to improved student outcomes and that family and community involvement can have a major impact on student learning, regardless of the social or cultural background of the family. (DEEWR, 2004, p. 2)

It is obvious to anyone who gives it any thought that this is even more important in the case of Aboriginal education, because family and community are so important in Aboriginal society. As the mother said in the *Bringing Them Home* video: 'We're family people. We're family people.' This is why educators who are involved in Aboriginal education are continually told to consult with and involve their local Aboriginal or Torres Strait Islander community. However, due to deficiencies in teacher education until very recently, and the general ignorance of most of the wider community, people often are not sure what consultation means in this context and do not know how to go about it.

Questions that tend to dominate this area include:

- What is consultation?
- What is participation? What is involvement?
- Why consult Aboriginal and Torres Strait Islander communities?
- How do we involve an Aboriginal or Torres Strait Islander community?
- What if . . . ?

What is consultation?

Consultation is an ongoing partnership that is mutually beneficial. Consultation and participation constitute a two-way process—a partnership based on mutual respect and understanding. For the partnership to achieve effective outcomes, it must be:

- open communication (as a two-way process);
- listening (not just hearing);
- negotiation (open and honest discussion by all involved based on equality);
- learning (all participants learning as a result of the consultative process);
- sharing (a two-way process from which all learn); and
- flexibility (discussing and negotiating, not trying to impose preconceived ideas).

We often take each of these skills for granted; however, few people have mastered them as they take considerable time and practice to develop. Fortunately they can be learnt 'on the job'—as each consultative situation takes a new focus, new skills are developed.

To be beneficial, consultation has to involve the active participation of community members in discussing the activities that students will undertake across the curriculum, and being involved in the implementation and evaluation process. Consultation is not a 'rubber stamp' activity; rather, it must involve active involvement in planning, design, implementation and evaluation across the curriculum.

Before catching a ride on the 'consultative process train', you should carefully assess your personal understandings and think about what you hope to achieve, what strategies you are going

Know the country and community

All new teaching staff have the right to know and the obligation to find out what First Nation country they will be teaching in after obtaining their teaching qualifications. The same applies to teaching staff who have been out in the field through their teaching careers, yet still many have no idea of which Nation's country they are teaching in or who are the custodians belonging to this country.

Teachers need to be careful about whom they talk to and trust in the community. There can be confusion around Aboriginal identity, country and culture, around which people belong to which country, when some Aboriginal people attach labels and misappropriate country. But in the process they may lose their own real connectedness to their own country. This is where proper cultural awareness is paramount in aligning new staff to country, people and the protocols for each country.

Active membership of the local AECG—or other Indigenous Education Consultative Body (IECB)—is the best way for teaching staff to learn about the local area they are teaching in, as well as the diversity of cultures within their community. Teachers can also be directed to resources, both human and material, to support Aboriginal studies programs in schools—not only during Reconciliation Week and NAIDOC Week—but all year round, with an all-inclusive involvement.

Born at the Menindee Mission in 1935 and a mother of ten, Aunty Beryl Carmichael (Yungha Dhu) of the Ngiyeempaa people has devoted her life to ensuring that Aboriginal culture is not lost to the Aboriginal and wider community: holding cultural immersion camps, publishing a book, and working in and with schools to pass on her knowledge and encourage recognition of Aboriginal perspectives in the curriculum. Having received countless awards for her decades of dedicated educational and community service, Aunty Beryl is a respected role model and advocate, whose views on Aboriginal education issues are sought and valued.

to use, and how this is likely to affect everyone involved. To achieve real involvement, you need to consider your level of understanding of Aboriginal and Torres Strait Islander peoples, cultures and the issues affecting people's lives. Your professional education needs to be an ongoing process.

Why involve Indigenous communities?

The development of genuine partnerships between schools and Indigenous communities remains the primary platform to productive, stimulating and responsive highly effective schools servicing Indigenous students. (MCEETYA and the Curriculum Corporation, 2006, p. 21)

The Commonwealth government and all states and territories are committed to Aboriginal community involvement in Aboriginal education. The Parental and Community Engagement Program (PaCE), which has replaced the program that in turn replaced ASSPA in 2005, aims to make it easier for schools and communities to establish real partnerships, but at the same time insists that systems and schools must live up to their responsibilities. This means, for example, that strategies to encourage Aboriginal students to attend school would not be funded, as this is the school's responsibility; however, PaCE would fund strategies to encourage parent and community involvement in the school. So systems fund 'outreach', while PaCE funds 'reach-in' strategies, supporting the capacity of families and the community to participate in school-level decisions and reciprocate the school's outreach activities. The focus is on thinking and innovation—new ways to foster real relationships.

It is universally acknowledged that in all education the involvement of the school community is an important factor in the effectiveness of the school's programs. Such involvement is even more essential for Indigenous Australian Studies programs—only Indigenous community members can teach their culture and convey their experience. The real impact of historical events on the lives of real people can readily be brought to life in the classroom by inviting Indigenous community members to share their experiences. Discussing issues that affect people today with community members will enable students to understand how these issues impinge on people's lives. The Indigenous community may also advise teachers on appropriate pedagogy for Indigenous students and Indigenous Studies activities.

Due to the failure of teacher education in the past, and the general conspiracy of silence on Indigenous Australia, most teachers know little or nothing about Indigenous Australia. Too often we still hear remarks like: 'I don't want to offend Aboriginal people, so I won't do it.' Effective consultation overcomes this problem by ensuring that only information acceptable to Aboriginal and Torres Strait Islander communities will be used in the classroom. A partnership is formed, developed and maintained, ensuring a collaborative approach to all the issues involved. Only through the consultative process will mutual knowledge and understanding be achieved that benefits all participants.

Local area Indigenous Australian Studies will always be the most appropriate focus, and the active involvement of local Indigenous communities is essential for the authenticity and success of all such studies. Interest in Indigenous Australian cultures, histories, perspectives and issues has grown dramatically over recent years. At the same time, it has been found that students are particularly receptive to and interested in Indigenous input, and in the viewpoints, knowledge and experiences of Indigenous people. Such input ensures that Indigenous Studies is taught as a real issue that affects the lives of Indigenous people and is relevant to all Australians today.

Indigenous people have knowledge and experience in their culture and history, so they can help children to realise they are learning content that has an effect on contemporary Indigenous Australians. Local people should be involved in the planning, implementation and evaluation of units of work that aim to teach students about the culture and history of the local community. Local communities can also provide guidance for teachers about what aspects of their history and culture need to be taught in schools. In addition, members of the local community can help to evaluate teaching resources to support the school curriculum.

For government schools with Indigenous students, the school Indigenous Education Worker can direct you to useful resources. Local, regional or state/territory Aboriginal Education Consultative Groups (e.g. the New South Wales AECG) also know what resources are appropriate for their communities. All state/territory Education Departments have Indigenous Education Units and district Aboriginal education resource personnel and consultants to provide advice to teachers in schools. Other systems, such as Catholic Education Commissions, also employ Aboriginal education resource personnel.

Some of the most useful resources teachers use are produced by local Indigenous community members. Across Australia, these communities have assisted schools with developing a wealth of important resources, such as:

- propagating, planting, and maintaining a bush garden in the school so that children can learn about environmental studies from Aboriginal perspectives;
- writing and illustrating 'big books' that inform children about local culture and the experiences of some of the members of the local community;
- murals and other artworks; and
- developing culturally appropriate mathematics materials.

Local community members have also taught children about:

- their life experiences;
- community initiatives and aspirations;
- current issues and ways forward;
- their culture today;
- how to play Aboriginal instruments;
- how to perform Aboriginal dances;
- bush survival skills; and
- how to understand and create Aboriginal inspired artworks.

While consultation is always vital, it is important to be aware of the age and stage of the students who will be learning from this input. This is where the importance of protocols becomes really evident. The communication should be two way, but non-Indigenous teachers need to be sensitive to the knowledge and beliefs of the communities with which they are engaging.

Books that have been examined by Indigenous people for appropriateness can be obtained from Indigenous book publishers and distributors (e.g. Magabala Books <www.magabala.com> or Black Ink Press, <www.blackinkpress.com.au>). Annual catalogues are also produced by commercial publishers, and they are happy to advise teachers on the resources available and which ones have been written by Aboriginal people.

Sources of advice

Indigenous organisations and Aboriginal education resource personnel can give guidance to teachers on where to locate appropriate and up-to-date material. For example, Aboriginal Land Councils often employ education officers who can assist teachers by giving talks to schools

Make your community proud. *Break dancer and VIBE role model Jason Campbell performing at a VIBE 3on3 Basketball and Hip-Hop Challenge at Taree. Note the Rio Tinto sign, an example of the sponsorship by big Australian companies. Courtesy Vibe Australia.*

and advising teachers about resources they have available. The New South Wales AECG markets resources (see <www.aecg.nsw.edu.au>).

The Australian Institute of Aboriginal and Torres Strait Islander Studies holds the largest Australian collection of Aboriginal Studies and Torres Strait Islander Studies materials, and can provide useful advice to teachers. The Institute also has an Aboriginal Education Officer.

What are the outcomes of community involvement?

Consultation and involvement in partnership with Indigenous communities in designing, teaching and evaluating programs ensures that:

- the knowledge, skills, and experiences of local Indigenous communities can be accessed to support Indigenous Studies in the classroom and school;
- teaching programs are authentic and presented in appropriate depth;
- appropriate pedagogy is utilised for the teaching of Indigenous Studies and the teaching of Indigenous students;
- information conveyed is accurate and appropriate to be taught to students, with a proper understanding of local history and culture;

- teaching resources are readily accessible, sensitive and appropriate;
- Indigenous people have control over what students are taught, how they are taught, and what resources from the community will be utilised;
- students can readily comprehend that they are learning about real people and how people have been affected by government policies and community attitudes; and
- the self-concept and pride in culture of Indigenous students is promoted and supported.

The role of Aboriginal Education Consultative Groups

Aboriginal Education Consultative Groups (AECGs) began in 1976 when the Commonwealth Schools Commission provided funds to state and territory Education Departments to consult Aboriginal people on education matters. AECGs or equivalent bodies, now widely known as Indigenous Education Consultative Bodies (IECBs), exist in each state and territory. They are composed of Aboriginal people who are committed to appropriate education for Aboriginal students.

The role of AECGs is to involve Aboriginal people and communities in educational decision-making in all sectors of Aboriginal education and training. AECGs' involvement and expertise extend from early childhood education through to higher education. They also advise all education providers from government systems, such as Education Departments and TAFE, to Catholic systems and independent schools, to universities and independent Indigenous providers. AECG services include:

- dissemination and networking of information relating to Aboriginal education;
- design, implementation and monitoring of policies and programs to meet the objectives of Aboriginal education;
- appropriate curriculum development; and
- advice on the development of appropriate teaching materials.

Community artist Chris Edwards working with students at Penshurst West Primary to paint a huge boomerang about the Georges River in Aboriginal designs for the school's Reconciliation Day, May 2009. Photo: Lisa Car.

How do we consult an Indigenous Australian community?

> There are cultural rules operating in Aboriginal communities that are very different to non-Aboriginal society. It is important to be sensitive to this. It is important to listen and learn. (Brady, Bennett and Phillips, 1993)

How do we consult any community? As teachers, we foster positive relationships with community members and seek their assistance in developing the curricula offered by the school. As community participation becomes an integral part of the school program, it is imperative that the Indigenous Australian community be actively consulted. This applies to all schools, irrespective of their Aboriginal or Torres Strait Islander student population. All Australian students have the right to learn about the history and celebrate the cultures of Indigenous Australian peoples.

A cautionary tale

Carpentaria is set in the fictional Gulf town of Desperance, said to be named after Captain Matthew Desperance Flinders. It was supposed to be a great port, but the river moved! It is told in the voice of a leader of the Pricklebush mob outside 'Uptown' boundaries—the kind of voice author Alexis Wright says white Australia has never wanted to hear. Uptown is where the 'respectable' white people live, then there are the Eastside and Westside Aboriginal mobs, and also the Gurfurrit mine up the country. This extract is about one of the main characters, Normal Phantom, and his youngest son Kevin—a brain at school, a menace anywhere else. With no thought to a career befitting his intellect; Kevin goes down the mine, suffers a horrific accident and damages his brain beyond repair:

None smarter than your Kevin, the white people used to say all the time about Kevin. Before, schoolteachers just about wore the road away, tramping down to the Phantoms' place every other day just to make sure Kevin was alright. *Mr Phantom, you must keep on encouraging Kevin with his schoolwork now won't you?* They would tell Norm, and he said he was starting to wonder what school teaching was all about. 'Well! What will you be doing if I have to teach him?' Norm asked. He said the family already knew how smart Kevin was. That was the reason he was going to school. *He has to amount to something*, the teachers wailed, biting their tongues, trying to make the family understand that Aboriginal people needed to succeed, and to succeed they needed to be educated.

Norm Phantom reiterated how proud he already was of Kevin but nobody needed to make a trophy of the boy either. 'You do your job and I will do mine.' By agreeing, he wanted those teachers to make sure they did their job to help, since nobody wanted more than Norm Phantom for Kevin to be able to get the hell out of Desperance, and away from family too, for that matter. 'Kevin thinks he is way too smart to be tied down to school,' Norm explained, wondering why the teachers had failed to capture his imagination by telling him straight that, like them, he could have a good life with lots of money.

'I don't even feel I belong here anymore,' Kevin complained about why he had to sit around uselessly trying to do essays about books talking about *them* white people's lives. He would look out the window from the kitchen table strewn with pencils, paper and books, and see his best friends enjoying the good life, standing around in the sun, preparing to go fishing down on the foreshore, talking to the teachers going fishing. Later, he would look up again from a pile of Tim Winton books, to look on a last glimpse of their boats crossing the seascape horizon, or would be out of range of their laughingly spent hours, tinkering over improvised outboard motors. He became the silent non-participant, listening to epic tales of sea journeys he kept missing out on. He was the warrior most unlikely. *Only in your dreams Kevin*. They told him of expeditions. Where renowned sharks were preyed upon in nocturnal hunts. Finally, Kevin was left only to hear stories. His essay on Tim Winton scored an A plus, but you tell me, who on earth cared?

Then, school days were finished for Kevin. When he left with his friends, they hung around town for months looking for something to do. At home, Kevin grew into the role of being the unchallenged brains trust of the family. He and Norm sat around for hours discussing television news, the political state of the nation, the way the country stuffed up the wool industry, who was who in the wars in countries nobody else in the family knew existed or were interested in, because they left the television for something in the fridge whenever the news came on.

But that was alright. Nobody in any case, including Norm, expected Kevin would actually get a job. 'No, look at Kevin,' the brothers teased, and Norm let his eyes slip over his thin son. He was all skin and bone. 'Aren't he the most unco kid you ever come across?' Norm refused to have Kevin on his boat even if he begged to be taken because he was too clumsy. All the family knew that if there was something to drop, Kevin was going to drop it.

> Gradually, all of his school mates were recruited into the road gangs working on the yellow roads. Up the track for weeks at a time mending chopped-up roads after the Wet, Brahman-cross cattle for company, they drove graders and trucks for the Town Council. They joined the crew sitting on their heavy machinery on the side of the road., waving at passing traffic, waiting for the foreman to arrive. There was plenty of work. Too much work. A perpetual round of work, repairing flood-damaged roads hacked to pieces by road transports carrying heavy machinery and grinding their way up to the mine, then loaded, returning to the coast, hauling the country away to pour into ships destined for overseas refineries.
>
> 'Kevin? You got to be joking!' The works supervisor was a straight-up-and-down kind of man who grew up with Kevin's older brothers and uncles. 'The Council has no use for Kevin.' Everyone in the town and down to the Pricklebush knew that Kevin, the fidget, would be useless on a job on the road. Over on Westside, Kevin's hands had already destroyed thousands of dollars worth of torches, electric appliances, motors. He must have had a little devil inside his head telling him to take other people's precious things apart. Even though the whole world could accept the fact that a table must have four legs, if you left Kevin alone, it would be on its side with three. *Kevin! Kevin! Why did you do that?* Unguarded machinery, instruments strung, screwed or balanced, or anything that operated on fuel, electricity or battery, was no place for Kevin. It would kill Kevin. Kevin would injure himself. But Kevin went down the mine for the money and the bosses took him on because how would they know? They did not even pretend to know who fronted up for work from Pricklebush. (pp. 105–7)

However, there are some considerations that must be taken into account when consulting Indigenous communities and people. In practice, there are a number of levels and types of consultative process:

- none ('We know best');
- dictatorial ('You will do this or else');
- tokenism—'I don't really care what you have to say, I'm only going through the motions', 'This is what we are going to do, starting tomorrow. What do you think?' ('We had better consult and make it look good');
- consultation—a bit of give and take ('But don't forget I'm paying you');
- effective consultation and involvement.

> I would say that government departments pay lip service. I do not think they value what we bring to the table. They talk about partnerships all the time. The partnership is actually, 'We will have a conversation with you, and we hear what you say but we do not listen.' They hear what we say but they do not listen. As someone mentioned before, the rhetoric is there and the commitment is there, but the practice and the action are not there. It is the value of working together.
> —Cindy Berwick, President, New South Wales AECG Inc., in New South Wales Legislative Council Standing Committee Final Report (2008) p. 21

Be warned: if you consult Indigenous communities, they will expect you to listen to what they have to say, and if you do not act they will want to know why.

Some strategies

Consultation with Indigenous communities is an ongoing process, which means considerable effort and time for all involved. Some strategies for achieving effective consultation include the following:

- Keep Indigenous parents and the Indigenous community informed about what is happening in your school at all levels through newsletters, meetings, informal discussions, and so on. Do not focus on negative aspects—instead, highlight the positive things that are happening in Indigenous education.
- Invite Indigenous community members to functions held at the school.
- Become actively involved in the Indigenous community. A familiar face is more easily and openly approached.
- Consult Indigenous parents from your school about what is happening in the school and how you may support each other.

- Consult key Indigenous education organisations (e.g. AECGs or IECBs).
- Discuss issues with Indigenous educators in your school (e.g. Indigenous teachers, Indigenous Education Workers (I/AEWs) and ancillary staff). Do not expect these people to do your work for you (they have their own roles within the school), but they may be able to assist you in getting started.
- Discuss issues with Indigenous parent organisations in the school, such as Indigenous members of the School Council.
- Other Indigenous organisations such as Aboriginal Land Councils, the Aboriginal Medical Service or the Aboriginal Legal Service can provide advice on issues in their fields; some have education officers. These organisations can also be a good way to introduce yourself to your community.
- Other government and non-government agencies such as local councils, National Parks and Wildlife, the police, museums, galleries, and so on may have Indigenous employees and/or contacts who may be able to assist in the consultative process.
- Hold meetings away from the school premises.
- Organise informal functions with the Indigenous community.
- Negotiate appropriate times and venues for meetings/discussions with Indigenous parents and community members. Do not assume that what suits you will also be appropriate for the community.
- Arrange child care for meetings/functions you hold.
- Celebrate National Aboriginal and Torres Strait Islander Week in the school, inviting Indigenous people to be involved.
- Invite Indigenous people to be involved in all aspects of the consultative process and take direction from them.
- In-service your staff about issues in Indigenous education, with the help of Indigenous educators and community members.
- Arrange payment for Indigenous community members to speak to students and staff.
- Promote Indigenous education and Indigenous Studies in the whole school community.
- Encourage Indigenous people to be members of school committees.

> **Considerations for effective consultation**
> Consider:
> - your level of understanding of Indigenous people and communities and of the issues that affect them daily;
> - your understanding of Aboriginality or Indigenous identity;
> - how much time and effort you prepare to put into developing effective consultative process;
> - developing your knowledge of Indigenous history and cultures;
> - developing the genuine friendship, mutual respect and trust of Indigenous people and communities;
> - being sensitive to events and issues in the community;
> - allowing appropriate time for Indigenous people to respond to your request or proposals (this may need to be negotiated);
> - being prepared to make changes to your program/s and approaches as a result of consultation;
> - sharing what you are doing, your skills and expertise with the Indigenous community;
> - recognising and respecting Indigenous people's skills and knowledge;
> - being clear about what you are asking for. Questions involving anything and everything about Indigenous people and cultures are inappropriate, so be focused;
> - being realistic with your requests; Indigenous people may have other commitments that take priority over your request;
> - being aware of the type of language you are using, as educational jargon often excludes people from being actively involved in consultative and decision-making processes; and
> - being careful not to stereotype Indigenous people and communities.
> —Rhonda Craven

None of these strategies will work in isolation. You need to try a number of combinations in order to develop effective consultative processes that will enable positive and proactive Indigenous community involvement and participation in the school. Commitment, time and being prepared to listen and learn are the strategies that will eventually lead to effective outcomes.

What if . . . ?

What if:

- you don't succeed?
- you offend someone?
- you make a mistake?
- you run out of time?

The list of 'What-ifs' is endless. If you don't succeed, there is always an opportunity to try again. You can learn a lot about what not to do the next time around. Commitment to consultation creates the determination to succeed.

If you make a mistake—so what? Everyone learns from their mistakes. Indigenous community members are familiar with Australia's inadequate schooling practices in relation to Indigenous Australian Studies, so it will not surprise them if you make an inadvertent mistake. In fact, the community will usually take the time to educate you about the facts to correct mistakes in an educative, amicable manner.

Many teachers worry needlessly about offending Indigenous community members by making mistakes. Community members are not easily offended, and—as is the case for other schooling issues that may cause offence—a simple apology goes a long way towards mending fences and addressing the issue of concerns together.

If you run out of time and just cannot do any more, remember you are an individual with limited time, resources, understanding and contacts. This is no reason to be disillusioned or defeated. But there is every reason to become more determined to make things work and to learn more about effective community consultation for yourself, your school, your students and the Indigenous community with which your school is involved.

What if there really is no local community?

This is the most commonly asked question in Aboriginal Studies. In some places, there will be no easily identifiable local Indigenous community. There are some schools that have no Aboriginal or Torres Strait Islander students; this means no AEW, no committee, no local AECG—apparently nowhere to go for advice and input, no one to consult, and hence no prospect of local community involvement. There may be few Indigenous people in your school's area, and for a range of reasons they may be unable to assist your school. None of this means that you should not teach Indigenous Australian Studies, or that you cannot have Indigenous involvement in your program. Aboriginal Studies is not just for Aboriginal and Torres Strait Islander students—it is a must for *all* Australian students.

Even without a local Aboriginal or Torres Strait Islander community, you can still have Indigenous involvement in your Aboriginal Studies program. This Indigenous involvement is essential. All state and territory education systems have Aboriginal education resource personnel. Community educators are available in all areas, and many Aboriginal organisations in other fields see themselves as performing an educative role.

Approaching the local community

The strategies presented in the following text box were developed by James Wilson-Miller. Together with common sense, they can help you approach your school's Indigenous community to establish effective links in the consultation process.

Guest speakers

Inviting Indigenous community members to share their experiences is the best way for students to learn. Students can see that what they are learning is about real people, real events that have adversely affected people today and real current concerns.

It is important to negotiate the topics to be covered with each guest speaker. A common mistake made by beginning teachers is to ask the guest speaker to cover too much. Try to be specific about the aspects of the topic you want covered. Avoid expecting the guest speaker to be your only form of intake for a content area—students should have the opportunity to learn from a variety of source material. Note also that at least three to four intake activities are needed to cover a particular content area in appropriate depth (see Chapter 15).

It is also important to ensure that your students are prepared for a visit from a guest speaker. There is usually little point in inviting a guest speaker to introduce a completely new

Some tips for approaching Indigenous school communities

- Get to know as much as you can about Indigenous communities before you go there, (i.e. do your own 'situational analysis'—especially on all the positive aspects of local Indigenous communities.
- Get to know and work with your local Indigenous community organisations (e.g. local and regional AECGs or IECBs, local Aboriginal Land Councils, medical services, employment services, legal services and local Indigenous Elders' organisations).
- Be aware that every Indigenous community differs from every other community.
- Be aware of the 'differing factions' within Indigenous communities. Keep an impartial position with all of them.
- Remember, it is professionally negligent for any non-Indigenous or Indigenous professional to be totally unaware of Indigenous Australian issues, given the amount written on Indigenous people and issues today.
- Greet people with a smile and warm, friendly gestures.
- Never try to impress Indigenous people with your professional level of education. They know you are an educated person or you would not be there.
- Be aware of the difference between the 'well-educated' and 'wisely educated' person. Both will know the meaning of educational jargon and how to use key educational terms, but a wisely educated person knows when *not* to use them.
- Become involved in community social events, if invited. These are good icebreakers.
- Never be swayed by the 'self-fulfilling prophecies' of others (e.g. longer-term teaching colleagues or local community members—both Indigenous and non-Indigenous) find out for yourself where 'problems' may exist and work with appropriate others to alleviate them.
- Liaise with your Indigenous colleagues and your principal, remembering that they may know more than you about the community you are in.
- Never assume that Indigenous colleagues and community members are expert historians, anthropologists, archaeologists, linguists or social commentators. They are knowledgeable people but have their job to do, as do you.
- Above all, be approachable, understanding, flexible, empathetic, not sympathetic; be *yourself*, and be prepared to listen and learn from Indigenous communities.
- The above dot points are for your benefit; if you choose not to use them, then for your sake, please let common sense prevail.

—James Wilson-Miller

area of study, as students will be ill-prepared to gain the most value from such a visit. As with any special visit, students should have undertaken preparatory work before the arrival of the guest speaker.

Also be aware of the potential for uninformed backlash. If the audience is racist, or holds misconceived or stereotypical views, Indigenous people's input can be seen negatively. We have experienced students in Year 3 holding views that were obviously transmitted to them from their parents. Careful pre-visit preparation and sequencing of lessons to explore each content area in depth can help to avoid such difficulties.

Tips for organising a visit from culture educators

Pre-visit preparation

- Seek advice and involve your local community.
- Send an official written invitation and be specific about what you want the culture educator to do. Follow your invitation up with a phone call.
- Negotiate the program with the culture educator and listen to what they can offer you.
- Find out whether the culture educator would like to bring along other support people.

Beyond Empathy

Beyond Empathy (BE) was set up in Armidale, northern New South Wales, in 2004 to use the arts as an individual and community development tool. It is based on the belief that arts can facilitate individual and community dialogue, development and change, and that arts practice can be delivered in a way that helps strengthen local support networks and promotes long term individual and social change.

BE has received awards for its community arts programs and was one of ten community arts organisations awarded long-term funding by the Australia Council in 2008. With a dedicated administration team, about ten permanent staff and a pool of 70 contracting artists and community workers, BE's $1.9 million annual budget is funded by a mix of government grants, philanthropic funding and individual donations.

BE arts programs in disadvantaged, regional and remote communities provide youth with experiences to help them build support networks to make positive changes in their lives. With backgrounds of recurring, often inter-generational hardship, many of the young people BE works with have dropped out of school, are jobless or never had a job, have an unstable home environment, have been in (or are highly likely to get into) trouble with the law, have multiple health issues and/or misuse drugs and alcohol. They often have limited contact with local support agencies and health and education services and distrust or dismiss them. A high number are Aboriginal or Torres Strait Islander.

BE runs long-term or repeat-intensive arts workshops over long timeframes (up to three years) to give time to build rapport and broker relationships between young people and support workers. A range of different art forms are used; BE workers select the form most likely to resonate with each group. A development program for youth who engage strongly in workshops encourages them to set positive aspirations and take advantage of mentoring and intensive training camps. Transition programs help young people 'graduate' from BE and move into more formal study or employment options based on the skills they have developed.

BE uses the arts to build confidence and skills in youth, develop support networks, and build communities' awareness of the needs of youth and programs that can help them. The arts engage young people and provide a fun, safe space to explore the issues of their lives and trial new ways of being. Arts activities connect young people with support workers and grow relationships. BE aims to help youth develop skills, build a sense of what they are capable of, and take responsibility for themselves and their future. BE also collaborates with local agencies and support workers to support the young people it works with. This dual focus makes BE's practice different from many other arts-based organisations.

Each of us has a way of looking at the world. Throughout our lives we build up sub-conscious mental models or frames of reference to interpret what goes on around us. Mental models can fast-track judgements, but they can also trip us up; they can limit us to familiar ways of thinking and acting, and lead us to make assumptions about ourselves, and others, that aren't true.

Getting involved with something like the programs BE runs can build skills and transform how young people think about themselves and their world through engagement in a creative process and through the artistic work produced. Often people make assumptions about others based on what they think their behaviour means, without realising what may have led to these actions (or their own role). Many disengaged youth have negative experiences with support services and may adopt a defensive, non-compliant attitude as self-protection. Support workers are often inadequately resourced; they try to help and feel frustrated, hurt and unappreciated when repeatedly rebuffed by those they seek to help—or when they believe young people aren't making an effort. Frustrated emotions on either side can lead to a failure to engage with one another. BE uses double-loop learning to get people to bring to the surface and then challenge the mental models that block them: both doing the activity and learning the skills, and then being encouraged to reflect on their mental models and view of the world.

BE programs explore individual and community issues: identity, place, difference and acceptance, drug and alcohol use/management, mental health, parenting and social space. BE staff work one-on-one with youth to explore how these issues affect their lives, families and communities. Public exhibitions and performances allow BE to translate one-on-one dialogue into a community discussion. The aim is to shape attitudes and encourage the community to engage with their young people in a more constructive way.

- Where necessary, provide transport to and from the school.
- Place a reminder to staff on your noticeboard to alert them to the visit, and tell people about it.
- Ensure that children have undertaken some activities on the topic so that the visit is not an isolated learning experience. It might also be useful to help students to develop some workshop questions prior to the visit.

During visit

- Provide morning tea and/or lunch.
- Introduce culture educator/s to the school executive.
- Coordinate informal meetings (e.g. morning tea) with other staff members.
- Organise students to assist in showing your visitor the school (e.g. Indigenous students could be asked to undertake this task to reinforce their identity, or non-Indigenous students could undertake this as a learning experience, or both an Indigenous and non-Indigenous student could escort the visitor).

Post-visit follow-up

- Remember to forward a letter of thanks and payment for services.
- Remember to engage your class in a debriefing session and follow-up activities.

Organising a community member visit

Community educators are Indigenous people who teach about their culture in schools. They are usually, though not always, drawn from the local community. Culture educators have many varied skills, and many specialise in a specific area—for example, storytelling, art, dance or even a variety of areas such as bush tucker, language or culture. Your local community and local consultation sources can advise you on appropriate and available educators for your school.

Organising a visit from a community member involves the same processes as organising other visits. Common sense and courtesy are the key requirements, but some awareness of Indigenous Australian protocol is also essential.

Koori Kids Don't Need Fixing

In 23 years of working in Aboriginal education I've never met a Koori kid that wanted to be 'fixed'. That's not to say they didn't want their circumstances to be better—they do want better opportunities and more options.

So surely our responsibility as teachers is to find the right tools that build on and draw from their incredible life experience. I've found that Koori kids are the most resilient, resourceful and entrepreneurial kids in any classroom or workshop setting I've been in. So, we need to start where they are and approach them with an asset-focused mindset.

What they've said to me, again and again, is: 'If you've come to preach to me or fix me, you're in the wrong place, Aunt. But if you wanna work with me, then right on; I'm up for it.'

Be aware that Koori kids are the best BS detectors. If they see a real, genuine relationship they'll embrace it every time; they'll do pretty much anything you want. They'll have a go.

Our duty as educators is to find the right tools to make that happen. And very likely those right tools will be found outside the box.

Kim McConville has a Diploma of Education focusing on Aboriginal Studies and Behaviour Disorders—a natural double, she says. She has worked with New South Wales Aboriginal communities for 23 years: working at the New South Wales AECG, then with the Aboriginal Curriculum Unit of the Board of Studies. Working at Tranby Aboriginal College after that, she co-wrote the first VETAB-accredited Aboriginal Studies course with Jack Beetson.

For the past fifteen years, Kim has used community arts and cultural development to build up individual and whole-community capacity to change people's lives. In 2004, she co-founded Beyond Empathy to deliver empowerment programs across the country for individuals and their communities. Her main focus has always been Aboriginal kids and their families. In 2006 she was recognised by Social Ventures Australia as Social Entrepreneur of the Year.

As with other visitors to your school, community members should be provided with some background information for their visit so they know what they are expected to do on arrival at the school.

—Rhonda Craven

> **Information that Indigenous community members may need to have before visiting the school**
> - Are there any Indigenous students or staff at the school?
> - What staff member do they deal with?
> - What is the age range and gender breakdown of the audience?
> - What is the size of the audience?
> - What previous experiences has the audience had in Indigenous Studies?
> - Have there been any particular misinformed views expressed by the audience?
> - Have any other Indigenous resource people or groups presented to this audience? Who were they? What did they talk about?
> - Does the Indigenous culture educator need the school to purchase some resources for their visit (e.g. paint).
> - Is this lesson to be followed up with another?
> - Where will they meet you when they arrive?
> - What is the venue like?
> - What equipment is available for the venue (microphone, interactive board, access to a computer)?
> - Are you setting up the guest speaker(s) in one room? Are groups being brought to the guest speaker(s) or do they need to visit more than one classroom or venue? How many classes are involved? If moving, who will be available to assist with moving resources? What is the timetable for the visit?
> - Overall, embrace this as a learning opportunity and ensure professional engagement takes place at all stages: negotiation, implementation and evaluation.
>
> —Rhonda Craven

Sources of assistance

Teachers can obtain help from a range of sources when trying to access the local Indigenous community. The most important sources are local, but regional and state/territory organisations can help you to contact your community.

Initial contacts can be made through Indigenous people associated with your school—for example, Aboriginal and Torres Strait Islander teachers working in your school, Indigenous education workers, parents of Indigenous students, local community members, the local AECG. If you are having difficulty contacting your local community or if no local Indigenous community is in your area, you can seek assistance from regionally based Aboriginal education personnel. Most education systems now have regional or district consultants in Aboriginal education. The role of these consultants is to help teachers to implement the education system's Aboriginal education policy.

An important source of district advice is regional AECGs. If you cannot identify a local AECG, you may find that a regional AECG exists. This can clarify whether a local AECG exists and provide advice and assistance when there is none. At the state/territory level, there are also a range of sources of assistance. Every state and territory has an AECG. If you cannot locate your local or regional AECG or if such organisations do not exist for your area, you can always contact your state/territory AECG for advice and assistance. Aboriginal education units also often exist within state/territory education systems, and can provide important advice on how to get started.

Procedures and ethics of consultation

It is critical to consult your local community from the beginning when school policy or teaching units is to be developed. There may be little point in attempting to consult the community to seek its approval of and participation in something you have already decided to do. Rather, a partnership between the school and community should be forged to develop school policy and units of work so that your local community can give you guidance on appropriate content and pedagogy. At the same time, it is important not to make members of the local community feel pressured to be involved in school activities. Consultation is a partnership, not a power relationship.

Often, meetings with the local community operate in a different way from staff meetings. For example, many Aboriginal communities conduct meetings on the basis of consensus: agreement is reached by all members of the group by talking through rather than voting on issues. Adequate time needs to be allowed for these decision-making processes to reach consensus. Teachers must respect the validity of Indigenous language styles. The fact that community people may not use educational jargon does not mean that they do not know about Indigenous education. Teachers also need to show respect for Aboriginal English without being patronising. It is not 'bad' English—it is just a different form of language and has its own expressive power.

Be aware that viewpoints will at times differ within the local Aboriginal or Torres Strait Islander community. As in the wider community, members of Indigenous communities reserve their right to hold individual opinions. It is also possible for different groups within the Indigenous community to hold different viewpoints. One way of addressing a variety of viewpoints is to meet a wide sample of the community so all are represented. Often consensus can be reached on most issues through discussion. Where it seems difficult to obtain consensus between opposing views, it can be useful to convene a special meeting of the consultative group and ask that the issue be addressed in such a way that you are advised on how to proceed. Once Indigenous community members are aware that you are experiencing difficulties, a compromise position might be reached.

Teachers need to avoid consulting or identifying with only one faction, one family or one individual in the community. If the teacher interacts with only one member or one group in a community, the teacher's effectiveness is greatly reduced because members of the other groups may feel under-valued and offended. One strategy for avoiding this problem is to be proactive in seeking the viewpoints of the entire local Indigenous community. Personal contact with a number of Indigenous members of the community is helpful. Likewise, inviting all the groups you are aware of (e.g. Aboriginal education resource people, local AECGs, parents) to advise the school is an important inclusive strategy.

Teachers should try to meet members of the local community in an environment that is culturally appropriate or comfortable for them. Teachers should understand that, due to previous negative experiences, some Aboriginal or Torres Strait Islander people may not be comfortable in schools or other learning institutions. Your community consultation and involvement program should be about making Indigenous community members feel at home in the school, so that they and their children can feel that it is their school too.

When the community offers information to teachers, it is professional courtesy to recognise their ownership of information by

Storyteller Tanya Ellis with students. Photo: Caroline Davy. Courtesy University of New South Wales.

acknowledging sources and seeking the community's permission to publish or photocopy any information conveyed. Any future use of this information should also be negotiated with and agreed to by the community.

In some communities, it is important for teachers to respect specific cultural beliefs and practices. For example, it may be culturally appropriate in a particular community to avoid mentioning the names or showing any images of deceased people.

When employing culture educators, schools should recognise their moral responsibility to pay these people for their services. Teachers are paid to teach, and guest teachers should be paid when they come to teach your students. Payment is recognition of the value of their knowledge and experience.

Also, it cannot be assumed that any community member is competent to teach children in a class. We do not assume that non-Indigenous community members are competent to teach children without our professional assistance, and the same applies to Indigenous community members. Failure to recognise this can lead to misconceptions about the role community members should be asked to perform in the school. For example, we cannot expect Indigenous community members to write entire Indigenous Australian Studies units of work, as only teachers have the expertise to do this.

Possible difficulties and possible solutions

Possible difficulty	Possible solutions
No local Indigenous community is available.	• Contact your state/territory AECG to ascertain whether a regional or local AECG can assist you or relevant counterparts in other systems. • Contact educational authority Aboriginal education personnel (e.g. community liaison officers, Aboriginal education consultants).
Members of the local Indigenous community seem reluctant to consult with the school.	• Realise that many Indigenous people have had negative experiences with schools. • Seek assistance from the school's Aboriginal Education Worker or relevant counterparts in other systems. • Where the school has no AEWs, contact AECG or systems Indigenous personnel to assist. • Organise experiences that Indigenous parents may be interested in attending to provide non-threatening opportunities for parents to feel comfortable visiting the school (e.g. cultural day, flag-raising ceremony, guest speakers, morning tea).
Only a few Indigenous pupils attend the school and their parents are too busy to assist the school.	• Seek assistance from local, regional, and state/territory AECGs. • Support children's pride in their Aboriginality in both the classroom and school (e.g. celebrate NAIDOC Week, invite guest speakers, form an Indigenous children's group, display Aboriginal murals, literature and art around the school). • Seek assistance from the Aboriginal education consultants, Aboriginal community liaison officers and relevant counterparts in other systems to develop Indigenous Australian Studies units and perspectives across the curriculum. • Recognise that Indigenous education involves the education of all students, both Indigenous and non-Indigenous, about the history, cultures and issues of Australia's Indigenous peoples.
A teacher wishes to invite a guest speaker on a specific topic but does not know who to ask or who would be available.	• Seek advice from your local Indigenous community, Aboriginal education consultants or local/regional AECG.
Differing viewpoints on what is to be taught are expressed to the teacher.	• Hold a community consultation meeting to decide what approaches the community would like to be used. Seek assistance from AEWs, regional Aboriginal education consultants and regional/local AECGs. • Recognise that Indigenous communities are diverse and made up of individuals with different views; hence one person's view should not be taken as constituting community consultation or necessarily representing the views of the community. • Note that community consultation should take place at all stages, and is the first step in deciding what to teach about local studies and how this is best achieved.

—Rhonda Craven

Similarly, Indigenous community members should not be expected to teach all Indigenous Australian Studies lessons; teachers need to structure and sequence the delivery of activities and contribute to the academic content of the subject.

Ask a representative group of the community to identify community members with the expertise to teach children about different topics. For example, some secret/sacred aspects of ceremonial life cannot be taught to non-Indigenous children or certain age groups of Indigenous children. Other aspects may not be taught to members of the opposite gender. Sensitive issues and cultural studies are usually taught by Elders, as Elders know which content is appropriate for specific groupings of children. With proper consultation, the Indigenous community can assist you to identify members with the expertise to teach specific topics.

Young Aboriginal dancers at an Aboriginal Education Council Family and Community Fun Day at Alexandria Park Community School, 2009. Photo: MYLC Photography. Courtesy Aboriginal Education Council (NSW).

White Child

White child I thank you
for giving me the time
to tell you how life is
in a hard white racist world.
You sat and listened
with open mind and open heart
devouring my words of life.
Cynicism has not destroyed your soul
nor dulled your shining eye
you still dream
dreams of justice and equality.
Don't forget that day we spoke
and how you felt for me
remain a beacon in the dark recess
of bigotry.
For it's you who looks at you
when you stand at the mirror each day.
    —Norm Newlin (1986, reproduced with permission)

What research can tell us

Rhonda Craven and
Gawaian Bodkin-Andrews

Students with faces painted, 2004 Croc Festival at Derby, Western Australia. Evaluations found improved attendance and participation; again and again previously unengaged or 'problem' students flourished at the Croc. Courtesy Indigenous Festivals of Australia.

Unfortunately for Australia, the full benefits of education have yet to be realised for the Indigenous peoples. At the beginning of the 21st century, ameliorating Indigenous educational disadvantage was presented as 'an urgent national priority' by MCEETYA (2000a, p. 1). Although the rate of Indigenous students' access to, participation in, and retention in education has shown improvements in some recent decades, equitable outcomes are not being achieved (Hunter & Schwab, 2003). Improvements in Indigenous education remain dwarfed by the magnitude of the discrepancy between Indigenous and non-Indigenous educational achievements (Ridgeway, 2002). (Mellor and Corrigan, 2004, pp. 1–2)

Mellor and Corrigan summarised the dire state of Indigenous disadvantage in 2002; it is still much the same almost a decade later (see Steering Committee for the Review of Government Services Provision, 2009). Indigenous Australians are arguably the most disadvantaged of Indigenous nations across all developed countries (Cooke et al., 2007; Hill, Barker and Vos, 2007; Ring and Brown, 2003) and the most educationally disadvantaged group in Australia. There is a shocking dearth of empirical research in Indigenous education, particularly in the schooling sector, as acknowledged by leading Indigenous educators in this field (e.g. Bin-Sallik in Craven, 2005). Furthermore, Professor Paul Hughes has noted:

> While our community still thinks that we are over-researched, the Advisory Committee and I do not agree, and we call for a substantial increase in research in the area of Indigenous education. This review so excellently and objectively done ... supports the contention that much more focused and longitudinal research is needed. (Hughes, quoted in Mellor and Corrigan, 2004)

This lack of quality research is unfortunate, as such research is fundamental and vital to effective intervention. Compounding this is a plethora of widely held assumptions about what seeds success for Indigenous students—everyone seems to think they know the solutions, so many have been tried and have failed to produce systemic change. Research has also tended to focus on deficit models—learning more about what is wrong rather than building on what actually works. This lack of empirical Indigenous education research impedes our progress in addressing the educational disadvantage suffered by Indigenous children in the development of new solutions.

Recent syntheses of educational research studies (Hattie, 2009) have identified promising aspects of excellence in educational practice that impact on educational outcomes (e.g. having high expectations, setting tasks of high intellectual challenge). In this chapter, it is argued that we need to capitalise on what is known about what factors actually impact on educational outcomes from research with both Indigenous and other students. We present a review of research evidence in order to identify potential factors that will seed success.

What research with non-Indigenous students says

To begin to identify what may seed success, we need to access the very best available educational theory, research and practice to inform Indigenous education. Given the dearth of empirical research—particularly in schooling—that targets Indigenous students, our journey needs to commence with what we already know about what makes a difference in all education. The best place to start is to examine some findings of leading education researchers who have devoted their careers to answering this question by utilising state-of-the-art theory, research and practice.

Hattie's synthesis of meta-analyses

> We need a barometer of what works best, and such a barometer can also establish guidelines as to what is excellent—too often we shy from using this word thinking that excellence is unattainable in schools. Excellence is attainable: there are many instances of excellence, some of it fleeting, some of it aplenty. (Hattie, 2009, p. ix).

John Hattie advocates that what we should be looking at is those attributes that have marked as opposed to minor effects on student achievement to identify a barometer of excellence. Given that excellence in teaching is vital to closing the gap for Indigenous students, this research has important implications for enhancing the teaching of Indigenous students.

Hattie (2009) analysed over 800 meta-analyses incorporating 52 637 studies targeting many millions of students, and in the process identified six primary factors that have been found to influence the achievement patterns of students: the child, home, school, curriculum, teacher and teaching approaches. Hattie (2003) synthesised five of these six major sources of variance in achievement and found that, overall, the two most substantive areas of contribution towards student achievement were the students themselves (e.g. motivation, self-concept) and excellent teaching practice. This led Hattie to conclude that it is not all teachers who make the difference, but it is excellent teachers that make the most difference:

> It is what teachers know, do, and care about which is very powerful in this learning equation . . . the

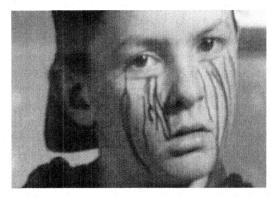

A young Aboriginal boy with tears of blood down his face. Still photo from the film Hurt, *scripted and filmed by 250 youth from five northwest NSW towns with BighART. Founded in west-coast Tasmania in 1992, BighART is a non-profit organisation that pilots arts projects to re-engage marginalised youth.* HURT *won the 2000 AFI Best Concept award. Courtesy BighART.*

person who gently closes the classroom door and performs the teaching act—the person who puts into place the end effects of so many policies, who interprets these policies, and who is alone with students during their 15,000 hours of schooling. (2009, p. 2)

Hattie (2009) produced a detailed examination of the criteria encouraging student excellence, and identified what variables have a stronger than average effect size ($d = .40$) over student achievement: 'a level where the effects of innovation enhance achievement in such a way that we can notice real-world differences, and this should be a bench mark of such real-word change' (2009, p. 17). In the following section, we review some of these findings as it is highly likely that, even though these findings have not been validated with Indigenous students, they are relevant to developing excellence in the Indigenous Studies classroom—and they certainly provide one benchmark of what is most likely to constitute excellence for Indigenous education.

The student
Hattie (2009) identified key student-learning-background influences on achievement, which included: students' *self-reported grades* (Rank 1), their awareness of ability to succeed; *Piagetian stage programs* (Rank 2), which incorporate an understanding of children's cognitive and emotional stages of development; and *levels of prior achievement* (Rank 17). These results resonate with Indigenous research (see Craven and Tucker, 2003), which has long emphasised the need for teachers to ensure that Indigenous students hold positive conceptions of themselves as successful learners. Hattie's findings offer empirical evidence to support this Indigenous community viewpoint. An understanding of how best to match learning strategies to children's cognitive and emotional development clearly is a key attribute of all excellent teachers and as critical for Indigenous students as it is for other Australian students. The influence of prior levels of achievement on later achievement resonates with the need to close the gap for Indigenous students (see Chapter 12). However, given that prior achievement is ranked at 17, clearly there are also other attributes of excellence that can influence achievement.

Outside of students' learning background, Hattie (2009) also found other factors to have an above-average effect on student achievement: *initial birth weight* (Rank 38); *concentration/engagement* (Rank 49); enhanced *motivation* (Rank 51); specific *pre-school interventions* targeting a variety of learning outcomes (Rank 52); *access to pre-school and kindergarten programs* (Rank 55); a stronger sense of *self-concept* (Rank 60); and *anxiety-reduction techniques* (Rank 66). Initial birth weight remains an issue of concern in Indigenous Australia, given Indigenous people are so disadvantaged in health status. Recently, we have advocated (Craven and Bodkin-Andrews, 2006) that a real turning point in Indigenous education could take place if a positive psychology approach could be applied by teachers fostering the development of adaptive psychological tools (e.g. engagement, enhanced self-concept, motivation and anxiety reduction), which research shows lead to desirable educational outcomes. Hattie's findings offer further support for this way forward. Also, Indigenous community members have long called for better access for Indigenous students to quality pre-school education programs, and some improvements in this regard are being made.

For the purposes of this chapter, it is also useful to note that Hattie (2009) found that ethnicity had minimal effects, which led him to conclude:

> What seems more important is that students have a positive view of their own racial group, and that educators do not engage in the language of deficit theorizing. Accepting that students come to school and have difference in cultural heritages and that they can be allowed and encouraged to have positive image of their own racial group or heritage is an acknowledgement of the importance of culture, and can show the students that they are accepted and welcomed within the learning environment. (2009, p. 58)

Researchers (e.g. Purdie et al., 2000; Craven and Tucker, 2003) and Indigenous community members have long advocated that the respect and promotion of Indigenous students' identity self-concepts are critical in the learning equation for Indigenous students.

The home

Hattie (2009) found key predictors of achievement related to the home included: *home environment (Rank 31)*, the socio-psychological environment and level of intellectual stimulation in the home; *socio-economic status* (Rank 32); and *parental involvement in learning* (Rank 45)—that is, parents who set positive expectations and involve themselves in the learning of their children. Clearly, positive parenting is critical for both Indigenous and other Australian students, and parents of Indigenous children are particularly keen to see their children do well at school.

The school

Hattie (2009) also identified individual school practices that influence student achievement. These include: *accelerated instruction* (Rank 5) for gifted students; *classroom cohesion* (Rank 39), promoting a sense of the students and teachers working together to achieve higher learning goals; *peer influences* (Rank 41), school policies emphasising class cooperation, peer tutoring, emotional support and peer feedback; *classroom management* (Rank 42), specific school-wide strategies for classroom management and discipline; *small-group learning* (Rank 48); and *school size* (Rank 59), with 600 to 900 students being optimal. These strategies could work equally well for Indigenous and other Australian students.

The curriculum

Hattie (2009) identified effective reading strategies including: *vocabulary programs* (Rank 15), definition and contextual information in tandem with deeper learning strategies; *repeated reading* (Rank 16), students repeatedly reading passages until fluency is achieved; *phonic instruction* (Rank 22), strategies such as phonic isolation; *comprehension programs* (Rank 28), strategies to ensure students understand what they read, categorisation blending, segmentation and deletion; *visual perception* (Rank 35), techniques for early learning readers; and *second/third-chance programs* (Rank 47). Identifying these programs surely is the way to establishing strategies for excellence in Indigenous literacy programs.

Hattie also identified a number of other effective programs, including: *creativity programs* (Rank 17), instructional materials and techniques to facilitate and enhance creative thinking; *outdoor education programs* (Rank 43); *mathematics programs* (Rank 54), with constructive feedback; and *writing programs* (Rank 57), teaching students how to structure compositions by planning/summarising, revising, editing their work and writing for a particular audience. Overall, Hattie (2009, p. 159) argues that 'it is less the content of the curricula that is important than the strategies teachers used to implement the curriculum'. In Indigenous education, it has been often emphasised that what fundamentally seeds success is engaging Indigenous students in schooling both actively and creatively.

The teacher

Hattie (2009) also identified effective teaching practices that have marked effects on student achievement. These include: *teaching clarity* (Rank 8), clear organisation and explanation in communicating with students; *teacher–student relationships* (Rank 11), teachers developing strong reciprocal relationships and valuing students' background and experience; *labelling students* (Rank 21), self-fulfilling labels such as 'able'/'disabled', 'special'/'regular', potentially influencing the quality of teaching students receive; *quality of teaching* (Rank 56), an openness to review of a teacher's teaching styles by students; and positive *expectations of students* (Rank 58). Overall, Hattie concludes:

> teachers [should] enter the classroom with certain conceptions about progress, relationships, and students. It requires them to believe that their role is that of a change agent—that all students *can* learn and progress, that achievement for all is changeable and not fixed, and that demonstrating to all students that they care about their learning is both powerful and effective. (2009, p. 128)

All of these predictors of achievement, along with Hattie's conclusion, resonate with what we know is best practice when it comes to Indigenous students. Community members have always emphasised the importance of developing positive relationships with Indigenous children and the critical nature of teachers holding high expectations for Indigenous students.

Teaching approaches

One recurring theme throughout this chapter is the paramount role of the teacher. This role is not limited to what teachers bring into the classroom in the form of expectations and prior learning, but is also what they actually *do* in the classroom. Considering the enormous amount of research into what constitutes quality teaching, it is no surprise that not only did Hattie split quality teaching practices into nine sub-categories, but also across two chapters. Here we summarise some of his findings with regard to three of the categories he mentions.

Successful strategies emphasising learning intentions that have a moderate effect include *concrete mapping* (Rank 33), providing students with a clear structure of what is to be learnt, and allowing students to identify components and themes of lessons; *setting challenging goals* (Rank 34); and *advance organisers/explaining specific behavioural objectives* (Rank 61).

Strategies about success criteria include *mastery learning* (Rank 29), giving students clear instructions about what it takes to master the learning; *Keller's Personalised System of Instruction* (Rank 40), individualised and sequentially structured teaching designs where students proceed at their own pace and progress when mastery is achieved, while teachers provide motivational and tutorial support rather than whole-class teaching approaches; and finally, *worked examples* (Rank 30), providing students with clear examples of how to complete a given task in a stepwise fashion. All of these attributes of excellence could readily be applied to enhance excellence in Indigenous education.

Implementations that *emphasise feedback* are a most powerful influence on student achievement. Hattie (2009) argues that *feedback* (Rank 10) is a reciprocal process whereby a teacher not only provides clear and informed feedback to the students, but is also open to feedback from students as an unbiased indication of how well teaching strategies are being received. This is a critical finding: too often in Australian classrooms, Indigenous students are not asked to provide teachers with critical feedback, yet such feedback is critical to developing excellence in teaching practice. Clear feedback as a tool to enhance teacher excellence could easily and readily be applied to Indigenous students.

The influence of varying teaching strategies over student outcomes is very much apparent in the large number of above-average positive effects identified in Hattie's (2009) meta-analysis, leading him to conclude that it is the strategies used by excellent teachers that have the greatest impact, rather than resources and top-down teaching reforms: it is 'the differences in the teachers that make the difference in student learning' (2009, p. 236). Clearly, the implication of Hattie's research for Indigenous education is that excellence in teaching Indigenous students is highly likely to enhance achievement outcomes and as such should be viewed as a prime catalyst for change.

The importance of teacher quality: Rowe (2003)

We continue this journey by looking at some of the work of another leading scholar and a valued colleague of ours—the late Ken Rowe. Like Hattie (2009), Rowe (2003) emphasises the importance of teacher quality as a key determinant of schooling outcomes. Rowe advocates that prevailing dogmas about presumed determinants of schooling outcomes:

> are now understood to be products of methodological and statistical artefact, and amount to little more than 'religious' adherence to the moribund ideologies of *biological* and *social determinism*. Moreover, post-modernist perspectives espoused by academics promoting the de-construction of *gender-specific pedagogy* and *'middle-class' curricula*, are equally unhelpful. Above all, a good deal of this 'discourse' is not supported by findings from evidence-based research. (2003, p. 1)

Rather than touting dogmas or post-modernist perspectives that have rarely impacted anywhere near the classroom door, Rowe advocates that we need to be focusing on '"real" effects from recent and emerging local and international research on educational effectiveness' (2003, p. 1).

Rowe highlights advances in school effectiveness research emanating from a small number of second-generation state-of-the-art studies (Bosker, Kremers and Lugthart, 1990; Brandsma, 1993; Mortimore et al., 1988; Hill et al., 1996; Hill and Rowe, 1996; 1998; Rowe, 1991; 1997; Rowe and Hill, 1998; Rowe and Rowe, 1992a, 1992b; 1999; Teddlie and Stringfield, 1993). For example, the *Victorian Quality Schools Project* (VQSP) (see Hill and Rowe, 1996, 1998; Hill et al., 1996; Rowe and Hill, 1998; Rowe et al.,

1993, 1995; Rowe and Rowe, 1999) examined variance in student achievement data for literacy and numeracy, taking into account the hierarchical nature of the data, for 13 700 students in primary and secondary schools. Table 11.1 notes the estimates of the proportion of residual variance due to school and class/teacher differences. Variation at the class/teacher level for literacy ranged from 38 to 45 per cent and for Numeracy from 53 to 55 per cent whereas variation at the school level was small. These results clearly demonstrate that quality teachers make the difference to specific achievement outcomes in numeracy and literacy in Australian schools.

These results are consistent with the findings of research in other countries. For example, in Canada both achievement and affective constructs were examined for all students in Grades 6 and 8 (Willms, 2000). Table 11.2 shows the proportion of variation in student outcomes, at the district (0.1–1.8 per cent), school (0–4.7 per cent), and student/class levels (93.5–99.2 per cent). Importantly, this research demonstrates that teachers make a difference both to specific academic outcomes and important affective domains.

Summing up the findings of next-generation school effectiveness studies, Rowe (2003) notes that these studies 'consistently find that differences between schools, when relevant prior achievement and "intake" characteristics of students are taken into account, are important but not especially large' (p. 6) (around 9 per cent of the variance is explained, which is consistent with the findings of Hattie (2009)). Furthermore, Rowe (2003, p. 6) notes that these studies have consistently found that at the class level there are 'larger proportions of between-class/teacher variance'. On the basis of this body of research findings, Rowe emphasises:

> whereas students' literacy skills, general academic achievements, attitudes, behaviors and experiences of schooling are influenced by their background and intake characteristics—the magnitude of these effects pale into insignificance compared with class/teacher effects. That is, the *quality of teaching and learning provision* are by far the most salient influences on students' cognitive, affective, and behavioral outcomes of schooling—regardless of their gender or backgrounds. (2003, p. 1)

Table 11.1 Proportional class/teacher and school effects for Victorian schools

Achievement Adjusted for Prior Achievement* (13,700 students in 90 government, Catholic, and independent primary and secondary schools)

Class/teacher effects (%)	School effects (%)
Literacy	
Primary:	Secondary:
45.4	37.8
8.6	7.4
Numeracy	
Primary:	Secondary:
54.7	52.7
4.1	8.4

Source: Rowe (2003, p. 19).

Table 11.2 Variation among school districts, schools, and classes for eight schooling outcomes

	Per cent of variation		
Measured outcomes	Between districts	Between schools	Among students Within classes
Reading	0.3	0.8	98.9
Writing	1.0	3.4	95.5
Mathematics	1.8	4.7	93.5
Science	0.4	3.8	95.8
Self-esteem	0.1	3.0	96.8
Sense of belonging	0.3	1.0	98.7
General well-being	0.4	1.6	98.1
General health	0.8	0.0	99.2

Source: Adapted from Willms (2000, p. 241).

Thus Rowe's findings and conclusions are markedly similar to Hattie's. Furthermore, findings from both local and international evidence-based research concur with their views, and demonstrate that excellent teachers *do* make a difference to desirable schooling outcomes.

What research with Indigenous students says

Craven and Marsh (2004) argue that although there has been considerable effort

School achievement: Aboriginal kids have the same capacity as all kids

There are a lot of widely held beliefs about Aboriginal motivation to learn and interest in learning. Many of these beliefs are stereotypes—and wrong.

The apparent lack of investment by Aboriginal kids in school and their poor achievement predominantly reflects their lack of opportunity, location and—most importantly—lack of perceived payoff from education for their future. For most Aboriginal kids, especially in remote locations, what's the point of going to school? For remote and very remote communities in the Northern Territory, for example, Maningrida, Wadeye, Ramingining, Gapuwiyak and others like them—and in other parts of Australia—one defining constant of lack of achievement is that the utility value of schooling may be stripped away. So many factors undermine the value of school that an adaptive response of many kids is to not go. For a start there are few jobs in the local area, so young people have to leave their community to get work or to get qualified for work. But there is huge resistance to the idea of leaving family and community, so the kids don't leave.

The way to fill the hole is for kids to see the utility value of school and learning for an improved future for themselves and their future families. An improved future means an improved quality of life which has material, intellectual and spiritual elements. This is not just an issue for Aboriginal kids. It is the same situation for all at-risk students and dropouts. There has to be a strong link between schooling and a valued future.

Persistent stereotypes about Aboriginal learning problems are based on erroneous beliefs about Aboriginal kids' capacity, interest and cultural differences. The reality is that lack of achievement for Aboriginal kids has nothing to do with capacity and cultural difference. Aboriginal kids have the same capacity as all kids, and their cultural background can and should be used to facilitate learning.

All societies value education to transmit culture. Effective teaching must build on and be embedded in culture. Effective schooling for Aboriginal kids, therefore, even when dealing with Western knowledge, can and should be embedded in Indigenous culture. Good education builds on culture—it is not either-or; it is both-and. Incompatibility is a straw man built up by inadequate theorists.

In summary: Education has to have utility and value, and must be seen to have these qualities by the communities and the kids for whom the education is being provided. The effective engagement of many Aboriginal kids at school is undermined by a whole lot of factors that have nothing to do with Aboriginal kids' capacity or interest. It is about **opportunity** and **location** and **resourcing** and **valuing**.

Dennis McInerney is Chair Professor of Educational Psychology and Associate Vice President (Research and Development) at the Hong Kong Institute of Education. Prior to this he was Research Professor and Associate Dean (Education Research) at the National Institute of Education, Nanyang Technological University Singapore, having served for a period as Vice-Dean (Research and Methodology) within the Centre for Research in Pedagogy and Practice. Before that Professor McInerney was Research Professor and Associate Director of the Self Research Centre at the University of Western Sydney.

Professor McInerney has published book chapters and over 150 research articles in refereed journals and edits two international research monographs. He has written a number of textbooks including Educational Psychology: Constructing Learning *(Pearson 5th Edition, 2010), a bestselling educational psychology text in Australia;* Developmental Psychology for Teachers *(Allen & Unwin, 2006);* Helping Kids Achieve Their Best: Understanding and Using Motivation in the Classroom *(Information Age Publishing, 2005), and* Publishing Your Psychology Research *(Sage and Allen & Unwin, 2001).*

Professor McInerney's major areas of research interest are cross-cultural studies of learning and motivation, self-processes and adaptive psychological determinants of school behaviour (such as self-regulation, self-concept, metacognition, learning styles etc), and instrument design and validation.

by Commonwealth and state governments to address Indigenous disadvantage, such efforts have been too 'often based on presumed collective wisdom rather than as a result of research, [therefore] the outcomes produced have not resulted in effective solutions' (2004, p. 18). This lack of effective outcomes, according to Craven and Marsh, stems from a lack of quality Indigenous educational theory, research and practice (see also Ainley, 1994; Bin-Sallik et al., 1994; Purdie et al., 2000), particularly in relation to key psycho-social drivers of life potential and desirable educational outcomes. In the following section, we highlight some of the research undertaken to date to elucidate what research with Indigenous students tells us.

Mental health

One area often overlooked within educational research is the mental health of students and their families, and factors that may threaten students' adaptive psychological functioning, which in turn will impact on school engagement, achievement and other desirable educational outcomes (Craven and Bodkin-Andrews, 2006). A notable exception in 1995 was a national report, *Ways Forward* (Swan and Raphael, 1995). This report highlights a number of critical and complex outcomes pertaining to Indigenous mental health, with attention focused on trauma and grief suffered by Indigenous Australians; suicide and self-harm; alcohol and other drug use; and forensic and justice issues. The report also notes that the complex range of mental health issues does not mean Indigenous mental health issues cannot be understood by conventional research, but rather that careful consideration must be given to the myriad of cultural and societal influences, too often traumatic, by which Indigenous Australians are affected.

A recent examination of the health and welfare of Indigenous Australians found that the rate of hospitalisation for Indigenous people due to mental or behavioural difficulties was two to three times higher than for other Australians (Australian Bureau of Statistics and Australian Institute of Health and Welfare, 2008). It is here that we can begin to see a web tying mental health to the variety of circumstances and situations mentioned by Swan and Raphael (1995). Specifically, the ABS-AIHW report argues that mental illness or emotional distress may be associated with more contact with the criminal justice system. This in turn increases the likelihood of incarceration, which research has shown to be associated with depression and suicide. The segregation of Indigenous Australians from their communities and culture has had a profound impact above and beyond that experienced by non-Indigenous Australians (Burdekin, 1993). Two factors that have been associated with behavioural and emotional difficulties suffered by Indigenous adults and youth are increased rates of trauma and the unique experiences of forced separation of children from parents and communities.

Trauma

In the *Ways Forward* report, Swan and Raphael (1995) highlight the diversity and severity of trauma and grief to which Indigenous Australians may be exposed, identifying important causal stressors such as dispossession of land, cultural genocide, mortality rates, higher levels of contact with the justice system, segregation and family separation, and various forms of abuse—all of which parallel Indigenous suicide research. More recently, the Social Health Reference Group (SHRG) (2004) stressed the need to closely examine Indigenous Australians' social and emotional well-being. Arguably, one of the most immediate and critical issues for understanding trauma and grief suffered by Indigenous Australians is the impact of bereavement in Indigenous communities. This sense of loss can be identified as being intrinsically tied to land and cultural suffering, but its most immediate and extrinsic cause can be seen in the lowered life expectancy of Indigenous Australians. Depending on the sources, this lowered life-expectancy is calculated to be around thirteen to seventeen years less than for the average non-Indigenous Australian (Hill, Barker and Vos, 2007; Ring and Brown, 2003). The higher mortality rate of Indigenous Australians has long been acknowledged as a critical issue (Cooke et al., 2007). Yet it is only recently that it has it been considered that the higher mortality rate among Indigenous Australians leads to Indigenous people experiencing the negative emotional and cognitive effects of loss both earlier and more often than other Australians (SHRG, 2004; Vicary and Westerman, 2004).

Forced separation

One often cited and comprehensive report on the effects of government policies on the lives and health of Indigenous Australians, both historically and today, is the *Bringing Them Home* report (HREOC, 1997), which sought to assess the impact of forced separation of Indigenous Australian children from their families and communities from 1910 to 1970. Obtained through interviewing over 500 Indigenous Australians about their experiences of forcible removal as children, the evidence overwhelmingly suggested that the conditions the children were forced to undergo did little to improve their lives and resulted in long-term adverse consequences. Such conditions included harsh living environments and shelters, where only the most rudimentary of education was received. An increased likelihood of excessive physical and sexual abuse within shelters, and also in later placements in foster homes and workplace environments, was also apparent. Acknowledgement was also given to the impact on the health and morale of Indigenous communities, and the ways in which forcible removal significantly contributed to the loss of language, culture and heritage, which were all essential for the survival of traditional laws, practices and the well-being of Indigenous nations.

An analysis of the later living conditions of those directly affected by forced removal also highlighted the unethical nature of the separation policies. In 1997, it was found that those taken *were not* better educated, *not* more likely to be employed and *not* receiving significantly higher incomes than Indigenous Australians who were raised in their original community. Moreover, for those taken away, 29 per cent rated their health status as poor or fair compared with 15.4 per cent of Indigenous Australians who were not taken away (HREOC, 1997). *Bringing Them Home* concluded that:

> Indigenous families and communities have endured gross violations of their human rights. These violations continue to affect Indigenous peoples' daily lives. They were an act of genocide, aimed at wiping out Indigenous families, communities and cultures, vital to the precious and inalienable heritage of Australia. (HREOC, 2002, p. 14)

A more recent study on Indigenous Australians affected by the forced separation policies, carried out by De Maio et al. (2005) extended the findings of the *Bringing Them Home* inquiry by seeking to understand whether forced separation had a cross-generational effect. The researchers found that Indigenous children brought up by carers who were forcibly removed were significantly more likely to be at high risk of clinically significant emotional or behavioural difficulties (e.g. emotional symptoms, conduct problems, hyperactivity and peer problems) than Indigenous children whose carers were not forcibly removed (32.7 per cent and 21.8 per cent respectively were at high risk). These were significantly greater rates than for non-Indigenous children, of whom 15 per cent were likely to be rated as being at high risk for clinical emotional and behavioural problems. De Maio et al. (2005) emphasise that not only must trauma and grief be recognised and understood for Indigenous Australians who were forcibly removed from their families, but the ongoing impact must also be considered for the generations that follow. The 'cycle of damage' referred to in the *Bringing Them Home* report is not limited to those directly subjected to forced removal, but it is a continuum that needs intervention.

Western Australian Aboriginal Child Health Survey (WAACHS)

To date, what is arguably the most comprehensive quantitative study of Indigenous youth mental health is the second volume of the Western Australian Aboriginal Child Health Survey, titled *The Social and Emotional Wellbeing of Aboriginal Children and Young People* (Zubrick et al., 2005b). This extensive survey was conducted throughout urban and rural Western Australia, targeting 3993 Aboriginal and Torres Strait Islander children aged between 4 and 17 years. A number of important mental health findings can be drawn from this study, as it gathered valuable information on emotional and behavioural symptoms, suicidal tendencies, bullying, self-esteem and racism. In addition to this, a sample of non-Indigenous children was also utilised for valid group comparisons.

Emotional and behavioural problems

Of the Indigenous children sampled, for the ages of 4 to 11, 26.3 per cent were at high risk of clinically significant emotional or behavioural difficulties and 20.5 per cent of Indigenous children aged from 12 to 17 were at high risk. In comparison, 16.9 per cent of non-Indigenous children aged from 4 to 11 and 12.5 per cent aged from 12 to 17 were at high risk. One of the more interesting statistics from these findings is that Indigenous children seem to be progressively less at risk from these psychological difficulties as their areas of living become more isolated (Zubrick et al., 2005b). Some caution should be directed at any conclusions regarding these findings, however, as cultural difficulties in interpretation may influence the results (e.g. language barriers and even relevancy of problem behaviours). Nevertheless, a number of authors have linked Indigenous ties to traditional lands and culture as an important factor in emotional well-being and healing (e.g. Elliot-Farrelly, 2004; Ganesharajah, 2009; HREOC, 1997; Swan and Raphael, 1995).

Within Zubrick et al.'s (2005b) analysis, a number of significant influences on emotional and behavioural problems were found, the factor most strongly associated with greater psychological risk being stressful life events such as illness, financial difficulties and family difficulties. Of Indigenous children, 22 per cent reported more than seven stressful life events in the twelve-month period, and these children were five and a half times more likely to be at a higher risk of clinical emotional and behavioural difficulties. Other factors included poor parenting, which contributed to a four times higher risk; poor family functioning, which resulted in Indigenous children being twice as likely to be at high risk; sole parenting, which also doubled the risk; and living in five or more homes since birth, leading to a one and a half times higher likelihood of being at high risk. Two protective factors identified were households with a high level of occupation and, as previously mentioned, extreme isolation.

Bullying and racism

Nearly one-third of Indigenous youth were bullied at some time at school, with the patterns of bullying being very similar for males and females. The most frequent ages for being bullied occurred at 12 and 17 years, and it was also found that if the Indigenous youths' primary carers were both non-Aboriginal, they were significantly more likely to be bullied. With regard to problematic behaviours, it was found that bullying was associated with increased levels of smoking and marijuana use.

One in five Indigenous youth reported being discriminated against because of their Aboriginality. Like bullying, racism was associated with increased smoking and marijuana use, and also with alcohol consumption. These results led Zubrick et al. (2005) to stress that a significant proportion of Indigenous youth have been significantly harassed in some manner, and the negative consequences, even within the limitations of this study, point to serious health-risk behaviours.

Self-esteem

In investigating a general measure of self-esteem, Zubrick et al. (2005b) found that Indigenous females were more likely to suffer from low self-esteem, especially as they grew older. Additionally, lower self-esteem was related to greater incidence of regular smoking, and also to a lack of exercise. Racism was also related to self-esteem, and Indigenous youth who reported they had suffered from racism also more frequently reported higher self-esteem. This was especially pertinent for males. For Indigenous females, family violence had a unique relationship with lowered levels of self-esteem. In summarising the findings on self-esteem, Zubrick et al. (2005b) highlight the need to further understand how self-esteem develops in Indigenous children, and how it may be related to a number of other factors such as cultural identification.

Suicidal behaviour

One in six Indigenous youth had seriously considered suicide in the twelve months prior to the survey, with 39 per cent of those actually attempting suicide. Although these figures did not differ significantly from the non-Indigenous sample, a number of important variables were found to be associated with suicidal thoughts. Notably, self-esteem acted as a potential protective mechanism, whereas family violence, emotional or behavioural difficulties and knowing an acquaintance who also had thought about suicide increased the risk of suicidal thoughts. Based on these findings, Zubrick et al. (2005b) once again stressed the need for higher self-esteem, not only through physical activity, but also through effective parenting programs.

Academic performance
Zubrick et al. (2005b, pp. 326–9) also identified a range of factors that were associated with low academic performance. Amongst these they identified three important drivers of low academic performance: poor school attendance; low education level of primary carers; and students at risk of clinically significant emotional or behavioural difficulties. Zubrick et al. emphasise that: 'What education systems are presently doing to improve educational outcomes of Aboriginal children is not working because the drivers of educational disparity are not being addressed.' (2005b, p. 506)

Summary
Despite research only recently emerging with regard to the varying mental health inequities faced by Indigenous Australians, the disadvantaged status of Indigenous Australians is clearly evinced. One of the more interesting findings of Indigenous mental health research is that many of the influences behind disadvantaged status are unique to Indigenous Australians. Swan and Raphael (1995) argue that factors such as increased experience of bereavement, obstacles to self-determination, the ongoing impact of the Stolen Generations, racism and increased levels of incarceration of family members could all be associated with the mental health discrepancies that are observed between Indigenous and non-Indigenous Australian students. In addition, it is clear that the drivers of educational disparity are not being addressed.

Improving the educational experiences of Aboriginal children and young people

In a follow-up study, Zubrick et al. (2006) linked family, health, emotional and social health, and schooling factors to outcomes in education for Indigenous youth, most notably, school attendance and educational achievement.

School attendance
Indigenous youth were found to have a median average of around 26 days absent from school per year. Zubrick et al. (2006) note that in comparison to an earlier 1993 Western Australian child health survey, this rate of absence was much higher than that found for the non-Indigenous students, who had a median of around eight days absent from school. Although Zubrick and colleagues also found substantial variation in rates of absenteeism with regard to relative state isolation for the Indigenous students (ranging from 20 days for Perth metro students to 42 days for highly isolated students), the rates of absenteeism were still substantially higher for Indigenous students compared with non-Indigenous students, regardless of their level of isolation.

In attempting to identify factors that may contribute to this higher rate of absenteeism, Zubrick et al. (2006) found fifteen separate factors that independently contributed to a greater likelihood of showing higher than average rates of absenteeism (attesting to the complexity of Indigenous disadvantage). The six most impacting of these factors were:

- Indigenous students who spoke an Aboriginal language (6.09 times more likely);
- Indigenous students who attended schools that were listed in the highest quartile of socio-economic disadvantage (2.82 times more likely);
- Indigenous students who spoke Aboriginal English (1.98 times more likely);
- Indigenous students who lived in rented housing rather than a home owned outright or under a mortgage (1.95 times more likely);
- Indigenous students whose family had experienced seven or more stressful life events in the previous year (1.90 times more likely); and
- Indigenous students who attended schools without Aboriginal and Islander Educational Workers (1.81 times more likely).

Academic performance
Although Zubrick et al. (2006) tap a number of performance indicators within their main report,

It's all about respect

It's all about respect, respect and the Law. Law governs our lives, the land, our environment, and our relationships with everything. You have to respect this.

Aunty Beryl Carmichael, 2009.

Knowledge is not a commodity that can be purchased and exploited at will. Because knowledge carries with it power to do good or ill to the knower and the community, many Elders decline to have their knowledge recorded in writing or electronic media. They want to be assured that the seeker is properly instructed and compliant with the ethical obligations that will be assumed.

(Castellano 2004:12)

Undertaking research with Indigenous communities must be understood as not a 'god-given right'. Instead, it must be appreciated as a gift and an opportunity to build relationships through respect and responsible action. Respect has not been considered in much of past research; this breached Indigenous people's ethics and protocols. Such unethical practice in research has resulted in problematic constructions that are maintained through poor policy development and then perpetuate a vicious cycle of 'problems' to be 'solved'.

Research can lead to positive outcomes when Indigenous community values and protocols are acknowledged, respected and followed. Respect must be the core of developing a meaningful and sustainable relationship. Law and knowledge through respect embodies our ethical conduct. What we mean by respect differs from mainstream academic formulations. Respect in the Indigenous sense means to listen and hear and value what we have to say about ourselves and our experiences, even if what we say challenges your ways of knowing. Respect means you're open enough to acknowledge that there are many ways of being in this world, and that all have their own authority.

A reflective model for decolonising research

1. *Respect.* A deep acknowledgement that you do not know it all, allowing you to not fear what you don't know. Once that fear has left you, you can be respectful of others.

2. *Being respectful gives you an openness that enables you to listen; you have to listen deeply so you can hear. It is a new 'power' dynamic.* Not knowing can be a fearful space; some people may 'cover' by pretending to know. Community can read people like a book. They will see that straightaway, and question the value of responding, knowing that this researcher will not listen deeply and hear. But if the researcher is respectful and acknowledges they don't know, community then sees this person is open to know and knowledge will be shared. The researcher should sit quietly and listen, not interrupt the flow of knowledge being shared. If your mind is busy thinking of the next question to ask, you are not listening deeply. You have to listen deeply to really hear what is being shared, the gift of knowledge you are being given.

3. *Once you comprehend what you are being told, you are connected to the person speaking to you; this creates a space for mutuality and inclusion.* Fully understanding what you are told is not immediate. It requires thoughtful reflection and later discussion with the person who shared this information with you to clarify that you have got the story right. Thus research is not a process that happens in an hour and is then finished. It is about establishing a communicative connection with your informant. Connecting to the person who is sharing with you is ethical practice; you are establishing a space in which truths can be shared without fear of 'put down'. If you try to be 'objective' by maintaining distance from your informants, you will violate the Aboriginal ethos of reciprocal relationships and collective validation.

4. *Once in this 'respect' zone you can collaborate effectively and work together.* This is a mutual space that honours the spirit of both persons' integrity and honours all worldviews. In every sense this is what we must all work towards, honoring everyone's worldview.

5. *Working together can facilitate a relationship*. Working together can only occur on a level playing ground. Community needs control of the process—otherwise their circumstances remain subservient to the power of the researcher. Building proper relationships means making a shift from coloniser and colonised, 'superior' and 'inferior' knowledge systems, to a more balanced equation of knowledge seeker and knowledge holder.

6. *Relationships come with embedded responsibilities that are complex and multi-faceted. Law within country has established the framework for these protocols. A key doctrine of the Law is to do no harm to any person, being or place. These responsibilities are what are known as reciprocity, the obligations that come with relatedness.* Relationships and related responsibilities fit within the framework of transparency and accountability. Relationships developed through proper processes are not extinguished once data collection is completed; accountability, your responsibility to the community, will remain a priority in the transfer of this data and especially in its publication.

The ethics of Indigenous research lie within a charter of social justice: collective self-determination, empowerment and emancipation with a core of cultural survival. Decolonising research challenges the power of Western institutions. This is critical because for over two hundred years Western perceptions of justice and beneficence have worked against us.

Juanita Sherwood *is a Wiradjuri woman, daughter, mother, sister, and Aunty. She has worked and lived in Aboriginal health and education for over 25 years, and recently completed her PhD on Indigenous health research,* Do No Harm: Decolonising Indigenous health research. *From 1989, with the New South Wales AECG, she led the fight to address otitis media (middle ear disease, 'glue ear') in Aboriginal students—'Can't hear, can't learn'. Her experiences, responsibilities and varied environments have shaped her worldview and ways of knowing, being and doing. Her worldview informs her approach to research, with rich insights into why research has not improved social justice for Indigenous Australians. Her life journey in Aboriginal health education has been enriched by peers, communities, Elders, academic supervisors and rich Indigenous and non-Indigenous textual dialogues. She is currently Senior Lecturer/Academic Co-ordinator at the Nura Gili Centre, University of New South Wales.*

---

for the purposes of this chapter we focus on the overall academic performance of Indigenous students as rated by their teachers ('far below age level', 'somewhat below age level', 'at age level', 'somewhat above age level', 'far above age level'). Overall, 18.6 per cent of Indigenous students were rated as far below average, and another 38.6 per cent were rated as somewhat below average. Also, only 6.4 per cent were somewhat above average and just 0.7 per cent far above average. Zubrick et al. again sought to identify factors that may contribute to the rating of students' performance, and once again found a diversity of influences. The six factors that most strongly contributed to lowered levels of performance for Indigenous students were as follows:

- Indigenous students with functional limitations (e.g. needing special help to carry out basic personal functions due to illness or disability—roughly 2 per cent of the Indigenous sample) were 6.93 times more likely to have a low level of educational performance.
- Indigenous students attending independent (community) schools were 3.9 times more likely to have a lower level of academic performance when compared with government schools.
- Indigenous students who had repeated a grade were 3.57 times more likely to have a low level of educational performance when compared with Indigenous students who had not repeated a grade.
- Indigenous students suspended from school at least twice were 3.45 times more likely to have a low level of educational performance when compared with Indigenous students who were never suspended.

- Indigenous students at high risk of clinically significant emotional or behavioural difficulties (as rated by teachers) were 2.42 times more likely to have a low level of educational performance.
- Indigenous students who spoke Aboriginal English were 2.42 times more likely to have a low level of educational performance compared with students who spoke Standard English in the classroom.

In their discussion of the findings, Zubrick et al. (2006) cite two key over-arching principles that may aid in improving educational outcomes for Indigenous students. First, they suggest that education systems and schools need to engage the carers of Indigenous students and the communities in which they live. Second, they recommend that the early childhood and learning experiences of Indigenous children must be drastically improved in an effort to break the early momentum of disadvantaged educational status. From this foundation, Zubrick et al. (2006) recommend diverse points of action ranging from education systems implementing early school, evidence-based programs and curricula, to better support for Indigenous students (reminiscent of Hattie's 2009 work), to establishing a national research agenda to charting and evaluating programs that have achieved educational outcomes. It was also suggested that, as a natural part of human development, people must be given the utmost ability to survive, to be knowledgeable, to access resources for a necessary standard of living, and to participate in the life of a community. In recognising this, Zubrick et al. emphasise that:

> The level of relative disparity in the educational outcomes of Aboriginal children and young people represents a principal barrier to their onward survival, access to resources, and participation in the most fundamental activities of social and civic life. Education systems are uniquely positioned among all other human service agencies to initiate changes as well as lead other sectors to undertake actions that would break the cycle of disadvantage that Aboriginal people experience. (2006, p. 497)

Indigenous students' aspirations: Dreams, perceptions and realities

In a large-scale study (involving 524 Indigenous and 1149 non-Indigenous students across three states) funded by the Department of Education, Science and Training (DEST), Craven et al. (2005) sought to better understand the educational dreams and aspirations of Indigenous high school students. In doing so, they identified the barriers Indigenous and other Australian students face when attempting to pursue their future aspirations, and also compared and contrasted Indigenous and other Australian students' academic and non-academic self-concepts, schooling and post-schooling aspirations, and the relationship of socio-economic status (SES) and academic self-concept to educational outcomes.

Craven et al. (2005) found that significantly more Indigenous students compared with other Australian students aimed to leave school before completing Year 12; for the most part, Indigenous students (37.1 per cent) aimed to get a job after leaving school, whereas most other Australian students (78.6 per cent) aimed to go to university—although a large proportion of Indigenous students (30.1 per cent) shared this aspiration. It was also found that over 48 per cent of Indigenous students, when compared with 36.3 per cent of other Australian students, reported either not knowing what they would do after they left school or thinking about getting advice in the next six months, suggesting that significantly more Indigenous students were unaware of their future options when compared with other Australian students.

In examining nine distinct barriers to students' post-school aspirations, Craven et al. (2005) found that all potential barriers were significantly more detrimental for Indigenous students compared with other Australians. Possibly reflecting the results of Zubrick et al. (2006), Indigenous students identified a lack of family support as the key barrier to achieving their goals, followed by the amount of career advice they had been given, their knowledge of what further education or job training they needed to do, and their academic achievement. Another major focal point of the investigation was the varying levels of self-confidence or self-concept possessed by Indigenous and non-Indigenous students. The results suggested that Indigenous students, compared with non-Indigenous students, had significantly *higher* levels of appearance, overall self-esteem, physical abilities and art abilities self-concepts, yet significantly *lower* levels of confidence for academic facets of self-concept (maths, school, verbal), peer relations (opposite-sex and same-sex relations) and honesty and emotional stability self-concepts.

Finally, Craven et al. (2005) sought to understand how a sense of academic self-concept and students' SES background influenced their educational outcomes. Of considerable interest was their finding that a good part of the effect of SES on outcomes was indirect and mediated through academic self-concept, especially for Indigenous students. That is, Indigenous students with a high level of academic self-concept and a higher level of SES wanted to stay on at school for longer, had a higher sense of efficacy in achieving future goals, showed more enjoyment at school and reported higher perceptions of teacher ratings of their ability. The direct and positive effects of academic self-concept tended to be as large or even larger for the Indigenous students when compared with the non-Indigenous students.

Craven et al. (2005) suggest a number of detailed practical strategies to address the results above, and we present here some of the key broad implications of the study. The study implies that more effective strategies need to be put in place to assist Indigenous students to set and attain higher aspirations, including strategies to encourage more Indigenous students to aspire to a higher level of education, such as university. Furthermore, in considering the potential impact of barriers reported by Indigenous students, Craven et al. suggest that there is a need for a more concerted strategic approach by a diversity of agencies to address barriers Indigenous students perceive as limiting the achievement of their aspirations.

For seven of eleven facets of self-concept measured, Indigenous students had a lower self-concept compared with their non-Indigenous peers. Previous research has established the causal relation between self-concept and educational outcomes, including academic achievement (e.g. Marsh and Craven, 2006).

In addition, Judge and Bono (2001) present a meta-analysis showing that components of a positive self-concept construct are among the best predictors of job performance and job satisfaction. Enhancing Indigenous students' self-concepts therefore offers a research-based new solution for intervention.

The impact of academic self-concept: Bodkin-Andrews et al. (2009)

Bodkin-Andrews et al. (2009) undertook a longitudinal causal ordering study examining the impact of academic self-concept on levels of academic disengagement across Indigenous and other Australian students. First, although they found that Indigenous students reported higher levels of academic disengagement when compared with non-Indigenous students, these differences were negated by a positive sense of academic self-concept. They also found that academic self-concept causally predicted subsequent lower levels of later academic disengagement. These results offer evidence to suggest that, for both Indigenous and other Australian students, academic self-concept is causally predominant over academic disengagement, and thus a key point for intervention, for:

> By creating a school and classroom environment that will foster both Indigenous and non-Indigenous students' value and confidence in education, it is logical to argue that not only will there be improvements in the educational outcomes of underachieving students, but also for students who may be achieving even though they may be at greater risk of later disengagement... Thus the school and classroom environments should recognise, nurture and promote students' academic self-confidence as a critical factor for increasing student resiliency. (Bodkin-Andrews et al., 2009, p. 20)

A positive self-identity for Indigenous students

In partnership with the Commonwealth Department of Education, Training and Youth Affairs (DETYA), Purdie et al. (2000) conducted an investigation into the nature and development of Indigenous students' positive sense of self-identity, and how this identity may be related to schooling outcomes. From this, Purdie et al. found that Indigenous students' sense of self-identity was a diverse, multifaceted, contextually sensitive and complicated construct. Some of the most important markers found for a positive sense of identity were a strong sense of identification with kinship groups, an understanding of true history, languages and traditional practices, and a strong sense of place. Indigenous students' sense of identity was found to be far deeper than overly simplistic notions of 'pan-aboriginality', where:

> Indigenous Australians have often been referred to as a single entity . . . [this] was not a reality in the various settings in which interviews and focus groups were conducted. Through their responses, Aboriginal people and Torres Strait Islander people demonstrated their individuality within the specific social and cultural sub-groups of which they are members, although there was some evidence of unique features of Indigenous cultures that were relative to location according to remote, regional and urban areas. These included strength of cultural identity, language group and career aspirations. (Purdie et al., 2000, p. x)

Purdie et al. (2000) also found a vast number of sources that may, positively or negatively, influence Indigenous students' sense of identity. These included direct family and community, Indigenous role models and—of considerable importance—people of authority within their schools (e.g. principals, teachers, AIEWs, peers) and social institutions within the wider Australian community (e.g. police, media, politicians). Of these influences, direct family and teachers themselves were found to be the strongest influences.

In their attempt to investigate how Indigenous students' sense of identity was related to the schooling system, it was found that although Indigenous students showed a positive sense of themselves, their family and their culture, their perceptions of themselves as students were generally ambivalent, and as a result their positive sense of identity was not linked to academic success. In considering these results, Purdie et al. argue that:

> The challenge for educators is to ensure that schools are places where Indigenous students want to be, where their presence and participation is valued, where they feel successful, and where they see value in completing their schooling. The participants in the present study have provided many insights about the kind of schooling that appeals to them. For example, they respond positively to teachers who are warm, encouraging, respectful, and make realistic demands. (2000, p. 39)

Strengthening identity

The strengthening of Indigenous learners' identity is an important goal. Students' well-being is supported by a strong sense of self, of heritage and culture, and a strong place in the world in interactions with others.

In part, the sense of identity comes from recognising and affirming the qualities and beliefs that establish Indigenous students as Indigenous. However, if students are to be successful at school, their sense of identity needs to expand so that students develop a self-concept that includes an affirmation of themselves as successful readers, writers, and speakers in a wide range of settings, where they have confidence that they have control of a wide range of language and behavioural resources.

—Ainsworth and McRae (2009, p. 3)

What Works

Despite increasing research pointing towards possible interventions that may strengthen Indigenous students' educational outcomes, it can be argued that little has been done to utilise these results for effective intervention strategies, which are then evaluated by directed empirical research. This is not to state that Indigenous educational research has not already identified successful interventional practices, at least with regard to smaller scale research settings. *What Works* (see Ainsworth and McRae, 2009; McRae et al., 2000) is a collection of case studies of interventions that produced positive effects on Indigenous students' schooling engagement and achievement. Overall, these case studies sought to directly tackle pedagogical practices, including cultural inclusion, school engagement, participation, community partnerships, self-confidence, feedback strategies, development of achievement skills, discrimination and racism, and peer and teacher relationships (McRae et al., 2000). By visiting the *What Works* website (<www.whatworks.edu.au>), researchers and teachers have the opportunity to review over 50 research projects that had positive effects on Indigenous students' educational experiences, and that will provide invaluable insights on successful strategies.

In reviewing the overall trends associated with these projects, McRae et al. (2000) suggest it is imperative that Indigenous students themselves be given respect, that their culture be respected and included in the school curriculum, that Indigenous students have the benefit of quality teaching, and that the students themselves regularly attend school to experience these benefits. From this, they argue that:

> A platform for marked and significant improvement in outcomes is beginning to emerge. The structural and cultural impediments are not as strong as they once were. The time for making improvement really is now (McRae et al., 2000, p. 180).

If outcomes for Indigenous students are to be improved:

- They must be given respect—self-esteem and pride in successful work are the starting points for becoming an effective learner.
- Their cultures and the relevant implications of those cultures must be respected—cultural dispossession can reduce people to shadows, a state of near invisibility; aspects of culture must be recognised, supported and integrated in the processes of education, not just for their own success, but for the general quality of Australian schools.
- They must be taught well—good teaching practice, applied with determination to achieve success for all involved. Good relationships, trust, flexibility, individual concern and problem-solving, perseverance, thoughtful observation and careful investigation of best teaching strategies and possibilities, and knowledge of students' backgrounds. That is good teaching. That is what teachers can do.
- They must participate consistently—the business of improving outcomes is a shared task; regular attendance and consistent participation are key ingredients. In some cases, additional support and encouragement from school personnel, from parents and carers and from other members of communities will be essential for this to occur.

The time for making improvement a reality is now

Over 150 years Australian teachers have achieved amazing results—near universal basic literacy by 1900, and 75 per cent completing Year 12 by 2000. But 20 per cent of the school population miss out on the benefits of education. More than 90 per cent of students who fail to complete Year 10 will be on welfare support for the rest of their lives—Indigenous students are way over-represented in this group.

What Works is part of the national effort to improve Indigenous student outcomes. It evolved from the Strategic Results Projects of the Australian Government's Indigenous Education Strategic Initiatives Program (IESIP).

In 1997 the Commonwealth gave education providers across the country—pre-school to TAFE—the chance to show that Indigenous education outcomes could be improved in a short time by planning and concerted efforts. Over 1998 and 1999, IESIP funded 84 Strategic Results Projects at a total cost of $12.7 million. At the same time the Commonwealth commissioned a consortium involving the Australian Curriculum Studies Association and National Curriculum Services to review and evaluate the projects. A team of educational consultants analysed reports, interviewed project staff on-site and conducted two conferences for the people involved. Their final report was *What Works: Explorations in Improving Outcomes for Indigenous Students*. It summarised what was learned about how outcomes could be improved. It is now available, together with a teacher resource booklet, *What has worked (and will again)*.

Our people have the right to a good education. Our children need the skills, experiences and qualifications to be able to choose their futures. Our communities need young people coming through with the education and confidence to be effective leaders. We need young people who can be advocates for our people, able to take their place in Australian society and still keep their culture strong.

It is clear that more needs to be done to support our people's educational opportunities. It is also clear that we need to ensure that Indigenous Australian young people succeed in schooling and have the skills to enjoy a more secure economic and cultural future.

—The Indigenous Education Ambassadors

The report showed that, in the main, successful projects had site-based performance targets and combined a relentless approach with high expectations and sound teaching-learning practices. Successful projects were based on three principles:

- recognition, acknowledgement and support of Indigenous culture and culturally appropriate approaches to teaching;
- teaching techniques that successfully develop requisite skills; and
- effective participation by the Indigenous community and students.

Projects found that a key barrier to improving literacy levels was the cultural bias of standard mainstream literacy practices, plus failure to take account of hearing impairment. Other negative factors included:

- low expectations by teachers, students and parents;
- low levels of academic activity in the classroom;
- a focus on behaviour management rather than teaching;
- difficulties in dealing with the diversity of student learning needs; and
- irregular attendance—at least partly as a result of all of the above!

Clearly these findings would apply to any other subject area or competency—across the board.

The NSW Aboriginal Education Review

In 2004, a major review of standards in Indigenous education within New South Wales was published. This report, titled *Yanigurra Muya: Ganggurrinyma Yaarri Guurulaw Yirringin gurray* [Freeing the Spirit: Dreaming an Equal Future] (New South Wales AECG and New South Wales Department of Education and Training, 2004), used a range of qualitative and quantitative methodologies to collect raw data from over 200 submissions in an extensive consultation process with Aboriginal communities, organisations, teachers and educational leaders, and reviewed past and previous initiatives with regard to policy and practice in Aboriginal education in New South Wales government schools.

The inequities highlighted between Indigenous and non-Indigenous students are consistent with previous research highlighting the disadvantaged status of Indigenous students across all levels of education. Indeed, in reviewing the findings, although there was evidence for many strong 'pockets' of systemic and community commitment to righting the inequities suffered by Indigenous students, most schools and TAFE institutes displayed a mixture of both improvements and failures. This inconsistency in effort and results was attributed to a lack of directed leadership quality within such educational systems:

> The Review indicated that all levels of the education system require inspired leadership and support if they are to move forward. Leadership and support with determination to tackle the barriers to success that are faced by too many Aboriginal students. Leadership and support with wisdom to make worthwhile contributions to Reconciliation between Aboriginal and non-Aboriginal peoples in Australia. (NSW AECG and NSW DET, 2004, p. 181)

Largely as a result of this overall observation and the detailed analysis of the many factors that contribute to Indigenous students' educational success, the report put forward a total of 71 recommendations that could be split into nine general areas of concern:

1. strengthening policy, planning, and implementation;
2. extending quality teaching and learning;
3. fortifying identities of Aboriginal students;
4. engaging Aboriginal students;
5. applying Aboriginal cultural knowledge;
6. collaborating in partnerships;
7. building community capacity;
8. challenging racism; and
9. advancing leadership and accountability.

Most of these recommendations are supported by the research we have reviewed in this chapter.

The research foundation for the future

In this chapter, we have tried to present a snapshot of what at least some of the research can tell us. Hattie's (2009) work makes a phenomenal contribution to the education literature in that we now know which factors are most likely to influence achievement and importantly, which ones have the greatest impact. Similarly, Rowe's (2003) findings indicate that it is excellent teachers who most influence desirable educational outcomes. While these findings have not been validated with Indigenous students specifically, they provide us with the benchmarks for excellence—very clearly, excellence is what we need to attain in Indigenous education. We advocate that we need to take the very best available theory, research and practice and apply it to the teaching of Indigenous students. Hattie's and Rowe's work shows us the way—we need to focus on the factors that have the most impact, and clearly excellent teachers are the prime catalyst for change in Indigenous education.

The Zubrick et al. (2005, 2006) and Craven et al. (2005) studies also offer important insights. Indigenous children are unlikely to succeed if the drivers of educational success are not addressed. In addition, Craven and Bodkin-Andrews (2006), in their review of Indigenous mental health, have emphasised that there is a dire need to capitalise on the psychology of success to strengthen Indigenous students' adaptive psychological functioning and well-being. Enhancing self-concept, along with other psychological constructs that have been demonstrated to make a tangible difference (e.g. motivation, resilience), is a potentially potent key to intervention and fundamental to seeding and driving success.

The many successful approaches in *What Works* offer teachers important insights on what has worked and what is likely to work in their own classrooms. Finally, the New South Wales Education Review (2004) offers a suite of recommendations to enhance Indigenous education.

Unfortunately, in the absence of a strong body of scholarly evidence-based research on schooling for Indigenous students, we can only presume, at best, beginning points to advance Indigenous education. It is puzzling to us why education systems collect data on achievement, but so often fail to collect data to elucidate its determinants. Such data collection could expedite our search for what seeds success for Indigenous students. However, we trust that this chapter has demonstrated that:

> Scholarly research can make an important difference and identify much needed fresh insights on how to address critical educational issues of our time... there is indeed a dire need to establish a concerted national programme of Indigenous Education research to develop a body of scholarly literature that can really put to the test presumed successful strategies, identify causal mechanisms that make a difference, and generate new solutions that are demonstrated by research to result in tangible outcomes. (Bin-Sallik, 2005)

12 Closing the gap
John Lester and Geoff Munns

The Dawn is at Hand

Dark brothers, first Australian race,
Soon you will take your rightful place
In the brotherhood long waited for,
Fringe-dwellers no more.
Sore, sore the tears you shed
When hope seemed folly and justice dead.
Was the long night weary? Look up, dark band,
The dawn is at hand.
Go forward proudly and unafraid
To your birthright all too long delayed,
For soon now the shame of the past
Will be over at last.
You will be welcomed mateship-wise
In industry and in enterprise;
No profession will bar the door,
Fringe-dwellers no more.
Dark and white upon common ground
In club and office and social round,
Yours the feel of a friendly land,
The grip of the hand.
Sharing the same equality
In college and university,
All ambitions of hand or brain
Yours to attain.
For ban and bias will soon be gone,
The future beckons you bravely on
To art and letters and nation lore,
Fringe-dwellers no more.
—Oodgeroo Noonuccal (2008, p. 44)

Gavin Mallard, Yamatji-Nhanda student at Wesley College, holding his Western Australian Trainee of the Year 2008 award. Gavin has since worked as a full-time trainee with Noongar Sports Association, completing his Certificate IV in Sport and Recreation, and now plans to study at university to be a primary sports teacher. Photo courtesy Lynn Webber, Indigenous Student Coordinator Wesley College.

The package for educational change

by John Lester

In the above poem, Oodgeroo points out the current movement and hope of equity in education and training for Indigenous peoples in this country. These same peoples have long practised very successful complex holistic educational systems for life. Effective, efficient, systemic and sustainable education of Aboriginal people was practised and proven overwhelmingly productive since time immemorial, or BC (Before Cook), in Australia. It is only since the invasion of non-Indigenous educational forces that the concept of an Indigenous deficit in education was born and the concept of a 'gap' in educational attainment commenced. Indeed, the first real recorded 'gap' in this relatively brief engagement with the invading educational endeavours in this country actually was the 'gap' between a young Aboriginal girl, Maria Lock, topping the earliest known tests of non-Indigenous knowledge bases in this country in 1819, surpassing her non-Indigenous rivals of the day (Parry, 2005, pp. 236–7). Unfortunately, this was to be both the first and last time that the 'gap' was so placed in favour of Indigenous peoples in this country and from this point on Western education would prove to be one of the prime drivers of mass cultural genocide and social injustice across Australia. So successful would be this attack that in the twenty-first century the 'gap' between Indigenous and non-Indigenous educational outcomes in the state of New South Wales is at crisis levels and unfortunately very much a national trend (Steering Committee for the Review of Government Service Provision, 2007). The difference at Year 7 of schooling was 'as much as 58 months and nearly 60 months behind in writing and language skills respectively' (NSW Aboriginal Education Consultative Group and NSW Department of Education and Training, 2004, p. 23) compared with their non-Indigenous peers).

The Australian government's *National Report to Parliament on Indigenous Education and Training, 2005* (Department of Education, Employment, and Workplace Relations, 2007) highlights the continuing 'gap' between Indigenous and non-Indigenous students. This is further supported in *Australian Directions in Indigenous Education 2005–2008* (Ministerial Council on Education, Employment, Training, and Youth Affairs, 2006), which states:

> Most Indigenous students, regardless of their completion year, leave school poorly prepared relative to their non-Indigenous counterparts. These outcomes limit the post-school options and life choices of Indigenous students, perpetuating intergenerational cycles of social and economic disadvantage. (MCEETYA, 2006, p. 4)

Australian Directions articulates a focused effort over the 2005–08 quadrennium to accelerate the pace of the change through processes that will 'engage' Indigenous students in learning. Its focus is on the key domains of early childhood education; school and community educational partnerships; school leadership; quality teaching; and pathways to training, employment and higher education. These domains form the basis of what I have termed 'the package', which is the culmination of the key elements of the change that must take place in the most effective environment for education change: the classroom.

The failure of basic principles

Past policy and practices in Indigenous education have fundamentally been flawed on a few basic principles. First, the continuing approach to Aboriginal students has placed them in the 'others' category of schooling. Reference here to 'other' is very much in Edward Said's (1979) interpretations around 'orientalism'. Indigenous students are interpreted similarly. This means that Indigenous students are to be treated differently. As such, many teachers and principals assume that Aboriginal children require additional externally funded resources and programs. In general terms, I refer to this as the *'sustainable' principle*, as it infers that without these additional resources Aboriginal education cannot exist. Second, again in categorising our children as 'others', schools ultimately have not accepted responsibility for Indigenous students' outcomes. Partly this is due to an overall lack of schools being held accountable by systems for effectively teaching our children. This I refer to as the *'systemic' principle*. Third, schools and systems have continually 'blamed the victims'—Indigenous students, their families and culture—for the poor schooling outcomes of Aboriginal children, and through this deficit theorising (Deyhle and Swisher, 1997) have once more taken the school's and teachers' accountability out of the equation. I refer to this as the *'ownership' principle*. The final principle is the 'Indigenous business' principle, where if any education issue involves any mention of the words 'black', 'Aboriginal', 'Indigenous', or anything remotely hinting at these, then the issue is the sole responsibility of Indigenous people and quite often this means Indigenous staff employed at the school. These failings have continually hampered the very positive work and direction needing to be taken in Indigenous education from the beginnings of the first real policy and practice in the 1980s to current times. It is only now that we are seeing some breakthroughs in realisations that Indigenous students are students in their own right and should be accessing mainstream resources, and that classroom teachers in schools are largely responsible for Indigenous students' outcomes from schooling.

The reality of all of these principles—sustainability, systemic responsibility, ownership and Indigenous business—is the fact that if we are to spark an educational revolution in Indigenous education (and, given the 'gap', this is what is required), its focal bonfire must be ignited in all classrooms with Indigenous students across Australia. Hattie (2003) clearly indicates that it is teachers who have the power and capacity to change the outcomes of students. The above principles also dictate that Indigenous education is certainly the ultimate responsibility of the classroom teacher. To effect the required shift in outcomes in Indigenous education, our primary focus must be on assisting teachers to engage with Indigenous students in normal inclusive classroom interactions and, crucially, to engage Indigenous students in learning. This is no more than we ask or would demand and expect for all students.

The sustainability principle
Compounding the difficulty surrounding the 'sustainability principle' is the concept that schools and teachers are not responsible for the poor outcomes of Indigenous students: the 'systemic principle'. It is as though Indigenous

---

Personal narrative of my schooling journey

Education has always been a major part of my life, largely because my mother is a teacher. Throughout my life she has always reinforced to me, and others, how important gaining an education is. From the outset I have learned about the different sacrifices that are made by families regarding schooling. Whilst my mother was training to be a teacher, my grandparents and extended family helped care for me.

My schooling began at the community school at Walhallow Primary School at Caroona in the northwest of NSW. Whilst reflecting on my journey I don't remember a lot about my early primary school days, although I do remember my mother working as the Aboriginal Education Assistant (AEA) and feeling that some of the kids thought that I may have been favoured (even though I never was). I always loved sport and being active at school which was probably the result of living on the Mission and there not being much to do. Arts and crafts were favourite activities at school due primarily to the fact we always got to take things home. Another vivid memory is we always went on school excursions to a different destination each year; these trips were probably the most fun because our parents always came with us. In hindsight it was probably also enjoyable because we never went anywhere on holidays except to visit family. During my latter school years at Walhallow a wonderful teacher named James (Jim) Miller came to teach. Mr Miller was an Aboriginal man from Armidale, and the first and only Aboriginal teacher I ever had during primary school. To this day I believe he inspired me to learn about my culture and ignited a passion of reading in me which I still have today. Athletics was another enjoyable experience as I got to represent the school and region, which entailed travelling and meeting other people outside my little circle.

Secondary school for me was quite different because there are no high schools at Walhallow; we all had to travel on the bus which came from Spring Ridge to Quirindi High. In many ways I found this extremely scary as I was not only leaving my little safe haven of an all-Indigenous primary school, but also travelling with non-Indigenous students to this new and quite large environment. In 1991 I moved with Mum to Moree where she got her first teaching position. This was actually confronting at first because I felt I might have been judged by the colour of my skin and wondered if I would be accepted within the Aboriginal schooling community. A great love of mathematics was somehow formed here and I was the only one in Year 10 who got an "A" on their School Certificate for this subject which made me very proud. To this day I still have a special talent for retaining numbers in my mind!

Lastly I am now currently studying at the Koori Centre. I first came here in 2004 but due to personal reasons I stopped after the first year. The desire to come back never waned, it actually grew stronger and that is why I'm back and loving it. As a mother I now understand what my Mum would have gone through when she went off to learn to be a teacher. I am realising there are a lot of similarities between my mum's journey and my own.

—Hayley Saunders

students don't count in the school system and there is a level of acceptance of this situation. As the MCEETYA Taskforce (2000) put it:

> lingering perceptions and mindsets in some quarters of the Australian community that the gap in educational outcomes between Indigenous and non-Indigenous Australian students is 'normal' and that educational equality for Indigenous Australians is either not achievable, or if possible, only achievable over a long period of time (i.e. decades or generations). (2000, p. 10)

The systemic principle

The issue of lack of responsibility or the 'systemic principle' demands not only that the curriculum and policy be put in place, which has been the avid pursuit of educators since the 1980s with a general level of success as shown in New South Wales (Lester and Hanlen, 2004), but Departments of Education in each state must clearly push down and spread the area of responsibility across the whole organisation, and particularly to the operative levels of delivery in the schools and their teachers. *Australian Directions in Indigenous Education 2005–2008* (MCEETYA, 2006) clearly spells out this responsibility to principals (2006, 7.1, p. 24) and teachers (2006, 9.2, p. 26). Closely aligned to the abdication of responsibility for Indigenous student outcomes in schools is the perception that the blame lies out of the school and in the Aboriginal community itself, through the general perception that Indigenous people's indifference to education is the reason behind poor Indigenous performance: the 'ownership principle'.

The ownership principle or deficit theorising of Indigenous peoples

Deficit theorising of Indigenous peoples stretches across international waters and was a subject of research in the United States with Native Americans (Trimble and Medicine, 1976; Trimble, 1977). Deficit theorising has also found fertile ground and allies in Australia (manifesting in perceptions of lower levels of cognitive capacity or lack of the required educational nurturing home environments). This has resulted in pockets of the broader community, and particularly some teachers, holding ethnocentric views about Indigenous families and their communities as lacking educationally conducive lives, and not accepting the richness of Indigenous cultural backgrounds. Laying the blame for poor educational attainments at the feet of Indigenous parents and their communities provides a seemingly plausible excuse to not look at the school, its teachers and its curriculum for levels of accountability when it comes to a lack of positive Indigenous student outcomes (Nurcombe, 1976; Nicklin Dent and Hatton, 1996; Harslett et al., 1998, p. 3).

The Indigenous business principle

The 'Indigenous business principle' often comes into play when a school has access to Indigenous human resources, and generally this relates to Aboriginal Education Workers or those few schools fortunate enough to have access to the limited pool of Indigenous teachers. Quite often, Indigenous people working specifically in Indigenous education will readily recognise this principle because basically anything that can be even remotely associated with Indigenous education ends up being assigned as their responsibility. It is as though as soon as you have an Indigenous worker, most of the non-Indigenous workers appear to have no responsibility for Indigenous

---

The importance of this book cannot be overestimated

We have been insisting for years that pre-service teachers be required to learn about Aboriginal history, culture and identity, and that it be regarded as integral to qualifying for their education degrees. In fact, the National Aboriginal Education Committee initiated this conversation back in the 1970s.

All teachers need to have a good understanding of Aboriginal people and Aboriginal issues before they enter the classroom, because what teachers know and do has a significant influence on student outcomes. If I had to outline what I want teachers to know before they walk in the school gate, I would say it is knowledge of the true history and culture of this country that we now call Australia.

Lionel Bamblett is a Wiradjuri man who in 1985 became the first General Manager of the newly formed Victorian Aboriginal Education Association Incorporated (VAEAI). Lionel has played a significant role in negotiations with different Ministers for Education about development and implementation of policy that impacts Koori students throughout Victoria.

> **Our kids deserve the best**
>
> One of the main things I am passionately opposed to is the practice of sending first-year-out teachers to remote and difficult schools. It seems to me that systems use these kids as factory fodder in order to keep a steady supply of teachers in those schools and the carrot that entices them to accept the deal is no more than double teaching credits in one year, which I think is a paltry reward for being thrown to the wolves. The whole process is flawed as first-year-outs do not have the experience of classroom/schoolyard dynamics necessary to deal with difficult situations with the result that there is enormous turnover of teachers in remote areas and a lack of teaching continuity for the students. It would be better by far to offer seasoned teachers incentives to undertake three-to-five year secondments to remote and difficult schools as I believe this would have positive impact on drop-out and truancy rates, which in turn would help to ameliorate poor levels of education. This is a real issue for me.
>
> When teaching history, teachers should always ensure that they include Aboriginal-authored texts as primary sources of information. Furthermore, students should be encouraged to do likewise when researching.
>
> Teachers should endeavour to consult with local Elders and people of importance in community when developing local history modules as their knowledge is most relevant to such projects.
>
> It would be helpful for teachers to build relationships with local communities as this translates into a trust relationship with invaluable outcomes for students and hence school and community morale.
>
> All teachers should undergo cultural awareness training and undertake refresher courses every two years and at each change of school, the latter to accommodate regional variations in protocols.
>
> Above all, teachers need to demonstrate respect for cultural differences and accept them as rich components of the school and community fabric.
>
> Our kids deserve the best, let's not fail them, give them the best.
>
> *A Wadi Wadi woman, **Aunty Barbara Nicholson** is a long-standing executive member of Link-Up, and has served in various capacities with numerous Aboriginal organisations, including on the executive of the former Aboriginal Deaths in Custody Watch Committee.*
>
> *She has been a lecturer in Aboriginal Studies at the University of New South Wales and the University of Wollongong, and was contracted by Southern Cross University to teach course work to prison inmates in Goulburn.*
>
> *For the last ten years she has been Senior Honorary Research Fellow in the Law Faculty of Wollongong University. In this position she delivers guest lectures, chiefly cross-cultural training modules in the post-graduate Practical Legal Training course. She also mentors and supports Aboriginal law students and other students who undertake research into Aboriginal issues. For nearly five years she has served on the university's Ethics Committee.*
>
> *Aunty Barbara is a member of the South Coast Writers Centre and active on the steering committee for 'Celebrating the Voice', the Aboriginal arm of the Writers Centre. She is a published poet with work in a number of anthologies. She is currently preparing to publish her own volume of poetry.*

matters or students. While Indigenous people have fought hard to gain access to educational employment and community input through consultative bodies, the reality is that Aboriginal education is everyone's business. It is certainly not the sole domain of Indigenous employees in schools. This is clearly spelled out in the *Australian Directions* document:

The recommendations in this paper are systemic to ensure that Indigenous education and the lessons learnt from strategic intervention programs are '*built in*' to core business to become everyone's business: departmental staff, principals, teachers, school staff, Indigenous students, parents/caregivers, families and communities. (MCEETYA, 2006, p. 16)

Harnessing the goodwill of teachers and the basic principles in action

The *Review of the NSW Aboriginal Education Policy* (Lester and Hanlen, 2004) indicated that the goodwill of teachers in general towards Indigenous education was significantly high, but they were hesitant about getting involved in Indigenous education because they did not want to offend Indigenous people or make mistakes in a domain where they had little knowledge. It could be argued that one effect of the positive work of many Indigenous educators and supportive non-Indigenous educators in the latter part of the last century in forcefully and successfully arguing a position for Indigenous Studies and education in the Australian syllabus has been to inadvertently disable many teachers. While significantly moving to improve outcomes for Indigenous students, perhaps these efforts have played a role in 'mystifying' Indigenous education, and ultimately have led to the paralysing inaction of some of the teachers who were the focus of this attention during this time. Yet it is paramount that teacher goodwill is harnessed and supported to provide inclusive engagement of Indigenous students in classrooms.

While teachers rightly remain the primary focus of both policy and strategic efforts across Australia in Indigenous education, the key principles of sustainability, systemic responsibility, ownership and Indigenous business must simultaneously be addressed. In 1967, the Referendum made Indigenous education—like all Indigenous issues—the responsibility of the federal government. Education is also a state government responsibility and the federal government's primary vehicle for influencing the Indigenous education agenda was via targeting additional tied-grant funding to states. In later developments, the federal government utilised agencies such as MCEETYA to create a united policy framework in Indigenous education. The government also began to tie funding to performance and outcomes measurements against the National Aboriginal and Torres Strait Islander Education Policy (Commonwealth of Australia, 1989) through grant funding supplied under the Indigenous Education Strategic Initiatives Programme (IESIP). This approach unfortunately led to a school mentality of 'Indigenous education equals additional support dollars', and ultimately led to the wrong conclusion that schools could only respond to Indigenous student needs if additional resources were forthcoming.

This was clearly echoed at a recent Quality Teaching Framework conference, when a school's response to the question, 'What has the school done for the 25 per cent of Indigenous students in the school's seemingly positive implementation of the Framework?' was: 'We haven't got an Aboriginal Education Assistant and when we get one, we will address the issue'. The 'sustainability principle' is clearly at work here—the school cannot sustain an effort in Indigenous education unless it gets additional resources!

For all these reasons, 'the package' therefore must be delivered to where it can best make a difference: at the classroom door. The job is to define that package and to guarantee that teachers will pick it up and make it a '*built-in*' component of their daily teaching practice. We need to unpack the package and discover what are the key classroom practices it can deliver to reduce the 'gap' between many Indigenous students and their non-Indigenous peers.

Unpacking 'the package' arriving at your classroom door

There is now ample research and many educational programs that have proven significant results for Indigenous students in our schools. The real challenge is how to package these positive results so that teachers in classrooms can pick up 'the package' and run with it. There may be some debate about what would constitute the content of 'the package', although the *Australian Directions* document (MCEETYA, 2006) has highlighted its key components where it directs specific action across the broader areas that are inclusive of prior-to-school (early childhood) and post-school destinations. However, this section will concentrate on the difference that can be made specifically in schools and with classroom teachers, which is in tune with the direction of the overall text in this book.

There are six key factors that will have the greatest effect on closing the gap for Indigenous

Stronger Smarter

In 1998 a new principal started at Cherbourg Aboriginal School. Cherbourg is a former mission about 300 kilometres north-west of Brisbane; one of the places Aboriginal people from all over Queensland who had been rounded up were sent to make them less Aboriginal. This principal was different—Dr Chris Sarra was Aboriginal, and determined to change the way the school ran.

Cherbourg was known to have high rates of alcoholism and domestic violence. The school was in chaos with a double status quo: teachers would say kids didn't value education or the community didn't support the school, and the community would blame the school. Teachers often said their lives were transformed by being in an Aboriginal community, but kids' lives were not transformed at all—research found 4260 Cherbourg kids going on to Murgon State High School over the previous 30 years had lasted in high school for an average of nine months.

Student behaviour at Cherbourg was extremely poor and this was tolerated: kids literally ran up and down on the top of two-storey buildings; the school grounds were a mess from weekend litter and vandalism; attendance was very low; kids would cruise home after lunch; and they were taught a watered-down version of the state curriculum. These Aboriginal kids were being failed miserably.

Under Chris Sarra the Cherbourg School adopted a motto of 'Strong and Smart' and the school now aims to nurture a positive sense of what it means to be Aboriginal in today's society (strong) and to generate good academic outcomes comparable to other schools around Queensland (smart). 'Strong and Smart' was, and is, about Aboriginal students being 'strong in our hearts, proud of our identity, solid in our community—and smart in the way we do things; focused on high achievement, determined to succeed'.

The Strong and Smart motto allowed Chris Sarra and his new team to hook the kids, the staff and the community—people were the most important resource. For example, one of the most powerful women in the community was a teacher's aide in the school, photocopying and doing colour-in sheets. Dr Sarra took her out into the community so that he could learn who was who; she became his 'right hand' at the school.

At the 'new' Cherbourg State School classes monitored their own absences, Aboriginal Studies was the centre of the curriculum, there was a school uniform and school song, and local Elders were invited to forge a school vision. The result of these changes was a 94 per cent drop in absenteeism and hikes in literacy and numeracy.

Every day in the new Cherbourg School, being Aboriginal was celebrated. Kids signed up to the new vision with their new school song:

Jingle bells, jingle bells,
Cherbourg School is here.
We're young and black and deadly—
Come and hear us cheer.
Bring on every challenge,
Put us to the test.
We're from Cherbourg State School,
And you know we're the best.

Dr Sarra says: 'It is just too easy to assume Aboriginal children are broken and need fixing. The new motto for our school was about being strong and smart. Every Friday on parade I would say to children: "When we leave school what are we going to be?" and they would say, from the bottom of their guts: "Strong and Smart".' He believes the key issue is addressing what makes a child want to come to school and makes their parents want to be involved in the school? He told new teachers before they started at Cherbourg they were not coming to rescue children—the kids didn't need rescuing.

Next, Chris Sarra founded the Indigenous Education Leadership Institute at Queensland University of Technology's Caboolture campus. It's aim is 'changing the tide of low expectations in Indigenous

> education', and it is supported by the Telstra Foundation, the Sydney Myer Fund and Jobs Australia. At the Stronger Smarter Summit held at the Institute in September 2009, the federal government announced a new Australia-wide Indigenous Education Action Plan. This included $16.4 million for the renamed Stronger Smarter Institute to set up 60 Stronger Smarter learning hubs with up to 1200 affiliated schools over three years. Stronger Smarter is schools and individuals creating stronger, smarter realities for Indigenous children. Dr Sarra says there would be more progress if English-as-a-second-language teachers worked in remote schools where local languages predominate—as they do in metropolitan schools with high migrant or refugee intakes.
>
> Chris Sarra says: 'At the Institute we maintain that acknowledging and embracing Aboriginal community leadership in education is one of the best ways of enabling Indigenous Australian children to succeed at school. Many Indigenous community leaders . . . are often described as the most valuable asset in their school. Having worked with many schools throughout Australia, I can say with certainty that, in school communities where principals and community leaders work respectfully together in the interests of stronger smarter futures for their children, great things happen.'

students: relationships; school/community partnerships; school/community leadership; effective prescriptive literacy and numeracy intervention; high expectations; and the vehicle to deliver most of this—creating a quality teaching environment. These primarily interrelated factors will create a classroom environment that will engage Indigenous students. I would also maintain that all these factors will work for all students—or, as I have put it on many occasions, 'If it works with Indigenous students it will work for the rest as well!' A great background resource for this package can be found in the readily available *What Works* series of resources (<www.whatworks.edu.au>).

Relationship and respect

The bottom line is that teaching is a relationship game. Without good and productive relations between students and their teacher, the act of learning will be compromised. There has been much written about what makes an effective teacher, and primarily the biggest asset relates to building rapport with the students under your care, which is well picked up in Geoff Munns' section later in this chapter. Fundamentally, to build a relationship you first must earn a level of respect. This is no different from our own personal relationships, nor is it different across the oceans for our native American brothers, the Cherokee (Dumont and Wax, 1976). It is often not achieved quickly, and in many instances will require working at and taking care not to force the equation:

> Non-Aboriginal teachers should be mindful of the complexity of Aboriginal society and respectful of the opportunities given by community members to establish relationships. However, it is important not to force the interaction beyond the scope of the invitation. (Heslop, 2003, p. 231)

I have maintained that the three 'Rs' of Indigenous education are 'respect, respect and respect'. It is the most fundamental component of relationships and involves a significant factor in Indigenous society, the concept of reciprocity.

Former NBL player and Sydney Kings coach Claude Williams demonstrates the finer points of basketball etiquette to young participants at a Vibe 3on3 Basketball and Hip-Hop Challenge. Claude is now Vibe's 3on3 Coordinator. Courtesy Vibe Australia.

Respect is a two-way process involving reciprocity. When I explained my '3 Rs' of Indigenous education to a non-Indigenous high school principal, he commented that this was the same for all kids, black or white! I begged to differ, as in reference to Indigenous kids it is often the 'cross-cultural respect' that brings a very different dimension to the equation. In a same or monocultural relationship, the respect is within the same cultural framework and the reciprocity requires limited or no differential cultural understanding. In an Indigenous framework, we are talking across two cultures and, rather than a parallel reference point, we have juxtaposed positioning. Cross-cultural respect requires each party to take the time and space to understand the other's cultural perspective and positioning. This is a relatively easy task for the Indigenous player, as most have lived their lives under a dominant non-Indigenous culture so more ably understand the foundation of this culture. The non-Indigenous teacher in this situation has to go out of their way to learn about Indigenous culture. When this is successfully achieved through taking the time, making the effort to get to know Indigenous people and taking a genuine interest in their culture, then cross-cultural respect has a foundation on which to develop.

In many instances, just by taking an interest the teacher can clearly give the genuine impression of working towards this level of respect required with their students. This can be as simple as acknowledging Indigenous people you pass in the town, taking an interest in the after-school activities of Indigenous students, or creating space for the teacher to meet with their Indigenous parents/carers in a comfortable place outside of the school. You know you have made it when you get to share a 'cuppa' on a well-worn laminated kitchen table in an Indigenous household. Getting to know your students and their cultural and home background is fundamental to developing relationships, and unfortunately this has resulted in many Indigenous students having 'fallen through the educational engagement cracks'; thus, while attending school regularly, many have not been engaged in the process. State Departments of Education and the Commonwealth government are strongly advocating that all Indigenous students have personalised learning plans in place to ensure they do not fall through these cracks, which are discussed in the following section.

Personalised learning plans

The New South Wales report of the *Review of Aboriginal Education* (NSWAECG and NSWDET, 2004, pp. 198–200) emphasises the importance of 'getting to know Aboriginal students' to ensure engagement in learning takes place. Both the Review in New South Wales and *Australian Directions in Indigenous Education 2005–2008* (MCEETYA, 2006) advocate moving this 'getting to know Aboriginal students' to a very formal approach. Both strongly recommend that schools establish the equivalent of 'personalised learning plans' (PLPs) for every Indigenous student, as discussed in recommendation 5.5:

> ensure that schools, in partnership with parents/caregivers, deliver personalised learning to all Indigenous students that includes targets against key learning outcomes and incorporates family involvement strategies. (MCEETYA, 2006, p. 22).

In strategic pursuit of this recommendation, states are implementing personal plans for every Indigenous student, and in New South Wales this required around 36 000 plans in operation by 2012 with an intermediary target of 10 000 by 2008 (NSWDET, 2006a, p. 6). Critical to effective implementation of these learning plans is recognising the need to work in genuine partnership with parents and caregivers. Ideally, these plans should be trilateral agreements negotiated between classroom teachers, parents/caregivers and the students. Remembering that our first key factor is based on building relationships through respect, the primary function of these learning plans is to put teachers and parents/caregivers on an equal footing to discuss the positive collaboration required to improve outcomes for each Indigenous student. Such plans are not founded on the paperwork involved, but unequivocally require building shared relationships between the school (teacher) and Indigenous community (parents/caregivers). This provides the clear opportunity to begin the '3Rs', as previously discussed.

All PLPs must involve a positive shared vision based on the personal best potential of the student. The process is designed to explore the positive background of the student and their family, and clearly articulate how, collectively, the teacher, parents/caregivers and the student can deliver their personal bests. In early assessments of the introduction of PLPs in New South Wales schools in situations where they have effectively been implemented, both teachers and parents are singing their praise, as indicated by this teacher:

> PLP meetings provided opportunity to welcome parents into schools, to share understandings, to discuss common goals and expectations, and to access parental expertise so as to help teachers and students. (Davies, 2007, p. 23)

These personal approaches to planning Indigenous students' futures are an important part of developing the critical relationships required and assisting in bridging the cultural chasm between many teachers and Indigenous communities. One must be careful that these formal opportunities are not used to reinforce stereotypical behaviours, for behavioural modification purposes only or as a process of just filling out more forms! When sensitively and professionally done, they provide a unique opportunity for building those important shared bonds between school, community and students—achieving these outcomes is the motivation behind such personalised planning.

Genuine community partnerships

> Engaging the local community in the future of Indigenous education is vital if there is to be a significant shift towards equity of educational outcomes. (MCEETYA, 2006, p. 21)

The MCEETYA Taskforce on Indigenous Education highlighted the importance of genuine community partnership in the education process in the release of its *Statement of Principles and Standards for More Culturally Inclusive Schooling in the 21st Century* (MCEETYA, 2000, pp. 15–17). Principle 2.2 states that schooling should acknowledge the role of Indigenous parents as the first educators of their children by:

> actively increasing public confidence in education and training through the process of explicit involvement of Indigenous parents/caregivers and community in the achievement of equitable and appropriate educational outcomes.

In every policy forum on Indigenous education, the Indigenous community partnership is an essential fundamental and over-arching condition that has prominence in all negotiations. Its prominence is predicated on the fact that the vast majority of non-Indigenous people do not have the required community background, cultural understanding or empowerment to articulate the needs and desires of the Indigenous community. Indigenous people are in the best possible position to provide such input, but this alone—without clearly defined educational expertise—cannot in itself provide the required answers on how to 'close the gap'. It is the movement to genuine partnership between community knowledge and educational expertise that will provide the required mix to facilitate a quantum movement in Indigenous educational outcomes.

Genuineness of the partnership

The use of the term 'genuine' in the above heading has important connotations. I have heard many an Indigenous parent flippantly remark about being involved in their schools only for 'Kodak moments'. This implies—in

Engagement: Rhoda Roberts reading with Aboriginal kids at the launch of Indij Readers at the Art Gallery of NSW. Photo: Robert Pearce. Courtesy Fairfax Photo Library.

many instances rightly—that Indigenous involvement was not genuine but only used to 'dress up' the supposed involvement of Indigenous community members. Often Indigenous people are called on at the latter stages of a submission for their signature on the document or for those important occasions when the school is on show or has special visitors, where the impression is to be of community involvement and the opportunity for that 'black and white' photo. Now Indigenous communities, through their various education consultative bodies throughout the state education systems, are rightfully demanding a shared planning role in the development of schools and their educational programs.

Indigenous communities want meaningful engagement with schools based on partnership. This high-level partnership *can* be achieved, as is readily exemplified by the partnership of the New South Wales Department of Education and Training (DET) and the New South Wales AECG in undertaking an extensive Review of Aboriginal Education (NSWAECG and DET, 2004) in the state in 2004. The AECG was intimately involved in designing the development, implementation and outcomes of the review, and rightfully had equitable ownership of the process. This ensured the outcomes of the review were relevant and representative of the broad community and educational environment.

Australian Directions in Indigenous Education 2005–2008 (MCEETYA, 2006) clearly spells out its call for genuine partnership with community through the development of formal partnership agreements between schools and local Indigenous communities. This, among other things, demands that Indigenous communities be involved in school planning and decision-making processes, even going to the length of preparing an 'agreement template' in an attempt to hasten the process (MCEETYA, 2006, pp. 21–2). States are currently rolling out these agreements: in Victoria this has occurred through Wannik, an education strategy for Koori Students (State of Victoria, 2006, p. 17); Queensland has commenced the process at Mornington Island, with local Indigenous partnership agreements being the first in this state (Queensland Government, 2008, p. 59); and finally in New South Wales, a major push known as Schools in Partnership involves 30 schools with high-density Indigenous numbers, which have nominated to become formal partners with the school's local community (New South Wales Department of Education and Training, 2006b).

In its simplest form, the genuine nature of a partnership requires equity between the partners at all stages of an effective educational planning process: the development, implementation and evaluation of the school's macro planning processes. To be truly equal, the school and the community will have to develop reciprocity of expertise. The school is obviously well versed in educational opportunities, and the community in its culture and environment. This will require each party to educate the other about their strengths, so that the appropriate mix of educational responses will maximise outcomes for Indigenous students. This may well involve the school in providing the community with professional development opportunities in governance matters such as meeting procedure, decision-making, accountability and more general structural matters surrounding such formal processes. Such genuine partnership involvement from the community will greatly assist with large numbers of transient school staff—as is the case in many isolated or rural school communities—and ensure the continuity of programs, as while teachers and principals move on the community becomes the stable influence on the school during such change. Newly arriving principals and their staff should value-add to an already established responsive syllabus and curriculum continuum.

> AECG President Cindy Berwick told the New South Wales Legislative Council Inquiry into Indigenous Disadvantage in 2008:
>
> It is not about doing things to Aboriginal people, it is about doing them with Aboriginal people. If the gap is to be closed or if there is to be any improvement in whatever it is, Aboriginal people have some responsibility. You have to make sure that they are able to do it and that they have the skills to do it.
>
> There are successful places and successful programs. Where they have been successful is when it involves the principles of governance and effective leadership, and valuing what people bring to the table and having a say in the decision making process. I think government departments—and I will say the education department because that is the one I know—fall down on it all the time, because they just do things that they think they need to do. (Legislative Council Standing Committee on Social Issues, 2008, p. 32)

Often the process of engaging community can be enhanced significantly by an already established Indigenous education group that can be accessed readily. If such a group does not exist, then it is important for the school to liaise with the diverse groupings in the Indigenous community to establish an advisory body for the school. Often in schools with significant numbers of Indigenous students, Indigenous staff are available (e.g. Aboriginal Education Workers or community liaison officers), who can be drawn upon to ensure the appropriate groups in the community are involved. The complexity of Indigenous communities and the importance of setting up effective consultative mechanisms were covered in more detail in the preceding chapter. Of critical importance to genuine community partnership is the capacity of leadership available within the school and community to drive this shared responsibility agenda.

School/community leadership

In genuine school–Indigenous community partnerships, the leadership is a shared responsibility, with both partners—as indicated earlier—sharing one another's expertise and knowledge bases, ensuring secured positive outcomes of Indigenous students (McRae et al., 2000, p. 6). This level of equity might not initially be shared in establishing such a relationship, and either party may need to show leadership to the other in moving to this equilibrium. It is here that true educational leadership is enhanced. The sometimes shy, reluctant and less empowered community member needs to be nurtured into an equitable partnership, and good school leadership will produce this. Similarly, the newly arrived school executive staff member, in an Aboriginal community for the first time, will need to be carefully and thoughtfully guided in the ways of the new community and culture in which they now find themselves. Obviously this is fertile ground for a nurturing Indigenous leader.

School leadership

Masters (2004; also see Groome and Hamilton, 1995; Collins, 1999) sees strong, effective school leaders with a primary focus on establishing a culture of learning throughout the school as a key component of any quality program for Indigenous students. While it is openly acknowledged that teachers remain the primary facilitators of school success of students (Hattie, 2003), the capacity of teachers to achieve such success is heavily influenced by the leadership being demonstrated by school executives, in particular principals.

School leadership which is driven by the principal provides direction to quality educational programs and ensures teachers are equipped with current best practice to provide opportunities for Indigenous students to flourish. Leadership on key policy, curriculum direction and quality teaching can significantly influence the school environment, and ultimately Indigenous student outcomes.

Racism, in both its overt and covert forms, is still a pervasive element in our community and schools, as is clearly articulated in the New South Wales Review of Aboriginal Education (NSWAECG and NSWDET, 2004, pp. 211–12). Another issue that consistently raises its head is the need to challenge stereotypical beliefs about and associated deficit labelling of the Indigenous community (see Chapter 3). These two issues on their own require considered and determined leadership within a school if an inclusive learning environment is to be achieved. Leadership of the principal and their executive staff can rise above these inherent debilitating circumstances and focus a school on inclusive practices based not on deficit models but rather on high expectations. Principals confronting such difficulties will not revert to behaviour modification processes, but will champion best practice and positively promote the virtues of engaging Indigenous students through systemic embodiment of quality teaching practices in their schools.

> School leaders play a crucial role in encouraging their colleagues to examine their practice and bring about cultural change within schools. Leaders are not there just to affirm good practice when they see it, but also to examine entrenched practices and attitudes that may be contributing to disparity in educational outcomes of Indigenous and non-Indigenous students. (MCEETYA, 2006, p. 23)

Good school leaders will clearly understand that their role is not a solo performance but is directly related to building a sound partnership with the community and its leadership.

Community leadership

Unlike the school system, which has a built-in process for the procurement and development of its school leadership, the Indigenous community currently is reliant on the evolution of its leadership through normal community processes or through active involvement in Indigenous issues and in particular education—often through consultative groups formed at school, regional and state levels across Australia.

The primary apprenticeship for educational community leadership often arrives in the form of taking part in either local community groups or through employment in schools, usually in casual positions such as Aboriginal Education Workers or tutors in the school. Many of these casual workers gain a new appreciation of education and often move into further training, with many ending up as teachers. Indigenous educational consultative bodies in each state/territory provide valuable opportunities for Indigenous community members to be exposed to the broader policy domains of education and the various programs for Indigenous students. For example, the New South Wales AECG has been in operation for over 30 years and has a long list of life members with nearly as many years' experience in Indigenous education. These groups across Australia have provided the backbone of support to Indigenous education and have remained at the forefront of Indigenous educational change.

While the various Indigenous consultative bodies are available at the local, regional and state levels, many communities do not come within the reach of these groups. In these circumstances, schools need to work collaboratively with their local communities to establish community advisory groups. As mentioned earlier, Indigenous staff within schools might be the best point at which to start this process. Schools need to understand that Indigenous communities are diverse (Beresford and Partington, 2003, pp. 12–13; Bourke, Rigney and Burden 2000, p. 20; NSWAECG and NSWDET, 2004, p. 95), and ensure that their invitation to participate in an advisory role covers all the key Indigenous stakeholder groups in the community.

School and community leadership must focus on the primary task of engaging Indigenous students in high-quality education. Paramount to this is the continued pursuit of the students' personal bests and the commitment to high expectations by school leadership, teachers, parents and community respectively.

High expectations

In my 30-plus years of work in Indigenous education, I have yet to run into an Indigenous parent who did not want the best from the education system for their children. However, such an expectation from the system was quickly followed up by the parents with the comment 'but not at the expense of their Aboriginality'. This is no different for other Indigenous groups like Native Americans (Deyhle and Swisher, 1997) or the Maori of New Zealand (Bishop et al., 2006), and is borne out by the following excellent community explanation of parenting in the two worlds of Indigenous culture and Western education from an Indigenous perspective by one-time Chairman of the Ngaanyatjarra Council, Bernard Newberry (quoted in Heslop, 2003, p. 233):

> My children are walking along the edge. They have to learn traditional knowledge and skills because they are Maru [Aboriginal] and will always belong to that culture. But, if the kids are going to help us [Yarnangu] to control our lives and run the businesses in the Lands, then they must learn Western knowledge, behaviour, and skills. They have to be able to mix with white people in business and through friendships, and so they need good English, good Maths, good writing skills, and a knowledge about the rest of the world.
>
> It's not easy to know where the balance between Western and traditional ways lies. If the children go one way, they will be skilled in whitefeller ways but might forget about their traditions. They might even leave [the community]. I don't want that, but if [his son] wants to be a pilot, then I have to give him the values of my family so that he will never forget where he belongs and what is important, no matter where he lives. That way, he will always come back. I lived down south for... must be fifteen years. But I came back. I was well taught by my uncle to value my culture.

Maori speak of the *Mannaakitang* (caring for the well-being of the child—or, as they refer to it, the soft element) and the *Mana motuhake* (caring for the performance of the student, or the hard element). Under their approach, *Te Kotahitanga* is their view of how to improve outcomes for Maori students. This holistic approach to Maori education simultaneously ensures that the students' personal and cultural needs are carefully looked after and maintained in the education process while the *Mana motuhake* demands that they are challenged in their education through high expectations and personal demands placed on the students (Bishop et al., 2006). These issues are no different from Indigenous Australian demands on our schooling system, and are very much incorporated in the New South Wales *Dimensions Regarding Quality Learning Environments and Significance in the Quality Teaching Framework* (Ladwig and King, 2003).

Exorcising the deficit demons

Earlier, I briefly introduced the concept of deficit theorising associated with predicating blame on to the victim—in this case, the Indigenous child and their family. In a study of teachers, Jane Dent and Elizabeth Hatton (1996) highlight the effect of holding deficit views of students' backgrounds in a school with a broad ethnic mix, including an 18 per cent Aboriginal school population, in a low socio-economic environment. Their research demonstrates how deficit modelling creates low expectations and also provides an opportunity for teachers to abdicate their accountabilities for performance of students and to develop coping mechanisms to 'survive' their teaching experiences. As Dent and Hatton show, this quite often leads to teacher absences and ineffective classroom practices best exemplified by reams of photocopied activity sheets often having little if anything to do with programmed classroom activities but rather used to fill in free time. (I have recently heard teachers refer to these sheets of work as 'shut-up sheets' or, as Dent and Hatton (1996) describe them, 'non-work, non-academic activities'). Furthermore, Dent and Hatton contend that many teachers in schools in low socio-economic areas with mixed racial groupings often resort to survival strategies of regular teacher absences from school, lowered academic expectations and a non-work, non-academic classroom. The focus for these teachers is on survival and limited responsibility, due to deficit demonising about the majority of parents and community of the students they teach, rather than on highlighting quality teaching and high expectations for all students in their care. These stereotypical and ethnocentric attitudes then permeate the school environment. Schools subject to such forms of racism often concentrate their efforts on 'student welfare' and 'behaviour modification' when the real answers lie in high expectations and engaging students through quality teaching programs (Newmann et al., 1996). There is little point in finally understanding the answers to improving Indigenous student outcomes if we can't successfully deliver these proven answers to teachers and schools where formal education takes place. This delivery is discussed in the following section.

The vehicle for delivery of the package

The Quality Teaching Framework

If we are to affect the outcomes of Indigenous students, we must—as previously argued—focus our efforts on the classroom practices of teachers, for they, as Hattie (2003) rightfully points out, will have the greatest potential impact on students. In the past, there has not been a coordinated capacity to address systemic and sustainable change in classroom practice to meet the specific needs of Indigenous students. Past practices and current continuing ones concentrate effort primarily where such effort can have the most perceived impact: in schools with significant Indigenous enrolments. Wrongly, the perception has been that targeting high-density Indigenous schools will resolve significantly the issues in Indigenous education. In fact, the majority of Indigenous students are found not in isolated or remote Indigenous communities but in provincial and metropolitan centres across Australia (Senate Employment, Workplace Relations, Small Business, and Education References Committee, 2000, p. 2). For example, in the highest Indigenous populated state in Australia—New South Wales—in 2003, some 89 per cent of schools with Indigenous students enrolled had 50 or fewer Indigenous students (NSWAECG and NSWDET, 2004, pp. 19–20). If we are to improve Indigenous outcomes in school education significantly, we must develop strategies that will target the whole Indigenous student base. Fundamentally, this can be achieved by piggy-backing on the general thrust currently in schooling to improve classroom teaching practice, pedagogy, through the national priority Australian Government Quality Teaching Programme (Department of Education, Employment and Workplace Relations, 2007).

States have each actively sought improvements in pedagogical practice. For example, in Queensland the School Reform Longitudinal Study (QSRLS) was undertaken and subsequently the Productive Pedagogy initiative (Queensland Department of Education and Training, n.d.) was implemented. In New South Wales the development of the Quality Teaching

Table 12.1 Productive pedagogies characteristics

High-scoring teachers	Low-scoring teachers
• Acknowledged that they could not force students to learn	• Expressed the belief that students were responsible for their own learning
• Considered themselves responsible for providing opportunities for student learning	• Held that factors totally outside the teacher's control largely 'determined' student outcomes
• Viewed all learners as capable of improving	• Aimed instruction at the 'middle level' of the class
• Spoke of themselves as facilitators of learning	• Assumed that some students would learn, others would not—it was up to the student
• Saw it as their task to set up environments where students could explore and where there was some openness about what students would produce	• Saw themselves as explainers of information
• Focused on the development of skills and concepts, more than transmission of content	• Complained of the lack of time to get through the curriculum
• Were more prepared to 'subvert the curriculum' to create spaces for learning activities they valued	• Appeared to have a strong focus on content, rather than on skills or concepts
• Problematised assessment practices more often than the low-scoring group	• Did not discuss assessment limitations so readily
• Tended to have high levels of extra-curricular involvement	• Seemed to be largely in the dark about the pedagogical work of their colleagues
• Engaged in professional conversations with colleagues about their teaching	• Were more guarded than their high-scoring colleagues about their own work
• Were willing to talk about their failings and about changes they had made to their teaching	• Reported a greater sense of feeling under surveillance in conducting their work.

Source: Queensland Department of Education and Training (n.d.).

Framework (Ladwig and King, 2003) built on the work of Queensland. The QSRLS initiative highlighted differences of ratings on lessons as high, average or low scales, and differentiated between high-scoring and low-scoring teachers based on classroom observations, that quite clearly indicate fundamental differences in approaches to teaching (see Table 12.1).

In examining Table 12.1, correlations can readily be drawn with previous issues raised in this chapter with regard to deficit theorising, teacher expectation, and teacher responsibility and capacity to make a difference to Indigenous students. Quality Teaching pedagogy provides a much-needed systemic platform to form a basis for inclusive classrooms and the mandate for teachers to ensure high expectations and subsequent improved outcomes for Indigenous students. As the system moves considerable resources into improving how teachers teach, we will experience the collective benefits of inclusive classrooms for Indigenous students—and of course others from non-dominant cultures. 'The package' can thus be delivered.

A cautionary note: Both the Queensland and New South Wales approaches to improving classroom practice appear problematic in relation to the implementation of elements of 'recognition of difference' and 'cultural knowledge' respectively in each system. These important elements of classroom practice proved to be missing in classrooms in both states (Mills and Goos, 2007). It is of particular concern that non-dominant cultures, such as Indigenous cultures, are not being introduced in any significant way in these classrooms. This in turn highlights how relatively recent developments with regard to Indigenous perspectives to syllabus and curriculum in both these states have been mainly implemented in a concerted way only over the past decade. It also raises once again the 'invisibility' of Aboriginal students, who are generally found in small numbers in individual classrooms, and the importance of PLPs for these students. Obviously there is more work to be done in this area if Quality Teaching models are to be demonstrably inclusive of difference/culture. The focus must now be on ensuring that these elements appear in teachers' lessons and that teachers are supported in this process through appropriate curriculum resources and demonstrable practice.

Effective literacy and numeracy intervention

It is not my intention here to enter into any significant discourse on either literacy or numeracy, but rather to position the importance and fundamental principles behind good practice in these areas and briefly outline some projects that are currently getting good results. In my 30-plus years of leadership in Indigenous education, I have been amazed how many quick-fix, high-cost programs have been implemented for Indigenous students. It seems that every couple of months someone seeks me out to sell me the next answer to Indigenous literacy and numeracy needs. Furthermore, a couple of years ago I addressed an advisory committee on Indigenous literacy in New South Wales. I openly asked them what the answer was to solving Indigenous low literacy rates. I was dumbfounded to not get a definitive answer, or at least a response. After 30 years of focusing on Indigenous education, the experts gathered could not offer me a collective answer. It became obvious at this time that all options should be canvassed. It also became very obvious in a scan of departmental activity in the area that there were numerous approaches being undertaken across the state, and in general confusion reigned, with little if any semblance of significant increase in outcomes for Indigenous students on statewide testing in either literacy or numeracy. In fact, numeracy at this time was not my primary focus—something I later regretted, as Indigenous results in the area crumbled around me and experience quickly proved that a simultaneous focus should have been placed on this area.

Essential elements of Indigenous literacy

The literacy team within the Directorate of Aboriginal Education and Training in New South Wales set about looking at options which had good success with Indigenous students. To guide their journey, they developed in a workshop the following elements that needed to be addressed in an effective literacy program for teachers of Indigenous students:

- literacy theory based on a social view of language and addressing the skill of code-switching;

- cultural education that involves processes of cultural exchange between schools and Aboriginal communities, and understands and values the use of local Aboriginal English dialects;
- syllabus requirements and standards, and the explicit teaching of a social view of language, code-switching and Standard Australian English;
- pedagogical approaches that address teacher talk, relationships with Aboriginal students, working with Aboriginal people in classrooms and the Quality Teaching framework;
- the value of community partnerships developed through exchanging cultural understandings and recognition of different expertise, and based on extended conversations with Aboriginal communities.

The Directorate literacy team was confident that literacy training addressing these five elements would produce comparable outcomes for Aboriginal students. These elements also worked within existing syllabus requirements, and recent research on a bi-dialectal pilot program developed and conducted in a small sample of New South Wales schools (NSWAECG and NSWDET, 2004, p. 71) also suggested these elements were effective. The literacy team then assessed the variety of programs that permeated the literacy domain to ascertain which programs most closely addressed the five elements they had identified. They deemed that the best fit came from the foundation work of Brian Gray (1998) and his follow-up work with David Rose and Wendy Cowey (Rose, Gray and Cowey, 1999) on Scaffolding Literacy, later known as Accelerated Literacy and mounted as the major literacy program extensively funded by the Australian and Northern Territory governments in the Northern Territory. Hence the later work of Gray and Cowey in the National Accelerated Literacy Program (<www.nalp.edu.au>), run through Charles Darwin University, was the closest match to the elements required for an effective Indigenous literacy program. This was integrated with the cultural lessons learnt in the bi-dialectal project and the capacity of the program to mesh with Quality Teaching and syllabus requirements. Given all of this, the required match with the Directorate's five elements was readily apparent.

The Directorate developed a strategic approach that provided substantial support to programs already proving successful with Indigenous students, and began the systemic roll-out of these programs across New South Wales in 2006. It is too early to judge the results for Indigenous students at this stage but it is anticipated that the impressive student growth from the National Accelerated Literacy Program will be replicated (Dunn, 2008).

It should be noted that the Accelerated Literacy approach is a whole-class exercise that does not involve the withdrawal of students to do intensive work. It is conducted as a normal literacy lesson on a daily basis. One of its reported strengths is the rigour around its consistency, predictability and the programming of lessons (Cowey, 2005). It is my strong view that Indigenous students are best served by working collaboratively in classroom groups and actively participating in whole-class projects in inclusive classrooms.

Essential elements of Indigenous numeracy

There has been substantially less effort and development in numeracy than in literacy for Indigenous students, and this is now manifesting itself in the flat-line persistence of a significant gap in national numeracy results (Steering Committee for the Review of Government Service Provision, 2007, pp. 6.16, 7.11, 7.16). To a far lesser degree than Indigenous literacy, the discipline of numeracy has lacked any systemic program that has proven its results with Indigenous students, although this trend is changing and programs are beginning to emerge (Morris and Moroney, n.d.).

Research into the essential elements of Indigenous numeracy by Frigo and Simpson (n.d.) and more recently Watson et al. (2006) has placed strong emphasis on successful programs being heavily reliant on genuine community partnership in any numeracy undertaken in schools and on the integral relationship of literacy specific to numeracy conceptual frameworks (see also Morris and Moroney, n.d. on the close link to literacy and the potential of Accelerated Literacy). Both areas have been well recognised in 'the package' in this chapter, and therefore do not come as a surprise.

Of particular note in the domain of detecting literacy needs in numeracy has been the work of Anne Newman (1983), in particular the relationship to diagnosis of literacy errors through the use of the 'Newman error analysis procedure' which provides the structure to determine between literate and numerical error through the child's processing involved in mathematics. Alan White (2005, p. 15) highlights the critical processes involved in Newman's work:

> Newman (1977)... maintained that when a person attempted to answer a standard, written, mathematics question then that person had to be able to pass over a number of successive hurdles: Reading (or Decoding), Comprehension, Transformation, Process Skills, and Encoding. Along the way, it is always possible to make a Careless error. While there are many other theoretical approaches available to teachers, Newman's [is] one of the easiest to use and adapt and has proven popular among teachers.

Inclusive of the two important critical elements of teaching numeracy to Indigenous students were other important factors that were highlighted in the work of Watson et al. (2006b, p. 2); these were:

> Where communities felt that students were achieving well by their own standards (i.e. the school was meeting the needs of its community):
>
> - The school and its classrooms were more culturally inclusive/responsive.
> - There had been consistent and strong leadership, with clear goals and processes fully supported by the Aboriginal community, over a number of years (5–10).
> - The Aboriginal community had real influence in decision-making, including purposeful recruitment, and therefore: there were committed teachers (including Aboriginal teaching staff), who knew their students and also had knowledge about their communities; and the school and community were less *separate*;
> - Schools where Aboriginal students were achieving well according to community standards were generally also those where students were achieving well by external standards.

Again, the importance of school–community partnerships tended to be the primary background required to improve numeracy outcomes for Indigenous students. These are the critical findings in the Indigenous numeracy domain; more specific details on programs and more specific pedagogical approaches can be found through the references used in this section.

Unpacking 'the package'

In this section of the chapter, the initial explorations of four misguided principles were explored: the sustainability principle; the systemic principle; the ownership or deficit principle; and the Indigenous business principle. These four principles have wrongly underpinned Indigenous education over at least the past two decades, and arguably some of these principles still very much cloud Indigenous education today for some people, and in particular teachers and school management. If we are to succeed in delivering the right 'package' on Indigenous education, then education systems, schools and teachers must actively dispel these false foundation principles. If Indigenous education is to flourish and gaps are to be closed between Indigenous and non-Indigenous outcomes from education, then we must establish a new base to work upon. The first step in this process is to recognise these incorrect and debilitating principles and then build on what we know is fact and can work.

Once we have established the facts and genuine background of Indigenous people's desire to assume their equitable and special place as Indigenous peoples of Australia, we can provide the proven educational programs that will emancipate Indigenous peoples and enable them to reach this equitable platform with their fellow Australians. These programs start with some basic fundamentals that have been outlined in this chapter, commencing with harnessing the current goodwill that exists amongst the majority of teachers across Australia and then providing them with the basic instruments and programs—or, as it is referred to here, 'the package'. No longer do we need to search for the guiding lights in Indigenous education; they are now packaged up and sitting at the door of classrooms ready to be taken up, opened and utilised.

The new foundation of Indigenous education is the 'relationship game', where teachers, parents

Dare to Lead

Dare to Lead <www.daretolead.edu.au> is a national project dedicated to improving educational outcomes for Indigenous students and promoting reconciliation. It is an initiative of Principals Australia acting on behalf of its members and their associations. It is funded by the Department of Education, Employment and Workplace Relations.

Fundamental to the project's strength and viability is the *Dare to Lead* Coalition: schools—primary, secondary, early learning centres, post-secondary, and alternative learning sites; Catholic, government and independent; in every state and territory—where principals make a commitment to addressing outcomes for Indigenous students and/or working towards reconciliation.

The *Dare to Lead* Coalition currently has more than 5150 member schools, more than half of all Australian school leaders have joined up. A key source of strength for *Dare to Lead* is partnerships. Foremost among these are those with school leaders' professional associations, and with key Indigenous groups. *Dare to Lead*'s most fundamental partnerships are with Aboriginal and Torres Strait Islander educators, leaders and community members. Nine high-profile Indigenous educators sit on the *Dare to Lead* National Steering Committee, while other eminent figures are ambassadors and patrons of the project. At a grassroots level, *Dare to Lead* encourages and guides school leaders towards more meaningful engagement with local Indigenous communities.

Dare to Lead has a host of other important alliances. For example, it has a crucial connection with the Senior Officers' National Network of Indigenous Education (SONNIE), a formal relationship with Reconciliation Australia and a partnership with the Stronger Smarter Institute. It operates symbiotically with the educational tool *What Works: The Work Program*.

The cornerstone of the project is the personal and professional challenge that school leaders take on when they 'dare to lead'. This is a collegial project, principals working with principals. It is not a program in the traditional sense but rather seeks to work through existing programs and with a diverse range of strategies to achieve results. *Dare to Lead* is not a service delivery model. Rather, it is a call for school leaders to engage on a personal and professional level to drive sustainable change in their schools, and to be catalysts for this change. This commitment reflects the underpinning belief of the project: that principals are pivotal to positive change not just in schools but in communities.

The project arose from a series of national gatherings supported by the main principals' associations in 2000. It was formally launched in 2003. The first phase was called 'Taking it on' and emphasised building a coalition of committed schools and school leaders. The second phase was 'Making the difference', dedicated to data-measured improvement in key indicators of literacy and school completion. The third phase, 'Partnership builds success' commenced in mid-2009 and emphasises that sustainable change cannot be generated in isolation, but only through cooperative work and the forging of genuine, ongoing partnerships.

All *Dare to Lead* schools are clustered geographically into Action Areas. There are currently 120 Action Areas across Australia, with between 30–50 schools in each. These are led by experienced and willing school principals who are supported by *Dare to Lead* to play an integral role in identifying the professional development needs of their colleagues and providing opportunities for leadership engagement.

An aspect of *Dare to Lead* often cited as a major positive by principals and teachers is the provision and recommendation of resources. Some are generated by the project itself, such as the *L5 School Leadership Frame: An Indigenous Focus*, a DVD on community connectedness at Yule Brook College in Western Australia, and the *Dare to Lead* website with stories and insights of effective educators across the country. Others are externally sourced, such as the *Our Mob* interactive resource, *Moorditj* and *The Little Red Yellow Black Book*.

Committed educators are recognised through the *Dare to Lead* Excellence in Leadership in Indigenous Education Award, which began in 2004 and which acknowledge schools and school leaders who work in a focused and strategic way to achieve excellence in improving Indigenous student outcomes.

> *Dare to Lead* is a national project, but it emphasises local action tailored to local school contexts, recognising that school leaders have to respond to unique sets of circumstances while working towards a shared goal: improved student outcomes. *Dare to Lead* is about leadership—in all its facets, and at every level. The project's most crucial work occurs in individual schools where principals and all school leaders develop and promote awareness and provide the drive to address educational needs of Indigenous students.

and students build mutual cross-cultural respect for each other. To achieve this, we must have personal, genuine and honest respect built on the reciprocal trust that can develop through the tripartite partnership between teacher, parent/carer and student—a process that is currently proving both a very powerful alliance and a fruitful one. In addition to this very personal approach must come the foundation of schools and Indigenous communities working together in genuine partnership on the issues that make a difference in school outcomes for students.

To achieve these personal and school partnerships, we must develop and promote leadership within the school and within the Indigenous community, for it is this strength that will drive the new 'packaged' agenda.

Achievements under this package should be limitless and underwritten through high expectations and all students achieving their 'personal best' results. Pleasingly, the package has a very legitimate and proven inclusive delivery service in Quality Teaching, where schools, teachers and Indigenous communities can focus their efforts on proven teaching practices (pedagogy) that work. Complementing the Quality Teaching delivery are very positive and promising developments of key literacy and numeracy strategies and programs, which again are proving we can provide equitable outcomes from education.

The packages are now packed, the delivery van booked and we have a teaching force that wants to make a difference. Let's get the show on the road and into your classroom.

Unpacking the 'relationship game'

by Geoff Munns

The poem that opens this chapter is both a plea and a challenge. The words of Oodgeroo Noonuccal echo with the longed-for hope for and promise of equality of access and educational outcomes for Indigenous students across all stages and places of schooling. Research has consistently shown that quality of teaching is central in delivering such a promise of a socially just education (Newmann and Associates, 1996; American Council on Education, 1999; Hayes et al., 2006; Hattie, 2008). In the previous section of this chapter, John Lester placed the

One Arm Point Remote Community School, a K-11 school 100 km north of Broome, Western Australia, 95 per cent Indigenous. Its Bardi Cultural Program involves: Elders being consulted to help weave community knowledge into its curriculum; transforming a classroom into a cultural museum, cultural activities every week, culture camps and a culture concert at the end of each term. The school produces books and DVDs in Bardi, Aboriginal English and 'school English'; these can be adapted by other Kimberley schools. In 2008 the school won a Partnership Acceptance Learning Sharing (PALS) Award. Courtesy Dare to Lead.

relationship at the heart of effective teaching for Indigenous students. Again, this has long been supported in the Indigenous education literature in Australia (e.g. Partington, et al., 2000; NSWAECG and NSWDET, 2004; Munns, 2005). The aim of this section of the chapter is to unpack the kind of teaching relationships that offer real hope for Indigenous students. While there is almost universal acceptance of the importance of the development of positive relationships between teachers and their Indigenous students, it is not always clear how this relationship plays out across community, school and classroom contexts. What follows is an attempt to capture the key elements of this relationship.

A framework is presented that proposes the shape and processes of a positive pedagogical relationship between teachers and their Indigenous students. This framework is reached in two ways. First, it picks up on a number of recurring themes in the Aboriginal education literature in Australia. Second, it illustrates these themes through research data collected from interviews with 'exemplary' teachers in schools recognised for their success in enhancing social and academic outcomes for Indigenous students in their classrooms. The data were collected in rural and urban primary schools in New South Wales. The schools were all government schools. For this study, there were four key over-arching criteria used to define an exemplary school for Indigenous students. The first of these was related to academic outcomes and involves measuring student achievement across the system (for example, standardised statewide testing results) and school-based (for example, work samples, class tests) data. Exemplary schools were those where Indigenous students' achievements were showing narrowing gaps between their performance and that of non-Indigenous students. The second criterion was based upon social outcomes and referred to significant numbers of motivated and engaged students, as shown through classroom observations and attendance and behavioural data (e.g. fewer Indigenous students being recorded in detention and suspension records). The standing the school had within the local educational and Indigenous community was the third criterion. It was reasoned that an exemplary school would have a good reputation for achieving success with students of all backgrounds, and particularly Indigenous students. Finally, the fourth criterion, the successful transition of Indigenous students from primary to secondary school, was seen to be important, given that research has consistently shown that this transition is a hazardous step (e.g. Munns, 2005). Schools were selected against these four criteria by consulting Aboriginal Education Consultants (working within school districts to improve outcomes for Indigenous students), the New South Wales Department of Education's Aboriginal Programs Unit (responsible for the delivery of Aboriginal Education across New South Wales public schools) and the New South Wales AECG (representing Aboriginal communities in advising about Indigenous education at local, regional and state levels). Within each school, teachers were interviewed whom Indigenous community members, Indigenous school workers and the school principal identified as the most effective in their teaching and in the development of positive relationships with Indigenous students.

The *pedagogical relationship*

The pedagogical relationship (see Figure 12.1) is proposed as a composite picture of the ways in which teachers of Indigenous students might construct their personal and pedagogical relationships with their students. A couple of points need to be made here. The first is that there is an emphasis on the importance of the pedagogical nature of the relationship. While not downplaying the need for teachers to develop a personal rapport with students, the argument is that it is the teaching relationship that really counts. Personal relationships alone are not enough if the classroom pedagogies do not help students to engage individually and culturally, and achieve the outcomes needed to open up productive future educational pathways. The second point is that this figure is not intended to represent all the qualities and actions of one 'ideal' teacher, but rather a way of showing the commonalities of teacher actions and practices across all the school contexts. Such a representation could be a valuable device through which educators might consider the nature of teachers' curricula, pedagogies and relationships with Indigenous students. This has the potential to offer further insights into what kinds of

AIME—A Unique Educational Mentoring Program

Studying at the University of Sydney, Jack Manning Bancroft was asked by corporate scholarship providers why so few Indigenous students applied for university scholarships. Having been surrounded by strong role models in high school, Jack realised there was a need to mentor Indigenous high school students through Years 9 to 12 and into university.

Research into mentoring in Australia and overseas showed that programs for teenagers during the formative ages of 13–15 have a lasting impact into adulthood. Jack believed that encouraging students to remain at school at this crucial stage could help them achieve their goals. He was determined to develop a mentoring program to improve the self-esteem, capacity and opportunities of young Indigenous Australians—the Australian Indigenous Mentoring Experience (AIME).

In 2005, with the support of the Koori Centre, he recruited 25 Indigenous and non-Indigenous university student mentors to partner one-on-one with 25 Alexandria Park Community School students in a pilot program, with intensive mentor and cultural awareness training. The pilot was delivered in two six-week blocks: activity-based workshops followed by weekly one-on-one tutoring sessions focused on goal setting; dealing with racism and bullying; and working in partnerships. The school worked closely with AIME in monitoring attendance and participation.

The AIME pilot was a huge success, reinforcing the relationship between the university and the school. The pilot attracted some students who otherwise rarely attended class, and there was a steady increase in attendance: 15 per cent in Year 10 and 40 per cent in Year 9.

The following year students from Leichhardt Secondary College were invited to join the Alexandria Park students for the Year 9 sessions. Each year since the pilot, AIME has expanded and refined the program in response to student, teacher and community feedback and set up Homework Centres at schools in each region. By 2009 AIME was at five university campuses[1] in New South Wales, mentoring more than 500 Indigenous high school students from over 40 high schools.

The AIME program consists of: numeracy and literacy in Years 7 and 8; interactive programs in Year 9; leadership for Year 10; tutoring and future pathways for Years 11 and 12. At the beginning of 2009 AIME conducted student voice workshops, platforms for Indigenous students to discuss issues related to their learning experiences. Students were asked what makes a good education program and what makes a good educator. They also provided feedback on learning environments and what they felt helped students learn in AIME sessions. The students found AIME highly appealing: fun activities; high expectations; personal mentors; high-energy and varied activities; student-directed learning. This was empowering for the students, enabling them to help AIME develop sessions which would have the greatest impact.

AIME's aim is for all participating schools and students to:

- increase Year 10 completion rates to greater than 90 per cent (currently 69 per cent nationally);
- increase Year 12 completion rates to greater than 75 per cent (currently 39 per cent nationally);
- increase university admission rates to 30 per cent (currently 1.25 per cent nationally).

As well as gaining knowledge and skills to achieve better educational outcomes, enhanced self-confidence and raised awareness of life possibilities, AIME provides: free tutoring and mentoring; culturally relevant, beneficial and fun programs; resources such as AIME texts; pathways to scholarships; introductions to university life; meetings with AIME partners, potential employers. Non-Indigenous mentors learn about Indigenous Australia in a personalised way; there is both-ways learning with very little effort; stereotypes are broken down; and all involved learn greater understanding, tolerance and respect.

AIME helps universities foster relationships with their local schools. Focused leadership training requires undergraduates to be role models and reflect on their lives at a critical stage of their own development. AIME is the chance to volunteer in a program that speaks their own language, and

---

1 University of Sydney, Camperdown and Cumberland campuses; University of Wollongong, Wollongong campus; Southern Cross University, Coffs Harbour campus; and Macquarie University.

passes on a critical life-lesson, the gift of giving, thus helping produce well-rounded graduates with a sense of learning and experience beyond the classroom.

AIME outcomes have surpassed expectations and generated interest among corporations and community groups, many of whom have formed partnerships with AIME. AIME is part of a coalition to change education for Aboriginal students: GenerationOne, Dare to Lead, What Works and others.

One big factor holding back Indigenous students is the idea of shame, not wanting to stand out ('Nah, that shame!'). In December 2010 AIME initiated its 'Strut the Streets' program in Sydney's Martin Place, with its partners in changing Aboriginal education.

Aboriginal student (left) with his university mentor, who is talking with an Aboriginal mentor sitting down in front. Courtesy AIME.

The AIME Patron-in-Chief is Her Excellency Professor Marie Bashir AC CVO, Governor of New South Wales. Its National Leadership Council is made up of: the Hon. Linda Burney, MP, Tom Calma, Andrew Denton, Greg Hutchinson, Dr Chris Sarra, Julianne Schultz and Ian Thorpe.

<www.aimementoring.com>

teachers might make a difference and help to address persistent inequitable outcomes across Aboriginal communities.

Figure 12.1 is an attempt to capture the complexity of this personal and pedagogical relationship. At the centre of the figure is the relationship that these exemplary teachers develop with their Indigenous students. Its central position recognises that strong relationships with these students are pivotal to the success teachers have in bringing forward enhanced social and academic outcomes. So while relationships sit at its heart, there is an argument that the whole figure represents the all-embracing cultural, personal and pedagogical relationship.

Above the central axis are critical umbrellas: the teacher's position in the community (particularly within the Indigenous community) and the ways that the Indigenous students are positioned as members of the school student body. There is a view within the data and the literature (see Chapter 1) that the teacher has a vital role to play in this positioning. Without either of these umbrellas, the suggestion is that the personal relationships between student and teacher are likely to be compromised, and that this in turn will have negative impacts on the quality of classroom practices.

The lower segments of the figure focus closely on the nature of exemplary teachers' classroom practices. At the group (left) side there is a consideration of whole-class approaches that will benefit all students, including those from

Figure 12.1

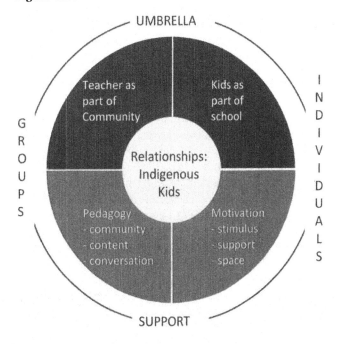

Indigenous backgrounds. On the other (right) side is a depiction of the individual support strategies that these teachers employ to assist the Indigenous students and build their self-concept and motivation. These strategies work alongside, and within, the whole-class pedagogical approaches. All segments of the figure are meant to be seen as highly interdependent. Each of these is now discussed and illustrated through research data.

The relationship

There are a number of critical aspects to the relationship between teachers and Indigenous students. It has consistently been shown that a positive relationship depends on teachers bringing high levels of caring, respect and trust to the learning relationship, and these have to be built patiently at a cultural level. A teacher's comments from the interviews capture this idea:

> Take in as much culture from the kids as you can. Because if you learn a little bit about their culture, you can build on that and work with the kids and pretty much get them to do anything you want them to do. Because they know that you've got a respect for their culture and their background. You've got to build that respect up with the kids and through their culture's a good way to do it.

This part of the relationship has most resonance with the umbrella (upper) segments of the figure. Vital to the support (lower) segments is the very strong understanding of the needs and issues of Indigenous students in the classroom. While the danger of essentialising these students is acknowledged (see *Education Australia*, 1996, 1997), it is arguably the case that teachers must still recognise the importance of appreciating how Indigenous students respond culturally to their school and classroom experiences (see Munns, 2005).

Achievement of Indigenous students ranges across different academic levels. In most research schools, there was a polarisation of these levels—that is, across all contexts there were students who are achieving well academically compared with their non-Indigenous peers, and another group who were not doing well at all. Both these groups have to be strongly supported in the classroom, as the research shows an awareness among teachers that Indigenous students are strongly aware of how they are achieving in relation to each other, and this awareness impacts on their school learning (see discussion of risk and shame below).

There is also a recognition that pride in cultural identity needs to be nurtured through the processes of schooling. When Indigenous students feel there is a cultural price to pay for school success (for example, being seen as different or 'acting white'—see Simpson, McFadden and Munns, 2001) there are negative impacts on social and academic outcomes. Shame continues to be a shaper of Indigenous students' responses in classrooms (see Munns, 2005). Avoiding shame associated with being singled out in the classroom was still seen by the teachers and Aboriginal officers in the research schools to influence behaviour. In particular, wanting to avoid shame is resulting in a reluctance of many students to take risks in their classrooms.

Finally, the research interviews consistently brought forward the need for teachers to understand the cultural resources that Indigenous students employ at school, while at the same time rejecting the stereotyping of these students. Time after time, the teachers talked about how they have to treat the Indigenous students 'the same' while still understanding that they have special cultural needs. Treating them 'the same' in this sense is the positive pedagogical stance of not lowering expectations or standards for this group. Consider, for example, this comment from an interview:

> We run on a policy of trying to treat them all the same. We're not trying to single particular groups out. We do different activities, we have our cultural groups and Aboriginal groups and different talent groups with them, but we still try and involve other kids with them at school and I don't think they stand out and think, 'Oh well I'm Aboriginal, I'm different.' Which I think really works here.

The teacher as part of the community

The upper left segment of the pedagogical relationship points to the importance of teachers taking an interest in and associating with the Indigenous community. It is interesting (and perhaps alarming) that when this happens it is considered noteworthy. Among the teachers interviewed, the significance of teachers' involvement with the Aboriginal community for school and classroom relationships was repeatedly mentioned. An Aboriginal officer talked about this:

> No he spends a lot of time out with the Aboriginal kids as well. He's musical, so he's got the kids taking his guitar and you know, Kooris love the guitar, love the music, so he's got them in that way as well. Also, our school environment, he just acknowledges the kids out of the school as well. He'll pass them on the street and say, 'Hi'.

This personal involvement and interest doesn't on the face of it seem like a 'big deal'. However, as one teacher explained, it is really important to treat people on a personal level and sometimes this means putting aside the school teacher role:

> Being interested and when I see their Mums, Dads, whatever down the street, I don't act like a school teacher. Just say 'G'day, how you going mate?'

Being part of the community might also mean becoming involved with some of the local and wider national struggles with which the Indigenous community is dealing. Standing alongside people over issues like land rights or legal justice can help to cement relationships and break down 'us versus them' feelings.

The student as part of the school

On the other side of the umbrella segment, the proposal is that the pedagogical relationship is strongly dependent on how the students are positioned within the school community. It is arguably the case that positive and effective teachers work hard to make Indigenous students feel valued and accepted. Sport and cultural activities (dance and art) are still seen as pathways in this process:

> Some of the Aboriginal kids are seen as icons in the school I guess, probably to do with their sporting ability, and so very much looked up to by the other kids and respected... like the kids are always at the front of assemblies, congratulated and recognised for it in the school. So I guess that's where the kids see it coming from... Anything positive that builds up confidence, is respectful, any responsibility or anything like that.

But these kinds of activities should not be seen as the only way that Indigenous students are helped to become part of the school. Schools and teachers need to identify the dangers of Indigenous students being 'sidetracked' into activities that are seen to be motivating and culturally appropriate for them, but which might interfere with their academic performance by taking them away from classroom instruction time and/or showing them that these areas are what they should concentrate on (see Simpson, McFadden and Munns, 2001). Research into schools that successfully enhance motivation and engagement among Indigenous students has shown that it is possible to provide students with a wide range of educationally worthwhile, enjoyable and culturally appropriate experiences in extra-curricular areas that will support and not interfere with the achievement of academic outcomes (Munns et al., 2006).

Classroom pedagogy

At a whole-class level, there were common approaches to classroom pedagogies that interviewees felt were conducive to enhanced outcomes for Indigenous students. These approaches are summarised as the '3Cs': community of learning, content and conversation. Each of these is now discussed in detail.

Community of learning

A community of learning indicates that teachers encourage an environment where students continuously support each other. Implicit here is that students are not pitted strongly against each other in a competitive classroom. They are given confidence through classroom discussions to feel comfortable about admitting when they cannot do something. Such an atmosphere works energetically against the shame issues identified above and challenges the negative impact of peer pressure. Frequent opportunities for reflection about learning (oral, written) help promote self-regulated learners—a key component of motivation (Martin, 2002)—as well as student engagement (Fair Go Team, 2006) and self-concept (Hattie, 2002). A teacher interviewed during the research talked about how she developed a team approach where no student felt left behind:

I say, 'We are like the marines, we don't leave anyone behind' and we keep working on things till we get it right... we're a team and this is our job to get through these outcomes and these objectives through the year and we do it together and that's when I turn into the marine sergeant and—we leave nobody behind.

Community and cooperative approaches to learning have continuously been recognised as culturally sympathetic to the learning needs of Indigenous students (see Harris, 1980, 1984; Hughes and More, 1993; Malin, 1990; NSW DET, 2008).

Content (Aboriginal Studies and perspectives)

The content focus in the classroom strongly acknowledges the importance of sensitivities to Indigenous content while simultaneously structuring learning experiences that are authentic, contextualised and motivating. A key learning approach is in the recognition within learning experiences that Indigenous students are bi-dialectal learners, frequently code-switching between Aboriginal English and Standard Australian English (Malcolm, 1998). There are implications here for classroom communications and assessment processes.

Closely associated with this is the place of Aboriginal Studies within the classroom curriculum. Effective teachers shared how they used this in 'powerful ways', meaning they involved students in serious and big ideas and issues (for example, land rights and the Stolen Generations). This is in contrast to the trivialising of Aboriginal Studies found in classrooms where students learn remote, sanitised and 'safe' content (see Chapter 1). The teachers in the research said Indigenous students were motivated by sport and creativity (for those interested in these activities), but these were not undertaken at the expense of other critical curriculum areas. Classroom content outside the highly integrated Aboriginal perspectives and topics tends to be shaped towards the authentic, the practical, the exciting and the contextualised. Such approaches were seen by the teachers interviewed as particularly effective for Indigenous boys, and this is consistent with findings by Munns et al. (2006) in a report to the Australian government on the motivation and engagement of Indigenous students.

Alongside these curricular orientations is a deliberate pedagogical approach that focuses students towards the outcomes to be learned. Teachers interviewed talked about a 'visibility' of outcomes, and these are made to be achievable for all without compromising standards. During interviews, teachers talked of 'backtracking', a process of constantly going back to earlier outcomes and then moving all students through to their appropriate level. This complements the 'nobody left behind' tactic mentioned above.

Conversation

The third of the '3Cs' refers to teaching as conversation. This is about teachers conducting classrooms as a running dialogue. Such a discursive environment is characterised by positive supportive feedback (particularly focused on self-regulation) and humour. Classrooms are quiet places where students are not confronted and there is little struggle over pedagogical spaces. (See Bernstein, 1996 for the debilitating consequences of such struggles.) A principal interviewed during the research explained the effectiveness of teaching as conversation, which he termed 'walking and talking':

> Constantly moving round the classroom, she's not the sort of a teacher who sits, she's a walker and talker. She moves around the classroom and she'll walk past you: 'Fantastic Joe'. That's the bottom line; I'm a great believer in walking and talking... to get out, she can be at the front of the classroom, she can be at the back, she can be sitting on the floor and those are Year 6 kids and she just has that ability, that good rapport with kids.

Research literature on student engagement (Fair Go Team, 2006; Nanlohy and Bull, 2006) shows that when classroom discourse is characterised as a form of mutual conversation, then students are encouraged to be 'insiders' in the culture of the classroom and learning is enhanced for all (see also Durrant and Green, 2000). We are also reminded through the seminal research of Cazden (2001) that marginalised students are advantaged when classrooms free themselves from interactions dominated by teachers using initiation-response-evaluation (IRE) discourses.

Stimulating motivation

The '3Cs' aspect of the pedagogical relationship discussed above is clearly aligned with ideas about 'authentic instruction' (Newmann and Associates, 1996), 'productive pedagogy' (Hayes et al., 2006) and 'quality teaching' (NSWDET, 2003). Within each of these frames a supportive and nurturing classroom environment is critical. However, the next part of the relationship acknowledges that teachers need also to supplement this whole-group environment with culturally appropriate and sensitive individual support strategies. These strategies are summarised as the '3Ss': stimulus, support and space. Each of these is now discussed in detail.

Stimulus

Stimulus refers to the different ways that teachers can encourage motivation in the classroom. In the research discussed in this chapter, teachers talked about being 'cheerleaders' for the students, building their self-concept through positive affirmation about their achievements while still holding high expectations for the attainment of learning outcomes. There is a fine balance here between having work that is achievable for the students without 'dumbing down' the curriculum. Holding high expectations was mentioned above, and it is worth repeating that it is at the point of expectations that teachers clearly need to hold on to a 'treating them the same' policy. Indeed, this section of the figure is about how teachers give particular individual support (that is, treating Indigenous students differently) in order to reach these expected outcomes. Interview data showed that teachers encouraged motivation and higher self-concept by providing challenges, setting goals and encouraging persistence. There is consistency here with Martin's (2002) adaptive thoughts and actions, the kind of classroom responses that are the hallmarks of motivated students. Principals spoke in interviews about their hopes for motivating students and having positive thoughts about their classrooms:

> I want them to come out of the end of it thinking that I can do this for me and I'm a good person and that I can actually say that about myself. And I know this way for this reason. It seems like a big ask. But it's not, because I've done it and I've seen other people do it and you can do it. And I want kids at the end of the day, to go out of the school with a smile on their face. And say to them after school: 'Did you have a good day?' 'Yeah!' That's what I want to hear.

When such positive feelings are linked with achievement across quality and intellectually rigorous learning activities, there are clearly defined benefits for learning self-concept and future educational success.

Support

Supporting students in classrooms can take many forms. Within the current study, support is perhaps best summed up by an attitude expressed by many of doing 'whatever it takes': finding any way that will help Indigenous students to become more confident and motivated learners. Doing whatever it takes is underpinned by the knowledge of the learners as both individuals and Indigenous students. This helps them read the signs: when students are feeling threatened by the work, are frustrated or need extra support. Offering safety nets to allow students to deal with these feelings is a common support strategy. Teachers talked of the importance of being fair and mentoring and nurturing students. Often this means being physically close to students to model the learning and offering productive help. This is the kind of help that shows ways to success, and it is different from unproductive help that merely gives students answers. Consider the way an Indigenous teacher interviewed in the research discussed this support:

> My class is very open and receptive to giving them an instruction and they can follow it. I spend a lot of time sitting next to my Koori kids and guiding them through the process that we need to go through. There are other kids in the class that I do need to do that with too, but mainly my Koori kids. Sometimes, I slip out of teacher mode without even realising it because... I'm just with the Koori kids and we just yarn and I'll use Aboriginal English often and the kids will know what I'm talking about. But when I'm in the classroom I do slip into the out-the-front teacher mode and sometimes I need to go back and revisit and sit down next time and say, 'Look you just do it like this', and break it down in a way that they can totally understand.

Space

Space, the third of the '3Ss', is about the pedagogical spaces that are opened up for students in classrooms. Many teachers of low socioeconomic status and Indigenous students have a view that tight routines within highly structured classrooms are needed. Often these are restricted and dull places, where low-level impoverished learning is the norm. Structure then stands in place of productive and useful teacher planning. By contrast, the relationships suggested in the chapter are not built within such constrictions. The argument is that students should not be 'crowded'—that is, pressured physically, emotionally and cognitively. Rather, they should be given time and space to work within the support systems set up within the lower segments of the figure. This pedagogical space operates within and outside the classroom. Quite a few of the teachers in the research reported ways that gave Indigenous students opportunities to talk through any issues they were facing, rather than the teacher being quick to judge and sanction. Here is an example of this:

> And I say to them too, 'Look mate, if something's coming your way and it doesn't look good, duck. Then when the rubbish has stopped flying around, come out of your hole and see if you can sort it out. Don't make it worse, just stop, whoa.' I just say, 'If something's wrong, you know you can talk to me about it, let me know if something's not right. It won't make you doing something wrong right, but it might change what we can do about it. Sometimes I just need to know if something's happened to you and maybe we can just lighten up, give you a bit of space.' I just say, 'Look, walk down the stairs with me for a minute. You're really not behaving like yourself. Is there anything I can help you with or is there something I can do? Is something wrong, what's happening?' Sometimes I think they're not game to tell me, but sometimes they do.

Other teachers said they made it a habit to always be in a certain place during break times, where Indigenous students knew they could find them and talk through any school and classroom issues (within Child Protection guidelines). It is vital to appreciate that space in the pedagogical relationship is not only about discipline matters. Space also refers to the daily learning experiences where students are given freedom to work, communicate and achieve without unnecessary pressures surrounding competition, time imperatives, structural constraints and traditional teacher–student relations. An Indigenous teacher summed up the kinds of classroom interactions that create this sense of supportive space:

> It's about the way teachers interact. Interaction is the most important thing. How they perceive you. You have to have a laugh, have humour. Koori kids love to laugh at themselves or you.

Looking ahead

From the outset, this chapter has acknowledged that the models presented are not intended to be definitive 'answers'. Educators are well aware that the important work of schools and classrooms occurs when teachers respond professionally and reflexively to their own contexts and develop their own solutions. However, theoretically framing the pedagogical relationship developed by respected and successful teachers of Indigenous students provides important insights to help educators consider what might make an educational difference for these students and give hope and realised promise to their communities.

> The future beckons you bravely on
> To Art and letters and nation lore,
> Fringe-dwellers no more.
>
> —Oodgeroo Noonuccal (2008, p. 44)

Diane McNaboe graduating with Masters in Indigenous Language Education, an Aboriginal-only course set up by the Koori Centre of Sydney University for teachers of Aboriginal languages in schools. Photo: Lyn Riley.

13 Working with Aboriginal students

Christine Halse and Aunty Mae Robinson

The Aboriginal Flag

Walk tall, my child, you walk real tall,
And hold your head up high,
Look around you at your people,
and see with untainted eyes.
Look in the mirror and look at yourself,
Not the picture of world holds before you,
See the spirits of your fathers,
and sisters and brothers,
And the strength of our mothers that bore you.
Who will deny that we are strong,
Have we not suffered, yet still survive,
The worst crimes that could be committed
By human beings against their own kind.
Haven't we lived and reared our young
Long as any race on earth,
Look at your history, your people,
And never deny their worth.
The value and life of living things;
Has been maintained since time began,
Ministered as part of a sacred trust.
By your people of this land,
'Aboriginaland' yes, your birthright,
No matter what some name it,
So dig your fingers deep in the soil
And feel it, and hold it, and claim it.
Your people fought and died for this
The history books distort it all,
But in your veins run that same
Aboriginal blood,
So walk tall, my child,
Walk tall . . .

—Maureen Watson, in Yabbastick (2003), p. 4

Inseparable: Charlotte and Tiffany, the only Aboriginal kids in their class at Penshurst West Public School and two of only four Aboriginal students at the school in 2009; the other two were their older sisters. More than half of Aboriginal students are more or less isolated in schools. Photo: Lisa Car.

Supporting Indigenous identities and cultures in schools

Like children from other cultures and backgrounds, the cultural identities of Aboriginal and Torres Strait Islander children are perpetuated through contemporary child-rearing practices, common historical experiences, kinship, value systems and community affiliation. How students express their cultural identity varies widely across Australia according to the nature and extent of their interaction with non-Aboriginal society.

More than 50 per cent of Indigenous people live in urban and regional Australia and have high levels of interaction with non-Indigenous cultures (Steering Committee for the Review of Government Service Provision, 2009, p. 2). The cultural identity of Indigenous students in these areas is likely to be subtle, highly diverse, localised and strongly based on interactions with their immediate family, peers and communities. In contrast, an estimated 31 per cent of Indigenous people live in remote areas and a further 15 per cent live in very remote areas, where there is little direct interaction with non-Indigenous communities (Steering Committee for the Review of Government Service Provision, 2009, p. 2). Indigenous students in these areas are more likely to have a very strong cultural identity rooted in traditional customs, extended family relations and close spiritual connections with land and country.

Recognising and addressing the cultural diversity of Indigenous students is a challenge for teachers and schools. The practices and curriculum of schools reflect Western intellectual traditions, and work to maintain and reinforce the knowledge, understandings, values and priorities of Western cultures. Students are required 'to conform with the Western social expectations which are embedded within conventional teaching practice' (Howard, 1994, p. 48). In such an environment, it can be difficult for Indigenous students to feel comfortable or be engaged with learning and committed to achieving. Teachers can facilitate student engagement and learning by building a supportive environment that respects and honours the cultural background of all students and by using a *repertoire* of teaching and strategies to help *all* students to feel comfortable in the classroom.

Government policy

Three decades of government policies and reviews have reinforced the importance of positively affirming Indigenous culture and the cultural identity of Indigenous students in schools. The Victorian Ministerial Review of Post-Compulsory Education (1985, p. 23) argued that the culture of schools needs 'to acknowledge the contribution of all major social groups to the collective experience, identity and operation of the society'. Recommendation 290 of the Report of the Royal Commission into Aboriginal Deaths in Custody (1991) stated that:

> curricula of schools at all levels should reflect the fact that Australia has an Aboriginal history and Aboriginal viewpoints on social, cultural and historical matters. It is essential that Aboriginal viewpoints, interests, perceptions and expectations are reflected in curricula, teaching and administration of schools.

The National Aboriginal and Torres Strait Islander Education Policy (DEST, 1993), endorsed by all federal, state and territory governments, identifies 21 goals for Indigenous education. A key priority is the importance of building understanding of and respect for traditional and contemporary Indigenous cultures amongst all Australians. More than a decade later, the Ministerial Council on Education, Employment, Training and Youth Affairs (MCEETYA, 2006) emphasised the importance of cultural understanding and the use of pedagogical approaches that result in high levels

---

> Much of the norms and values portrayed in what I read and heard from White teachers bore little relation to what I experienced at home. This meant that at school I was continually thrust into a state of confusion and anxiety. School education was important but in learning to read and write I learnt of the disrespect with which Aborigines were held by white society. Schooling constantly forced upon me a choice between education and my identity as an Aboriginal. Most Aboriginal people can tell a similar story of discomfort in school: only the details vary.
>
> —Terry Ngarritjan-Kessaris (1994, p. 5)

of academic expectation and achievement if schools and teachers are to significantly improve Indigenous outcomes across all learning areas. Reflecting the trend in most states and territories, the New South Wales Aboriginal and Education Training Policy advocates an integrated, whole-of-school approach to Indigenous education which "incorporate[s] the cultural contexts, values and practices of local Aboriginal communities into the mainstream delivery of education and training' (NSW DET, 2008). As others have argued:

> Indigenous education has come to be seen as peripheral rather than integral to core business... [it] has been 'bolted on' rather than 'built in' to mainstream effort, becoming the province of specialists and committed individuals instead of systems as a whole (MCEETYA, 2006, p. 16; see also NSW AECG and NSW DET, 2004)

Scholars and policy-makers stress the importance of eliminating a 'deficit' view that attributes poor Indigenous education outcomes to the innate shortcomings of individual children, families and communities, and the importance of 'developing systems and schools that *engage* all students in learning, including Indigenous students' (MCEETYA, 2006, p. 16).

Why is engagement important?

Engaging Indigenous students in school is essential for improving educational outcomes. Indigenous leaders have emphasised that 'education needs to be exciting and culturally engaging to encourage parental and community interest' (Pearson, 2004). Indigenous students remain one of the most disadvantaged minorities in Australian education systems (Bradley et al., 2007). Completing school significantly enhances young people's future employment opportunities and life chances but there has been no improvement in the Year 12 completion gap between Indigenous and non-Indigenous students (Steering Committee for the Review of Government Service Provision, 2009, p. 4). In the last three international testing (PISA) cycles, Indigenous students have received significantly lower scores in literacy, numeracy and scientific knowledge than their non-Indigenous peers (DeBortoli and Thomson, 2009) and there has been no significant change in Indigenous students' reading, writing and numeracy, or closing of the gaps between Indigenous and non-Indigenous students' performance in the past ten years (Steering Committee for the Review of Government Service Provision, 2009).

In the 2008 National Assessment Program—Literacy and Numeracy (NAPLAN), a lower proportion of Indigenous than non-Indigenous students at all year levels achieved national minimum standards in reading, writing and numeracy. However, a more nuanced analysis shows that: Indigenous students in mainstream schools in Victoria, Tasmania, and the Australian Capital Territory perform at the same literacy and numeracy levels as non-Indigenous students; New South Wales, South Australia, Western Australia and Queensland have non-performing remote Indigenous schools; and poor student achievement is a 'serious and systemic' problem in the remote Indigenous schools of the Northern Territory (Hughes and Hughes, 2009, p. vii).

Engagement is a construct involving three dimensions: behavioural (involvement); affective (personal attachment to others, such as teachers and classmates); and cognitive (application to learning). Engagement makes a critical difference to academic achievement, and fosters a sense of belonging and self-worth in students. Children who are engaged in school develop lifelong skills in learning, participation and communication.

The Ministerial Council on Education, Employment, Training and Youth Affairs report, *Australian Directions in Indigenous Education 2005–2008*, states that research indicates positive outcomes result when the school culture and philosophy acknowledge and affirms students' Indigenous cultures and identities, and when instructional and learning programs 'challenge, develop and embrace this positive sense of Indigenous identity' (MCEETYA, 2006, p. 23). This report emphasises that students are placed 'at risk' of failing school not just by:

> circumstances of birth or environment, but the school itself... because the school has not adequately engaged them... when we make needed improvements in the way we educate all students, we won't need special programs for some students (MCEETYA, 2006, p. 16).

Personalised learning, high expectations

Good morning delegates. I'm Joyce Woodberry, representing the New South Wales AECG—Aboriginal Education Consultative Group. I'm a founding member, a Life Member, and on the Executive. We advise the government on Aboriginal education and training. We are a community-based volunteer network. I'm known as Aunty Joyce—in our society 'Aunty' and 'Uncle' respect the life experience of senior people, and stand for the connectedness of Aboriginal life.

On behalf of the AECG, I'm proud to welcome you to the country of the Gadigal people of the Eora nation, and to wish you every success in your deliberations in this important conference. I also take this opportunity to pass on a few thoughts on learning and expectations from our perspective.

Some of you may know that Aboriginal education is in a state of crisis. A review has found that an Aboriginal student can be up to three years behind in literacy by Year 8—one reason why so many of our kids are high-school dropouts—with all that that implies. There has to be a better way.

I see some hope in the idea of personalised learning because that must mean teachers getting to know their students. Some research that we at the AECG have been involved in tells us that relationships with teachers are absolutely fundamental—if our kids don't like the teachers, they won't learn. And it works the other way too—the teachers have to know our kids and like them. Personalised learning means a focus on the students as individuals, getting to know them. And if there's one thing Koori kids are, let me tell you, it's individuals!

Your conference brochure tells us that high expectations bring better results, better discipline, higher self-esteem and self-confidence, and more satisfaction being at school. That may seem obvious. But think for a moment about what low expectations might therefore be expected to produce—worse results, worse discipline, lower self-esteem, lower self-confidence, no satisfaction being at school. And then think of what generations of our kids have been put through in mainstream education.

Twenty years ago when they called the dummy classes 'OA' (Other Activities) we used to say that 'OA' really meant 'Only Aboriginal', because so many of our kids were in those classes. That is the context we have been working in. And we call TAFE second-chance education because it does such a good job rescuing so many of our people who have been failed by schooling. And that's because TAFE treats its students as people.

We want to get educators to think about what our kids can do if they get a fair go. The world has seen what us blackfellas can do in sports and arts. Let me tell you there is so much more that we can do. Our kids can do anything if we can make education work for them—not against them.

One final story: when the AECG was involved in the Teaching the Teachers project and we researched Aboriginal pedagogy as part of teaching teachers how to teach Koori kids, we found some experts who said it was hard to tell the difference between Aboriginal teaching styles and best practice!! So maybe we could teach you a thing or two.

I hope I've given you something to think about.

Welcome to Aboriginal country, and every success in your conference.

Thank you.

Aunty Joyce Woodberry

Born Joyce Ralph 1940, she grew up at La Perouse, enrolling herself in La Perouse Public School because she didn't like the Catholic school across the road. She left school at 15 to work at the Wills tobacco factory, and in 1962 married Syd Woodberry. Times were tough and the young family moved to New Zealand for work but returned to Sydney in 1974 to be with her family.

In 1975 she started work as an Aboriginal Teachers Aide (ATA) at La Perouse school, and in the same year was one of the first group of ATAs to complete the training course at Sydney University. Moving to southwest Sydney, she worked at Campbelltown High School in 1977, but returned to La Perouse in 1978 and worked at the school there until she retired in 1998.

> *A founding member of the New South Wales AECG, one of the strong women who were its backbone, she was known across the state as Aunty Joyce for the way she looked after everyone—'a mother to all of us', one member said. She represented Met East region for years, served on the executive committee and was made a Life Member in 1986. She represented the AECG on a national taskforce on conditions of Aboriginal and Islander Education Workers (AIEWs) and with the national Federation of AECGs. She was featured in the Older Women's Network book,* Steppin' Out, Speakin' Up.
>
> *Aunty Joyce was a strong believer in Aboriginal Studies for all students and passionate about opportunities for Aboriginal kids. Her advocacy for Aboriginal kids was legendary—'Koori kids can do anything!' She founded the La Perouse school Aboriginal dance troupe and was so proud when they performed for Sydney's bid for the 2000 Olympic Games. She could never have achieved so much in Aboriginal education without the total support of her husband Syd.*
>
> *She would never back down from her beliefs; she was a strong role model, proud in her culture, loyal and loved, a solid friend. She would say, 'It's not what you get out; it's what you put in'. Another favourite saying was, 'You can't put brains on a monument'. For her family she was a devoted wife and parent and doting grandmother.*
>
> *After battling cancer and beating it, she was carried off years before her time in October 2005. Her funeral was one of the biggest seen at her beloved 'La Pa'. Among many tributes, Dr Brendan Nelson, federal Minister for Education, Science and Training, wrote to her family. La Perouse school principal Caterina Robertson described her as a true believer in the potential of every child: 'Joyce was a fireball of love and inspiration to all those who were fortunate enough to be touched by her enthusiasm'. She 'achieved what most people strive for—she made a positive difference to the lives and futures of many people', and left the community a better place for having been in it.*
>
> *Aboriginal educator and writer Sue Hodges wrote to the Woodberry family: 'I will always be grateful for the work she did in her lifetime to make it easier for me and many others on our journeys.'*

The child as the pedagogical starting point for engagement

As with non-Indigenous communities, there is tremendous diversity *within* and *between* Aboriginal and Torres Strait Islander children and communities according to their personal and collective histories, geographic location, socio-economic circumstances, kinship ties and belief systems, as well as past and present engagement with non-Aboriginal society and culture.

Pedagogy is the 'art and science of teaching', and consists of a complex amalgam of elements that shape teaching and learning and define the educational environment of the classroom. Because each child is unique, the child is the starting point in making decisions about an appropriate pedagogy. Each child brings to the classroom a diverse range of abilities and talents, cognitive, affective and physiological behaviours, as well as developmental and cultural experiences that have been moulded by home, school and the wider society. This is true for *all* children.

Many teachers use the pedagogies with which *they* are most comfortable, but *effective* teachers recognise the importance of using approaches that are appropriate to the backgrounds and needs of their students. The pedagogical approach employed by teachers will vary according to the learning activity, but the sorts of pedagogies a teacher uses will decide whether the classroom climate may be competitive or cooperative, formal or informal, personal or impersonal, friendly or unfriendly, supportive or unsupportive of students, and so on.

The debate about learning styles

The idea that children have different 'learning styles' grew out of the field of cognitive psychology (Linard, 1994, p. 58) and developed as a theory during the 1970s. Learning style advocates maintain that it is possible to generate a taxonomy of children's preferred learning styles, and that learning outcomes are improved when there is a match between a child's culturally preferred learning style and the pedagogy or teaching styles used in classrooms (Dunn, Dunn and Price, 1984, cited in Linard, 1994, pp. 62–3).

Learning style theory emerged as a theme in Indigenous education in the 1980s as a result of Stephen Harris's research in Milingimbi in the Northern Territory. Harris (1984) identified five main methods of Yolngu (Aboriginal) learning: learning by observation; learning by trial and error; learning in real-life situations; context-specific learning; and person-oriented instruction where knowledge is valued because of who gives it.

The debate about whether there are appropriate classroom pedagogies for Indigenous students, and whether Indigenous students have specific cultural ways of processing, learning and producing knowledge, has been highly contentious. On the one hand, advocates of culturally different learning styles maintain that we can generalise about how Indigenous students learn. Hughes (1987), for instance, argues that Aboriginal learning styles tend to favour the group over individuality, spontaneity rather than structure, repetition rather than inquiry, uncritical rather than critical approaches, personal versus impersonal strategies, listening rather than verbalising, and indirect rather than direct questioning techniques.

Advocates of culturally specific learning styles contend that matching teaching to children's learning styles has produced 'statistically significant increases in academic achievement, improved attitudes towards school, less classroom tension, and significantly increased school retention' (Dunn, 1990, p. 16; also see Milgram, Dunn and Price, 1993), and that it is necessary for teachers to understand and accommodate the cultures, values and lifestyles of Indigenous students in order to reduce disengagement from schooling, absenteeism and poor retention rates, and to improve achievement levels (Groome, 1994).

Critics argue that it is unclear what constitutes an individual's learning style or how it can be identified (Claxton and Murrell, 1987; Snider, 1990), and that taxonomies of learning styles are reductionist and obscure important differences between individuals, schools and communities. A key weakness with learning styles theory is that it attributes differences *within* classrooms and *between* individual children to a generalised and static notion of culture and identity. The idea that individuals and cultures are unchanging is contrary to our everyday experience of the world. Individuals and cultures constantly adjust, develop and change in response to broader social and cultural developments as a result of the global influence of new ideas and cultural practices, or experience lifestyle changes as a result of technology, economic development, changes in income, travel, and cross-cultural engagement and relationships. The idea of unchanging individuals and cultures also fails to acknowledge the diversity *within* and *between* different Indigenous groups, and implies that the 'solution' for any education 'problem' lies in finding the 'right' pedagogy or learning style for a specific cultural group. As Nakata (2003) argues, emphasising cultural difference draws attention away from teachers' practice and is a convenient justification for poor student outcomes.

While the notion of learning styles alerts teachers to the different ways in which students learn, researchers caution against the rigid application of learning styles because this labels and stereotypes students, ignores the diversity within Indigenous groups and can result in a 'narrow and unchallenging education' that fails to prepare Indigenous students for strong competence in both Indigenous and non-Indigenous worlds (Guild, 1994; Stairs, 1994).

Guild (1994) surveyed the 'observation-based' and 'data-based' research on the links between culture and learning styles and found that research generally agrees that:

- students of any particular age will differ in their ways of learning;
- learning styles are a function of both nature and nurture;
- learning styles are neutral; and
- both the observational and data-based research on cultures agree that, within a group, the variations among individuals are as great as their commonalities.

In addition, many authors recognise that cultural conflict exists between some students and the typical learning experiences in schools, and that some can have difficulties adjusting to their teachers and school when they have been socialised in ways that are inconsistent with the school culture. Guild concludes that the complexity and limitations of learning styles as a diagnostic tool severely restricted the drawing of generalisations.

Recent research has demonstrated that using a particular pedagogical approach or 'learning style' will only be successful when broader cultural issues are taken into account, including the responsiveness of the school to the needs of the Indigenous students and to community input (Chodkiewicz, Widin and Yasukawa, 2008; Donovan, 2007; Mander and Fieldhouse, 2009; Watson et al., 2006). Recognising the broader context of schooling, the OECD (2007) argues that effective engagement of Indigenous students in schooling involves mutual learning and parental and community participation, and must:

- honour cultural distinctiveness—start with a recognition of, and respect for, the culture and identities of Indigenous peoples;
- focus on aspiration, success and innovation—explicitly promote high expectations;
- understand the purpose of learning from the perspective of Indigenous peoples—finding answers to the question 'Learning for what?';
- emphasise community ownership—'community based' and 'community paced'; and
- build 'demand-side' expectations (students and parents), while ensuring a high quality of practical and focused responses from the 'supply side' (teachers and schools) (OECD Steering Group, 2007, pp. 1–2).

Explicit pedagogies

Contemporary research indicates that 'explicit pedagogy' (Hudspith, 1997) is crucial for the effective teaching and learning of Indigenous *and* non-Indigenous children. Explicit pedagogy involves students understanding and reflecting on what is being asked of them, how it is encoded, and their own methods of learning (Harrison, 2005). Explicit pedagogy requires students to think about *what* and *how* they are taught, and to negotiate what is *said* and *meant* in different contexts, specifically the classroom as opposed to the home/community (Harrison, 2005).

Scaffolding is a pedagogic technique based on notions of explicit pedagogy, which has had significant success when used with Indigenous students. Although the concept of educational scaffolding originated in the mid-1970s (Wood, Bruner and Ross, 1976), David Rose and others developed the concept for use with Indigenous students in Australia (Martin and Rose, 2005; Rose, 2004; Rose, Gray and Cowey, 1999). Scaffolding describes 'the temporary assistance that teachers provide for their students in order to assist them to complete a task or develop new understandings so that they will later be able to complete similar tasks alone [and] to help learners to work with increasing independence—to know not only *what* to think and do, but *how* to think and do, so that new skills and understandings can be applied in new contexts' (Hammond and Gibbons, 2001, pp. 3–5).

Scaffolding involves 'clearly articulated goals and learning activities which are structured in ways that enable learners to extend their existing levels of understanding [and] located within the broader framework of a planned program with its own clearly articulated goals' (Hammond and Gibbons, 2001, p. 7). Experts describe scaffolding as consisting of three key components:

1. careful preparation of learners so that they can respond successfully;
2. feedback on students' responses that extends beyond merely evaluation or comment but *elaborates* on shared knowledge; and
3. positive affirmation of students' responses, even if they are incorrect, to build students' sense of belonging and preparedness to take risks by participating in class (Martin and Rose, 2005, p. 8).

Scaffolding has been used most commonly to teach literacy, but evidence indicates that it is an effective strategy for teaching other subjects, including mathematics (Warren and Young, 2008; Zevenbergen, Mousley and Sullivan, 2004). Furthermore, Cresswell et al. (2002, p. 22) concluded that 'the results of the introduction of scaffolding procedures observed in the schools in this study are little short of sensational'.

Langwij Comes to School: Promoting Literacy Among Speakers of Aboriginal English and Australian Creoles, *published by Social Change Media in 1994. Teachers need to know that Aboriginal English is now accepted as a legitimate dialect of Australian English. As such, and as the home language of Aboriginal kids, it needs to be respected in schools. The teacher's role is to enable students to be able to switch codes when appropriate, remember that Aboriginal people have been linguists since the beginning of the Dreaming, and to be aware that Aboriginal kids love to play with words. Courtesy Social Change Media.*

Creating a positive classroom environment for learning

Like all children, Aboriginal and Torres Strait Islander children learn best in a non-threatening environment. A culturally sensitive classroom uses pedagogies that are meaningful and that support students' Indigenous identity. The following list offers some examples of strategies for creating a positive classroom climate that respects and honours the identities, cultures and communities of Indigenous students:

- Focus on content areas that develop cross-cultural themes (e.g. Indigenous and Western dance; Aboriginal and Western land use; history of the local area).
- Incorporate Aboriginal perspectives into all curriculum areas (e.g. Aboriginal designs into art, craft and drawing; Aboriginal experiences into history studies; Aboriginal life-science into science lessons; Dreaming trails as the basis for geography lessons; Aboriginal herbal medications in health studies).
- Be sensitive to Anglo-European bias and values in books and resources (see Chapter 14).
- Use teaching resources that are culturally familiar and relevant to Aboriginal students (e.g. Dreaming stories, resources decorated with Aboriginal designs, productions by Aboriginal media companies and filmmakers; contemporary Aboriginal literature and poetry).
- Establish links with Aboriginal parents and local Aboriginal organisations and community groups. Draw on their expertise and help in the classroom (see Chapter 10).
- Invite Aboriginal guest speakers and artists (visual artists, dancers, storytellers, etc.) into the classroom on a regular basis.
- Draw on the expertise of Aboriginal personnel employed in the school, region or school system.

Pedagogies for engaging students and scaffolding learning

Translating the three key steps of scaffolded learning into positive student outcomes requires teachers to take careful account of the diversity within the class and to attend to a range of different elements in the classroom. There is enormous diversity across *individual* children and there is no 'best way' of learning for all situations. A child might learn language more effectively using collaborative group work but prefer to work independently when studying mathematics. As those entrusted with meeting the educational needs of each student, teachers need to connect with the diverse ways of learning present in each class. This entails modifying the selection of learning strategies and teaching style, the tone of the classroom and the physical character of the learning environment. The key features of successfully engaging students and scaffolding learning is to acknowledge that individual students need different forms of support and that a 'one-size-fits-all' approach does not work.

Aboriginal English as a springboard for learning

Indigenous students' home language is central to their cultural identity. Effective engagement and scaffolded learning require effective two-way communication between teachers and students, and between schools and communities. When students' home language is Aboriginal English and/or one or more Indigenous languages, children may have only limited understanding of, or ability to communicate effectively using, Standard English. Warren warns that:

> the importance of spoken language as the foundation for all learning is often not fully recognised and many young Indigenous Australian students are not able to make a strong start in the early years of schooling as the discourses of their family often do not match those of the school. (Warren and Young, 2008, p. 129; also see Cairney, 2003)

Acknowledging that some Indigenous students do not speak English as their first language and that dialect use is intimately connected to identity (Mellor and Corrigan, 2004) is necessary to ensure that children 'feel secure at school or make a commitment to learning other forms, registers and genres of English' (Cambourne and Turbill, 1990, pp. 3–4). It is also necessary that teachers and schools do not 'put standard

Australian English in an oppositional relationship to the home language' (MCEETYA, 2006, p. 17). Doing so will invite students' resistance, discourage participation in classroom activities, impede effective learning and inhibit the formation of harmonious social relations at school.

Teachers need to develop an informed understanding of Aboriginal English to enable them to understand and communicate effectively with Indigenous students (MCEETYA, 2006, p. 17). Teachers will increase the likelihood of successful literacy and language learning among Indigenous children if they accept Aboriginal English and use it as a basis for building confidence, understanding and skill in Standard English (see 'Using Aboriginal English' box later in the chapter). Such an approach also contributes to students' learning in other subject areas, such as mathematics (Warren and Young, 2008; Zevenbergen et al., 2004).

Teachers also need to be aware that up to 80 per cent of Aboriginal children suffer from otitis media (glue ear)—a rate nearly ten times higher than for other Australians (Sherwood and McConville, 1994). This condition can damage the eardrum and hearing bones, and lead to permanent hearing loss. The combination of hearing loss and the incompatibility of school English and home language can seriously impede a child's learning development. If hearing loss is suspected, the teacher should seek the advice of the school counsellor, school executive and Aboriginal support teacher.

Person-centred teaching

Children are person centred rather than information oriented, and will assess their teachers on the basis of how they relate to them as individuals rather than according to their qualifications or performance as instructors in the classroom (see Chapter 11). Children of all cultural backgrounds recognise when their teachers genuinely and consistently *care* about their development and well-being.

Teachers who care and take a personal interest in their students earn the respect of their students, establish a positive, trusting relationship and build a classroom environment in which students feel safe, positive about learning, and willing to take risks and attempt new tasks.

Fitzroy Crossing students on stage at the Halls Creek Croc Festival, 2005, showing the flair, spirit and focus that can be harnessed when Aboriginal kids are engaged (one boy wanted to live at the Croc!). Courtesy Indigenous Festivals of Australia.

Teachers can improve student achievement by using simple strategies such as smiling regularly at the children, warmly welcoming them to class, building self-esteem through positive reinforcement, and showing consistent interest in the child's family, friends and activities outside the classroom.

Encourage risk-taking

Reticence to take public risks is a constraint on formal learning (Coombs, Brandl and Snowden, 1983), yet Western academic traditions emphasise the individual through teaching techniques that single out individuals to perform tasks, answer questions and demonstrate mastery or understanding. Such a pedagogical approach can be threatening and isolating for all but the most self-confident and extroverted student.

Such approaches are inappropriate for all children, but Aboriginal and Torres Strait Islander students can be particularly 'sensitive and susceptible to criticism and ridicule used in classrooms' (Enemburu, 1985, p. 5). The experience is described as 'a shame job'. Fear of being singled out and publicly humiliated may make children reticent to participate in class, and fear of criticism may lead them to reject a teacher's advice, regardless of how positive the criticism may be (Enemburu, 1985, p. 5). For some children, the fear of being shamed is so strong that they will truant to avoid the classroom or school altogether. Effective scaffolding of learning requires the teacher to create a non-threatening classroom environment that fosters risk-taking.

Appropriate methods of questioning

Because Aboriginal and Torres Strait Islander families often have an extensive kinship network and a high degree of interaction with family and friends, an individual's activities are generally open and well known. Despite this, privacy is important, and it is maintained by controlling possession of the reason or explanation for actions. Direct interrogation or 'why' questions can be regarded as extremely rude and as an invasion of privacy. Some Indigenous students are likely to ignore the question or to give a deliberately uninformative answer. Non-Indigenous teachers may incorrectly interpret such behaviour as evasive, uncooperative or defiant. Questions can also be intimidating for Aboriginal students. To avoid being shamed, they respond with silence. A more appropriate way of eliciting information than asking direct questions is to:

- observe;
- draw assumptions based on the observation; and
- indirectly inquire about motive and reason by proffering an explanation based on observation and assumption. Your explanation will be accepted, rejected or elaborated on, depending on the individual's willingness to share their reasons.

The amount of time that is acceptable between hearing a question and answering is socially and culturally constructed. In some communities, responding to a question quickly is not a high priority. In urban, rural and remote Indigenous communities, for example, more time is allowed to answer a question than may be the norm in school or non-Indigenous society. Teachers should be careful not to misread the delay between question and answer as a signal that the student is intellectually 'slow'.

In school, teachers often use questions to test *existing* knowledge and comprehension. A scaffolded approach uses questions for the specific purpose of building *new* knowledge and understanding. Indigenous languages and Aboriginal English do not use 'either/or' questions (Metropolitan East Region, 1992, p. 13), and such questions can confuse Indigenous students, who may even find multiple-choice assessment tasks problematic. In other circumstances, a student will give the answer they anticipate the teacher wants, even if they do not understand or agree with it. This concurrence is part of an endeavour to maintain 'smooth and co-operative social relationships' (Metropolitan East Region, 1992, p. 13), and illustrates that it is unproductive for teachers to rely solely on direct questioning to evaluate knowledge and understanding.

Effective questioning involves using open-ended questions, which help create a secure, risk-taking environment that allows individual students to capitalise on their existing knowledge while also leaving room for the negotiation of cultural difference. Because multiple answers may be 'correct', the use of open-ended questions allows for cultural diversity within a single classroom as well as offering encouragement to students with different knowledge and skill levels. Open-ended questions stimulate high-order thinking while also allowing students to provide responses that can vary in quality and quantity, depending on students' knowledge. Open-ended questioning is 'powerfully inclusive', particularly for students who have experienced limited success in traditionally oriented classrooms (Zevenbergen et al., 2004, pp. 392–403).

Supporting integrated learning and understanding

The rigid divide between academic disciplines is a historical construct that often bears little relationship to the way the learning styles of the various disciplines interconnect, both in the classroom and in real life. For instance, language skills are important in all areas of study—not just during English lessons. An integrated approach to learning does not artificially compartmentalise learning according to academic disciplines or apparently unrelated skills. Rather, areas of study are integrated so that learning flows smoothly across discipline areas and the interrelationship between knowledge and skills is apparent.

Integration across disciplines of learning areas can avoid fragmented learning, accommodate an overcrowded curriculum, and prepare students for a world where it is necessary to transfer common knowledge and skills across a range of different areas (Fogarty, 1991a, 1991b).

Facilitating visual and concrete learning

Traditional Aboriginal societies had a strong oral tradition, and learning often occurred in informal, unstructured situations through observation and imitation rather than through verbal instruction or written texts (Harris, 1980, 1984; Malin, 1990; Sansom, 1980). Artwork and rock paintings were used to record events, information, legends and history. Today, because of the extensive use of visual communication in everyday life (television, computers, simulation games), children from all cultural backgrounds are highly skilled at absorbing visual information.

A pedagogy that capitalises on students' visual skills can enhance learning by utilising modes of learning that students use extensively outside of the classroom. It entails the use of visual images, symbols and diagrams to impart new information and understandings. Lessons constructed so that concrete examples precede abstract understanding or that use a shared experience (film, excursion, role-play, story) followed by modelling, reflection and performance will support the visual learning of all students in the classroom.

Supporting 'learning by doing'

Children of all backgrounds and cultures have a seemingly endless supply of physical energy. Yet, if the pedagogy of the classroom requires students to remain confined to their desks and immobile,

> **Integrated learning strategies**
> A range of models exist for designing integrated curricula (see Fogarty 1991a, 1991b). The following suggestions provide a starting point for thinking about this useful approach.
> - Integrate SOE/HSIE with language, maths and science.
> - Integrate reading, writing, spelling and grammar by using stories as the basis for language activities.
> - Emphasise a whole-language approach to reading rather than a phonics approach.
> - Draw on the student's own world as a starting point for lessons.
> - Illustrate the transferability of knowledge and skills by applying learning across subject disciplines and in 'real-life' contexts (e.g. teach measurement, or maths, as part of a cooking class; write letters, or language, to pen-friends in Asia as part of English or SOE).
> - Build lessons across the curricula using common themes or concepts (e.g. bias as a concept can be addressed in maths as bias in graphics, or in SOE through propaganda, or in language through newspaper studies).

clashes can occur that teachers regard as a behaviour problem but are merely because students find sitting still in class difficult and frustrating. A pedagogy that employs 'learning by doing' gives children the opportunity to move around, be physically active, and learn through movement, by manipulating objects and by 'doing'.

Facilitating cooperative learning

The contemporary work environment emphasises teamwork and collaboration in order to draw on and utilise the expertise of the group. Such strategies can have value as part of a teacher's repertoire. Collaboration and cooperative learning in small groups has the potential to provide all students with peer support, thereby creating a less threatening learning environment and encouraging risk-taking while also allowing opportunities for the informal growth of social and leadership skills (Howard, 1994).

Contextualising learning

Schools are artificial, human-made environments where the content often has little apparent application to daily life. By contextualising learning, students discover that education is meaningful and relevant to their own lives.

Responsibility and independence

Schools generally allow students little autonomy, responsibility or control over decision-making. School rules are rarely open to negotiation and teachers structure, direct and pace all students' learning and activities. Many students have considerably more responsibility at home than at school, and older students are often responsible for dressing, feeding and caring for younger siblings, particularly in Indigenous families where there is a strong emphasis on care and responsibility for others.

Regardless of their cultural heritage, many young children do not feel obligated to automatically obey the rules and instructions decreed by adults, and consider that deference and respect are things teachers need to earn rather than an automatic right bestowed by their position. Rather than interpreting such behaviour as a 'problem' to be 'fixed', teachers and schools need to develop strategies that address the diverse needs of all students. Extra time and effort may be required to explain and negotiate school expectations concerning behaviour, completion of work and silence, while learning and classroom management may be enhanced if students are allowed a greater degree of autonomy and responsibility in decision-making and complying with the new, negotiated standard.

Body language

Body language is a subtle but powerful form of communication, and a vital part of any learning environment. Both students and teachers use non-verbal communication to assess importance, understanding, interest and involvement. Because different cultures have a variety of forms and expressions of non-verbal communication, the engagement behaviour of students may not accord with teachers' expectations. This behaviour is exemplified in such social practices as eye and body contact:

In non-Aboriginal culture eye contact is often assumed to be an indicator of attention, interest or as a way of showing respect. Some Aboriginal students may lower their eyes when being spoken to by a teacher; this is in fact, a culturally determined sign of respect but can be misinterpreted as being disrespectful, evasive or, in extreme circumstances, guilty. For Aboriginal students, active participation in the learning process may occur without direct eye contact which does not necessarily mean lack of engagement or attention. (Metropolitan East Region, 1992, p. 11)

In Aboriginal society, lowered eyes can be a sign of politeness and respect. A child will rarely look an older person directly in the eye. It does not follow, therefore, that Aboriginal children are inattentive or disrespectful if they do not look directly at the teacher.

In addition, when children from any background feel embarrassed or ashamed, they may hang their heads, refuse to move and avoid eye contact. Or they might try to defuse a tense situation by giggling, smiling or walking away. Such behaviour has implications for classroom management. It is inappropriate to demand that a child look at you when you are speaking or to interpret 'shame' behaviour as insolence.

Broadening the base of respect

Teaching is a complex process. Respecting and honouring students' cultural background, engaging students learning and scaffolding learning are important for *all*. The pedagogies appropriate for Indigenous students are equally effective for other students, particularly those who have difficulty learning from teacher-centred lessons or who find the status differential in teacher–student relationships problematic. Being culturally sensitive and using pedagogies that are appropriate to the needs of individual students will facilitate cultural understanding and foster a positive classroom climate that improves outcomes. This will be of benefit to Australia and all Australians.

Visual and concrete learning strategies

- Use pictures, charts, diagrams and models to convey information and concepts.
- Emphasise 'showing' or modelling rather than explaining (e.g. model counting and spelling patterns by writing them on the chalk board or whiteboard).
- Set activities, assessment tasks and assignments that allow students to demonstate their knowledge visually (e.g. a picture or model).
- Use interactive media resources, particularly computer simulation games.
- Use film and video to demonstrate concepts, introduce new language and convey information.
- Foster verbal skills by using environment and immersion language techniques, and by drawing on students' own experiences to stimulate discussion and writing.
- Demonstrate the meaning of words in context before teaching the meaning of individual words.
- Use geometric shapes to provide a concrete understanding of fractions before proceeding to written works.
- Give examples to demonstrate concepts.
- Use experiments and concrete demonstrations as the basis of science lessons (e.g. put celery sticks in coloured water to demonstrate capillary action; grow one plant in sunlight and another in a paper bag to demonstrate the importance of light in photosynthesis).
- Use 'real-life' objects (fruit, marbles, tennis balls) to teach counting, addition, subtraction, multiplication and division.
- Use field trips as a basis for learning. These need not be expensive or difficult to organise (e.g. walk around the local area to explore the variety and form of local businesses, the type of vegetation and to identify traffic problems).
- Use Lego letter boards to teach spelling.
- Teach word recognition using lotto games.

Kinaesthetic learning strategies

- Allow students to move around the classroom, to explore and observe.
- Provide opportunities to 'learn by doing'.
- Incorporate the manipulation of materials in lessons (e.g. use containers to teach spatial concepts; buttons or balls for counting; movable alphabet letters for reading and spelling).
- Incorporate role-plays, drama, improvisations and simulation games into lessons.
- Teach geometry by having students measure and draw geometric shapes in the playground.
- Teach songs with hand and body movements.
- Pretend to 'moonwalk' to demonstrate the lack of gravity.
- Draw a clock on the playground, have each student adopt the role of part of the clock (e.g. numbers, and hour, minute and second hands) and re-enact the clock's movement across time.
- Collect items from the school grounds (leaves, rocks, sand) as a basis for artwork, teaching about the senses, development of stories.
- Use 'whispers' to learn new words and words in context.
- Teach verbs by performing the actions.
- Learn spelling by clapping out the letters (a more complex version is to perform the vowels in semaphore).
- Assess comprehension by having students retell a story using movement and facial expressions.

Cooperative learning strategies
- Build lessons around learning that can be performed as joint projects (e.g. construction of models, joint research assignments, shared story-writing, group problem-solving).
- Use assessment tasks that reward teamwork.
- Recognise the physical learning environment to foster group work by clustering desks; creating separate corners for reading, writing, puzzles and model-building; using the open floor space for large-group work.
- Allow children to work in friendship groups for certain tasks.
- Accept that group work means a higher noise level in the classroom and introduce non-verbal strategies for regaining attention (e.g. moving to a particular location to indicate that silence is needed).
- Use outside space for group discussion and class activities.

Contextualising learning strategies
- Conduct learning in relevant, real-life situations (e.g. visit a river to learn about water life; visit a factory to learn about production; go to a farm to learn about irrigation, farm animals).
- Emphasise the practical applications of learning (e.g. science in the kitchen, functional literacy).
- Use dressing up and role-play as the starting point of lessons (e.g. going shopping to learn counting and currency).
- Discuss the pictures in books before reading.
- Encourage contextualised thinking by using jigsaws, games and modelling tools like Mobilo, Lego, etc.
- Use themes over a series of weeks so that students who were absent can contextualise knowledge.

Building responsibility and independence strategies
- Provide opportunities for students to choose and/or negotiate content, assessment tasks, assignment formats, time required to complete tasks, etc.
- Give students responsibility for jobs within the classroom (e.g. collecting books, distributing pencils, setting up display tables, organising group work).
- Make students responsible for their own learning by using research assignments, a self-paced learning and study program, and so on.
- Organise the classroom furniture with separate areas for group work and quiet work, so that students can control their own learning.
- Remember that effective learning is more important than 'good' behaviour or unquestioning obedience.

Encouraging risk-taking strategies
- Create a secure, comfortable, relaxed learning environment.
- Use positive reinforcement to acknowledge student achievement.
- Allow students to work in small groups.
- Introduce a peer tutoring scheme.
- Do not insist on answers to questions.
- Introduce self-assessment of work to avoid alienating students through criticism.
- Avoid public confrontation and reprimands.

Questioning Techniques

Inappropriate questioning technique
Teacher: 'Why are you late for class?'
Student: 'Don't know.'

Appropriate questioning technique
Teacher: 'We couldn't start without you. Did you need to get your books?'
Student: 'Yes, and Mr Smith wanted to see me about maths.'

Questioning strategies
- Avoid personal questions.
- Be explicit about the purpose of the question.
- Avoid direct questions to individuals.
- Use small-group questioning to reduce shaming.
- Allow students time to respond to questions.
- Ask broad, open questions such as 'Tell me what you know about . . . ?' that are directed to the whole class, rather than closed questions such as 'In what year was . . . ?' that are directed to specific individuals.

Using Aboriginal English as a basis for learning
- Avoid over-correction.
- Accept and demonstrate both verbally and visually that there is a variety of equally acceptable ways of saying the same thing.
- Model contextually appropriate language by gently translating Aboriginal English into Standard English when children are speaking or writing.
- Encourage children to do their own translations from Aboriginal to Standard English and vice versa.
- Provide a non-threatening, interactive learning environment that fosters literacy through immersion in reading, writing and listening.
- Capitalise on verbal skills to develop written work.
- Use 'big books' to model language and print conventions.
- Allow students to make their own 'big books' by substituting their own words for parts of a known story. Display these and make them accessible. Language skills will be consolidated because students will read them repeatedly.

Variations between the language of the child, the language of the teacher and the language of the school have been identified as a source of cross cultural communication breakdown and a barrier to effective teaching and learning.

—Royal Commission into Aboriginal Deaths in Custody (1991, p. 350)

A teacher made an announcement at school assembly about head lice: 'the number of parents ringing up has been substantial so please be on the alert. A note will go home this afternoon regarding prevention and treatment.' The class mumbles and a student asked the question: 'What did she say?' Another student translated into Aboriginal English. 'Kids have got munnas again: munnas goin' round so look out, eh.'

—Metropolitan East Region (1992, p. 7)

Danny Eastwood's cartoon in the Koori Mail *illustrates the sense of fun of Aboriginal kids—too often seen as 'cheeky' by teachers. Years ago, Aboriginal kids in western Sydney defined a good teacher as 'Someone that likes us and is fair'. Courtesy* Koori Mail.

A Poem About Me

Me is the black I'll always be,
Me is the way I want to see
The day the white man sees my way
And understands the things I say.

Me is the pride I haven't lost
I will not lose at any cost.
For without pride I am done,
there is no battle to be won.

Me is the freedom like the wind
To sing and dance through the darkest sting
Freedom loved is freedom enjoyed
Things that hinder we must avoid.

Me is the people I represent
To fight my cause with no repent
To overcome the white man's chide
And learning to live side by side.

—Greg Strong (1989)

14 Teaching resources

Rhonda Craven, Mark d'Arbon and Sharon Galleguillos

This chapter is about some of the Indigenous Studies teaching resources available today. Thirty years ago, resources suitable for primary and secondary classrooms were few and far between. They were usually of an anthropological nature, relying on traditional stories and lifestyle experiences. Today, resources for the teaching of Indigenous Studies have become much more relevant to the reality of the contemporary Indigenous experience. Now, more than ever in our history, there is recognition and valuing of the nature and diversity of Indigenous culture and experience. This is reflected in the resources that are available to teachers who are interested in and committed to the honest representation of the place of Indigenous peoples in the making of Australia.

Resources that adopt a superficial 'anthropological' approach and that do not acknowledge developmental issues associated with learning are always going to be inadequate, misleading, stereotypical—or all of the above. Selecting appropriate resources can be a difficult task, because teachers attempting Indigenous Studies at any stage of the K/P–12 continuums across states/territories often have to organise their resources from a wide and sometimes confusing range. This chapter offers advice for teachers on appropriate resources and identifies some resources that we have found to be useful. It is

Cover of Network Educational Australia's Australian Indigenous Studies Resources Buying Guide 2010. *There have always been more books and graphics about Aboriginal Australia than anyone knew. Now, books, kits, videos, CDs, DVDs—you name it—there are more resources for Aboriginal education than most people can keep up with. Courtesy Network Educational Australia.*

hoped that this chapter will increase teachers' awareness of:

- some available resources;
- how to critically evaluate resources; and
- how to begin to locate a range of stimulating materials.

As this publication goes to press, the Australian Curriculum and Assessment Authority (ACARA) is finalising a national curriculum that will override extant state and territory curricula:

> ACARA is responsible for the development of Australia's national curriculum from Kindergarten to Year 12, starting with the learning areas of English, mathematics, science and history, for implementation from 2011. As a second phase of work, national curriculum will be developed in languages, geography and the arts. The development of continua for literacy and numeracy skills and ICT will be a foundation of the curriculum. The curriculum will outline the essential skills, knowledge and capabilities that all young Australians are entitled to access, regardless of their social or economic background or the school they attend. (ACARA, 2008, <www.acara.edu.au/curriculum.html>)

The National Curriculum Board (NCB), which has oversight of this process, has made the following important statement:

> The advent of a national curriculum also offers a unique opportunity to ensure that all young Australians learn about the history and cultural background of the nation's Aboriginal and Torres Strait Islander peoples, of the contribution that has been made to Australia, and of the impact that colonial settlement has had on Indigenous communities, past and present. For Indigenous people and Torres Strait Islanders, a national curriculum provides the opportunity to establish and pursue excellence within education settings that respect and promote their cultural identity. (NCB, 2009, p. 6)

This means that the resources selected to enhance student experience in the area of Aboriginal Studies will remain relevant, however the national curriculum is shaped.

Indigenous input: An essential resource

Indigenous involvement in Indigenous Studies activities is the best resource available to teachers. Indigenous people know their culture, their history, the effects of that history and the current issues. Local Indigenous people are the custodians of their culture and history. Their cultures are dynamic and changing, and those with the keenest insight into these cultures are Indigenous people. For these reasons, the best resource available to teachers of Indigenous Studies is the life experiences and expertise of Indigenous people (see Chapter 10).

Many museums and art galleries have Aboriginal curators and/or education officers (e.g. the Australian Museum, the Art Gallery of New South Wales, the Powerhouse Museum, the Museum of Sydney). For example, the Australian Museum has a movie gallery on its website (<http://australianmuseum.net.au/Stories-from-New-South-Wales>), where you can play students Dreaming stories told by Indigenous people. Museums will often provide teaching strategies and lesson plans online to enhance excursions or visits. There are also local resource centres run by Indigenous education officers and local or regional museums.

Indigenous media

Indigenous media can be a useful source of current information:

- *Koori Mail* (<www.koorimail.com>);
- *National Indigenous Times* (<www.nit.com.au>);
- *Land Rights News* (<www.nlc.org.au/html/wht_lrn.html>);
- *Torres News* (<www.torresnews.com.au>).

We now have an Indigenous TV channel, NITV (<http://nitv.org.au>), where teachers can access a range of high-quality films and up-to-date information. There are also Indigenous units within ABC TV and Radio, as well as SBS. Often when a new program such as *The First Australians* is produced, it will come with teaching resources and lesson plans. The Aboriginal Program Exchange, based in Melbourne, networks tapes of programs from a wide network of Indigenous community broadcasters across Australia.

Vibe Australia Pty Ltd is a dynamic Aboriginal media, communications and events management agency, which specialises in implementing, producing and networking targeted, culturally sensitive communication products and services for Aboriginal and Torres Strait Islander communities, with a strong education focus. Vibe produces:

- *Deadly Vibe*—a national Aboriginal and Torres Strait Islander health, sport, music and lifestyle magazine, with a monthly distribution of 57 000;
- *In Vibe*—a dynamic, accessible and culturally sensitive sixteen-page full-colour magazine for Indigenous people in secure rehabilitation care and at risk;
- *Deadly Sounds*—a weekly radio program syndicated to over 250 Aboriginal community stations around Australia, featuring music, culture and health information in an upbeat magazine format;
- The Vibe 3on3™—a national music and sporting event to promote health, well-being, identity and sportsmanship;
- The Deadlys—the National Aboriginal and Torres Strait Islander Music, Sport, Entertainment and Community Awards, held every year at the Sydney Opera House, and broadcast nationally on SBS;
- <www.vibe.com.au>—an extensive website that consolidates all of Vibe's activities, which attracts approximately 5000 visits per day;
- Living Strong, on NITV—all the latest good news on healthy living and positive futures; and
- Vibe Alive—two-day festivals for young Indigenous Australians who like to dance break, rap, sing, paint and play sport; celebrating culture and encouraging tolerance and teamwork.

Resources

Virtual libraries

If it is possible to find a site that is regularly updated and provides a list of resources that is appropriate for a variety of Aboriginal Studies purposes, then the search for resources can be less difficult than it might be. One such resource site can be found at: <www.ciolek.com/WWWVLPages/AborigPages/Koori.html>, which has a list of 'safe' resources. It is a subsection of the Aboriginal Studies WWW Virtual Library, which can be found at: <www.ciolek.com/WWWVL-Aboriginal.html>.

Teacher references

Several outstanding collections of Aboriginal writings are available. These are invaluable teaching resources for conveying a variety of Indigenous people's perspectives on a wide range of issues. They include the following:

- *Voices of Aboriginal Australia: Past Present Future* was edited by the late Irene Moores (1995). It is a collection of writings by Aboriginal people over the past 50 years.
- *Paperbark: A Collection of Black Australian Writings*, edited by Jack Davis, Stephen Muecke, Mudrooroo Narogin, and Adam Shoemaker (1990), features the work of 36 Indigenous authors.
- *The Wailing: A National Black Oral History* edited by Stuart Rintoul (1993) is a collection of oral histories from across Australia.
- the *Macquarie PEN Anthology of Aboriginal Literature*, edited by Anita Heiss and Peter Minter (2008), contains samples from Bennelong's letter in 1796 to Indigenous writers now, journalism, petitions and political letters from the nineteenth and twentieth centuries, bits of major works that reflect the blossoming of Aboriginal poetry, prose and drama. The book is accompanied by a website that includes resources and links for students and teachers (<www.macquariepenanthology.com.au>). It is a priceless teaching resource!
- *Dharawal Seasons and Climatic Cycles*, compiled by Frances Bodkin (2008) is the first in a series aimed at sharing knowledge and understanding of the Dharawal people of the Sydney region's environment, resources, seasons and climates. It has beautiful full-colour illustrations by the artist Lorraine Robertson plus a free poster of the Dharawal seasons. This book is ideal for teachers, ecologists or meteorologists, or indeed anyone interested in Aboriginal culture and the Indigenous relationship with the natural environment. It gives students an understanding of the complexity of Aboriginal knowledge and science of observation and experience.
- *Heartsick for Country: Stories of Love, Spirit, and Creation* by Sally Morgan, Mia Tjaliminu and Blaze Kwaymullina (2008), is an anthology of personal accounts about

the love between Aboriginal peoples and their land. Each account speaks of a deep connection to land and of feeling heartsick because of the harm that is being inflicted on country today. It would be suitable for lower secondary students, but also for senior students who are critically engaging with Aboriginal experience. For a review, see <www.nla.gov.au/openpublish/index.php/ras/article/viewFile/815/1086>.

- 'Using the Right Words: Appropriate Terminology for Indigenous Australian Studies', from *Teaching the Teachers Indigenous Australian Studies for Primary Pre-Service Teacher Education* (Craven, 1996), a booklet containing information on appropriate terminology for the Indigenous Studies classroom that avoids inadvertently conveying misconceptions and stereotypes—a must for every teacher's bookshelf.
- The *Report of the Royal Commission into Aboriginal Deaths in Custody* (1991). While this is a large document (which can be found at <www.austlii.edu.au/au/other/IndigLRes/rciadic/#national>), the education recommendations—Educating for the Future (found in Volume 5 of the Report <www.austlii.edu.au/au/other/IndigLRes/rciadic/national/vol5/5.html#Heading28>) provide useful insights into how equity of educational opportunity is a powerful springboard for Aboriginal self-determination.
- The report *Bringing Them Home* (HREOC, 1997) is an essential reference resource for teaching students about the Stolen Generations. The full report is out of print but available in libraries, and there is a free summary version available on the Human Rights Commission website (<www.hreoc.gov.au/social_Justice/bth_report/report/index.html>). Also available from this website is a free DVD (see below) and teaching and learning materials and activities about the *Bringing Them Home* report, along with recent speeches (<www.hreoc.gov.au/education/bth/teaching_materials/t_DVD_activity.html>).
- *Addressing the Key Issues for Reconciliation* (Council for Aboriginal Reconciliation) is a series of nine books dealing with information on the key issues of: understanding country, improving relationships, valuing cultures, sharing histories, addressing disadvantage, responding to custody levels, agreeing on a document, and controlling destinies. The first book of the series is a useful summary of each of the eight key issues. These are available from Reconciliation Australia, which has up-to-date information about reconciliation today. The site for both the Council for Aboriginal Reconciliation and Reconciliation Australia can be found at <www.austlii.edu.au/au/orgs/car>. The archive, which contains a huge set of publications and resources, can be found at <www.austlii.edu.au/au/other/IndigLRes/car>. Reconciliation Australia is the organisation that took over from the Council after 2000.
- *Mabo: A Symbol of Sharing* by Sean Flood (1993), is highly recommended for Years 7–12. Available from E. Fink, PO Box 937, Glebe, NSW, 2037. Can be adapted for upper primary: <http://speednet.com.au/~abarca/mabo>.
- *Survival: A History of Aboriginal Life in New South Wales* by Nigel Parbury (2005) is a particularly useful teacher reference with a wealth of information and powerful images that can be adapted to create stimulating activities. *Survival* can be ordered from New South Wales Board of Studies and New South Wales AECG, <www.aecg.nsw.edu.au> or <www.boardofstudies.nsw.edu.au/links/shoponline.html>.
- *Telling It Like It Is: A Guide to Making Local Aboriginal and Torres Strait Islander History* (1992), a boxed set produced by Marcia Langton, contains the video *Back Trackers: Aboriginal and Torres Strait Islander People Making History* and two books, *Lookin' for Your Mob: A Guide to Tracing Aboriginal Family Trees* by Diane Smith and Boronia Halstead and *Telling It Like It Is: A Guide to Making Aboriginal and Torres Strait Islander History* by Penny Taylor. Contains useful information that teachers can adapt readily.
- *Too Many Captain Cooks* by Alan Tucker (Omnibus Books, 1994), tells the story of fourteen Captain Cooks who came to Australia; it conveys European impressions of Aboriginal people as well as some Aboriginal impressions of the Europeans. *Side by Side* by Alan Tucker (Omnibus Books, (1999) is also an excellent resource with fourteen stories

demonstrating the diversity of race relations in Australia in the colonial era. Gives some examples of non-Indigenous Australians who maintained good relations with Indigenous Australians.

- *Possession: Settlers, Aborigines and Land in Australia* by Bain Attwood (Melbourne University Press, 2009) tells the story of the only treaties made between Aboriginal and non-Aboriginal people. It also describes how Aboriginal people and some other Australians have ensured this history is remembered.
- *Working with Aboriginal Communities: A Guide to Community Consultation and Protocols* (New South Wales Board of Studies, 2001) provides strategies for educators for building relationships with Aboriginal communities. Available from New South Wales Board of Studies at <http://ab-ed.boardofstudies.nsw.edu.au/files/working-with-aboriginal-communities.pdf>.
- *Carpentaria*, by Alexis Wright (Giramondo, 2006), is set in the Gulf country of Northwestern Queensland, from where her people come. 'This is the kind of writing in which a reader can put their entire trust in the narrator, put the weight of their doubt in the narrator's hands . . . Of all this novel's wonderful inventions, the narrator may be the most remarkable. *Carpentaria* is a big book, more than 500 pages, big enough to enter a world, to feel as if you once lived in a town called Desperance.' (*The Age* 19 August 2006).
- *Telling The Truth About Aboriginal History* by Bain Attwood (Allen & Unwin, 2005). One of Australia's leading historians of Aboriginal Australia takes us to the heart of the 'history wars' over our Aboriginal past. Bain Attwood argues that controversy over interpretations of our Aboriginal past has never been so intense, and never mattered more.
- *Aboriginal Victorians: A History Since 1800* by Richard Broome (Allen & Unwin, 2005). The fascinating and sometimes horrifying story of Aborigines in Victoria since white settlement, from one of Australia's leading historians.
- *Seven Seasons in Aurukun: My Unforgettable Time at a Remote Aboriginal School* by Paula Shaw (Allen & Unwin, 2009). A well-crafted memoir of a young woman who spends two years teaching at the school at Aurukun in Cape York. A colourful picture of life in a remote Aboriginal community in the sweltering tropics. Available from New South Wales AECG.

Internet resources

- The Aboriginal Website Directory is a useful starting point to browse a selection of sites: <www.koori.usyd.edu.au/register/main.html>.
- Ernabella Anunga School from Central Australia has its own website (<www.edu.au/schools/ernabella/staff.htm>), as does Roebourne Primary School from West Pilbara (<www.kisser.net.au/roebourneps/rpsframes.htm>).
- The ABC website has a wide range of information (<www.abc.net.au>), including: Education for Schools (<www.abc.net.au/schoolsstv>), information about Aboriginal Studies on the World Wide Web, information about Aboriginal and Torres Strait Islander issues and history (<www.abc.net.au/learn/links.htm>), civil rights and the Stolen Generations (<www.abc.net.au/m/talks/ bbing/bb960211.htm>), and the ABC documentary series Frontier (<www.abc.net.au/frontier>). The ABC also has a dedicated Indigenous site at <www.abc.net.au/indigenous>, which contains a collection of media resources on Indigenous issues and experience. It also contains a daily update that can be accessed easily.
- *What is Black Words?* at <www.austlit.edu.au> is a searchable database and a forum for the communication of information about the lives and work of Australian Indigenous writers and storytellers. It provides access to both general and specific information about Indigenous literary cultures and traditions.
- Other useful sites include those of the Council for Aboriginal Reconciliation (CAR) (<www.austlii.edu.au/car>), which contains CAR's Social Justice Library, and the Human Rights and Equal Opportunity Commission (HREOC) (<www.hreoc.gov.au>).

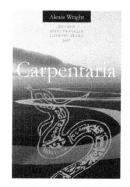

Indigenous Education Resources Update

Published regularly by Dare to Lead and the What Works program, supported by the Australian Government. In June 2010 the following resources were profiled:

Make it count: Numeracy and Mathematics for Indigenous Learners

Enables teachers and educators to communicate and collaborate on-line; Interactive Numeracies: Maths Situations in Everyday Indigenous Family and Community Life and the 'Numeracy Circle' approach.

8 ways Aboriginal Pedagogy Research Review

Designed for teachers to embed Aboriginal perspective by using Aboriginal learning techniques, produced by a partnership of James Cook University School of Indigenous Studies and DET Western Aboriginal Education team between 2007 and 2009.

rightsED

A resource from the Australian Human Rights Commission distributed to schools in April 2010; includes Bringing Them Home – teaching activities for students to understand the history and the issues.

Closing the Gap Clearinghouse

Australian Government clearinghouse for evidence-based research on overcoming disadvantage – quality information on what works in all areas; includes a collection on schooling.

National Gallery of Victoria (NGV) Tradition and Transformation website

A dynamic dialogue between artists, artworks, students, teachers and the wider community. Includes an education unit Identity about art and cultures with film clips, interviews and information about connection to country and Dreaming.

NGA Indigenous Art

About visual art and the creative process; cultural sensitivity to differences and identity. Online resources include education kits, teacher notes and slide shows.

Astronomy

Australia's first astrologers, thousands of years before the Greeks, Includes a Message Stick video 'Before Galileo'.

The site includes access to previous issues.
<www.edna.edu.au>
ieru@edna.edu.au

Statistics

- *Census—Australia's Aboriginal and Torres Strait Islander People* by the Australian Bureau of Statistics (ABS) gives statistical profiles of Aboriginal and Torres Strait Islander Australia. The ABS can also generate statistics for specific regions if you require a profile of your area. Some statistics contrast social indicators for Indigenous and non-Indigenous Australians, with a breakdown for each state/territory—an important resource. Given the depth of Indigenous social disadvantage, up-to-date statistics are an essential teaching resource. The ABS website also provides links to reference material to assist with understanding and using Aboriginal and Torres Strait Islander statistics, plus other relevant sources and contacts.

- *Closing the Gap on Indigenous Disadvantage: The Challenge for Australia*, produced by the Council of Australian Governments (COAG, 2009); (<www.ahmrc.org.au/Downloads/CTG.pdf>) contains statistics and useful graphs about Aboriginal and Torres Strait Islander health. It also includes a comparative analysis of national health data for Indigenous populations in Australia, New Zealand, Canada and the United States, with Australia ranking bottom in this table of developed nations. For example, Aboriginal and Torres Strait Islanders die years younger than non-Indigenous Australians, whereas in the United States, Canada and New Zealand, life expectancy for Indigenous people is approximately seven years less than for the non-Indigenous population. COAG has set key areas for targeting in this report.

- The *National Report to Parliament on Indigenous Education and Training* is produced regularly and tracks progress in Indigenous education and training at all levels, from pre-school through to higher education. Priority areas for improving outcomes for Indigenous students are identified (e.g. professional development of teachers, involvement of Indigenous parents and communities in education, and the need for culturally inclusive curricula). Interspersed through this report are the activities of eleven education providers. Their stories provide insights into how they are meeting the needs of their communities and how they are achieving outcomes for their students. Developments in other Australian government programs that assist Indigenous students are also outlined.

- *Overcoming Indigenous Disadvantage: Key Indicators* by the Productivity Commission is a series of reports commissioned by heads of Australian governments since 2002, to provide regular reporting against key indicators of Indigenous disadvantage. It is the report card on how well COAG's *Closing the Gap* targets are being met. The report also includes references to programs that are considered successful in addressing disadvantage. Across nearly all the indicators in this report, there are wide gaps in outcomes between Indigenous and non-Indigenous Australians. The reports include graphs, statistics and programs that work.
- *The Achievement of Australia's Indigenous Students in PISA 2000–2006* (De Bortoli and Thomson, 2009). Available from the Australian Council for Educational Research (<www.acer.edu.au/documents/PISA2006-Indigenous.pdf>). In 1997, the OECD (Organisation for Economic, Cooperation, and Development) launched the triennial Program for International Student Assessment (PISA). PISA monitors the outcomes of education systems and measures how well students who are approaching the end of their compulsory schooling are prepared to meet the challenges they will face. Data collected also allow detailed analysis and comparison of the performance of Australian Indigenous and non-Indigenous students and enable teachers and students to access up-to-date statistics.
- *Face the Facts*, produced by the Australian Human Rights Commission (<http://www.humanrights.gov.au/education/face_facts/index.html>) is updated regularly and provides a snapshot of aspects of the social realities of Australia for Indigenous Australians, including statistics. For teachers, *Face the Facts* is also produced as an education resource that complies with national curriculum standards and has sample online activities for secondary students (see Chapter 1). A valuable teaching resource that is also accessible to students.

DVDs

A DVD can often convey higher-order concepts more quickly than other teaching resources. Not only do DVDs capture the interest of students, they also provide teachers with a ready resource for conveying a diversity of Indigenous viewpoints. They can provide a springboard to explore a range of issues.

- *Apology to the Stolen Generations of Australia* (120 minutes, ABC Shops, 2008) is a DVD every Australian should see. It presents a defining moment in Australia's history—the apology in federal Parliament to the Stolen Generations of Australia by Prime Minister Kevin Rudd in 2008. It was a moment in time when crowds gathered at big screens all over Australia and Australians—young and old, Aboriginal and non-Aboriginal—were glued to their TVs. Includes complete coverage of the speeches and proceedings, with expert analysis and reactions from members of Australia's Stolen Generations.
- *Jimmy Little's Gentle Journey* (2003)—tells the remarkable story of one of Australia's living treasures, a great human being and Australia's first Aboriginal popstar.
- *First Australians* (SBS, 2003) (383 minutes, ABC Shops) documents the untold story of Australia's history from the perspective of our first Australians from Bennelong in 1788 to Koiki Mabo's challenge to *terra nullius* in 1992. Seven documentaries depict true stories of individuals—both Aboriginal and non-Aboriginal—caught in the epic drama of Australia's transformative history.
- *The Journey's Just Begun: Enhancing Schools' Capacity to Partner Aboriginal Communities* (2008). The 30-minute DVD plus book (available from New South Wales Board of Studies <http://ab-ed.boardofstudies.nsw.edu.au/go/partnerships>) demonstrates the far-reaching benefits of genuine partnerships by focusing on the journeys of four schools.
- *Winangaylanha Dhayn-gu Gaay: Understanding Aboriginal Languages* (2004) (CD-ROM) is aimed at schools and communities who want to work together to set up Aboriginal languages programs. It offers tips and advice on successful teaching of languages in schools.

- *Ripples from Wave Hill Part 1 and 2—Message Stick* (ABC, 2009) is the definitive account of Australia's first successful land rights campaign as told by the Gurindji people of the Northern Territory, who took on one of England's richest men, the beef baron Lord Vestey. Their 1966 strike on Australia's biggest cattle station became one of Australia's longest industrial disputes and gave rise to a national movement. Their victory was a pivotal event in Indigenous land rights and as such is crucial to convey to Australian students.
- *Bringing Them Home* (2007) is a must-see DVD for every Australian student to understand the history and the impact of past government policies on the children of the Stolen Generations. A moving experience that sensitises students to the key issues. Available free from the Australian Human Rights Commission at <http://www.hreoc.gov.au/education/bth/teaching_materials/t_DVD_activity.html>.
- *Walking Together* (Council for Aboriginal Reconciliation) is an introduction to the role of the Council. *Talkin' Business* (Council for Aboriginal Reconciliation) explains the Council's consultation program, vision, and key issues. *Talking Together* (Council for Aboriginal Reconciliation) records the views of four Australian women on the importance of healing the relationship between Indigenous Australians and other Australians. A compilation video of all three of these videos is also available. It also shows the historically significant Redfern Park Statement by Paul Keating, which is vital for every Australian student to see and critically analyse. May be available in school and council libraries, but otherwise can be difficult to find.
- *Mabo—Life of an Island Man* (Screen Australia, 1997). This documentary on the life of Eddie Mabo screened nationally on ABC TV on 12 November 1997 after an extended national theatrical release viewed by over 7000 people. The film has been invited to screen at many international film festivals, most recently to much acclaim at Australia Week at the Denver Film Festival. On 3 June 1992, six months after Eddie 'Koiki' Mabo's tragic death, the High Court of Australia upheld his claim that Murray Islanders held Native Title to land in the Torres Strait; the legal fiction that Australia was empty when first occupied by Europeans had been laid to rest. It tells the private and public stories of a man so passionate about family and home that he fought an entire nation and its legal system. Though his great victory was won only after his death, it has forever ensured his place on Murray Island and in Australian history. A study guide can be downloaded from Screen Australia's website at <www.screenaustralia.gov.au>. There is also a catalogue section that contains a range of related resources.
- *Best Kept Secret* (Blackout, ABC TV, 1991) is the profile of award-winning Aboriginal singer/songwriter Archie Roach and his late wife Ruby Hunter. Archie was part of the Stolen Generations. His life is told through narrative, music and re-enactments.
- *Black Man's Houses* (Ronin Films, 1992) is the a story of racism, survival and the revision of history. It explores the meaning of being Aboriginal and whether or not the Tasmanian Aboriginal people really died out with the death of Truganini in 1876.
- *1967—Citizens at Last?* (ABC, 1997) describes the struggle of Indigenous Australians to lobby the government to hold the referendum that would give them citizenship.
- *Stolen Children* (ABC, 1997): two Indigenous Australians talk about their experiences of being separated from their families and culture.
- *Lousy Little Sixpence* (Ronin Films, 1982) portrays aspects of the lives of five Aboriginal Elders who lived in New South Wales from 1900 to 1946 and illustrates Aboriginal political history. Includes the 1938 First Fleet re-enactment.
- *Women of the Sun* by Hyllus Maris and Sonia Borg (Ronin Films, 1981) (57 to 60 minutes per part), is a series of four videos that re-enacts aspects of Australia's history. Much dialogue in Episode 1 is spoken in an Aboriginal language with English subtitles.
- *An Act of Justice: The Mabo Judgment and the Native Title Act* (10 minutes, ATSIC) provides a useful introduction to the historical background and issues involved in the *Native Title* decision. Available at <www.

- glc.edu.au/AnActOfJustice.html> on <http://nla.gov.au/anbd.bib-an21360824>.
- *Frontier* (ABC TV, 1997) is a series of five episodes examining Australia's history from primary resource material. This is a superb classroom resource that can provide a springboard for a wealth of activities.
- *Koori: A Will to Win* (50 minutes) (Screen Australia, 1987) visually depicts Australian history through the experiences of James Miller's family. Available at <www.afc.gov.au/filmsandawards/filmdbsearch.aspx?view=title&title=KOORIA>.
- *Munyarl Mythology* (20 minutes) (University of New South Wales, 1996) is designed to introduce and debunk some of the myths about Indigenous Australia.
- *You Can Do It Too* (Curriculum Corporation, 1996) comprises a video and booklet that demonstrate how urban, rural and remote Australian schools have incorporated Aboriginal Studies and perspectives across the Key Learning Areas.
- *Babakiueria* (30 minutes, re-released on DVD) is a satirical presentation that examines questions concerning past and present treatment of Aboriginal people. The video begins with an Aboriginal captain landing in Sydney amidst a group of non-Aboriginal people having a barbecue and claiming the country as 'Babakiueria' (i.e. barbecue area). Shows the other side of the fence in a hilarious manner. One of our favourite resources.
- *French Connection*: Musee Du Quai Branly is a new museum featuring Australia's Indigenous artworks in Paris, France. This DVD follows key Aboriginal artists as they prepare their works to be featured in this new museum.
- *Message Stick—Lest We Forget*. This DVD pays tribute to the contribution of Indigenous servicemen and women—many of whom earned highly distinguished honours—who have served in every conflict since the turn of the nineteenth century.
- *Intervention, Katherine, NT* (Ronin Films, 2008) (52 minutes). A one-year-on record of the impact of the federal government's Emergency Intervention in the Northern Territory region of Katherine and the surrounding communities of Beswick, Barunga, Eva Valley and Binjar.
- *Intervention: Stories From The Inside* (Ronin Films, 2009), (46 minutes). An incisive inside look at the historic Intervention by the federal government in Aboriginal communities in the Northern Territory, made with the participation of Alice Springs town-campers.
- *Kabbarli* (Ronin Films, 2003) (50 minutes). Kabbarli explores the extraordinary life of Daisy Bates and her passionate involvement with Australian Aborigines. The film interweaves fiction and biography, history and memory to explore Daisy Bates's life—a dramatic map of the colonial imagination, and a portrait of a remarkable and wily old woman.
- *Lest We Forget* <http://shop.abc.net.au/browse/product.asp?productid=901456>
- *French Connection*: Musee Du Quai Branly. <http://shop.abc.net.au/browse/product.asp?productid=900856>
- *Intervention*, Katherine, Northern Territory. <http://www.roninfilms.com.au/feature/1087.html>

Films

- The *Chant of Jimmie Blacksmith—30th Anniversary Edition*. Producer and Director: Fred Schepisi. The Film House Pty Ltd. Based on a novel by Thomas Keneally, which was inspired by real events, this Australian classic film is the shocking tale of an oppressed Indigenous man driven to madness and revenge.
- *Rabbit-Proof Fence*. A clip with teachers' notes is available at <http://australianscreen.com.au/titles/rabbit-proof-fence/clip1>. Producer and Director: Phillip Noyce. Screen Australia.

  Following is an excerpt from <www.eniar.org/pdf/Rabbit-proofFence.pdf>, a study guide for the film.

  > *Rabbit-Proof Fence* is a powerful film based on the true story and experiences of three young Aboriginal girls, Molly, Gracie and Daisy, who were forcibly taken from their families in Jigalong, Western Australia in 1931. The film puts a human face on the

> **Plenty Stories**
>
> *Plenty Stories* is a collaboration between Pearson Australia educational publishers and the National Museum of Australia (NMA). A pack of specially written books for primary schools includes: *Discovering Aboriginal Australia; Keeping Strong Through Art; Keeping Language Alive; Celebrating Survival Day; Fighting for Rights; Special Objects; Indigenous Sporting Greats; Caring for Country; Our Stories Through Art; Making A Difference; Unsung Hero*, and many others. Also included in Plenty Stories class packs are Teacher Resource Books, with curriculum links for all States and Territories, background information and advice on further research, learning activities; and poster packs. <www.nma.gov.au>

'Stolen Generations', a phenomenon which characterised relations between the government and Aborigines in Australia for much of the twentieth century. The girls were taken away to be trained as domestic servants at the Moore River Native Settlement, north of Perth. This was consistent with official government assimilationist policy of the time decreeing that 'half-caste' children should be taken from their kin and their land, in order to be 'made white'.

- *Ten Canoes*. This is an acclaimed comedy about forbidden love and Aboriginal life before Europeans arrived, narrated by Australian icon David Gulpilil and starring his son, filmed in the Arafura Wetlands of Central Arnhem Land. Producers: Rolf de Heer and Julie Ryan. Palace Films.
- *Samson and Delilah* (2009). Producer: Kath Shelpin. Footprint Films. Samson and Delilah are teenagers living in a remote community in central Australia. Delilah cares for her Nanna, an artist who has been exploited by art dealers; Samson leads an aimless, petrol-sniffing existence. The two leave the community for Alice Springs on a road trip conducted first in a stolen car and then on foot; they are under the permanent threat of violence, alcohol and drugs even as they learn to care for each other. Won the Camera d'Or Prize at Cannes 2009, nominated for an Oscar 2010.

Books

- *Talk Softly, Listen Well: Profile of a Bundjalung Elder* by Uncle Charles Moran as told to Glennys Moran (2004). As a young boy growing up in Northern New South Wales, Uncle Charles Moran was taught the traditional ways of his people, including the need to 'listen well'. By listening to the Elders who were there to guide him, he learned about resourcefulness, initiative, responsibility, self-reliance and respect—ways to live in harmony with the natural and cultural environments he inhabited. Now, as a respected Bundjalung Elder himself, he shares his wisdom and experience and is especially renowned for his work with youth and the sufferers of asbestos mining-related diseases. This is a rare book that gives insight into the wisdom of a highly respected Elder.
- *Portraits From a Land Without People* (2009)—is a pictorial anthology of Indigenous Australia 1847–2008. A history of Indigenous Australia through photography.
- *Treading Lightly: The Hidden Wisdom of the World's Oldest People* by Karl-Erik Sveiby and Tex Skuthorpe (2006). This book shows how traditional Aboriginal stories and paintings were used to convey knowledge from one generation to the next, about the environment, law and relationships. The book offers a powerful and original model for building sustainable organisations, communities and ecologies.
- *Conversations with the Mob* by Megan Lewis and Kate McLeod (2008). Photojournalist Megan Lewis went to live with the Martu people—one of the last Indigenous groups in Australia's vast Western Desert to come into contact with Europeans. Through a stunning collection of photographs and oral stories, this book captures the beauty, humour, sadness and friendship of a traditional Aboriginal tribe at odds with Western culture.
- *Riding the Black Cockatoo* (for teenagers) by John Danalis (2010). The inspiring true story of one man's reconciliation journey based on the author's reflections. All through his growing-up years, John Danalis's family had an Aboriginal skull on the mantelpiece; yet only as an adult did he ask where it came from and whether it should be restored to its rightful owners. This book is about his journey to return Aboriginal remains to the community and sends a powerful message about reconciliation and Indigenous culture.

Teachers' notes and reviews of the text are available on Allen & Unwin's website.
- *Freedom Ride* by Ann Curthoys (2002). The story of Australia's historic Freedom Ride, the 1965 bus journey into the heart of the country to fight racism, from one who was there.
- *Maralinga: The Anangu Story* (for children) (2009) is an illustrated history told from the Indigenous perspective and created through a series of workshops, extensive research and community consultation. In words and pictures, Yalata and Oak Valley community members, with author Christobel Mattingley, describe what happened in the Maralinga Tjarutja lands of South Australia before the bombs and afterwards.
- *The Education Movement: A people's history of the AECG* by Nigel Parbury. A history with pictures of the growth of the New South Wales AECG, with chapters on Aboriginal education before the invasion and before the AECG. The book includes the words of people who were and are involved and a timeline history. It is richly illustrated with great photos. <www.aecg.nsw.edu.au>.
- *Yirra and Her Deadly Dog, Demon* by Anita Heiss, Adam Hill and the kids of La Perouse Public School (2007) is a story about a very naughty dog called Demon owned and loved by Yirra. This book is madcap fun and gives young readers a contemporary view of urban Indigenous life in Sydney.
- *Where is Here?—350 Years of Exploring Australia* by Tim Flannery (2007) traces the history of the exploration of Australia starting with Indigenous Australians. This book is great because it is designed for school children and is often told through the diaries of explorers.
- *An Australian 1, 2, 3 of Animals* by Bronwyn Bancroft (2009a) is a stunning book beautifully illustrated by one of Australia's leading Aboriginal artists. It provides an introduction to the numbers 1 to 15.
- *An Australian ABC of Animals* by Bronwyn Bancroft (2009b) is a must-have book for classrooms. It introduces the alphabet and some Australian wildlife through lavish illustrations.
- *Malu Kangaroo* by Judith Morecroft and Bronwyn Bancroft (2008) is a poignant story about how people first learn to surf. This one has become a classic in classrooms around Australia.
- *Possum and Wattle* by Bronwyn Bancroft (2009c) contains over 100 words about Australia and is aimed specifically at children. The book is designed to celebrate the uniqueness of our country and words.
- *Deadly Australians* by Rhonda Craven and James Wilson-Miller (2003). Deadly is a word many Aboriginal Australians use to mean cool, tops, great or outstanding. *Deadly Australians* is a book about some very deadly, successful Aboriginal Australians. It provides inspirational role models.
- *First Australians: An Illustrated History* by Rachel Perkins and Marcia Langton (2009) is an illustrated history of Australia that accompanies a major seven-part television series broadcast on SBS TV. This is the story of the violent clash of cultures at the heart of Australia's history, drawing on a rich collection of historic documents and haunting images.
- *Darby: One Hundred Years of Life in a Changing Culture* by Liam Campbell (2006). Born in the bush, Darby Jampijinpa Ross lived through a time of great change for his people and died the day after his hundredth birthday. He survived the deaths of his family in the 1928 Coniston massacre before travelling widely around Australia. He was a successful artist and strong advocate for Aboriginal law and culture. This book provides fascinating insights into his life and achievements.
- *Issues in Society* (The Spinney Press, <www.spinneypress.com.au>) is a most valuable series, featuring up-to-date information on contemporary social issues including Indigenous and race issues. Each volume is a compilation of news, facts, opinions and statistics relating to a specific social issue, ideal for student use for essays, assignments, debates and as teaching aids. Contents include news, fact sheets, website material, magazine features, lobby group publicity, journal and book extracts, graphics, cartoons, photographs, government report extracts, statistics, opinion and newspaper features. Titles include: *Indigenous health; Multiculturalism in Australia; Aboriginal Reconciliation; Indigenous Australians and the Law;*

- *Native Title and Land Rights; Indigenous Disadvantage & Racial Discrimination;* and *Stolen Generations—The Way Forward*.
- *The Encyclopaedia of Aboriginal Australia*, edited by David Horton (1994), is a comprehensive reference on all aspects of Australian Aboriginal and Torres Strait Islander history, society and culture. It is also available on CD-ROM. Australian Institute of Aboriginal and Torres Strait Islander Studies (AIATSIS).
- *Father Sky and Mother Earth* by Oodgeroo Noonuccal (2007) is a delightful conservation story that can readily be converted into a performed play for younger students. Also available in a 'big book' version.
- Life stories are an invaluable resource: *My Place* by Sally Morgan (1999) and *My Place for Young Readers* by Sally Morgan (2005), edited by Barbara Ker Wilson, a useful adaptation of the original book; *Oodgeroo: A Tribute*, edited by Adam Shoemaker (1994), and *Oodgeroo* by Kathie Cochrane (1994) are invaluable for gaining an insight into the remarkable achievements of Oodgeroo Noonuccal. *Don't Take Your Love to Town* by Ruby Langford Ginibi (2007) is a powerful, true story of an Aboriginal woman's struggle to raise a family of nine children in a divided society; many Aboriginal women have similar stories.
- *The Rainbow Serpent* by Oodgeroo Noonuccal and Kabul Noonuccal (1995) is a retelling of a Dreaming story about the Rainbow Serpent. Could be adapted for a drama activity in your school.
- *Our Land Is Our Life: Land Rights—Past, Present and Future*, edited by Galarrwuy Yunupingu (2008) is a collection from the 1996 20th anniversary 'Our Land Our Life' land rights conference at Old Parliament House, Canberra. These essays present both insight and visions for the coexistence of Indigenous and non-Indigenous Australians, as well as living history from people who made history, highly esteemed leaders including Noel Pearson, Marcia Langton and Galarrwuy Yunupingu. It has an introduction from the then Governor-General, Sir William Deane.
- *The Way We Civilise: Aboriginal Affairs— The Untold Story* by Rosalind Kidd, (1997) does not just tell a history of 'savages' and 'natives', but restitutes Aboriginal people as human beings with a knowable and known past.
- *The Fat and Juicy Place* by Diana Kidd (1992), illustrated by Bronwyn Bancroft, is endorsed by the New South Wales AECG. Ideas for this book came from Aboriginal people's stories through the author's attendance at community meetings and the final draft of the text was edited by the AECG. It was shortlisted in 1993 by the Children's Book Council of Australia and won the Australian Multicultural Children's Book Award. Still one of the best books for upper primary and junior secondary classes. Also available as an audiotape.
- *Black Chicks Talking* by Leah Purcell (2004) features nine successful young Aboriginal women telling their stories to Leah Purcell.
- *From Little Things Big Things Grow* book (2008) shares the title of the iconic song by Paul Kelly and Kev Carmody about the historical events of 1966, when Vincent Lingiari led his people to walk off the job at Wave Hill station. A nine-year struggle ensued to get their land back, until 1975 when Gough Whitlam poured earth into Vincent's hands as a symbol of giving the land back. This book is a tribute to Vincent, and to Frank Hardy, the writer who told the story.

Reading kits

- *Indij Readers Series*. Indij Readers is a not-for-profit company that develops and publishes contemporary, Indigenous literacy materials for Indigenous and non-Indigenous students who are learning to read and write. *Indij Readers for Big Fullas and Little Fullas* is a collection of literacy acquisition classroom stories, accompanying teachers' guides and other support materials (CD/audio, VHS/DVD film). The collection comprises stories from urban and rural communities around New South Wales and Victoria.

  The aim of the Indij Readers stories is twofold: to help students learn to read; and to encourage and support teachers to explore with their students contemporary Indigenous perspectives and issues, and thus progress reconciliation in Australia. The stories deal in a relaxed and often amusing way with issues that affect the lives of all children: culture, family, self-esteem, pride, setting goals and working towards them, good health, humour, tolerance and school attendance.

Indij Readers is currently building on the success of the established school-based stories and lesson notes by developing a Community Writers' Kit (CWK). This will enable communities to develop their own culturally relevant, engaging and authentic reading resources. The professional development training delivered by Indij Readers with the CWK, 'How to make good story publication', will also give community education workers valuable expertise and skills. The elegance of this initiative is that it can grow independently in a community to reflect its unique attributes, and deliver more pragmatic outcomes such as an increase in capacity and social capital.

The Indij Readers include Series 1 (eleven books plus a teacher's guide), Series 2 (nine books—six of them also available in 'big book' format), plus a teacher's guide, an audio CD (raps), a ten-minute film (*Nan and Dad and Me at the Zoo*), and Series 3 (nine books and a teacher's guide). Each teacher's guide includes cultural notes, guided reading lesson plans and blackline masters for every book in the series.

- *Reconciliation (Scholastic Australia)*. Scholastic's 'Reconciliation' series incorporates an Indigenous perspective into the curriculum for lower, middle and upper primary. Its goal is to assist teachers and students in developing an appreciation of Indigenous culture and the process of reconciliation between Indigenous and non-Indigenous Australians.

Years of planning and research plus collaboration with various Indigenous bodies have helped Scholastic to produce this comprehensive resource, which includes inspiring stories, amazing photographs and artwork, as well as simple-to-follow activities. The complete program includes:
  – 33 student titles;
  – five big books;
  – eight high-quality glossy posters;
  – three audios, and
  – three teacher resource books (TRBs).

The series won the 2003 **Australian** Awards for Excellence in Educational Publishing.

Upper primary consists of:
  – ten student titles;
  – four high-quality glossy posters;
  – a Teacher Resource Book; and
  – an audio CD.

Poetry and plays

Our student teachers are constantly amazed at the insight they have gained from reading Indigenous people's poetry and plays. Like other Indigenous writings, these are resources that can stimulate discussion and convey a wealth of Indigenous viewpoints. Poetry and plays deal with a wide range of topics:

- *Little Eva at Moonlight Creek and Other Aboriginal Song Poems*, edited by Martin Duwell and R.M.W. Dixon (1994);
- *The Honey-Ant Men's Love Song and Other Aboriginal Song Poems*, by R.M.W. Dixon and Martin Duwell (1990);
- *Black from the Edge*, by Kevin Gilbert (1998);
- *Inside Black Australia*, edited by Kevin Gilbert, (1998) the first anthology of Aboriginal poems and a must for every teacher's resource shelf;
- *My People* (2007) by Oodgeroo Noonuccal, a must for every teacher's resource collection. Oodgeroo's hard-hitting poetry provides an Aboriginal perspective to many historical events and current issues;
- *Ngalga Ngalga* (Let's Talk) by Burraga Gutya (Canning, 1990), a collection of poems on contemporary issues;
- *Where There's Life There's Spirit* by Norm Newlin (1988), a collection of poems on various issues;
- *Mother's Heartbeat* (Ngudjung Yugarang) (2005): a collection of poems—The late Uncle Bobby McLeod was well known as a singer, songwriter, performer, writer and political activist, and now this book proves he was a talented poet as well; and
- *Plays from Black Australia* (Davis, 1989): by Jack Davis, Eva Johnson, Richard Walley and Bob Maza.

Cartoons

Students enjoy learning higher-level concepts from examining cartoons. Cartoons make learning fun and can stimulate the exploration of a range of issues. No teacher of Aboriginal Studies should be without the following (be warned—you won't be able to put these books down).

- *Beyond a Joke: An Anti-Bicentenary Cartoon Book*, edited by Kaz Cooke (1988), a humorous but hard-hitting look at issues that have affected Aboriginal people by a number of well-known Australian cartoonists.
- *200 in the Shade,* edited by David Swain (1988) is another excellent resource of cartoons from history.

Kits and other resources

- The *Australians for Reconciliation Study Circle Kit*, produced by the Council for Aboriginal Reconciliation and developed by the Australian Association of Adult and Community Education, is available from Reconciliation Australia. The kit contains a wealth of discussion activities examining the issue of reconciliation. It can readily be adapted for the classroom.
- *The Aboriginal Program Exchange Tape* distributes Aboriginal radio programs across Australia.
- *Frontier: Stories from White Australia's Forgotten War* is an ABC history CD-ROM based on the highly acclaimed ABC TV series. It shows the secret history of our country. The two-CD-ROM set is also available as an education edition that includes teachers' notes. Available from ABC shops—a synopsis is available online at <www.abc.net.au/frontier/stories/default.htm>.
- *Growin' Up Strong*—a lower to middle primary resource kit inspired by songs directly relating the experiences of Aboriginal children in Australia. The kit includes a teachers' resource book with blackline masters, a comprehensive map of Aboriginal Australia, six laminated posters, sixteen storybooks (four copies of four titles) and a music CD. Available from Scholastic Education.
- *Whole School Anti-Racism Project Resource Materials* help school communities challenge racism; they are 'designed to equip students, parents, teachers, administrators and local communities with practical strategies to actively speak out and challenge racism' (John Aquilina, New South Wales Minister for Education and Training, 1995). Available from New South Wales Department of Education and Training.
- *Invasion and Resistance: Untold Stories* (Board of Studies New South Wales). This kit is designed for secondary students and includes four booklets with information and teaching activities: *The Myth of Terra Nullius*; *Invasion and Resistance: Untold Stories*; *I Give This Story: Life Stories and the Telling of Aboriginal History*; and *Talking LaPa: A local History of La Perouse*. It also includes the video *Discovering Australia's Aboriginal History* and timeline maps depicting key historical events.

Songs and music

Music CDs by Indigenous musicians are an invaluable resource. Often the lyrics of songs are a form of poetry and express Indigenous viewpoints on a range of issues. Try writing a class play based on a sequence of different songs to tell a part of Australia's history from Indigenous perspectives.

- *Making Waves Hip Hop*. This is a compilation of contemporary black Australian hip-hop music through the eyes of some of our best hip-hop artists, who are determined to take a stance and make a difference.
- *Cannot Buy My Soul: The Songs of Kev Carmody* (2009) is a two-CD set—the first disc features Australian musicians paying tribute to Kev Carmody; the second is Kev Carmody singing his original songs. The album was put together by Paul Kelly, who describes Kev Carmody's body of work as one of our 'great cultural treasures, incorporating oral history, the ongoing hurt of dispossession and the healing power of nature... influential and highly regarded in all corners of the country'.

- *Overnighter*, by Neil Murray. Neil Murray is one of Australia's respected non-Indigenous songwriters. He has written countless classic songs, including the iconic 'My Island Home' made famous by Christine Anu, which was APRA Song of the Year. He was a member of the pioneering Aboriginal rock group the Warumpi Band and has forged a solo recording career, including the release of his album *Overnighter* in 2007.
- *Ngarraanga* by Emma Donovan. Emma was an original member of the vocal trio Stiff Gins. She includes her traditional Gumbayngirr language through her songs and educates people to help them understand more about Aboriginal culture and spirituality.
- *The Rough Guide to Australian Aboriginal Music*. This CD was compiled by leading Australian music journalist Bruce Elder. It provides a musical overview of the key issues faced by Aboriginal Australians, from country through to rock music. This album is dedicated to the memory of Alan Dargin, who passed away suddenly in 2008.

Helping students to detect bias

Despite recent advances in the development of resources, a plethora of readily available resources still reinforce misconceptions and stereotypes (see Chapter 3) about Indigenous Australia. These encourage students to adopt misunderstandings based on stereotypical generalisations. Such materials usually do not acknowledge the diversity of Indigenous Australia and often focus on a mythical view of past societies—what might be described as a 'boomerang and gunya' approach—whereby the vitality and richness of living cultures today is not considered (see Chapter 2). Such resources are not only insensitive but often highly offensive and insulting to Aboriginal communities. They can easily be identified, as they tend to examine Aboriginal Studies in a superficial manner, and facts are rarely included as the focus of content. Resources that are targeted at 'time-saving' and 'syllabus outcomes' are particularly dangerous. For example, some sets of blackline masters that purport to provide in-depth information for the use of teachers of Aboriginal Studies need to be regarded with deep suspicion and carefully evaluated.

The National Aboriginal and Torres Strait Islander Studies (NATSIS) project developed selection criteria for the evaluation of Aboriginal Studies and Torres Strait Islander Studies materials: questions to ask, things to look for and action to take when evaluating materials. In some instances, examples of words and phrases found in unsuitable material have been given. It is also useful to have a developed selection criterion for Aboriginal Studies resources. Examples can be found at the following sites: <www.aboriginaleducation.sa.edu.au/pages/Educators/criteria/> and <www.neutralbay-p.schools.nsw.edu.au/library/infobias.htm>. A more general set of protocols for dealing with issues associated with Indigenous people can be found at: <www.cdu.edu.au/library/protocol.html>.

Of all of the issues that confront teachers of Aboriginal Studies at whatever level, perhaps the most vital (and this is not limited to this area—it can infuse a school curriculum) are those associated with bias, stereotype and prejudice. This can be evident in a variety of ways, in terms of behaviour, structure and text. Teachers need to be aware of the potential for all of the above to be evident in resources. It is vital that students be provided with the skills to be able to detect bias in resources—and for teachers to have the skills to teach them.

Text needs to be read *critically* by both teacher and student in order for intention to be identified. A useful and general book that provides a background in this area is Burnett, Meadmore and Tait (2004): *New Questions for Contemporary Teachers taking a Socio-cultural Approach to Education*. A useful website for critical questioning of text, titled *Cultural Bias—Can You Recognise it?* can be found at: <www.neutralbay-p.schools.nsw.edu.au/library/infobias.htm>.

This site provides a comprehensive set of critical questions that will enable students to develop a critical stance towards resources that claim to support Indigenous Studies. As a useful 'value-added' approach, these questions can be modified to assist students to identify bias in other areas as well.

When students have become familiar with the critical skills necessary to be able to effectively evaluate a resource, it means that they can be presented with resources that are culturally biased and historically narrow, so that they can begin to develop understandings about the ways in which Indigenous peoples have been constructed by powerful external groups over time, and begin to consider ways in which these inappropriate and harmful biases can be negated (also see box below).

Finally, it is important to remind ourselves that it does not matter how well developed, sensitive and engaging a resource is, it can only have limited value if the context in which it is made available to students is inappropriate. A resource is much more than the sum of its parts, because it can only be effective if the learning environment in which it is made available is one that provides students with opportunities to make the best possible use of it. This means that teachers need to consider the relationships that are developed, the way in which the learning space is organised and the atmosphere that is fostered within it, as well as the sorts of resources that are to be made available to students.

Importantly, teachers need to be aware of the developmental context within which resources are being introduced. All effective learning must take into account the capacity of students to engage effectively with learning activities. To be worthwhile, any resource must be relevant to the developmental stage of the learner, presented in such a way as to stimulate interest, provide opportunities for students to develop positive values about their learning, and to develop and enhance the critical skills necessary for positive engagement with Indigenous Studies. This is critical in the primary years of schooling, but remains vitally important in the secondary years as well.

Summary

In this chapter we have examined a sample of the teaching resources available. Indigenous community members are often the best 'resources' for up-to-date information based on real-life experiences. Community members bring the content to life for students and readily convey the consequences of our history. This helps students to understand the relevance of the subject area for understanding critical contemporary social concerns and empathise with Indigenous people's viewpoints. Community-devised resources provide invaluable local studies perspectives to the curriculum and are usually inexpensive to create. Appropriate multimedia resources are becoming increasingly available and, with the advent of the internet, a wealth of information can be accessed almost instantly. This is where critical approaches to resources become vital.

As mentioned, the resources we have mentioned are only a sample of those available. Every competent and sensitive teacher can teach Indigenous Studies effectively by using the best available resources to design relevant activities according to the needs of their students and Indigenous communities.

Sample activities for detecting cultural bias

Students can:

- act out/rewrite a scene/event from an alternative viewpoint (e.g. Captain Cook's landing at Botany Bay as viewed by Aboriginal people);
- rewrite dialogue in a more realistic/authentic way;
- offer alternative endings or resolutions to conflict;
- attempt to correct bias by further research, comparing different accounts of the same event, using primary sources;
- survey the diversity within the school community—how do the results compare with the information given in materials?
- compare materials in use now with those used ten years ago and, if possible, with those used by parents and grandparents;
- bring in examples of cultural bias that they have found: circulars, advertisements, photos of graffiti. Record it, keep a file, make a film or slide set;
- help to develop school-based resources—films, photoboards, slide sets, class books, case studies, community archive collections;
- develop their own list of criteria for detecting cultural bias;
- contact bodies such as the Anti-Discrimination Board or the Ethnic Affairs Commission. Find out what they do, what sorts of complaints they receive and how they attempt to resolve them;
- write to authors, publishers or producers expressing concern about bias or discriminatory materials;
- invite authors/filmmakers to come to the school to discuss their work.

Source: Extracted from McIntosh (1984)

15 Developing teaching activities

Rhonda Craven, Mark d'Arbon and James Wilson-Miller

Being able to develop worthwhile teaching activities based on sound learning principles is just as important as being knowledgeable about subject-matter and available teaching resources. In this chapter, we explore how to develop stimulating teaching activities based on sound principles of learning.

The role of the teacher as a facilitator

Two major historical events have had a significant impact on the role of the teacher in the European educational tradition. First, the printing press provided a much wider range of the population with access to texts; and second, the Age of Enlightenment proposed that all human beings were capable of guiding their own destinies.

The impact of these two events began the shift away from the idea of the teacher as controller and director towards the concept of the teacher as mentor and guide—a participant with learners in the process of education. Other influences and pressures have acted on cultural perceptions of 'the teacher' to the point where there are no longer any clear boundaries to the role. It could almost be said that the role of teacher is subject to the teacher's environment.

Bush Tragedy, late 19th century postcard photo by Star Photos. Aboriginal-subject photo postcards were highly popular at the time. Classes can be asked to 'read' the photo: what does it really show? Can the white man use his gun to shoot? as a club? Look at the Aboriginal man's left arm with the spear; who will win? Is this what the image was meant to convey? Courtesy Mitchell Library, State Library of New South Wales.

This 'freeing up' of perceptions of the teacher has allowed for the development of a range of learning environments, in which a teacher can make available to learners a variety of learning experiences that take into account individual learning styles. While direct instruction still has

> **Aboriginal kids reaching dreams**
>
> Given the attention, the human and practical resources and the belief in their ability to achieve in the classroom—in all areas of learning—Aboriginal kids have the same chance of reaching their dreams and goals as any other children. Teacher encouragement, support, nurturing and the willingness to understand that our kids want to learn and live complete lives once they know their options are the key to ensuring that they *will* be able to do just that. Don't write a child off without giving them the FULL capacity to learn from your end. Appreciate that they may be on the field but the playing ground is not level due to life situations and histories. Treat every child as an individual who needs to laugh, play, sing and have fun, while also needing the essentials of literacy and numeracy. Use their own role models to inspire them—local Aboriginal heroes in the community and national heroes from all walks of life—actors, musicians, painters, authors, doctors, lawyers, journalists, sporting heroes, and so on. Use resources that show Aboriginal characters, stories and ways of thinking.
>
>
>
> *Dr Anita Heiss has published non-fiction, historical fiction, chicklit, poetry, social commentary and travel articles. She is a regular guest at writers' festivals and travels internationally performing her work and lecturing on Indigenous Studies. From 1998 to 2004 she was on the executive of the Australian Society of Authors, and president 2008–09. She is an Indigenous Literacy Day Ambassador, a Books in Homes Ambassador, a board member of National Aboriginal Sporting Chance Academy and Adjunct Associate Professor at the University of Western Sydney, attached to the Badanami Indigenous Studies Centre. In 2007 and 2008, her works won Deadly Awards for Outstanding Contribution to Indigenous Literature:* Not Meeting Mr Right *in 2007, and the* Macquarie PEN Anthology of Indigenous Literature, *co-edited wih Peter Minter, in 2008. Her poetry collection,* I'm not racist, but . . . , *won the Scanlon Award for Indigenous poetry. She is a proud member of the Wiradjuri nation of Central New South Wales. Anita divides her time between writing, public speaking, MCing and as a workshop facilitator. She lives in Sydney.*

a place in the pedagogical quiver of strategies, it is no longer the foundation on which schooling is built.

The fierce questioning to which schooling has been put, as exemplified by Illich (1973), Freire (1972) and Neill (1971), has further diversified the perceived role of the teacher. In conjunction with developments and discoveries in the areas of child development, learning and curriculum theory, this has provided a window of opportunity for teachers to participate directly in the development of individual approaches to the teaching/learning environment.

Teaching as facilitating

The concept of the teacher as facilitator has emerged from the above influences, but there is significant debate regarding what is meant by the term 'facilitator'. Detractors of the facilitation model argue that a 'facilitator' is someone who 'lets things happen' and that, within this framework, learning structures, directions and outcomes become 'chancy' at best. Adequate and useful planning, they say, cannot occur within such a framework, and ultimately standards of educational achievement must suffer.

In fact, the task of facilitator in an educational setting requires a great deal of planning and preparation for success. A facilitator is not someone who 'lets things happen', but someone who organises the environment in a way that will enable students to learn as effectively as possible. Facilitation requires that the teacher has not only a sound understanding of learning theory but an intimate knowledge of the learners, including their prior experiences, home background within a cultural, social and environmental setting, and preferred learning styles. Obviously, it would be impossible for such a teacher to develop an effective teaching procedure in isolation from the communities from which learners come. Community participation in the development of appropriate learning environments must be fostered.

Stepping back

An important part of the role of the facilitator is the suspension of personal judgement. We cannot fully escape our backgrounds, particularly our cultural backgrounds. However, if the classroom is to be an environment where the range of experiences of students is to be valued, including the range of world-views expressed by children, the teacher needs to be able to step back from their own judgement.

Vital to the facilitation model is a secure and accepting environment in which a diversity of views can be explored and in which conflict resolution is encouraged, so that children have the opportunity to see an issue from perspectives other than their own. Within such an environment, children are encouraged to take responsibility for their own learning and to value the contributions of others.

By involving community members in the development of a non-judgemental environment, children can see that they are integral to a learning community that extends beyond the walls of the classroom. Sensitive and important issues that are significant not only to the children but to their communities can become learning experiences that permit children to become active participants in the search for preferred futures, while developing a balanced view of the actions of the past.

The teacher as a facilitator of Indigenous Studies

Teachers are not expected to be—and in fact should not be—the experts on Indigenous Studies; rather, their role is to facilitate children's understanding of the subject. In the Indigenous Australian Studies classroom, the role of the teacher as facilitator includes:

- recognising that teachers are not experts but co-learners. What distinguishes the teacher from other members of the learning community, apart from the requirements of the duty of care, is the ability to guide and advise. Through the creation of a learning environment based on trust and mutual respect, the teacher is able to facilitate understanding about issues under critical investigation;
- understanding that community involvement is essential to the development of a learning community. The traditional view of the teacher as controller has no place here, only a recognition of and respect for the expertise of Indigenous people;
- recognising that there are differences in learning styles and that, before designing activities that cater to these differences, teachers need to be aware of the children's backgrounds through consultation with their families, in the context of their communities;
- recognising the importance of matching pedagogy and methodology to the learner's needs;
- respecting Indigenous forms of knowledge and ways of knowing;
- recognising the diversity of views of Aboriginal and Torres Strait Islander peoples;
- allowing a diversity of views based on rational argument;
- fostering commitment for taking responsibility for the future; and
- being aware of world-views and value systems, and how these affect the ways we view and react to others.

Appropriate teaching strategies within a facilitation model

It is important to realise that education is not simply teaching—that in fact, within a facilitation model, the term 'teacher' is not necessarily attached to one person. It is a holistic, eclectic and continuous process that maintains a progress and life outside both the classroom and the school. The teacher's role within this setting is to enhance the educational possibilities by, as much as possible, ensuring that what happens in the classroom supports the educational setting.

Inevitably, teachers will need to be aware of the learning styles of students and, wherever possible, of the teaching strategies with which the student is familiar outside the class environment. While this is not an easy task, by establishing and maintaining effective two-way communication with students' families and communities, the teacher can gain important insight into a range of educational environments and even add to their own teaching repertoire. Negotiation within and outside of the classroom becomes an integral element of the learning process.

The prime rule to be observed in the development of appropriate teaching strategies is that there are no constants. The relationship between student, content, knowledge, skills, attitudes and values is constantly changing, and no one strategy is sufficiently flexible to cope with all the circumstances that arise during a normal teaching day—let alone a normal teaching year.

Positive modelling

As an educator, you will be key to our children's future. Call on local and regional role models, parents and community representatives to share their life's stories. Discuss Indigenous education challenges with your colleagues and community, brainstorm solutions and share positive education outcomes that are needed to unlock our children's potential for long-term career investments.

Life skill cycle

I believe there are three stages in the cycle of life skill development. The period from birth to 20 years is the foundation period of establishing the necessary learning values required for life. Stage 2 of the cycle, incorporating ages 21 to 40 years, makes up the refinement or enhancement periods of the life skill cycle. The third and final stage, ages 41 to 65 years, is the implementation period where you put into practice all that has been learnt in the previous 40 years of the life skill cycle.

Investing in our future

Indigenous heritage is not only culture, it is rich in tradition and history. Embark on your own cultural enrichment program. Learn to appreciate the humanity and connectedness of Indigenous culture. Invest your time in understanding Indigenous history, especially at the local and/or community level. This will be your cultural preparedness program to work with our children. At the same time, you will enrich yourself. From here you as an educator will be able to help improve outcomes for our children and be an agent of change to enhance the future for Indigenous people, and for Australia.

Bamboo direction and guidance

All children need direction and guidance, particularly in their early learning periods of life. It is from here that I feel that the life skills and learning values in education are developed. Like bamboo: if proper direction and training is not provided the bamboo will bend and grow in a manner that will make it difficult to straighten later.

Tat Whaleboat is a Torres Strait Island man, with family from Mer, Erub and Ugar Islands. Raised in Brisbane, he completed Year 12 at Coorparoo State High School, completed a trade in building and construction and began in 1990 as a Workplace Health and Safety Investigator with Queensland Industrial Relations. He has also been a workplace trainer for Indigenous community projects and managed inspector teams. He is an OHS consultant and workplace trainer for United Group Resources working in Western Australia. In his spare time he puts time and effort into sports management, has been an Indigenous Education Ambassador for DEST and is involved with Croc Festival.

Inquiry learning

Inquiry learning, in our view, is not so much an educational strategy as something all learners do naturally. It is the foundation of any program in which the learner 'owns' what is learnt. At its nub is the recognition that:

- for effective learning to take place, children need to see a reason (purpose) for the learning activity;
- the process of learning is as important as the product (and, at times, more so);
- learning processes are open ended—there may be no single 'correct' answer to a question, or solution to a problem; and
- there is more than one path to understanding.

An inquiry approach allows students to range across all learning areas in the search for solutions, and recognises that knowledge is a unity. It enables students to discover the range of learning tools emerging from particular disciplines, such as history and mathematics, while allowing the use of these specific tools in a holistic fashion. In fact, when an inquiry approach is adopted, the apparent boundaries between what we think of as 'disciplines' begin to collapse. Also, it permits the recognition of alternative ways of learning about the world, as the inquiry itself sets the parameters of what is useful. Teachers actively engage with issues to do with the nature of knowledge. This strategy fosters the development of perspectives, such as gender perspectives and Aboriginal and Torres Strait Islander perspectives, as it encourages paths to understanding and values development that are accepting of a variety of points of view.

It has long been recognised that learning is an integrated, if eclectic, activity. James Welton, in his foundational work published in 1914, puts it very well:

> As the child is gradually led into . . . wisdom, he [sic] is gradually enabled to understand his environment, is made acquainted with the typical relations of life, and is inspired with clear and generous ideas about them; he becomes capable of entering into the thoughts, and aspirations, and activities of his fellow-men, both as individuals and as smaller or larger communities; he reaches understanding of the physical world, and appreciation of its forms and beauty. And in this ever-widening process, his own individuality grows and develops: his powers are realised *only as they are exercised on appropriate material.* [our emphasis] (1914, p. 13)

This message has been repeated throughout the history of education, but is often ignored because of the perceived difficulty, particularly from a political point of view, of maintaining control of the learning process and the learner (and teacher). Adopting an inquiry learning approach requires that the teacher, while not relinquishing responsibility, relinquishes ownership of what is learnt and, to a certain extent at least, of how it is learnt.

The value of role-play

Role-play is one of the most powerful generators of understanding, and of attitude and value development. It provides a context within which children can engage, as completely as possible within a contrived environment, with social issues. Role-play is *not* impromptu acting. Participants attempt, based on input, to work through an issue in as real a fashion as possible. Insight gained through this activity can be transforming.

Because of its power, teachers need to be familiar with the processes and procedures of this strategy (see Role-play box). Because children particularly identify strongly with the roles they adopt, sensitivity is vital. Issues and situations that cause obvious distress or discomfort should be avoided. Children also need to be briefed before the role-play and debriefed after it.

Cooperative group techniques

Cooperative group techniques within the context of inquiry learning are strategies to encourage the development of a range of desirable skills and values. They include providing an environment in which children are encouraged to cooperate in the achievement of shared goals, and which allows them to recognise and use individual talents.

It is an area that lends itself to negotiated learning and fosters both group and individual ownership of work (see Group strategies box). Children share the responsibility of negotiating appropriate roles according to the activity or task in which they are engaged. With guidance, children are capable of selecting groups to which they would want to belong, although teachers need to be aware of classroom politics.

Cooperative group techniques can help teachers to negotiate the curriculum with students—to make learning activities relevant, enjoyable, purposeful and meaningful to them. When developing units of work, it is generally good practice for teachers to plan, structure and negotiate learning tasks and activities with students. This allows teachers to use a methodology that immerses students in relevant activities across the curriculum, and at the same time maintains student interest.

Teaching approaches

Indigenous Australian Studies can be taught in many ways. Up to the 1990s, most teacher educators advocated the use of a chronological approach—starting with the Dreaming/s and

Role-play lesson: model

Description

Role-play is the taking on and acting out of roles of real or imaginary individuals in varied, non-threatening simulated situations in order to clarify values and develop empathy with other people.

Strategies

Planning
1. Identify the objectives of the role-play—for example, to explore an issue using an inquiry method.
2. Select or design a role-play to achieve the desired objectives.
3. Consider the casting of students.
4. Arrange for necessary props.
5. Select a suitable venue for performing the role-play.

Managing
1. Explain the role-play to the whole class so that all begin from a common understanding of the situation.
2. Cast students, beginning with learners who are competent and relaxed. Acceptance of the role-play by some will give others more confidence. Avoid placing children in their usual life role as this can be self-defeating and will limit possible experiences for the child.
3. Brief the students:
    (a) Discuss the roles and how they might be played as a class.
    (b) Explain the audience role (i.e. effective observers of human behaviour).
4. Be prepared to intervene where necessary.
5. Redirect if an actor steps out of their role.
6. Stop the drama after main behaviours and points have been observed.
7. Re-enact parts of the role-play. A role-play may be stopped at any point and one or more new players, who have other ideas about certain roles, can be introduced.
8. Check that 'audience' class members are on task.
9. Question players (in character) immediately after role-play. The class may question players thus: How were you feeling? Why did you respond as you did? This leads to debriefing.
10. Debrief role-play participants. This is an essential step, as it helps players out of their roles. They must be disassociated from the role, both in their own eyes and the eyes of other children.
11. Include the role-play and subsequent discussion, and encourage students to reach certain conclusions leading to the formation of a class generalisation.

Evaluation of activity/strategy

Reflect on the following questions:

- Were the explanations adequate?
- Were the students placed in appropriate roles?
- Did the planned activities keep the audience involved?
- Was the classroom climate conducive to the exploration of issues and values?

Special considerations for this activity

- Role-play can occur through:
    (a) body language—particularly miming, which is valuable if students have limitations with language;
    (b) puppets—children can take on roles they may be reluctant to play as themselves.

progressing through various historical events up to the present. This was favoured as the traditional and 'right (logical) way' of teaching history. The fundamental defect of this approach is that Indigenous Australian Studies is not solely about history. The subject focuses on the complexity, diversity and dynamic nature of Indigenous issues and societies today, and investigates how they emerged by exploring the past. Also, Indigenous people have a different view of history. The multidisciplinary subject Social Studies incorporates studies of history but also draws on a wide range of disciplines, and is the main discipline from which Indigenous Australian Studies units are developed.

Social Studies is a useful basis from which to develop Indigenous Australian Studies units of work because, by its inclusive nature, it takes in such important disciplines as sociology, geography, economics, psychology, anthropology, cultural studies, sociology and history. Such an approach allows teachers to draw on a range of disciplines to explore significant content in appropriate depth and to reach understanding. Using Social Studies as a basis for developing activities also facilitates the examination of Indigenous Australian Studies in a holistic manner, which much more accurately reflects Indigenous world-views and pedagogy.

National consultations during the course of developing *Teaching the Teachers: Indigenous Australian Studies* materials have stressed that Indigenous educators generally prefer teachers to focus on units of work that examine Indigenous Australia now. This does not mean there is no need to develop a central core of activities to empower children to comprehend historical events; rather, history is used to critically analyse the forces that have shaped Indigenous Australia, and as such are the origins and basis of contemporary Indigenous issues. The purpose of this focus on Indigenous society and where it has come from is to provide an informed basis from which to predict more socially just futures for all Australians.

Indigenous Australian Studies, like Social Studies, involves teaching children to think, feel, value and act. The process of learning is just as important as the products of learning. Children need to think about contemporary issues. In today's schools, children want to learn about things happening in their world today, and in

---

Group strategies

Description

Group work is a teaching and learning strategy that encourages students to participate in achieving a shared goal. A range of grouping strategies is possible, the appropriateness of each dependent on the nature of the shared goal and the needs of the students. Successful group work gives students the opportunity to interact with each other and to value each member's contribution.

Strategies

1. Planning
   (a) Identify the task or purpose of the activity.
   (b) Decide on the structure of the group to suit the task or purpose (e.g. mixed homogeneous ability, friendship, interests or talents, needs).
   (c) Decide on the size of the group to suit the task or purpose and the students' level of group work skills (e.g. individuals, pairs, threes).
   (d) Consider students who should be grouped in certain ways to meet their particular needs and to foster positive group dynamics (e.g. students who are quiet, dominant, disruptive; students with special talents or disabilities; and students with diverse socio-cultural backgrounds).
   (e) Ensure that adequate resources are accessible to all groups.
   (f) Consider using additional spaces available inside or outside the classroom.
2. Managing
   (a) Ensure that the students are comfortable with initially working in pairs and smaller groups.
   (b) Ensure that students have experienced a variety of roles within various groups (e.g. leader, recorder, observer, researcher, artist) before being expected to negotiate their own roles.
   (c) Communicate the overall goal and the necessary tasks to be performed.
   (d) Clarify the parameters of the task (e.g. time available, conventions of group work, resources to be used).
   (e) Monitor group dynamics and progress; be flexible and be prepared to intervene and restructure if necessary.
   (f) Provide feedback to groups as they are working and at the completion of the activity.

Evaluation of activity/strategies

Analyse the students' interactions to determine the suitability of the size of the group and the tasks set, the clarity of the directions, and further experiences needed for individuals and groups.

Special considerations for this activity

Students gain significant academic and social benefits from being placed in mixed-ability groups. Avoid the use of homogeneous groups unless for specific purposes.

Adapted from New South Wales Board of Studies (1994).

Classroom display resulting from Koori Day at Mayfield West Demonstration School (NSW). Courtesy Mayfield West Demonstration School.

Indigenous Australian Studies there is a wealth of content of interest to children.

It is not enough merely to think about the complexity of key content examined; children need to explore their feelings in relation to the content explored. Reading newspaper articles about appalling health conditions in remote communities may provide children with knowledge, but knowledge alone does not guarantee students' empathy. If children feel nothing about an issue, they are unlikely to explore it in appropriate depth and unlikely to be motivated to recognise their power as individuals who can make a difference to Australian society.

We also want children to develop values as they progress through Indigenous Australian Studies units of work. For example, a child experiencing a ten-week unit of work with a range of stimulating activities should emerge with positive values that include respect for and appreciation of Australia's Indigenous cultures and an understanding of some Indigenous issues.

Similarly, if all we do is teach children to think, feel and value, we have only half-completed what we set out to do, for without commitment to social action, all the knowledge and positive feelings in the world will not be used to create a better Australia. Enabling children to develop and explore social action skills is a critical objective in the Indigenous Studies classroom.

What topics can non-Indigenous teachers teach?

Non-Indigenous teachers can develop stimulating teaching activities based on a wealth of content (see Examples box). Non-Indigenous teachers can help children to recognise that many people hold limited world-views that focus only on their own life experiences or hearsay about Indigenous society. By providing students with a factual knowledge base from which they can make informed decisions about society today, teachers can provide children with the foundations from which they can critically analyse Australian contemporary society. They can assist children to 'take the blinkers off' by

---

Examples of topics that can be taught by non-Indigenous educators

Wherever possible, activities should be developed, implemented and evaluated in consultation and with the participation of the local Indigenous community:

- contemporary issues;
- economic, political and social relationships;
- about belonging to the land;
- land rights;
- educational pedagogy and historical practices;
- futures perspectives;
- gender roles;
- historical events;
- about kinship;
- land and water usage and management;
- conservation;
- technology.

Examples of Cultural Studies topics that should only be taught by Indigenous people

The following topics should not be taught in schools except by appropriately qualified Indigenous educators if they deem it appropriate:

- ceremonial life, sacred symbolism, ritual, mystic language, sacred stories;
- spirituality;
- information about sacred artefacts;
- men's business and women's business.

facilitating knowledge and understanding about how Australian society came to be the way it is.

Just about every aspect of Indigenous Studies apart from the secret/sacred can and should be taught by teachers in Australian schools with maximum Indigenous involvement (see Examples box). Activities should always be developed in consultation and with the participation of the local Indigenous community wherever possible.

What topics should be taught only by Indigenous educators?

There are aspects of Indigenous culture that should be taught only by Indigenous educators (see Examples box). For example, many older texts contain information about ceremonies. Often this information is of a secret/sacred nature and only general aspects of the ceremony can be mentioned rather than the details of it. In the past, non-Indigenous texts and teachers have focused on ceremonies to emphasise the 'exotic' features of Indigenous society. Indigenous educators know the cultural parameters of teaching about culture and the social ethics involved when implementing activities associated with them.

Some aspects of Indigenous cultures can be taught only by women and other aspects can be taught only by men. Many aspects of Indigenous Studies reflect certain degrees of profoundness, such as men's business and women's business. Indigenous people of either gender can give an overall picture of these cultural aspects, but only the appropriate gender can qualify more fully the issues to do with their gender's specific business. Sometimes aspects of this knowledge can be shared only with children of the same gender as the Indigenous educator.

There are aspects of Indigenous culture that should not be taught to non-Indigenous children. For example, spiritual matters that are of a secret/sacred nature are not taught to non-Indigenous children and are often not taught to Indigenous children until they reach a certain age or stage of knowledge. Indigenous people are the custodians of their culture, so only Indigenous people can teach their culture. Cultural Studies includes topics of a sensitive nature that describe cultural beliefs and practices; as such, it should be taught only by Indigenous educators. Activities that involve students learning about ceremonial life are inappropriate if they are taught by a person with little or no knowledge of the specific purpose of the ceremony. Teachers need to have intimate knowledge of content before it is possible to teach students about it. Cultural Studies is best left to the experts. This will ensure that both Indigenous and other children are taught the appropriate aspects of Indigenous Cultural Studies according to their age and their right to know.

A theoretical model

In the Indigenous Australian Studies classroom, two key approaches are often used to develop units of work. One involves starting with a theme such as land rights and exploring contemporary and historical events in relation to this theme. Another involves developing units of work based on one or more key concepts. For example, focusing on the key concept *caring* could lead students to explore what Indigenous and non-Indigenous people care about today in the light of what people—Indigenous and non-Indigenous—cared about in the past. Both approaches are worthwhile and can be used as a springboard for developing stimulating activities.

Figure 15.1 is a theoretical model which reflects a holistic approach to developing Indigenous Australian Studies units of work. Three circle figures are depicted in an interconnected model to demonstrate the interactive nature of subject matter from each of the three circles—present, past, and futures perspectives. Futures perspectives are placed at the top of the model to denote the importance of developing teaching activities that will enable children to contribute to creating a better future for all Australians. The central arrow demonstrates that all aspects of the model need to be examined in the context of local, state/territory and national perspectives.

The model is designed to focus on contemporary society by designing units of work with a present perspective. Each unit of work should then deal with finding out how today's society was affected by past perspectives so that children

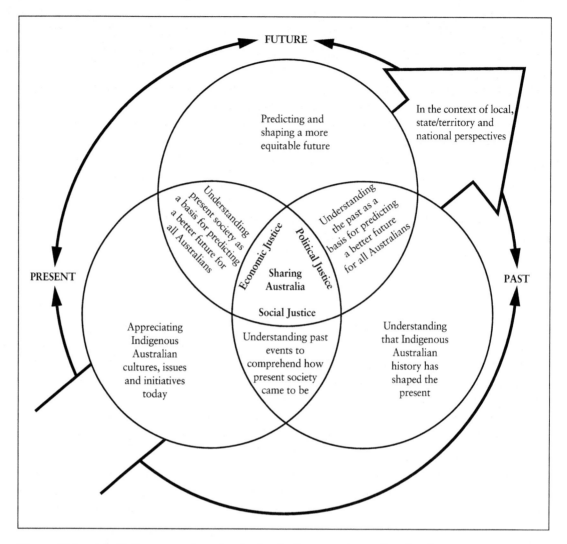

Figure 15.1 A holistic approach to developing Indigenous Australian Studies units of work

can understand how society came to be what it is. The model is based on the premise that in order to appreciate Indigenous culture and issues today, children need to understand the impact of history on Indigenous Australian societies. Understanding and respect for living cultures and knowledge and appreciation of Indigenous issues form the basis for planning and shaping future directions.

Within each circle of Figure 15.1, examples of content that could be incorporated in a unit of work are listed. The *present perspectives* circle depicts the need for children to appreciate Indigenous culture and issues today. While the content could be ordered in many ways to suit specific regional needs, it is depicted in this order to show the need for teachers to devise activities to enable children to:

- focus on Indigenous culture today and the achievements of Indigenous peoples today both at the beginning and throughout the unit of work; and
- examine any stereotypes or misconceptions they hold about Indigenous societies.

The *past perspectives* circle denotes the importance of integrating historical perspectives, stressing pre-invasion history as part of the full range of Indigenous experience in Australia, and chronologically exploring invasion and post-invasion history as the genesis of today's experience. Dreamings and the nightmare of invasion and colonisation need to be seen together as the full Indigenous history. In the past, there has been an over-emphasis on developing teaching activities that relate to pre-invasion history—as safely remote in time and space, and nothing to do with Indigenous people and issues now—rather than articulating content to incorporate invasion and post-invasion history. Aspects of history and all teaching activity topics should not be explored in isolation but related to present and future perspectives, as depicted by the overlapping nature of the circles in the model.

The *futures perspectives* circle advocates teaching activities that enable children to:

- understand the need for a real new partnership between Indigenous and non-Indigenous Australians;
- understand the importance of Indigenous self-determination—and why it is essential to a new partnership and for reconciliation; and
- contribute to predicting and thinking about how to create more equitable outcomes in Australian society.

The interaction of all elements of the model—present, past and future—leads children to understand the importance of all Australians sharing in social, political and economic justice. The model's interactive nature stresses that teaching activities need to be developed in a holistic way to explore present, past and futures perspectives rather than to isolate each area. This approach leads to a focus on society today rather than to a sole 'content' approach, and provides the foundation for children to be empowered to contribute to the creation of better futures for all Australians.

Ideas for a unit of work based on a theoretical model

The model can be used a basis for developing ideas for a unit of work. It is a helpful tool in assisting teachers to check that units of work contain a balanced approach in relation to the three key perspectives. Both thematic and key concepts-based approaches can easily be accommodated by the model.

Starting with a theme

There is a wealth of themes teachers could use as a basis for an Indigenous Australian Studies unit of work (see Themes box).

Here are some useful ways of starting:

- Choose your theme—where possible in consultation with your local Indigenous community.
- Write down as many ideas for activities with maximum community involvement using the theoretical model (Figure 15.1) as a trigger for ideas that relate to:
  - present perspectives;
  - past perspectives, making sure pre-invasion, invasion and post-invasion events are presented in a balanced approach; and
  - futures perspectives.
- Gather as many multimedia resources as possible that relate to the theme and add to your activities list.
- Write a summary of the order in which you will develop activities.
- Write up your unit of work in detail for your teaching program.

Figure 15.2 depicts some ideas for a Social Studies unit based on the theme of land rights. Such a unit could begin by examining land rights legislation today and some of the misconceptions and stereotypes related to this issue. Initiatives undertaken by Aboriginal Land Councils could also be explored. Historical events can be used to explain how land rights emerged as a crucial

---

Themes as a basis for developing units of work—examples
- Education
- Employment
- Health
- Housing
- Art
- Land management
- Land rights
- Local community studies, including local area history
- Maintaining culture
- Political activism
- Special treatment
- Technology

issue in today's society. Futures perspectives could consider what directions need to be undertaken to fully implement native title legislation, equitable outcomes in terms of land rights, how social justice is to be achieved, and how all these relate to *terra nullius*, native title and the *Wik* decision. Ideas for other units based on a theme could be developed in this manner (see Figure 15.3).

Starting with a key concept

Similarly, one can start with a key concept (see Key concepts box) as the basis for unit development. The concept can be used to link activities together. It is useful to ask students to define the key concept in the first activity to ensure they understand its meaning. Mentioning the key concept in every activity also helps children to relate each content area to understanding the concept under investigation more fully.

Getting started is just a matter of brainstorming ideas, but this time the ideas relate to a sequence of key areas. For example, in Figure 15.4 the concept *caring* is used as a basis for developing a unit; in Figure 15.5 it is the concept *belonging*.

Checking units

When beginning to develop units of work, it is important to check the overall unit structure. Beginning teachers can fall into the trap of getting lost in the detail of activity development rather than examining the overall structure of the unit to ensure the stated outcomes of the unit. A common mistake is to focus units on traditional societies. Such an inappropriate approach ignores the reality of our history and the consequences of our history for today's Indigenous peoples. Another common error is to not explore every content area in adequate depth: a 30-minute activity examining the role of the Council for Aboriginal Reconciliation is not going to be adequate for students to comprehend the range and complexity of issues associated with the process of reconciliation. Isolated activities that do not explore each content area in depth are highly unlikely to lead to students comprehending the full complexity of the subject-matter.

Balance is also needed when examining history. It is not enough solely to explore traditional pre-invasion history without addressing invasion and post-invasion history. A balanced approach, whereby an appropriate number of teaching activities are devoted to pre-invasion, invasion and post-invasion history, is needed to ensure students gain an appreciation of our actual history and comprehend how it has adversely affected Indigenous Australians today.

Teachers need to consider reflecting on the total unit structure before implementation to ensure stated outcomes are achieved. Activities need to be checked to make sure that they are interesting and pertinent to the topic under investigation, and that they explore content areas in depth. All activities need to be presented in such a way that learning *from* and *with*

Key concepts—examples
- Belonging
- Caring
- Respect
- Independence
- Responsibility
- Sharing
- Tolerance

Checklist for unit writing
- ☐ Is every activity interesting? Would I enjoy doing this task?
- ☐ Do I have maximum community involvement in teaching about present, past and futures perspectives to ensure that students are learning from Aboriginal people?
- ☐ Does every activity explore the content area in depth? (For example, only one teaching activity on reconciliation would not convey the meaning of reconciliation.)
- ☐ Do my activities begin with the present?
- ☐ Do my activities teach children about past events and relate them to today's society?
- ☐ Do my activities contain a balance of invasion, pre-invasion and post-invasion activities?
- ☐ Do my activities contain a balance of present, past and futures perspectives?
- ☐ Have I included activities that can help children to create a better future for all Australians?

DEVELOPING TEACHING ACTIVITIES • 301

Figure 15.2 Ideas for a unit of work based on a land rights theme

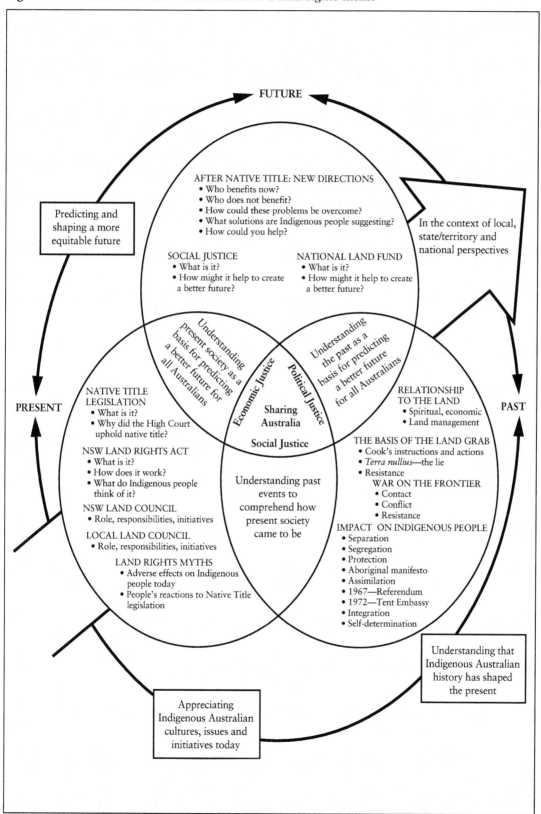

302 • TEACHING ABORIGINAL STUDIES

Figure 15.3 Ideas for a unit of work based on a special treatment theme

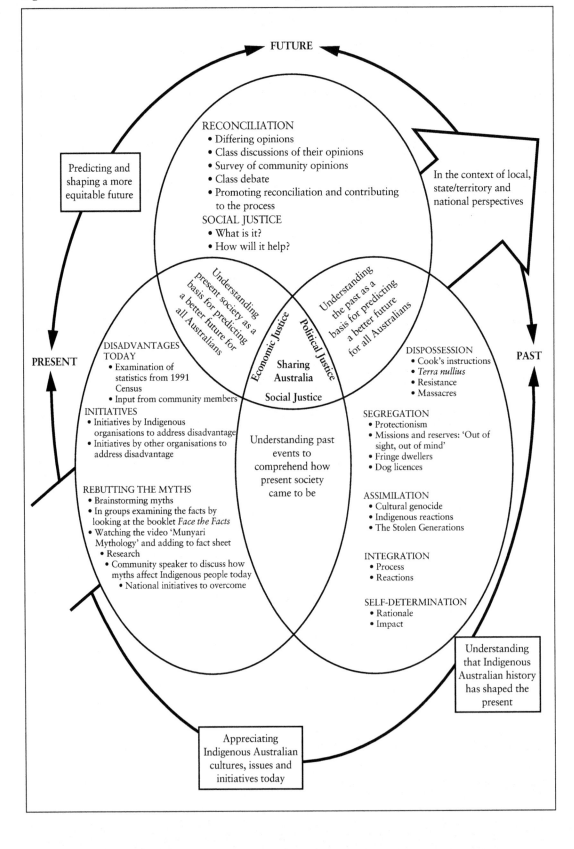

Figure 15.4 Ideas for a unit of work based on the key concept of *caring*

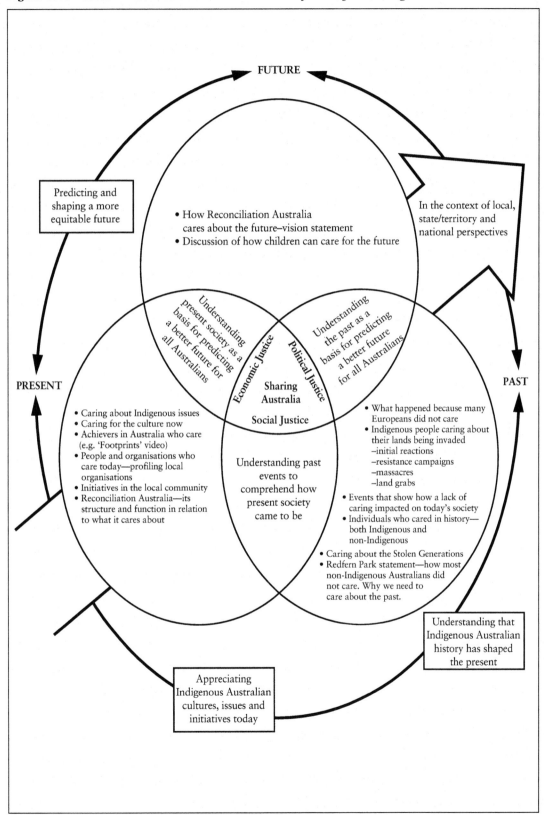

Figure 15.5 Ideas for a unit of work based on the key concept of *belonging*

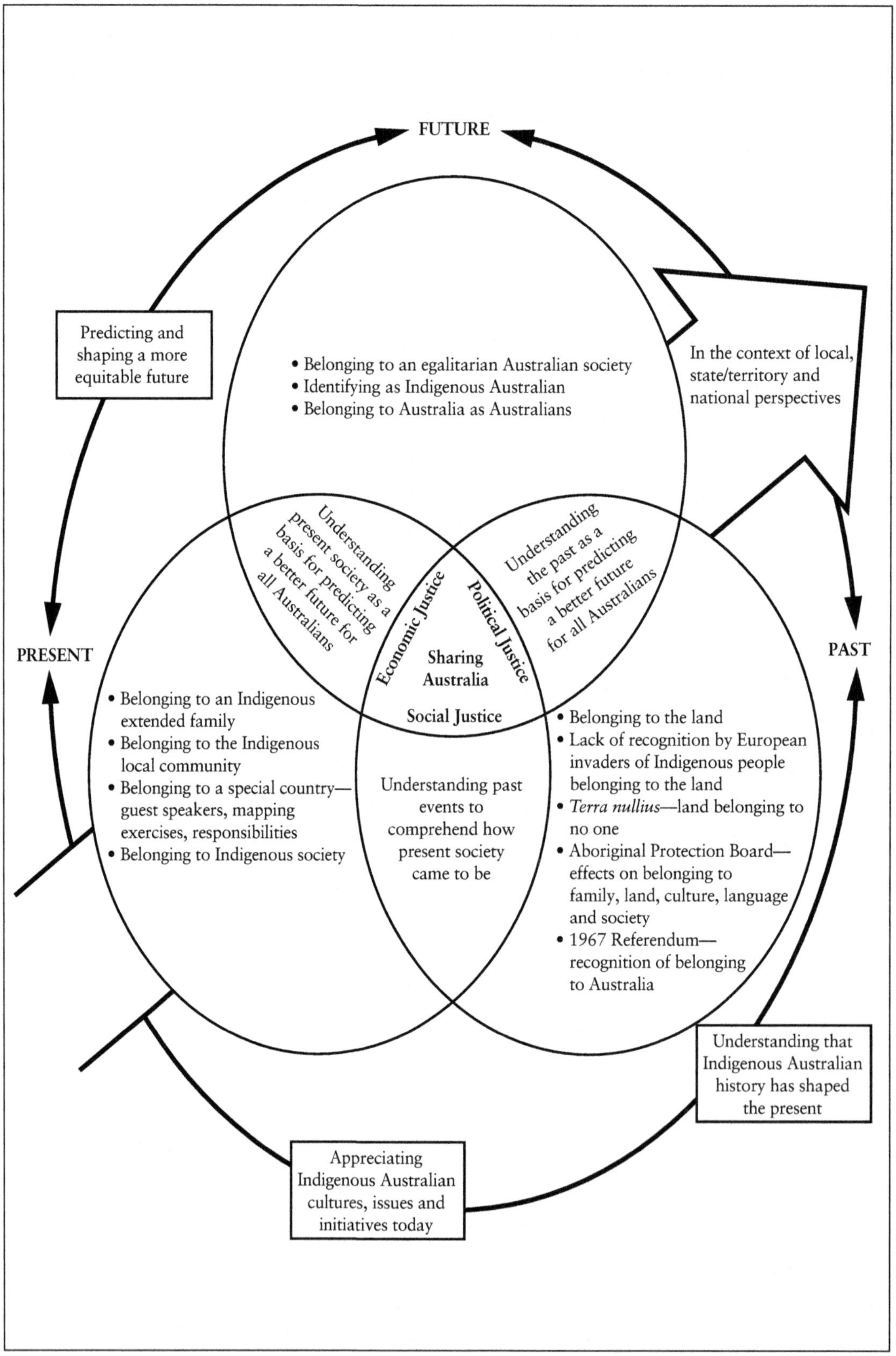

FUTURE
- Belonging to an egalitarian Australian society
- Identifying as Indigenous Australian
- Belonging to Australia as Australians

Predicting and shaping a more equitable future

In the context of local, state/territory and national perspectives

Understanding present society as a basis for predicting a better future for all Australians

Understanding the past as a basis for predicting a better future for all Australians

Economic Justice · Political Justice

Sharing Australia

Social Justice

Understanding past events to comprehend how present society came to be

PRESENT
- Belonging to an Indigenous extended family
- Belonging to the Indigenous local community
- Belonging to a special country—guest speakers, mapping exercises, responsibilities
- Belonging to Indigenous society

PAST
- Belonging to the land
- Lack of recognition by European invaders of Indigenous people belonging to the land
- *Terra nullius*—land belonging to no one
- Aboriginal Protection Board—effects on belonging to family, land, culture, language and society
- 1967 Referendum—recognition of belonging to Australia

Understanding that Indigenous Australian history has shaped the present

Appreciating Indigenous Australian cultures, issues and initiatives today

Indigenous people—as opposed to learning *about* Indigenous people—is maximised.

Structuring activities

In too many classrooms, children are engaged in the same kinds of activities each day—reading, writing and listening to teachers talk. But students learn in different ways, and many students do not learn by listening and reading; rather, they prefer to be actively engaged in the learning task (e.g. problem-solving, field trips, role-plays and predicting solutions). The activities that adults recall undertaking during their schooling are often of the type that engage learners in a specific task. Any active inquiry will often mean that children remember what they have learnt.

Understanding that different kinds of learning activities serve different functions can help teachers to design learning activities that will assist students to learn in a variety of ways, and therefore take account of individuals' preferred learning styles.

Intake activities

Some activities provide for intake of new information (see Table 15.1). These kinds of activities are essential for students, as they must have information to work with or think about before they can engage in action. Intake activities should be varied so that students can learn from as many information sources as possible. More than one intake activity should be included in a teaching unit for each content area under exploration. For example, if students are exploring the role of Reconciliation Australia, possible sources of information include:

- local reconciliation groups;
- views of members of the local Indigenous and non-Indigenous community on the rationale and process of reconciliation;
- Kevin Rudd's apology to the Stolen Generations;
- the Redfern Park statement;
- the *Encyclopaedia of Aboriginal Australia* on CD-ROM;
- the DVDs *Walking Together* and *Talking Together*;
- the *Australians for Reconciliation Study Circle Kit*; and
- information on the Reconciliation Australia website.

The nature of intake activities also means that teachers must actively locate information with which students will be working. Aboriginal Studies is not about students going out and finding out all the answers themselves. It is about teachers fostering high-quality learning by directing children to information sources. This means that before you write units you will need to find useful web resources, newspaper articles, primary source material, DVDs, posters, photographs, books, poems, etc. Discuss with your local Indigenous community the sources of information that are available, appropriate guest speakers and useful excursions. Surf the web to identify useful resources.

Organising

It is not enough for children just to take information in. When adults are listening to a lecture, some learn by listening, others by writing, others by reading handouts and others by looking at PowerPoint slides. Some adults organise information in summary notes.

Data must be organised in some way so that they can be understood. You cannot expect children to watch a DVD and assume that they understand its contents. Like adults, children need time to organise this new information. This means that after every intake activity, an organising activity needs to be included (see Table 15.1).

Demonstrative activities

Students need to display the skills they possess to demonstrate how well they can think, and to indicate how well they understand the actions, problems and feelings of others. This helps teachers to evaluate student progress. Demonstrative activities involve students showing that they understand what they have learnt (see Table 15.1).

Table 15.1
Types of learning activities

Intake	Organise	Demonstrate	Express
Reading	Outlining	Role-playing	Solving problems
books	Chart-making	Discussing	Inventing new uses for things
magazines	Graphing	Writing	Composing songs or poetry
articles	Mapping	Drawing	Writing reports or stories
newspapers	Timelines	Question-asking	Role-creating
labels	Building	Reporting	Miming
advertisements	Diagramming	Explaining	Painting
pamphlets	Arranging	Analysing	Question-forming
posters	Note-taking	Generalising	Cartooning
handbills	Filing	Building	Hypothesising
Observing (looking, watching, seeing, photographing)	Question-answering	Singing	Predicting
films	Question-asking	Dancing	Drawing
slides	Stating	Modelling	Singing
videotapes	Restating	Describing	Dancing
pictures	Summarising	Debating	Photographing
drawings	Writing	Photographing	Proposing
paintings	Identifying	Reacting	Building
photographs	Categorising	Storytelling	Creating a mural
people	Choosing	Preparing murals	
buildings	Recording	Applying	
television	Ordering	Sketching	
different environments	Sorting	Choosing	
Listening to			
records/cassettes			
guest speakers			
lectures			
music			
debates			
discussions			
radio			
Touching			
objects			
artefacts			
buildings			
natural environments			
Interviewing			
speakers			
friends			
parents			
other adults			
Tasting			
foods			
liquids			

Expressive activities

A fourth type of activity enables children to express themselves by creating or producing an original product (see Table 15.1)—for example, writing a poem/song/report, building a model, illustrating an idea.

Though demonstrative and expressive activities overlap, demonstrative activities ask students to demonstrate the degree to which they understand the data they have previously acquired and organised. Expressive activities encourage students to use their newly acquired understanding to produce a new and different product or to render an original performance.

Ordering and setting out activities

Intake activities should always be followed by one or more further activities to enable students to organise the new knowledge they have acquired. Generally, organising activities are followed by demonstrative or expressive activities, so that students have the opportunity to show that they understand the new information conveyed.

Combinations to avoid include following an intake activity with another intake activity, or with a expressive activity or demonstrative activity. These sequences do not allow the students to organise the new information they have learnt.

All teachers develop their own way of setting out activities in a unit of work based on their personal teaching philosophy. One approach that has successfully been used by student teachers appears in the IODE activities box, and some hints for setting out activities using this approach appear in the box on this page.

Assessment and evaluation

Assessment and evaluation are a vital part of the educator's toolkit. They are carried out in order to determine the effectiveness of both teaching and learning, and are vital in establishing the relationship between what has been learnt and what will be learnt next.

Girls at the Vibe Alive festival in Port Augusta 2009 working together on their Vibe Alive Putting It Together *workbook. Courtesy Vibe Australia.*

IODE activities: setting out

Contributing question: _____
Outcomes and pointers:
Knowledge and understandings
Skills
Values and attitudes

- Write the four IODE activities as headings.
- Intake activities are always followed by one or more organisational activities.
- Organisational activities can be followed with intake, demonstrative or expressive activities.
- Demonstrative and expressive activities must be preceded by organisational activities.

Intake	Organise	Demonstrate	Express
1. Activity	2. Activity	NB: Activity 4 is not written here to aid readability.	
	3. Activity	4. Activity	
5. Activity	6. Activity		7. Activity

Generalisation:
- Write here the generalisation that children will make based on the above activities.
- Make sure the generalisation relates to the contributing question.

Table 15.2 Some helpful hints for writing IODE Social Studies activities

Helpful hints	Rationale
Intake activities are always followed by one or more organisational activities	New information must be organised in some way to facilitate understanding
Avoid sequencing activities as follows: —intake, intake —intake, demonstrate —intake, express	Inappropriate sequencing of activities does not provide students with the opportunity to organise new information gleaned from intake activities
Organisational activities are followed by intake, demonstrative or expressive activities	After organising information the next planned activity might enable students to demonstrate their understanding, express their knowledge in a new way, or in the case of a complex organisational activity be followed by a new intake activity
It is useful to number each teaching activity	Facilitates referencing in evaluating specific teaching activities
It is useful to provide a one- to three-word summary heading for each teaching activity (e.g. newspaper writing, mapping)	Provides a succinct reminder of the nature of the next teaching activity for quick reference
Summarise the nature of the teaching activity in one or two sentences, providing enough detail to outline student expectations	Helps teachers to recall planned activities and facilitates the implementation of planned activities when the regular classroom teacher is absent
Write each activity in formal teacher-directed language and clear English	Units of work are professional documents, and as such should be written in a formal style
Consider including diagrams of sample formats for student-produced work (e.g. sample layout for project findings)	Diagrams assist teachers to plan and document expectations of students
Double-checking every activity contributes to the answering of the question	Provides a check on coherent unit structure
Check that enough teaching activities have been written to explore the contributing question in depth	Ensures all contributing questions are being explored in appropriate depth
Provide adequate teacher-located sources of intake	Provides students with a variety of rich sources of information
Break complex tasks down into a number of teaching activities	Allows teachers to plan each stage of a series of activities. For example, documenting project activities often involves: —intake—reading to locate information —organise—writing summary notes —demonstrate—setting out and writing up findings based on summary notes
Devise enough intake activities to explore each contributing question in depth	Provides an adequate information base from which to explore the question
Check that activities enable students to generate the generalisation for each contributing question	Provides a means of checking that activities enable students to generalise

Assessment is defined as the process of gathering evidence and making judgements about students' needs, strengths, abilities and achievements. Evaluation is the process of gathering data and making judgements about the effectiveness of teaching programs, policies, procedures and resources. In the past, assessment and evaluation were used for a variety of purposes which did not relate to effective teaching and learning. Neither of these processes should be used as methods of punishment.

Effective assessment of progress and evaluation of programs should be developed cooperatively between teachers, students and other stakeholders, and utilised as a method of communication between all those engaged in the learning process. In this way, *reflection* on what has taken place is encouraged, *understanding* of the process of learning—as well as what has been learnt—is fostered, and *future directions* that are relevant, interesting and rewarding can be identified and planned for.

What to evaluate

Effective, ongoing evaluation should be undertaken on a regular basis before, during and after implementing Indigenous Australian Studies units of work and perspectives across the curriculum. All aspects of the processes involved in unit development and implementation should be examined (see Course evaluation box).

What to assess

Assessment provides a variety of methods of imparting vital information that enhances the opportunities for effective learning to take place. It allows the teacher to gain insight into the level of understanding of students after engaging in a learning activity, as well as insight into the learning styles of students, and the opportunity to reflect upon and adjust, if necessary, the teacher's own teaching style. Assessment should focus on the achievements of the student, teacher or others involved.

A wide range of assessment practices could be appropriate to establishing achievement. All of them should be positive and take into account the purpose for which the assessment is intended, the nature of the individual or group to which it is directed, and the intended audience.

A vital element of assessment is teacher judgement. A student may be able to demonstrate competence in a particular activity, but understanding is sometimes a more difficult achievement to identify empirically. Teachers, by knowing their students through close and

---

Course evaluation

1. Schools should regularly evaluate the course to ensure that the teaching strategies, learning experiences, content, resources and assessment procedures are appropriate. Evaluation procedures ought to be implemented before, during and after course introduction. Outcomes other than those anticipated in the objectives should be taken into consideration. In particular, Aboriginal perspectives need to be included.
2. Schools should design effective ongoing evaluation that addresses such questions as:
   - Does the teaching program provide for genuine community consultation and participation?
   - Have teachers and students developed an awareness of Aboriginal rights and concerns when negotiating with communities?
   - Are the learning opportunities and teaching strategies compatible with the aims and content?
   - Are the objectives of the teaching program clear and precise?
   - Are they achievable?
   - Is the teaching program organised in a logically appropriate way?
   - Does the teaching program cover all relevant concepts?
   - Is there opportunity for flexibility, adaptation and open-endedness?
   - Does the teaching/learning program provide for development of appropriate skills, attitudes and values?
   - Does the teaching program adequately cater for a variety of student needs, interests and ability levels?
   - Are suitable, adequate and contemporary resources being used?
   - Are the selected assessment procedures appropriate and varied?
   - What unintended outcomes can be identified?
   - Does the teaching program include a variety of teaching methods and student activities?
   - Will it be possible for teaching/learning strategies and student assessment procedures to be modified in relation to outcomes of evaluation?
3. What has been the student, community and overall school response to the course before, during and after its introduction?
4. Have Aboriginal people been involved in the course evaluation?
5. What has been the response of students to the course?
6. Have both qualitative and quantitative dimensions of evaluation been taken into account?
7. What resources and teaching materials were most useful, and why?

Source: New South Wales Board of Studies (1993, p. 53)

Table 15.3 Stage 1 assessment

Investigating	Not yet	Making progress	Achieved	Achieving beyond

Identifies information from a number of sources
    level 1
    level 2
    level 3				

Gathers information from a number of sources
    level 1
    level 2
    level 3				

Records information in a variety of ways
    level 1
    level 2
    level 3				

Analyses different sources of data
    level 1
    level 2
    level 3				

Uses data to explain findings
    level 1
    level 2
    level 3				

accepting contact, can develop a 'feel' for the way in which they are learning, which is not only valid in the assessment process but integral to really effective assessment. Without assessment, evaluation cannot take place.

Sometimes teacher-devised checklists can be useful assessment tools. Table 15.3 shows a possible checklist for assessing student skills based on a stage approach, which is compatible with outcomes-based assessment.

Why evaluate?

Evaluation of programs, policies and procedures is essential if the learning environment is to become effective and accepting. It is an integral part of the teaching/learning cycle and is the process that allows stakeholders to reflect on what has happened, make judgements about it and plan future directions based on past experiences.

The major concern when evaluating learning experiences—as expressed in programs, procedures and policies—should be enhancing the possibilities for students to learn more effectively. It should take into account what has been successful and unsuccessful, what students have responded to positively, and what has been difficult for them or incomprehensible. Positive and successful elements of past experiences should be incorporated into future planning and adjustments made to marginal experiences to make them useful.

Unsuccessful or negative aspects should not immediately be discarded. Reflection on experiences is sometimes more valuable for learning than the experiences themselves. Teacher-devised evaluation formats can be useful to guide aspects of evaluation (see Tables 15.4 and 15.5).

Collaborative assessment

Collaborative assessment allows the teacher and student to work together to assess individual progress and formulate the next step in the learning process. It may be used as a tool to individualise and improve the curriculum. Allowing students an active role in assessment can assist them to identify the goals of a task, recognise their successes, and identify areas in which new skills need to be developed and utilised. Thoughtful, reflective learning can be produced by encouraging pupils to co-assess tasks with the teacher and monitor their own performance.

Co-assessment involves: co-selection of the tasks; co-determination of the scope, demands and expectations of the task; collaborative setting of criteria for assessment; and co-assessment. Before collaborative assessment can take place, participants must have clear understanding of why they are assessing, what they are assessing and how they are assessing. Collaborative assessment and evaluation should grow naturally out of established collaborative learning models. It is difficult, if not impossible, to add collaborative assessment on to an autocratic structure.

Some features of collaborative assessment include:

- positive comments about the person;
- discussion is about the work, not the person;
- discussion is based on the agreed purpose of the activity;
- everyone has the opportunity to contribute to the discussion; and
- the results of assessment are recorded in an agreed-upon way.

Recording sheets are useful for upper primary students experienced in collaborative assessment practices (see Group assessment box). For less experienced or younger children, a more directed or more clearly explained format should be developed (see What have I learnt? box).

It should be emphasised that, in a collaborative structure, the teacher becomes one of the participants, and should be prepared to have their own work subjected to similar practices. In a collaborative model, where the 'bottom line' is honesty and acceptance, no one should feel threatened by assessment procedures.

Evaluation is directed towards making judgements about the effectiveness of programs, policies and procedures. It can be conducted in a similar fashion to collaborative assessment. Teachers need to be prepared to be the focus of scrutiny in evaluation procedures. They need to clarify with students their professional responsibility and how much of their educational activity can be subject to collaborative evaluation. Collaborative evaluation of, for example, school policy as it applies to student work and behaviour may need to be in a different forum.

In the Indigenous Australian Studies classroom, the role of the teacher is to facilitate learning rather than be the expert on Indigenous Studies. This is best achieved by creating experiences that allow children to learn *from* Indigenous people as opposed to learning *about* Indigenous people. Utilising appropriate teaching strategies can ensure that students are actively engaged in the learning process and exploring the full complexity of Indigenous Australian Studies.

Stimulating teaching activities can be developed when teachers consult their local Indigenous community and seek members' participation in the planning, delivery and evaluation of activities. Careful planning needs to be undertaken to ensure that units of work explore Indigenous Australian Studies in appropriate depth. It is important for teachers to consider: maximising Indigenous viewpoints and perspectives in teaching activities; the critical nature of learning from Indigenous people; and the idea that successful units are not dependent on *teaching about* Indigenous people but *learning from* Indigenous people. Assessment and evaluation are critical to maximise the potential of the learning experience and measure outcomes.

Table 15.4 Example format for evaluating teaching activities

Activity	Comments
1. Video viewing: *Warriors*	Aimed at correct level for my class. Students need to be directed to take summary notes on Pemulwuy's actions as they view the video
2. Role-playing	Samantha and Robert experienced difficulty relating factual information to the role-play
3.	
4.	
5.	

Key strengths of teaching activities were:

_____

_____

Key weaknesses of teaching activities were:

_____

_____

Table 15.5 Example format for evaluation of teaching behaviours

Teaching behaviour	Yes	No	Comments
Did I use a variety of instructional media and techniques?			
Did I pose questions to probe for higher-level responses?			
Did I provide positive reinforcement for appropriate behaviour?			
Did I ensure that children recognised the achievements they gained from the unit?			
Did I ensure that children understood the next steps in various learning processes they would need to master?			

School must be cool

At Croc Festival we told students:

> If you ever looked out the window, fell asleep, laughed with your friends, ignored your teacher or wagged school—think again. The ONLY reason you are at school is YOU! You are there for YOU—not your parents, not your friends, not your teachers—just YOU!
>
> The school, the teachers, the buildings, all the staff, the equipment, the bureaucracy—all are there for YOU.
>
> If you don't have a go, if you don't try your best—you are not going to be the success you COULD be. YOU are there to gain the best set of skills you can so you can market those skills when you leave school, OR have the best options to do what YOU want and achieve what YOU want to achieve—and be happy in YOUR life.
>
> It is that simple.

We all know that if school is boring, if teachers are uninspiring, or hurtful, or disappointing—it can be hard for students to see the point of being there every day. And we know they need to be at school every day to be the best they can be.

The joy of Croc Festival was seeing young people switch on and blossom. We all want all our young people to fulfil their potential, to dream and make it. It will be your job as teachers to create the conditions for our young people to be engaged and unlock their potential. YOU must be there for THEM.

Years ago, Aboriginal students in Western Sydney described a good teacher as 'Someone that likes us and is fair'. You need to know your students and like them. And they need to like you. Or they won't achieve. It is that simple.

So much of our young people's talent goes to waste in this country—especially in the back-blocks—and especially Indigenous youth. At Croc Festival we saw them do amazing things. YOUR mission is to unearth that talent and help it bloom. YOU can help make this great country the best it can be. It is YOUR job.

It's that simple.

—Peter Sjoquist

Peter Sjoquist with a student at Aurukun, Cape York. Courtesy Indigenous Festivals of Australia.

Peter Sjoquist AM has over 30 years' experience in film and TV production and events, including Crocodile Dundee, the openings of the Bicentennial and Expo 88, TV specials on John Farnham and Mick Jagger and the opening and closing telecasts of the Sydney 2000 Olympics. He produced the Rock Eisteddfod from 1988 and from 1998 to 2007 produced 57 Croc Festivals, the magical and engaging music-culture-sport-education event for bush kids across Australia, especially Aboriginal students, to be the best they could be. The festivals were tragically cancelled in 2008. He was awarded the Centenary Medal and in 2004 was appointed to the Order of Australia.

A child's Aboriginal identity must be secured and celebrated

A sense of self comprises many identities including racial identity, which is the most important contributor to an individual's self-esteem. In the case of Aboriginal children, there is a relationship between their personal self-esteem, Aboriginal identity and sense of self because those who have high group esteem of their race (Aboriginal identity) will possess a high regard of their personal self-esteem. Furthermore, a relationship between self-esteem and academic outcomes has also been found by researchers, and therefore it is vital to the success of Aboriginal student achievement and retention that schools develop a culturally secure environment where students can freely express their Aboriginal identity, feel accepted and gain equality. A culturally secure environment can be achieved by schools who actively engage with their AIEO. Schools need to recognise that AIEOs are the cultural experts who can access the local Aboriginal community. Schools need to work with the AIEO in order to encourage the Aboriginal community to be active contributors to the ongoing cultural security of the school.

Some of the things that assist in the cultural security of schools are:

- traditional Aboriginal welcomes and acknowledgements for all school official events such as assemblies;
- more active and visible participation of Elders and other Aboriginal people in aily school activities;
- more appropriate library books/videos/CDs and other resources about Aboriginal people and culture;
- more excursions and incursions of Aboriginal culture, history, etc.;
- more posters, paintings and pictures hanging around the school;
- the Aboriginal flag flown at the school which is hung by Aboriginal students;
- a welcome sign at the school reception that is written in the local appropriate Aboriginal languages;
- more Aboriginal school community involvement in the larger Aboriginal community events, activities, etc.;
- Aboriginal language to be taught at school by local Aboriginal people;
- more involvement of the larger Aboriginal community in the school community;
- Aboriginal history to be taught at school by local Aboriginal people.

—Dr Cheryl S. Kickett-Tucker

Dr Cheryl Kickett-Tucker is a postdoctoral Research Fellow at the Telethon Institute for Child Health Research. In 1999, Cheryl completed her PhD which explored the sense of self, identity and self-esteem of urban Aboriginal children. Cheryl is particularly interested in continuing this research to further explore how Aboriginal children think and feel about themselves in the world in which they live and how this affects their lives. As well as completing her PhD, Cheryl also has a Master of Science, a Bachelor of Applied Science and an Associate Diploma of Applied Science. She has also received numerous awards, including National NAIDOC Scholar of the Year in 2001 and the Queen's Trust Award for Young Australians in Western Australia in both 1992 and 1995.

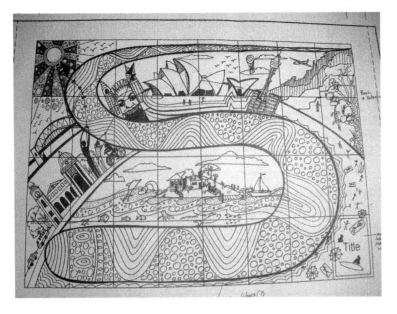

Line drawing for class activity by Bronwyn Bancroft, leading artist and author-illustrator of children's books. Not just a colouring-in exercise—students can be asked, what does the image convey? © Bronwyn Bancroft. Courtesy the artist.

16 Together we can't lose

Rhonda Craven

The image of Cathy Freeman and Melinda Gainsford-Taylor carrying the Australian and Aboriginal flags on their victory lap at the 1994 Commonwealth Games illustrates a watershed in Australian sporting history. It also graphically depicts the real possibility of a new beginning in race relations in Australia—with its message that together we can't lose. 'Together we can't lose' is the message of this final chapter.

Key messages

This text began by presenting a rationale for you to consider why teaching Aboriginal Studies is a national priority. Hopefully you have now developed your own rationale and commitment to teach Indigenous Studies. Respected Indigenous Elders and community members showed how Indigenous culture today continues to be diverse and vibrant and how Indigenous achievers enrich Australia. Their wisdom shows us the way—we need to teach our students about the dynamic culture and life of contemporary Indigenous Australia and make them aware of the rich contributions Indigenous Australians are making to our nation.

We also have shown how teachers can teach Australian students the facts to dispel misconceptions and stereotypes. Indigenous students will not thrive in an environment that continues to promote or condone racism. The enduring nature of these inaccuracies also prevents other Australians from understanding the truth about our history and celebrating the achievements of Indigenous Australians today—interfering with reconciliation and denying its perceived benefits to the nation. Clearly, we need to enable our students to be informed of the facts so that they can form their own attitudes and understandings, and form a commitment to reconciliation based on accurate information.

Subsequent chapters demonstrated how the need for reconciliation has emerged because of our history and how it has affected Indigenous Australians. *Terra nullius* was defined as legal fiction, a white lie—in the words of the High Court, 'wrong in fact and in law'. Clearly this is an important aspect of Australian history to convey to students. The impact of *special treatment* government policies on successive generations and on Indigenous Australian families today was graphically demonstrated, and we stressed the importance of teaching all Australian students the truth about this disgraceful and painful aspect of our shared history. New insights were also provided into why all Australian students should experience their right to be taught the truth about our history, and we illustrated a new way of looking at Australia's history: as a shared history. An overview of the history of Aboriginal education policies was provided to convey how history has shaped education today and how Indigenous people have been denied schooling. We, as

Respect, *poster by Australians for Native Title and Reconciliation (ANTaR). The good-looking young Aboriginal woman recalls the 1990s 'Racism Sux' poster campaign by the New South Wales Aboriginal Land Council. One poster had the headline 'They Say I'm Too Pretty to be Aboriginal'. Courtesy ANTaR.*

> **Aboriginals and the rest of us may be a fair bit closer than we think**
>
> They say culture-influence is one-way—the impact of Europe. But as Germaine Greer noted in *Jump Up Whitefella*, Australians are quite distinct from the British, and just as different from all the other ex-colonies. The difference, the 'x-factor', I reckon, is Aboriginal.
>
> White Australia was racist by definition; appalling things happened. The statistics of disadvantage are appalling. But at the same time, Aboriginal Australia has shaped Aussies in ways that have rarely been noticed, let alone acknowledged.
>
> Governor Phillip named Manly for the 'confident and manly bearing' of Aboriginal men there. Colonial-born whites were 'Cornstalks' – taller than their parents with a straight-up way of walking. Aboriginal men in 1830s Sydney were 'lords of the soil', walking around as if they owned the place (!). Then the Anzacs were hailed for their long confident stride.
>
> Tom Roberts spoke of the 1890s artists camps, where Australian School painting began, as 'blackfellow days'. Australia identified by Aboriginal symbols. Waves of Aboriginal-design advertising. Not to mention the boomerang.
>
> Why has Australia fought so above its weight in arts: more pianos per head of population in the late 19th century than anywhere in the world; two ten-a-page volumes of Australian artists in major galleries, each as thick as a man's arm?
>
> Is it coincidence that Australian arts flowered from the early 1960s when Aboriginal people were admitted to society? Think of the galaxy of Aboriginal stars in sport. And Aussie sporting dominance. Is there really no connection?
>
> We all know Aboriginals are the 'real Australians'. About time to celebrate the 'aboriginality' of being Australian. Where do we think the creativity of Australian artists comes from? The power of our actors? The go-for-it daring of the *Sydney 2000* designers?
>
> The irony and friendly 'take-the-piss' mockery of Aussie humour; enduring the inevitable: droughts, floods, axle-deep in sand in the backblocks—what can you do but make a joke of it (and anything else)!
>
> Popular speech owes a huge debt: 'big smoke' (city), 'pussy-cat hair' (fine and falling out). 'Deadly', 'mob' with its sense of belonging, and 'durri' (smoke) passing into mainstream speech. Vivid images in street-talk ('off like a bride's nightie')—often so referential, it's unintelligible to outsiders.
>
> It was the power of the Dreaming that dazzled the world at the *Sydney 2000* opening: the giant mask, the dancers, the infusion of spirituality—but also the power of imagination. And the party spirit, the friendly humour and tolerant irony of the volunteers, crowds on their feet cheering the swimmer who nearly drowned finishing the 100 metres and the last man to finish the marathon.
>
> The happy ending of Jimmy Chi's vibrant musical *Bran Nue Dae*—now a knockout film by Rachel Perkins—is that everyone is Aboriginal.
>
> What we can be. Hopefully, the future.
>
> About . . . time.
>
> —Nigel Parbury

teachers, need to comprehend both the failures and triumphs of our education history to see the ways forward, and to lift the bar. We rounded off the historical section with a history of the reconciliation movement and example activities and ideas to help teachers get started educating for the future. We emphasised that, in order to forge a new future, we all have to know about our past as a basis for understanding Australia today and, more importantly, determining, creating and shaping a new future.

The later chapters of the text attempted to provide teachers with a range of strategies to begin to teach Indigenous Studies effectively. We provided a summary of some recent research findings and identified the implications of these findings for delivering excellence in the teaching of Indigenous students—noting that many of these quality practices are also useful for other Australian students. The critical nature of community consultation and involvement at all stages of the schooling process was emphasised. Finally, useful teaching strategies for developing Indigenous Studies units of work and some examples of teaching resources were discussed.

Overall, the content of this text was designed to begin to equip teachers with knowledge of Indigenous Studies subject-matter and pedagogical skills. We trust that the key messages conveyed in each chapter have planted the seed for a passion for teaching Indigenous Studies, teaching the truth, and really educating both Indigenous and other Australians for the future.

Challenges and ways forward

> We . . . are never going to be at peace with ourselves until it is done, till the Aboriginal community's sense of injustice is purged and . . . our sense of what is right is satisfied. Our failings, the terrible wrongs of the past, have to be acknowledged. I think that the sense of pain within the Aboriginal community will not be exorcised until we accept that it is a product of our arrival. That pain will be unbearable until it is recognized . . . Aborigines must feel they have an equal stake in the future of this country. Only then can we move forward.
>
> —Leon Davis, Westpac Chair, *The Australian*, 4 June 2002

We simply cannot afford as a nation to lose the challenge of reconciliation. We have already lost way too many Indigenous youth to hopeless lives and early deaths. They have been the ones who have bravely dealt with social, physical and mental health issues that no young person or family should have to deal with by virtue of simply being born an Indigenous Australian—too often, they have also been the ones to pay the ultimate price.

It also needs to be appreciated that Indigenous students do not fail to educate themselves. Quite simply, teachers have failed to teach them. In doing so, we fail our precious charges, fail their parents, fail their communities, fail our profession—and fail our nation. Too many Australian teachers have failed too many generations of Indigenous youth. We need to draw a line in the sand now and take action. And there are actions outlined in this text that we can all implement in classrooms tomorrow that cost not one cent of additional funding.

Given that Indigenous Australians still remain the most disadvantaged group of Australians on all socio-economic indicators, and in particular are the most educationally disadvantaged Australians, we have an enormous challenge ahead of us. However, as Australians, we are always up to a challenge. And we take great pride in supporting the underdog. Let's just do it.

Harnessing Indigenous talent

The breathtaking breadth and depth of Indigenous Australian talent from youth to Elders never ceases to amaze me (see Chapter 2). Just take one look at the increasing number of talented Indigenous artists, poets, writers, dancers, musicians, sports stars, community leaders, academics, doctors, educators and lawyers who feature prominently on the local, national and international stage.

This breadth of talent is also attested to by the multiple talents many Indigenous people deftly pursue. I have Aboriginal friends and colleagues who are not only leading professionals in their respective fields but are talented artists, musicians, storytellers or poets as well. James Wilson-Miller is a great example of this.

Why Aboriginal Education?
Lynette Riley

I remember being sent to my first school to teach; I was Infants/Primary trained and then was sent to a High School, because the staff there wanted an Aboriginal teacher to help solve the school community problems!

What that situation taught me was what I didn't know and how easy it is to become a racist. I started to intensely dislike some of the non-Indigenous staff for their lack of understanding and their inflexibility to learn about Aboriginal people. Even though they were in a school teaching Aboriginal students, they felt the kids and community needed to conform to their ideologies. I didn't like their attitudes or what I was turning into. But I also didn't know how to respond—what I could say? How could I argue when I didn't really understand what had happened or what was currently happening?

What did I do? I went back to my old college in Armidale, now the University of New England and did a Graduate Diploma in Aboriginal Education. This was probably one of the most important decisions in my life. Why? Because it taught me two key lessons:

1. The first being, you need to understand what has taken place before, so you can recognise why we are in the current cultural, social, economic and political situations as Aboriginal and non-Aboriginal people in this country; and
2. Secondly, how these situations have affected each of us as a person and our inter-relationships in our communities.

I also recognised that this means we all need to learn about the real history of development in this country, if we are to have a true Australian identity. Aboriginal education has strengthened who I am as an Aboriginal person; it has given me greater skills to teach non-Indigenous people and to better assist my communities.

Aboriginal Studies is unlike many other subjects; it actually challenges and helps you learn about yourself and how to be a better communicator. I think this makes me a better person in this society called Australia.

Lynette Riley is a Wiradjuri-Kamilaroi woman from Dubbo and Moree; she is currently Senior Lecturer and Academic Coordinator at the Koori Centre, University of Sydney.

Lynette has over 30 years' experience in Aboriginal education and administration. She was one of the first Aboriginal people to work in the Aboriginal Education Unit, where she organised the first statewide meeting of the New South Wales Aboriginal Education Consultative Group (AECG). She has also been principal of Dubbo College of TAFE, and manager of the Aboriginal Programs Unit of the Department of School Education. As an Aboriginal person, Lynette has been required not to just theorise about what was occurring to Aboriginal children and communities or the interwoven interactions with non-Aboriginal people, communities and organisations; but rather to be actively involved in researching new solutions and effecting lasting change for Aboriginal students and their communities.

> **Generation One**
>
> For me, this is personal. I grew up with Aboriginal kids and at age nine attended a hostel with my Aboriginal mates in Carnarvon, WA. I was blessed with education and opportunity but as I hit adulthood my mates were left behind, lost eventually to welfare and addiction. I went to the last fella's funeral last year. His name was Ian Black, one of the nicest, most talented youngsters I'd ever met. His premature death was too much and now the future of his kids keeps me awake at night.
>
> Growing up with Aboriginal people I saw them go from stock shepherds to stockmen to head stockmen to overseers. Then I watched them become just as adept at handling motorbikes as mechanics, then four-wheel drives, then aeroplanes. I realised they were just as smart as us, perhaps even smarter at adapting to new skills and new professional demands.
>
> —Andrew Forrest

In March 2010 GenerationOne (with an aim to wipe out Indigenous disadvantage in one generation) was formally launched at Circular Quay, Sydney, with speeches by Prime Minister Kevin Rudd, Premier Kristina Keneally, 2007 Young Australian of the Year Tania Major, mining entrepreneur Andrew Forrest and New South Wales 2010 Young Australian of the Year Jack Manning-Bancroft (founder of AIME). Also present were businessmen James Packer, Kerry Stokes and Lindsay Fox, actors Cate Blanchett and Russell Crowe, and a host of others. Handprints of all present were beamed across to the Opera House, the first projections onto a World Heritage building.

Spokeswoman Tania Major said this was for all Australians to get together to eliminate Indigenous disparity in this generation. 'As I get around this country I find that Australians really are unified around a desire to ensure that this is the last generation to suffer Indigenous disparity,' Ms Major said. Jack Manning-Bancroft says GenerationOne is 'different from previous attempts to fix this problem because it isn't just calling on governments to act; it's calling on business, governments and all Australians to act. I think the GenerationOne campaign has huge potential for this nation because to make a real difference we need to all do this together'.

The launch led into a five-month business breakfasts and community events roadshow around Australia, finishing in August 2010 at the National Centre of Indigenous Excellence in Redfern. Over 40,000 people have signed up to wipe out Indigenous disadvantage in this generation.

GenerationOne is a movement, not a campaign; in partnership with the Indigenous community, working holistically—jobs, education and training all together. It is grassroots led and driven, and all about action. It is post-partisan, post 'black-and-white', post-bureaucratic. It is every Australian on the same page, to get rid of disparity in one generation.

GenerationOne works hand-in-glove with the Aboriginal Employment Strategy, which has placed 5000 Aboriginal people in work over the last three years.

In July 2010, SBS *Insight* presenter Jenny Brockie moderated a live-online debate, bringing together business and Aboriginal leaders to workshop how to generate more Indigenous jobs, and to discuss the gap between school leavers and work-ready employees, practical workplace training, and how to convince parents that real chances exist for their children. Andrew Forrest says the elephant in the room is the welfare culture (what Noel Pearson famously called 'welfare poison'), responsible for at least one lost generation: 'If things are given to you, you lose your drive. We need to demand more of our Aboriginal brothers and sisters.'

The forum heard about many ideas and actions taking place, such as that: more businesses are now working to grow Indigenous employment; the ANZ's Aboriginal training and employment scheme (they plan for 10 per cent of their inductees to be Indigenous) is 'business as usual' and has inspired non-Aboriginal workers to want to know about Aboriginal cultures; the bar should be set higher for what Aboriginal kids learn at school; it is critical to help young people complete Year 12 and build career-path mindsets; real change will come when government can convince Aboriginal people the end of disparity is in sight; and a collective decision needs to be made on what skills industry and employees need.

> The day following the forum the First Australians Business Awards were launched at a bush-food lunch at Aunty Beryl Van-Oploo's Yaama Dhiyaan catering and hospitality school at Redfern. Aunty Beryl stood up in her apron and told guests: 'My main focus is training young people in getting an education, getting them into jobs, making their dreams come true... Having choices. Because we never had those choices. We need to bust the myth, not just because it's not true, but because it's an essential part of breaking the chains of the welfare mentality that has stifled Indigenous economic development for too long.'
>
> The Indigenous Chamber of Commerce initiated the business awards and is working to train 1000 Aboriginal accountants: learning accounting is not just learning a profession but 'changing the way people think'. *The Australian* is a partner in the awards, also the Minerals Council of Australia, GenerationOne, Rio Tinto, BDO Accountants, and DEEWR (federal Department of Education, Employment and Workplace Relations).
>
> Andrew Forrest says GenerationOne is 'the most important thing I do'. The private sector, not government, should drive Indigenous employment: 'We need to make the employers of Australia, the people who will be providing the jobs, responsible for the training.' Actively encouraging Indigenous people to set up their own business is even more game-changing.

James is Australia's first published Aboriginal historian (he says Koori), is Curator of Koori History and Culture at the Powerhouse Museum, knows most if not everything about his culture and seems to know most Kooris in New South Wales; sang in one of the first Aboriginal bands, Silver Linings, can still entertain a whole party with his guitar and songs, and writes poetry. The life of the late Oodgeroo Noonuccal is another prime example. She was one of Australia's national treasures as the country's first published Aboriginal poet, but not so many Australians would know that she was also a leader of her people; she could teach any class of students from pre-school to university as well as any professionally trained teacher; she was an artist in her own right, a playwright, and on top of this had a wealth of knowledge about herbs, cooking and gardening! I know of few Australians who could boast such a breadth of talents.

Some positive moves are also continuing to emerge. Our Indigenous talent has started to become more visible to mainstream Australia as new films with Indigenous actors are reaching out to mainstream Australia. Who could forget the moving performance of young Brandon Walters in Baz Luhrmann's *Australia*, or the education about Australia's real history in *Rabbit-Proof Fence*. In 2009 the multi-award-winning *Samson and Delilah*, *Stone Bros* and *Bran Nue Dae* lit up the big screen, showing for all to see the fun and the deadly humour of Indigenous life. Then there is NITV.

Break-off entrant in the VIBE 3on3 Basketball and Hip-Hop Challenge at Rockhampton performing her hip-hop entry. Note the total focus of all the audience—excellence in dance appeals to all Australians. Courtesy Vibe Australia.

Our Indigenous politicians are also demonstrating that they can bring to the political arena an intelligence, wisdom, sensitivity and respect for others to make a real difference that is valued by all Australians, as seen in the work of the Hon. Linda Burney, New South Wales Minister for Community Services and Women, lead Minister for Human Services and Minister for the State Plan. Or the work of the 'Father of Reconciliation', Patrick Dodson, and 2009

Ray Martin AM: Walking together on the Journey of Healing

Following is an edited version of the third Lowitja O'Donoghue Oration delivered by veteran broadcaster Ray Martin AM for the Don Dunstan Foundation in Adelaide in June 2010. Ray Martin has approved this edit.

Saying that journalists are essentially storytellers, Ray Martin told some Aboriginal stories. As a member of the Council for Aboriginal Reconciliation, he helped organise the walk over Sydney Harbour Bridge that kickstarted this journey of healing.

People know Aboriginals are seven times more likely to have diabetes. But the details are horrific: in the 25–49 age group they are 27 times more likely to have minor amputations (fingers, toes, feet); 38 times more likely to have major amputations (above or below the knee); and, five years on, half of these same people are dead, or had the other leg amputated.

The Council for Aboriginal Reconciliation deliberately aimed its messages at Australian women through the women's magazines—'Because women are ultimately the ones in our society who finally decide our attitudes and our morality.' Now he tells women the Lowitja story: taken and sent to the home in Adelaide with her brother and sister, worked for white families, became a nurse; 30 years later flew into Oodnadatta as a District Nurse and was recognised at the airport by two old Aboriginal women as her mother's long-lost daughter. A much better story than saying 10,000 Aboriginal boys and girls were taken. Or Lowitja leaving a Reconciliation Council dinner in Adelaide to walk down to the station where Aboriginal kids were hanging round 'looking for trouble': 'She barked at them and herded them onto their trains, to at least get them out of the clutches of the city's predators. Caring and healing is in her blood.'

On one of his first assignments in Meekatharra, he was speaking to an old Aboriginal man who'd been thrown out of the Whites-Only pub, for being Aboriginal, who told how as a ten-year-old boy he was picked up by the police, accused of spearing cattle, then chained to a boab tree for three days until the police returned with the culprits. No bitterness in the old man, just telling it like it was. The anger was all Ray's!

In Narrandera to launch Bryce Courtenay's book *Jessica*, told by the librarian of an old white man looking at a display of 1930s photos of Aboriginal people in the town and shaking his head because as a six-year-old boy he'd been taken by his father one Sunday on a 'shooting party' down the Murrumbidgee. That would have been the 1930s, the same time as those photos.

That's before he tells people proudly that his great-great grandmother was a Kamilaroi woman from Keepit Station in north-east NSW.

> Indeed, I like to tell white Australians how leaders like Lowitja, Noel Pearson and Charlie Perkins (when he was around) used to harangue and harass and tongue-lash blackfellas for not picking up their garbage. For not sending their kids to school. For not getting off their 'black asses' and getting a job. For living off welfare. For not setting an example to their kids.
>
> Let me underline this. It's clearly time for a change in the message being sent out to white Australia. This is a two-way street. Indigenous leaders must get smarter in bringing about change, in capitalising on this positive mood, this healing process. The days of endlessly bashing up whitefellas for being racist, insensitive and not caring are over . . . it's no good trying to make Australians still take the blame for policies that go back 50 or 100 years. And it's too late for blackfella excuses.
>
> Clearly, blackfellas have to show strong new leadership. More than ever before. And get fair dinkum about the raging problems in their communities . . . and stop denying that it exists. That gives them no credibility at all.

At the same time, it's about time for honesty about the tens of billions of dollars that has gone into Aboriginal affairs over the last ten years:

> It's a question I get asked all the time. And it makes me smile. Because it's the same question I asked Charlie Perkins 25 years ago. Back then Charlie threw back his head and laughed out loud. And said he bloody wished he knew what happened to it.

> Well, today taxpayers are slugged over TWO billion dollars a year to help 'close the gap'. And still the same story—no one can explain properly where all that money ends up:
>
>> ... if you somehow follow the Aboriginal money trail you'll find that it bypasses the shanty towns and the camp dogs and Diabetes Row ... [and] ends up in the deep pockets of 'the Aboriginal Industry'.
>
> These days he tells people of the 90 very nice, but basic, houses on Tiwi Islands built by contractors—$1 million each, paid by taxpayers. 2000 Indigenous people jobless and not one maintenance tradesman being trained: 'What will these million-dollar houses be like in ten years time?'
>
> On Bathurst and Melville Islands, there are AFL coaching programs that respect families, culture and tradition. If anyone thinks that's just football, it's about life. Think of Nicky Winmar and Michael Long: 'Racism was rampant in sports. Especially football. That's now stopped.' And it's not just about the next fleet-footed high-flying black superstar, or teaching kids to kick both-feet—they do that almost from birth; 5- and 6-year-olds can bounce empty Coke bottles hand-to-ground-to-hand like proper footballs! It's about life choices. The Ozkick rule is: No class, no footy.
>
> A flag debate in a western Sydney high school. A class of Year 10 16-year-olds, many wanting to keep the flag, *but* all agreeing any change has to include Aboriginal recognition, and just one Aboriginal girl in the class: 'Don't tell me nothing is changing in Indigenous Australia.'
>
> The Business Council of Australia report labelling our failure to improve Indigenous education as 'our greatest national shame'—and promising to do something about it. In tandem with that is the Australian Employment Covenant, to create 50,000 Indigenous jobs. Andrew Forrest and Australia's richest men have made an unequivocal commitment of time, energy and money to Australia's poorest people—'Nothing like this has ever happened in Australia before.'
>
> To finish, two success stories. The first started sixteen years ago when Dick Estens, a successful Moree cotton farmer, decided to get young blackfellas into work, and hopefully save Moree from the stagnant fate of other wild-west towns. 'Doomed to fail', said the know-alls. Now, staffed by blackfellas, the Aboriginal Employment Strategy he kicked off is in every state, 1500 jobs this year and 500 traineeships, and more blackfellas on its books than Centrelink!
>
> The second is the Australian Indigenous Education Foundation, to create 2000 Indigenous scholarships at private schools. Getting a good education is a no-brainer, which is why the Federal Government gave the AIEF $20 million to be matched by corporations, families and philanthropists. By the end of 2010 there will be 200 scholarships. Building on the work of schools like St Joseph's College in Sydney, which now has 40 Aboriginal boys on scholarship.
>
> Two Joey's success stories: Craig Ashby came from Walgett, illiterate at 16 and has just graduated as a teacher from Sydney University; Ricky McCourt from Nambucca Heads is a Law graduate from Bond University; his ambition is to be the first Indigenous Prime Minister, and Ray reckons no one who knows Ricky would rule that out. 'Imagine for a moment hundreds of young, well-educated Indigenous leaders!'
>
> We all know there is no silver bullet, but as patron Sir William Deane says, education is the key.
>
> As Fred Hollows used to say: 'The alternative is to do nothing. And that is not an alternative.'

Australian of the Year Mick Dodson. Imagine how much better Australia could be with more leaders of this extraordinary calibre.

This wealth of Indigenous talent, coupled with the continuing failure of education to deliver to Indigenous Australians, shows clearly that we as a nation have not maximised all of our pool of valuable human capital. How much Indigenous talent has been wasted in the past? How much is being wasted even now? Imagine how different Australia could be if we put an end to the sheer wastage of talent by ensuring every Indigenous person reaches their full human potential. This would surely result in the Australian dream of Australia as a clever nation. In one of the most prosperous and successful multicultural nations on earth, surely this is achievable. I, for one, believe we have the best teachers in the world in our land and it is this quality of our teachers working collaboratively with Indigenous communities that can make such a goal a reality, particularly if we start implementing educational excellence in every Australian classroom today (see Chapter 11). Working together to achieve this, we can't lose—only gain:

> Blackfellas are 'people people', naturally gifted in human professions, making a difference in social work, nursing, teaching, hospitality. Aboriginal services break ground for the mainstream, establishing the first women's refuges, the first community legal service, first work-for-the-dole and inaugurating community consultation. And they add value: the best of Aboriginal education, for example, works better for all kids, while the connectedness and compassion of Aboriginal thinking could transform government. (Parbury, 2005, p. 216)

Improving relations

In this book, we have discussed the need to improve relations between Indigenous and other Australians (see Chapter 8). We also reported on the first Australian Reconciliation Barometer research (Reconciliation Council, 2009). This research suggests that other Australians clearly want to learn more about Aboriginal history and culture. Imagine how much having more opportunities to genuinely work with and learn from Indigenous Australians could do for our nation. Respect, trust and mutual understanding can be achieved if Indigenous and other Australians could have more opportunities to develop a relationship based on mutual respect and understanding. This can be started in Australian classrooms tomorrow without any additional funding. Let's just do it!

Djakapurra Munyarryun of Bangarra Dance Theatre playing didgeridoo at Bondi Beach in March 1988 among a Sea of Hands signed by supporters of native title. This public event was organised by Australians for Native Title and Reconciliation (ANTaR). Photo: Robert Pearce; courtesy Fairfax Photo Library.

Portrait of Brandon Walters, one of the stars of the 2008 film Australia, *which was used as a poster around Sydney to promote the Archibald Prize exhibition at the Art Gallery of New South Wales. The portrait by Vincent Fantauzzo was a finalist in the Archibald Prize and won the People's Choice award. Courtesy Art Gallery of New South Wales.*

NCIE: No more deficit language—'excellence and profound outcomes'

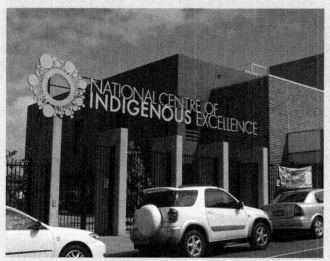

Main entrance and street-front of the National Centre of Indigenous Excellence, Redfern. Courtesy National Centre of Indigenous Excellence.

In 2006, the Indigenous Land Corporation (ILC) bought the old Redfern Public School in inner Sydney from the New South Wales government. Over four years it was transformed into a cutting-edge facility, with a state-of-the-art gym, oval, swimming pool, basketball stadium and 100-bed camp. The site also features corporate conferencing facilities, dance and art studios, a rope course and an outdoor basketball court.

Prime Minister Kevin Rudd opened the National Centre of Indigenous Excellence (NCIE) on 26 February 2010. He quoted CEO Jason Glanville, formerly of Reconciliation Australia, saying it was time to get away from the 'deficit language of disadvantage' and focus on 'excellence and profound outcomes'. The $50 million investment in the NCIE was a social investment for the 5000 young people who will come to the Centre each year from all over the country.

The Centre aims to become a hub of Indigenous excellence that creates an environment of learning and opportunity to foster talents and pave the way to brighter futures through its four pathways: arts and culture; learning and innovation; health and well-being; and sport and recreation.

The NCIE is an outstanding model of the collaboration that can improve the life chances of Indigenous young people and adults. The Centre works with its Pathway Partners to deliver programs around its four pathway areas:

- The **YMCA** runs gym, conferencing and camp facilities and local community programs.
- The **Exodus Foundation** provides intensive tutorial programs developed with Macquarie University.
- The **National Aboriginal Sporting Chance Academy** (NASCA) runs inspirational sporting and development programs for young Indigenous people from all over Australia and the local community.
- The **Lloyd McDermott Rugby Development Team** helps youth achieve their sporting dreams through development camps, sport tours, educational scholarships and mentoring.
- The **Australian Indigenous Mentoring Experience** (AIME) provides interactive leadership, mentoring, and numeracy and literacy programs for secondary students.

Local Aboriginal and Torres Strait Islander residents are highly engaged at the gym—70 per cent of gym membership is Indigenous. CEO Jason Glanville notes that 900 people, Aboriginal and non-Aboriginal, signed up in the first month and says:

> 'Having blackfellas and whitefellas—particularly older Aboriginal men and women—training alongside each other is a powerful experience for both. This is true grassroots reconciliation in action.'

As the Prime Minister said on the day he officially opened the Centre, no wonder NCIE marks what many are calling the 'Renaissance of Redfern': what can be achieved with hard work, having good people, and grasping the opportunities that are available. At long last, through the National Centre of Indigenous Excellence, the critical idea of Indigenous excellence across the board is up in lights for all to see.

Daring to reimagine our future

Imagine if every teacher was taught how to teach Indigenous Studies effectively to all students. Our teachers would serve as an unstoppable tide of change. Our youth would be inspired to contribute their talents and creativity to relationship and nation building—forging sustainable and productive change.

Imagine if every teacher implemented strategies based on educational excellence with all Indigenous students. The wastage of Indigenous talent would cease; Indigenous students and communities would thrive—building materially national well-being.

Imagine if all schools worked in close partnership with their Indigenous communities—we would foster reconciliation and together educate a nation based on genuine and respectful relationships.

Imagine if every non-Indigenous Australian understood the real history of Australia and became familiar with the devastating impact this history has had on Indigenous people today—think how much mutual respect and understanding would be fostered.

Imagine if all Australians could learn about and celebrate the sheer beauty of the heart of Indigenous Australia—to hold dear the commonalities we share as Australians, value the special place of Indigenous Australians, and in so doing mature as a nation.

Imagine if we closed the gap and encouraged all Aboriginal students to set high aspirations and attain their dreams—the socio-economic benefits that would flow are incalculable.

Imagine if we could maximise Indigenous students' self-concepts so every Indigenous

A roll-call of the best of Australians stand up for decency and reconciliation. Heritage Council chair and wife of former PM Hazel Hawke signs a Sorry Book at Circular Quay, Sydney, 1998. She said: 'It is . . . impossible for us even to imagine the wound, and the despair of children being stolen . . . unthinkable.' Next to sign is best-seller Bryce Courtenay, whose novel Jessica *was launched by the Reconciliation Council's Ray Martin that year in Narrandera where the story was set. Photo: Sahlan Hayes, courtesy Fairfax Photo Library.*

Full-page ad by Commonwealth Bank in National Indigenous Times *2 April 2009 to celebrate Bangarra Dance Theatre's twentieth anniversary: 'The Commonwealth Bank is proud to be an Anniversary Partner of the Bangarra Dance Theatre. Congratulations on twenty years.' The bank is a major sponsor of Bangarra. Courtesy Commonwealth Bank.*

student left school feeling good about themselves and their abilities. Research has demonstrated that self-concept drives educational achievement (see Chapter 11)—think about the talent this would harness and grow to full potential.

Imagine if we could encourage businesses to employ Indigenous people, provide work experience during schooling and become involved in mentorship. Research shows most Indigenous youth aspire to a good job (see Craven et al. 2005).

Before they get in the school gate – teaching teachers what's what

In 2010, Australian education ministers agreed in principle to a blueprint on how they will tackle disadvantage in schooling, with the aim of halving literacy and numeracy gaps by 2018.

Under the Indigenous Education Action Plan (IEAP), teachers would need to learn how to teach Aboriginal children as part of their training before they could register to work in public and private schools.

Education providers would need to ensure that trainee teachers completed 'core components on good practice in Indigenous education'. One recommendation was to mandate teaching Indigenous students in pre-service teacher education courses as a condition of registration.

The strategy would also aim to drive the recruitment of high-performing principals and teachers in hard-to-staff schools so students with the poorest outcomes would be taught by the best teachers.

Another key recommendation is to establish about 900 'focus schools' to help close the gap by creating a culture of high expectations. Focus schools will be responsible for improving attendance – strategies to be published, schools to report annually.

But leading Indigenous educators have criticised the draft, saying it fails to recognise the crucial importance of cultural pride to success at school. The Indigenous Education Consultative Bodies (IECBs) argued that there is a growing body of evidence that Indigenous students need 'cultural affirmation' to perform well in school: 'Closing the Gap has the danger of being described as a policy of assimilation if it does not explicitly articulate building on the cultural identity/capability of the learners and parents/caregivers as the first educators.'

Stronger Smarter Institute head Chris Sarra said the plan 'appears to be the subset of an assimilation policy where things are being done TO Aboriginal communities to make them more like mainstream society not WITH and this is disturbing.' Such assumptions 'can only result in more of the same.' He said the draft plan of holding principals accountable is 'problematic'; senior officials in the systems should be responsible.

The Australian Institute of Aboriginal and Torres Strait Islander Studies (AIATSIS) said there was insufficient emphasis on indigenous languages and the plan should stress that mastery of English literacy and numeracy should not come at the expense of the child's 'home culture'.

The Australian College of Educators warned that to children's schooling may be undermined if families feel that a Western-style education is being imparted at the expense of 'community ways of knowing'; educators must explicitly link the importance of school attendance with the community's vision for their children:

> 'Linking success at school to getting a job may carry less weight than linking success at school to nurturing and developing strong leaders who will be able to negotiate with government and other bodies on behalf of their community or contribute to the social goals of the community such as caring for country.'

A spokesperson for Minister Julia Gillard stated that in endorsing the plan ministers acknowledged that collaborative action must be responsive to local needs.

Meanwhile in New South Wales the AECG and the Minister negotiated a package of reforms including five-day community-controlled immersion induction, on full pay, for new teachers appointed to targeted schools with high Aboriginal enrolments. Other IECB chairs could barely believe their ears.

What these programs show is that, at last, education authorities and Aboriginal community bodies are negotiating on a level playing field and finding common ground – together we can't lose.

—Nigel Parbury

The knowing and caring profession

A close friend of mine, Dr Paul Brock, quotes the OECD *Quality in Teaching* report, describing teachers as belonging to the 'knowing and caring' profession. Trust the truth of that quote; it makes it easier to withstand the roller-coaster ride that day-to-day teaching is—full of joy one day and sadness and worry the next.

Every group of children is diverse and being with them can be exhilarating and at times gut-wrenching. Teaching Indigenous students requires non-Indigenous teachers to be conscious of even more: we are teaching students whose ancestors had a spiritually and culturally rich culture, deeply rooted in Australia for 60 000 years.

Given that many of these children are coming from disadvantaged communities and circumstances brought about by two hundred years of deprivation and marginalisation requires teachers to be more reflective, more generous, to be their advocate, sounding board, and at times their ally.

Margaret Cossey is a non-Aboriginal Australian who is recognised as one of Australia's most important figures in encouraging Aboriginal writers to write for young Australians. For sixteen years from 1993 she led a remarkable innovation in Australian publication through the publishing company she founded, Indij Readers Ltd. Most of the 50 or so Indigenous authors Margaret worked with had not been previously published. In addition to the stories, Margaret, with a small group of dedicated literacy teachers, developed AV materials, lesson notes and professional development materials for teachers.

Margaret resigned from Indij Readers in 2009 and is currently continuing her work promoting literacy acquisition through story. Her new company TwoWay Talk Pty Ltd is focused on making stories and songs in Aboriginal communities, to teach the competencies of literacy while emphasising the enjoyment and satisfaction literacy learners gain by putting story at the centre of the experience.

Together for Humanity

These edited extracts from the chapter 'Together for Humanity' in *Hand in Hand: Jewish and Indigenous people working together* (2010), by Dr Anne Sarzin and Lisa Miranda Sarzin, are reproduced with the kind permission of the publisher, the New South Wales Jewish Board of Deputies. Based on 80 in-depth interviews, *Hand in Hand* tells the powerful stories behind 40-plus initiatives linking Indigenous and Jewish Australians in past and continuing endeavours to support reconciliation in health, education, culture and social justice. The full story about 'Together for Humanity' can be found in *Hand in Hand*, available for purchase from the New South Wales Jewish Board of Deputies, 146 Darlinghurst Road, Darlinghurst NSW 2010, 02 9360 1600. <www.nswjbd.org>.

The Together for Humanity Foundation is an inter-faith non-profit organisation that conducts programs in Australian schools that challenge stereotypes and misconceptions and emphasise the shared values and common humanity of all people, seeking to promote behaviours that contribute to a more harmonious society.

Students engage with role models from Christian, Jewish and Muslim faiths. Since 2007, Together for Humanity has recognised the importance of including an Indigenous presenter, particularly in schools with high Aboriginal enrolments. National Director Rabbi Zalman Kastel says:

> It was important for Aboriginal students in the schools that we visited to see someone from their heritage represented in the context of people from different walks of life and groups bringing different gifts to Australia with their values. We saw Aboriginal students sitting up straighter and feeling prouder and standing up and speaking about the 'Blackfella's way', so in terms of fostering belonging and reinforcing the idea that we can work together, it was quite effective.

Working with student leaders in Orange, students were asked to build something together out of small building blocks and toys. Rabbi Kastel recalls:

> One group of Aboriginal student leaders built a little plastic box filled with black pieces and all around it were colourful things and they said 'this is how we see Australia, all this diversity and everyone having a great time around us and, in the middle, there is this segregated group that is us, separated from everyone else, the Blackfellas. We are in this box and completely separate from everything else that is going on in this wonderful multicultural Australia.'
>
> And then they said they didn't want to talk about it and we chose to respect their wishes. But later, we opened it up to the whole group of about 70 student leaders from around western NSW and asked what they thought about the way Aboriginal and non-Aboriginal Australians interact—and it was an absolute explosion. I mean the room just came alive with students who said they felt silenced and concerned about these issues and this relationship but they were fearful they would be labelled as 'racist'. And, in this context, when they were given permission to talk about it, there was a very constructive and very powerful heartfelt discussion about how those connections and the relationship could be improved. It was a meaningful moment in our contribution to reconciliation or integration.

Heather Laughton, an Arrernte woman in Alice Springs, was asked by a friend to help Rabbi Kastel run the program there. She was deeply impressed by what she saw and is now Northern Territory coordinator for the program. She says:

> I have worked for many years in dealing with racism in school programs and raising awareness in government agencies and the community and I was absolutely floored by the power of the . . . workshops. It has everything that we need to help children navigate through racism and deal with assumptions . . .
>
> . . . It gives kids an opportunity to interact with each other, to have deep and meaningful conversations and you see a bonding which is really quite phenomenal.
>
> . . . It has given me hope in my own country. Because I see that given the right opportunity and support, phenomenal changes can be made. Because you deal with racism every day. You walk into it no matter what and no matter how hard you try you get knocked down again and fall in a well and you are like a drowned cat trying to climb out the side of the well because you lose hope. And you know, one day you are just going to let go.

Together For Humanity also runs a 'Sister Schools' program in which a class that lacks diversity, for example, one that comprimises a single ethnic or religious group, is linked with a class comprising students from different and diverse backgrounds.

Rabbi Kastel hopes that Together for Humanity programs will become tailored more specifically to the inclusion of Indigenous people in society. He says:

> We are looking at opportunities to take the basic ideas we have developed in a multi-faith context and look specifically at how those can be developed to address the relationship between Indigenous and non-Indigenous Australians.

Working with Aboriginal people has enriched Rabbi Kastel's understanding of Australia and of Australia's history:

> It has also challenged me much more deeply than almost anything else to think about my own prejudice and my own assumptions about what 'normal' is and how things should be. It's brought home to me some of the complexity of the way people with conflicting stories clash with each other and the challenge and importance of reaching across.

Heather Laughton would like to see the Government take a more serious look at the program and include it as a compulsory component of the curriculum. In fact, she foresees that the program could benefit Government officers, enabling them to understand better and to challenge some of their own personal assumptions.

At a personal level, Heather's interaction with Jewish people has given her new insights:

> People are in the same boat as us, people who are here and who are equally marginalised but their skin is not black. So it opens up a whole range of issues. It's wonderful to understand a different faith and different culture and it gives you so much strength, we can be strengthened by our diversity. Understand the cultural differences and respect them, that's the greatest thing. That is what I have learnt from all this, and it's transferable.

© NSW Jewish Board of Deputies

Writing *Carpentaria*: How our spirits might be reconciled

I have had to deal with history all my life and I have seen so much happen in the contemporary Indigenous world because of history, that all I wanted was to extract my total being from the colonising spider's trapdoor.

[Writing,] I might contribute something to disrupting the stagnating impulse that visualises the world of Aboriginal people as little more than program upon countless program for 'fixing up problems'. Surely we are more than that. Perhaps, too, the drive in the Indigenous world to endlessly accomplish more is equally the internalised consequence of being members of a people who are so scrutinised and unvalued, and the by-product of the extreme pressures of oppression and relentless, ongoing colonisation.

Carpentaria imagines the cultural mind as sovereign and in control, while freely navigating through the known country of colonialism to explore the possibilities of other worlds... I think it is important to at least try to write something of ourselves of what has been unwritten, so as to affirm our existence on our terms... without settling for one explanation for the novel while others could be imagined, *Carpentaria* is the land of the untouched: an Indigenous sovereignty of the imagination.

'My countrymen up in the Gulf country and also Clarence Walden, they would always say "We're of one heartbeat," and I hope the book is of one heartbeat. Not only for us, but for anybody in Australia as we move towards the future and try to understand better.'

I also carry in my heritage the remnants of a Chinese cultural background, and what I believe I have of an Irish ancestry, which makes me, I am told, the kind of person that might be mistaken as a native on most continents.

When I read the fine Chinese writer Chi Zygian's *Figments of the Supernatural*, I also see another side of the ancestral stories from my grandmother. Or, if I look at Michael Demes' *Mythic Ireland*, I wonder what I might have learnt from my father's family had I known them, and what of them I might have inherited.

I have often thought about how the spirits of other countries have followed their people to Australia and how these spirits might be reconciled with the ancestral spirits that belong here. I wonder if it is at this level of thinking that a lasting form of reconciliation might begin and if not, how our spirits will react.

I think there's great efforts on our side to try to reconcile the spirits and to think about those ideas, 'cause we're quite spiritually minded people and we're dealing with spirits of our country all the time and trying to honour the spirits of the ancestors.

I think there's a lot of writing about Australia to be done in many different ways. Australia really is a country that's made up of lots of different people, Indigenous people and those who have made Australia home from all over the world.

What songs should be sung in recognition of our national collectivity?

Alexis Wright was born in Cloncurry, North West Queensland. She is a member of the Waanyi nation of the southern highlands of the Gulf of Carpentaria. A writer, researcher and social commentator, she has been widely published in magazines and journals. She has worked for many years on campaigns for Aboriginal land rights, Indigenous self-government and constitutional change in the Northern Territory, and for the prevention of Indigenous injury.

Her books include Grog War *(Magabala Books, 1997, 2009), a study of the problems associated with the excessive availability of alcohol in the outback town of Tennant Creek, and she was the editor and compiler of* Take Power *(Jukurrpa Books, 1998), an anthology of essays and stories exploring Aboriginal land rights in Central Australia. Her novel* Plains of Promise *(University of Queensland Press, 1997) was short-listed for the Commonwealth Prize, the* Age *Book of the Year Award, and the NSW Premier's Award for Fiction.*

Her novel Carpentaria *(Giramondo, Sydney, 2006) won the 2007 Miles Franklin Literary Award, the Australian Literature Society Gold Medal, the Victorian Premier's Vance Palmer Prize for Fiction, the Queensland Premier's Award for Fiction, and the ABIA Literary Fiction Book of the Year. The novel has been translated and published in Italy, France and Poland, and further translations are being developed for publication in Spain and China.*

She is a Distinguished Research Fellow of the University of Western Sydney Writing and Society Research Group, College of the Arts, and holds an honorary doctorate in communications from RMIT University.

This would help make that goal a reality and ensure Indigenous youth truly have a place in Australia and a stake in our prosperity.

Imagine if we got our very best researchers to identify what seeds success and tangible outcomes—we would have more answers on what can make a real difference now and foster further educational excellence.

Imagine if we could get this right for Indigenous students—how we could transfer this knowledge to maximise the full human potential of other disadvantaged youth nationally, strengthen Australia's socio-economic fabric and prove to ourselves that together we can't lose. It would be a giant step for humanity and an achievement of which all Australians could be truly proud.

If together we can imagine these things, then together we can't lose. United we can create a more socially just Australia for all Australians, which will ultimately enrich us all in all facets of our lives. *All* of us.

Together we can be:

> A united Australia that respects the land we share, values the Aboriginal and Torres Strait Islander heritage, and provides justice and equity for all.
> —Vision, Council for Aboriginal Reconciliation, 1991

In conclusion

In the end, learning from each other and walking together, we can journey in genuine friendship based upon mutual respect, pride and understanding to forge a new and stronger Australia. Such an achievement would be of enormous benefit to all Australians and humanity. Clearly teachers have a central role in forging the way forward. We trust this text helps to inspire you to be one person who can make a real difference. Together we can't lose.

Song of Hope

Look up, my people,
The dawn is breaking,
The world is waking,
To a new bright day,
When none defame us,
Nor colour shame us,
Nor sneer dismay.
Now brood no more
On the years behind you,
The hope assigned you
Shall the past replace,
When juster justice
Grown wise and stronger
Points the bone no longer
At a darker race.
So long we waited
Bound and frustrated,
Till hate be hated
And caste deposed;
Now light shall guide us,
And all doors open
That long were closed
See plain the promise,
Dark freedom-lover!
Night's nearly over,
And though long the climb,
New rights will greet us,
New mateship meet us,
And joy complete us
In our new Dream Time.
To our father's fathers
The pain, the sorrow;
To our children's children
The glad tomorrow.

—Oodgeroo Noonuccal (2008)

Sisters of Our Land. *Photo by Jaime Maria Bridge, student at Canobolas Rural Technology High School (NSW), of an Aboriginal and a non-Aboriginal girl, shown in the 1997 schools Reconciliation Week exhibition at the Art Gallery of NSW. Courtesy* Koori Mail.

References

ABC (2009). *ABC Radio News*, 10 July, Retrieved 30 July 2009 from <www.abc.net.au/radio/news>.

Aboriginal and Torres Strait Islander Commission (ATSIC) (1993). *ATSIC Current Issues: The Mabo Judgment*. Canberra: ATSIC.

——(1998). *As a Matter of Fact: Answering the Myths and Misconceptions about Indigenous Australians*. Canberra: ATSIC.

——(2003). *Submission to the Senate Legal and Constitutional References Committee Inquiry into the Progress Towards Reconciliation*, <www.aph.gov.au/Senate/committee/legcon_ctte/Reconciliation/index.htm>.

——(2008). *Social Justice Report 2008*. Sydney: HREOC.

Aboriginal Consultative Group (1975). *Report to the Commonwealth Government*. Canberra: Commonwealth of Australia.

Adorno, J. W., Frenkel-Brunswick, E., Levinson, D. J. and Sanford, R. (1950). *The Authoritarian Personality*. New York: Harper.

Ainley, J. (1994). *School Achievement Among Aboriginal and Torres Straight Islander Students*. Melbourne: Australian Council for Educational Research.

Ainsworth, G. and McRae, D. (2009). *What Works: The What Works Program—Improving Outcomes for Indigenous Students. Successful Practice*. Canberra: Commonwealth of Australia.

Akerman, P. (1996). Pauline Speaks for the Majority. *Sunday Telegraph*, 30 June, p. 139.

Altman, J. C. and Hunter, B. H. (2003). *Monitoring 'Practical' Reconciliation: Evidence from the Reconciliation Decade 1991–2001*. Discussion paper no. 254. Canberra: Centre for Aboriginal Economic Policy Research.

American Council on Education (1999). <www.acenet.edu/resources/presnet/report.cfm>.

Anderson, M. (2009). Come Out With the Numbers, Macklin and Rudd. *Indigenous Media*, 8 July, <www.sydney.indymedia.org.au>.

Atkinson, W., Langton M., Wanganeen, D. and Williams, M. (1983). Introduction: A Celebration of Resistance to Colonialism. In M. Hill and A. Barlow (Eds.), *Black Australia 2*, Canberra: AIATSIS.

Attwood, B. (1989). *The Making of the Aborigines*. Sydney: Allen & Unwin.

——(1994). *A Life Together, A Life Apart*. Melbourne: Melbourne University Press.

——(1999). *The Struggle for Aboriginal Rights: A Documentary History*. Sydney: Allen & Unwin.

——(2003). *Rights for Aborigines*. Sydney: Allen & Unwin.

——(2005). *Telling the Truth About Aboriginal History*. Sydney: Allen & Unwin.

——(2009) *Possession: Settlers, Aborigines and Land in Australia*. Melbourne: Melbourne University Press.

Australian Bureau of Statistics (2004). *National Aboriginal and Torres Strait Islander Social Survey, 2002*. Cat. No. 4714.0. Canberra: ABS.

——(2006). *Self-employed Aboriginal and Torres Strait Islander People*. Cat. No. 4722.0.55.009. Canberra: ABS.

——(2008a). *Population Characteristics: Aboriginal and Torres Strait Islander Australians*. Cat. No. 4713, Table 2.3.

——(2008b). *Deaths Australia*. Cat. No. 3302.0. Canberra: ABS.

——(unpublished) *Deaths Australia*.

Australian Bureau of Statistics and Australian Institute of Health and Welfare (2008). *Australians*. Canberra: AGPS.

Australian Council of Deans of Education (1998). *Preparing a Profession: Report of the National Standards and Guidelines for Initial Teacher Education Project*. Canberra: Australian Council of Deans of Education.

Australian Curriculum Assessment and Reporting Authority (ACARA). (2008). <http://www.acara.edu.au/curriculum.html>.

Australian Educator. (1993). Winter.

Australian Human Rights Commission (AHRC) (2006). *Your Guide to the Racial Discrimination Act, 2006*, <www.unhcr.org/refworld/docid/49997af50.html>.

——(2008). *Face the Facts: Some Questions and Answers About Indigenous Peoples, Migrants and Refugees and Asylum Seekers*, <www.humanrights.gov.au/education/face_facts/index.html>.

Australian Medical Association (2007). *Northern Territory Intervention: Help or Hindrance?* <www.ama.com.au/node/2911>.

Australians for Native Title and Reconciliation (2008). *NT Intervention*, <www.antar.org.au>.

Bancroft, B. (2009a). *An Australian 1,2,3 of Animals*. Sydney: Little Hare Books.

——(2009b). *An Australian ABC of Animals*. Sydney: Little Hare Books.

——(2009c). *Possum and Wattle*. Sydney: Little Hare Books.

Bannister, S. (1830). *Humane Policy or Justice to the Aborigines of New Settlements?* London: Thomas and George Underwood.

Barnett, K., McCormick, J. and Conners, R. (2001, December). *Leadership Behaviour of Secondary School Principals*. Paper presented at the Australian Association for Research in Education Annual Conference, Fremantle.

Barton, G. B. (1889). *History of New South Wales From the Records*. (Vol. 1). Sydney: Government Printer.

Barwick, D. (1972). Coranderrk and Cumeroogunga: Pioneers and Policy. In T. Epstein and D. Penny (Eds.), *Opportunity and Response, Case Studies in Economic Development* (pp. 10–68). London: C. Hurst & Co.

Beaglehole, J. C. (Ed.) (1955). *The Voyage of the Endeavour 1768–1771*. Cambridge: Cambridge University Press.

Beresford. Q. (2003) The Context of Aboriginal Education. In Q. Beresford and G. Partington (Eds), *Reform and Resistance in Aboriginal Education: The Australian Experience* (pp. 12–13). Perth: University of Western Australia Press.

Berndt, R. M. & Berndt, C. H. (1964) *The World of the First Australians*. Sydney: Lansdowne Press.

Bernstein, B. (1996) *Pedagogy, Symbolic Control and Identity: Theory, Research, Critique*. London: Taylor & Francis.

Berwick, C. (2008). Aboriginal Education and Training Policy Launch. Quoted in New South Wales AECG, *Pemulwuy*, no. 3. Sydney: New South Wales AECG.

——(2009). Vision # 1, 2009: The Professional Voice of the Independent Education Union, quoted in AECG, *Pemulwuy*, no. 3. Sydney: New South Wales AECG.

Bin-Sallik, M., Blomeley, N., Flowers, R. and Hughes, P. (1994). *Review and Analysis of Literature Relating to Aboriginal and Torres Strait Islander Education. Part 1—Summary*. Canberra: DEET.

Bishop, R., Berryman, M., Cavanagh, T., Teddy, L. and Clapham, S. (2006) *Te Kotahitanga Phase 3—Whakawhanaungatanga: Establishing a Culturally Responsive Pedagogy of Relations in Mainstream Secondary Schools*. Report to the Ministry of Education. Wellington, New Zealand: Ministry of Education.

Biskup, P. (1973). *Not Slaves Not Citizens: The Aboriginal Problem in Western Australia, 1898–1954*. Brisbane: University of Queensland Press.

Blainey, G. (1976). *The Triumph of the Nomads*. Melbourne: Sun Books.

——(1991). *Eye on Australia*. Melbourne: Schwartz and Wilkinson.

——(1993a, July–August) Drawing Up the Balance Sheet of Our History. *Quadrant*, 10–15.

——(1993b). A Nascent Spectre of Black–White Cleavage, *Sydney Morning Herald*, 10 November.

Bodkin, F. (2008). *Dharawal Seasons and Climatic Cycles*. Illustrated by Lorraine Robertson. Sydney: F. Bodkin and L. Robertson.

Bodkin-Andrews, G. H., O'Rourke, V., Dillon, A., Craven, R. G. and Yeung, A. S. (2009, January). *Explaining Away Aboriginality: Causal Modelling of Academic Self-Concept and Disengagement for Indigenous and Non-Indigenous Australian Students*. Paper presented at the Fifth Global SELF International Biennial Conference, United Arab Emirates University, Al Ain.

Bonwick, J (1869). *The Last of the Tasmanians or the Black War of Van Diemen's Land*. London: Sampson, Low, Son and Marston.

Bosker, R. J., Kremers, E. J.J., and Lugthart, E. (1990). School and instructional effects on mathematics achievement. *School Effectiveness and School Improvement 1*, 213–248.

Bourke, C. J., Rigney, K. and Burden, J. (2000). *Better Practices in School Attendance: Improving the School Attendance of Indigenous Students*. Report Commissioned by Department of Education, Training and Youth Affairs, July. Canberra: AGPS.

Bradley, S., Draca, M., Green, C. and Leeves, G. (2007). The Magnitude of Educational Disadvantage of Indigenous Minority Groups in Australia. *Journal of Population Economics*, 20(3), pp. 547–69.

Brady, M. (2008). *First Taste: How Indigenous Australians Learned About Grog* (a set of resources in six parts). Book Two: 'The First taste of Alcohol'. Canberra: The Alcohol Education & Rehabilitation Foundation Ltd.

Brady, W., Bennett, E. and Phillips, S. (1993) *Local Area Studies: Guide for Teachers of Aboriginal Studies*. Sydney: The Koori Centre, University of Sydney.

Brandsma, H. P. (1993). *Characteristics of primary schools and the quality of education*. Groningen: RION

Breen, S. (2003). *Re-inventing Social Evolution*. In R. Manne (ed.), *Whitewash: On Keith Windschuttle's Fabrication*. Melbourne: Black Inc. Agenda.

Brett, J. (2000/01, December–January). Why John Howard Can't Say Sorry. *Arena Magazine*, 35–41.

Broome, R. (1982). *Aboriginal Australians: Black Response to White Dominance, 1788–1980*. Sydney: George Allen & Unwin.

——(2005). *Aboriginal Victorians: A History Since 1800*. Sydney: Allen & Unwin.

Burdekin, B. (1993). *National Inquiry into the Human Rights of People with a Mental Illness: Findings and Recommendations*. Canberra:

Burnett, B., Meadmore, D. and Tait, G. (Eds.) (2004). *New Questions for Contemporary Teachers Taking a Socio-cultural Approach*

to Education. Sydney: Pearson Education.
Burridge, N. (2003) The Implementation of the Policy of Reconciliation in NSW Schools. Unpublished PhD Thesis. Macquarie University, Sydney.
——(2006). Meanings of Reconciliation in the School Context. *Journal of Indigenous Education* 35(2), 68–77.
Cairney, T. (2003). Literacy Within Family Life. In N. Hall, J. Larson and J. Marsh (Eds), *Handbook of Early Childhood Literacy*. London: Sage.
Calder, J. (1875). *Some Accounts of the Wars, Extirpations, Habits etc. of the Native Tribes of Tasmania* (facsimile edition). Hobart: Fuller's Bookshop.
Cambourne, B. and Turbill, J. (1990). *Aboriginal Reflections from ELIC*. Sydney: NSW Department of School Education.
Campbell, L. (2006). *Darby: One Hundred Years of Life in a Changing Culture*. Sydney: ABC Books.
Canning, Ken (Burraga Gutya) (1990). *Ngali Ngalga (Let's Talk): Poetry*. Sydney: Breakout Press.
Carrington, K. (1991) The Death of Mark Quayle: Normalising Racial Horror in Country Towns & Hospitals. *Prisons & Punishment, Journal for Social Justice Studies*, 4.
Castellano, B., Marlene. (2004). Ethics of Aboriginal Research. *Journal of Aboriginal Health*, 98–114.
Catholic Commission for Justice and Peace (1978). *Aborigines. A Statement of Concern*. Sydney: Catholic Commission for Justice and Peace.
Catholic Commission for Justice and Peace, Uniting Church in Australia Social Justice and Responsibility Commission, & Commission for Church and Society (1987). *A Just and Proper Settlement*. Melbourne: Collins Dove.
Cavanagh, P. (2002). The Arts of Contact. Unpublished PhD dissertation. Macquarie University.
——(2005). Silences, Secrets and Little White Lies: Reflections on the Representation of Aboriginal People in Australian Schools. In G. Cant (Ed.), *Discourses and Silences: Indigenous Peoples, Risks and Resistance*. Christchurch: Department of Geography, University of Canterbury.
Cawley, E. and Jarrett, P. (1993). *Home: The Evonne Goolagong Story*, Sydney: Simon & Schuster.
Cazden, C. (2001). *Classroom Discourse: The Language of Teaching and Learning*. Portsmouth: Heinemann.
Centre for Public Law (2002). *Submission to the Senate Legal and Constitutional References Committee Inquiry into the Progress Towards Reconciliation*, <www.aph.gov.au/Senate/committee/legcon_ctte/Reconciliation/index.htm>.
Chodkiewicz, A., Widin, J. and Yasukawa, K. (2008). Engaging Aboriginal Families to Support Student and Community Learning. *Diaspora, Indigenous, and Minority Education*, 2(1), 64–81.
Clark, M. (1963). *A Short History of Australia*, Melbourne: Macmillan.
——(1980a). A Discovery of Australia. In M. Clark, *Occasional Writings and Speeches*. Melbourne: Fontana/Collins.
——(1980b). Rewriting Australian History. In M. Clark *Occasional Writings and Speeches*. Melbourne: Fontana/Collins.
——(1980c). Writing History in Australia. In M. Clark *Occasional Writings and Speeches*. Melbourne: Fontana/Collins.
Claxton, C. S. and Murrell, P. H. (1987). *Learning Styles: Implications for Improving Educational Practices*. Washington: Clearinghouse on Higher Education.
Clendinnen, I. (1999). *ABC Boyer Lectures*. Sydney.
——(2005). *Dancing with Strangers*. Melbourne: Cambridge University Press.
Cochrane, K. (1994) *Oodgeroo*. Brisbane: University of Queensland Press.
Cokley, K. O. (2002). Ethnicity, Gender and Academic Self-concept: A Preliminary Examination of Academic Disidentification and Implications for Psychologists. *Cultural Diversity and Ethnic Minority Psychology*, 8(4), 378–88.
Collins, R. (Chair) (1999). *Learning Lessons: An Independent Review of Indigenous Education in the Northern Territory*. Darwin: Northern Territory Department of Education.
Commonwealth of Australia (1989). *National Aboriginal and Torres Strait Islander Education Policy—Joint Policy Statement*. Canberra: Department of Education, Employment and Training.
——(1992). *Aboriginal Deaths in Custody: Response by Governments to the Royal Commission*, vol. 3. Canberra: AGPS.
——(1997) *Rebutting the Myths: Some Facts About Aboriginal and Torres Strait Islander Affairs*. Canberra: AGPS.
——(2003). *Senate Legal and Constitutional References Committee Report into National Reconciliation*. Canberra: AGPS.
Cooke, K. (1988) *Beyond a Joke: An Anti-Bicentenary Cartoon Book*. Melbourne: McPhee Gribble/Penguin.
Cooke, M., Mitrou, F., Lawrence, D., Guimond, E. and Beavon, D. (2007). Indigenous Well-being in Four Countries: An Application of the UNDP'S Human Development Index to Indigenous Peoples in Australia, Canada, New Zealand, and the United States. *BMC International Health and Human Rights*, 7(9), 1–39.
Coombs, H., Brandl, M. and Snowden, W. (1983). *A Certain Heritage*. Canberra: Centre for Research and Environmental Studies, Australian National University.
Council for Aboriginal Reconciliation (1990). *Three Strategic Plans 1991–94*. Canberra: AGPS.
——(1992). *Walking Together*, 1. Canberra: Australian Government Publishing Service.
——(1993a). *Exploring Common Ground: Aboriginal Reconciliation and the Mining Industry*. <www.austlii.edu.au/au/other/Indig.Res/car/pubs/html#reports>.
——(1993b). *Making Things Right: Reconciliation After the High Court Decision on Mabo*. <www.austlii.edu.au/au/other/Indig.Res/car/pubs/html#reports>.
——(1994a). *Together We Can't Lose*. <www.austlii.edu.au/au/other/Indig.Res/car/pubs/html#reports>.
——(1994b). *Walking Together: The First Steps*. Canberra: AGPS. <www.austlii.edu.au/au/other/Indig.Res/car/pubs/html#reports>.

——(1994c). *Weaving the Threads*. <www.austlii.edu.au/au/other/Indig.Res/car/pubs/html#reports>.

——(1994d). *Three Strategic Plans 1995–98*. Canberra: AGPS.

——(1997a). Addressing the Key Issues for Reconciliation series: *Improving Relationships; Valuing Cultures; Sharing History; Addressing Disadvantage; Responding to Custody Levels; Agreeing on a Document; Controlling Destinies*. Key Issues Papers 1–8. Canberra: Australian Government Publishing Service.

——(1997b). *Proceedings from the Australian Reconciliation Convention, May 26–28, 1997*. Books 1–5. Canberra: Commonwealth of Australia.

——(1997c). *The Path to Reconciliation: Building a People's Movement*. NSW Regional Meetings Summary, March 4–27.

——(1997d). *Strategic Plan (1998–2000)* <www.austlii.edu.au/au/other/IndigLRes/car/1998/5>.

——(1998). *Towards Reconciliation. Activities for Reconciliation Week*. Canberra.

——(2000a). *Road Map for Reconciliation*. <www.austlii.edu.au/au/other/IndigLRes/car/2000/10/index.htm>.

——(2000b). *Walking the Talk: Commitments to Reconciliation*. Proceedings from Corroboree 2000. Canberra: Pirie Printers.

——(2000c). *Reconciliation: Australia's Challenge. Final Report of the Council for Aboriginal Reconciliation*. Canberra: AGPS.

——(2001). *Reconciliation Over to You. Walking Together*. Canberra: AGPS

Council of Australian Governments (COAG) (2009). *Closing the Gap on Indigenous Disadvantage: The Challenge for Australia*. Canberra: AGPS.

Cowey, W. (2005). A Brief Description of the National Accelerated Literacy Program. *TESOL in Context*, 15(2, 3–14.

Craven, R. (ed.). (1996a). *Teaching the Teachers: Indigenous Australian Studies for Primary Pre-Service Teacher Education*. Sydney: DETYA, University of New South Wales.

——(ed.) (1996b) *Using the Right Words: Appropriate Terminology for Indigenous Australian Studies*. Sydney: School of Teacher Education, University of New South Wales in association with the Council for Aboriginal Reconciliation.

——(ed.) (1996c). *Why teach Aboriginal studies?* [DVD]. Australia: University of New South Wales.

——(1999). *Teaching Aboriginal Studies*, Sydney: Allen & Unwin.

——(2005). *Turning Points in Indigenous Education. New Findings that Can Really Make a Difference and Implications for the Next Generation of Indigenous Research*. Paper presented to the national conference of the Australian Association for Research in Education, Sydney. <www.aare.edu.au/05pap/abs05.htm>.

——(2006). Turning Indigenous Secondary Students' Educational Disadvantage Around: How Psychologists Can Begin to Make a Real Difference. *The Australian Community Psychologist*, 18(1), 14–22.

Craven, R. G., & Bodkin-Andrews, G. (2006). New solutions for addressing Indigenous mental health: A call to counsellors to introduce the new positive psychology of success. *Australian Journal of Guidance and Counselling*, 16(1), 41–54.

Craven, R. G. and Marsh, H. W. (2004). The Challenge for Counsellors: Understanding and Addressing Indigenous Secondary Students' Aspirations, Self-concepts and Barriers to Achieving Their Aspirations. *Australian Journal of Guidance and Counselling*, 14(1), 16–33.

Craven, R. G., & Tucker, A. (2003). *Enhancing self-concept and educational outcomes for Indigenous students: AECG members' views and suggestions for strategic research directions*. NSW: NSW Aboriginal Education Consultative Group.

Craven, R. G., Tucker, A., Munns, G., Hinkley, J., Marsh, H. W., and Simpson, K. (2005). *Indigenous Students' Aspirations: Dreams, Perceptions and Realities*. Canberra: Commonwealth of Australia.

Cresswell, J., Underwood, C., Withers, G. and Adams, I. (2002). *Evaluation of the University of Canberra Programme for Advanced Literacy Development Scaffolding Literacy Programme with Indigenous Children in School*. Report prepared for DEST. Melbourne: ACER.

Crowley, F. (ed.) (1974). *A New History of Australia*. Melbourne: Heinemann.

Cunningham, P. (1966 [1834]). *Two Years in New South Wales* (facsimile edition). Brian Fletcher (Ed.) Sydney: A. H. and R. W. Reed.

Curriculum Corporation (1995). *Guidelines and Principles for the Development of Aboriginal Studies and Torres Strait Islander Studies*. Melbourne: Curriculum Corporation.

Curthoys, A. (2002) *Freedom Ride*. Sydney: Allen & Unwin.

Cyclops Press (2009) *Portraits from a Land Without People*. Sydney: Cyclops Press.

Danalis, J. *Riding the Black Cockatoo*. Sydney: Allen & Unwin.

Dare to Lead (2005). *Dare to Lead . . . Taking it on: Report on the second phase of Dare to Lead April 2003–March 2005*. <www.daretolead.edu.au/servlet/Web?s=169694&p=DTL08_ProjHist_Main>.

Davies, O. (2007). Evaluation of the Schools in Partnership Initiative: The First Ten Schools 2006. Unpublished, prepared 2007 from research collected in Term 4, 2006 for the NSW Department of Education and Training.

Davis, J. (1989). *Plays from Black Australia*. Sydney: Currency Press.

Davis, J., Muecke, S., Nagogin, M. and Shoemaker, A. (Eds.) (1990). *Paperbark: A Collection of Black Australian Writings*. Brisbane: University of Queensland Press.

De Bortoli, L. and Thomson, S. (2009). *The Achievement of Australia's Indigenous Students in PISA 2000–2006*. Melbourne: ACER.

De Maio, J. A., Zubrick, S. R., Silburn, S. R., Lawrence, D. M., Mitrou, F. G., Dalby, R. B., Blair, E. M., Griffin, J., Milroy, H. and Cox, A. (2005). *The Western Australian Aboriginal Child Health Survey: Measuring the Social and Emotional Wellbeing of Aboriginal Children and Intergenerational Effects of Forced Separation*. Perth: Curtin University of Technology

and Telethon Institute for Child Health Research.
Deane, W. (1996). *Signposts from Daguragu*. Vincent Lingiari Lecture. Canberra: Council for Aboriginal Reconciliation and Australian Government Publishing Service.
——(1997) Speech delivered at the Australian Reconciliation Convention, 26–28 May. <www.austlii.edu.au/au/other/IndigLRes/car/1997/3/Con%20speeches.htm>.
Dent, J. and Hatton, E. (1996) Education and Poverty: An Australian Primary School Case Study. *Australian Journal of Education*, 40(1), pp. 46–64.
Department of Aboriginal Affairs. (1981). *Report on a review of the administration of the working definition of Aboriginal and Torres Strait Islanders*. Canberra: DAA.
Department of Education, Employment and Training (1989). *Discipline Review of Teacher Education in Mathematics and Science*, Vol. 1. Canberra, AGPS.
Department of Education, Employment and Workplace Relations (DEEWR) (2007). *National Report to Parliament on Indigenous Education and Training, 2005*. Canberra: DEEWR.
Department of Education, Science and Training (DEST). (1993). *National Aboriginal and Torres Strait Islander Education Policy (AEP)*. Canberra: Department of Education, Science and Training. <www.dest.gov.au/archive/schools/indigenous/aep.htm>.
——(2002). *Achieving Equitable and Appropriate Outcomes: Indigenous Australians in Higher Education*. Canberra: Commonwealth of Australia.
——(2005). *National Report to Parliament on Indigenous Education Science and Training*. Canberra: Commonwealth of Australia.
——(2007). *Guide to the Teaching of Australian History in Years 9 and 10*, Canberra: DEST. <www.dest.gov.au/NR/rdonlyres/0B8BB929-AD4F-4A1E-8CDB-F73AB8E312A4/18868/Guidetoteachinghistory.pdf>.
Department of Education and Training (2004) *Report on the Review of Aboriginal Education in NSW.*

Yanigurra Muya: Ganggurrinyma Yaarri Guurulaw Yirringin.gurray. Canberra: AGPS. <www.det.nsw.edu.au/reviews/aboriginaledu/language.htm>.
Department of Education, Training and Youth Affairs (2000). *Nallawa: Achieving Reconciliation in NSW Schools*. Sydney: Macquarie University.
——(2000) *What Works: Explorations in Improving Outcomes for Indigenous Students*. Canberra: Curriculum Studies Association of Australia. <www.acsa.edu.au/publications.whatworks_sections.htm>.
Devine, M. (2006). How intolerance can turn the tide. <http://www.smh.com.au/news/opinion/how-intolerance-can-turn-the-tide/2006/09/27/1159337220004.html>.
Deyhle, D. and Swisher, K. (1997). Research in American Indian and Alaska Native Education: From Assimilation to Self-Determination. *Review of Research in Education*, 22, 113–194.
Dixon, R. M.W. and Duwell, M. (1990). *The Honey-Ant Men's Love Song and Other Aboriginal Song Poems*. Brisbane: University of Queensland Press.
Dodson, M. (1993). *Aboriginal and Torres Strait Islander Social Justice Commission: First Annual Report 1993*. Canberra: AGPS.
——(2000). Speech delivered at Corroboree 2000 Conference, Sydney, 27 May. <www.austlii.edu.au>.
Dodson, P. (1992). *Walking Together*. Council for Aboriginal Reconciliation Newsletter no. 1.
——(1996). Reconciliation at the Crossroads. *Koori Mail*, 22 May, p. 12.
Donovan, M. (2007). Can Information Technological Tools Be Used to Suit Aboriginal Learning Pedagogies? In L. E. Dyson, M.A.N. Hendriks and S. Grant (Eds.), *Information Technologies and Indigenous Peoples* (pp. 93–104). Sydney: Idea Group Inc.
Dumont, R. V. Jr. and Wax, M. L. (1976) Cherokee School: Society and the Intercultural Classroom. In J. Roberts and S. Akinsanya (Eds.), *Schooling in the Cultural Context: Anthropological Studies*

of Education. New York: David McKay.
Dunn, B. (2008) *National Accelerated Literacy Program: Student Progress 2008—Accelerated Literacy in NT Schools—System Level Summary*. Darwin: Education Systems Reform, School for Social and Policy Research, Charles Darwin University. <www.nalp.edu.au/datareports2008.htm>.
Dunn, R. (1990). Rita Dunn Answers Questions on Learning Styles. *Educational Leadership*, 48(2), pp. 15–19.
Dunn, R., Dunn, K. and Price, G. E. (1984). *Learning Style Inventory*. Lawrence, KS: Price Systems.
Durack, M. (1959). *Kings in Grass Castles*. London: Constable.
Durrant, C., and Green, B. (2000). Literacy and the new technologies in school education: Meeting the li(IT)eracy challenge. *Australian Journal of Language and Literacy Education* 23(2), 89–108.
Duwell, M. and Dixon, R. M.W. (1994). *Little Eva at Moonlight Creek and Other Aboriginal Song Poems*. Brisbane: University of Queensland Press.
Edmund Rice Centre (2002). *Submission to the Senate Legal and Constitutional References Committee Inquiry into the Progress Towards Reconciliation*. <www.aph.gov.au/Senate/committee/legcon_ctte/Reconciliation/index.htm>.
Education Australia (1996). Issue 33.
——(1997). Issue 35.
Education Department of Victoria (1985). *Report of the Ministerial Review of Post-compulsory Schooling: Information Kit*. Melbourne: Education Department of Victoria.
Edwards, C. and Read, P. (Eds.) (1989). *The Lost Children: Thirteen Australians Taken from Their Aboriginal Families Tell of the Struggle to Find Their Natural Parents*. Sydney: Doubleday.
Elliot-Farrelly, T. (2004). Australian Aboriginal suicide: The need for an Aboriginal suicidology? *Australian e-Journal of the Advancement of Mental Health*, 3(3), 1–8.
Enemburu, I. G. (1985). *Koori English*. Melbourne: Ministry of Education.
European Network for Indigenous Australian Rights (ENIAR) (2008). *NT Intervention a Lemon: 28*

Medical Specialists Give Their Diagnosis. <www.eniar.org/news/health>.

Fair Go Team (2006). *School is for Me: Pathways to Student Engagement.* Sydney: Priority Schools Funding Program, NSW Department of Education and Training.

Fesl, E. M. D. (1993). *Conned: Eve Mumewa D. Fesl Speaks Out on Language and the Conspiracy of Silence.* Brisbane: University of Queensland Press.

Flannery, T. (2007). *Where is Here? 350 Years of Exploring Australia.* Melbourne: Text.

Fletcher, J. J. (1989a). *Clean, Clad and Courteous: A History of Aboriginal Education in NSW.* Melbourne: J. J. Fletcher.

——(1989b). *Documents in the History of Aboriginal Education in NSW.* Melbourne: J. J. Fletcher.

Flood, S. (1993) *Mabo: A Symbol of Sharing.* Sydney: Fink Consultancy.

Fogarty, R. (1991a). *The Mindful School: How to Integrate the Curricula.* Palatine, IL: IRI/Skylight Publishing.

——(1991b). Ten Ways to Integrate the Curriculum. *Educational Leadership,* October, 61–5.

Freire, P. (1972). *Pedagogy of the Oppressed.* Harmondsworth: Penguin.

Frigo, T. and Simpson, L. (no date). Research into the Numeracy Development of Aboriginal Students: Implications for NSW K–10 Mathematics Syllabus. <www.boardofstudies.nsw.edu.au/aboriginal_research/pdf_doc/aboriginal_num_k10_math.pdf>.

Ganesharajah, C. 2009. *Indigenous Health and Wellbeing: The Importance of Country, Native Title Research Report No. 1/2009.* Canberra: Native Title Research Unit, Australian Institute for Aboriginal and Torres Strait Islander Studies.

George, R. (1787). *Historic Records of New South Wales.* London: Public Record Office. 25 April 1787, Vol. 11, pp. 89–90.

Gibson, M. (1998). Sorry Day … I'll Send My Regrets. *Daily Telegraph,* 26 May, p. 9.

Gilbert, K. (1988). *Inside Black Australia: An Anthology of Aboriginal Poetry.* Ringwood: Penguin.

——(1998). *Black from the Edge.* Brisbane: University of Queensland Press.

Gilmore, M. (1934). *Old Days, Old Ways.* Sydney: Angus & Robertson.

——(1935). *More Recollections.* Sydney: ETT Imprint.

Ginibi, R. L. (2007). *Don't Take Your Love to Town.* Ringwood: Penguin.

Goodall, H, (1996). *Invasion to Embassy.* Sydney: Allen & Unwin.

Grattan, M. (Ed.) (2000). *Reconciliation: Essays on Australian Reconciliation.* Melbourne: Black Inc.

Gray, B. (1998). Accessing the Discourses of Schooling: Language and Literacy Development with Aboriginal children in Mainstream Schools. Unpublished PhD thesis, University of Melbourne.

Gregory, J. B. and Wicks, J. M.C. (1969). *New Effective Social Studies: Grade 3.* Sydney: Horwitz Martin.

Greene, N. (1983). *Desert School.* Fremantle: Fremantle Centre for the Arts Press.

Grenville, K. (2006). *The Secret River.* Melbourne: Text.

Groome, H. (1994). *Teaching Aboriginal Studies Effectively.* Wentworth Falls: Social Science Press.

Groome, H. And Hamilton, A. (1995). *Meeting the Educational Needs of Aboriginal Adolescents.* Canberra: National Board of Employment, Education and Training.

Guild, P. (1994). The Culture/Learning Style Connection. *Educational Leadership,* 51(8), pp. 16–22.

Halse, C. (2002). *A Terribly Wild Man: The Life of the Rev. Ernest Gribble.* Sydney: Allen & Unwin.

Hammond, J. and Gibbons, P. (2001). What is Scaffolding? In J. Hammond (Ed.), *Scaffolding: Teaching and Learning in Language and Literacy Education* (pp. 1–14). Sydney: Primary English Teaching Association.

Hancock, W. K. (1961 [1930]). *Australia.* Brisbane: Jacaranda.

Harris, S. (1980). *Culture and Learning: Tradition and Education in Northern Arnhem Land.* Darwin: Professional Services Branch, Northern Territory Education Department.

——(1984). Aboriginal Learning Styles and Formal Schooling. *The Aboriginal Child at School,* 12(4), 3–23.

Harrison, N. (2005). The Learning is In-between: The Search for a Metalanguage in Indigenous Education. *Educational Philosophy and Theory,* 37(6), 867–80.

Harslett, M., Harrison, B., Godfrey, J., Partington, G. and Richer, K. (1998, November–December). *Aboriginal and Islander Education Workers' Perceptions of Schooling.* Paper presented at the 1998 Annual Conference of the Australian Association for Research in Education, Adelaide. <www.eddept.wa.edu.au/abled/quality/Aboriginal%20Ed%20Workers%20Ref%20chang.html>.

Hattie, J. (2002, August). *Why is It So Difficult to Enhance Self-concept in the Classroom? The Power of Feedback in the Self-concept–Achievement Relationship.* Paper presented at International SELF-Conference, Sydney.

——(2003). *Teachers Make a Difference: What is the Research evidence?* Auckland: University of Auckland, Australian Council for Educational Research. <www.acer.edu.au/documents/RC2003_Hattie_TeachersMakeADifference.pdf>.

——(2008). *Visible Learning.* London: Routledge.

——(2009). *Visible Learning: A Synthesis of Over 800 Meta-analyses Relating to Achievement.* New York: Routledge.

Hayes, D., Mills, M., Christie, P. and Lingard, B. (2006). *Teachers and Schooling: Making a Difference.* Sydney: Allen & Unwin.

Heiss, A., Hill, A. and La Perouse Public School students (2007). *Yirra and Her Deadly Dog, Demon.* Sydney: ABC Books.

Heiss, A. and Minter, P. (2008). *Macquarie Pen Anthology of Aboriginal Literature.* Sydney: Allen & Unwin.

Heslop, J. (2003) Living and Teaching in Aboriginal Communities. In Q. Beresford and G. Partington (Eds.), *Reform and Resistance in Aboriginal Education: The Australian Experience* (pp. 208–237). Perth: University of Western Australia Press.

Hill, K., Barker, B. and Vos, T. (2007). Excess Indigenous Mortality: Are Indigenous Australians More Severely Disadvantaged Than

Other Indigenous Populations? *International Journal of Epidemiology*, 36(3), 580–9.

Hill, P. W., & Rowe, K. J. (1996). Multilevel modeling in school effectiveness research. *School Effectiveness and School Improvement*, 7 (1), 1–34.

——(1998). Modeling student progress in studies of educational effectiveness. *School Effectiveness and School Improvement*, 9 (3), 310–333.

Hill, P. W., Rowe, K. J., Holmes-Smith, P., & Russell, V. J. (1996). *The Victorian Quality Schools Project: A study of school and teacher effectiveness*. Report to the Australian Research Council (Volume 1 – Report). Centre for Applied Educational Research, Faculty of Education, The University of Melbourne.

Hirst, J. (1988–89). The Blackening of Our Past. *Institute of Public Affairs (IPA) Review*, December–February, pp. 49–54.

——(1993). Black Land, White Light, *The Weekend Australian Review*, 17–18 July.

Historical Records of Australia (1914). Canberra: Library Committee of the Commonwealth Parliament.

History Teachers Association of NSW (HTANSW) (2009). *Response to the National Curriculum, February 2009*. Sydney: HTANSW. <www.htansw.au>.

House of Representatives Select Committee on Aboriginal Education (1985) *Aboriginal Education*. Canberra: AGPS. <http://www.aph.gov.au/House/committee/atsia/education.pdf>.

Horner, J. (1974). *Vote Ferguson for Aboriginal Freedom*. Sydney: Australia & New Zealand Book Company.

Horton, D. (Ed.) (1994). *The Encyclopedia of Aboriginal Australia*. Canberra: AIATSIS.

Howard, D. (1994). Culturally Responsive Classrooms: A Way to Assist Aboriginal Students with Hearing Loss in Urban Schools. In S. Harris and M. Malin (Eds), *Aboriginal Kids in Urban Classrooms*. Wentworth Falls: Social Science Press, pp. 37–50.

Howard, J (1988). *Future Directions*. Canberra: Liberal Party of Australia.

——(1996a). Speech in Parliament, 30 October 1996, *Hansard*. Canberra: Commonwealth of Australia.

——(1996b). *Sir Thomas Playford Lecture*, Adelaide, 5 July.

Hudspith, S. (1997). Visible Pedagogy and Urban Aboriginal Students. In S. Harris and M. Malin (Eds), *Indigenous Education: Historical, Moral and Practical Tales*. Darwin: Northern Territory University Press.

Huggins, J. (2009). *Civics and Citizenship*. Canberra: DEEWR. <www.civicsandcitizenship.edu.au/cce/default.asp?id=9319>.

Hughes, H. (2007). *Lands of Shame: Aboriginal and Torres Strait Islander 'Homelands' in Transition*. Sydney: Centre for Independent Studies.

Hughes, H. and Hughes, M. (2009). *Revisiting Indigenous Education*. : Centre for Independent Studies.

Hughes, P. (1987). *Aboriginal Culture and Learning Styles: A Challenge for Academics in Higher Education Institutions*. Armidale, NSW: University of New England.

Hughes, P., and More, A. J. (1993). *Aboriginal Ways of Learning: Learning Strengths and Learning Patterns*. Adelaide: Education Department of South Australia.

Human Rights and Equal Opportunity Commission (HREOC) (1997). *Bringing Them Home: Report of the National Inquiry into the Separation of Aboriginal and Torres Strait Islander Children from Their Families*. Canberra: AGPS. <www.austlii.edu.au/au/journals/AILR/1997/36.html>.

——(2002). *Bringing Them Home: A Guide to the Findings and Recommendations of the National Inquiry into the Separation of Aboriginal and Torres Strait Islander Children and their Families*. Sydney: Commonwealth of Australia.

——(2006). *Annual Report 2006–2007*. Sydney: Commonwealth of Australia.

Hunt, S. (1997). *Towards Tomorrow, Youth Reconciliation Convention*. Report of the 1997 Youth Reconciliation Convention, Darwin.

Hunter, B. H. and Schwab, R. G. (2003). Practical Reconciliation and Continuing Disadvantage in Indigenous Education. *The Drawing Board: An Australian Review of Public Affairs*, 4(2), 83–98.

Hunter, E., Hall, W., and Spargo, R. 1991, *The Distribution and Correlates of Alcohol Consumption in a Remote Aboriginal Population*, Sydney: National Drug and Alcohol Research Centre, University of New South Wales.

Illich, I. (1971). *Deschooling Society*. Harmondsworth: Penguin.

Innovative Research Universities Australia (IRUA). (2006). *Response to DEST Knowledge Transfer Project: Developing a Culture of Engagement in Australian Universities through the Formation of Sustainable Partnerships*. <http://www.irus.edu.au/policy/policy-20060131.pdf>.

Issues Deliberations Australia (2001). *Deliberative Poll on Reconciliation—Executive Summary of Results*. <www.i-d.a.com.au/recon_report.htm>.

Johns, G. (1999). Reconciliation: Read the Fine Print. *Quadrant*, 53(11), pp. 16–24.

Johns, G. and Brunton, R. (1999). *Reconciliation: What Does it Mean?* Institute of Public Affairs Backgrounder 11. 4. Canberra: IPA.

Johnston, E. (1991) *Report of the Royal Commission into Aboriginal Deaths in Custody*. Canberra: AGPS.

Judge, T. A. and Bono, J. E. (2001). Relationship of Core Self-evaluation Traits—Self-esteem, Generalized Self-efficacy, Locus of Control, and Emotional Stability—with Job Satisfaction and Job Performance: A Meta-analysis. *Journal of Applied Psychology*, 86, 80–92.

Keating, P. (1992). Paul Keating's Redfern Speech. *The Millenium Project*. <http://www.ratbags.com/rsoles/comment/redfern.htm>.

——(1993). *Redfern Park Statement*, 10 December 1992, to Launch the International Year of the World's Indigenous People. In *International Year Speeches*. Canberra: ATSIC.

Kelly, P., Carmody, K. and Hudson, P., with the children of Kalkarinji School (NT) (2008). *From Little Things Big Things Grow*. Darwin: One Day Hill.

Kidd, D. (1992). *The Fat and Juicy Place*. Sydney: HarperCollins.

Ladwig, J. and King, M. (2003) *Quality Teaching in NSW Public Schools: An Annotated Bibliography*. Sydney: NSW Department of Education and

Training, Professional Support and Curriculum Directorate.

Langton, M. (ed.) (1992). *Telling It Like It Is: A Guide to Making Local Aboriginal and Torres Strait Islander History* (boxed set). Canberra: IATSIS.

Lester, J. and Hanlen, W. (2004). Report on the New South Wales Aboriginal Education Policy Review. Unpublished report for the NSW Department of Education and Training.

Lewis, M. and McLeod, K. (2008). *Conversations with the Mob*. Perth: University of Western Australia Publishing.

Linard, M. (1994). From learner's style to learner's activity: lessons from various learner-centred research. In R. Lewis & P. Mendelsohn (Eds.), *Lessons from Learning* (pp. 57–79). North Holland: Elsevier Science.

Lippman, L. (1989). *Generations of Resistance*. Melbourne: Longman.

Loos, N. (1982) *Invasion and Resistance: Aboriginal–White Relations on the North Queensland Frontier 1861–1897*. Canberra: Australian National University Press.

Lounsbury, J. H. (1996). Please, Not Another Program. *The Clearing House*, 69, 211–13.

Lovejoy, A. (1976). *The Great Chain of Being*. Cambridge: Harvard University Press.

Macintyre, S. and Clark, A. (2003). *The History Wars*. Melbourne: Melbourne University Press.

Malcolm, I. (1998). You Gotta Talk the Proper Way: Language and Education In Partington, *Perspectives on Aboriginal and Torres Strait Islander Education*. Katoomba: Social Science Press.

Malin, M. (1990a). The Visibility and Invisibility of Aboriginal Students in an Urban Classroom. *Australian Journal of Education*, 34(3), 312–29.

——(1990b). Why is Life so Hard for Aboriginal Students in Urban Classrooms? *The Aboriginal Child at School*, 18(1), 9–29.

Mander, D. and Fieldhouse, L. (2009). Reflections on Implementing an Education Support Programme for Aboriginal and Torres Strait Islander Secondary School Students in a Non-Government Education Sector: What Did We Learn and What Do We Know? *The Australian Community Psychologist*, 21(1), 84–101.

Mann, D. (1811) *The Present Picture of New South Wales*. London: John Booth.

Manne, R. (2001). Right and Wrong. *Sydney Morning Herald, Spectrum*, 31 March, pp. 11–12.

——(2003). *Whitewash: On Keith Windschuttle's Fabrication*. Melbourne: Black Inc Agenda.

Marett, A., Barwick, L. and Ward, G. K. (Eds.) (2007). *Studies in Aboriginal Song*, special edition of *Australian Aboriginal Studies, Journal of the Australian Institute of Aboriginal and Torres Strait Islander Studies*, 2.

Marsh, H. W. and Craven, R. G. (2006). Reciprocal Effects of Self-concept and Performance from a Multidimensional Perspective: Beyond Seductive Pleasure and Unidimensional Perspectives. *Perspectives on Psychological Science*, 1(2). pp. 133–63.

Masters, G. (2004). Beyond Political Rhetoric: The Research on What Makes a School Good. In NSWAECG and NSWDET, *The Report of the Review of Aboriginal Education—Yanigurra Muya: Ganggurrinyma Yaarri Guurulaw Yirringin.gurray—Freeing the Spirit: Dreaming and Equal Future*. <www.onlineopinion.com.au/view.asp?article=2100&page=0>.

Martin, A. J. (2002). Motivation and Academic Resilience: Developing a Model of Student Enhancement. *Australian Journal of Education*, 47, pp. 88–106.

Martin, J. R. and Rose, D. (2005). Designing Literacy Pedagogy: Scaffolding Asymmetries. In J. Webster, C. Matthiessen and R. Hasan (Eds.), *Continuing Discourse on Language* (pp. 251–80). London: Continuum,.

Mattingley, C. and Hampton, K. (1988). *Survival in Our Own Land: Aboriginal Experiences in 'South Australia' Since 1936*. Adelaide: Wakefield Press.

Maynard, J. (2004, 18th November). *For Liberty and Freedom: Fred Maynard and the Australian Aboriginal Progressive Association*, Paper delivered at State Library for the History Council of NSW.

——(2007). *For Liberty and Freedom: Fred Maynard and the Australian Aboriginal Progressive Association*. Canberra: Aboriginal Studies Press.

McEwen, J. (1939). *The Northern Territory of Australia: Commonwealth Goverment's Policy with Respect to Aboriginals*. Canberra: Minister for the Interior.

McGrath, A. (1987). *Born in the Cattle*. Sydney: Allen & Unwin.

——(Ed.) (995). *Contested Ground*. Sydney: Allen & Unwin.

McGuinness, P. (1999). Who Will Rid Us of the Bleeding Hearts? *Sydney Morning Herald*, 20 February, p. 41.

——(2000). Time to Bury the Stolen Myth Forever. *Sydney Morning Herald, Features*, 6 April, p. 6.

McIntyre, S. (2004). *A Concise History of Australia*, 2nd ed. Melbourne: Cambridge University Press.

McKenna M. (1997–98). *Different Perspectives on Black Armband History*, Parliamentary Research Paper 5 1997–98. Canberra: Parliament of Australia.

——(2002). *Looking for Blackfellas' Point: An Australian History of Place*. Sydney: UNSW Press.

McLeod, B. (2008). *Mother's Heartbeat (Ngudjung Yugarang)*. Nowra, NSW: BMAC Publishing.

McQueen, H. (1970). *A New Britannia*. Harmondsworth: Penguin.

McRae, D. (no date) *School and Community Working Together: What Works. The Work Program: Improving outcomes for Indigenous Students*. Abbotsford, Victoria.

McRae, D., Ainsworth, G., Cumming, J., Hughes, P., Mackay, T., Price, K., Rowland, M., Warhurst, J., Woods, D. and Zbar, V. (2000a). *Education and Training for Indigenous Students. What Has Worked (and Will Again)*. The IESIP Strategic Results Project. Canberra: Australian Curriculum Studies Association and National Curriculum Services.

——(2000b). *What Works? Explorations in Improving Outcomes for Indigenous Students*. Commonwealth of Australia: Australia.

Mellor, S. and Corrigan, M. (2004). *The Case for Change: A Review of Contemporary Research on Indigenous Australian Outcomes*. Melbourne: Australian Council for Academic Research.

Metropolitan East Region. (1992). *Causerie: Aboriginal English*. Sydney: Department of School Education.

Middleton, H. (1977). *But Now We Want the Land Back*. Sydney: New Age Publishers.

Milgram, R. M., Dunn, R. and Price, G. E. (Eds.) (1993). *Teaching and Counselling Gifted and Talented Adolescents: An International Learning Style Perspective*. Westport, CT: Praeger.

Miller, J. (1985). *Koori: A Will to Win—the Heroic Resistance, Survival and Triumph of Black Australia*. Sydney: Angus & Robertson.

Mills, M. and Goos, M. (2007, November). *Productive Pedagogies: Working with Disciplines and Teacher and Student Voices*. Paper presented at the Annual Conference of the Australian Association for Research in Education, Fremantle. <www.aare.edu.07pap/mil07399.pdf>.

Ministerial Council on Education Employment, Training and Youth Affairs (MCEETYA) (2000a) *Report of MCEETYA Taskforce on Indigenous Education*. Melbourne: MCEETYA.

——(2000b). *A Model of More Culturally Inclusive and Educationally Effective Schools*. Canberra: Curriculum Corporation. <www.curriculum.edu.au/mceetya>.

——(2000c) *A Statement of Principles and Standards for More Culturally Inclusive Schooling in the Twenty-First Century*. Melbourne: MCEETYA.

——(2006). *Australian Directions in Indigenous Education 2005–2008*. Melbourne: MCEETYA.

——(2008). *Melbourne Declaration on Educational Goals for Youth Australians*. Melbourne: MCEETYA.

Molony, J. (1988). *The Penguin Bicentennial History of Australia*. Ringwood: Penguin.

Moorehead, A. (1966). *The Fatal Impact*. Harmondsworth: Penguin.

Moran, A. (1982). *Women of the Sun*, Sydney: ABC.

Moran, C. (2004). *Talk Softly, Listen Well: Profile of a Bundjalung Elder*, as told to Glennys Moran. Lismore, NSW: Southern Cross University Press.

Morecroft, J. and Bancroft, B. (2008). *Malu Kangaroo*. Sydney: Little Hare Books.

Morgan, A. (1982). *Lousy Little Sixpence*. Canberra: Ronin Films.

Morgan, S. (1999). *My Place*. Fremantle: Fremantle Arts Centre Press.

——(2005). *My Place for Young Readers*, Barbara Ker Wilson (Ed.). Fremantle: Fremantle Arts Centre Press.

Morgan, S., Tjaliminu, M. and Kwaymullina, B. (2008). *Heartsick for Country: Stories of Love, Spirit and Creation*. Fremantle: Fremantle Arts Centre Press.

Moores, I. (1995). *Voices of Aboriginal Australia: Past Present Future*, compiled for the Aboriginal Deaths in Custody Watch Committee. Springwood, NSW: Butterfly Books.

Morris, C. and Moroney, W. (no date) *What Works: The Work Program: Core Issues 4—Numeracy*. <www.whatworks.edu.au/docs/Core4numeracy.pdf>.

Mortimore, P., Sammons, P., Stoll, L., Lewis, D., & Ecob, R. (1988). *School matters: The junior years*. Wells: Open Books.

Moses, A. (2003) *Revisionism and Denial*. In R. Manne (Ed.), *Whitewash: On Keith Windschuttle's Fabrication*. Melbourne: Black Inc. Agenda.

Multicultural and Community Affairs Group (2004). *Facing up to Racism: A Strategic Plan addressing Racism and Unfair Discrimination 2004–2008*. Canberra: ACT Government.

Mulvaney, D. J. (1958). The Australian Aborigines 1606–1859. *Historical Studies, Australia and New Zealand*, 8, 135.

Munns, G. (2005). School as a Cubbyhouse: Tensions Between Intent and Practice in Classroom Curriculum. *Curriculum Perspectives*, 25(1), 1–12.

——(2007). A Sense of Wonder: Pedagogies to Engage Students Who Live in Poverty. *International Journal of Inclusive Education*, 11(3), 301–15.

Munns, G., Arthur, L., Downes, T., Gregson, R., Power, A., Sawyer, W., Singh, M., Thistleton-Martin, J. and Steele, F. (2006). *Motivation and Engagement of Boys: Evidence-based Teaching Practices*. Report submitted to the Commonwealth Department of Education, Science and Training. DEST. Canberra: Commonwealth of Australia.

Munns, G.., Martin, A. J. and Craven, R. G. (2006, July). *What Can Free the Spirit? Motivating Indigenous Students to be Producers of their Own Educational Futures*. Paper presented at the 4th International SELF Research Conference, Self-concept, Motivation, Social and Personal Identity for the 21st Century. Ann Arbor: University of Michigan.

Nakata, M. (2003). Some Thoughts on Literacy Issues in Indigenous Contexts. *Australian Journal of Indigenous Education*, 31(2), 7–15.

National Aboriginal Education Committee (NAEC) (1986). *Policy Statement on Teacher Education for Aborigines and Torres Strait Islanders*. Canberra: AGPS.

National Accelerated Literacy Program (no date), <www.nalp.edu.au>.

National Assembly of the Uniting Church of Australia (2002). *Submission of the National Assembly of the Uniting Church in Australia to the Senate Legal and Constitutional References Committee Inquiry into Progress towards National Reconciliation*. Sydney. Uniting Church. <http://www.aph.gov.au/SEnate/committee/legcon_ctte/completed_inquiries/2002–04/reconciliation/submissions/sublist.htm>.

National Board of Employment, Education and Training (NBEET) (1992). *Aboriginal and Torres Strait Islander Education in the Early Years*. Canberra: AGPS.

National Curriculum Board (2008). *National History Curriculum Framing Paper*. Canberra: NCB. <www.ncb.org.au>.

——(2009). *The Shape of the Australian Curriculum*. <www.acara.edu.au/verve/_resources/Shape_of_the_Australian_Curriculum.pdf>.

National Health and Medical Research Council (2003). *Values and Ethics: Guidelines for Ethical Conduct in Aboriginal and Torres Strait Islander Health Research*. Canberra: NHMRC.

National Times (1986). 18–24 April.

Neill, A. S. (1971). *Children's Rights*. London: Granada.

Neville, A. O. (1937). Quoted in *Aboriginal Welfare: Initial*

Conference of Commonwealth and State Aboriginal Authorities. Canberra: Commonwealth of Australia.

Newlin, N. (1988). *Where There's Life There's Spirit.* Sydney: Norm Newlin.

Newman, M. A. (1977). An Analysis of Sixth-grade Pupils' Errors on Written Mathematical Tasks. *Victorian Institute for Educational Research Bulletin*, 39, 31–43.

—— (1983). *Strategies for Diagnosis and Remediation.* Sydney: Harcourt, Brace Jovanovich.

Newmann, F. and Associates (1996) *Authentic Achievement: Restructuring Schools for Intellectual Quality.* San Francisco: Jossey-Bass.

New South Wales Aboriginal Education Consultative Group (NSW AECG) Inc. and NSW Department of Education and Training (NSW DET) (2004). *The Report of the Review of Aboriginal Education. Yanigurra Muya: Ganggurrinyma Yaarri Guurulaw Yirringin.guray. Freeing the Spirit: Dreaming an Equal Future.* Sydney: NSW AECG and NSW.

New South Wales Board of Studies (2001). *Working with Aboriginal Communities: A Guide to Community Consultation.* Sydney: New South Wales Board of Studies.

New South Wales Department of Education and Training (NSW DET) (1995). *Whole School Anti-Racism Project Kit.* Sydney: NSWDET.

——(2003). *Quality Teaching in NSW Public Schools: Discussion Paper.* Sydney: NSW DET.

——(2006a). *NSW Aboriginal Education and Training Strategy 2006–2008: A Direct Response to the Aboriginal Education Review.* Sydney: Aboriginal Education and Training Directorate, NSW DET.

——(2006b). A Further 20 Schools to Join the 'Schools In Partnership' Initiative. News Room NSWDET. <www.det.nsw.edu.au/newsroom/yr2006/sep/partnersh_init.htm>.

New South Wales Legislative Council Standing Committee on Social Issues (2008). *Overcoming Indigenous Disadvantage: Final Report.* Sydney: New South Wales Government.

Newspoll Market Research (2000). *Quantitative Research into Issues Relating to a Document of Reconciliation.* Canberra: Council for Aboriginal Reconciliation. <www.austlii.edu.au/au/other/IndigLRes/car/2000/3>.

Ngarritjan-Kessaris, T. (1994). Talking properly with Aboriginal parents. In S. Harris and M. Malin (Eds.), *Aboriginal Kids in Urban Classrooms* (pp. 117–123). Wentworth Falls: Social Science Press.

Nicklin Dent, J. and Hatton, E. (1996). Education and Poverty: An Australian Primary School Case Study. *Australian Journal of Education*, 40(1), 46–64.

Noonuccal, O. (1995). *Rainbow Serpent.* Midland, WA: Narkaling Inc.

——(2007a). *My People* (4th ed.). Brisbane: John Wiley and Sons.

——(2007b). *Father Sky and Mother Earth.* Melbourne: John Wiley and Sons.

——(2008). *My People.* 4th ed. Milton: John Wiley and Sons.

Norrington, B. (2007). Keating Scorns 'Deathbed Repentance'. *The Australian*, 12 October.

Nurcombe, B. (1976). *Children of the Dispossessed.* Honolulu: East-West Centre.

OECD Steering Group (2007). *Communiqué from the OECD Seminar on Indigenous Education: Effective Practice, Mutual Learning.* Cairns: OECD.

Office for Aboriginal and Torres Strait Islander Partnerships). (2008). Queensland Closing the Gap Report: 2007–08; Indicators and Initiatives for Aboriginal and Torres Strait Islander Peoples <http://www.atsip.qld.gov.au/partnerships/partnership-qld/documents/closing-the-gap-report.pdf>

Osborne, J. W. (1997). Race and Academic Disidentification. *Journal of Educational Psychology*, 89(4), 728–35.

Parbury, N. (2005). *Survival: A History of Aboriginal Life in New South Wales.* Sydney: New South Wales Department of Aboriginal Affairs.

Parliament of Australia (2002). *Terms of Reference: Inquiry into the Progress of Reconciliation.* <www.aph.gov.au/Senate/committee>.

Parry, N. (2005). 'Lock, Maria (c. 1805–1878)', *Australian Dictionary of Biography*, Supplementary Volume (pp. 236–7). Melbourne: Melbourne University Press.

Partington, G. (Ed.) (1998). *Perspectives on Torres Strait Islander Education.* Katoomba: Social Science Press.

Partington, G., Godfrey, J., Harslett, M. and Richer, K. (2000, July). *Can non-Indigenous Teachers Succeed in Teaching Indigenous Students.* Paper presented at Australian Indigenous Education Conference, Fremantle.

Partington, G. and Richter, K. (1999, November–December). *Barriers to Effective Teaching of Indigenous Students.* Paper presented to the Australian Association of Research in Education Conference, Melbourne. <www.eddept.wa.au>.

Pearson, N. (1991). *Sydney University Gazette*, June.

——(2004). We Need Real Reform for Indigenous Public Schooling. *The Australian*, 25 August. m digenous%20public%20schooling.pdf

——(2007). Many Paths to Reconciliation, *The Australian*, 14 October.

——(2007). No More Victims. *New Statesman*, 27.

——(2009). A People's Survival. *Weekend Australian, Review*, 3–4 October, p. 1.

Peating, S. (2009). Sorry Mick, but Australia Day Date Stays: Rudd, *Sydney Morning Herald*, 26 January.

Penfold, A. (2006). *One of the Boys: St Joseph's College Indigenous Fund Annual Report, 2006.* Sydney: St Joseph's College.

Perkins, R. and Atkinson, W. (2009). *First Australians: An Illustrated History.* Melbourne: Melbourne University Press.

Pilger, J. (1986). *A Secret Country.* Melbourne: Vintage.

Poad, D., West, A. and Miller, R. (1990). *Contact: An Australian History*, 2nd ed. Melbourne: Heinemann Educational.

Pratt, A., Elder, C., and Ellis, C. (2000, December). *Reconciliation: Origins, Policy, Practice, Representations, Meanings, Futures.* Paper presented to the Diversity Conference—Imagining Ourselves: Reconciliation in the National Imagination. University of Technology Sydney.

Reprint in M. Kalantzis and W. Cope (Eds.) (2001). *Reconciliation, Multiculturalism, Identities: Difficult Dialogues, Sensible Solutions* (pp. 135–47). Adelaide: Common Ground.

Productivity Commission (2007). *Overcoming Indigenous Disadvantage: Key Indicators 2007*. Canberra: AGPS.

——(2009). *Overcoming Indigenous Disadvantage: Key Indicators 2009*. Canberra: AGPS.

Purdie, N., Tripcony, P., Boulton-Lewis, G., Fanshawe, J. and Gunstone, A. (2000). *Positive Self identity for Indigenous Students and Its Relationship to School Outcomes*. Queensland University of Technology and Department of Education, Science and Training.

Queensland Department of Education and Training (no date). *Queensland School Reform Longitudinal Study*. Brisbane: Queensland DET. <http://education.qld.gov.au/public_ media/reports/curriculumframework/qsrls/html/abt_ppc.html>.

Queensland Government (2008). *Quarterly Report on Key indicators in Queensland's Discrete Indigenous communities July–September 2008*. <www.atsip.qld.gov.au/government/programs-initiatives/partnerships/quarterly-reports/report-july-sep-2008.asp>.

Read, J. (1982). *The Stolen Generations; the Removal of Aboriginal Children in New South Wales 1883–1969*. Sydney: New South Wales Ministry of Aboriginal Affairs.

Reconciliation Australia (2001). Reconciliation: Australia takes the next step. Melbourne: Reconciliation Australia.

——(2002). *What is Reconciliation?* <www.reconciliationaustralia.org./graphics/info/whatis.html>

——(2009) *Australian Reconciliation Barometer*. <www.reconciliation.org.au/home/reconciliation-resources/facts--figures/australian-reconciliation-barometer>. Accessed 20 December 2009.

Reece, R. H.W. (1974). *Aborigines and Colonists*. Sydney: Sydney University Press.

Resolution of the Conference of Commonwealth and State Aboriginal Authorities, Canberra, 1937. Excerpt. (1996). In J. Thompson and A. McMahon (Eds.), *The Australian Welfare State: Key Documents and Themes* (pp. 156–157). South Yarra: Pan Macmillan.

Reynolds, H. (1981). *The Other Side of the Frontier*. Brisbane: University of Queensland Press.

——(1987). *Frontier*. Sydney: Allen & Unwin.

——(1989). *Dispossession: Black Australians and White Invaders*. Sydney: Allen & Unwin.

——(1994). Invasion versus settlement debate wears on. *The Weekend Australian*, 13–14 August.

——(1995). *Fate of a Free People*, Ringwood: Penguin.

——(1996). *Frontier: Aborigines, Settlers and Land*. Sydney: Allen & Unwin.

——(1998). *This Whispering in Our Hearts*. Sydney: Allen & Unwin.

——(2003). *Terra Nullius Reborn*. In R. Manne (Ed.), *Whitewash: On Keith Windschuttle's Fabrication* (pp. 109–138). Melbourne: Black Inc. Agenda.

——(2004). *Fate of a Free People*, rev. ed. Ringwood: Penguin.

Ridgeway, A. (1999). Maiden speech in the Australian Senate. Parliament of Australia. <www.aph.gov.au/senate/senators/homepages/web/sfs-8g6.htm>.

Ring, I. and Brown, N. (2003). Aboriginal and Torres Strait Islander Health Implementation, Not More Policies. *Journal of Australian Indigenous Issues*, 6(3), 3–12.

Rintoul, S. (1993). *The Wailing: A National Black Oral History*. Melbourne: Heinemann.

Roberts, J. (1981). *Massacre to Mining*. Melbourne: Collins Press.

Robinson C., Tobin C. and Connolly T. (1993). *1788: The Great South Land: A music-based Integrated Resource Kit*. Calga, NSW: Creative and Musical Resources.

Rose, D. (2004). Sequencing and Pacing of the Hidden Curriculum: How Indigenous Learners are Left Out of the Chain. In J. Muller, A. Morais and B. Davies (Eds.), *Reading Bernstein, Researching Bernstein* (pp. 91–107). London: RoutledgeFalmer.

Rose, D., Gray, B. and Cowey, W. (1999). Scaffolding Reading and Writing for Indigenous Children in School. In P. Wignell (Ed.), *Double Power: English Literacy and Indigenous Education* (pp. 23–60). Melbourne: National Language and Literacy Institute of Australia (Languages Australia).

Rowe, K. J. (1998, July). *What's so good about Reading Recovery?* Invited keynote address presented at the International Reading Recovery Institute Conference, Cairns, Queensland, Australia.

—— (2002). The Importance of Teacher Quality. *Issues Analysis, Centre for Independent Studies*, 22, 28 February.

——(2003). The Importance of Teacher Quality as a Key Determinant of Students' Experiences and Outcomes of Schooling. Keynote Address for the ACER Research Conference, Melbourne, October.

——(2006). *Effective Teaching Practices for Students With and Without Learning Difficulties: Constructivism as a Legitimate Theory of Learning and of Teaching?* Melbourne: ACER.

Rowe, K. J., and Hill, P. W. (1998). Modeling educational effectiveness in classrooms: The use of multilevel structural equations to model students' progress. *Educational Research and Evaluation*, 4 (4), 307–347.

Rowe, K. J., Hill, P.W. and Holmes-Smith P. (1995). Methodological issues in educational performance and school effectiveness research: A discussion with worked examples. *Australian Journal of Education*, 39 (3), 217–248.

Rowe, K. J., Holmes-Smith, P. D. and Hill, P. W. (1993, November). *The link between school effectiveness research, policy and school improvement: Strategies and procedures that make a difference*. Paper presented at the 1993 Annual Conference of the Australian Association for Research in Education, Fremantle, W.A.

Rowe, K. J. and Rowe, K. S. (1992a). The relationship between inattentiveness in the classroom and reading achievement (Part A): Methodological Issues. *Journal of the American Academy of Child and Adolescent Psychiatry*, 31 (2), 349–356

Rowe, K. J. and Rowe, K. S. (1992b). The relationship between inattentiveness in the classroom and reading achievement (Part B): An Explanatory Study. *Journal of the American Academy of Child and Adolescent Psychiatry*, 31 (2), 357–368.

Rowe, K. J. and Rowe, K. S. (1999). Investigating the relationship between students' *attentive inattentive* behaviors in the classroom and their literacy progress. *International Journal of Educational Research*, 31 (1/2), 1–138 (Whole Issue). Elsevier Science, Pergamon Press.

Rowley, C. D. (1972). *The Destruction of Aboriginal Society*. Harmondsworth: Penguin.

Ruddock, P. (2002). *Commonwealth Government Submission to Senate Legal and Constitutional References Committee Inquiry into the Progress Towards National Reconciliation*. Canberra: Parliament of Australia. <www.aph.gov.au/Senate/committee/legcon_ctte/Reconciliation/index.htm>.

Ryan, L. (1981). *Aboriginal Tasmanians*. Brisbane: University of Queensland Press.

——(2003). Who is the Fabricator? In R. Manne (Ed.), *Whitewash: On Keith Windschuttle's Fabrication*. (pp. 230–257). Melbourne: Black Inc. Agenda.

Said, E. (1979). *Orientalism*. New York: Vintage.

Sansom, B. (1980). *The Camp at Wallaby Cross: Aboriginal Fringe Dwellers in Darwin*. Canberra: Aboriginal Studies Press.

School for Social and Policy Research (SSPR) Charles Darwin University, 2008, Student Progress 2007, Accelerated Literacy NT Schools, System Level Summary, <http://www.nalp.edu.au/documents/AL_Student_Progress_2007_web_release.pdf>.

Scott, E. (1998). Reconciliation Council Media Release. 27 May.

Senate Employment, Workplace Relations, Small Business, and Education References Committee (2000). *Katu Kalpa: Report of the Inquiry into the Effectiveness of Education and Training Programs for Indigenous Australians*. Canberra: Parliament of Australia.

Shanahan, D. (2007). Howard's 'New Reconciliation.' *The Australian*, 12 October.

Shaw, P. (2009). *Seven Seasons in Aurukun*. Sydney: Allen & Unwin.

Sherwood, J. and McConville, K. (1994). *Otitis Media and Aboriginal Children: A Handbook for Teachers and Communities*. Sydney: NSW Board of Studies.

Shoemaker, A. (Ed.) (1994). *Oodgeroo: A Tribute*. Brisbane: University of Queensland Press.

Simpson, L., McFadden, M. G. and Munns, G. (2001). Someone Has to Go Through: Indigenous Boys, Staying on at School and Negotiating Masculinities in W. Martino and B. Meyenn (Eds.), *What About the Boys? Issues of Masculinity in Schools*. Buckingham: Open University Press.

Smith, B. (1960). *European Vision and the South Pacific 1768–1850*. London: Oxford University Press.

Smith. D. (1992). *Lookin' for Your Mob: A Guide to Tracing Aboriginal Family Trees*. Canberra: IATSIS.

Snider, V. E. (1990). What We Know About Learning Styles from Research in Special Education. *Educational Leadership*, 48(2), 50–56.

Social Health Reference Group (2004). *Social and Emotional Wellbeing Framework: A National Strategic Framework for Aboriginal and Torres Straight Islander Peoples' Mental Health and Social and Emotional Wellbeing 2004–2009*. Canberra: Commonwealth Department of Health and Aging.

Stairs, A. (1994). Indigenous Ways to Go to School: Exploring Many Visions. *Journal of Multilingual and Multicultural Development*, 15(1), 63–74.

Stanner W. E. H. (1968). *After the Dreaming: Black and White Australians—an Anthropologist's View*, ABC Boyer Lectures. Sydney: ABC.

State of Victoria (2008). *Wannik: Learning Together—Journey of Our Future. Education Strategy for Koorie Students, Victoria 2008*. Melbourne: Koorie Education Strategy Branch, Department of Education and Early Childhood Development.

Steering Committee for the Review of Government Service Provision. (SCRGSP) (2007). *Overcoming Indigenous Disadvantage: Key Indicators 2007*. Canberra: Productivity Commission.

——(2009). *Overcoming Indigenous Disadvantage: Key Indicators 2009*. Canberra: Productivity Commission.

Stevens, F. (1980). *The Politics of Prejudice*. Sydney: Alternative Publishing Cooperative.

Streetwize (1997). *Reconciliation*. Sydney: Streetwize Communications.

Summers, A. (2000). An Olympic Icon Signals Australia's Awakening. *Sydney Morning Herald*, 28 September, p. 18.

Strong, G. (1989). A Poem About Me, *Pemulwuy: Journal of the New South Wales AECG*.

Sun-Herald (1991). Editorial: An Opportunity to Heal Wounds, 28 April, p. 26.

Sveiby, K.-E. and Skuthorpe, T. (2006). *Treading Lightly: The Hidden Wisdom of the World's Oldest People*. Sydney: Allen & Unwin.

Swain, D. (1988). *200 in the Shade*. Sydney: Collins.

Swan, P. and Raphael, B. (1995). *Ways: National Aboriginal and Torres Strait Islander Mental Health Policy—National Consultancy Report*. Canberra: AGPS.

Sweeney, B. and Associates (1996). *Unfinished Business: Australians and Reconciliation*. Canberra: Council for Aboriginal Reconciliation.

Taylor, P. (1992). *Telling It Like It Is: A Guide to Making Aboriginal and Torres Strait Islander History*. Canberra: IATSIS.

Teddlie, C. and Stringfield, S. C. (1993). *Schools make a difference: Lessons learned from a 10-year study of school effects*. New York: Teachers College Press.

The Australian. (2000). Editorial, 8 December, p. 12.

Tickner, R. (1991). *Council for Aboriginal Reconciliation Bill. Second reading by the Minister Assisting the Prime Minister in Aboriginal Affairs, the Hon. Robert Tickner*. Canberra: AGPS.

——(1993). *Rebutting Mabo Myths*. Canberra: ATSIC.

Toohey, Paul (2009). Roadblock on Remote Housing as Progress Stalls on Indigenous Response. *The Australian*, 4 July.

Trimble, J. E. (1977). The Sojourner in the American Indian Community:

Methodological Issues and Concerns. *Journal of Social Issues*, 33, 159–74.

Trimble, J. E. and Medicine, B. (1976). Development of Theoretical Models and Levels of Interpretation in Mental Health. In J. Wesermeyer (ed.), *Anthropology and Mental Health* (pp.161–200). The Hague: Mouton.

Tucker, A. (1994). *Too Many Captain Cooks*. Adelaide: Omnibus Books.

——(1999). *Side by Side*. Adelaide: Omnibus Books.

United Nations General Assembly, *International Convention on the Elimination of All Forms of Racial Discrimination*. 21 December 1965. United Nations, Treaty Series, vol. 660, p. 2. <www.unhcr.org/refworld/docid/3ae6b3940.html>.

Vicary, D. and Westerman., T. (2004). 'That's Just the Way He Is': Some Implications of Aboriginal Mental Health Beliefs. *Australian e-Journal of the Advancement of Mental Health*, 3(3), pp. 1–10.

Warren (1998). Wake Up—Time to Say Sorry [Cartoon]. *Daily Telegraph*, p. 10.

Warren, E. and Young, J. (2008). Oral Language, Representations and Mathematical Understanding: Indigenous Australian Students. *Australian Journal of Indigenous Education*, 37, 130–7.

Watson, M. (2003). The Aboriginal Flag. Yabbastick, Vol. 7 (6), 4.

Watson, P., Partington, G., Gray, J. and Mack, L. (2006a). *A Research Project Commissioned by the Aboriginal Education and Training Council of Western Australia*. Perth: Aboriginal Education and Training Council. <www.etcwa.org.au/files/pdf/aborignal_students_numeracy.pdf>.

——(2006b). *Aboriginal Students and Numeracy*. Perth: Edith Cowan University.

Welton, J. (1914). *Principles and Methods of Teaching*. Oxford: University Tutorial Press.

West, J. (1852). *History of Tasmania*, 2 vols. Launceston: Henry Dowling.

White, A. (2005). Active Mathematics in Classrooms: Finding Out Why Children Make Mistakes—and Then Doing Something to Help Them. *Square One*, 15(4), 15–19. <www.curriculumsupport.education.nsw.gov.au/primary/mathematics/assets/pdf/sqone.pdf>

Wignell, P. () (1999). *Double Power: English Literacy and Indigenous Education*. Melbourne: NLLIA.

Wild, R. and Anderson, P. (2007). *Little Children are Sacred: Exploring Accountability to Australia's Aboriginal Children*. Darwin: Northern Territory Board of Inquiry into the Protection of Aboriginal Children from Sexual Abuse.

Willey, K. (1972). *When the Sky Fell Down*. Sydney: Collins.

Williams, P. (2001). Deaths in Custody: 10 Years on from the Royal Commission, *Trends & Issues in Crime and Criminal Justice*, 203. <www.aic.gov.au/documents/F/1/6/%7BF163D8C1–79C4–48DE-BB14–0782100695B9%7Dti203.pdf>.

Willms, J. D. (2000). Monitoring school performance for standards-based reform. *Evaluation and Research in Education*, 14, 237–253.

Windschuttle, K. (2000). *The Myths of Frontier Massacres in Australian History*, Parts 1–3. Quadrant, October, November, December, pp. 8–21, 17–24, 6–20. [accessed 10 August 2009]

——(2002). *The Fabrication of Aboriginal History: Volume One: Van Diemen's Land, 1803–1947*. Sydney: Macleay Press

——(2003). Doctored Evidence and Invented Incidents in Aboriginal Historiography. In B. Attwood and S. Foster (Eds.), *Frontier Conflict: The Australian Experience*. Canberra: National Museum of Australia.

Wood, D., Bruner, J. and Ross, G. (1976). The Role of Tutoring in Problem Solving. *Journal of Child Psychology and Psychiatry and Allied Disciplines*, 17(2), 89–102.

Woolmington, J. (1973). *Aborigines in Colonial Society, 1788–1850: From 'Noble Savage' to 'Rural Pest'*. Australia: Cassell.

Wright, A. (2006) *Carpentaria*. Melbourne: Giramondo.

Yalata and Oak Valley Aboriginal Communities and Mattingley, C. (2009). *Maralinga: The Anangu Story*. Sydney: Allen & Unwin.

Yarwood, A. T. and Knowling, M. J. (1982). *Race Relations in Australia: A History*. North Ryde: Methuen.

Yunupingu, G. (2008) *Our Land is Our Life: Land Rights Past Present and Future*. Brisbane: University of Queensland Press.

Zevenbergen, R., Mousley, J. and Sullivan, P. (2004). Making the Pedagogic Relay Inclusive for Indigenous Australian Students in Mathematics Classrooms. *International Journal of Inclusive Education*, 8(4), 391–405.

Zubrick S. R., Silburn S. R., De Maio J. A., Shepherd C., Griffin J. A., Dalby R. B., Mitrou F. G., Lawrence D. M., Hayward C., Pearson G., Milroy H., Milroy J. and Cox A. (2006). *The Western Australian Aboriginal Child Health Survey: Improving the Educational Experiences of Aboriginal Children and Young People*. Perth: Curtin University of Technology and Telethon Institute for Child Health Research.

Zubrick, S. R., Silburn, S. R., Lawrence, D. M., Mitrou, F. G., Dalby, R. B., Blair, E.M, Griffin, J., Milroy, H., De Mino, J. A., Cox, A. and Li, J. (2005a). *The Western Australian Aboriginal Child Health Survey: Vol. 1—Forced Separation from Natural Family*. Perth: Curtin University of Technology and Telethon Institute for Child Health Research.

——(2005b). *The Western Australian Aboriginal Child Health Survey: Vol. 2—Social and Emotional Wellbeing of Aboriginal Children and Young People*. Perth: Curtin University of Technology and Telethon Institute for Child Health Research.

——(2006). *The Western Australian Aboriginal Child Health Survey: Improving the Educational Experiences of Aboriginal Children and Young People*. Perth: Curtin University of Technology and Telethon Institute for Child Health Research.

Zyngier, D. (2005). Listening to Teachers—Listening to Students. Substantive Conversations About Resistance, Empowerment and Engagement. Translation of Research into Practice. Paper presented to national conference of the *Australian Association for Research in Education*, Sydney. <www.aare.edu.au/05pap/abs05.htm>.

Index

Page numbers in *italics* refer to figures and illustrations.

ABC, 274, 277
Aboriginal Australia – To the Others (poem), 68, 190
Aboriginal Charter of Rights (poem), 1–2
Aboriginal Children's Advancement Society, 139
Aboriginal Consultative Group, 16, 138, 140
Aboriginal Education and Training Directorate, 14
Aboriginal Education Consultative Groups
  demise of national federation, 146
  establishment of, 139
  in New South Wales, vii, 17, 239, 241, 249
  as researchers and lobbyists, 39
  review of Aboriginal education, 239
  role of, vii, 17, 198
  as a source of advice, 59, 206, 208
Aboriginal Education Council, 139
Aboriginal Education Council Family and Community Fun Day, *209*
Aboriginal Education Policy, 116
Aboriginal Education Workers, 148, 208, 232–3, 241
Aboriginal Employment Strategy, 13, 318, 321
Aboriginal English, 254, 264–5, 271
The Aboriginal Flag (poem), 257
Aboriginal Land Council network, 38
Aboriginal Land Councils, 82, 197
Aboriginal Land Rights (Northern Territory) Act 1976, 81, 84
Aboriginal languages, 144–5
Aboriginal Program Exchange, 274

Aboriginal Sharers of Knowledge program, 14
Aboriginal Student Support and Parent Awareness program, 40, 143, 146–7, 189
Aboriginal Studies
  anti-racist teaching strategies, 66–7
  assessment and evaluation, 307, 309–12
  benefits to all children 18, 19
  benefits to Indigenous children, 19–20
  calls for establishment of courses, 16
  checking units of work, 300, 305
  consulting Indigenous communities, 195–209
  content of, 3, 5, 254
  demonstrative activities, 305–6
  expressive activities, 306, 307
  first courses in NSW, 118
  harnessing goodwill of teachers, 234
  Indigenous involvement in, 274
  intake activities, 305, 306
  key concepts, 300, *303–4*
  ordering and setting out activities, 307
  organising information for students, 305, 306
  as part of reconciliation, 20, 39
  politics of, 5
  reasons for teaching, 2, 17–21
  role of the teacher, 209
  Royal Commission recommendations, 181–2
  structuring activities, 305
  syllabus developed in NSW, 140
  teachers as facilitators, 289–91
  teaching resources for, 273–88
  teaching strategies, 291, 293–6

  teaching suggestions, 186–7, 190–3
  terminology in, 59–62, 276
  testimony by student of, 4
  themes in, 299–300, *301*, *302*
  theoretical model of, 297–9, *298*
  topics for Indigenous teachers only, 297
  topics for non-Indigenous teachers, 296–7
  see also history; students, Indigenous; teachers
Aboriginal Studies Association, ix, 39
Aboriginal Teacher Aides, 139
Aboriginal Tent Embassy, 37
Aboriginal Tutorial Assistance Scheme, 142, 146
Aboriginal Website Directory, 277
Aborigines *see* Indigenous Australians
Aborigines Progressive Association, 79, 80, 104
Aborigines Protection Boards, 74, 78, 79, 92–3, 99–100, 105
Aborigines Protection Society (UK), 75
Aborigines Welfare Board, 78, 92–3, 100, 106, 133, 136, 141
absenteeism, 7
Abstudy, 146, 177
academic achievement, 5, 7–11, 14–16, 220, 222–3, 279
academic self-concept, 224
ACARA, 274
Accelerated Literacy, 245
Accor Asia Pacific Corporate Leaders for Indigenous Employment Project, 13
ACT Indigenous Traineeship Program, 13

Addressing the Key Issues of Reconciliation, 183
Adorno, J.W., 44
Advance Australia Fair (poem), 182
AECGs *see* Aboriginal Education Consultative Groups
AEP, 142
AIME, 250–1, *251*, 323
Ainsworth, G., 225
Akerman, Piers, 121
Albert Namatjira (linocut), *90*
alcohol, and Indigenous people, 49, 51, 145
Alexandria Park Community School, *209*, 250
Altman, J.C., 164
Anangu-Mara people, 92
Andrews, Auriel, 33
Andrews, Gavin, *38*, *194*
Annan, Kofi, 33
anthropology, 47, 62
Anyone for a Bit of Reconciliation? (cartoon), *85*
ANZ Bank, 162
Anzac Legend, 111
An Appeal (poem), 21
Aquilina, John, 63
Archibald Prize, *322*
ARIA Awards, 34
armed services, Indigenous Australians in, 104, *110*, 130–1
Around the Kitchen Table (kit), 157
art and artists, 32–3, *41*, 52, 54, 77, 204, 253
art galleries, 274
Arthur, George, 73
Ashby, Craig, 321
Ashfield Public School, 188–9
assessment, in Aboriginal Studies, 307, 309–12
assimilation, 78–9, *79*, 98, 114, 135, 137, 325
ASSPA, 40, 143, 146–7, 189
ATAS, 142, 146
Atkinson, Stuart, 123
Atkinson, Wayne, 117
ATSIC, 82, 84, 85, 87, 146
attitudes, towards Indigenous people, 174, *175*, 176
Attwood, Bain, 123
Auspoll, 172
Australia (Crawford), 113
Australia (film), 319
Australia, British invasion of, 47, 70, 70–5, 93–7, 110–11
Australia Day, 27
Australia Post stamps, *165*
The Australian, 163
Australian Aboriginal Fellowship, 105
Australian Aborigines League, 79, 80
Australian Aborigines Progressive Association, 79

Australian Broadcasting Corporation, 122
Australian Bureau of Statistics, 2, 25, 108, 185, 278
Australian Constitution, 125
Australian Council of Deans of Education, 16
Australian Curriculum and Assessment Authority, 274
Australian Directions in Indigenous Education, 232, 233, 234, 237, 239, 259
Australian Education Council, 16
Australian Film Industry Awards, 35
Australian Football League, 162
Australian Government Quality Teaching Programme, 242–4
Australian Hall, Sydney, 80, *80*
Australian Human Rights Commission, 49
Australian Idol (television program), 34
Australian Indigenous Education Foundation, 321
Australian Indigenous Mentoring Experience, 250–1, *251*, 323
Australian Indigenous Resources Buying Guide 2010, 273
Australian Institute of Aboriginal and Torres Strait Islander Studies, 197, 325
Australian Labor Party, 77, 106
Australian National Opinion Polls, 82
Australian Opera Company, 33–4
Australian Reconciliation Barometer, 172–80, *175*, *178*, *179*, 187
Australian Reconciliation Convention, 86, 186
Australians for Native Title and Reconciliation, 87, *315*
Australia's Language..., 144
awareness, of Indigenous history, 173–4, *174*

Babakiueria (video), 190
'backtracking', 254
Balloderree, 74
Bamblett, Lionel, 232
Bancroft, Bronwyn, 32, 54, *314*
Bancroft, Jack Manning, 250
Bangarra (poem), 22
Bangarra Dance Theatre, *322*, *324*
Banks, Sir Joseph, 75
Bannister, Saxe, 97–8
Barambah rugby league team, *103*
Barefoot Rugby League Show (television program), 36
Bark Petition, 80
Barker, June, 138
The Barometer, 172–80, *175*, *178*, *179*, 187
Barton, G.B., 111–12
Barwick, Diane, 117

Bashir, Marie, 28, 156, *156*, 251
Bateman Report on Survey of Native Affairs..., 137
Batman, John, 74
BE, 204
Bedford, Paddy, 33
Beetson, Jack, 14, 189
behavioural problems, 219
Bellear, Kaye, 116
Bendigo Senior Secondary College, 14
Bennelong, 40, 129
Bennett, E., 198
Bennett, John, 4
bereavement, 217
Berndt, R.M & C.H., 47
Berwick, Cindy, 4, 14–15, 17, 200, 239
Beyond a Joke (Cooke), 190
Beyond Empathy program, 204
BHP Billiton, 162
bias, in teaching resources, 287–8
Bicentennial History of Australia (Molony), 119
Bicentennial of Australia, 82, 118, 119
BighART, *211*
Biko, Steve, 105
bilingual schools, 144–5
Bin Bakar, Mark, 35
Bin-Sallik, Mary Ann, 25, 228
Biskup, Peter, 117
'black armband' approach to history, 121
Black Chicks Talking (Purcell), 36
Black Lace (band), 34
'black money' syndrome, 142
Black, Sir Hermann, 139
Black War, 71, 74
Blacktracks (poem), 24
Blainey, Geoffrey, 29, 111, 117, 118, 120, 160
Blair, Harold, 33–4
Blair, Noel, 138
Blanchett, Cate, 318
Blanket Day, 97
Bleakley, J.W., 137
Blek Bela Mujik (band), 34
Bligh, William, 73
boarding schools, 177, 184–5
Bodkin-Andrews, G.H., 224, 228
body language, 268
Bolt, Andrew, 121
Bomaderry Infants' Home, 99, 100
Bonner, Neville, 80
Bonwick, J., 111–12
Boomerangs Rugby League Football Club, 103
Borbidge, Rob, *85*
Born in the Cattle (Mcgrath), 122
Boughton, Bob, 14
Boyce, James, 122
Boyd, David, *71*
Brady, W., 198
Bran Nue Dae (film), 35, 319
breastplates, *91*

Brennan, Justice, 83
Bridge, Jaime Maria, *328*
Brindle, Ken, 139
Bringing Them Home, 87, 107–9, 158, 160, 190, 218, 276
Brisbane Courier, 76
British invasion, of Australia, 47, 70, 70–5, 93–7, 110–11
Brock, Paul, 326
Brockie, Jenny, 318
Brodie, Veronica, 57
Broome, Richard, 117
Bropho, Robert, 36
Broulee Public School Dhurga Djamanji language program, 14
Brown, Maquilla, *4*
Bulletin, 77
bullying, 219
Bungaree, 40
Burgoyne, Joe, 137
Burney, Linda
  on Aboriginal Studies, 18, 144
  biography of, 159, *159*
  contribution of, 319
  on council of mentoring project, 251
  criticises education policy, 116
  desire for shared history, 129
  MCs book launch, ix
  member of Teaching the Teachers project, *ix*
  at presentation, *4*
  on schools, 194
Busby Marou (band), 34
Business Council of Australia, 321

Cadigal Clan, 92
Calder, J., 111
Calma, Tom, 58, 176, 251
Cambourne, B., 264
Campbell, Jason, *197*
Campbell, Preston, 28
Cannes Film Festival, 35
Canobolas Rural Technology High School, *328*
Canowindra Club, 103
Cape York Institute, 10
Cape York Welfare Reform Trial, 8
CAR *see* Council for Aboriginal Reconciliation
Carmichael, Beryl, 195, 221
Carmichael, Stokely, 105
Carmody, Kev, 34
Carowra Tank Aboriginal School, *132*
Carpentaria (Wright), 36, 199–200, 277, 328
Carrington, Kerry, 58
Carrol, Esther, *80*
Carroll, Luke, 36
cartoons
  Anyone for a Bit of Reconciliation?, 85
  A Curiosity in Her Own Country, 78
  Expo '88, 83
  Robbery Under Arms, 68
  Stolen History, 122
    as a teaching resource, 286
  You are a repeat offender, 149
Cartwright, Reverend Robert, 97
case studies, 225–6
Casey, Dawn, 122
Cassar-Daley, Troy, 34, 86
Catholic Commission for Justice and Peace, 31, 115
Catholics, 115
Cavalier, Rodney, 118
Cawthorne, W.A., 73
Census, 278
Centenary of Federation, 87
Central Land Council, 81
Centrelink, 162
ceremonies, 297
Certificate Level III, 11, *11*
Chambers, Thomas, *112*
Champion, Brian, 102
Charles Sturt University, 38
Cherbourg Aboriginal School, 136, 235–6
Chi, Jimmy, 35
child abuse, 12, *12*, 218
child mortality, 5, 6–7, *7*
children, forced removal of, 37, 86–8, 97–102, 104, 107–9, *109*, 133, 218
  see also Stolen Generations
Chirac, Jacques, 33
Choolburra, Sean, 35
Christian, Dan, 36
Christianity, 95, 133
civil rights movement, 105
clan gatherings, 40
Clark, Manning, 112, 113, 125
Clark, Geoff, 164
Clarke, Henry 'Banjo', 136
Clendinnen, Inga, 122
Closing the Gap campaign, 5–6, 278
COAG, 5, 84
Coghlan, Damien, 194
Colbee, 129
collaborative assessment, 310
Collingwood Football Club, 32
Collins, Bob, 148, 149
colonisation, 47, 70–5
Coloured Progressive Association, 123
Coloured Stone (band), 34
comedy, 35
Commonwealth Department of Aboriginal Affairs, 82
Commonwealth Department of Education, 137
Commonwealth Department of Education, Science and Training, 223
Commonwealth Department of Education, Training and Youth Affairs, 224

Commonwealth Native Welfare Conference (1937), 135
Commonwealth Schools Commission, 138
communities of learning, 253–4
Community Development Employment Projects, 38, 52
community educators, 205–6
community involvement
  community leadership, 241
  in education policy, 238–40
  outcomes of, 197–8
  procedures and ethics of consultation, 206–7
  reasons for, 195–7
  school and community leadership, 240–1
  sources of advice, 197
  sources of assistance, 206
  strategies for effective consultation, 200–3
  troubleshooting checklist, 208
  visits from culture educators, 203, 205–6
  ways of consulting the community, 198, 200
concrete learning, 267, 269
Connecting the Country, Culture and Community program, 14
conservation, 29
consultation, 195
Consultative Committee on Aboriginal Education, 139
content, in the curriculum, 254
Contested Ground, 122
contextualised learning, 267–8, 270
conversation, in class, 254
convicts, 110–11
Cook, James, 47, 69, 92, *93*, 94, 97, 110, 116
Cook, Lois, 123
Cook, Patrick, *83*
Cooktown, 69
cooperative group techniques, 293, 295
cooperative learning, 267, 270
Cootamundra Home, 99, 100
Copacabana Club, New York, 33
Corrigan, M., 210
Corroboree 2000, 87
Cossey, Margaret, 326
Council for Aboriginal Reconciliation
  Burney as member of, 159
  chairpersons of, 56, 155
  created by Keating government, 82–3, 119, 153, 155
  disbanded, 87
  emphasis on education, 168
  Keating government consults with, 84
  produces roadmap for reconciliation, 161
  reports of, 87
  role of, 155
  targets women, 320

teaching resources produced by, 183, 185–6, 191
vision of, vii, 166
work of, 157
Council for Aboriginal Reconciliation Act 1991, 186
Council of Australian Governments, 5, 84
Councils of Elders, 26
Counihan, Noel, 90
Country Areas Program, 139
Country Outcasts (band), 34
course evaluation, 309
Courtenay, Bryce, 324
Coutts-Trotter, Michael, 17
Cowey, Wendy, 245
Craddock, Laurie, 147
Craven, R., 215, 223–4, 228
Crawford, R.M., 113
Creation Stories, 61
Creswell, J., 263
cricket team (1867), 37
Croc Festival, *150*, 150–1, *193*, *210*, *265*, 313
Croft, Brenda, 33, 36
Cross, Stan, *48*
Crowe, Russell, 318
Crowley, Frank, 114
Cultural and Indigenous Research Centre Australia, 10
culture *see* Indigenous culture
Culture Wars, 121, 125, 130, 160
cultures, classifying of, 62
Cummeragunja, *117*
Cunningham, Peter, 96
A Curiosity in Her Own Country (cartoon), *78*
curriculum content, 254
curriculum development, 274
Curtin University, 11
Curtis, Dave, 152
Cynical Song (poem), 106–7

Daily Telegraph, 161
Dampier, William, 95
Dan, Seaman, 35
dance, 33, *41*, *209*, 253, *322*
Dare to Lead program, 14, 15–16, 247–8, 251, 278
Darling, Ralph, 71, 72
Darug people, 26, *26*
Darwin, Charles, 75, 76
Davey, Thomas, *70*
Davies, O., 238
Davis, Angela, 105
Davis, Jack, 36, 68, 190
Davis, Leon, 316
Davison, Charlene, *156*
The Dawn is at Hand (poem), 229
Day of Mourning (1938), 123
De Maio, J.A., 218
Deadly Awards, 36, 275

Deadly Funny (comedy), 35
Deadly Sounds (radio program), 28, 275
Deadly Vibe (magazine), 10, 28, 275
Deane, Sir William, 83, 87, 122, 150, 184, 186, 321
deaths in custody, 48, 56–8, 82, *109*, 119
see also Royal Commission into Aboriginal Deaths in Custody
deficit theory, 135–6, *140*, 232, 242, 246
Dent, Jane, 242
Denton, Andrew, 251
The Destruction of Aboriginal Society (Rowley), 117
detention centres, 9
Devine, Frank, 121
Devine, Miranda, 121
Dharawal people, *38*
Dharug people, 73
diabetes, 320
Dimensions Regarding Quality Learning Environments..., 242
Dingo, Ernie, 32, 35, 36
Disadvantaged Schools Program, 139
Discovering a Living Culture (painting), *41*
disease, 75, 93
Djerkurra, Gatjil, 109
Djilpin Arts Festival, 22
Dodson, Mick, 2, 84, 88, 109, 126, 163, 321
Dodson, Patrick
  on Aboriginal deaths in custody, 56
  on Aboriginal stereotypes, 59
  calls for 'people's movement', 87
  as chair of CAR, 155
  contribution of, 319
  gives Vincent Lingiari Lecture, 186
  with John Howard, *159*
  on the meaning of the land, 31
  on reconciliation, 158
  on social justice, 193
Domain, Sydney, 79
domestic violence, 219
Donovan, Casey, 28, 34
Doomadgee people, 101
Doyle, Matthew, *41*
The Dreaming, 26, 30, 33, 39, 61
Dreaming Stories, 61
Duffy, Michael, 121
Duncan, Alan, 139, 141–2, 143
Dunstan, Don, 105
Durack, Mary, 71
Durham, Judith, 183
Dusty, Slim, 34
DVDs, as a teaching resource, 279–81
dying race ideology, 75–6, 134

Eastwood, Danny, 272
education, of Indigenous Australians
  Aboriginal languages, 144–5

academic achievement, 5, 7–11, 14–16, 220, 222–3, 279
at boarding schools, 177, 184–5
boys' education, 148
Carowra Tank Aboriginal School, *132*
communities of learning, 253–4
community involvement, 146, 238–40
conversation in class, 254
curriculum content, 254
deficit theory, 135–6, *140*
exclusion from mainstream schools, 133, 134–5
failure of basic principles, 230–3
gap in educational outcomes, 230
government policy, 258–9
harnessing goodwill of teachers, 234
methods of Aboriginal learning, 262
on missions, 133–4
national Aboriginal education policy, 142–4
parent and student expectations, 241–2, 248
participation rates, 38
personal experiences, 136, 137, 138
personalised learning plans, 237–8
poor standards in reserve schools, 135
primary students, 230
promotion of, 177
Quality Teaching Framework, 242–4, 248
the right to be Aboriginal, 149
role in addressing disadvantage, 181–3
role in reconciliation, 15, 159, 168, 170
school and community leadership, 240–1
secondary students, 138, 146, 250
stereotypes of Aboriginal students, 216
stimulating motivation, 255–6
supporting Indigenous culture, 258
teacher education, 151
teacher-student relationships, 236–7, 248–9, 252–6
tertiary students, 146, 250
two-way schooling, 144–5
see also Aboriginal Education Consultative Groups; Aboriginal Studies; educational research; learning; literacy; numeracy; students, Indigenous; teachers
educational research
  case studies, 225–6
  decolonising research, 221–2
  on educational experiences, 220, 222–3
  Hattie's synthesis of meta-analyses, 211–14
  on Indigenous mental health, 217–20
  Indigenous students' aspirations, 222–6

lack of effective outcomes, 215, 217
review of standards in NSW, 227, 228
Rowe's work on teacher quality, 214–15
students' self-identity, 224–5
Edwards, Christopher (Wirriimbi), 33
Eggington, Dennis, 125
Elcho Island, 144
Elders, 26–7, 30, 32
Ella, Mark, 119
Ellington, Duke, 33
Ellis, Tanya, *207*
emotional distress, 7
emotional problems, 219
employment, of Indigenous Australians, 5, 11–12, *12*, 51–2
Endeavour (ship), 69
Enemburu, I.G., 265–6
Eora people, 92
Ernabella, 144
Estens, Dick, 321
ethnocentrism, 43–4
Eulo, Max, 189
Eurocentricity, 53–5, 60, 113
European Vision and the South Pacific (Smith), 117
Exemption Certificates, 60, 135, 136
Exodus Foundation, 8, 323
explicit pedagogy, 263
Exploring Common Ground, 157
Expo '88 (cartoon), *83*
The Expulsion (painting), *113*
eye contact, 268

The Fabrication of Aboriginal History (Windshuttle), 121–2
Face the Facts..., 48, 50–1, 190, 279
Fair Skin–Black Soul (poem), 56
Family and Community Healing Program, 13
The Fatal Impact (Moorehead), 117
FATSIL, 145
FCAATSI, 2, 81, 105
Federal Council for the Advancement of Aborigines and Torres Strait Islanders, 2, 81, 105
Federation of Aboriginal and Torres Strait Islander Languages, 145
Ferguson, William (Bill), *80*, 104, 131
Fesl, Eve, 136
Festival of the Dreaming, 40, *41*
festivals, 40
film, 35
films, as a teaching resource, 281–2
Finding Your Pathway into School and Beyond program, 8
Finnan, Sharon, 37
Finniss Springs Mission, *133*
firestick farming, 29
'fire-water theory', 51

The First Australians (television program), 274
First Fleet, 86
Fischer, Tim, 120
Fisher, Frank, 103, *103*
fishing, 29–30
flags, 84
Flick, Isabel, 136
Foley, Fiona, 32
Foley, Gary, 130
Follow The Dream program, 12
forced labour, 102, 104
Forrest, Andrew, 318–19
Foundation for Aboriginal Affairs, 105
Fourmile, Henry, 101
Fox, Lindsay, 318
Frankland, Richard, 35, 131
Fraser government, 114
Fraser, Malcolm, 81, 186
Freedom Rides, 81, 105, 137
Freeman, Cathy, 36–7, 164, *168*, 315
French, Darryl, *65*
Fringe Dwelling Man (poem), 76–7
Frontier (television program), 73
'full-blood', 60
funding, for Aborigines, 320–1
Future Directions statement, 119

Gadigal people, 75
Gainsford-Taylor, Melinda, 315
Gallagher, Brendan, *154*
Gardner, Furley, 57
Garma Festival, 40
Garma theory, 146
Garrett, Peter, 34
Garvey, Marcus, 123
Gaudron, Justice, 83
Gawura (Whale) Song Ceremony, *38*
Gemes, Juno, 123
GenerationOne, 251, 318–19
genocide, 70–3, *72*, 84, *111*, 159
George III, King of England, 94
Gibbons, P., 263
Gibbs, Pearl, 104
Gibson, Mike, 161
Gilbert, Kevin, 36, 41
Gillard, Julia, 89, 127–8
Gilmore, Dame Mary, 29, 72, *114*
Gipps, Sir George, 72, 133
Girri Girri Sports Academy, 192
Glanville, Jason, 323
Goanna (band), 34
Gondwanaland (band), 34
Goodall, Heather, 74, 122
Goolagong-Cawley, Evonne, 36–7, 116, 119, 150
Goold, Sally, 131
Gordon, Sir Arthur, 72
Gordon, Sue, 145, 166
Gorton, John, 105
Gove case, 80
government policy, on education, 258–9

Graham (Polly) Farmer Foundation, 16
Grant, Ernie, 130
Grant, Karla, 36
Grant, Stan, 36
Gray, Brian, 245
Great Australian Silence, 77, 111, 113, 115–16
Great Chain of Being, 95
Greer, Germaine, 316
Gregory, J.B., *115*
Gringai Clan, 102
Grog Wars (Wright), 152
Groom, Ray, 120
Grosvenor, Helen, *80*
Groves, Bert, ix, 105, 139
guest speakers, 202–5
Guide to the Teaching of Australian History..., 123–5, 127, 129
Guild, P., 262–3
guilt, 129
Gulargambone, 136
Gumala Mirnuwarni Project, 16
gumleaf bands, 34
Gurindji people, 80
Gutya, Burraga, 56

Hall, W., 51
Halls, Bronwyn, 49
Hammersley Iron, 16
Hammond, J., 263
Hancock, W.K., 112–13
Hand in Hand..., 326
Hanson, Pauline, 64, 85, 121, 159
Hardcastle, Joseph, 97
Harradine, Brian, 87
Harris, Stephen, 262
Hattie, John, 211–14, 227, 231, 242
Hatton, Elizabeth, 242
Hawke government, 81, 119
Hawke, Hazel, *324*
Hayden, Bill, 53
hearing difficulties, 144, 145, 265
Heiss, Anita, 36, 290
Henderson, Gerard, 121
Henry, William, 95
Hermeston, Wendy, 109
Heslop, J., 236
Hewson, John, 120
High Court of Australia, 52–3, 85–6
Higher Expectations Program, 10
Hillston Central School, 141
Hirst, John, 119, 120
historiography, development of, 114–15, 117–18
history
  in Aboriginal Studies, 5, 293, 295
  awareness of Indigenous history, 173–4, *174*, 178
  Howard criticises teaching of, 121
  Howard launches guide to teaching of, 123–5
  Labor commits to national curriculum, 125

myths about, 59–60
racism in, 65
reaction to new histories, 118–23
recent curriculum developments, 127–9
teaching of prior to 1980, 110–17
teaching resources, 276–7
History Wars, 121, 125, 130
Hough, Paul, 177
House of Representatives Standing Committee on Aboriginal and Torres Strait Islander Affairs, 16, 144
Howard government
   abandons social justice package, 84
   abolishes ATSIC, 87
   attitude towards reconciliation, 153, 160–1, 165
   loses 2007 election, 88
   Northern Territory Intervention, 88, 126, 166
   refuses to recognise racism, 64
   scraps employment initiatives, 38
   wins 1996 election, 85
Howard, John
   criticises 'black school of history', 119
   launches guide to teaching history, 123–5, 127, 129
   loses seat in 2007 election, 88
   promises referendum on reconciliation, 167
   receives Reconciliation Council report, 87
   at Reconciliation Convention, 158–9, *159*
   refuses to apologise, 87, *106*, 108, 159
   rejects 'black armband' view of history, 121
   with Young Australian of the Year, *19*
Hudspith, S., 263
Huggins, Jackie, 15, 16
Hughes, Helen, 149
Hughes, P., 262
Hughes, Paul, 142, 210
Hughes Report, 142
human remains, 25
Human Rights and Equal Opportunity Commission, 87, 107–8, 109, 158
humanitarianism, 97
Hunt, Sonia, 165
Hunter, B.H., 164, 210
Hunter, E., 51
Hunter, John, 71
Hunter Valley, 96, 97
Hurt (film), 211
Hutchinson, Greg, 251
Hutchinson, Robyn, 188, 189

identity, of Indigenous Australians, 23–4, 53–6, 176, 313–14

IECBs, 39, 142, 195, 198, 203, 325
immigration, 79
Immigration Restriction Act, 77
Imparja, 36
In Vibe (magazine), 275
Indigenous Advisory Council, 39
Indigenous Australians
   achievements by, 32–7
   child mortality, 5, 6–7, *7*
   cultural identity of, 258
   defined, 23
   depiction of in early histories, *112*
   diversity of, 207
   employment of, 5, 11–12, *12*, 51–2
   harnessing Indigenous talent, 317, 319, 321–2
   impact of British invasion on, 93–7
   involvement in decision-making, 142
   life expectancy, 5, 6
   misconceptions and stereotypes of, 46–56
   myth of a dying race, 75–6, 134
   political action by, 79–80, *80*, 104–6
   population of, 2, *3*, 75
   self-perceptions, 176–7, *178–9*
   state of residence, 55
   see also children, forced removal of; community involvement; education, of Indigenous Australians; reconciliation
Indigenous business principle, 231, 232–3, 246
Indigenous culture, 24–7, 297
Indigenous Education Action Plan, 325
The Indigenous Education Association, 226
Indigenous Education Consultative Bodies, 39, 142, 195, 198, 203, 325
Indigenous Education Forum, Alice Springs, 148
Indigenous Education Leadership Institute, 235–6
Indigenous Education Policy, 142–4
Indigenous Education Strategic Initiatives Program, 226, 234
Indigenous Festivals of Australia, 151
Indigenous Land Fund Act 1994, 84
Indigenous media, 274–5
Indigenous Studies, 3–4
   see also Aboriginal Studies
Indigenous Youth Leadership Program, 9
Indij Readers, *238*
Industrial revolution, 111
Inglis, Greg, 45
Ingram, Abe, *80*
Ingram, Joyce, *29*
Ingram, Philip, *80*
initiation-response-evaluation, 254
inquiry learning, 292–3

Institute of Teachers' Policy for Approval of Initial Education Programs, 17
intake activities, 305, 306
integrated learning, 266–7
integration, 137
International Year of the World's Indigenous People, 83, 119
internet resources, for Aboriginal Studies, 275, 277
The Intervention, 88, 126, 166
Intolerance (poem), 42
Invasion Day, 27
Invasion to Embassy (Goodall), 122
Islam, 326

Jarvis, Patricia, *26*
Johns, Andrew 'Joey', 45
Johnson, Colin, 36
Johnson, Eva, 36, 67
Johnson, Jack, 123
Johnson, King Mickey, *91*
Johnson, Patrick, 36
Johnston, Elliott, 58, 84
Jolliffe, Eric, *62*
Jones, Gavin, 35
Journey of the Spirit (DVD), 156
Judaism, 326
Judgement by His Peers (painting), *105*
Jump Up Whitefella (Greer), 316
Justice and Equity (CD-ROM), 186
juveniles, 9

Kahlin Home, *101*
Kalparrin Spirited Men's Project, 13
Kamilaroi people, 320
Kastel, Zalman, 326–7
Keating government, 84, 119–20
Keating, Paul, 63, 83, 119, 125, 129
Kelly, Clive, 34
Kemp, Darren, *69*
Kemp, David, 148
Keneally, Kristina, 318
Kickett, John, 134
Kickett-Tucker, Cheryl, 314
Kija people, 122
Kilgour, Jack, *92*
kinaesthetic learning strategies, 269
Kinchela Boys Home, 98, 99, 102, 104
Kinchela, Jack, *80*
Kinchela School, *134*
King, Martin Luther, 105
King, Philip Gidley, 73
kinship, 26–7
Kirinari Hostel, 139
kits, 286
Kngwarrye, Emily Kame, 33, 131
Kong, Kelvin, 131
Koori: A Will to Win... (Miller), 117, 190
Koori Centre, 250
Koori Mail, 36, 274
Koori people, 91

Koori, use of term, 91–2
Kormilda College, 165
Kropinyen, Kevin, 35
Kruger, Alexx, 108
Kuckles (band), 34, 35
Kulkarriya Comunity School, 8
Kunoth-Monks, Rosalie, 29, 137

Lambert, George, *112*
the land, 28–31, 47
land rights, 37, 38, 73–5, 80–2, 106, 114, 299–300, *301*
Land Rights Act 1983 (NSW), 81–2
Land Rights News, 274
Lands of Shame (Hughes), 149
Lane, William, 77
Langford-Ginibi, Ruby, 36
Langton, Marcia, 117
language
    Aboriginal language groups, 60
    in Aboriginal Studies, 58–9, 276
    as a barrier, 14
    retaining Aboriginal languages, 325
    teaching of Aboriginal languages, 40, 144–5, *256*
Langwij Comes to School, 264
Lanne, William, *75*
Laughton, Heather, 327
Laura Dance Festival, 40
Lawson, Henry, 77
laziness, as a stereotype, 51–2
Leah Flanagan Band, 34
Leak, Bill, *85*
learning
    Aboriginal perspectives, 278
    contextualised learning, 267–8, 270
    cooperative learning, 267, 270, 293, 295
    cultural sensitivity in, 268
    by doing, 267
    explicit pedagogies, 263–4
    inquiry learning, 292–3
    integrated learning, 266–7
    kinaesthetic learning, 269
    learning styles, 261–3
    person-centred teaching, 265
    positive classroom environments, 264
    risk-taking in, 265–6, 270
    visual and concrete learning, 267, 269
    see also scaffolding; teachers
Learning Lessons, 148, 149
learning styles, 261–3
Learning to Earning program, 13
The Legends, 61
Leichhardt Secondary College, 250
Lennis, John, 189
Leonard, G., *110*
Lethbridge, Brett, *88*
Lewis, Tom, 131
life expectancy, 5, 6
life skill development, 292

A Life Together, a Life Apart (Atwood), 123
lime kilns, 30
Lingiari, Kadidjeri Vincent, 80, 131
Link-Up NSW, 107–8
Link-Up (video), 190
Lismore RSL, 135
literacy, 5, 7–8, 244–5, 259
literature resources, for Aboriginal Studies, 275–7, 282–4
Little Children Are Sacred, 88, 166
Little, Jimmy, 33, 34, *154*
Living Black (television program), 36
Living Strong (television program), 275
Lloyd McDermott Rugby Development Team, 323
Lock, Maria, 40, 133, 152, 230
Locke, John, 95
Long, Michael, 321
Looking for Blackfellas' Point (McKenna), 122–3
Loos, Neal, 117
The Lost Children (Morgan), 149
Lousy Little Sixpence (Morgan), 117, 190
Lucy, Judith, 35
Luhrmann, Baz, 319
Lyons, Ricky, *156*

Mabo case, 52–3, 83, 119–20, 123, 276
Mabo, Eddie, 131
Macdonald, Gaynor, 14
Macintyre, Stuart, 127
MacMahon government, 106
MacMahon, William, 105
Macquarie, Lachlan, 74, 111, 133
Madden, Charles, *156*
Magabala Books, 36
Mailman, Debra, 36
Major, Tania, 19, *19*, 318
The Making of the Aborigines (Attwood), 98, 123
Making Things Right, 186
Malangi, David, 32
Malin, Merridy, 151
Mallard, Gavin, *229*
Mandela, Nelson, 105
Mann, David, 97
Manne, Robert, 160
Manning-Bancroft, Jack, 318
Maori, 241, 242
Maralinga Tjaruta people, 81
Marder, Kurt, 143
Marn Grook Show (television program), 36
Marsh, H.W., 215
martial law, 70
Martin, Ray, 320
Marxism, 117
Mason, Tiarna, *36*
massacres, 71–3, *72*
A Matter of Survival, 144

Matterson, Neil, 79
Mauboy, Jessica, 10, 34
Mawurndjul, John, 33
May, John, *156*
May, Phil, *78*
Mayfield West Demonstration School, *296*
Maynard, Fred, 123, 131
Maynard, John, 123, 130
MC Wire (band), 34
McConville, Kim, 205
McCourt, Ricky, 321
McEwen, J., *78*
McGrath, Ann, 122
McGree, Barry, 94
McGuiness, Denise, 35
McGuiness, Paddy, 121, 160
McInerney, Dennis, 216
McIntyre, Stuart, 123
McKenna, Mark, 122
McKenzie, Kerrie, 156, *156*
McKew, Maxine, 88
McLaren, Phillip, 36
McMillan, Faye, 38
McMullen, Jeff, 45, 130–1
McNaboe, Diane, *256*
McQueen, Humphrey, 113
McRae, D., 225–6
McRae, David, 16, *16*
media, 36
medicine, 38
The Medics (band), 34
Meeks, Arone Raymond, 32
Melbourne City Council, 162
Melbourne Declaration, 15
Mellor, S., 210
Menindee Central School, *193*
men's business, 297
mental health, 217–20
mentoring, 250–1
Message Stick (television program), 36
Meston, Archibald, 135
Meyrick, Henry, 72
Microwave Jenny (band), 34
Middleton, Hanna, 117
Midnight Oil (band), 34
Miles Franklin Award, 36
Milestone Events, 123
Miller, James, 91, 117, 190, *see also* James Wilson-Miller
Miller, Jean, 99–100
Mills Sisters, 33
Ministerial Council on Education, Employment, Training, and Youth Affairs, 15, 230, 232–4, 237, 238, 240, 258–9
Minns, B.E., *120*
missionaries, 95–8
missions, *96*, 98, *101*, 102, 133–4, 137
Mistake Creek, 122
Mixed Relations (band), 34
modelling, 292
Moffatt, Tracey, 36

Molony, John, 119
Moonahcullah Aboriginal Reserve, 141
Moorditj Mob students, 8–9, *9*, 11, *11*
Moorehead, Alan, 117
Mop and the Drop Outs (band), 34
Moran, Charles, 138
Morgan, Hugh, 119, 120
Morgan, Sally, 32, 36, 149, 190
Mornington Island, 239
Mornington Island elders, *27*
Morris, Shellie, 34
mortality, 5–7, *7*, 217–18
motivation, stimulation of, 255–6
Mowaljarlai, David, 31
MULTILIT program, 8
multiple choice questions, 266
Mulvaney, John, 75
Mundine, Anthony, 36, 37
Mundy, Godfrey, 72
Munkimunk, 28
Munns, Geoff, 248
Munro, Jenny, 116
Munyarl mythology, 42, 67
Munyarl Mythology (video), 187
Munyarryun, Djakapurra, *322*
Murray, Neil, 154, *154*
Murray, Stewart, 169–70
Murri people, 92
museums, 274
music and musicians, 33–5, 286–7
musical theatre, 34–5
Must This Be Their Fate (painting), 92
My Land, My Tracks (Grant), 130
My Place for Young Readers (Morgan), 190
Myall Creek massacre, 72–3, 123

Nabalco, 80
NAEC, 16
NAIDOC, 118
NAIDOC Week, 185
Nakata, M., 262
NALP, 8, 245
Namatjira, Albert, 32, *90*
NAPLAN, 259
Narrogin, Mudrooroo, 36
National Aboriginal and Islanders Day Observance Committee, 118
National Aboriginal and Torres Strait Islander Education Policy, 142, 234, 258
National Aboriginal and Torres Strait Islander Studies project, 287
National Aboriginal and Torres Strait Islander Survey (2004), 25
National Aboriginal Education Committee, 16, 138–9
National Aboriginal Sporting Chance Academy, 323
National Accelerated Literacy Program, 8, 245

National Apology, 87–8, *88*, 123, 126, *126*, 151, 153, 167–8, 183
National Assessment Program—Literacy and Numeracy, 259
National Australia Bank, 162
National Board of Employment, Education and Training, 16
National Centre of Indigenous Excellence, 323, *323*
National Committee to Defend Black Rights, 82
National Congress of Australia's First Peoples, 88
National Curriculum Board, 274
National History Curriculum Advisory Group, 127
National History Curriculum Framing Paper, 127–8
national identity, 176–7, *178*
National Indigenous Higher Education Network, 39
National Indigenous Television, 36, 274, 319
National Indigenous Times, 36, 274
National Inquiry into the Separation of Aboriginal and Torres Strait Islander Children from their Families, 107–9
National Museum, 122, 282
National Native Title Tribunal, 84
National Reconciliation Convention, 158–9
National Reconciliation Week, 91, 183, 185
National Report to Parliament on Indigenous Education and Training, 230, 278–9
National Rugby League, 45
National Sorry Day, 108, 151
National Statement and Profile of Studies of Society and Environment, 140
National Tertiary Education Union Indigenous Policy Committee, 39
National Times, 82
Native Americans, 241
Native Institution, 133
native title, 52–3, 119–20
Native Title Act 1993, 53, 84, 87
Native Title: Making Things Right, 157
Natives Driven to the Police Courts for Trespassing (painting), 73
NATSIEP, 142
natural selection, 75
neck chains, 66
Neville, A.O., 78
A New Britannia (McQueen), 113
New Effective Social Studies Grade 3 (Gregory & Wicks), 115
A New History of Australia (Crowley), 114
New South Wales Aboriginal Education Policy, 144

early histories of, 111
land rights, 81–2
syllabus in Aboriginal Studies developed, 140
New South Wales Aboriginal and Education Training Policy, 258–9
New South Wales Board of Education, 133
New South Wales Board of Secondary School Studies, 118
New South Wales Department of Education and Training, 14, 17, 116, 239, 249, 259
New South Wales Directorate of Aboriginal Education and Training, 244–5
New South Wales Education Review, 227, 228
New South Wales Jewish Board of Deputies, 326–7
New South Wales Legislative Council Select Committee, 133
New South Wales Legislative Council Standing Committee on Social Issues, 17, 46, 239
New South Wales Reconciliation Council, 160
New South Wales Review of Aboriginal Education, vii, 237, 240
New South Wales Select Committee on the Native Police, 133
New South Wales Teachers Federation Survey, 138
New Tomorrow (poem), 30
Newberry, Bernard, 241
Newlin, Norm, 148, 209
Newman, Anne, 246
Ngarritjan-Kessaris, Terry, 258
Nicholls, Sir Douglas, 32, 36, 104
Nicholson, Barbara, 233
Nicholson, Peter, *85*
Nilsen, Laurie, *118*
NITV, 36, 274, 319
No Fixed Address (band), 34
'noble savages', 94–5
Noffs, Ted, 81
non-verbal communication, 268
Noongah people, 33, *see also* Nyoangah people
Noonuccal, Oodgeroo
  artist-in-residence at UNSW, viii
  breadth of talent of, 319
  defines racism, 45–6
  passion for education, viii–ix
  poems by, 1–2, 21, 42, 132, 171, 187, 190, 229, 248, 256
  portrait of, v
  speaking at Oatley campus, viii
  as a writer, 36, 131
Norseman Mission, 102
Northern Land Council, 81
Northern Territory Emergency Response, 126

Northern Territory Intervention, 88, 126, 166
Northern Territory, land rights in, 81
numeracy, 5, 7–8, 244, 245–6, 259
Nunn, Major, 73
Nyadbi, Lena, 33
Nyoongah people, 92

octoroons, 60
O'Donoghue, Lowitja, 125, 320
OECD Steering Group, 263
Office of Aboriginal Affairs, 105
Office of the Aboriginal and Torres Strait Islander Social Justice Commissioner, 84
O.H.M.S. (drawing), 69
Old Days, Old Ways (Gilmore), 29, *114*
Olympic Games, Sydney, 164
On the Origin of Species (Darwin), 75
One Arm Point Remote Community School, *248*
One Nation Party, 64, 85, 87, 121, 159
'Only Aboriginal' classes, 144
open-ended questions, 266
O'Shane, Pat, 46, 144
'other', 230
The Other Side of the Frontier (Reynolds), 117
otitis media, 144, 145, 265
Overcoming Indigenous Disadvantage: Key Indicators, 5–6, 14, 18
ownership principle, 230–1, 232, 246
Oxfam Australia, 162

PaCE program, 40, 147, 196
Packer, James, 318
Page brothers, 36
Palawa people, 92
Parbury, Nigel, 18, 26, 37, 316, 322
Parental and Community Engagement program, 40, 147, 196
Parent-School Partnership Initiative, 147
Parkes, Sir Henry, 74
Parramatta Native Institutions, 97
'part-aborigine', 60, 78
Pascoe Crook, W., 97
pastoral industry, 137
pastoral leases, 86
Pat, John, 82
paternalism, 115
Patten, Herb, 34
Patten, Jack, *80*, 104
Patten, Selina, *80*
Peachey, David, *193*
Peacock, Andrew, 119
Peardon, Annette, 137
Pearson, Christopher, 121
Pearson, Noel, 14, 74, 125, 166, 259, 318
pedagogy, 242–4, 249, *251*, 251–6, 261, 263–4, 268
Pederson, Aaron, 36

Pemulwuy, 129
Penfold, Andrew, 184
Penshurst West Public School, *190*, 257
Pepper, Phillip, 36
perceptions, 176–7, *178–9*
Peris, Nova, 37
Perkins, Charles, 48, 81, 105, 114, 320
Perkins, Hettie, 33, 36
Perkins, Rachel, 35, 36
Perron, Marshal, 120
personalised learning plans, 237–8, 260
person-centred teaching, 265
Petty, Bruce, *20*, *68*, *122*, *163*
Phillip, Arthur, 70, 75, 92, 94, 110, 316
Phillips, S., 198
Pigram Brothers (band), 34
Pike, Jimmy, 32
Pilger, John, 129
Pitjantjatjara people, 81
plays, 285
Plenty Stories, 282
A Poem About Me (poem), 272
poetry, 285
Polding, Bede, 115
political correctness, 58–9, 85, 127
The Politics of Prejudice (Stevens), 44
population, 2, *3*, 75
Possession Island, 69, 94
posters, 186, *315*
Preston, Margaret, *113*
Principals Australia, 15–16, 247
privacy, 266
Productive Pedagogy initiative, 243
Productivity Commission, 13
Proof: Portraits from the Movement (exhibition), 123
Pryor, Geoff, *109*
Puggy Hunter Memorial Scholarship Scheme, 38
Punch, 93
punishment, 66, 70, 94, 102
Purcell, Leah, 36
Purdie, N., 224

Qantas, 162
Quadrant, 121, 160
Quality in Teaching (OECD), 326
Quality Teaching Framework, 243–4, 248
'quarter-caste', 60
Quayle, Mark, 56–8
Queensland School Reform Longitudinal Study, 243
questioning methods, 266, 271

Rabbit-Proof Fence (film), 319
racial discrimination, 43, 46
Racial Discrimination Act 1975, 88, 126
racism
    anti-racism strategies, 63–7
    causes of, 43–6

    defined, 42, 46
    examples of, 43, *44*, *48*
    in the Great Chain of Being, 95
    impact of, 43
    institutionalised racism, 116–17
    recognition of impact of, 62–3
    in schools, 148, 151
    in sport, 45, 103, 321
    in the WAACH survey, 219
Radiance (film), 36
Randall, Bob, 190
Raphael, B., 217, 220
Read, Peter, 117
reading, 7
    see also literacy
reading kits, 284–5
Reading, Wilma, 33
'real Aborigines', 55–6
Rebutting Mabo Myths, 52–3
Rebutting the Myths…, 48
ReconciliACTION Network, 166
reconciliation
    Aboriginal Studies as part of, 20, 39
    attitude of Howard government, 85, 87, 121, 125, 158–9, 160–1
    attitude of Keating government, 119, 155
    barriers to, 42
    council for established, 82–3, 155, 157, 161–2
    defined, 162–4
    future for, 166–7
    national convention, 158–9, *159*
    policy of, 155
    proposed statement in Constitution, 125
    The Reconciliation Barometer, 172–80, *175*, *178*, *179*
    role of education in, 15, 159, 168, 170
    role of teachers in, 181
    Senate inquiry into, 163–4
    and the Stolen Generations, 160
    teaching resources, 276, 285
    types of, 162–4
    UWS statement on, 166
    for youth, 165–6
    see also Council for Aboriginal Reconciliation; National Apology
Reconciliation Action Plan, 162
Reconciliation and Schooling Strategy, 148
Reconciliation Australia, 87, 161–2, 165, 176, 183, 185–6, 187
Reconciliation: Australia's Challenge, 157, 186
Reconciliation Councils (state), 165
Reconciliation Day, *1*, *190*
Reconciliation News, 185
Reconciliation Week, 83, 160, 183, 185
Red (poem), 28
Redfern Aboriginal Medical Service, 37
Redfern Legal Service, 37

Redfern Park Statement, 83, 119
Redfern Tutorial Centre, 8
Referendum (1967), viii, 48, 81, 91, 114, 123, 138, 185
Reid, Janice, 166
Rekindling Indigenous Family Relationships in the Riverland program, 13
relationships, 26–7, 27
relevance, in education, 147
remote missions, 136–7
remote regions, Indigenous Australians in, 258
Renewal of the Nation strategy, 158
research *see* educational research
reserves, 74, 98, 138, 141
respect, 221–2, 236–7
responsibility, of students, 268, 270
Review of Education for Aboriginal and Torres Strait Islander Peoples (1994), 140
Review of the NSW Aboriginal Education Policy, 234
Reynolds, Henry, 73, 74, 78, 117, 119, 120, 122, 129
Richards, Fay, 26
Ridgeway, Aden, 36, 87, 160
Right To Be (poem), 67
Riley, Lynette, 116, 317
Riley, Michael, 33
Rio Tinto Indigenous employment programs, 13
risk-taking, in learning, 265–6, 270
rituals, 26–7
Roach, Archie, 34, 100, 190
Road Map for Reconciliation, 157, 161
Robbery Under Arms (cartoon), 68
Roberts, Rhoda, 23, 27, 28, 33, *238*
Roberts, Tom, 316
role models, 9, 292
role-play, 293, 294
Rose, David, 245, 263
Ross, Joshua, 36
Rousseau, Jean-Jacques, 94
Rowe, Ken, 214–15, 228
Rowley, C.D., 77, 78, 117, 122, 129, 134
Royal Commission into Aboriginal Deaths in Custody
  on destruction of Aboriginal culture, 58, 84
  documents death of Mark Quayle, 56–8
  encourages questioning of attitudes, 82
  establishment of, 82, 119
  findings on education level of victims, 132, 149
  on language, 271
  recommendations of, 82–3, 140, 153, 181–2, 258, 276
Rudd government, 125–7

Rudd, Kevin
  apologises to Aborigines, 37, 88, *88*, 151, 153, 160, 167
  becomes leader of Labor Party, 87
  launches GenerationOne, 318
  opens National Centre of Indigenous Excellence, 323
  promises to close the gap, 88–9
  supports Howard's referendum proposal, 125
  takes pains not to offend mainstream, 126–7
Ruddock, P., 164
Russell, W. Les, 28
Ryan, Lyndall, 117, 122

sacred places, 31
Said, Edward, 230
Salt Pan Creek, ix, 79
Samson and Delilah (film), 35, 36, 319
Samuels, Charlie, 36
Samuels, Jeffrey, 32
Sand Goanna Man (poem), 25–6
Sarra, Chris, 235–6, 251, 325
Saunders, Hayley, 231
SBS, 274
scaffolding, 263, 264, 266
Scaffolding Literacy Program, 8, 245
schools
  Aborigines excluded from, 133, 134–5, 136
  anti-racism initiatives in, 63–5
  attendance at, 220
  deficit theory of Indigenous students, 135–6, *140*
  exclusion of Aboriginal children from, 78–9
  Indigenous students at boarding schools, 177, 184–5
  school and community leadership, 240–1
  students as part of the school, 253
  supporting Indigenous culture in, 258
  visits from culture educators, 203, 205–6
  see also education, of Indigenous Australians; students, Indigenous; teachers
Schools Commission, 16
Schools in Partnership, 239
schools programs, 40–1
Schultz, Julianne, 251
Schwab, R.G., 210
Scott, Evelyn, 87, 155
Scott, Kim, 36
Sea of Hands, *322*
Seaman Inquiry, 81
segregation, 136
Select Committee of the House of Commons (UK), 73
self-concept, 224
self-determination, 74, 115

self-esteem, 219
self-identity, 224–5
self-management, 115
self-perceptions, 176–7, *178–9*
Sen, Ivan, 36
Senate Committee on Reconciliation, 164–5
Senate, motion on dispossession, 80
Senior Officers' National Network of Indigenous Education, 247
servicemen, Indigenous, 104, *110*, 130–1
Sesquicentenary of Australia, 79–80
1788: The Great South Land (play), 182, 190
sexism, 36
Shakaya, 28
shame, 251, 252, 265–6, 268
shared history, 125–6, 129
shared pride, *175*, 176
shell middens, 29–30
Shelley, Reverend, 97
Sherwood, Juanita, 222
Shewring, Terry, 29
Short History of Australia (Clark), 113
'shut-up sheets', 242
Simms, Ruth, 173
Simon, Ella, 36
Simon, James P., *41*
Six O'Clock...Outa Bed (poem), 90–1
Sjoquist, Peter, 150, 313
Slaughterhouse Creek, 73
smallpox, 75
Smith, Bernard, 117
smoke ceremonies, 27
The Social and Emotional Wellbeing of Aboriginal Children... (Zubrick), 218–20
social Darwinism, 75–6, 134, 135
Social Health Reference Group, 217
social justice, 18, 84
Social Studies, 295, 308
socio-economic status, 223–4, 242
songs, as a teaching resource, 286–7
Sorry Books, 108, 160, *324*
Sorry Day, 87, 161
South Australia, land rights in, 81
space, in the classroom, 256
Spargo, R., 51
Speaking Out (radio program), 36
Spencer, Sir Baldwin, 135
Spigelman, Jim, 81
Spirit Festival, 40
spirituality, 23, 61, 62
sport, 32, 36, *37*, 45, 103, 253, 321
St Clair mission, 99
St Joseph's College, Sydney, 10, 177, 184–5
St Joseph's Indigenous Fund, 10
St Kilda Football Club, 32
Stage 4 Aboriginal language program, 14
stamps, *165*

Standard English, 254, 265
Stanner, W.E.H., 31, 77
Statement of Regret, 87
statistics, 278–9
Stephen, Ann, *111*
stereotypes, of Indigenous people, 42, 44, 46–56, 59, 151, 216, 287
Stevens, F., 44
Stewart, Emma, 4, *4*
Stiff Gins (band), 34
stimulus, in the classroom, *255*
Stokes, Kerry, 318
Stolen Generations
    effect on mental health, 218
    Howard refuses to apologise to, 87, 159
    National Inquiry into, 107–9, *109*
    personal stories of forced removal, 98–102, 104
    policy of forced removal, 97–8, 100–2
    political action by Aborigines, 104–6
    report on, 158
    Rudd apologises to, 37, 86, 88, 126, *126*, 167
    teaching suggestions, 189–90
Stolen History (cartoon), 122
Stone Bros (film), 35, 319
Street Warriors (band), 34
Streetwize (magazine), 157
Strong, Greg, 272
Stronger Smarter Institute, 236
Strut the Streets program, 251
students, Indigenous
    aspirations of, 222–6
    ASSPA program, 40, 143, 146–7, 189
    at boarding schools, 177, 184–5
    deficit theory of Indigenous students, 135–6, *140*
    engaging students, 259, 264
    expectations of, 241–2, 248
    helping students detect bias, 287–8
    Moorditj Mob students, 8–9, *9*, 11, *11*
    as part of the school, 253
    primary students, 230
    responsibility and independence of, 268, 270
    secondary students, 5, 7, 138, 146, 250
    self-identity of, 224–5, 264
    stereotypes of, 216
    student-teacher relationships, 236–7, 248–9, 252–6
    tertiary students, 146, 250
Studies of Society programs, 66
Study Circle (kit), 157, 186, 187
substance abuse, 219
suicide, 219–20
Sultan, Dan, 34
Summers, Anne, 164
Survival (Parbury), 74
Survival Day, 27

sustainability principle, 230, 231–2, 234, 246
Swan, Doug, 136
Swan, P., 217, 220
Sydney Bridge Walk, *163*, 164
Sydney Morning Herald, 108, 164
Syron, Gordon, *105*
systemic principle, 230, 231, 232, 246

TAFE, 11, 145, 148, 226
Tahu, Timana, 45
Talkin' Business (video), 186, 187
Talking Together (video), 186, 187
Tandberg, Ron, 149
Taplin, Reverend George, 133
Tasmania, 74, 111
Tasmanian Aborigines, 55, 71
Tatz, Colin, 143
teacher aides, 139, 234
Teacher Education Scholarship Program, 14
teachers
    appropriate questioning methods, 266
    education of, viii–ix, *ix*, 16–17, 59, 140, 182, 260, 295
    effect of deficit theory on, 242
    evaluating teaching activities, 312
    as facilitators, 289–91
    harnessing goodwill of, 234
    learning Aboriginal English, 265
    Quality Teaching Framework, 242–4
    resources for teaching Aboriginal Studies, 273–88
    role in community involvement, 207
    role in reconciliation, 181
    teacher-student relationships, 236–7, 248–9, 252–6
    topics for Indigenous teachers only, 297
    topics for non-Indigenous teachers, 296–7
    see also pedagogy
The Teachers (poem), 132
teaching kits, 286
Teaching the Teachers: Indigenous Australian Studies, viii–ix, *ix*, 59, 140, 260, 295
television, 35
The Ten Minute System, 180
Tench, Watkin, 94–5
Tennant Creek, 152
Tent Embassy, Canberra, 80, *82*, 106
terminology, in Aboriginal Studies, 59–62, 276
terra nullius, 5, 18, 47, 69, 74, 83, 94, 119, 122, 300
Thayorre people, 85–6
This Whispering in Our Hearts (Reynolds), 74
Thomas, Rover, 32, 131
Thornton, Warwick, 35, 36
Thorpe, Ian, 251

Three Cheers view of history, 111, 114, 121
Threlkeld, Lancelot, 70
Thursday Islanders, *35*
Tickner, Robert, viii, 19, 52–3, 85, 121, 155, 186
Tiddas (band), 34
timelines, 190
Tjakamarra, Michael Nelson, 32
Tjapaltjarri, Clifford Possum, 32
Together for Humanity Foundation, 326–7
Together We Can't Lose, 157
Too Dark for the Light Horse (poster), *120*
Torrens, Robert, 74
Torrens Title, 74
Torres News, 274
Torres, Pat, 36
Torres Strait Islanders *see* Indigenous Australians
Tosh, Peter, 34
trauma, 217–18
Treaty of Waitangi, 74
tree ceremony, *26*
Trindall, Charles, 24, 25–6, 30, 76–7, 106–7
The Triumph of the Nomads (Blainey), 29, 117
Trucaninni's Dream of Childhood (painting), 71
Truganini, 55, 75, 76
Tucker, Margaret, 36, 104
Tula, Papunya, 33
Turbill, J., 264
turtle dinner, *24*
Turtle Point, 138
Tweed Heads Football Club, 103
2020 Summit (2008), 185
200 in the Shade (Swain), 190
two-way schooling, 144–5, 146

Uluru, 82, 126–7
Uluru-Kata Tjuta National Park, 126
Unaipon, David, 36, 40, 131
unemployment, 51–2
United We Win (poem), 171, 190
Unity (poem), 41
Universal Negro Improvement Association, 123
University of Western Sydney, 166
Upton, Ken, *26*
urban regions, Indigenous Australians in, 258
Us Mob (band), 34
Using the Right Words in the Indigenous Australian Studies Classroom, 48

Van Der Kuyp, Kyle, 36
Van Leer Foundation, 138
Van-Oploo, Beryl, 319
VEGAS, 143, 146

Vesteys, 80
Vibe 3on3™, 275
Vibe Alive, 275, *307*
VIBE Australia, 36
Vibe Australia Pty Ltd, 10, 28, 274–5
VIBE Living Strong (television program), 24
VicRoads Indigenous Traineeship Program, 13
Victoria and Its Metropolis, 76
Victorian Ministerial Review of Post-Compulsory Education, 258
Vincent Lingiari Lectures, 186
virtual libraries, 275
Visiting Speakers Program, 148
visual learning, 267, 269
Vocational Education Guidance for Aboriginals Scheme, 143, 146
Voices of the Land, 145

Wadjularbinna, 30
Walgett Public School, 147
'walkabout', 52
Walker, Kath *see* Noonuccal, Oodgeroo
Walking Together (video), 157, 186, 187
Walking with Spirits Festival, 40
Walley, Richard, 36
Walters, Brandon, 319, *322*
Wangal Garden, Ashfield Public School, 188–9
Wannik, 239
Warakurna Artists, 13
Warren, E., 264
Warumpi Band (band), 34
Watson, Edna, *26*
Watson, Judy, 33
Watson, Maureen, 257
Watson, P., 246
Watson, Tommy, 33
Wave Hill station, 80
Ways Forward (Swan and Raphael), 217
Weaving the Threads, 157
websites, 275–9
Weller, Archie, 36
Welsh, Rob, 156, *156*
Welton, James, 293
Wentworth, Billy, 105
Wesley College, Perth, 8–9, *9*, 11, *11*
West, H., *110*
West, J., 111
Western Australian Aboriginal Child Health Survey, 218–20

Whaleboat, Tat, 292
What Works, 225–7, 228, 251, 278
When the Sky Fell Down (Willey), 117
White, Alan, 246
White Australia Has a Black History (poster), *118*, 119
White Australia Policy, 5, 44, 47–8, 69, 77–9
White Child (poem), 209
White, Patrick, 139
White, Peter, 75
Whitlam, Gough, 106, 186
Whitlam government, 47, 79, 80–1, 106, 114, 139, 144
Whole School Anti-Racism Project, 63–5, 148
Why Teach Aboriginal Studies? (video), 187
Wicks, J.M.C., *115*
Wik case, 85–6, 120, 159, 300
Wik people, 85–6
Wilcannia, 58
Wilcannia Aboriginal Settlement, *101*
Wilcox, Cathy, *106*
Wilkes, Ted, 33
Will and a Way program, 12
Willey, Keith, 117
Williams, Claude, *236*
Williams, Harry, 34
Williams, Neno, *80*
Willmot, Eric, 36
Willoughby, Bart, 34
Wilson, Sir Ronald, 159
Wilson-Miller, James, 19, 36, 47, 53, *190*, 203, 317, 319
Windeyer, Richard, 74
Windschuttle, Keith, 121–2, 123, 129
Winmar, Nicky, 32, 321
Winters, Tombo, 136
Woggan ma Gule mourning ceremony, 27–8
Women for Wik, 87
Women of the Sun (television series), 117, 134
women's business, 297
Wonnarua people, 96, 102
Woodberry, Joyce, 260–1
Woodenbong Aboriginal School, 141
Woodford Bay Reconciliation Memorial, 156

Woodward Royal Commission, 80, 106
Wootten, Commissioner, 57–8
work-for-the-dole schemes, 38, 52
Workstart Program, 13
World Indigenous Peoples' Conferences, 34
The World of the First Australians (Berndt & Berndt), 47
World War II, Indigenous Australians in, *110*, 117, 120
Wotton, Reverend Roy, 169, *169*
Wright, Alexis, 36, 152, 199, 328
writers and writing, 7, 32, 35–6, 52, 77, 275–7, 328
Wymarra, Pearl, 158

X, Malcolm, 105

Yabun, 27, *28*
Yachad Accelerated Learning Project, 180
YALP, 180
Yamatji people, 95
Yandel'ora Women's Dance Group, *38*
Yang, William, *163*
Yanigurra Muya..., 227
Yarnballa Cultural Festival, 40
Yass Public School, 134
Yate, Reverend W., 71
Year 12 attainment, by Indigenous students, 5, 7
Yirawala (artist), 32
Yirrkala Community School, 146
Yirrkala people, 80
YMCA, 323
Yolngu people, 92
Yorta Yorta people, 87
Yothu Yindi (band), 34, 35
You are a repeat offender (cartoon), *149*
Young, Dougie, 34
youth, 9, 165–6
Youth Reconciliation Convention, 165
Yugal Band (band), 34
Yule Brook College, 247
Yunupingu, Galarrwuy, 186
Yunupingu, Geoffrey Gurrumul, 34, 35
Yunupingu, Gulumbu, 33
Yunupingu, Manduwuy, 146

Zevenbergen, R., 266
Zubrick, S.R., 218–20, 222–3, 228